PAGE 44

ON THE ROAD

and insider tips

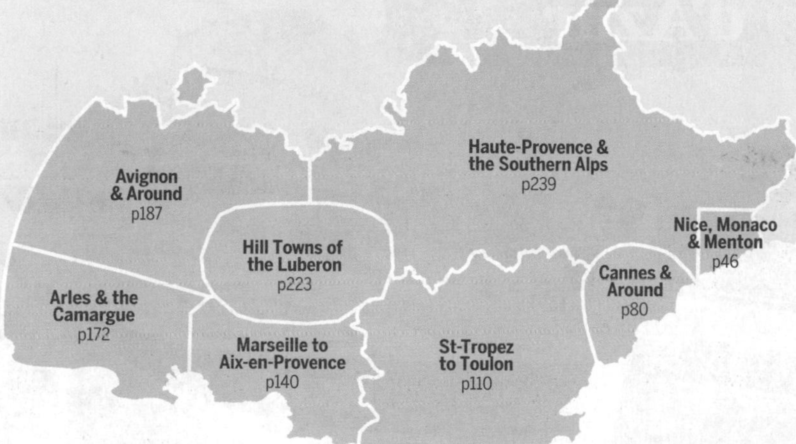

PAGE 285

SURVIVAL GUIDE

VITAL PRACTICAL INFORMATION TO HELP YOU HAVE A SMOOTH TRIP

THIS EDITION WRITTEN AND RESEARCHED BY

Emilie Filou,
Alexis Averbuck, John A Vlahides

welcome to Provence & the Côte d'Azur

Lyrical Landscapes

With their fields of lavender, olive groves, rolling hills, thick cork-oak and pine forests, vineyards, mountains and dazzling blue sea, Provence and the Côte d'Azur are an embarrassment of scenic riches. The region is blessed with almost year-round sunshine and a divine light, making travelling to Provence a delight whatever the season.

The diversity of landscapes is truly astonishing for such a small pocket: you can go from beach to snow-covered peaks in just an hour. There are many unusual gems: fossils trapped for eternity in rock formations; Europe's deepest canyon; hills of vibrant yellow and red ochres; rare wildlife; and crystalline Mediterranean coves.

Art Aplenty

The region's natural bounty didn't escape early settlers: the Romans built on Greek settlements and their phenomenal legacy has helped shape the landscape. Many of Provence–Côte d'Azur's towns and cities were first settled during antiquity; Provençal vineyards are millennia-old and the region is peppered with superb Roman monuments, from entire towns (Vaison-la-Romaine, Glanum) to the highest Roman structure still in existence (Pont du Gard) and the best preserved Roman theatre in the world (Orange's Théâtre Antique).

Impressionist and 20th-century artists were also drawn by the region's incredible light, which Matisse described as 'soft and

Scenic landscapes, azure seas, world-class modern art, wonderful food and incredible historical heritage – everything on offer in Provence and the Côte d'Azur exceeds expectations.

(left) Fishing boats, St-Tropez (p114)
(below) Cycling along a sandy track, Île de Porquerolles (p131)

tender, despite its brilliance'. Dozens of artists either drew inspiration from or settled in the region, the result being a phenomenal artistic legacy: Van Gogh painted some 200 oil canvases whilst in Arles and St-Rémy de Provence; Matisse designed and Picasso decorated chapels, and both left dozens of works to the cities of Nice and Antibes respectively; and art collectors Aimé and Marguerite Maeght amassed so many masterpieces from their friends that they opened the now world-famous Fondation Maeght in St-Paul de Vence.

The Sea

And then there is the Mediterranean, omnipresent, deep blue and turquoise in turns, vehicle of multiculturalism, and endless source of inspiration and fun. Even if you don't visit the coast (a mistake!), you'll feel its presence, and not just thanks to the abundant seafood everywhere, but because it defines the region's climate.

Spring and summer visitors can look forward to afternoons by the beach, snorkelling excursions and swimming in between sights, whereas autumn and winter travellers will have the chance to feast on seafood and marvel at moody seascapes. But whatever the season, you'll be able to go on boat trips, discover unspoilt islands and explore the shores along wonderful coastal paths.

› Provence & the Côte d'Azur

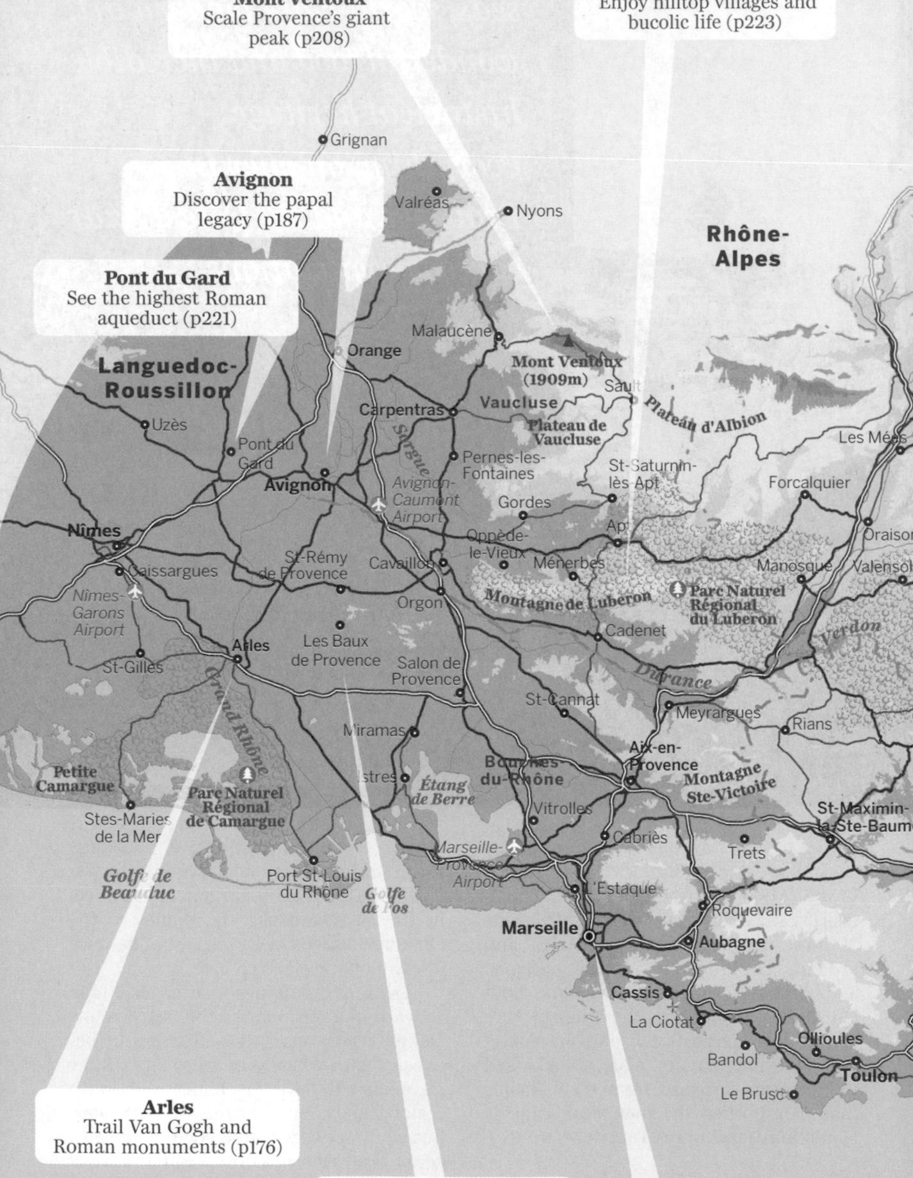

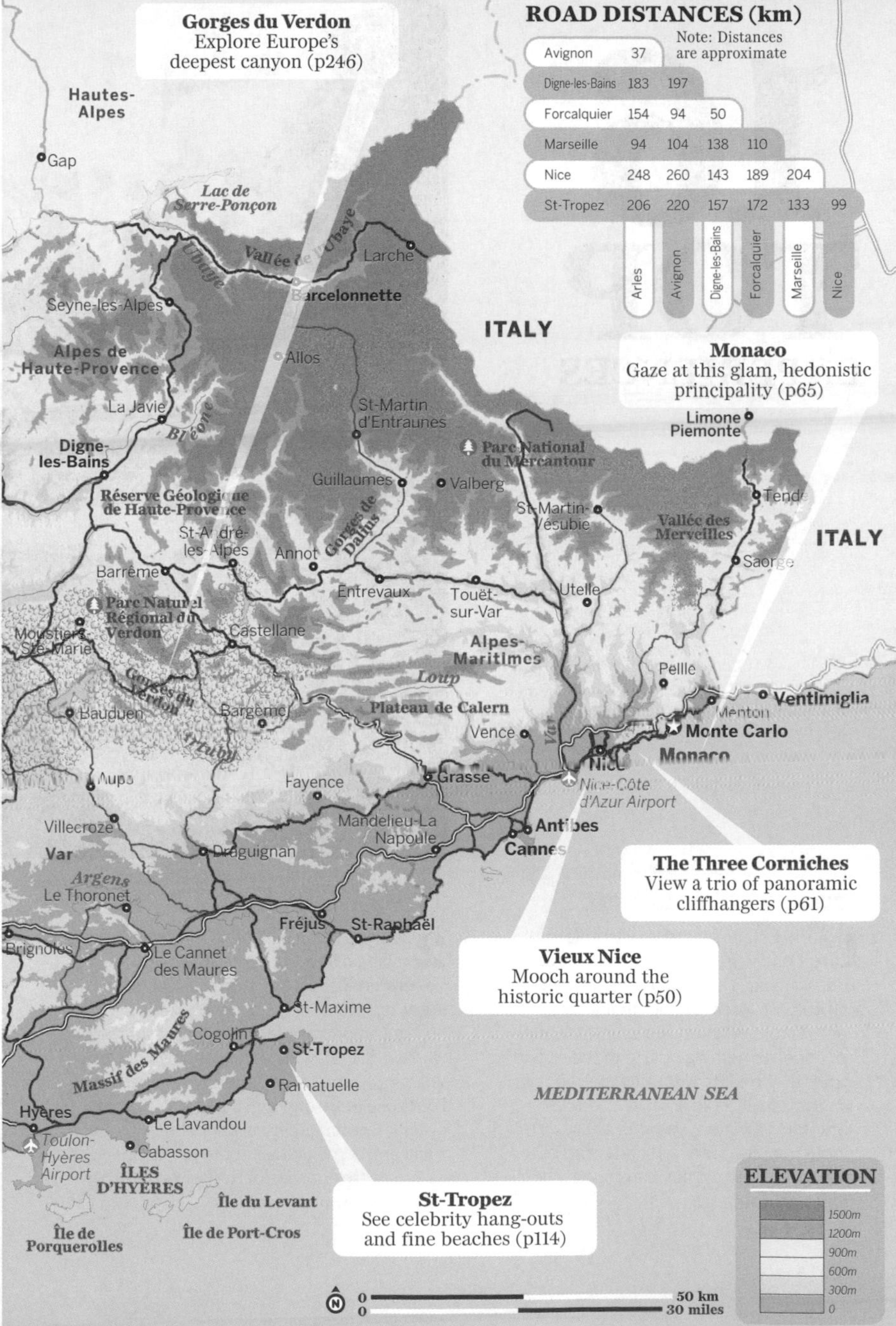

ROAD DISTANCES (km)

Note: Distances are approximate

	Arles	Avignon	Digne-les-Bains	Forcalquier	Marseille	Nice
Avignon	37					
Digne-les-Bains	183	197				
Forcalquier	154	94	50			
Marseille	94	104	138	110		
Nice	248	260	143	189	204	
St-Tropez	206	220	157	172	133	99

16 TOP EXPERIENCES

Provençal Markets

1 Market stalls groaning with colourful fruit and veg, trays of *saucisson* (dry cured sausage) and cheese to sample, stall holders loudly plying their wares – to most visitors, markets are quintessential Provence, something no trip to the region would be complete without experiencing. Villages usually hold at least one weekly market: it's always a cheerful affair, with people meeting for a drink after their big shop and plenty of gossip exchanged while queuing at the stalls.

The Luberon

2 With its hilltop villages, fields of lavender, rolling hills and bucolic lifestyle, the Luberon (p223) is the stuff of Provençal dreams. Attractions can be low-key – ambling in pretty villages, shopping at the weekly market, wine tasting, enjoying a long afternoon lunch on a panoramic terrace. For those more energetic, the area is prime cycling territory, there are dozens of hiking trails and some unique spots to explore, such as the ochre quarries of Roussillon (p228).

Stone village houses, Luberon

1

TONY BURNS/GETTY IMAGES ©

2

BARBARA VAN ZANTEN/GETTY IMAGES ©

Vieux Nice

3 The maze that is Vieux Nice (p50) is the most joyous part of this exquisite city. In the morning it teems with shoppers checking out the stalls of the market on cours Saleya or the town's numerous delis. In the afternoon tourists take over, lapping up ice creams, strolling along the atmospheric, boutique-lined alleyways and admiring the superb Baroque heritage. At night Vieux Nice runneth over with bars, pubs, fabulous restaurants and live-music venues, drawing a merry crowd of all ages. Crowds on cours Saleya, Vieux Nice

Marseille & Les Calanques

4 The vibrant, millennia-old port city of Marseille (p144) isn't just about its Vieux Port (p146) – stunning as it may be! Thanks to its multicultural background the city is an artistic hotspot, which translates into brilliant art galleries, bold new museums, a thriving music scene and the 2013 nomination for European Capital of Culture. Take a break from the city by going to Les Calanques (p161): this stretch of coast is famed for its numerous coves and the translucent turquoise colour of the water. Coastal views of Les Calanques

Jazz à Juan

5 Few festivals can claim to have lined up so many jazz greats: from Miles Davis to Ella Fitzgerald, Stan Getz, Norah Jones and Jamie Cullum. Antibes-Juan-les-Pins' annual event (p93) has become a seminal moment in the jazz calendar, and while the line-up is the star attraction, the setting comes a close second: among pine trees, overlooking the sea, with dreamy views of the coast. If you didn't get tickets in time, fear not, for the Off fringe festival will let you soak up the atmosphere. Anoushka Shankar performing on the sitar at the Jazz à Juan festival, Antibes-Juan-les-Pins

The Three Corniches

6 This trio of coastal roads offers the most outstanding overview (literally!) of the Riviera. The Corniche Inférieure (p61) skirts along the glittering shores, with numerous swimming opportunities. Up in the hills, the jewel in the crown of the Moyenne Corniche (p63) is the medieval village of Èze, spectacularly perched on a rocky promontory offering awe-inspiring views of the coastline. And then there is the Grande Corniche (p64), snaking along the 500m-high cliffs, with spectacular vistas at every bend and a regional park seemingly made for panoramic picnics. Town along the Riviera's coastal road

Pont du Gard

7 One of the most grandiose examples of Roman engineering genius, the Pont du Gard (p221) stands 50m tall and 275m across. In its day the top tier watercourse carried 20,000 cubic meters of water a day. The bridge's 35 arches majestically straddle the River Gard and whether you walk across it, or paddle underneath in a canoe, it is a magnificent sight. Make sure you visit the whizz-bang Museo de la Romanité (p222) for a full, interactive history of the site.

Les Baux de Provence

8 At the heart of the Alpilles, amid hills tumbling with vineyards, olive trees and orchards, Les Baux de Provence (p219) sits spectacularly perched on a rocky promontory. The village is best known for its ruined château, a rambling, evocative place, full of medieval weaponry, with fantastic panoramas. Foodies will no doubt know the place for its divine olive oil, the quality of which is protected under the sought-after *Huile et Olives de la Vallée des Baux* (AOP olives and oil from the Baux Valley label).

The Camargue

9 With its distinctive flat landscape, grasslands, wetlands and slanting light, the Camargue (p172) is unlike any other area of Provence. It's all about nature here: cycle through salt marshes, spend a couple of hours birdwatching, canoe down the Petit Rhône, or go horse-riding along the beach in the setting sun. The Camargue is also where former Spanish influences over Provence are most keenly felt: to wit, the *gitan* festivities of May and October, bullfights and Camargue's red rice.

8

GERARD GSELL/GETTY IMAGES ©

9

SAMI SARKIS/GETTY IMAGES ©

Monaco

10 With its forest of skyscrapers, unabashed hedonism, yacht-filled harbour and couture boutiques, Monaco (p65) is a beguiling place. It's not exactly beautiful – although Monte Carlo has some fine belle époque buildings, chief among them the casino (p68 and p73) – but it has attitude. Monaco has truly embraced its singularity, and so should you: watch the daily change of the guard at 11.55am, go celebrity spotting at the principality's most famous bars and restaurants, and dress up one night and head for the casino. Monaco's Casino de Monte Carlo

Riviera High Life

11 The Riviera really is all about the good life – and the good news is that you don't have to be a millionaire to enjoy it. Must-dos include hiring a lounger for the day at one of Cannes' exclusive beaches (p84); taking a punt at the Casino de Monte Carlo (p68 and p73); flying from Nice to Monaco by helicopter (p74); dining at Le Negresco's decadent restaurant Le Chantecler (p57); or attending the most glamorous event of them all, Monaco's Formula One Grand Prix (p71).

St-Tropez & the Peninsula

12 The hang-out of choice for superstars and party animals in summer – and a strangely quiet, pretty seaside town the rest of the year – St-Tropez (p114) is the Dr Jekyll/Mr Hyde of the Côte d'Azur. The town and surrounding peninsula are transformed from one season to the next, with throngs of holidaymakers in search of brilliant clubs, fine beaches (by far the best on the coast) and great eating. Come in June or September for atmosphere minus the crowds. Yachts lining the harbour at St-Tropez

Gorges du Verdon

13 What's special about Europe's deepest canyon (p246) is that there are so many ways to enjoy it. You can walk, you can cycle, you can drive along the cliffs or thunder down the river on a raft or kayak. However you do it though, you're guaranteed to be mesmerised by the water's ethereal green colour and the sheer scale of this natural wonder. It's not all rough-and-ready, however: gorge gateway Moustiers Ste-Marie (p249) is home to one of Provence's most fabulous *auberges*, La Bastide de Moustiers (p249).

Arles

14 Famed for its outstanding Roman architecture and for being the home of ill-fated impressionist Vincent van Gogh, Arles (p176) is a delight: it's small, you can walk everywhere, and there is something to see at every corner. There may not be any Van Gogh paintings to admire but there are informative walking tours and art galleries in honour of the master. And then there is the food: Arles has some of the finest restaurants in the region, so don't leave without indulging in an evening of gastronomic dining. Inside the Cloître St-Trophime (p178), Arles

13

14

HEINZ WOHNER/ALAMY ©

ANDREW BAIN/GETTY IMAGES ©

The Popes in Avignon

15 The seat of papal power for more than a century, Avignon (p189) has retained something regal about it: the Palais des Papes (p189) is indeed impressive, but there are many more historical buildings to discover, some of them now splendid hotels. The popes didn't just build a great city however – they also planted some fine vineyards: Châteauneuf-du-Pape (p200) is without a doubt one of the world's great reds, and going on a wine-tasting tour is part and parcel of discovering the popes' legacy. Palais des Papes, Avignon

Mont Ventoux

16 The defining feature of northern Provence, Mont Ventoux (p208) stands like a sentinel over the region's undulating landscape. Its reputation is mythical among cyclists, but everyone feels the pull of the *géant de Provence* (Provence's giant), be it for hiking, wildlife watching (the mountain's biodiversity is second to none), scenic drives or panoramas. On clear days, you can see from Camargue to the Alps. From November to April, the summit is snowed under. Cycling along the foothills of Mont Ventoux

need to know

Currency

» The euro (€)

Language

» French

When to Go

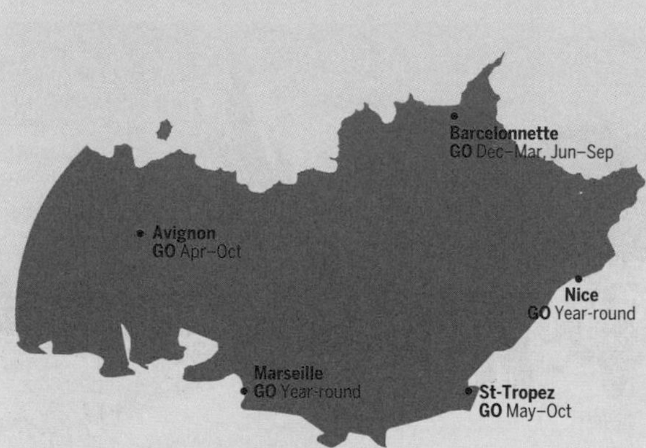

High Season
(Jul & Aug)

» Hotels are full, often booked months in advance and at their priciest.

» It is hot: 35°C is fairly common at lunch time.

» Alpine resorts fill up with snow-seekers during the ski season (Dec–Mar).

Shoulder Season
(Apr–Jun, Sep & Oct)

» Definitely the best time of year to travel, with good weather and no school holiday crowds.

» Spring blooms and autumn colours.

Low Season
(Nov–Mar)

» Very quiet, especially in rural areas and coastal resorts, where many hotels close.

» Attractions open shorter hours.

» Cities remain lively and offer great accommodation bargains.

Your Daily Budget

Budget under

€100

» Dorm bed: €20–30

» Double room in a budget hotel: €60–80

» Excellent markets and bakeries for picnics

» Good, affordable public transport

Midrange

€100–200

» Double room in a boutique hotel: €80–180

» Set menus in gourmet restaurants: €20–40

» Online deals for car rental

Top End over

€200

» Double room in luxury hotel: more than €180

» Meal à la carte in a top restaurant: €50–100

» Tickets to festivals, concerts

» Car rental, taxi when required

Money

» ATMs widely available. Most hotels and restaurants take credit cards; only larger establishments accept Amex.

Visas

» Generally not required for stays up to 90 days (or at all for EU nationals); some nationalities will require a Schengen visa (p292).

Mobile Phones

» Local SIM cards can be used in (unlocked) European and Australian phones. Other phones (US, Japan) must be set to roaming.

Accommodation

» Anything from campsites to luxury five-star palaces; *chambres d'hôte* (the French equivalent of a B&B) are also very popular.

Websites

» **Provence–Alpes–Côte d'Azur Tourisme** (www.decouverte-paca fr) Indispensable.

» **Provence-Hideaways** (www.provence-hideaway.com) Written by expats living in the region.

» **Côte d'Azur Tourisme** (www.cotedazur-tourisme.com) Riviera.

» **Visit Provence** (www.visitprovence.com) Marseille, Arles and the Camargue.

» **Visit Var** (www.visitvar.fr) St-Tropez to Toulon.

» **Lonely Planet** (www.lonelyplanet.com/france)

Exchange Rates

Australia	A$1	€0.85
Canada	C$1	€0.80
Japan	¥100	€1.03
New Zealand	NZ$1	€0.66
UK	£1	€1.25
US	US$	€0.80

For current exchange rates see www.xe.com.

Important Numbers

France country code	☎33
International dialling code	☎00
Europe-wide emergency	☎112
Ambulance (SAMU)	☎15
Police	☎17

Arriving

» **Nice-Côte d'Azur airport**

Bus – service to Nice every 15 minutes, to Cannes, Antibes, Monaco and Menton every 30 minutes

Taxi – allow €25 to Nice, €70 to Cannes or Monaco

» **Marseille Provence Airport**

Bus – Service to Marseille and Aix-en-Provence every 20 minutes

Train – direct services to Marseille, Arles, Avignon, Nîmes and Orange; dozens more with connection

Taxi – allow €50 to Marseille

Driving in Provence–Côte d'Azur

Driving in France is on the right-hand side of the road; the steering-wheel is on the left-hand side of the car.

Marseille, Toulon and Nice are a driver's nightmare but outside of the big cities, motoring is generally a pleasant affair and is an attraction in its own right in the most scenic places (Luberon, Gorges du Verdon, the Three Corniches etc). Roads are in good condition, and traffic is light, except in July and August and during rush hour in the more built-up areas.

Watch out for the treacherous 'priority to the right' rule (see p298).

In Alpine areas, note that some roads can be cut off by snow in winter – ask before you set off. Negotiating the hairpin bends of the smallest mountain roads can be hair-raising for inexperienced drivers.

Everyone needs a helping hand when they visit a country for the first time. There are phrases to learn, customs to get used to and etiquette to understand. The following section will help demystify Provence and the Côte d'Azur so your first trip goes as smoothly as your fifth.

Language

It is perfectly possible to travel in Provence–Côte d'Azur without speaking French, but you'll probably have an easier (and more pleasant) time if you learn a few basics. The French are proud of their language and will expect you to give it a try, if only with greetings. People in tourist offices and hotels tend to speak good English but don't expect fluency on market stalls, shops and rural areas. See also the language section of this book (p300) for useful phrases.

Booking Ahead

It is a good idea to reserve at least the first night of your stay to make arriving as smooth as possible. Booking online is the easiest way of doing it but if you have to do it over the phone, the following phrases should see you through the reservation.

Hello.	Bonjour.
I'd like to book a room.	Je voudrais réserver une chambre.
a single room	une chambre à un lit
a double room	une chambre avec un grand lit
My name is ...	Je m'appelle ...
from ... to ... (date)	du ... au ...
How much is it?	C'est combien?
per night/person	par nuit/personne
Thank you (very much).	Merci (beaucoup).

What to Wear

Outside of glamorous hotspots such as Monaco, Cannes and St-Tropez, fashion is pretty relaxed in the south of France. Jeans are as universal here as they are in most of Western Europe. In winter, you'll need to layer up as it gets cold. A waterproof coat and sturdy shoes are a good idea for all-weather sightseeing. In summer, shorts, skirts and dresses are fine.

For evening wear, smart casual is the norm. Upmarket places insist on shoes (not trainers) and trousers or dresses instead of jeans; jackets and ties are a prerequisite for men in Monaco, while high heels for ladies are the 'open sesame' to Cannes and St-Tropez' trendiest bars.

Bars and clubs usually have a cloakroom for bags and coats.

What to Pack

- Passport
- Driving license
- Credit card
- Adaptor plug
- Camera
- Sunglasses
- Suncream
- Hat
- Mosquito repellent
- Beach towel
- Swimsuit
- Pocket knife
- Smart clothes
- Corkscrew
- Refillable water bottle
- French phrasebook
- Sturdy shoes
- Regional map

Checklist

» Check the validity of your passport

» Book car rental online for the cheapest deals

» Reserve a table if you plan to eat at a famous restaurant

» Book courses or popular tours to avoid disappointment

» Check custom restrictions so that you can shop for food and drink souvenirs

» Organise travel insurance

» Check whether your mobile phone will work

Etiquette

» Greetings
Shake hands and say *bonjour Monsieur* or *bonjour Madame* (hello) to strangers; air kiss on both cheeks and say *comment ça va* (how are you) to friends.

» Conversation
Use *vous* (you) in polite company; use *tu* (also you) with friends and children. Only use first names if invited. Talking about money is seen as crass.

» Asking for help
Say *excusez-moi* (excuse me) to attract attention; say *pardon* (sorry) to apologise.

» Religion
Dress modestly and be quiet and respectful when visiting any religious building.

» Eating & Drinking
When dining in a French home, wait for your host to start first. Always clear the plate. When you're finished, line up your fork and knife on top of your plate towards the right.

» Waiters
Never call waitstaff garçon – use *Monsieur* (Mr), *Mademoiselle* (Miss) or *Madame* (Mrs).

Tipping

» When to Tip
Tipping is optional everywhere, although still customary in restaurants.

» Restaurants
A 15% service charge is usually included in the bill; tip if you've really appreciated the service.

» Taxis
Most people round up to the nearest euro.

» Bars
If you go to the bar to get drinks, there's no need to tip; if drinks are brought to your table, tip as for restaurants.

» Hotels
Rare, unless for concierge or valet car service in luxury hotels.

Money

Credit and debit cards can be used almost everywhere, though there may be a minimum purchase of €10. Visa and MasterCard are the most popular options; American Express is only accepted by major chains, and few places take Diners Club and JCB. Ask if bars and restaurants take cards before you order. Chip-and-pin is the norm for card transactions – few places accept signatures as an alternative.

ATMs are everywhere; you could also make cash advances on your credit card. Beware of high transaction fees when using your card.

what's new

For this new edition of Provence & the Côte d'Azur, our authors have hunted down the fresh, the transformed, the hot and the happening. These are some of our favourites. For up-to-the-minute recommendations, see lonelyplanet.com/France.

Marseille

1 Marseille (p144) has long been working on its renaissance, what with the re-development of its port and the preparations for its 2013 reign as European Capital of Culture. Numerous attractions have benefited from a facelift, the sensational Fonds Regional d'Art Contemporain has opened, and the city generally seems to ooze culture.

Musée d'Art Classique de Mougins

2 This outstanding collection juxtaposes antique artefacts and world-class modern art and illustrates in an artistic tour de force just how much ancient civilisations have inspired artists over the ages. (p104)

Les Jardins du MIP, Mouans-Sartoux

3 Pick, rub and smell your way around these fragrant gardens. Run by the outstanding Musée International de la Parfumerie in Grasse, they showcase the most common plants used in perfumery. (p104) (p101)

Musée Jean Cocteau Collection Séverin Wunderman

4 It's about time a museum dedicated itself to the genius of Jean Cocteau: from drawings to films, find out more about the artist and his legacy at this excellent museum in Menton. (p76)

Sea Sens, Cannes

5 It's not that Cannes lacked good restaurants, but the Sea Sens has found a niche in a town of stars: sensational fusion food, great views, and remarkably good-value prices. (p88)

Palais des Papes Interactive Audioguide

6 Avignon's star attraction has embraced 21st-century technology by adopting interactive PDA-style audioguides showing you how the palace's rooms used to be decorated. (p189)

Express cooking lessons

7 This is literally like having your cake and eating it too: at Les Apprentis Gourmets, cooking lessons are short and sweet (and tasty), leaving you time to do plenty more during your stay. (p89)

Carrières de Lumière

8 The new incarnation of Cathédrale d'Images in Les Baux de Provence opened in 2012 with a show on Cézanne and Van Gogh. (p219)

Mont Ventoux Bike Park

9 Forget slogging it up the hill on your bike: at this new bike park, you get towed up the mountain so that you can focus on the thrill of descent along ramps and jumps. (p208)

if you like...

Food

There are so many ways to enjoy Provençal food: from dining at one of the region's fine restaurants to trawling food markets or learning how to do it yourself.

Seafood Feast on freshly-caught fish or *plateaux de fruits de mer* (seafood platter) with a glass of white wine in Marseille (p156) or Cassis (p163)

Niçois cuisine A blend of Provençal and Italian cuisine, the best place to try Nice's celebrated cuisine is in Niçois restaurants (p56)

Fashionable gastronomy Dine at one of Arles (p180), Aix (p168) or Cannes' (p88) superb restaurants for a night of culinary style and substance

Markets Salivate over fresh products, take in the atmosphere and buy ingredients for the king of all picnics at Provence's numerous markets

Cooking courses Whether it's a whole day affair including a trip to the market, or a convivial one-hour blast, pick up a few tricks from Provençal chefs (p33)

History

Provence and the Côte d'Azur are like an open book, with history unfolding in every town and village.

Prehistory Marvel at the millennia-old drawings of the Vallée des Merveilles in the Mercantour (p257)

Roman times Be humbled by the sheer amount and grandeur of Provence's Roman ruins, starting with the Pont du Gard (p221) and Orange's Théâtre Antique (p202)

Religious legacy Religious communities thrived in medieval times, as magnificent buildings such as Monastère de la Verne (p129)and Abbaye Notre Dame de Sénanque p225) attest

Papal Provence Find out how Avignon fared as the capital of Christendom at Palais des Papes (p189)

Belle Époque The Riviera's golden age is chronicled in wonderful and highly evocative details at Musée Masséna in Nice (p51)

Beaches

It's not called the coast of azure for nothing: the Mediterranean is a tantalising presence, to which you'll be able to give in from April to October.

Calanque d'En Vau, Les Calanques The Calanques' most photogenic cove won't disappoint: yes, the water *really* is that colour (p162)

Plage de Notre Dame, Île de Porquerolles The Golden Islands' finest: long and curvy, with crystalline waters and a few sailing boats to complete the picture (p132)

Plage de Pampelonne, Péninsule de St-Tropez Soft buttermilk sand unfolding over 9km, this is Mediterranean beach-going at its best (p115)

Plage du Layet, Cavalière Nudist, beautiful and host to a very chic restaurant (p130)

Z Plage, Cannes Designer swimwear, oversized sunglasses and cocktails are *de rigueur* for a spot of sunbathing along La Croisette (p84)

» Route des Crêtes (p131)

Wine & Liqueurs

Provence is famed for its chilled rosé wine, the highlight of many a long lunch or alfresco dinner, but the region also produces characterful reds and unique liqueurs.

Maison des Vins Côtes de Provence The geographic and spiritual home of Provence's rosé, with tasting and advice galore (p125)

La Maison du Pastis, Marseille Provence's other beloved tipple is the aniseed-flavoured pastis, of which there are some 90 varieties to choose from at this boutique (p160)

Châteauneuf-du-Pape No wine has had a more tumultuous – and illustrious – history; find out more over the course of a few tastings (p200)

Beaumes-de-Venise Unearth your favourite vintage of this delicious sweet Muscat in the eponymous village (p208)

Distilleries et Domaines de Provence Try Provence's distinctive liqueurs – peach, thyme, almond – to spice up your aperitif (p244)

The Great Outdoors

The region's outstanding natural beauty is none more obvious than in its stunning protected areas, all of which are free, easily accessible and home to activities galore.

Parc National du Mercantour This is what the great outdoors look like: snow-capped mountains, fertile valleys, abundant (and rare) wildlife and immense skies (p252)

Île de Port-Cros Exceptional Mediterranean fauna and flora, an almost deserted island to discover (p133)

Parc Naturel Régional du Verdon Take to the green waters of the Verdon to explore the park's dramatic gorges, cliffs, rivers and lakes (p246)

Parc Naturel Régional du Luberon Hilltop villages, rolling hills and limestone gorges, with eagles and vultures circling the sky (p230)

Parc Naturel Régional de Camargue Weave between salt pans and paddy fields to admire Camargue's unique birdlife (p181)

Parc National des Calanques France's newest national park is well known for the exceptional turquoise colour of its rocky coves. (p161)

Dramatic Drives

Driving in Provence is not only convenient, it is also an attraction in its own right for the sheer beauty of its landscapes: try some of these routes for the drive of your life.

Grande Corniche Follow in the footsteps of Cary Grant and Grace Kelly and enjoy spellbinding views of the Med at every turn (p64)

Corniche Sublime Steel yourself for this jaw-dropping road along the Gorges du Verdon and catch a glimpse of the canyon's emerald green waters (p248)

Route des Crêtes, Cassis to La Ciotat Sweeping panoramas of the Calanques' distinctive mineral beauty (p131)

High Mountain Loop Take in three of Europe's highest *cols* (mountain passes) – Col d'Allos, Col de La Cayolle and Col des Champs – on this dramatic loop in Parc National du Mercantour (p255)

If You Like... Lavender
The quintessential image of Provence is one of rolling hills covered in bright purple lavender – follow this dreamy vision along the Routes de la Lavende (p138)

Festivals & Events

Provence and the Côte d'Azur have a packed calendar and planning your trip around one of these festivals is highly recommended.

Performing Arts Choose from opera in Orange (p202), theatre in Avignon (p194), classical music in Aix (p166), dance music in Cannes (p89) and circus in Monaco (p70)

Sports Support Marseille's legendary OM football team (p160), watch Monaco's Formula One Grand Prix (p70) or the principality's Masters Tennis series

Carnivals Join the floats and parades at Carnaval de Nice (p55), Carnaval de Marseille p154) and Menton's Fête du Citron (p78)

Folklore Watch bullfighting in Arles (p179) and Nîmes (p219), attend *gitan* celebrations in Stes-Maries de la Mer (p186), and join in truffle and chestnut celebrations in Aups (p126) and Collobrières (p128)

Hilltop Villages

Perched spectacularly on rocky outcrops, often commanding superb views, Provence's hilltop wonders are a testament to medieval builders – and a sight to behold.

Èze Spellbinding views of the Med and windy stone-pebbled lanes attract throngs of visitors and yet, Èze remains magical (p63)

Roussillon Famed for its distinctive red-ochre colour, beautifully offset by the vegetation tumbling down its promontory (p228)

Gourdon An austere eagle's nest towering above the Gorges du Loup; the village looks magical under the snow in winter (p98)

Ste-Agnès Europe's highest cliffhanger (780m) looms large over Menton and Italy (p79)

Bonnieux, Lacoste & Ménerbes This classic trio of hilltop villages in the Luberon really is as wonderful as everyone says it is (p233)

Les Baux de Provence Sitting atop a limestone *baou* (rocky spur) lie the dramatic ruins of the old Château des Baux (p219)

20th-Century Art

Many of the 20th century's great artists came here for inspiration and eventually settled.

Fondation Maeght, St-Paul de Vence One of the world's finest collections of 20th-century art, acquired by two art dealers over a lifetime of friendships (p96)

Cézanne in Aix Visit the master's studio, former home and favourite painting spot (p165)

Musée de l'Annonciade, St-Tropez Punching well above its tiny weight, with masterpieces by Signac, Braque and Picasso (p114)

Musée d'Art Moderne et d'Art Contemporain, Nice This modern art museum pays tribute to home-grown New Realists such as Yves Klein, Nikki de Saint-Phalle and Arman (p51)

Musée Granet, Aix-en-Provence The works on display are like a who's who of modern art: Matisse, Picasso, Cézanne, Van Gogh and co (p165)

Musée Jean Cocteau Collection Séverin Wunderman, Menton Discover the genius of the prolific Jean Cocteau, from illustrations to cinematography. (p76)

month by month

Top Events

1 **Truffle Celebrations**, January

2 **Monaco Grand Prix**, May

3 **Festival d'Avignon**, July

4 **Dance Music in Cannes**, August

5 **Transhumance**, October

January

Even in the depths of winter, Provence and the Côte d'Azur has its charms. The Provençal Alps are carpeted in snow whilst crisp winter days flatter the Riviera. Outside of ski resorts and large cities however, many hotels and attractions close, making travel harder.

Festival International du Cirque de Monte-Carlo

The world's best circus artists compete every year for the 'Golden Clown' Award in Monte-Carlo. Winners then put on a week of performances (www.montecarlofestival.mc).

On Your Skis!

Provence and the Côte d'Azur's ski resorts (p255) are excellent: small, family-friendly, peppered with trees, sunny and easily accessible by public transport (just €2 return from Nice).

Truffle Hunting

Provence's black diamond is picked from November to February (restaurants make the best of it, and so should you!), but the season culminates in January with the Messe de la Truffe in Richerenches (p207) and the Journée de la Truffe in Aups (p126).

February

February can be divine on the Riviera: the days are bright, the sky is blue and it's often mild. French school kids get two weeks off to tear down the pistes.

Carnaval de Nice

Both the decorated floats and the crowds are gigantic at this flamboyant Mardi Gras street parade in Nice, celebrated since 1293. Don't miss the legendary flower battles (www.nicecarnaval.com).

April

April weather is much the same in Provence as it is elsewhere in Europe: full of surprises. Easter holidays can be spent on the beach as much as on the slopes. Many towns and villages hold ancestral religious celebrations high in folklore and colour.

Féria Pascale

Held each Easter in Arles to open the bullfighting season (www.feriaarles.com), the *féria* is four days of exuberant dancing, music, concerts and bullfighting.

May

Spring may be well under way but the sea remains cold at this time of year, and the mistral (northern wind) can be howling in Provence. May is also bank-holiday-tastic in France, with no less than four bank holidays, so plan ahead for reservations.

Pèlerinage des Gitans

Roma from Europe pour into remote seaside outpost Stes-Maries-de-la-Mer to honour their patron saint on 24 and 25 May (and again in October): processions, street singing and dancing are all part of the celebrations (p186).

Monaco Grand Prix

Formula One's most anticipated race, the Monaco Grand Prix tears around the tiny municipality in a haze of glamour, champagne, VIPs and after parties (www.acm.mc).

Gardens in Bloom

Provence's gardens look lush at this time of year. Visit a flower farm (p103) or stroll in the sumptuous gardens of Villa Ephrussi de Rothschild (p63).

July

July is Provence at its most picturesque: the cicadas fill the air with their incessant song, lavender fields stretch in all their purple glory, it is hot and you have a choice of pool, sea or rosé to cool off.

Festival d'Avignon & Festival Off

Theatre in every guise takes to the stage at this renowned theatre festival in Avignon; fringe Off parallels the official fest. (www.festival -avignon.com)

Les Chorégies d'Orange

France's oldest festival stages operas at the incredible Roman theatre in Orange, an unforgettable night if you can get tickets (www. choregies.asso.fr).

Jazz on the Riviera

The Riviera swings to the music of two great jazz festivals: Jazz à Juan in Antibes-Juan-les-Pins (www. jazzajuan.com) and Nice Jazz Festival (www.nicejazz festival.fr). Book tickets well in advance.

Festival d'Aix-en-Provence

A month of world-class opera, classical music and ballet is what this prestigious festival offers (www. festivalaix.com).

August

Depending on how you look at it, this is either the worst or the best time to come to Provence. It is definitely the busiest, with every hotel fully booked, but also the liveliest, with events galore, night markets and an infectious party atmosphere.

Fireworks by the Sea

Cannes and Monaco both hold free international fireworks festivals in July and August when pyrotechnicians from around the world compete for the 'ooohs' and 'aaahs' of the crowd.

Dance the Night Away in Cannes

Cannes is *the* party spot in August. Le Palais nightclub opens for 50 nights of dancing under the stars, and two great dance music festivals set up shop: Festival Pantiero (www.festivalpantiero.com) and Les Plages Électroniques (www.plages-electroniques. com).

October

The days may be shortening but in the glow of the autumn sun, they're a delight. You can still swim on warm days, and what's more, you're likely to have the beach to yourself.

Chestnut a Go-Go

Head to Collobrières in the Massif des Maures to pick, feast on and learn about chestnuts (p128). The forest is at its loveliest for long walks too. Harvest celebrations culminate in the Fête de la Châtaigne.

Transhumance

Sheep and their shepherds descend from their summer pastures and crowd the roads of Haute-Provence, from the Verdon to Col d'Allos. The same happens in reverse in June.

December

Families celebrate Christmas with midnight Mass, Provençal chants, 13 desserts (yes) and nativity scenes full of santons (terracotta figurines). Outside of Christmas and New Year's Eve parties however, it is a quiet month.

Whether you've got a week or a month, these itineraries provide a starting point for the trip of a lifetime. Want more inspiration? Head online to lonelyplanet.com/thorntree to chat with other travellers.

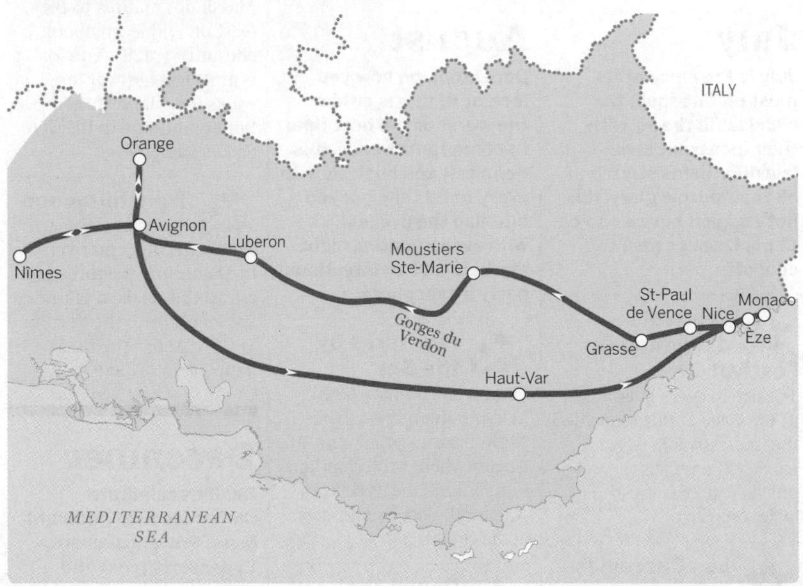

Two Weeks

Essential Provence-Côte d'Azur

Fly to **Nice**. On day two, mooch around Vieux Nice and amble along promenade des Anglais. On day three, catch a bus to stunning **Èze** to feast on views; head to **Monaco** for lunch and enjoy the rest of the day in the principality. Catch a train back to Nice. On day four, pick up a rental car and drive to the medieval wonder of **St-Paul de Vence** and its art galleries. On day five, drive to **Moustiers Ste-Marie** along the scenic N85, stopping in **Grasse** on the way for an insight into the town's perfume industry. Spend the following day in **Gorges du Verdon**.

On day seven, drive to the **Luberon**, stopping in villages on the way. Spend day eight enjoying the area and on day nine, head to **Avignon**. Enjoy the city for a day, and take a day trip to **Orange** or **Nîmes** on day 11. On day 12 and 13, head to the **Haut-Var** for hilltop villages and vineyards, before driving back to Nice on day 13, in time for your flight home.

DOUG PEARSON/GETTY IMAGES ©

ALAN COPSONL/GETTY IMAGES ©

» (above) View of Èze (p63), Moyenne Corniche
» (left) Les Arènes (p219), Nîmes

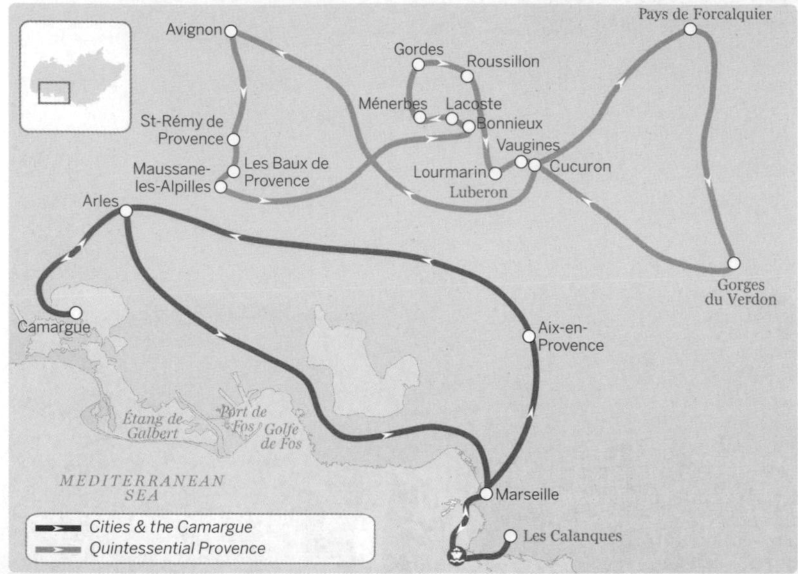

One Week
Cities & the Camargue

Spend your first day exploring **Marseille**; its Vieux Port, the historic Le Panier quarter and discovering the city's art scene. Go to cours Julien for a night out. On day two, take a boat trip to **Les Calanques** or visit Château d'If before heading up to Basilique Notre Dame de la Garde for panoramic views of the city and the sea. Go for dinner at the picturesque Vallon des Auffes. On day three, head to **Aix-en-Provence** to visit Cézanne's studio, family house and the Bibemus quarries where he painted. Treat yourself to dinner in one of Aix's fine restaurants.

On day four, head to **Arles** and discover the places that inspired Van Gogh. Book a table for dinner at one of Arles' Michelin-starred establishments. On day five, immerse yourself in the town's fine Roman heritage, the amphitheatre, theatre, baths and Musée Départemental Arles Antique to learn about life in Roman times. Take a day trip to **Camargue** on day six: hire bikes if you're game, and don't forget your binoculars for birdwatching. Head back to Marseille. This entire itinerary can be done by public transport.

One Week
Quintessential Provence

Spend day one in **Avignon**, visiting Palais des Papes and ambling the atmospheric town. On day two, drive down to **St-Rémy de Provence** in Les Alpilles and put your bags down for a couple of nights. Explore the town's stupendous Roman site Glanum and visit the asylum where Van Gogh spent the last – but most productive – year of his short life. On day three, take a day trip to **Les Baux de Provence**: visit the ruined castle and go olive oil tasting around **Maussane-les-Alpilles** in the afternoon.

On day four, drive to the **Luberon** (where you'll spend the next three nights) in the morning and spend the afternoon exploring the classic trio of villages **Bonnieux**, **Lacoste** and **Ménerbes**. On day five, visit **Gordes** and its Abbaye Notre-Dame de Sénanque (of postcard fame) and the ochre-coloured village of **Roussillon**. On day six, pack a picnic and set off to explore the gorges, forests and lavender fields around **Lourmarin**, **Vaugines** and **Cucuron**. Treat yourself to dinner at the gastronomic Auberge La Fenière. On day seven, drive back to Avignon or carry on to **Pays de Forcalquier** and the **Gorges du Verdon** for another three days.

SANDER SANDER/GETTY IMAGES ©

DAVID EPPERSON/GETTY IMAGES ©

» (above) Sailing boats, Les Calanques (p161)

» (left) View of Bonnieux (p233), the Luberon

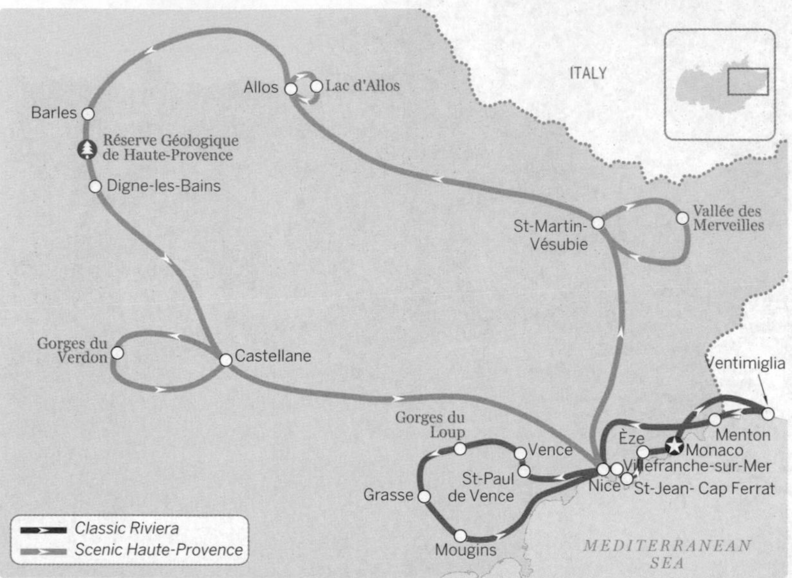

10 Days
Scenic Haute-Provence

Start in **Nice** – enjoy a day of urban delight in Vieux Nice, before hitting the road on day two. Drive to **St-Martin-Vésubie**. Visit wilderness park Alpha to learn more about the wolves inhabiting the mountains and plan your excursion in the **Vallée des Merveilles** the next day. On day three, discover with a guide the thousands of petroglyphs that have given the Vallée des Merveilles its name. On day four, drive to **Allos** through spectacular mountain scenery. Book for two nights at Alpine wonder La Ferme Girerd-Potin for a roaring fire inside and hot tub outside. On day five, hike around **Lac d'Allos**.

On day six, drive to **Digne-les-Bains**, stopping in **Barles** along the way for fossil hunting in the Réserve Géologique de Haute-Provence. Organise a lavender walk on day seven, and on day eight, drive down to **Castellane**, and take a scenic tour of the **Gorges du Verdon**. Explore the canyon in a different way on day nine: go rafting, canyoning or just trekking. On day 10, drive back to Nice or carry on along the Riviera.

10 Days
Classic Riviera

The first five days of this trip can be done from Nice by public transport. Dedicate your first couple of days to the belle of the Côte d'Azur: **Nice**. Stroll in Vieux Nice and browse the market stalls of cours Saleya; visit Cimiez's wonderful Musée National Marc Chagall and Musée Matisse; and party till dawn in Vieux Nice's numerous bars.

On day three, take a day trip along the Corniche Inférieure stopping at **Villefranche-sur-Mer** and **St-Jean-Cap Ferrat**. On day four, head to hilltop **Èze** for sensational views of the Med; carry on to **Monaco** for the rest of the day. The following day, venture into **Ventimiglia** in Italy (try to aim for a Friday, market day) in the morning and hop back into France for an afternoon in **Menton**.

On day six, rent a car and head for the hills: stop in **St-Paul de Vence** and **Vence**, and spend day seven motoring around the beautiful **Gorges du Loup**. On day eight, visit **Grasse**, its museums and perfumeries; leave your last day for the pretty village of **Mougins**. Drive back to Nice on day 10 or continue in Haute-Provence or head west along the coast.

Staying in Provence

Best...

Views
Château Eza (p64) Clinging dramatically to a rocky outcrop, on the edge of the medieval village of Èze, with plunging views of the Mediterranean.

Out & Out Luxury
Hôtel La Mirande (p195) Gold-threaded tapestry, marble staircases, antique furniture and chandeliers: life château style.

Design
Pastis (p117) Pop-art inspired interior, original artworks and an emerald-green pool.

Self-Catering
Nice Pebbles (p55) Boutique flats in Nice and the Riviera.

Hostel
Villa Saint-Exupéry (p56) Lovely grounds, great rooms, a packed schedule of activities and fantastic services, from bargain meals to free wi-fi.

At One with Nature
Moonlight Chalet (p256) An eco-lodge nestled in the mountains, with natural pool and cabins featuring living trees and river rocks.

Where to Stay

Accommodation in southern France is delightful, abundant and often expensive.

Hotels

Hotels have one to five stars; they run the gamut of the comfort spectrum, from simple pension to no-holds barred luxury. Pools are common in this sunny part of France but note that few are heated, which means you'll only really be able to swim from April to October. Most midrange and top-end hotels have air-con (which you'll only really need from June to September).

Irrespective of price range, single rooms are rare (smaller doubles are often sold as singles, but are more expensive than a real single). King-size beds are the exception rather than the rule (and often made up of two single beds). Triples and quads, frequently available, have two double beds or a double and one/two singles.

Chambres d'Hôte

An increasingly modish way to sleep, eat and dream Provence is in a *chambre d'hôte*, the French equivalent of a B&B. Many are on farms, wineries or a historic property and are highly sought after. They are limited by law to six rooms and therefore tend to be more convivial than hotels. Hosts are the cornerstone of the *chambre d'hôte* and their advice and company is a major draw for visitors keen to engage with the locals.

A feast of a homemade breakfast is included in the price, and many serve a delicious dinner around a shared table (known as *table d'hôte*) a few nights a week.

Self-Catering

Who hasn't dreamt of having his or her own century-old *mas* (traditional stone farmhouse) in a cherry-tree orchard, a designer pad in Nice or a villa with a magnificent pool? Self-catering accommodation in Provence–Côte d'Azur is a great option, particularly for families or those seeking to experience 'life as a local'. Amenities range from basic bathroom facilities and simple kitchenette (with oven, hot plates and fridge) to superb bathrooms, fully equipped kitchen with dishwasher and washing machine, TV, wi-fi, garden and pool. Linen can be rented.

Tourist offices generally keep lists of local studios, apartments and villas to rent.

Prices

Budget hotels usually charge the same rates year-round. Mid- and top-end lodgings typically use three sets of seasonally adjusted prices:

» Low season (October/November to February/March)

» Mid-season (March to May and September/October)

» High season (June to August)

With the exception of prices for *chambre d'hôte* and *maison d'hôte*, rates don't include breakfast, which costs anything from €7 to €30 per person.

Every hotel is obliged to charge a daily *taxe de séjour* (tourist tax) on each visitor in their jurisdiction; the daily tax (€0.20 to €1.50) is set by the local authority and can be applied year-round or seasonally.

All but the smallest hotels take credit cards; Visa and MasterCard are universally accepted but only larger establishments will take American Express.

See p286 for the budget range used in this book.

Special Events

Big-ticket events such as the Monaco Grand Prix, Festival d'Avignon, Cannes film festival or Nîmes *férias* bump up prices beyond belief. Rooms also get booked up fast so try to work around these dates – unless of course you're attending, in which case you should book as soon as you have tickets.

Reservations

Out of season, it is quite possible to snag a room in a drop-dead gorgeous property on the spot – although many addresses close for a few weeks for their *congé annuel* (annual closure) when no one's around. From Easter onwards, things hot up making advance booking essential. In July and August don't even contemplate the coast unless you have a reservation or are prepared to pay a fortune for the few rooms still available.

Tourist offices can invariably tell you where rooms are available; some run accommodation reservation services (often called *centrale de réservation*).

Smoking

Smoking is banned in public places in France, which includes communal areas in hotels. This doesn't apply to bedrooms however, which are considered private. It is therefore up to the hotelier to decide whether they allow smoking in rooms or not. Whatever your disposition, ask for a room that caters to your preference.

Resources

» **Guide de Charme** (www.guidesdecharme.com) Hotels and B&Bs with bags of charm.

» **Gîtes de France** (p287) For authentic self-catering accommodation.

» **Gîtes Panda** (www.gites-panda.fr) Green arm of Gîtes de France; self-catering and B&Bs near nature reserves.

» **Relais & Château** (www.relaischateaux.com) and **Châteaux & Hôtels Collection** (www.chateauxhotels.com) Two umbrella organisations representing the last cry in luxury.

» **Avignon & Provence** (www.avignon-et-provence.com) Hotels, B&Bs and self-catering options.

» **Fleurs de Soleil** (www.fleursdesoleil.fr) Quality *chambres d'hôte*.

» **Bienvenue à la Ferme** (www.bienvenue-a-la-ferme.com) Farmstays.

Eat & Drink Like a Local

Food Seasons

Winter

It may be cold and grey outside but inside, Provençal winter specialities will dazzle you: feast on pungent truffles, try all 13 desserts on Christmas day and add some zest to your food with Menton's lemons.

Spring

Lamb is the traditional Easter meat across Provence; in Camargue, bull meat (stewed or cured in *saucissons*) is another spring favourite. Fill up on olive oil from the harvest just gone.

Summer

Sun-ripened fruit and vegetables are at their very best: tomatoes, peaches, cherries and melon burst with sugar and taste. Grilled meat or fish are alfresco dinner staples.

Autumn

It's vintage time; wine makers celebrate with family meals and festivals. It's chestnut harvest in Collobrières, just in time to make the *marrons glacés* (glazed chestnuts) for Christmas.

Thinking, dreaming, living food is the norm in Provence, where days are geared around satisfying a passionate appetite for dining well. Some culinary traditions are upheld everywhere: oodles of olive oil, garlic and tomatoes find their way into dozens of dishes. Yet there are regional differences, which see fishermen return with the catch of the day in seafaring Marseille; grazing bulls and paddy fields in the Camargue; lambs in the Alpilles; truffles in the Vaucluse; cheese made from cows' milk in alpine pastures; and an Italianate accent to Niçois cooking.

Ultimately, the secret of Provençal cuisine lies not in elaborate preparation techniques or sophisticated presentation, but in the use of fresh local ingredients. In Provence it is the humble rhythm and natural cycle of the land that drives what you eat and when.

Food Experiences

Meals of a Lifetime

Provence and the Côte d'Azur are undoubtedly one of the finest food destinations in the world, so here is, after much hand-wringing, our crème de la crème for an unforgettable meal.

» **Restaurant Pierre Reboul, Aix-en-Provence** Chic, modern, inventive and utterly delicious – a homage to food. (p168)

» **L'Atelier, Arles** Food magician Jean-Luc Rabanel takes you on a culinary odyssey with

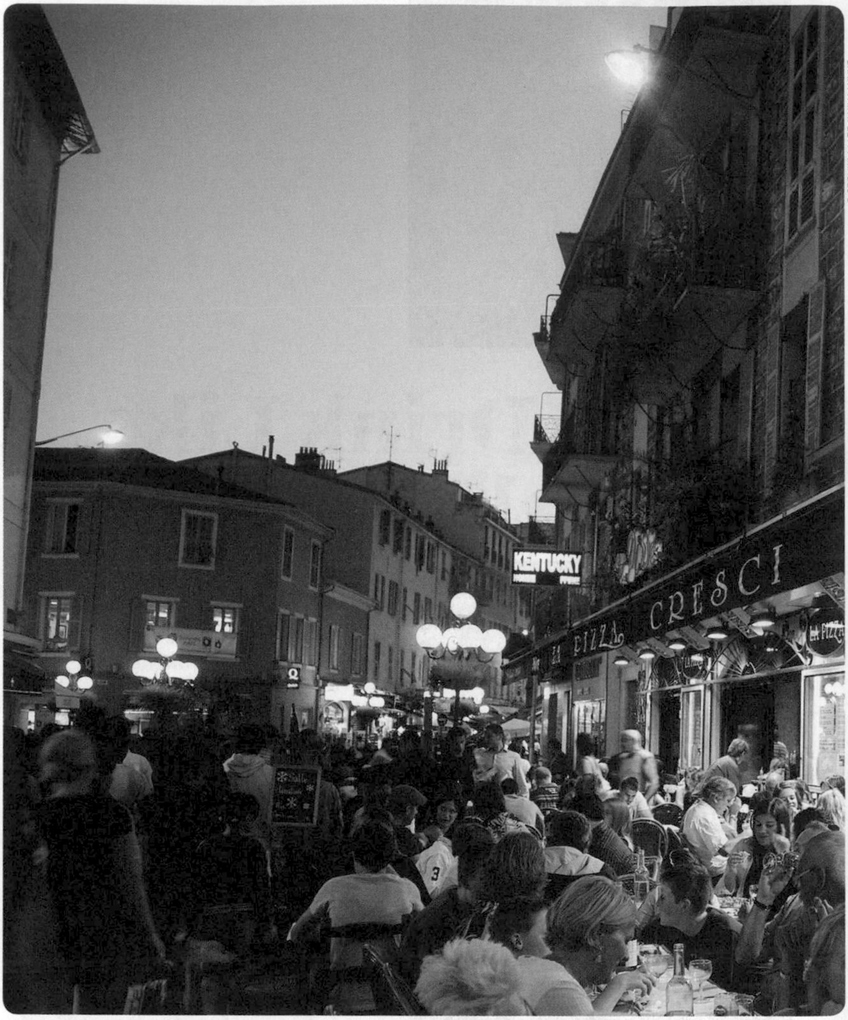

GRANT FAINT/GETTY IMAGES ©

MOIRENC CAMILLE/HEMIS.FR/GETTY IMAGES ©

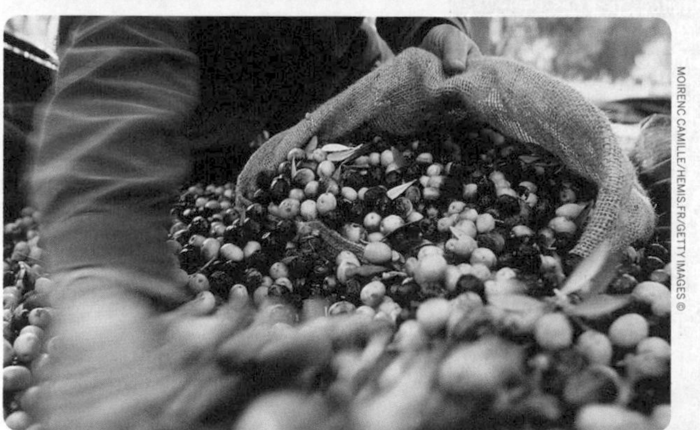

» (above) Outdoor dining, Nice
» (left) Olive harvest, Les Mées

L'APÉRO

L'apéro (short for *l'apéritif*, an alcohol drink taken before dinner) is a national pastime in France, particularly in Provence–Côte d'Azur where chilled rosé wine and croutons topped with *tapenade* (olive spread) were seemingly made to be consumed together. Other *apéro* favourites include pastis (an aniseed-flavoured alcohol), marinated olives and *socca* (a pancake made with chickpea flour and olive oil, a Nice speciality).

L'apéro is common practice amongst friends but many convivial *chambres d'hôte* that serve dinner uphold the tradition with their guests.

seven- or 13-course (nibble-sized) menus, each nibble a work of art. (p180)

» **Le Chantecler, Nice** Le Negresco's mythical restaurant, a pink antique confection with superb service and food truly worthy of its two Michelin stars. (p57)

» **Sanglier Paresseux, Caseneuve** The culinary equivalent of smart-casual, with stunning yet simple dishes and superb sunset views of the Luberon. (p233)

» **La Bastide de Moustiers, Moustiers Ste-Marie** French gastronomy heavy-weight Alain Ducasse's famed address, in the splendid settings of the Gorges du Verdon. (p249)

» **Sea Sens, Cannes** Fusion food has never looked or tasted so divine than at this rooftop bijou establishment. (p88)

» **Chez Bruno, Lorgues** Feast of black diamonds at France's most famous truffle restaurant. (p126)

Wine Tasting

No meal in Provence-Côte d'Azur would be complete without a glass of chilled rosé or aromatic red, and so a trip to a vineyard is a must. (For details on Provençal wine, their characteristics and the best places to buy them, see p283).

Wine can be bought direct from the *producteur* (wine producer) or *vignoble* (vineyard), most of whom offer *dégustation* (tasting), allowing you to sample two or three vintages with no obligation to buy. Lists of estates, *caves* (wine cellars) and cooperatives are available from tourist offices and *maisons des vins* (wine houses – generally the official representative of a vintage, for instance Côtes de Provence or Bandol).

Cook Up a Storm

You've tasted it, now do the same back home! Here are our favourite cooking courses to recreate these decadent meals.

» **Le Marmiton, Avignon** A roll-call of celebrity chefs impart their secrets on a weekly basis in the sumptuous 19th-century kitchen of this former château, now the prestigious Hôtel La Mirande. (p195)

» **L'Atelier de Cuisine Gourmande, St-Tropez** For authentic flavours and recipes, nothing beats local chef Mireille Gedda's cooking workshops. (p130)

» **Les Apprentis Gourmets, Cannes** A boutique kitchen serving express cooking courses, from 30 minutes watch-in-hand to more indulgent two-hour classes. (p89)

» **Auberge La Fenière, Cadenet** Learn the secrets of perfect puff pastry or how to have your way with asparagus at this idyllic auberge. (p237)

» **École de Dégustation, Châteauneuf-du-Pape** Not a cooking course but a wine-tasting school, the essential complement to cooking lessons. (p201)

Gourmet Shops

Whether you feel like treating yourself for your picnic or want to take fabulous foodie presents home, here are a few shops over which to salivate.

» **Joël Durand, St-Rémy de Provence** Exquisite chocolates with Provençal flavours: lavender, rosemary, violet or thyme. (p218)

» **Maison d'Olive, Bormes-les-Mimosas** Flavoured olive oils, unusual vinegars and liqueurs. (p130)

» **Place aux Huiles, Marseille** Olive oil, truffles, foie gras and retro beer La Cagole. (p160)

» **Au Bec Fin, Cogolin** Conserves of all things Provençal (from tomatoes to anchovies), perfect for picnics and souvenirs. (p123)

» **Chez Melchio, Banon** Cheese and sausage shop: picnics have never looked so good! (p245)

Goodies to Take Home

You'll be glad to hear that it's easy to take the taste of Provence home, so make sure you leave plenty of space in your suitcase. Visitors

AFFORDABLE GASTRONOMY

If you'd like to try a Michelin-starred or upmarket restaurant without breaking the bank, go for lunch. Top-end establishments invariably offer lunch menus (€30 to €50), a steal compared to à la carte evening dining.

from outside the EU, note that you may not be able to take fresh products home.

» **Olive oil** Some brands sell metal as opposed to glass bottles (lighter and unbreakable).

» **Tapenade** To recreate the perfect Provençal aperitif; sold in small glass jars.

» **Marinated olives** They don't need to be refrigerated; market stalls sell them in sturdy plastic tubs.

» **Fromage de chèvre, demi-sec or sec** Semi-dry and dry goat's cheese travel well.

» **Calissons d'Aix** Aix-en-Provence's signature cakes (hoover-packed assortments are available).

» **Wine** Buy direct from the producer for the best deals; ideal if you're driving to France, less so if you're flying (ship home instead).

Local Specialities

Many of Provence's specialities had humble beginnings: most were poor man's meals, using unwanted fish (bouillabaisse), cheap cuts of meat (daube) and dried instead of fresh fish (stockfish). But their stellar rise in the region's culinary folklore means they're now beloved traditions, so do try them out on your journey.

Bouillabaisse

King of regional dishes, bouillabaisse is a pungent yellow fish-stew, brewed by Marseillais for centuries. It requires a minimum of four types of fresh fish (favourites include scorpion fish, white scorpion fish, weever, conger eel, chapon and tub gurnard) cooked in a rockfish stock with onions, tomatoes, garlic, saffron (hence its colour), parsley, bay leaves, thyme and other herbs. Popular variations (heathen to the Marseillais!) call for lobster or potatoes.

The name bouillabaisse is derived from the French *bouillir* (to boil) and *baisser* (to lower, as in a flame), reflecting the cooking method required: bring it to the boil, let it bubble ferociously for 15 minutes, then serve it: the *bouillon* (broth) first as a soup, followed by the fish flesh, in the company of a local wine, a white Cassis or dry Bandol rosé.

Daube

The definitive recipe for this classic Provençal beef stew is as debated as that of the bouillabaisse – but then it wouldn't be Provence without a heated culinary argument!

Daube is basically beef braised in red wine, onions, celery, carrot, garlic and herbs; like all stews, it must cook slowly for several hours, and ideally, be prepared the day before it is served. Traditional accompaniments are gnocchi (potato dumplings) or boiled potatoes.

Oursinade

Oursin (sea urchin) is a delicacy that falls in the same love-it-or-hate-it sphere as oysters, which is reason enough to try it and decide which side of the fence you sit on!

Sea urchins are fished September to April; they are eaten raw, with a squeeze of fresh lemon on top, a piece of bread and a glass of chilled white Cassis. In winter, you'll see many locals in Carry-le-Rouet, Cassis or Sanary-sur-Mer enjoying an *oursinade* (a sea urchin tasting) in the port, straight from the fishermen's crates, but *oursinade* is also served in restaurants. They tend to be served like oysters by the dozen or half-dozen.

Brouillade de Truffes

Simple, timeless and delicious, *brouillade de truffes* (essentially scrambled eggs with truffle shavings) is a favourite in many a lavish three- and four-course *menu aux truffes* (truffle menu) served at several restaurants in season. Simplicity is key, allowing the palate to revel in the flavour (it's subtle) of Provence's most luxurious and elusive culinary product.

Stockfish (or Estocaficada)

The main ingredient of this Niçois dish – rehydrated dried cod – puts many people off, yet well prepared (and most restaurants that serve it are pros), it is up there with every regional speciality.

Dried cod is soaked in running water for several days, then stewed with onions, garlic, tomatoes, peppers, potatoes and fresh herbs (fennel, thyme and parsley). Olives are added towards the end of the cooking and the dish is normally served piping hot, splashed with a glug of olive oil. Nothing like it on a cold winter day!

Niçois Nibbles

Perfect for filling a hungry moment coming from the beach (or any time of day) are Nice's many snacks. Must-haves for every visiting palate include:

» **Socca** A savoury, griddle-fried pancake made from chickpea flour and olive oil, sprinkled with a liberal dose of black pepper.

» **Petits farcis** Vegetables (tomatoes, onions, courgettes, courgette flowers) filled with a stuffing made of meat, cheese, bread crumbs, egg yolk and herbs.

» **Pissaladière** A traditional onion tart topped with black olives and anchovies.

» **Salade niçoise** A green salad with boiled egg, tuna and anchovy.

» **Beignets** Fritters (aubergine and scampi in particular).

Practicalities

When to Eat

» Breakfast isn't the French's forte: most working people grab a coffee and some toast or cereal on their way out. *Viennoiseries* (croissant, *pain au chocolat* etc) tend to be weekend treats. Luckily for visitors, most hotels put on a spread including sweet and savoury treats (fruit, croissants, eggs, ham, cheese etc), usually for a cost (€8 to €20).

» Lunch is generally between 12.30pm and 2pm; long weekend lunches can stretch well into the afternoon. Even at work, many people tend to take at least an hour for lunch.

» Although most restaurants open around 7pm, diners generally start trickling in around 8pm. Few establishments have more than one seating, allowing ample time to linger over coffee and *digestif* (post-dinner drink).

Where to Eat

Dining *à la provençal* can mean spending anything from lunch in a village bistro with no tablecloths to dining in a star-studded gastronomic temple. Irrespective of price, a *carte* (menu) is usually pinned up outside, allowing for a price and dish check.

It is generally advisable to book for evening and weekend meals in restaurants and *auberges*, particularly if you'd like a table *en terrasse* (outside) – a must do in Provence-Côte d'Azur between April and October.

» **Auberge** Country inn serving traditional country fare, often in rural areas. Some also offer rooms.

» **Bistro** (also spelled *bistrot*) Anything from an informal bar serving light meals to a fully-fledged restaurant.

» **Brasserie** Very much like a cafe, except that it serves full meals (generally non-stop from 11am to 11pm) as well as drinks and coffee.

» **Cafe** Serves basic food (cold and toasted sandwiches), coffees and drinks.

» **Restaurant** Most serve lunch and dinner five or six days a week. For standard opening hours, see p287.

Navigating Menus

The length of a restaurant's menu (*la carte*) varies widely, from just a few rotating dishes to several pages of choice.

Set two- or three-course menus (known as *menu*) are commonplace, particularly for lunch; they generally offer less choice than ordering à la carte but tend to be cheaper.

Customs & Etiquette

» Forget balancing your bread on your main-course plate; crumbs on the table are fine.

» Using the same knife and fork for your starter and main is commonplace in many informal restaurants.

» *Santé* is the toast for alcoholic drinks; *bon appétit* is what you say before tucking in.

» The French generally end their meal with a short, sharp espresso coffee.

» Splitting the bill is seen as crass – except amongst young people.

» Service is generally included so leaving a tip is optional.

Outdoor Inspiration

The Best...

Snorkelling

Say hello to the Côte d'Azur's marine residents at Domaine du Rayol (p129).

Canyoning

Jump, slide and swim your way down the stunning Gorges du Verdon (p246).

Skiing

One of Provence–Côte d'Azur's winter joys, don your skis – or your snow shoes – to explore the Mercantour (p252).

Cycling

It is hard work but there is no better way to discover the sublime Dentelles de Montmirail (p206) and the great bulk of Mont Ventoux (p208).

Sea-kayaking

Keen to see the secluded coves of the Calanques? This is the way to do it! (p161)

Horse-riding

Saddle up on one of Camargue's sturdy white horses and venture out into this marshland (p181).

With its varied landscapes – alpine mountains and cavernous gorges, flamingo-pink wetlands, and a world-famous coastline of sparkling white sand and turquoise water – Provence has an outdoor activity to match every mood, moment and energy level.

Trail Finder

There are numerous resources to help you plan a day in the great outdoors. Here is a selection of the very best – note that many are in French only.

» Fédération Française de Randonnée Pédestre (p289) has the most comprehensive walking guides; some are now available as ebooks.

» The excellent **Guides RandOxygène** (www.randoxygene.org), published by the Alpes-Maritimes *département*, include three walking guides, as well as mountain-biking, canyoning and snow-shoe guides detailing itineraries of varying difficulty. Tourist offices stock the paper guides; electronic versions are available on the website.

» Non-French speakers will love *Walker's Provence in a Box* by Adrian Woodford, a collection of 35 illustrated walking itineraries, each printed on a card and presented in a box.

» Download cycling, mountain-biking or walking itineraries from **Escapado** (www.escapado.fr); it is also available as an app.

» The Var *département* (www.var.fr) publishes an excellent cycling topoguide for the St-Tropez

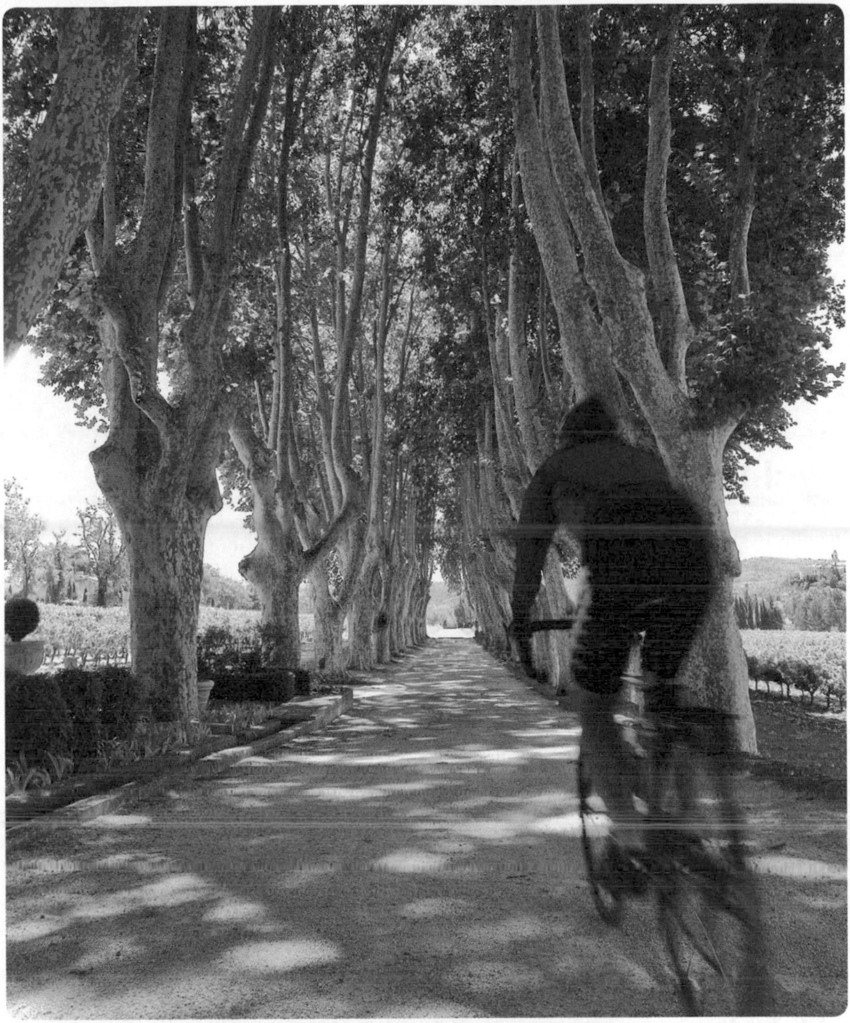

DAVID EPPERSON/GETTY IMAGES ©

DAVID C TOMLINSON/GETTY IMAGES ©

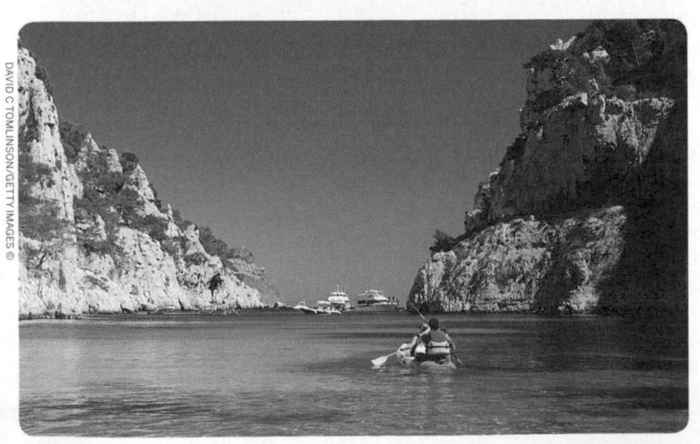

» (above) Cycling in the Provençal countryside
» (left) Kayaking the waters of Calanque d'En-Vau (p162)

to Toulon area containing 22 detailed itineraries, which you can download.

» **IGN** (www.ign.fr) is France's official mapping body and has a range of topographical maps.

Walking

The region is criss-crossed by a plethora of *sentiers balisés* (marked walking paths).

Between 1 July and 15 September paths in heavily forested areas are closed due to the high risk of forest fire. Always check with the local tourist office before setting off.

Tourist offices are also a good port of call for guided nature walks.

Cycling

With near-endless sunshine and some killing hills to climb, not to mention storybook scenery en route, Provence is ideal two-wheeling territory. Some walking trails are open to mountain bikes, and those keen to tackle the region's roughest mountain terrain should hightail it to Haute-Provence.

Cycling itineraries of various lengths and difficulties can be picked up at rental outfits and tourist offices.

Road and mountain bikes can be hired for around €15 a day including helmet, puncture-repair kit and suggested itineraries. Children's bikes (around €12 per day) and toddler seats (around €5 per day) are also widely available. Some outlets deliver to your door for free.

Water Sports

The Sea

With such a beautiful coastline, it's no surprise there is so much to do on the water. In summer, you'll find the usual jet skiing, waterskiing and wakeboarding (€30 to €50) rides at a number of beaches.

More mellow are the year-round sea kayaking (€35) forays around the turquoise rocky coves of the Calanques near Marseille.

Snorkelling and diving are popular, too. Underwater nature trails and guided tours (€30) make snorkelling a real discovery. Note, however, that the sea is only really warm enough to snorkel from June to October, unless you wear a wetsuit.

WEATHER CHECK

Before you set off, check the weather on **Météo France** (www.meteofrance.com). It has dedicated marine, snow and mountain forecasts.

Divers will love the diversity of dive sites off French coastal waters, including numerous shipwrecks. Most dive clubs offer courses (€300 to €500) as well as single dives (€50) and rental equipment.

Rivers & White Water

Canoeing is a tranquil way to discover the bucolic waterways of Provence. It is particularly popular around the Camargue and in the Vaucluse.

For an adrenalin rush, nothing beats the green waters of Gorges du Verdon or the mountain rivers of Haute-Provence for canyoning, floating, rafting and white-water kayaking. Allow €35/60 for a half/full day.

Snow Activities

The few ski resorts in Haute-Provence are refreshingly low-key. Slopes are best suited to beginner and intermediate skiers and costs are lower than in the Northern Alps.

Resorts include the lovely Pra Loup (straddled between 1500m and 1600m) and the concrete-block Isola 2000 (2450m), with direct bus services to Nice (just €2 return).

They offer the usual skiing and snow boarding but snow shoeing is increasingly popular too, notably amongst smaller (and lower altitude) resorts where you can track wildlife in snow-covered forests.

The ski season runs from December to March/April (depending on the snow conditions). Buying a package is the cheapest way to ski and/or snow board. Otherwise allow €25 to €30 for a daily lift pass, and about the same again for equipment rental.

Mountain Biking

Keen to make the best of their ski lifts and cable cars in summer, ski resorts have developed a brilliant mountain-biking infrastructure, whereby you and your bike are ferried up the mountain so that you can enjoy two hours of uninterrupted, thrilling descent.

Travel with Children

Best Regions for Kids

Arles & the Camargue

Quiet roads, bountiful nature, long beaches and activities-galore make Camargue one of the easiest places to visit *en famille*. Add evocative Roman ruins in Arles and you have the perfect holiday.

Nice, Monaco & Menton

Riviera glamour isn't just for grown-ups: skate or scooter along Nice's promenade des Anglais; hop on a boat for a scenic cruise or a dolphin excursion; and in Monaco, watch the change of the guard, ogle at the yachts and slurp on milkshakes at Stars 'n' Bars.

Haute-Provence

White-water activities in the Verdon, snow fun in the mountains, dinosaurs in Digne and the Vallée des Merveilles – nature is Haute-Provence's drawcard.

St-Tropez to Toulon

Buckets and spades, beach combing, swimming, snorkelling – it's all about the sea here. Too cold to swim? No problem: cycle in car-free Île de Porquerolles or pick chestnuts in Collobrières.

Provence & the Côte d'Azur for Kids

Provence–Côte d'Azur is a wonderful place to travel with children of all ages: buckets, spades and plenty of swimming are part and parcel of coastal travel but there is so much more to do than this well-rehearsed formula: cycling through lavender fields, trailing Romans, fossil-hunting, meeting local producers, trying out new ice-cream flavours and observing wildlife are just some of the highlights to try during your stay.

The French are big on family and the infrastructure is often excellent, with many dedicated children's activities. Note that children under four get free train travel.

Museums & Activities

Many museums and monuments are free for children: there is no rule about the age under which kids get free admission though – sometimes it's six, sometimes 12 or 18.

Food & Drink

Eating out *en famille* is commonplace, but note that it is frowned upon for children to run wild. If your children are used to eating lunch before 12.30pm or dinner before 7.30pm, brasseries, which serve food continuously, are a better bet than restaurants.

Menu enfant (fixed children's menus) are common, although they often cruelly lack imagination: *steak hâché-frites* (bun-less beef burger and fries) and spaghetti Bolognese

BREASTFEEDING

For all their topless sunbathing, the French are surprisingly uneasy about breastfeeding in public; consider using a shawl or a blanket.

are staples. Don't be shy about ordering a starter or a half-portion of a main, most restaurants will happily oblige.

Drinks can be pricey in restaurants (€5 for a soda is not unusual); save money by ordering *une carafe d'eau* (a jug of tap water) or *un sirop* (syrup; €2 at most), which is diluted with water.

Baby requirements are easily met. The choice of infant formula, soy and cow's milk, jarred baby food and so on is as good in France as it is in other developed countries.

Children's Highlights

Rainy Days

» Go Roman at Ludo, Pont du Gard (p222)

» Watch sharks and fish at Musée Océanographique de Monaco (p65)

» Test your sense of smell at Musée International de la Parfumerie (p101)

» Learn about space at Centre d'Astronomie (p244)

Animal Lovers

» See wolves at Alpha (p256)

» Meet a goat cheese producer – and the goats! – at La Ferme des Courmettes (p100)

» Go horse riding and birdwatching in the Camargue (p182)

» Snorkelling in Port-Cros (p134), Domaine du Rayol (p129) or Corniche de l'Estérel (p106)

Fun Times

» Clowns and acrobats at the Festival International du Cirque (p70)

» Burgers, shakes, arcade games and celebrity spotting at Stars 'n' Bars (p73) in Monaco

» Re-live medieval battles during demonstrations at Château des Baux (p219)

» Tackle the adventure course at Colorado Aventures (p228)

Planning

When to Go

Provence–Côte d'Azur is an easy destination year-round for families. The sea is off-limits from October to May but the warm Riviera sun will give you plenty more to do. Snow activities in Haute-Provence (easily accessible from Nice) are another winter favourite for kids and teenagers. And there is plenty to keep the family entertained on rainy days, from museums to cinemas.

Be mindful of the heat in summer.

Accommodation

Many hotels cater well to families. Babies and toddlers are generally accommodated for with an extra (free) bed in the parents' room. For kids, options include quadruple or family rooms, suites, or *chambres communicantes* (communicating rooms).

Chambres d'hôte are a great option; many offer dinner on the premises, which takes care of babysitting arrangements: just bring a baby-monitor to wine and dine in at peace.

Hostels are often a great bet for families keen to watch the pennies, with excellent half-board deals. Some upmarket establishments have kitchenettes; top-end hotels can also arrange baby-sitting services.

Camping is popular too. Book ahead as tent pitches and mobile homes get snapped up fast.

What to Pack

Don't panic if you forget something: you will find everything you need in French shops and supermarkets.

Babies & Toddlers

» A carry sling: strollers are a pain on cobbled lanes.

» A portable changing mat (changing facilities are a rarity)

» A screw-on seat for toddlers (restaurants don't always have high chairs)

» Inflatable armbands for the sea or pool

» Baby sunscreen lotion and mosquito repellent

Six to 12 Years

» Binoculars to zoom in on wildlife and panoramas

» Activity books, sketchpad and travel journal

» A plastic ball for the park or pool

regions at a glance

Provence and the Côte d'Azur pack in the most incredible diversity of sights, landscapes and activities.

The coast tends to be relatively built up, with heavenly exceptions such as Camargue, the Calanques and the unspoilt Îles d'Hyères. To get away from the crowds, head inland to the sparsely populated Haute-Provence, the majestic southern Alps, the vineyards of the Var or the storybook Luberon.

Back in town, Nice is utterly delightful, its old town teeming with life and the Mediterranean lapping the shores of its promenade, whereas Marseille, France's second biggest city, blends urban grit with culture on the rise.

And then there is Monaco, a law unto itself with its skyscrapers, tax haven residents, scandal-prone royal family and hedonist fun.

Nice, Monaco & Menton

Panoramas ✓✓✓
Gardens ✓✓✓
Architecture ✓✓

Panoramas
The coast rises abruptly from the sea along the Riviera, reaching 800m in places with mind-bending views along the way. Drive the Grande Corniche or visit Ste-Agnès or Èze for knock-out vistas.

Gardens
With its mild sunny climate, the Côte d'Azur has always been a gardener's heaven. Cue the region's many exotic, botanical and themed gardens, which reach their prime in spring.

Belle Époque legacy
The French Riviera was all the rage in the 19th century and we can thank wintering royals and high society divas for their legacy: meringue-like buildings, operas, casinos, and promenades.

p46

Cannes & Around

Art ✓✓✓
Perfumeries ✓✓
Walks ✓✓✓

20th-Century Art
Few other places have played host to so many seminal artists: Chagall, Matisse, Picasso, Renoir and Léger all spent much time here, and left plenty behind. Trail their legacy.

Perfumeries
From flower fields to factory, follow the making of a perfume around Grasse. The city is the world's leading perfumery hub and it has thrown its doors wide open to visitors.

Scenic Walks
From long coastal walks to ancient mule paths in the back country and breathtaking panoramas, make sure you don your boots to discover the area's most scenic spots.

p80

St-Tropez to Toulon

Wine ✓✓✓
Beaches ✓✓✓
Clubbing ✓✓

Wine

This is the home of Provence's signature rosé wines, so spare an afternoon to visit the vineyards of Côtes de Provence, Bandol or Correns' organic wine makers.

Beaches

If Côte d'Azur conjures up images of azure seas with golden sand fringed by pines and *maquis*, you've come to the right place. Take your pick from remote island beaches, nudist heavens and celebrity spots.

Clubbing

Nowhere parties quite as hard as St-Tropez in the summer. Dress to impress and bring plenty of cash to follow in the dance moves of BB, Kate Moss, Paris Hilton and more.

p110

Marseille to Aix-en-Provence

Culture ✓✓✓
Eating Out ✓✓✓
Outdoors ✓✓

Museums & Galleries

With its status as European Capital of Culture in 2013, Marseille has been buzzing with artistic activity, a legacy lasting well beyond its year of reign.

Eating Out

From gastronomic to traditional, all-out culinary magic to simple, straight-from-the-boat-to-your-plate grilled fish, Marseille and Aix-en-Provence have it.

Great Outdoors

The rugged, mineral beauty of the Massif de la Ste-Baume and the Calanques has captivated painters and writers; follow in their footsteps with a walk, a paddle or a long drive.

p140

Arles & the Camargue

Food ✓✓✓
Nature ✓✓
History ✓✓✓

Food

Camargue's specialities – its red rice, bull meat and seafood – are reminiscent of Spain. Try them, as well as Modern French cuisine, in one of the area's mighty fine restaurants.

Birdwatching

More than 500 species of birds regularly visit the Camargue, chief amongst them the colourful flocks of pink flamingoes. The mosquitoes seem just as abundant as the birds so pack repellent along with your binoculars!

Roman Sites

Arles flourished under Julius Ceasar and the town's past prosperity is still awe-inspiring: amphitheatre, theatre, necropolis and a leading mosaic renovation centre.

p172

Avignon & Around

History ✓✓✓
Wine ✓✓✓
Outdoors ✓✓✓

History

The Romans and the popes all decided to call the area home: find out why at Nîmes' phenomenal Roman heritage, the Pont du Gard and Avignon's imposing Palais des Papes.

Wine Tasting

With three of Provence's most famous wines – reds Châteauneuf-du-Pape and Gigondas, and Muscat Beaumes-de-Venise – the Avignon region is a must for wine connoisseurs.

Outdoors

Ascend giant Mont Ventoux, hike the stunning Dentelles de Montmirail, paddle below Pont du Guard or along the glassy Sorgue and breathe Provence's fresh air.

p187

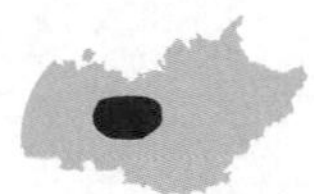

Hill Towns of the Luberon

Villages ✓✓✓
Cycling ✓✓✓
History ✓✓

Villages

Gordes, Ménerbes, Lacoste, Bonnieux, this is the Provence of dreams. There are 101 ways to enjoy these stunning villages: stroll, cycle, attend the weekly market or stop for a long lunch.

Cycling

With its rolling hills, postcard landscapes and light traffic, the Luberon is prime cycling territory. And happily, there is plenty of help out there to facilitate your journey, from itineraries to luggage-carrying services.

History

Long a Protestant stronghold in a Catholic country, the Luberon is steeped in religious history, from tragic massacres to the construction of glorious churches and *abbayes*.

p223

Haute-Provence & the Southern Alps

Activities ✓✓✓
Scenery ✓✓✓
Wildlife ✓✓

Activities

Adrenalin junkies, Haute-Provence is for you: you can go rafting, canyoning, skydiving, bungee-jumping, mountain biking, cycling, paragliding and climbing. Hiking, in comparison, will look meek, but make no mistake: trekking here is arduous.

Scenery

From Europe's deepest canyons to some of its highest peaks, Haute-Provence's Alpine scenery is majestic and unspoilt. Even the night sky will bowl you over with its incredible clarity.

Wildlife

The grey wolf made a much publicised comeback to the Mercantour from Italy in the 1990s but as well as wolves, you could see vultures, eagles, mountain ibexes and cute marmots.

p239

Every listing is recommended by our authors, and their favourite places are listed first

Look out for these icons:

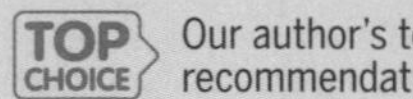

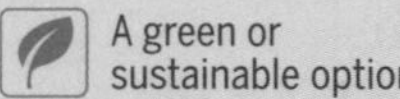

FREE No payment required

See the Index for a full list of destinations covered in this book.

On the Road

Nice, Monaco & Menton

Includes »

Best Places to Eat

» Le Bistrot d'Antoine (p56)
» La Montgolfière (p72)
» Pasta & Basta (p79)
» Luna Rossa (p57)
» Café de la Fontaine (p64)

Best Places to Stay

» Château Eza (p64)
» Hôtel La Pérouse (p55)
» Hôtel Victoria (p75)
» Nice Garden Hôtel (p56)
» Nice Pebbles (p55)

Why Go?

There may only be 30km between Nice and Menton, but what kilometres! Nice, with its atmospheric old town, great architectural heritage (from baroque to belle époque), fantastic nightlife and excellent restaurants is everyone's favourite city. As you head east, the Grande and Moyenne Corniches (coastal roads) will wow you with their mesmerising views of the Mediterranean, while the lower Corniche snakes along the shores from pretty beach to belle époque folly. Monaco will elicit mixed reactions: the concrete jungle won't be for everyone but this unique country, complete with scandal-prone monarchy, throngs of VIPs and casino glamour, endlessly fascinates: come and form your own opinion! And if it makes you run for the hills, what better place than the Arrière-Pays Niçois, an area of stark beauty so isolated that even the Niçois come here for mini-breaks.

Driving Distances (km)

	Beaulieu-sur-Mer	Èze	La Turbie	Menton	Monaco	Nice
Èze	5					
La Turbie	12	7				
Menton	19	19	15			
Monaco	11	10	8	10		
Nice	10	15	20	30	21	
Roquebrune-Cap-Martin	18	16	11	4	9	25

Getting Around

There aren't many places in this area that you can't access by public transport. The Arrière-Pays Niçois, the Grande Corniche and the villages around Menton are the only places where you'll really need a car; elsewhere, you should make the best of the fantastic - and very cheap - trains and buses. They also run at night, so you'll be able to keep the wine flowing!

THREE PERFECT DAYS

Day 1: Nice, Belle of the Côte d'Azur

Wake up to Vieux Nice's vibrant market scene (p50). Enjoy the buzz of the market from a cafe terrace on cours Saleya and get some picnic supplies from the groaning stalls. Head to the Parc du Château (p50) to feast on views and delicacies. In the afternoon, arty types shouldn't miss Nice's Musée Matisse (p51) or the Musée d'Art Moderne et d'Art Contemporain (p51). For something more active, rent out skates and zoom along the Promenade des Anglais (p51).

Day 2: Scenic Riviera

Make your way to Èze, the coast's most stunning perched village. Wander about Jardin d'Èze (p63) for breathtaking views of the coast, and lunch at Château Eza (p64) to revel in this exceptional panorama in style. Head back down to the coast and spend the afternoon at the eccentric Villa Ephrussi de Rothschild (p63) or admiring Jean Cocteau's frescoes at Villa Santo Sospir (p62) in St-Jean-Cap Ferrat.

Day 3: Hit Monaco

Start with a visit the Jardin Exotique (p70), from where there are stupendous views of the principality. Lunch at La Montgolfière (p72) before exploring Le Rocher (p65) for the afternoon. A couple of hours should do justice to Monaco's outstanding Musée Océanographique (p65). Start your evening at the Brasserie de Monaco (p72) and finish the day with a gamble at the casino (p73).

Advance Planning

» **Accommodation** Nice is a great place to base yourself to explore this part of the world. It has good nightlife and excellent transport to all places along the coast (even at night).

» **Monaco Grand Prix** Every hotel within a 50km radius of Monaco gets booked up months in advance and prices go up tenfold; if you're attending, book as soon as you have tickets.

» **Tours & Courses** These rarely run every day so make sure you check exact dates to avoid disappointment.

DON'T MISS

Nice and Menton's mineral *arrière-pays* (hinterland) is incredibly unspoilt and scenic, so make sure you leave the coast's razzmatazz one day and explore this unique hinterland.

Best Guided Tours

» Villa Santo Sospir (p62)

» Cabanon Le Corbusier (p74)

» Affrètement Maritime Villefranchois (p62)

» Nice Guided Walking Tours (p55)

Best Gardens

» Jardin d'Èze (p63)

» Jardin de la Serre de la Madone (p77)

» Villa Ephrussi de Rothschild (p63)

» Parc du Château (p50)

Resources

» **Guides RandOxygène** (www.randoxygene.org) Essential for anyone who loves walking. Also available in paperback in tourist offices across the region.

» **French Riviera Tourism** (www.frenchriviera-tourism.com) Advice and events schedule across the region.

» **Visit Monaco** (www.visitmonaco.com) Monaco's official website.

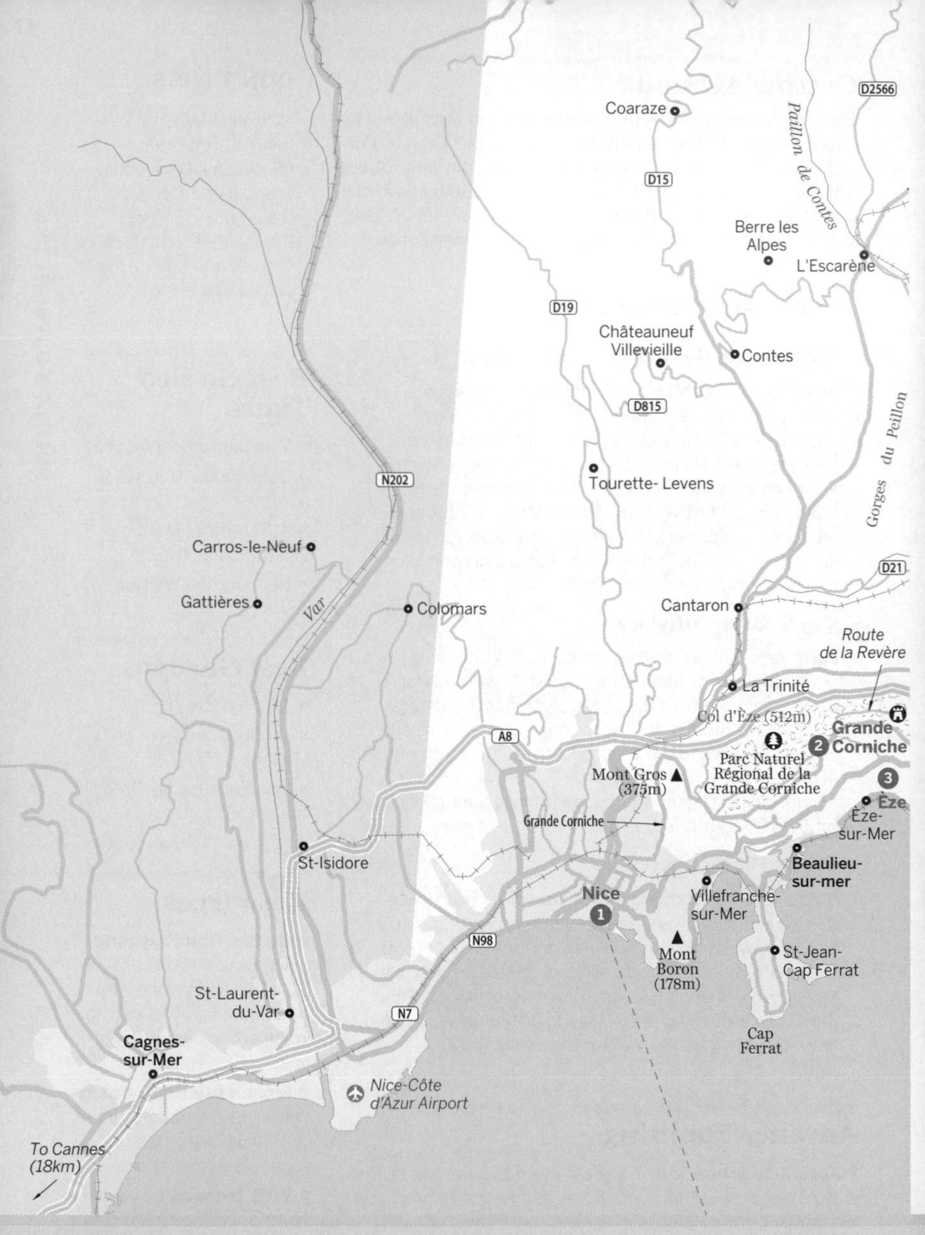

Nice, Monaco & Menton Highlights

1. Revel in **Vieux Nice**'s (p50) lively shopping streets and brilliant nightlife
2. Take a scenic drive along the **Grande Corniche** (p64) for jaw-dropping views of the Med
3. Enjoy a magical aperitif, meal or night at the exceptional **Château Eza** (p64) in Èze
4. Pop over to Italy for the day, filling up on fashion bargains and lunching on delicious pasta in **Ventimiglia** (p79)
5. Attend one of **Monaco's** (p65) great sporting events – circus, tennis or Formula One

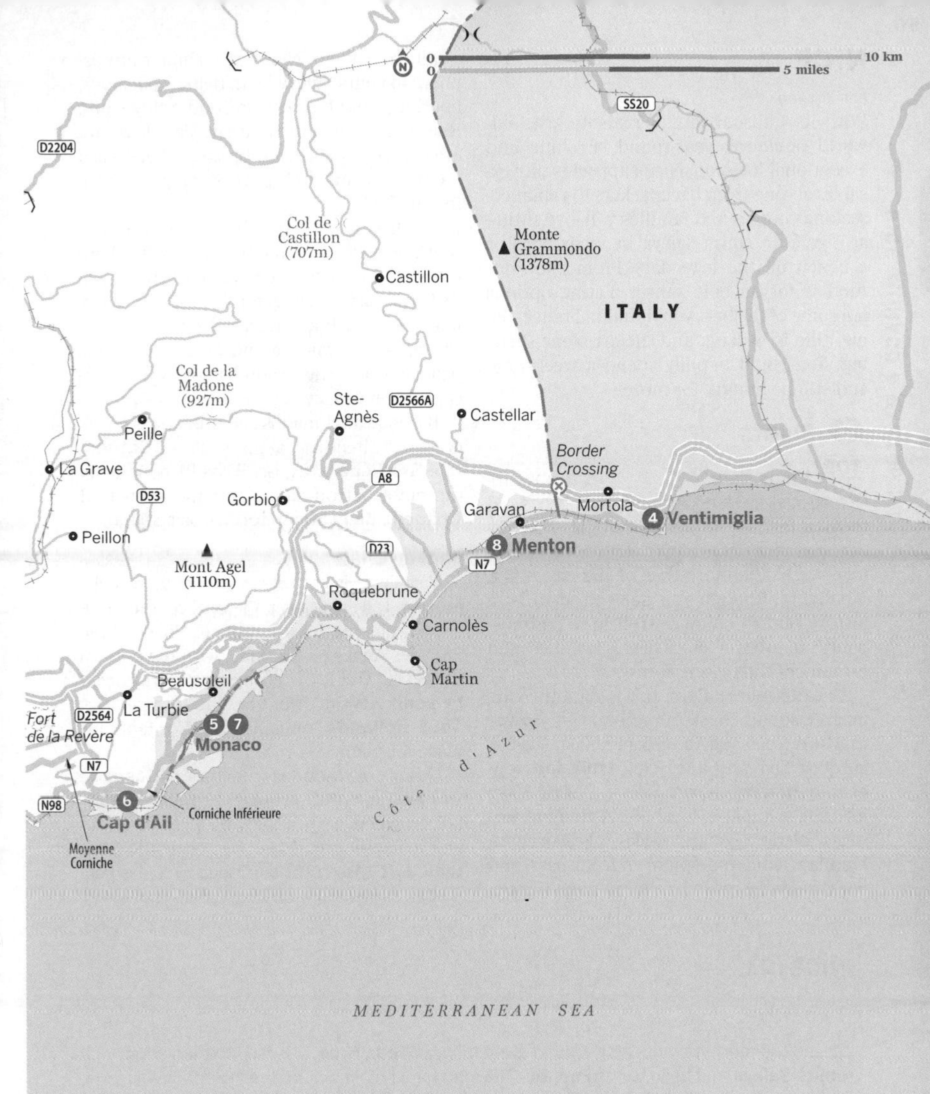

6 Walk from **Cap d'Ail** (p75) to Menton along the shores of the brilliantly blue Mediterranean

7 Try your luck at Monaco's opulent **casino** (p73)

8 Discover Cocteau's genius at Menton's new **Musée Jean Cocteau Collection Séverin Wunderman** (p76)

NICE

POP 344,460

With its unusual mix of real-city grit, old-world opulence, year-round sunshine and exceptional location, Nice's appeal is universal. Everyone from backpackers to romance-seeking couples and families will love sitting at a cafe on cours Saleya in Vieux Nice or a bench on the legendary Promenade des Anglais for an epic sunset. Eating options are some of the best you'll find in France, the nightlife is buzzing and the art scene thriving. You could happily spend a week here and still be hungry for more.

Sights

TOP CHOICE Vieux Nice HISTORIC QUARTER

(food markets 6am-1.30pm Tue-Sun) Nice's old town, a mellow rabbit warren, has scarcely changed since the 1700s. Retracing its history – and therefore that of the city – is a highlight, although you don't need to be a history buff to enjoy a stroll in this atmospheric quarter. Vieux Nice is as alive and prominent today as it ever was.

Cue the cours Saleya: this joyous, thriving market square hosts a well-known **flower market** (cours Saleya; 6am-5.30pm Tue-Sat, to 1.30pm Sun) and a thriving **fruit and vegetable market** (Cours Saleya; 6am-1.30pm Tue-Sun), a staple of local life. A **flea market** (cours Saleya; 8am-5pm Mon) takes over on Mondays, and the spillover from bars and restaurants seems to be a permanent fixture.

Much of Vieux Nice has a similar atmosphere to cours Saleya, with delis, food shops, boutiques and bars crammed into tiny lanes. Rue de la Boucherie and rue Pairolière are are excellent for food shopping. There's also a daily **fish market** (place St-François; 6am-1pm Tue-Sun).

Much harder to spot because of the narrow lane it sits on is the baroque **Palais Lascaris** (15 rue Droite; guided visit €3; 10am-6pm Wed-Mon, guided tour 3pm Fri), a 17th-century mansion housing a frescoed orgy of Flemish tapestries, faience and gloomy religious paintings. On the ground floor is an 18th-century pharmacy.

Baroque aficionados shouldn't miss Nice's other architectural gems such as **Cathédrale Ste-Réparate** (place Rossetti), honouring the city's patron saint, and the exuberant **Chapelle de la Miséricorde** (cours Saleya).

Parc du Château GARDEN

(8am-6pm winter, to 8pm summer) On a rocky outcrop towering over Vieux Nice, this park offers a cinematic panorama of Nice and the Baie des Anges on one side, with the port on the other. The 12th-century castle was razed by Louis XIV in 1706; only the 16th-century **Tour Bellanda** remains. It is a fabulous place for picnics.

Other attractions include **Cascade Donjon**, an 18th-century artificial waterfall crowned with a viewing platform, and kids' playgrounds. To get here, ride the **Château Lift** (Ascenseur du Château; rue des Ponchettes; single/return €1/1.30; 9am-6pm winter,

NICE IN...

Two Days

Spend the morning mooching around atmospheric **Vieux Nice**. Browse the market on **cours Saleya** and head to the **Parc du Château** for a picnic. Spend the afternoon on the **promenade des Anglais**, either at the beach or skating around. Settle down for dinner at the **Bistrot d'Antoine**. The following day, trace Matisse's artistic evolution at the **Musée Matisse**. Grab some Nice-style tapas at **Chez René Socca** for lunch before immersing yourself in Nice's belle époque history at the beautiful **Musée Masséna**. Finish your day with a long aperitif at **Les Distilleries Idéales** and a flamboyant dinner of Italian fare at **Luna Rossa**.

Four Days

Head to **Èze** for extraordinary views of the Riviera. Walk down **chemin de Nietzsche** to Èze-sur-Mer and catch the train to **Monaco** for a punt at the **Casino de Monte Carlo**, a tour of the aquarium at the **Musée Océanographique de Monaco** and a taste of the principality's culinary delights. On the fourth day, cruise the mighty heights of the **Grande Corniche**. Stop for lunch at **Café de la Fontaine** in La Turbie and spend the afternoon in **Roquebrune-Cap-Martin** or at the **Musée Cocteau** in Menton.

to 8pm summer) from beneath Tour Bellanda, or hike up the staircases on montée Lesage or the eastern end of rue Rossetti in Vieux Nice. From the port, follow montée Montfort.

Promenade des Anglais ARCHITECTURE
Palm-lined promenade des Anglais, paid for by Nice's English colony in 1822, is a fine stage for a stroll. It's particularly atmospheric in the evening, with Niçois milling about and epic sunsets over the sea. Don't miss the magnificent facade of **Hôtel Negresco**, built in 1912 for Romanian innkeeper Henri Negresco, or art deco Palais de la Méditerranée (p56), saved from demolition in the 1980s and now part of a four-star palace.

The promenade follows the whole Baie des Anges (4km) and has a cycle and skating lane. For a fantastic family outing, rent skates or scooters at **Roller Station** (www.roller-station.fr; 49 quai des États-Unis; ⏲10am-7pm) and whizz along the Prom. You'll need some ID as a deposit. Rentals include protective gear (helmet and pads).

FREE **Musée Matisse** GALLERY
(www.musee-matisse-nice.org; 164 av des Arènes de Cimiez; ⏲10am-6pm Wed-Mon) Located about 2km north of the centre, in the leafy quarter of Cimiez, the Musée Matisse houses a fascinating assortment of works by Matisse, documenting the artist's stylistic evolution. Its permanent collection is displayed in a red-ochre 17th-century Genoese villa overlooking an olive-tree-studded park. Temporary exhibitions are hosted in the futuristic basement building. Sadly, all explanations are in French only.

Matisse lived nearby in the 1940s, in the monumental **Régina** (71 bd de Cimiez) building. Originally Queen Victoria's wintering palace, it had been converted and Matisse had two apartments that he used as his home and studio. He died there in 1954 and is now buried at the cemetery of the **Monastère de Cimiez** (Place du Monastère; ⏲8.30am-12.30pm & 2.30-6.30pm), across the park from the museum.

Musée National Marc Chagall GALLERY
(www.musee-chagall.fr; 4 av Dr Ménard; adult/child €7.50/5.50; ⏲10am-5pm Wed-Mon Oct-Jun, to 6pm Jul-Sep) This small museum houses the largest public collection of works by Belarusian painter Marc Chagall (1887–1985). The main hall contains 12 huge interpretations (1954–67) of stories from Genesis and Exodus. In an antechamber, an unusual mosaic of Elijah in his fiery chariot, surrounded by signs of the zodiac, is viewed through a plate-glass window and reflected in a small pond.

The excellent audioguide is available in English (you will need ID as deposit). Smartphone users can also download the commentary as an app. It takes about 20 minutes to walk to the museum from the city centre (signposted from av de l'Olivetto).

SIGHT SAVINGS

The **French Riviera Pass** (www.frenchrivierapass.com) includes access to a number of sights and costs €26/38/56 for a one-/two-/three-day pass.

Sights included are, in Nice, the Musée Chagall, Nice Le Grand Tour bus and walking guided tours; along the coast, the Musée Renoir in Cagnes, the Musée National Fernand Léger in Biot, the Jardin d'Èze, and the Jardin Exotique and Musée Océanographique in Monaco. It is available online or at the Nice tourist office.

FREE **Musée Masséna** MUSEUM
(65 rue de France; ⏲10am-6pm Wed-Mon) The beautiful Musée Masséna, housed in a marvellous Italianate neoclassical villa (1898), retraces Nice and the Riviera's history from the late 18th century to WWII. It's a fascinating journey, with a roll call of monarchs, a succession of nationalities (British, Russians, Americans), the advent of tourism, the prominence of the carnival and much more.

History is told through an excellent mix of furniture, objects, art deco posters, early photographs, paintings and the lovely setting (note however that captions are in French only). The city of Nice still uses the ground-floor rooms for official occasions so it can sometimes close at short notice.

FREE **Musée d'Art Moderne et d'Art Contemporain** GALLERY
(Mamac; www.mamac-nice.org; Promenade des Arts; ⏲10am-6pm Tue-Sun) European and American avant-garde works from the 1950s to the present are the focus of this museum. Highlights include many works by Nice's New Realists, Christo, César, Arman, Yves Klein and Niki de Saint-Phalle. The building's rooftop

Nice

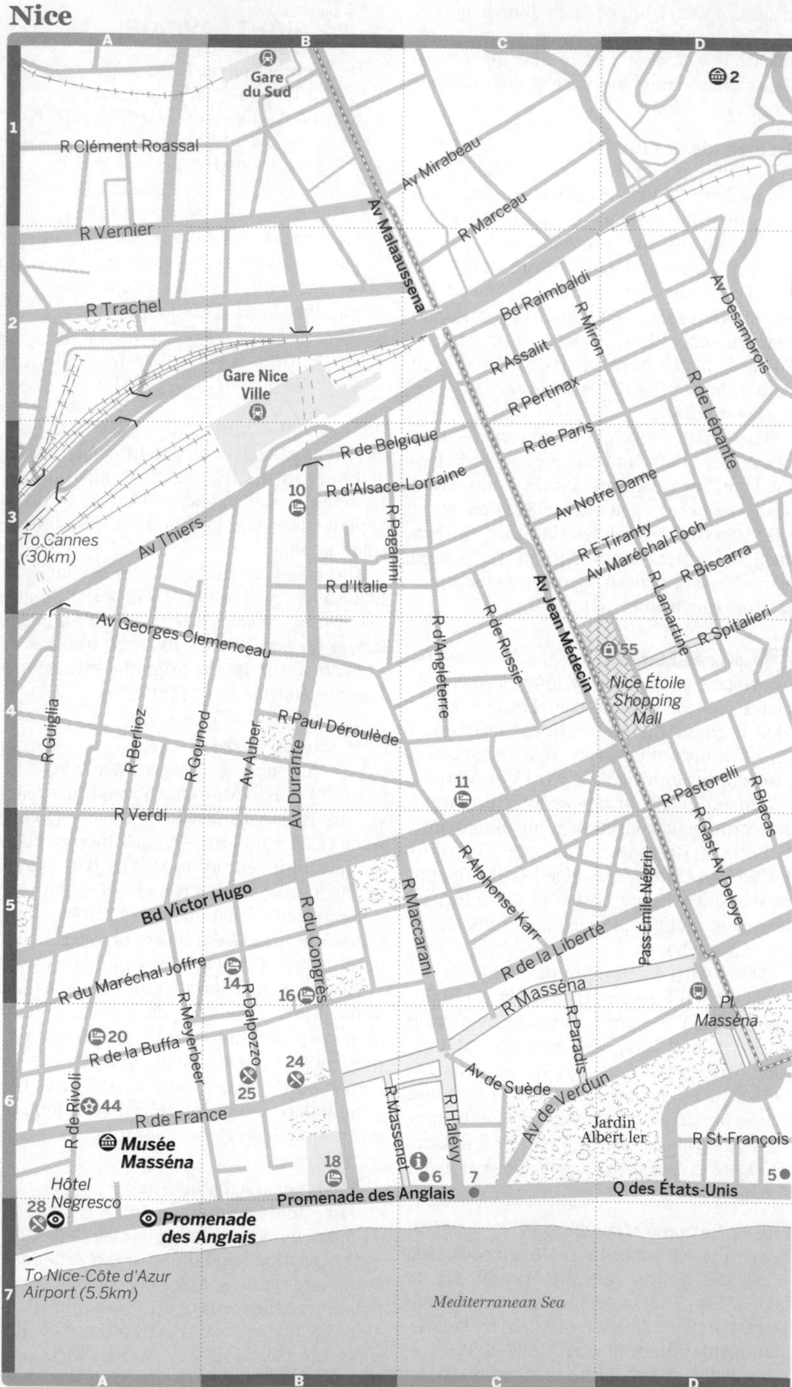

A
B
C
D
1
2
3
4
5
6
7
Gare du Sud
2
R Clément Roassal
Av Mirabeau
R Marceau
Av Malaussena
R Vernier
R Trachel
Bd Raimbaldi
R Miron
Av Desambrois
R Assalit
R de Lépante
Gare Nice Ville
R Pertinax
R de Belgique
R de Paris
R d'Alsace-Lorraine
10
Av Notre Dame
R Paganini
To Cannes (30km)
Av Thiers
R E Tiranty
Av Maréchal Foch
R Biscarra
R d'Italie
R Lamartine
Av Jean Médecin
R Spitalieri
Av Georges Clemenceau
R d'Angleterre
R de Russie
55
Nice Étoile Shopping Mall
R Guiglia
R Berlioz
R Gounod
Av Auber
R Paul Déroulède
Av Durante
11
R Pastorelli
R Blacas
R Verdi
R Gast Av Deloye
R Alphonse Karr
Pass Émile Négrin
Bd Victor Hugo
R du Congrès
R Maccarani
R de la Liberté
R du Maréchal Joffre
14
R Dalpozzo
16
R Masséna
R Paradis
Pl Masséna
20
R de la Buffa
R Meyerbeer
24
25
Av de Suède
Av de Verdun
R de Rivoli
44
R de France
R Massenet
R Halévy
Jardin Albert Ier
R St-François
Musée Masséna
18
6
7
5
Hôtel Negresco
Promenade des Anglais
Q des États-Unis
28
Promenade des Anglais
To Nice-Côte d'Azur Airport (5.5km)
Mediterranean Sea

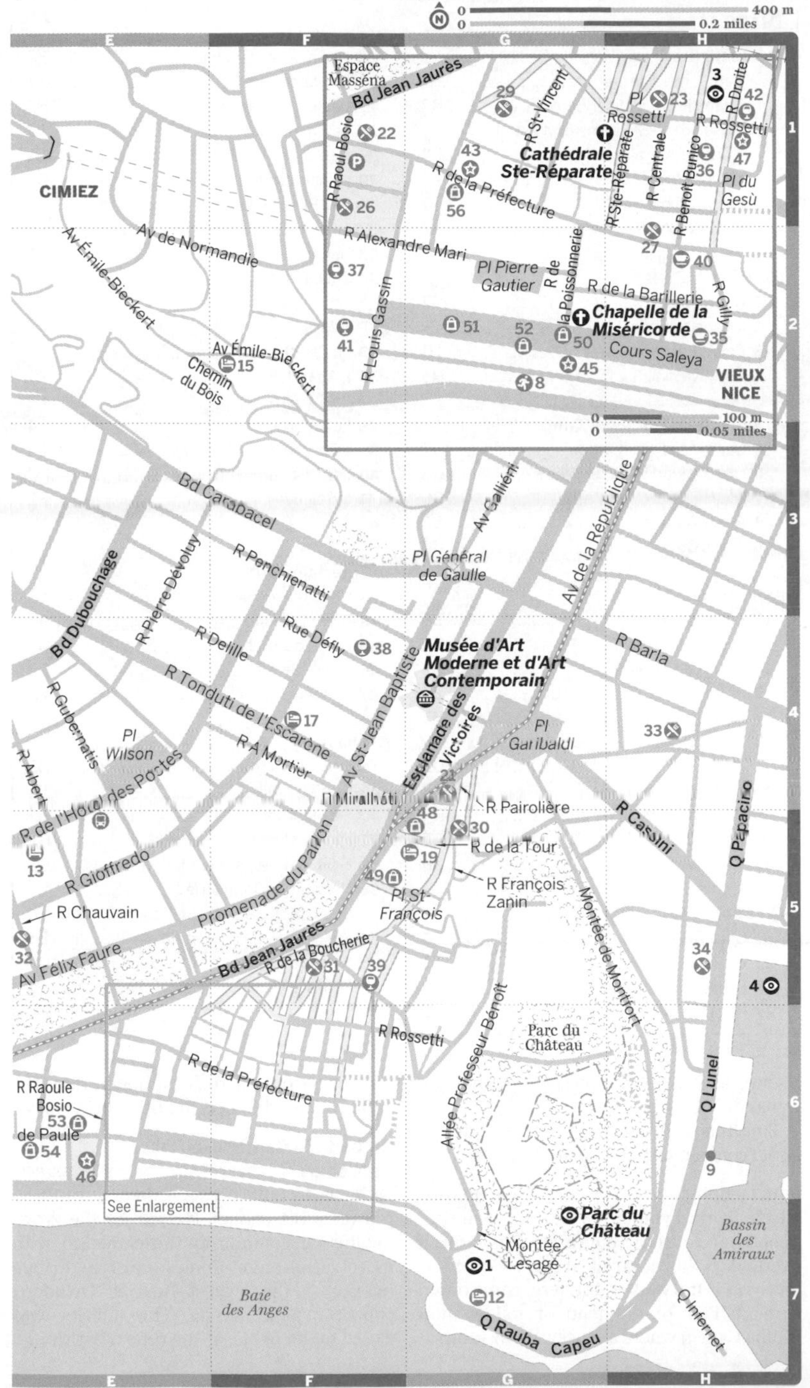

0 400 m
0 0.2 miles
E
F
G
H
Espace Masséna
Bd Jean Jaurès
R Raoul Bosio
R Louis Gassin
R St-Vincent
Pl Rossetti
R Rossetti
R Droite
Cathédrale Ste-Réparate
R Ste-Réparate
R Centrale
R Benoît Bunico
Pl du Gesù
R de la Préfecture
R Alexandre Mari
Pl Pierre Gautier
R de la Poissonnerie
R de la Barillerie
R Gilly
Chapelle de la Miséricorde
Cours Saleya
VIEUX NICE
0 100 m
0 0.05 miles
CIMIEZ
Av de Normandie
Av Émile-Bieckert
Chemin du Bois
Bd Carabacel
Av Gallieni
Av de la République
Pl Général de Gaulle
R Penchienatti
Bd Dubouchage
R Pierre Dévoluy
R Delille
Rue Défly
Musée d'Art Moderne et d'Art Contemporain
R Barla
R Tonduti de l'Escarène
R A Mortier
Av St-Jean Baptiste
Esplanade des Victoires
Pl Garibaldi
R Gubernatis
Pl Wilson
R Alberti
R de l'Hôtel des Postes
R Pairolière
R Cassini
Q Papacino
R de la Tour
R Gioffredo
Promenade du Paillon
Pl St-François
R François Zanin
R Chauvain
Montée de Montfort
Av Félix Faure
Bd Jean Jaurès
R de la Boucherie
R Rossetti
Parc du Château
Allée Professeur Benoît
R de la Préfecture
R Raoule Bosio
de Paule
Q Lunel
See Enlargement
Parc du Château
Montée Lesage
Bassin des Amiraux
Baie des Anges
Q Rauba Capeu
Q Infernet
1
2
3
4
5
6
7

Nice

Top Sights

	Cathédrale Ste-Réparate	G1
	Chapelle de la Miséricorde	G2
	Musée d'Art Moderne et d'Art Contemporain	G4
	Musée Masséna	A6
	Parc du Château	G7
	Promenade des Anglais	A7

Sights

1	Château Lift	G7
2	Musée National Marc Chagall	D1
3	Palais Lascaris	H1
4	Port Lympia	H5

Activities, Courses & Tours

5	Centre du Patrimoine	D6
6	Nice Guided Walking Tours	C6
7	Nice Le Grand Tour	C6
8	Roller Station	G2
9	Trans Côte d'Azur	H6

Sleeping

10	Belle Meunière	B3
11	Exedra	C4
12	Hôtel La Pérouse	G7
13	Hôtel Wilson	E5
14	Hôtel Windsor	B5
15	Le Petit Palais	F2
16	Nice Garden Hôtel	B5
17	Nice Pebbles	F4
18	Palais de la Méditerranée	B6
19	Villa la Tour	G5
20	Villa Rivoli	A6

Eating

21	Chez René Socca	G4
22	Emilie's Cookies	F1
23	Fenocchio	H1
24	Keisuke Matsushima	B6
25	La Cave de l'Origine	B6
26	La Merenda	F1
27	Le Bistrot d'Antoine	H2
28	Le Chantecler	A7
29	Le Comptoir du Marché	G1
30	L'Escalinada	G5
31	Lou Pilha Leva	F5
32	Luna Rossa	E5
33	Sapore	H4
34	Zucca Magica	H5

Drinking

35	La Civette du Cours	H2
36	L'Abat-Jour	H1
37	Le Six	F2
38	Le Smarties	F4
39	L'Effervescence	F5
40	Les Distilleries Idéales	H2
41	Ma Nolan's	F2
42	Snug & Cellar	H1

Entertainment

43	Chez Wayne's	G1
44	Cinéma Rialto	A6
45	Les Trois Diables	G2
46	Opéra de Nice	E6
47	Shapko	H1

Shopping

48	Cave de la Tour	G5
49	Fish Market	F5
50	Flea Market	G2
51	Flower Market	G2
52	Fruit and Vegetable Market	G2
53	Henri Auer Confiserie	E6
	Les Trois Étoiles de St-Paul	(see 30)
54	Moulin à Huile d'Olive Alziari	E6
55	Nice Étoile	D4
56	Pâtisserie LAC	G1

also works as an exhibition space (with panoramas of Nice to boot).

Smartphone users will be able to access audio commentary thanks to flashcodes.

Port Lympia ARCHITECTURE

Nice's Port Lympia, with its beautiful Venetian-coloured buildings, is often overlooked, but a stroll along its quays is lovely, as is the walk to get here: come down through Parc du Château or follow quai Rauba Capeu, where a massive **war memorial** hewn from the rock commemorates the 4000 Niçois who died in both world wars.

Cathédrale Orthodoxe Russe St-Nicolas CATHEDRAL

(Av Nicolas II) Built between 1902 and 1912 to provide a big enough church for the growing Russian community, this cathedral, with its colourful onion domes and rich, ornate interior, is the biggest Russian Orthodox church outside Russia. The interior was closed to the public at the time of writing.

Beaches BEACHES

Nice's beaches are all pebbly; sensitive behinds should therefore opt for a comfy mattress at one of its 14 private beaches (€15 to €20 per day). Out of the free **public sections of beach** (with lifeguards, first-aid posts and cold showers), **Plage Publique des Ponchettes**, opposite Vieux Nice, is the most popular (and don't worry about your bottom, many hotels lend you mats!).

Most beaches also offer a raft of activities, from beach volleyball to jet skis and pedalos.

Tours

Nice Guided Walking Tours WALKING TOUR

The best way to discover Nice's rich heritage is to take a guided walking tour. The **Centre du Patrimoine** (75 Quai des Etats-Unis; ⌚8.30am-1pm & 2-5pm Mon-Thu) runs a two-hour Vieux Nice Baroque tour (Tuesday afternoon), as well as themed tours, including art deco, neoclassical and belle époque Nice. The tourist office (p59) runs a 2½-hour Vieux Nice tour in English (adult/child €12/6) at 9.30am on Saturday.

Art With The Tram TRAM TOUR

(www.tramway-nice.org) As well as Jaume Plensa's glow-in-the-dark *Conversation* on place Masséna, there are 13 more works of art to discover along Nice's tram, including original sound bites at each stop, the calligraphy of the tram's stops and more visual works. The best way to appreciate this artistic input is to take the tourist office's two-hour **Art dans la Ville** (adult/child €8/3, plus €2 for transport; ⌚tours 7pm Fri) guided tour.

Trans Côte d'Azur BOAT TOUR

(www.trans-cote-azur.com; quai Lunel; ⌚Apr-Oct) To escape the crowds, take a scenic cruise along the coast. Trans Côte d'Azur runs one-hour trips along the Baie des Anges and the Rade de Villefranche (adult/child €16/10) from April to October. From mid-June to mid-September it also runs regular excursions to Île Ste-Marguerite (€35/25, crossing one hour), St-Tropez (€58/44, crossing 2½ hours) and Monaco (€34/25, crossing 45 minutes). Reservations are essential.

Nice Le Grand Tour BUS TOUR

(www.nicelegrandtour.com; 1-day pass adult/child €20/5) With headphone commentary in several languages, the open-topped Le Grand Tour buses (1½ hours) give you a good overview of Nice. You can hop on or off at any one of 14 stops.

Festivals & Events

Carnaval de Nice CARNIVAL

(www.nicecarnaval.com) Held each year around Mardi Gras (Shrove Tuesday) since 1294. Highlights include the *batailles de fleurs* (battles of flowers) and the ceremonial burning of the carnival king on promenade des Anglais, followed by a fireworks display.

Nice Jazz Festival MUSIC FESTIVAL

(www.nicejazzfestival.fr) France's original jazz festival has taken on a life of its own in its new promenade location, with fringe concerts popping up all around the venue, from Vieux Nice to Massena and the shopping streets around rue de France. The festival itself remains as highbrow as ever.

Sleeping

Accommodation is excellent and caters to all budgets. Most hotels will charge substantially more during the Monaco Grand Prix. Book well in advance for summer months.

TOP CHOICE **Nice Pebbles** SELF-CONTAINED €€

(☎04 97 20 27 30; www.nicepebbles.com; 23 rue Gioffredo; 1-/3-bedroom apt from €105/320;) Have you ever dreamed of feeling like a real Niçois? Coming back to your designer pad in Vieux Nice, opening a bottle of ice-cold rosé and cooking up a storm with the treats you bought at the market? Nice Pebbles' concept is simple: offering the quality of a four-star boutique hotel in holiday flats.

The apartments (with one to three bedrooms) are equipped to high standards (flat-screen TV, kitchen, linen bedding and, in some cases, wi-fi, swimming pool, balcony etc) and come with a useful starter pack (no need to rush to the supermarket). Nightly rates decrease for longer stays and are significantly cheaper during the low season.

Hôtel La Pérouse BOUTIQUE HOTEL €€€

(☎04 93 62 34 63; www.hotel-la-perouse.com; 11 quai Rauba Capeu; d from €195;) Built into the rock cliff next to Tour Bellanda, La Pérouse captures the vibe of a genteel villa. Lower-floor rooms face the lemon-tree-shaded courtyard and infinity pool; upper-floor rooms have magnificent vistas of the promenade and sea, many with balconies or terraces to make the best of the panorama. Smart accent colours add flair to the traditional decor. Guests can also enjoy the solarium and spa. Service is excellent.

Nice Garden Hôtel BOUTIQUE HOTEL €€
(☎04 93 87 35 63; www.nicegardenhotel.com; 11 rue du Congrès; s/d €75/100; ❄📶) Behind heavy iron gates hides this little gem of a hotel: the nine beautifully appointed rooms, the work of the exquisite Marion, are a subtle blend of old and new and overlook a delightful garden with a glorious orange tree. Amazingly, all this charm and peacefulness is just two blocks from the promenade.

Villa Saint-Exupéry HOSTEL €
(☎04 93 84 42 83; www.villahostels.com; 22 av Gravier; dm €25-30, s/d €45/90; @📶) Set in a lovely converted monastery in the north of the city, this is a great place to put down your bags for a few days. Chill out in the 24-hour common room, housed in the old stained-glass chapel, sip a €1 beer on the barbecue terrace and stock up on travel tips.

The villa staff will come and pick you up from the nearby Comte de Falicon tram stop, or St-Maurice stop for bus 23 (direct from the airport) when you first arrive. Rates include breakfast.

Villa Rivoli BOUTIQUE HOTEL €€
(☎04 93 88 80 25; www.villa-rivoli.com; 10 rue de Rivoli; s/d/q from 85/99/210; ❄📶) Built in 1890, this stately villa feels like your own pied-à-terre in the heart of Nice. A marble staircase leads to spotlessly clean, character-rich rooms, some with fabric-covered walls, gilt-edged mirrors and marble mantelpieces. Take breakfast in the garden's sun-dappled shade, or in the grand belle époque salon.

Palais de la Méditerranée LUXURY HOTEL €€€
(☎04 92 14 77 30; www.lepalaisdelamediterranee.com; 13-15 promenade des Anglais; d €345; ❄@📶🏊👪) This opulent edifice is spectacularly recessed behind the massive pillars of its majestic 1929 art deco facade. Rooms are well-appointed (king-size beds, separate shower and bath) and all have balconies, although it's worth noting that the sea views tend to be obstructed by the facade's pillars.

Villa la Tour BOUTIQUE HOTEL €€
(☎04 93 80 08 15; www.villa-la-tour.com; 4 rue de la Tour; s/d €79/91; ❄📶) Small but perfectly formed, the Villa la Tour is delightful, with warm, romantic Provençal rooms at the heart of Vieux Nice, and a diminutive flower-decked roof terrace with views of the Colline du Château and surrounding rooftops.

Hôtel Windsor BOUTIQUE HOTEL €€
(☎04 93 88 59 35; www.hotelwindsornice.com; 11 rue Dalpozzo; d €120-175; ❄@📶🏊) High-profile artists have decorated more than half the rooms here, with very bold, sometimes unsettling designs. Traditional rooms are more soothing yet still nod to the arts with hand-painted wall murals. Rooms facing the backyard tropical garden have lush views.

Hôtel Wilson BOUTIQUE HOTEL €
(☎04 93 85 47 79; www.hotel-wilson-nice.com; 39 rue de l'Hôtel des Postes; s/d €50/55; 📶) Years of travelling, an experimental nature and exquisite taste have turned Jean-Marie's rambling flat into a compelling place to stay. The 16 rooms have individual, carefully crafted decor and share the eclectic dining room.

The hotel is on the 3rd floor and there's no elevator. Unusually, people are allowed to smoke in some rooms, so ask to see a couple if you're concerned about the smell.

Exedra DESIGN HOTEL €€€
(☎04 97 03 89 89; www.boscolohotels.com; 12 bd Victor Hugo; d from €255; ❄@📶🏊) Totally gutted in 2008, the belle époque shell now houses one of Nice's most sexy establishments. Inside, the hotel is an ultra-modern ode to white, from furniture to fabrics, bathroom fixings and walls, with only the odd touch of colour breaking through the minimalist decor.

Le Petit Palais HOTEL €€
(☎04 93 62 19 11; www.petitpalaisnice.fr; 17 av Émile-Bieckert; d €150; ❄@📶) This belle époque lemon-meringue-pie hotel in upmarket Cimiez is an attractive choice. Views of Vieux Nice and the Baie des Anges are stunning, and the decor is understated elegance.

Belle Meunière HOSTEL €
(☎04 93 88 66 15; www.bellemeuniere.com; 21 av Durante; dm/d/tr/q €28/78/93/124, without bathroom dm/tr €22/66; 📶👪) This jovial hostel, in a 19th-century mansion, is great for families and groups of friends: rooms are very basic but the price is fair. Rates include breakfast.

Eating

The Niçois love eating out so booking is essential for weekend meals, particularly if you want to bag a table on a terrace (pretty much any time from April to October).

TOP CHOICE **Le Bistrot d'Antoine** MODERN FRENCH €€
(☎04 93 85 29 57; 27 rue de la Préfecture; mains

€13-18; ⌚lunch & dinner Tue-Sat) What's so surprising about this super brasserie is how unfazed it is by its incredible success: it is full every night (booking essential), yet the 'bistro chic' cuisine never wavers, the staff are cool as cucumbers, the atmosphere is reliably jovial and the prices incredibly good value for the area.

Le Chantecler GASTRONOMIC **€€€**
(☎04 93 16 64 00; www.hotel-negresco-nice.com; Le Negresco, 37 promenade des Anglais; menu €90, mains €55-68; ⌚dinner Wed-Sun, lunch Sun) In a sumptuous pink Regency dining room, the Negresco's two-Michelin-starred restaurant, run by locally trained chef Jean-Denis Rieubland, is no ordinary place. Ensure you're in a grand mood if you're going to splash out: every dish is an exquisite creation, both in cuisine and presentation, and there is a seemingly endless succession of appetisers, palate cleansers and petits fours.

All of this comes complete with the expertise of an exceptional sommelier, who will happily match every course with a wine or recommend a bottle for your meal. Service is truly stellar and you'll finish your evening feeling like royalty.

Luna Rossa ITALIAN **€€**
(☎04 93 85 55 66; www.lelunarossa.com; 3 rue Chauvain; mains €15-25; ⌚Tue-Fri, dinner Sat) Luna Rossa is like your dream Mediterranean dinner come true: fresh pasta, exquisitely cooked seafood, sun-kissed vegetables and divine meats. Try the Poêlée Luna Rossa, a seafood stir-fry with garlic, basil and fresh linguine, served in a cast-iron pan; simply divine. Wash it down with one of the excellent bottles of red or rosé from the cellar.

Fenocchio ICE CREAM **€**
(2 place Rossetti; ice cream from €2; ⌚9am-midnight Feb-Oct) Dither too long over the 70-plus flavours of ice cream and sorbet at this unforgettable *glacier* (ice-cream shop) and you'll never make it to the front of the queue. Eschew predictable favourites and indulge in a new taste sensation: black olive, tomato-basil, avocado, rosemary or lavender.

Keisuke Matsushima MODERN FRENCH **€€€**
(☎04 93 82 26 06; www.keisukematsushima.com; 22ter rue de France; 2-/3-course lunch menu €18/25, mains €30-46; ⌚lunch Tue-Sat, dinner Mon-Sat) Japanese hotshot Keisuke Matsushima, alias Kei, makes heads turn at a minimalist space dedicated to his trademark cuisine: Mediterranean (lots of Italian influence) with a subtle dash of the Orient. The presentation is a work of art and the content of the cellar is as stellar as the food (and exclusively French). Booking essential.

SNACKING À LA NIÇOISE

Perfect for filling a hungry moment coming from the beach (or any time of day) are Nice's many snacks. Essential tasting for every visiting palate is *socca*, a savoury, griddle-fried pancake made from chickpea flour and olive oil, sprinkled with a liberal dose of black pepper. Also typical are *petits farcis* (stuffed vegetables), *pissaladière* (traditional onion tart topped with black olives and anchovies) and the many *beignets* (fritters).

Try them at **Chez René Socca** (2 rue Miralhéti; dishes from €2; ⌚9am-9pm Tue-Sun, to 10.30pm Jul & Aug, closed Nov) or **Lou Pilha Leva** (☎04 93 13 99 08; 10 rue Collet; ⌚9am-midnight; 🖉), two informal joints where a merry crowd sits around shared outdoor benches with a glass of rosé.

L'Escalinada NIÇOIS **€€**
(☎04 93 62 11 71; www.escalinada.fr; 22 rue Pairolière; menu €24, mains €15-23; ⌚lunch & dinner daily) This enchanting old-town auberge has been one of the best places in town for Mediterranean favourites for the last half-century: melt-in-your-mouth homemade gnocchi with tasty *daube* (Provençal beef stew), grilled prawns with garlic and herbs, Marsala veal stew. The staff are delightful and the welcome kir is on the house. No credit cards.

La Cave de l'Origine MODERN FRENCH **€€**
(☎04 83 50 09 60; 3 rue Dalpozzo; mains €15-22; ⌚lunch & dinner Tue-Sat) This sleek new wine bar–restaurant has as much substance as style. As you would expect from a wine emporium, there is a great selection of wines by the glass, many of them local, and fantastic advice about what to try with your food (well-executed, modern French fare with a touch of fusion).

Le Comptoir du Marché MODERN FRENCH **€**
(☎04 93 13 45 01; 8 rue du marché; mains €13-15; ⌚lunch & dinner Tue-Sat) With its vintage kitchen decor and recession-proof prices, it's no wonder the Comptoir, which opened in early 2012, is off to a flying start. There are

five or six daily mains, scribbled on a chalkboard. The cuisine is a modern twist on French traditional recipes, with lentil stews, raviolis, confit rabbit and even *os à moelle* (bone marrow).

La Merenda NIÇOIS €€
(4 rue Raoul Bosio; mains €12-15; ⏲Mon-Fri) Simple, solid Niçois cuisine by former Michelin-starred chef Dominique Le Stanc draws the crowds to this pocket-sized bistro (you'll be rubbing back and shoulders with fellow customers). The tiny open kitchen stands proud at the back of the room, and the equally small menu is chalked on the board. No credit cards.

Sapore MODERN FRENCH €€
(☎04 92 04 22 09; www.restaurant-sapore.com; 19 rue Bonaparte; menu €32; ⏲dinner Tue-Sat) Inquisitive gourmets will love this place: the menu is a fixed eight-course meal of bite-size dishes, each a riot of taste inspired by the chef's culinary travels and the season's products (ratatouille samosa, chicken ginger kebabs etc). Booking essential.

Zucca Magica VEGETARIAN €€
(☎04 93 56 25 27; www.lazuccamagica.com; 4bis quai Papacino; menus €30; ⏲Tue-Sat; ✎) Bursting with vegetarian surprises, the 'Magic Pumpkin' serves a fixed five-course menu, dictated simply by the market and the chef's fancy. Seating is amid a fabulous collection of pumpkins and fairy lights. Bring along a gargantuan appetite.

Emilie's Cookies CAFE €
(www.emiliescookies.com; 1 rue de la Préfecture; cookies from €2, sandwiches & salads around €6; ⏲9am-6.30pm Tue-Sat, from 10am Sun; ᯤ) As the name suggests, Emilie does a mean cookie. But not only: there are also gorgeous salads, bagels and lattes if you fancy a change from standard espressos. Take it away on your city ventures, or eat in the pretty, retro cafe.

Drinking

Any of the cafe terraces on cours Saleya are lovely for an early evening aperitif. Vieux Nice's bounty of pubs attracts a noisy, boisterous crowd but there are also plenty of more sophisticated establishments.

TOP CHOICE **Les Distilleries Idéales** CAFE
(24 rue de la Préfecture; ⏲9am-12.30am) Whether you're after an espresso on your way to the cours Saleya market, or an aperitif (complete with cheese and charcuterie platters, €5.20) before trying out one of Nice's fabulous restaurants, Les Distilleries is one of the most atmospheric bars in town. Tables on the small street terrace are ideal for watching the world go by. Happy hour is from 6pm to 8pm.

Le Smarties BAR
(http://nicesmarties.free.fr; 10 rue Défly; ⏲6pm-2am Tue-Sat) We love Smarties' sexy '70s swirly orange style, which draws a hot-looking straight-gay crowd. On weekends the tiny dance floor fills when DJs spin deep house, electro, techno and occasionally disco; weekdays are mellower. Free tapas with happy hour (nightly 6pm to 9pm).

L'Abat-Jour BAR
(25 rue Benoît Bunico) With its vintage furniture, rotating art exhibitions and alternative music, l'Abat-Jour is all the rage with Nice's young and trendy crowd. The basement has live music or DJ sessions.

La Civette du Cours CAFE
(1 cours Saleya; ⏲8am-1am) Sprawling across cours Saleya, La Civette is *the* place to hang out if you're cool, regardless of age. Dark shades nurse a hangover with a cappuccino in the morning sun, locals kick back with a pre-lunch pastis at weekends and friends come here in the evenings for a kir or a beer.

Snug & Cellar PUB
(cnr rue Droite & rue Rossetti; ⏲noon-midnight) The cellar of this new pub hosts live music (Monday), a quiz (Wednesday) and giant screens for sports events. And when there is nothing special going on, it's just a great place for a drink! The atmosphere is more sophisticated than in Nice's other English/Irish pubs and the staff are charming.

L'Effervescence BAR
(www.leffervescence-nice.com; 10 rue de la Loge; ⏲6pm-midnight Tue-Sat) This champagne bar offers all the big names as well as small vintages from the Loire Valley, Spain and Italy. Many are available by the glass, and all by the bottle (or magnums). Make it a night with some of the bar's delicious nibbles. Happy hour is from 6.30pm to 7.30pm.

Le Six GAY BAR
(www.le6.fr; 6 rue Raoul Bosio; ⏲10pm-5am) Primped and pretty A-gays crowd shoulder to shoulder at Nice's compact, perennially popular 'mo bar. The thing to do: climb the ladder to the mezzanine (watch your head!).

Ma Nolan's PUB
(www.ma-nolans.com; 2 rue St François de Paule; ⏲noon-2am Mon-Fri, 11am-2am Sat & Sun) This Irish pub is big, loud and *the* pub of reference for all foreigners. With live music, pub quiz, big sport events and pub grub, it's a rowdy place. Happy hour is 6pm to 8pm.

☆ Entertainment

Nice has a strong live-music tradition, from pop rock to jazz and cabaret, and many bars regularly host bands.

Chez Wayne's LIVE MUSIC
(www.waynes.fr; 15 rue de la Préfecture; ⏲2.30pm-12.30am) Raucous watering hole Chez Wayne's is a typical English pub that looks like it's been plucked out of London, Bristol or Leeds. It features excellent live bands every night and has the best atmosphere in town. The pub is also sports-mad and shows every rugby, football, Australian football, tennis and cricket game worth watching.

Shapko LIVE MUSIC
(www.shapko.com; cnr rue Benoît Bunico & rue Rosselli; cover charge €5; ⏲7pm-12.30am Wed-Sun; 📶) The brainchild of Russian jazz musician Dimitri Shapko features plenty of fantastic local and international jazz, soul and R & B bands. Happy hour is between 7pm and 9pm and music generally starts around 9pm.

Les Trois Diables NIGHTCLUB
(☎04 93 62 47 00; 2 cours Saleya; ⏲5pm-2.15am) Music is a mix of trip-hop, house and electro at this small club. Thursday is student night (show your ID); Wednesday is karaoke.

Cinéma Rialto CINEMA
(http://lerialto.cine.allocine.fr; 4 rue de Rivoli) Non-dubbed films, with French subtitles.

Opéra de Nice OPERA
(www.opera-nice.org; 4-6 rue St-François de Paule) The vintage 1885 grande dame hosts operas, ballets and orchestral concerts. Tickets cost €10 to €90.

Shopping

Nice is a shopper's paradise: as well as the numerous little boutiques in Vieux Nice, you'll find designers around rue de France and the usual franchises at the enormous **Nice Étoile** (www.nicetoile.com; av Jean Médecin) shopping mall. Whether you're looking for original souvenirs or just fancy treating yourself during your stay, the following shops are guaranteed to delight foodies.

Moulin à Huile d'Olive Alziari FOOD
(www.alziari.com.fr; 14 rue St-François de Paule) Superb olive oil, fresh from the mill on the outskirts of Nice, for €17 per litre. Alziari also produces a dizzying variety of *tapenades* (olive spread), fresh olives (plain, stuffed, marinated etc) and other snacks.

Les Trois Étoiles de St-Paul FOOD & DRINK
(rue Pairolière) More great olive oil and a wonderful selection of liqueurs (anything from absinth to armagnac, raspberry liqueur and crème de cassis); all are sold in beautiful bottles of various shapes and sizes.

Cave de la Tour WINE
(3 rue de la Tour) Buy wine from *cavistes* (cellarmen) who know what they're talking about: Cave de la Tour has been run by the same family since 1947.

Pâtisserie LAC FOOD
(www.patisseries-lac.com; cnr rue de la Préfecture & rue St-Gaétan) Divine macaroons and chocolates from chef patissier Pascal Lac.

Henri Auer Confiserie FOOD
(www.maison-auer.com; 7 rue St-François de Paule) Sweet teeth will love the crystallised fruit sold at this traditional sweet shop; the recipes date back to 1820 and the shop is a sight in its own right.

ℹ Information

Hôpital St-Roch (☎04 92 03 33 33; www.chu-nice.fr; 5 rue Pierre Dévoluy) 24-hour emergency service.

Police Station (☎04 92 17 22 22; 1 av Maréchal Foch; ⏲24hr) Non-French speakers can call 04 92 17 20 31, where translators are on hand.

Tourist Office (☎08 92 70 74 07; www.nicetourisme.com; 5 promenade des Anglais; ⏲9am-6pm Mon-Sat) There's another tourist office (open 8am to 7pm Monday to Saturday) at the train station on av Thiers.

ℹ Getting There & Away

Air

Nice-Côte d'Azur Airport (NCE; ☎08 20 42 33 33; www.nice.aeroport.fr; 📶) is France's second-largest airport and has international flights to Europe, North Africa and the US, with regular as well as low-cost airlines. The airport has two terminals, linked by a free shuttle.

Bus

There are excellent intercity services around Nice. All journeys cost €1. The bus station was demolished in 2011 so bus stops are now scattered around the coulée verte. There are detailed maps all along the park to help you locate your bus stop. Smartphone users can also download the very useful Ligne d'Azur (p60) app or visit the company's office.

» Bus 100 goes to Menton (1½ hours) via the Corniche Inférieure and Monaco (40 minutes)

» Bus 200 goes to Cannes (1½ hours)

» Bus 400 goes to Vence (1¼ hours) via St-Paul de Vence (one hour)

» Bus 500 goes to Grasse (1½ hours)

There are also services to Alpine villages such as ski resort Isola 2000 (buses 740 and 750).

Eurolines (www.eurolines.com) serves long-haul European destinations.

Ferry

Nice is the main port for ferries to Corsica. **SNCM** (www.sncm.fr; quai du Commerce, ferry terminal) and **Corsica Ferries** (www.corsicaferries.com; quai Lunel) are the two main companies.

Train

DESTINATION	FARE	DURATION	FREQUENCY
Cannes	€6.40	40 minutes	hourly
Grasse	€9.20	1¼ hours	hourly
Marseille	€35	2½ hours	hourly
Menton	€4.80	35 minutes	half-hourly
Monaco	€3.60	25 minutes	half-hourly
St-Raphaël	€14	1¼ hours	hourly

Getting Around

Nice is relatively spread out but since the weather is often good and the city beautiful and pedestrian-friendly, walking is the best way to get around. For longer journeys, use the **Vélo Bleu** (☎04 93 72 06 06; www.velobleu.org).

To/From the Airport

Nice-Côte d'Azur airport is 6km west of Nice, by the sea. A taxi to Nice's centre from the rank outside the terminal will cost around €25.

» Buses 98 and 99 link the airport's terminal with Nice Gare Routière and Nice train station respectively (€4, 35 minutes, every 20 minutes).

» Bus 110 (€18, hourly) links the airport with Monaco (40 minutes) and Menton (one hour).

» Bus 210 goes to Cannes (€14.70, 50 minutes, half-hourly); bus 250 to Antibes (€9, 55 minutes, half-hourly).

Bus & Tram

Buses and trams in Nice are run by **Ligne d'Azur** (www.lignedazur.com; 3 place Masséna). Tickets cost just €1 and include one connection, including intercity buses within the Alpes-Maritimes *département*. A new tram line linking place Masséna with the airport along promenade des Anglais is planned for 2016.

Buses are handy to get to Cimiez and the port. Night buses run from around 9pm until 2am.

The tram is great for getting across town, particularly from the train station to Vieux Nice and place Garibaldi. Trams run from 4.30am to 1.30am.

Car, Motorcycle & Bicycle

Major car-rental companies (Avis, Budget, Europcar, Hertz etc) have offices at the train station. The best deals are generally via their websites. For taxis, call **Taxi Riviera** (☎04 93 13 78 78; www.taxi-nice.fr).

To go native, go for two wheels (and be prepared for hefty safety deposits).

» **Holiday Bikes** (www.holiday-bikes.com; 23 rue de Belgique) Rents out 50cc scooters/125cc motorcycles for €27/55 per day.

» **Vélo Bleu** (p60) A shared-bicycle service with over 100 stations around the city – pick up at one, return at another. One-day/week subscriptions costs €1/5, plus usage: free the first 30 minutes, €1 the next 30, then €2 per hour thereafter. Stations in the most popular parts of town are equipped with special terminals where you can register directly with a credit card; otherwise you'll need a mobile phone. The handy Velo Bleu app allows you to find your nearest station, gives real-time information about the number of bikes available at each and can also calculate itineraries.

ARRIÈRE-PAYS NIÇOIS

You'd never believe you're just 20km from Nice. This little-known corner of the Côte d'Azur is so quiet and unaffected by tourism that Niçois themselves come here to spend a weekend away from the urban rush.

Attractions are pretty low-key: a walk in the hills – check out the Guides RandOxygène (p289) for suggestions – a stroll in isolated villages, or a long lunch in an excellent restaurant.

Although there is a bus to Peille, the only way to really discover this area is with your own wheels.

Peillon

POP 1362

The hilltop village of Peillon has to be one of the most spectacularly perched villages in France. The remote location has long been prized by local populations for its defensive characteristics: the first houses date back to the 10th century.

What draws visitors from far and wide, however, is not so much the village (which is very small and low-key) as the village inn, **Auberge de la Madone** (☎04 93 79 91 17; www.auberge-madone-peillon.com; Peillon; menus from €30; ⊙lunch & dinner Thu-Tue Feb-Oct; 📶). In the grand dining room in winter, or on the panoramic terrace in summer, father-and-son chef-duo Christian and Thomas Millo serve divine Provençal cuisine, a refined mix of traditional staples with a dash of modernity (Swiss Chard tart with fresh herbs, cod fillet in spice crust, Muscat pan-fried strawberries with an almond biscuit and strawberry sorbet). The area is very popular with trekkers so the auberge also prepares gourmet sandwiches (€8). There are a handful of rooms (doubles €98 to €200) too, all with *tomette* (traditional terracotta tiles) floors, rustic furniture and cosy feel.

WORTH A TRIP

TRAIN DES PIGNES

Chugging between the mountains and the sea, the narrow-gauge railway **Train des Pignes** (Pine Cone Train; www.trainprovence.com) is one of Provence's most picturesque rides. Rising to 1000m, with breathtaking views, the 151km track between Nice and Digne-les-Bains passes through Haute-Provence's scarcely populated backcountry.

The service runs five times a day and is ideal for a day trip inland. The beautiful medieval village of **Entrevaux** is just 1½ hours from Nice (return €20.60), perfect for a picnic and a wander through its historic centre and citadel.

Peille

POP 2287

Peille may not be quite as spectacular as Peillon but it makes up in history what it lacks in wow factor. The village's excellent **Point Info Tourisme** (☎04 93 82 14 40; 15 rue centrale, Peille; ⊙ 10am-noon & 1-6pm Wed-Sun) offers free, tailor-made guided tours depending on how much time you have (available in English and Italian). Highlights include the medieval centre, the village museum, the church and old photographs of the village.

Peille is also renowned for its **via ferrata** (☎04 93 91 71 71; www.viaferratapeille.fr; ⊙9am-6pm), a mountain course equipped with ladders, fixed cables, rope bridges etc. No previous experience required, although you must be sure-footed, reasonably fit and, most importantly, not scared of heights. The entire course takes about four hours to complete. Admission must be paid either at the Point Info Tourisme, or at **Bar l'Absinthe** (Place du Serre, Peille), where you can also rent all the equipment you'll need (€18 for helmet, harness, ropes, carabiners etc). A guide costs €40 and must be booked the day before.

For sustenance, head to **Le Relais Saint-Martin** (☎04 93 41 16 03; www.chezcotton.com; Saint-Martin de Peille; mains €11-18; ⊙lunch & dinner Thu-Tue Apr-Oct, lunch only Nov-Mar), 6km south of Peille. This typical country inn serves hearty Provençal fare, prepared by the incomparable Gérard. Depending on the seasons, you'll feast on pit-roasted suckling pig, grilled fish, wild boar, polenta, *barbajuan* (fried ravioli from Monaco) and homemade ravioli. In summer, meals are served on the panoramic terrace.

Bus 116 (€1) links Peille with La Turbie (20 minutes) and Nice (one hour) three times a day.

THE THREE CORNICHES

This trio of *corniches* (coastal roads) hugs the cliffs between Nice and Monaco, each higher than the last, with dazzling views of the Med.

Corniche Inférieure

Skimming the villa-lined waterfront between Nice and Monaco, the Corniche Inférieure, built in the 1860s, passes through the towns of Villefranche-sur-Mer, St-Jean-Cap Ferrat, Beaulieu-sur-Mer, Èze-sur-Mer and Cap d'Ail.

ℹ Getting There & Around

Bus 100 (€1, every 15 minutes between 6am and 8pm) runs the length of the Corniche Inférieure between Nice and Menton, stopping at all the villages along the way, including Villefranche-sur-Mer (15 minutes), Beaulieu-sur-Mer (20 minutes) and Cap d'Ail (35 minutes). Bus 81 serves Villefranche (20 minutes) and St-Jean-Cap Ferrat (30 minutes).

Nice-Ventimiglia (Italy) trains (every 30 minutes, 5am to 11pm) stop at Villefranche-sur-Mer (€1.60, seven minutes), Beaulieu-sur-Mer (€2, 10 minutes) and Cap d'Ail (€3, 18 minutes).

VILLEFRANCHE-SUR-MER

POP 5888

Heaped above a postcard-perfect harbour, this picturesque village overlooks the Cap Ferrat peninsula and, with its deep *rade* (harbour), is a prime port of call for *Titanic*-sized cruise ships (Nice harbour isn't deep enough for the biggest cruise liners so they moor here and passengers get ferried to/from Nice in smaller boats).

Sights & Activities

Vieille Ville HISTORIC QUARTER

Villefranche's 14th-century old town, with its tiny, evocatively named streets broken by twisting staircases and glimpses of the sea, is reason enough to visit. Don't miss eerie, arcaded **rue Obscure**, a historical monument a block in from the water.

Chapelle St-Pierre CHURCH

(admission €2.50; 10am-noon & 2-6pm Wed-Mon) Villefranche was a favourite of Jean Cocteau (1889–1963), who sought solace here in 1924 after the death of his companion Raymond Radiguet. Several years, holidays and friends later, Cocteau convinced locals to let him paint the neglected, 14th-century Chapelle St-Pierre, which he transformed into a mirage of mystical frescoes.

Scenes from St Peter's life are interspersed with references to Cocteau's cinematographic work (notably the drivers from Orpheus) and friends (Francine Weisweiller, whose Villa Santo Sospir (p62) in St-Jean-Cap Ferrat Cocteau also decorated). The chapel keeper will give you fascinating explanations (in French) about the meanings of each scene.

COMBINED TICKETS

Combined tickets for the following local attractions offer good discounts.

» Villa Ephrussi + Villa Kérylos (adult/child €18/13.50)

» Villa Ephrussi + Jardin d'Èze (adult/child €13.50/9.50)

Tickets can be purchased at the relevant sights. They are valid for seven days.

Affrètement Maritime Villefranchois BOAT TOUR

(04 93 76 65 65; www.amv-sirenes.com; Port de la Santé; Jun-Sep) Offers regular two-hour boat tours to Monaco (adult/student/child €18/16/12) and four-hour dolphin- and whale-watching expeditions (adult/student/child €46/40/32). Since the creation of an international marine mammal sanctuary between France, Monaco and Italy in 1999, a number of cetaceans frequent Riviera waters. Dolphins are common; more occasional are sperm whales and fin whales.

Sleeping & Eating

Hôtel Welcome BOUTIQUE HOTEL €€€

(04 93 76 27 62; www.welcomehotel.com; 3 quai Amiral Courbet; d from €192;) Teetering over the water's edge at Villefranche's picturesque port, the Welcome is one classy establishment. The 35 rooms are all different: some Cocteau-themed, others Provençal, others art deco, but all share the same high-quality furnishings, sweeping sea views and fantastic location (the bus and train station are just five minutes' walk).

La Grignotière BRASSERIE €€

(3 rue Poilu; mains €16; lunch & dinner daily;) Cheap and cheerful, La Grignotière serves large portions of grilled fish and veg, lasagne, pizza and other crowd pleasers in charming and unpretentious surroundings.

La Mère Germaine SEAFOOD €€€

(04 93 01 71 39; www.meregermaine.com; 7 quai Amiral Courbet; mains €30-40; lunch & dinner Christmas-Nov) Opened in 1938, La Mère Germaine is a quintessential Villefranche address. Seafood, fish and more seafood is the order of the day. Bookings are essential for one of the prized tables on the water's edge. Fabulous selection of white wines.

BEAULIEU-SUR-MER & ST-JEAN-CAP FERRAT

The seaside holiday town of Beaulieu-sur-Mer (population 3370) is known for its well-preserved belle époque architecture. It sits at the beginning of Cap Ferrat, a wooded peninsula laden with millionaires' villas and home to the small village of St-Jean-Cap Ferrat (population 2047).

Sights & Activities

TOP CHOICE **Villa Santo Sospir** HOUSE MUSEUM

(04 93 76 00 16; www.villasantosospir.fr; 14 av Jean Cocteau, St-Jean-Cap Ferrat; guided tours €12) This villa belongs to the Weisweiller family,

who were patrons of Jean Cocteau. In 1950 Cocteau asked Francine Weisweiller (1916–2003) if he could paint the living room. He got carried away and soon the entire villa was covered in frescoes. You can see this unusual body of work in 45-minute guided tours; book at least the day before.

Tours are run by Eric Marteau, Francine Weisweiller's former nurse and now the villa's guardian. Weisweiller was a well-known Parisian socialite and Marteau got to know her well. His tours are therefore peppered with anecdotes about Cocteau, Weisweiller and their peers, which makes the visit compelling listening as much as viewing.

Villa Ephrussi de Rothschild HOUSE MUSEUM
(www.villa-ephrussi.com; St-Jean-Cap Ferrat; adult/child €12/9; ⏲10am-6pm Mar-Oct, 2-6pm Nov-Feb) An over-the-top belle époque confection, this villa was commissioned by the eccentric Baroness Béatrice Ephrussi de Rothschild in 1912. Béatrice was an avid art collector and the villa is filled with Fragonard paintings, Louis XVI furniture and Sèvres porcelain (multilingual audioguides take you through the collection). The villa is famous for its nine exquisite themed gardens, with wonderful sea views.

They look at their best in spring, but at any time of year you'll enjoy a stroll through Spanish, Japanese, Florentine, stone, cactus, rose and French gardens. They were landscaped to resemble a ship's deck when admired from the villa's balcony. The fountains in front of the villa 'dance' to classical music every 20 minutes.

Bus 81, which links Nice and St-Jean-Cap Ferrat, stops at the foot of the driveway leading to the villa (stop Passable).

Villa Grecque Kérylos HOUSE MUSEUM
(www.villa-kerylos.com; av Gustave Eiffel, Beaulieu-sur-Mer; adult/child €10/7.50; ⏲10am-6pm Mar-Oct, 2-6pm Nov-Feb) The Villa Kérylos is a reproduction of a 1st-century Athenian villa, complete with baths, stunning mosaic floors and furniture such as dining recliners. It was designed by scholar-archaelogist Théodore Reinach in 1902, at a time when the must-have for well-to-do socialites was an eccentric house on the Côte d'Azur.

Cap Ferrat WALKING
There are 14km of eucalyptus-scented walking paths around the cape, with magnificent views and wonderful coastline all the way. There are various itineraries but all of them are easy going; the **tourist office** (☎04 93 76 08 90; www.saintjeancapferrat.fr; 59 av Denis Séméria; ⏲9am-4pm Mon-Fri) has maps.

Sleeping & Eating

Hôtel Riviera HOTEL €€
(☎04 93 01 04 92; www.hotel-riviera.fr; 6 rue Paul Doumer, Beaulieu-sur-Mer; s/d/tr €70/80/100; ⏲Jan-Oct; ❄📶) A breath of fresh air, this tasteful two-star hotel with wrought-iron balconies and a hibiscus-laden summer patio perfect for breakfasting is really hard to resist. Rooms are immaculate and comfortable, and the owners charming. Probably the best value on the coast.

Le 35 FUSION €€
(☎04 93 91 30 00; 35 bd Marinoni, Beaulieu-sur-Mer; mains €17-25; ⏲lunch & dinner Tue-Sat) An elegant bistro decked out in lilac and designer grey, Le 35 has become a fixture in the local eating scene. The dynamic team serves perfectly executed fusion cuisine and original desserts using flowers (rose, violet etc).

Le Sloop SEAFOOD €€
(☎04 93 01 48 63; Port de Plaisance, St-Jean-Cap Ferrat; menu €32, mains €18-25; ⏲lunch & dinner Thu-Tue) With its elegant red-and-blue nautical decor and port-side terrace within grasp of the bobbing yachts, Le Sloop is a cut above the rest on this popular restaurant strip. Its seafood and shellfish are uberfresh and good value.

Moyenne Corniche

Cut through rock in the 1920s, the Moyenne Corniche takes drivers from Nice past the Col de Villefranche (149m), Èze and Beausoleil (the French town bordering Monaco's Monte Carlo).

Bus 82 serves the Moyenne Corniche from Nice all the way to Èze (20 minutes); bus 112 carries on to Beausoleil (40 minutes, Monday to Saturday).

ÈZE

POP 2865

This rocky little village perched on an impossible peak is the jewel in the Riviera crown. The main attraction is the **medieval village** itself, with small higgledy-piggledy stone houses and winding lanes (and plenty of galleries and shops), and the mesmerising views of the coast.

You'll get the best panorama from **Jardin d'Èze** (adult/child €4/free; ⏲9am-sunset), a cactus garden at the top of the village. It's also where you'll find the old castle ruins; take time to sit there or in the garden's Zen area to enjoy the view: few places on earth offer such a panorama.

At the bottom of the village, you'll find the factory of perfumery **Fragonard** (www.fragonard.com; admission free; ⌚8.30am-6.30pm Feb-Oct, 8.30am-noon & 2-6.30pm Nov-Jan), which offers free guided tours and has a shop.

The village gets very crowded between 10am and 5pm; if you'd prefer a quiet wander, come first thing in the morning or late in the afternoon. Or even better, stay in the village. La Bastide aux Camélias (p64) has an exquisite suite. Otherwise, the stunning **Château Eza** (☎04 93 41 12 24; www.chateaueza.com; rue de la Pise; d from €440; ❄📶) should see you right. The 10 regal rooms all feature sumptuous furniture, rich drapes and bathrooms to die for (spa, hydrojet showers, Japanese toilets, marble etc), but each is unique, some with parquet floors and wood panels on the walls, some with panoramic terraces, others cosy fireplaces for the winter.

Château Eza is also an excellent, Michelin-starred gastronomic restaurant (mains €39 to €65), where seasonal meats and fish will impress as much as the views. The panoramic bar is highly recommended for an unforgettable aperitif.

You can walk down from the village to Èze-sur-Mer on the coast via the *steep* **chemin de Nietzsche** (45 minutes); the German philosopher started writing *Thus Spoke Zarathustra* while staying in Èze and enjoyed this path.

Grande Corniche

Hitchcock was sufficiently impressed by Napoléon's cliff-hanging Grande Corniche to use it as a backdrop for his film *To Catch a Thief* (1956), starring Cary Grant and Grace Kelly. Ironically, the Hollywood actor, died in 1982 after crashing her car on this very same road.

Bus 116 links the town of La Turbie (population 3212) with Nice five times a day (€1, 35 minutes), and bus 114 goes to Monaco six times a day (€1, 30 minutes).

Sights

Views from the spectacular Grande Corniche are mesmerising and, if you're driving, you'll probably want to stop at every bend to admire the unfolding vistas.

TOP CHOICE Fort de la Revère VIEWPOINT

Sitting 675m above the sea, the fort is the perfect place to revel in 360-degree views. An orientation table helps you get your bearings. The fort was built in 1870 to protect Nice (it served as an allied prisoner camp during WWII).

There are picnic tables under the trees for an al fresco lunch and dozens of trails in the surrounding **Parc Naturel Départemental de la Grande Corniche**, a protected area that stretches along the D2564 from Col d'Èze to La Turbie; the Guides RandOxygène (p289) have suggestions.

Trophée des Alpes ROMAN SITE

(18 av Albert Ier, La Turbie; adult/student/child €5.50/4/free; ⌚10am-1pm & 2.30-5pm Tue-Sun) This triumphal monument was built by Emperor Augustus in 6 BC to celebrate his victory over the Celto-Ligurian Alpine tribes that had fought Roman sovereignty (the names of the 45 peoples are carved on the western side of the monument). The tower teeters on the highest point of the old Roman road, with dramatic views of Monaco.

Last admission is half an hour before closing time.

Sleeping & Eating

La Bastide aux Camélias B&B €€

(☎04 93 41 13 68; www.bastideauxcamelias.com; 23c rte de l'Adret, Èze; d €130-150, ste €240; ❄📶🏊) Spa, hammam, olive-tree-framed pool and sauna are among the lazy-weekend comforts to enjoy at this lovely *chambre d'hôte*. The four rooms are romantic and beautifully done, but the jewel in the crown is the suite that Fred and Sylviane renovated in the medieval village of Èze. Its rooftop terrace has plunging views of the Med.

Domaine Pins Paul B&B €€

(☎04 93 41 22 66; www.domainepinspaul.fr; 4530 av des Diables Bleus, Èze; d €175; ❄📶🏊) Swimming in the panoramic pool of the Domaine Pins Paul comes complete with views of the sea and Èze village. Rooms in the grand Provençal *bastide* (country house) are beautiful (each with their own little wine fridge), and the surrounding fragrant woods are perfect for a stroll.

Café de la Fontaine MODERN FRENCH €€

(☎04 93 28 52 79; 4 av Général de Gaulle, La Turbie; mains €13-18; ⌚lunch & dinner Tue-Sun) Those not in the know wouldn't give this inconspicuous village bistro a second glance. What they don't know is that it is Michelin-starred chef Bruno Cirino's baby – somewhere for him to go back to his culinary roots with simple yet delicious dishes. Try his *osso bucco à la Niçoise* (a beef stew).

MONACO

POP 32,350 / ☎ 377

Squeezed into just 200 hectares, this confetti principality might be the world's second-smallest country (the Vatican is smaller), but what it lacks in size it makes up for in attitude. Glitzy, glam and screaming hedonism, Monaco is truly beguiling.

Although a sovereign state, the principality's status is unusual. It is not a member of the European Union, yet it participates in the EU customs territory (meaning no border formalities crossing from France into Monaco) and uses the euro as its currency.

History

Since the 13th century, Monaco's history has been that of the Grimaldi family, whose rule began in 1297. Charles VIII, king of France, recognised Monégasque independence in 1489. But during the French Revolution, France snatched Monaco back and imprisoned its royal family. Upon release, they had to sell the few possessions they still owned and the palace became a warehouse.

The Grimaldis were restored to the throne under the 1814 Treaty of Paris. But in 1848 they lost Menton and Roquebrune to France, and Monaco swiftly became Europe's poorest country. In 1860 Monégasque independence was recognised for a second time by France and a monetary agreement in 1865 sealed the deal on future cooperation between the two countries.

Rainier III (r 1949–2005), nicknamed *le prince bâtisseur* (the builder prince), expanded the size of his principality by 20% in the late 1960s by reclaiming land from the sea to create the industrial quarter of Fontvieille. In 2004 he doubled the size of the harbour with a giant floating dyke as part of an ambitious project to place Port de Monaco (Port Hercules) among the world's leading cruise-ship harbours. Upon Rainier's death, son Albert II became monarch.

Sights & Activities

TOP CHOICE Musée Océanographique de Monaco AQUARIUM

(www.oceano.org; av St-Martin; adult/child €13/6.50; 9.30am-7pm) Stuck dramatically to the edge of a cliff since 1910, the world-renowned Musée Océanographique de Monaco, founded by Prince Albert I (1848–1922), is a stunner. Its centrepiece is its **aquarium**, with a 6m-deep **lagoon** where sharks and marine predators are separated from colourful tropical fish by a coral reef.

Ninety smaller tanks contain a dazzling 450 Mediterranean and tropical species, sustained by 250,000L of freshly pumped sea water each day. Kids will love the **tactile basin** (which runs during school holidays) – tickets (€3) for the 30-minute feel-the-fish sessions are sold at the entrance.

Upstairs, two huge colonnaded rooms retrace the **history of oceanography** and marine biology. Displays recount Prince Albert's explorations, and the cetacean skeletons, fossils and other pickled specimens give an insight into the trials of these now-established fields.

Visit the rooftop terrace for sweeping views of Monaco and the Med.

Le Rocher HISTORIC QUARTER

Monaco Ville, also called Le Rocher, thrusts skywards on a pistol-shaped rock. It's this strategic location, overlooking the sea, that became the stronghold of the Grimaldi dynasty. Built as a fortress in the 13th century, the **palace** is now the private residence of the Grimaldis. It is protected by the Carabiniers du Prince; **changing of the guard** takes place daily at 11.55am.

Le Rocher is the only part of Monaco to have retained small, winding medieval lanes; they tend to be overrun with souvenir and ice-cream shops but it does give a sense of what Monaco once was.

MONACO TRIVIA

» Citizens of Monaco (Monégasques), of whom there are only 7600, don't pay taxes.

» Monaco has its own flag (red and white), a national anthem and the national holiday is on 19 November.

» The traditional dialect is Monégasque (broadly speaking, a mixture of French and Italian).

Monaco

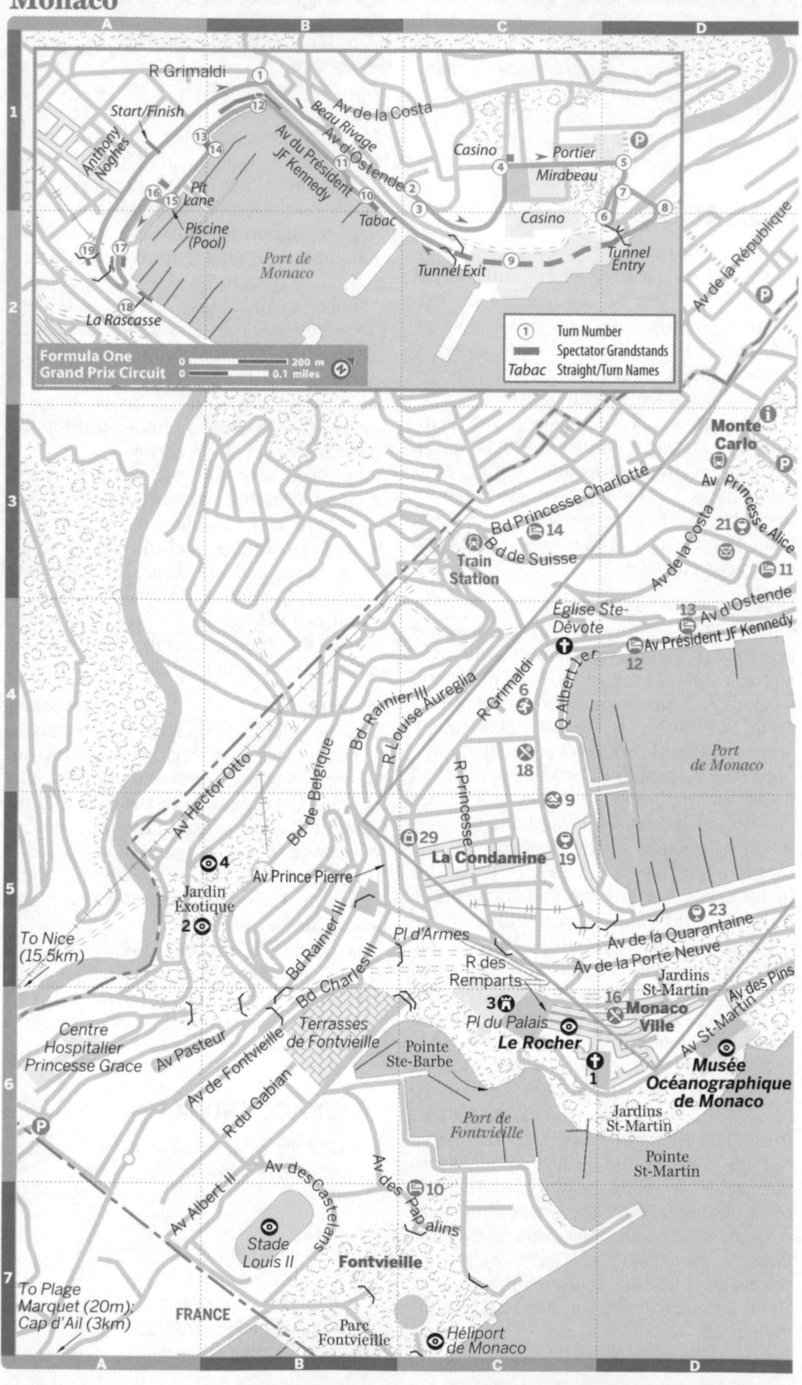

Formula One Grand Prix Circuit
R Grimaldi
Start/Finish
Anthony Noghes
Av de la Costa
Beau Rivage
Av d'Ostende
Av du Président JF Kennedy
Casino
Portier
Mirabeau
Pit Lane
Piscine (Pool)
Tabac
Port de Monaco
Tunnel Exit
Tunnel Entry
La Rascasse
Turn Number
Spectator Grandstands
Tabac Straight/Turn Names
Av de la République
Monte Carlo
Av Princesse Alice
Bd Princesse Charlotte
Bd de Suisse
Train Station
Église Ste-Dévote
Av d'Ostende
Av Président JF Kennedy
Q Albert 1er
R Grimaldi
Bd Rainier III
R Louise Aureglia
R Princesse
Port de Monaco
Av Hector Otto
Bd de Belgique
La Condamine
Jardin Exotique
Av Prince Pierre
To Nice (15.5km)
Pl d'Armes
Av de la Quarantaine
Av de la Porte Neuve
R des Remparts
Jardins St-Martin
Av des Pins
Bd Charles III
Monaco Ville
Av St-Martin
Pl du Palais
Le Rocher
Centre Hospitalier Princesse Grace
Av Pasteur
Av de Fontvieille
Terrasses de Fontvieille
Pointe Ste-Barbe
Musée Océanographique de Monaco
R du Gabian
Port de Fontvieille
Jardins St-Martin
Pointe St-Martin
Av des Castelans
Av des Papalins
Av Albert II
Stade Louis II
Fontvieille
To Plage Marquet (20m); Cap d'Ail (3km)
FRANCE
Parc Fontvieille
Héliport de Monaco

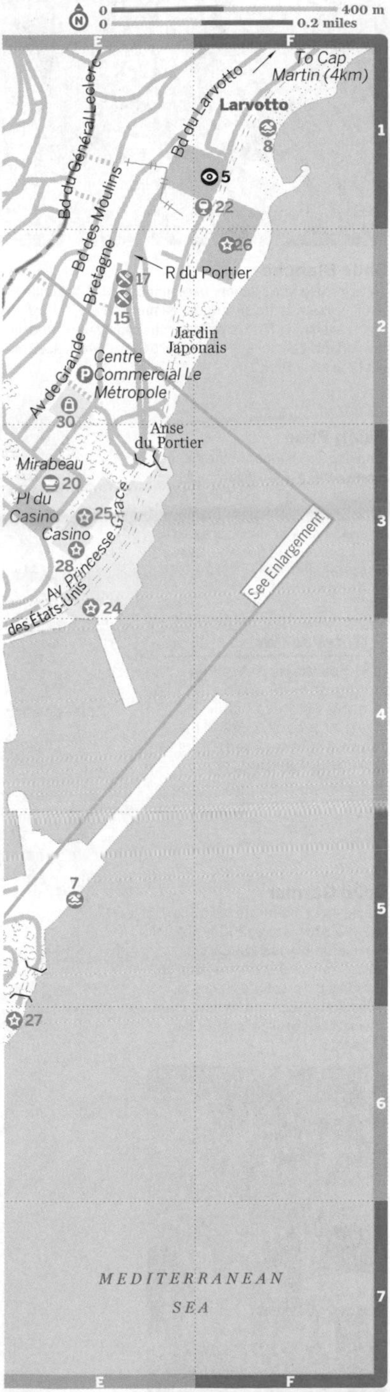

Monaco

Top Sights

Le Rocher C6
Musée Océanographique de Monaco D6

Sights

1 Cathédrale de Monaco C6
2 Jardin Exotique A5
3 Palais du Prince C6
4 Villa Paloma B5
5 Villa Sauber F1

Activities, Courses & Tours

6 Automobile Club de Monaco C4
7 Esplanade Stefano Casiraghi E5
8 Plage du Larvotto F1
9 Stade Nautique Rainier III C5

Sleeping

10 Columbus C7
11 Hôtel Hermitage D3
12 Hôtel Miramar D4
13 Hôtel Port Palace D4
14 Novotel Monte Carlo C3

Eating

Café Llorca .... (see 26)
15 Cosmopolitan E2
16 La Montgolfière D6
17 Mozza E2
18 Supermarché Casino C4
Tip Top .... (see 30)
Zelos .... (see 26)

Drinking

19 Brasserie de Monaco C5
20 Café de Paris E3
Cosmopolitan .... (see 15)
21 Flashman's D3
22 Sass Café F1
23 Stars 'n' Bars D5

Entertainment

Atrium du Casino .... (see 25)
24 Auditorium Rainier III E3
25 Casino de Monte Carlo E3
26 Grimaldi Forum F2
27 Open-air Cinema E6
28 Opéra de Monte Carlo E3

Shopping

29 Boutique Formule 1 .... C5
30 Métropole Shopping Centre E2

Monte Carlo Casino

TIMELINE

1863 Charles III inaugurates the first Casino on the Plateau des Spélugues. **The atrium** 1 is a room with a wooden platform from which an orchestra 'enlivens' the gambling.

1864 Hôtel de Paris opens and the area becomes known as the 'Golden Square'.

1865 Construction of **Salon Europe** 2. Cathedral-like, it is lined with onyx columns and lit by eight Bohemian crystal chandeliers weighing 150kg each.

1868 The steam train arrives in Monaco and **Café de Paris** 3 is completed.

1878–79 Gambling moves to Hôtel de Paris while Charles Garnier is charged with building a new casino with a miniature replica of the Paris Opera House, **Salle Garnier** 4.

1890 The advent of electricity casts a glow on architect Jules Touzet's newly added **gaming rooms** 5 for high rollers.

1903 Inspired by female gamblers, Henri Schmit decorates **Salle Blanche** 6 with caryatids and the painting *Les Grâces Florentines.*

1904 Smoking is banned in the gaming rooms and **Salon Rose** 7, a new smoking room, is added.

1910 **Salle Médecin** 8, immense and grand, hosts the high-spending Private Circle.

1966 Celebrations mark 100 years of uninterrupted gambling despite two World Wars.

TOP TIPS

- Bring photo ID
- Jackets are required in the private gaming rooms, and after 8pm
- The cashier will exchange any currency
- In the main room, the minimum bet is €5, the maximum €2000
- In the Salons Privés, the minimum bet is €10, with no maximum

Salle Blanche

Transformed into a superb bar-lounge in 2012, the Salle Blanche opens onto an outdoor gaming terrace, a must on balmy evenings. The caryatids on the ceiling were modelled on fashionable courtesans like La Belle Otero, who placed her first bet here aged 18.

Salon Rose

Smoking was banned in the gaming rooms after a fraud involving a croupier letting his ash fall on the floor. The gaze of Gallelli's famous cigarillo-smoking nudes are said to follow you around the room, now a restaurant.

Hôtel de Paris

Notice the horse's shiny leg (and testicles) on the lobby's statue of Louis XIV on horseback. Legend has it that rubbing them brings good luck in the casino.

Salle Garnier

Taking eight months to build and two years to restore (2004–06), the opera's original statuary is rehabilitated using original moulds saved by the creator's grandson. Individual air-con and heating vents are installed beneath each of the 525 seats.

Atrium
The casino's 'lobby', so to speak, is paved in marble and lined with 28 Ionic columns, which support a balustraded gallery canopied with an engraved glass ceiling.

Salon Europe
The oldest part of the casino, where they continue to play *trente-et-quarante* and European roulette, which have been played here since 1863. Tip: the bull's-eye windows around the room originally served as security observation points.

Café de Paris
With the arrival of Diaghilev as director of the Monte Carlo Opera in 1911, Café de Paris becomes the go-to address for artists and gamblers. It retains the same high-glamour ambience today. Tip: snag a seat on the terrace and people-watch.

Jardins et Terrasses du Casino

Place du Casino

1 2 3 4 5 6 7 8

Salles Touzet
This vast partitioned hall, 21m by 24m, is decorated in the most lavish style; oak, Tonkin mahogany and oriental jasper panelling are offset by vast canvases, Marseille bronzes, Italian mosaics, sculptural reliefs and stained-glass windows.

Terraces, gardens & walkways

Hexagrace mosaic

Fairmont Monte Carlo

Best Views
Wander behind the casino through manicured gardens and gaze across Victor Vasarely's vibrant op-art mosaic, *Hexagrace*, to views of the harbour and the sea.

Salle Médecin
Also known as Salle Empire because of its extravagant Empire-style decor, Monégasque architect François Médecin's gaming room was originally intended for the casino's biggest gamblers. Part of it still remains hidden from prying eyes as a Super Privé room.

To access Le Rocher, walk up the 16th-century red-brick Rampe Major from place aux Armes in the Condamine area. Alternatively, a path winds from the port up through the shady **Jardins St-Martin**.

Palais du Prince ROYAL PALACE
(www.palais.mc; adult/child €8/3.50; ⏲10am-6pm Apr-Sep) For a glimpse into royal life, you can tour the state apartments with an 11-language audio guide. The palace is what you would expect of any aristocratic abode: lavish furnishings and expensive 18th- and 19th-century art.

Cathédrale de Monaco CATHEDRAL
(4 rue Colonel) An adoring crowd continually shuffles past Prince Rainier's and Princess Grace's graves, inside the cathedral choir of this 1875 Romanesque-Byzantine cathedral. The Monaco's boys' choir, **Les Petits Chanteurs de Monaco**, sings Sunday Mass at 10.30am between September and June.

Jardin Exotique GARDEN
(www.jardin-exotique.mc; 62 bd du Jardin Exotique; adult/student & child €7/3.70; ⏲9am-dusk) Home to the world's largest succulent and cactus collection, from small echinocereus to 10m-tall African candelabras, the gardens tumble down the slopes of Moneghetti through a maze of paths, stairs and bridges. Views of the principality are spectacular and the gardens are delightful. Your ticket also gets you a 35-minute guided tour round the **Grottes de l'Observatoire**.

The caves are an important prehistoric network inside the hillside; strangely, they're the only caves in Europe where the temperature rises as you descend. They're full of stalactites and stalagmites. Bus 2 links the gardens with the town centre.

Nouveau Musée National de Monaco ART MUSEUM
(www.nmnm.mc; adult/child €6/free) The revamped national museum is housed in two different locations in Monaco. The museum hosts exhibitions on contemporary art, with each location focusing on a theme: performing arts (Serge Diaghilev, stage designs etc) at **Villa Sauber** (17 av Princesse Grace) and the environment (oceans, apocalypse etc) at **Villa Paloma** (56 bd du Jardin Exotique). Only one of the two villas is open at any one time.

Beaches BEACH
The beaches in Monaco are definitely not the best on the coast but there are a couple of nice – and surprisingly, free – options: **Esplanade Stefano Casiraghi** is a concrete solarium that has been installed on the back of the port's sea-defence wall. If you prefer sand, **Plage du Larvotto** has free as well as paying sections.

Stade Nautique Rainier III SWIMMING/SKATING
(quai Albert 1er; ⏲9am-6pm) Olympic-sized outdoor sea-water pool with a water slide (adult/child €5.10/3.20) from May to October, and an ice rink (€6) from December to March.

Festivals & Events

Monaco has a packed events schedule, and with a little planning ahead, it can be surprisingly accessible, both in price and availability.

Festival International du Cirque PERFORMING ARTS
(www.montecarlofestival.mc; ⏲late Jan) Hold your breath during world-class acrobatics, or laugh out loud at the clowns.

Tennis Masters Series SPORTS
(www.monte-carlorolexmasters.com; ⏲Apr) Fast becoming a key fixture on the professional circuit, with all the big players involved.

Formula One Grand Prix SPORTS
(Automobile Club de Monaco; www.formula1monaco.com; ⏲late May) One of Formula One's most iconic races. If you're dead keen, you can walk the 3.2km circuit; the tourist office has maps.

FREE **International Fireworks Festival** EVENT
(☎93 15 28 63; ⏲Jul & Aug) A showdown of pyrotechnic expertise in the port area. The winner gets to organise the fireworks on 18 November, eve of the national holiday.

Sleeping

MONACO

Accommodation in Monaco is expensive to say the least, reaching prohibitive levels during the Formula One Grand Prix.

Columbus BOUTIQUE HOTEL €€€
(☎92 05 90 00; www.columbushotels.com; 22 av des Papalins; d from €230; ❄@🛜≋) High-tech urban chic best describes this large boutique hotel in Fontvieille. Rooms are beautifully decorated in designer greys, elegant striped fabrics and 'back to nature' bathrooms with bamboo towel racks and elegant wooden

THE FORMULA ONE GRAND PRIX *TONY WHEELER*

If there's one trophy a Formula One driver would like to have on the mantelpiece, it would have to be from the most glamorous race of the season, the Monaco Grand Prix. This race has everything. Its spectators are the most sensational: the merely wealthy survey the spectacle from Hôtel Hermitage, the really rich watch from their luxury yachts moored in the harbour, while the Grimaldis see the start and finish from the royal box at the port. Then there's the setting: the cars scream around the very centre of the city, racing uphill from the start/finish line to place du Casino, then downhill around a tight hairpin and two sharp rights to hurtle through a tunnel and run along the harbourside to a chicane and more tight corners before the start/finish.

But despite its reputation, the Monaco Grand Prix is not really one of the great races. The track is too tight and winding for modern Formula One cars, and overtaking is virtually impossible. The Brazilian triple world champion Nelson Piquet famously described racing at Monaco as like 'riding a bicycle around your living room'. Piquet clearly rides a much faster bicycle than most of us; Monaco may be the slowest race on the calendar, but the lap record is still over 160km/h and, at the fastest point on the circuit, cars reach 280km/h. Even the corner in the gloom of the tunnel is taken at 250km/h.

The 78-lap race happens on a Sunday afternoon in late May, the conclusion of several days of practice, qualifying and supporting races. Tickets (€75 to €400) are available from **Automobile Club de Monaco** (ACM; ☎93 15 26 00; www.acm.mc; 15 rue Grimaldi).

furniture. Rooms have little balconies and views (the higher the better). The outdoor pool is heated from April to October.

Novotel Monte Carlo HOTEL €€€
(☎99 99 83 00; www.novotel.com/5275; 16 bd Princesse Charlotte; d from €218; @☎≈♿) Put all your chain-hotel preconceptions aside, for the Novotel Monte Carlo is no ordinary chain hotel. Rooms are bright, spacious and colourful, with bath and shower in every bathroom. Even better, up to two children under 16 can stay for free with their parents (and they throw the breakfast in too).

Hôtel Port Palace LUXURY HOTEL €€€
(☎97 97 90 00; www.portpalace.com; 7 av du Président JF Kennedy; r from €249; ☎♿) Built into the hillside overlooking the yacht harbour, this discreetly sexy boutique hotel is decked out in fine silks, soft leather and Carrara marble. All rooms have king-size beds, spa baths and super views of the port and Le Rocher. The hotel offers a 50% discount on the childrens' bedroom.

Hôtel Miramar HOTEL €€
(☎93 30 86 48; www.miramar.monaco-hotel.com; 1 av du Président JF Kennedy; d €145; ❄☎) This 1950s seaside hotel with rooftop terrace bar is a great option right by the port. Seven of the 11 rooms have fabulous balconies overlooking the yachts. All rooms were undergoing renovation at the time of writing.

Hôtel Hermitage LUXURY HOTEL €€€
(☎98 06 40 00; www.montecarloresort.com; square Beaumarchais; d from €412; @☎≈) The Hôtel Hermitage is one of Monaco's super-swish pamper palaces. The rooms are understated sophistication, with cool blues, classic golds or stylish crimsons.

CAP D'AIL

There is no such thing as budget accommodation in Monaco; there are however, two excellent budget-friendly options in Cap d'Ail, a mere 2km from Monaco.

Relais International de la Jeunesse Thalassa HOSTEL €
(☎04 93 81 27 63; www.clajsud.fr; 2 av Gramaglia, Cap d'Ail; dm €18; ⊙Apr-Oct) Cheapest of all, this youth hostel has an outstanding location right by the beach (and close to the train station): the dorms are simple but well-kept. Rates include sheets and breakfast; half-board is available.

Hôtel Normandy FAMILY HOTEL €€
(☎04 93 78 77 77; www.hotelnormandy.no; 6 allée des Orangers; d from €89; ☎) Run by a multilingual family of artists and it shows: original modern pieces adorn the walls and the rooms have charm with their simple, old-school furniture (although some of the bathrooms are very dated). Some rooms have sea views. It's just 50m from the bus 100 stop (for Nice, Menton and Monaco) and 20 minutes from the gorgeous beach of La Mala.

DRESS CODE

By law it's forbidden to inline skate or walk around town bare-chested, barefoot or bikini-clad. In the evening many restaurants, bars and entertainment venues will require smart outfits (jacket and tie for men).

Eating

Eating in Monaco is as diverse as its population. Everything from Monégasque (a variant of Niçois) to Italian, Japanese and gastronomic French cuisine is available, and like most things in the principality, it's rather expensive.

TOP CHOICE La Montgolfière FUSION €€
(☎97 98 61 59; www.lamontgolfiere.mc; 16 rue Basse; mains €21-30; ⏲lunch & dinner Mon, Tue, Thu, Fri, Sun, dinner Sat) This tiny fusion wonder is an unlikely find amid the touristy jumble of Monaco's historic quarter. But what a great idea Henri and Fabienne Geraci had to breathe new life into the Rocher. They have spent a lot of time in Malaysia, and Henri's fusion cuisine is outstanding, as is Fabienne's welcome in the pocket-sized dining room.

In winter, Henri cooks *bourride*, a salted cod stew typical of Monaco, every day.

Zelos FUSION €€€
(☎99 99 25 50; 10 av Princesse Grace, Grimaldi Forum; mains €25-30; ⏲dinner;) With enormous chandeliers, intensely blue walls, a ceiling fitted with hundreds of star-like lights and uninterrupted sea views, it's hard to say which makes more of an impression, the setting or the food (modern dishes such as a trio of Carpaccio – sea bass, king crab and salmon). The restaurant also has a huge terrace for magical summer dining.

Café Llorca MODERN FRENCH €€
(☎99 99 29 29; www.cafellorca.mc; 10 av Princesse Grace, Grimaldi Forum; mains €15-26; ⏲lunch;) This new restaurant is Michelin-starred-chef Alain Llorca's version of a traditional cafe: the menu is classic French fare (pork loin with sautéed potatoes; *daube*, a local beef stew) but elevated to new heights in taste and presentation. In summer, tables are set out on the terrace overlooking the sea.

Mozza ITALIAN €€
(www.mozza.mc; 11 rue du Portier; mains €16-29, lunch menu €14-24;) The clue to Mozza's speciality is in the name: mozzarella. You'll find all the traditional Italian fare here, but don't miss out on the mozzarella bar: the restaurant has about 10 different varieties, which it serves in platters or as starters.

Cosmopolitan INTERNATIONAL €€
(www.cosmopolitan.mc; 7 rue du Portier; mains €17-31, lunch menu €16-21;) The menu at this hip restaurant features timeless classics from all corners of the world, such as fish and chips, three-cheese gnocchi or veal cutlets in Béarnaise sauce, all revisited by Cosmo's talented chefs. Wash it down with one of the *many* wines on offer.

Supermarché Casino BOULANGERIE €
(17 bd Albert 1er; pizza slices & sandwiches from €3; ⏲8.30am-10pm Mon-Sat, to 9pm Sun;) It's not so much the supermarket that's worth knowing about as its excellent street-side bakery and pizzeria, which churn out freshly prepared goodies. A saviour for those keen to watch the pennies.

Tip Top PIZZERIA €
(11 rue Spélugues; mains €12-24; ⏲24hr;) This is where Monégasques gather all night long for pizza, pasta and gossip. At lunch there's a good-value €13 *menu*.

Drinking

Much of Monaco's superchic drinking goes on in its designer restaurants and luxury hotels. Otherwise, the following are pretty popular too.

TOP CHOICE Brasserie de Monaco MICROBREWERY
(www.brasseriedemonaco.com; 36 rte de la Piscine; ⏲11am-1pm Sun-Thu, 11am-3am Fri & Sat) Tourists and locals rub shoulders at Monaco's only microbrewery, which crafts rich organic ales and lager, and serves tasty (if pricey) antipasti plates. Happy hour is 5pm to 8pm.

Cosmopolitan BAR
(☎93 25 78 68; www.cosmopolitan.mc; 7 rue du Portier; ⏲5.45pm-1am;) Whether you're after cocktails or excellent wine, Cosmopolitan should see you right. With its chocolate-orange decor, contemporary furniture and *The Big Chill* music, it's a nice place to ease yourself into a night out.

Café de Paris CAFE
(www.montecarloresort.com; place du Casino; mains €17-53; ⏲7am-2am) Monaco's best-known cafe has been in business since 1882 and is *the* place to people watch. Service is brisk and rather snobbish but it's the price to pay for a front-row view of the casino's razzmatazz.

Stars 'n' Bars AMERICAN
(www.starsnbars.com; 6 quai Antoine 1er; ⏲noon-2.30am, closed Mon Oct-May) This Monaco party institution was undergoing a major facelift at the time of our visit but it promised to be back with a bang, with the same American sports-bar atmosphere.

Sass Café BAR
(11 av Princesse Grace; ⏲7pm-3am) The atmosphere at this popular piano bar is reminiscent of old-school cabarets, with its shiny bar counter, lacquered grand piano (live jazz every night) and padded red walls.

Flashman's BAR
(7 av Princesse Alice; ⏲9pm-5am Wed-Mon; 📶) The retro American-diner-style decor, with fluoro lights and chrome counter, is funky. DJs start playing around 10pm. Dress code is smart-casual.

☆ Entertainment

The Grimaldis have a long tradition of art patronage. Even back in the 18th century, the palace regularly opened its doors to offer music performances to its subjects.

Casino de Monte Carlo CASINO
(www.montecarlocasinos.com; place du Casino; Salon Europe/Salons Privés admission €10/20; ⏲Salon Europe noon-late daily, Salons Privés from 4pm Thu-Sun) The drama of watching the poker-faced gamble in Monte Carlo's grand marble-and-gold casino (p68) makes the stiff admission fees, stakes and obligatory cloakroom 'tips' almost bearable. To enter the casino, you must be at least 18.

The **Salon Europe** has English and European roulette and 30/40; the **Salons Privés** offer European roulette, blackjack and chemin de fer. A jacket and tie are required to enter the Salons Privés and the Salon Ordinaire in the evening.

Monte Carlo Philharmonic Orchestra CLASSICAL MUSIC
(☎98 06 28 28; www.opmc.mc) Going strong since 1856, the orchestra has maintained the tradition of summer concerts in the Cour d'Honneur (Courtyard of Honour) at the Palais Princier. Tickets (€18 to €80), sold at the **Atrium du Casino** (☎98 06 28 28; place du Casino; ⏲10am-5.30pm Tue-Sun) in the casino, are like gold dust. The orchestra performs in the principality's various auditoriums the rest of the year.

Open-air Cinema CINEMA
(Chemin des Pêcheurs) Nightly shows from June to September, specialising in crowd-pleasing blockbusters, mostly in English.

Les Ballets de Monte Carlo DANCE
(www.balletsdemontecarlo.com) The Monte Carlo Ballet is a word-class act. The company regularly tours internationally – performances in Monaco therefore sell out months in advance.

Auditoriums

There are three main auditoriums in Monaco that all stage ballet, opera, classical music and other performing arts:

Opéra de Monte-Carlo AUDITORIUM
(☎92 16 22 99; www.opera.mc; Place du Casino) Or Salle Garnier; an 1892 confection of neoclassical splendour adjoining Monte Carlo Casino and designed by Charles Garnier (who also designed the Paris opera).

DYNASTY

Monaco's longest-ruling monarch, reigning for 56 years, Rainier III (1923–2005) won the heart of the nation with his fairy-tale marriage to Grace Kelly in 1956. The legendary Philadelphia-born actress made 11 films in the 1950s, including Alfred Hitchcock's *To Catch a Thief* (1955). The movie took Kelly to Cannes and Monaco for a photo shoot, where she met Rainier. Tragically, she died in a car crash in 1982.

The soap-opera lives on with the couple's children, Prince Albert (b 1958), monarch since 19 November 2005, Caroline and Stéphanie. Prince Albert is as well known for his sporting achievements (he's a black belt in judo and played in the national soccer team) as he is for his two illegitimate children, neither of whom are in line for the throne. Pressure remains on him to produce a legitimate heir, one of the reasons why his marriage to South African swimmer Charlene Wittstock in July 2011 was so keenly anticipated.

Auditorium Rainier III AUDITORIUM
(☎93 10 85 00; blvd Louis II) This auditorium has a much larger but plainer stage.

Grimaldi Forum AUDITORIUM
(☎99 99 30 00; www.grimaldiforum.mc; 10 av Princesse Grace) The Salle des Princes here is another contemporary stage with a large capacity.

To find out what's on where, you can check the venue's schedule or that of the relevant companies (orchestra, ballet etc). Note that jacket and tie are generally compulsory for men for evening performances.

Shopping

Monaco's streets drip with couture and designer shops, many of which congregate in Monte Carlo. Av des Beaux Arts and av de Monte Carlo, close to the casino, are where to go for all your haute couture needs (from Chanel to Yves Saint Laurent). For chic boutiques and a few more designer brands, head to the **Métropole Shopping Centre** (www.metropoleshoppingcenter.com; 17 av des Spéluges; ⊙10am-7.30pm Mon-Sat). From mid-July to mid-August, boutiques are open on Sunday.

Information

Centre Hospitalier Princesse Grace (Hospital; ☎97 98 97 69; www.chpg.mc; 1 av Pasteur)

Police Station (☎112; 3 rue Louis Notari)

Tourist Office (www.visitmonaco.com; 2a bd des Moulins; ⊙9am-7pm Mon-Sat, 11am-1pm Sun) Download the tourist office's excellent Smartphone app, 'Monaco Travel Guide'.

Getting There & Away

AIR **Héli-Air Monaco** (☎92 05 00 50; www.heliairmonaco.com) runs helicopter flights between Nice and Monaco's **Héliport** (av des Ligures) several times a day (from €107, seven minutes).

BUS Bus 100 (€1, every 15 minutes from 6am to 9pm) goes to Nice (45 minutes) and Menton (40 minutes) along the Corniche Inférieure. **Bus 110** (€18, hourly) goes to Nice-Côte d'Azur airport (40 minutes). Both services stop at place d'Armes and the stop on bd des Moulins. There are also four night services (10pm to 3.45am) on Thursday, Friday and Saturday.

CAR Only Monaco and Alpes-Maritimes (06) registered cars can access Monaco Ville. If you decide to drive, park in one of the numerous underground car parks.

TRAIN Services run about every 20 minutes east to Menton (€2, 15 minutes) and west to Nice (€3.60, 25 minutes). Access to the station is through pedestrian tunnels and escalators from 6 av Prince Pierre de Monaco, pont Ste-Dévote, place Ste-Dévote and bd de la Belgique. The last trains leave around 11pm.

Getting Around

BUS Monaco's urban bus system has five lines, bizarrely numbered one to six without the three. Line 2 links Monaco Ville to Monte Carlo and then loops back to the Jardin Exotique. Line 4 links the train station with the tourist office, the casino and Plage du Larvotto. Tickets are €1.

NIGHT BUS The **Bus de Soirée** (9.20pm to 12.30am) follows one big loop around town; service is extended to 4am on Friday and Saturday. Tickets are €1.

LIFTS A system of escalators and public lifts links the steep streets. They operate either 24 hours or 6am to midnight or 1am.

TAXI Call **Taxi Monégasque Prestige** (☎08 20 20 98 98; www.taximonacoprestige.com).

ROQUEBRUNE-CAP-MARTIN

POP 13,335

Beautiful Cap Martin stretches its languid shores in a sea of crystalline water between Monaco and Menton. The village of Roquebrune-Cap-Martin is actually centred on the medieval village of Roquebrune, which towers over the cape (the village and cape are linked by innumerable *very* steep steps). The amazing thing about this place is that despite Monaco's proximity, it feels a world away from the urban glitz of the principality: the coastline around Cap Martin remains relatively unspoiled and it's as if Roquebrune had left its clock on medieval time.

Sights

Cabanon Le Corbusier ARCHITECTURE
(Promenade Le Corbusier; guided tours €8; ⊙guided tours only 10am Tue & Fri) The only building French architect Le Corbusier (1887–1965) ever built for himself is this rather simple – but very clever – beach hut on Cap Martin. The *cabanon*, a small beach hut that he completed in 1952, became his main holiday home until his death. The hut can be visited on excellent two-hour guided tours run by the Roquebrune-Cap-Martin **tourist office** (☎04 93 35 62 87; www.roquebrune-cap-martin.com; 218 av Aristide Briand).

Le Corbusier first came to Cap Martin in the 1930s to visit friend Eileen Gray, an Irish designer who had built a house here.

WALKING FROM CAP D'AIL TO MENTON

With the exception of in Monaco, you can walk the 13km between Cap d'Ail and Menton without passing a car. The **Sentier du Littoral** follows the rugged coastline from the hedonistic **Plage Mala** (a tiny gravel cove where a couple of restaurants double as private beach and cocktail bars) in Cap d'Ail to **Plage Marquet** in the Fontvieille neighbourhood of Monaco. The path then picks up at the other end of Monaco, in **Larvotto**, from where you can walk to Menton along the beaches and wooded shores of Cap Martin, including the beautiful **Plage Buse**.

The walk is easy going but visitors should note that the stretch of coast between Monaco and Cap d'Ail is inaccessible in bad weather. The path is well signposted and you can easily walk small sections or make a day trip out of it, including beach stops and lunch in Monaco. If you don't fancy walking through Monaco you can catch bus 6, which takes you from Larvotto to Fontvieille.

Le Corbusier loved the area and visited often. During one of his stays, however, Le Corbusier decided to paint the interior of Gray's villa without her permission. Gray was understandably furious: Le Corbusier's paintings had ruined the perspectives of her design, and she was offended by the subject matter (kissing women; Gray was a lesbian).

No longer welcome as a guest, Le Corbusier did come back to Gray's villa in 1949, but as a tenant. It was during that stay that he met Robert Rebutato, owner of **L'Étoile de Mer**, the next-door cafe where he ate his meals. Friendship blossomed between the two men and in 1951, they agreed on the construction of a beach house next door to L'Étoile de Mer so that Le Corbusier could have his own space.

The *cabanon* was designed using the Modulor, a mathematical benchmark based on the height of a man with his arms up.

Guided tours also take in L'Étoile de Mer, except during July and August (the Rebutato family still uses it as a holiday residence).

Roquebrune HISTORIC VILLAGE

The medieval half of the town of Roquebrune-Cap-Martin, Roquebrune sits 300m high on a pudding-shaped lump. The village is delightful, free of tacky souvenir shops. The **Château de Roquebrune** (www.roquebrune-cap-martin.com; place William Ingram; adult/child €4.50/2.50; ⊙10am-12.30pm & 2-6pm) dates back to the 10th century. It's an atmospheric place, with simple but evocative props of life in medieval times and the audio guide (available in English) is fascinating.

Of all Roquebrune's steep and tortuous streets, **rue Moncollet**, with its arcaded passages and stairways carved out of rock, is the most impressive. Architect Le Corbusier is buried in the **cemetery** at the top of the village (in section J – he designed his tombstone before he died).

There are sensational views of the coast from **Place des Deux Frères**.

Sleeping & Eating

TOP CHOICE **Hôtel Victoria** DESIGN HOTEL €€

(☎04 93 35 65 90; www.hotel-victoria.fr; 7 promenade du Cap Martin; s/d from €134/144; ❄@📶) Fans of Eileen Gray and Le Corbusier (or design in general) should make a beeline for this sensational hotel on the shores of Cap Martin. Here, everything from the frescoes in the stunning white and blue rooms to the custom made furniture draws from the designers' influences. All rooms are on the 1st floor and those facing the sea have balconies.

The lobby and restaurant also feature original furniture and lithographies. The hotel is located right next to the bus 100 stop (going to Menton, Monaco and Nice) and just 500m from the Carnolès train station (on the Nice–Ventimille route).

Les Deux Frères BOUTIQUE HOTEL €€

(☎04 93 28 99 00; www.lesdeuxfreres.com; place des Deux Frères; d €75-110; ❄📶) This gorgeous boutique hotel on the village square is a gem. Rooms 1 and 2 steal the show with their heart-stopping views of the Med, but the other eight rooms hold their own, with exquisite decor (themed, but gradually being replaced by a uniform but equally gorgeous pastel boutique interior). A bargain considering the location and standards.

Les Deux Frères MODERN FRENCH €€€

(☎04 93 28 99 00; www.lesdeuxfreres.com; place des Deux Frères; lunch/dinner menu €28/48; ⊙lunch Wed-Sun, dinner Tue-Sat; 📶) This gourmet restaurant, perched dramatically at the edge of the village on a panoramic terrace, is a stylish choice. Waiters wear formal black, and mains (huge pieces of meat or whole fish for two, delicate fish fillets in hollandaise sauce or spinach and basil olive oil) come hidden beneath silver domed platters.

In winter, guests lunch or dine in the minimalist dining room with its contemporary fireplace. The lunch menu, including a half-bottle of wine, is good value.

Fraise et Chocolat CAFE €
(place des Deux Frères; light meals €6; ⌚8am-6pm Sat-Thu; ☑) Fraise et Chocolat (Strawberry and Chocolate) is a lovely cafe with an old-fashioned-deli feel. Stop for a drink, an ice cream or a quick bite (sandwiches and quiches). There are two terraces, including one with sweeping sea views at the back.

Getting There & Around

BUS Bus 100 (€1) goes to Monaco (20 minutes), Nice (1¼ hours) and Menton (30 minutes); it stops on av de la Côte d'Azur, which lies below Roquebrune and above Cap Martin (you'll see steps near the bus stop).

TRAIN The Cap-Martin-Roquebrune train station is at the Cap Martin end of town; destinations include Monaco (€1.50, four minutes), Nice (€4.20, 30 minutes), Menton (€1.30, six minutes) and Ventimiglia (€3.40, 20 minutes); trains runs half-hourly.

WALKING It takes 30 to 45 minutes to walk from Cap Martin to Roquebrune, depending on your fitness level (a lot less the other way around since it's downhill) – you'll find several staircases linking the two parts of town.

MENTON & AROUND

A string of mountain villages peer down on Menton from the surrounding hills. The stunning **Parc National du Mercantour** (www.mercantour.eu), a prime walking area, is a mere 20km away. But make sure you start your explorations on Menton's doorsteps in Ste-Agnès and Gorbio.

Menton

POP 29,361

Menton used to be famous for two things: its lemons and its exceptionally sunny climate. We'd bet, however, that the city will soon add Cocteau as its third claim to fame, thanks to the opening of the fantastic Musée Jean Cocteau Collection Séverin Wunderman.

Sights

The town's epicentre is pedestrian rue St-Michel, where ice-cream parlours and souvenir shops jostle for space.

TOP CHOICE Musée Jean Cocteau Collection Séverin Wunderman GALLERY
(2 quai Monléon; adult/student/child €6/3/free; ⌚10am-6pm Wed-Mon) In 2005 art collector Séverin Wunderman donated some 1500 Cocteau works to Menton, on the condition that the town build a dedicated Cocteau museum. And what a museum Menton built: opened in 2011, the futuristic, low-rise building has breathed new life into the slumbering city and is a wonderful space to try and make sense of Cocteau's eclectic work.

The collection focuses on Cocteau's graphic works. Displays are organised chronologically and thematically, from Cocteau's early works as an illustrator to his cinematograpic swansong, the convoluted and abstract *Testament of Orpheus* (in which he stages his own death). There are poignant drawings from his rehab days (Cocteau was addicted to opium) in Villefranche-sur-Mer, beautiful photographs of Cocteau and his acolytes (actor and muse Jean Marais; Picasso, who introduced Cocteau to pastels and oil painting) and plenty of extracts from his films.

Explanations are in French, English and Italian; audio guides (€2) are also available. The admission fee lets you in at the Musée du Bastion, which Cocteau designed.

Musée du Bastion ART MUSEUM
(quai Napoléon III; combined admission with Musée Jean Cocteau adult/student/child €6/3/free; ⌚10am-6pm Wed-Mon) Poet, artist, novelist and filmmaker Jean Cocteau loved Menton. It was following a stroll along the seaside that he got the idea of turning the disused 17th-century seafront bastion into a monument to his work. Cocteau restored the building himself, decorating the alcoves, outer walls and reception hall with pebble mosaics. The works on display change regularly.

Vieille Ville HISTORIC QUARTER
Menton's old town is a cascade of pastel-coloured buildings. Meander the historic quarter all the way to the **Cimetière du Vieux Château** (montée du Souvenir; ⌚7am-8pm May-Sep, to 6pm Oct-Apr) for great views. From place du Cap a ramp leads to south-

Menton

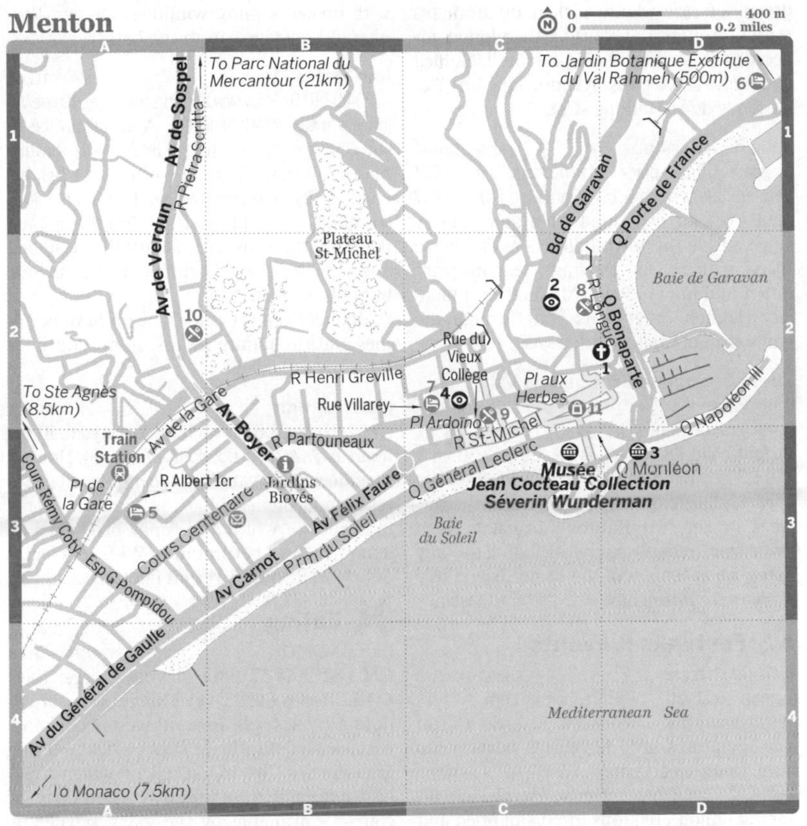

Menton

Top Sights

Musée Jean Cocteau Collection Séverin Wunderman C3

Sights

1 Basilique St-Michel Archange D2
2 Cimetière du Vieux Château C2
3 Musée du Bastion D3
4 Salle des Mariages C2

Sleeping

5 Hôtel Lemon A3
6 Hôtel Napoléon D1
7 Ibis Styles Menton C2

Eating

8 A Braïjade Méridiounale C2
9 La Table d'Oc C2
10 Sucre & Salés A2

Shopping

11 Au Pays du Citron C2

ern France's grandest baroque church, the Italianate **Basilique St-Michel Archange** (place de l'Église St-Michel; ⏲10am-noon & 3-5.15pm Mon-Fri, 3-5.15pm Sat & Sun), its creamy facade flanked by a 35m-tall clock tower and 53m-tall steeple (1701–03).

Jardin de la Serre de la Madone GARDEN
(☎04 93 57 73 90; www.serredelamadone.com; 74 rte de Gorbio; adult/student/child €8/4/free; ⏲10am-6pm Tue-Sun) Beautiful if slightly unkempt, this garden was designed by American botanist Lawrence Johnston. He planted

dozens of rare plants picked up from his travels around the world. Abandoned for decades, it is slowly being restored. Guided tours take place daily at 3pm. Take bus 7 to the Serre de la Madone stop.

Salle des Mariages ARCHITECTURE
(Registry Office; place Ardoïno; adult/child €2/free; 8.30am-noon & 2-4.30pm Mon-Fri) In 1957 Jean Cocteau decorated Menton's registry office, inside the town hall. It's a distinctive space, with swirly drawings, leopard-print carpet and no windows. An audio commentary (French only) runs you through the symbolism of Cocteau's designs.

Jardin Botanique Exotique du Val Rahmeh GARDEN
(www.jardins-menton.fr; Av St-Jacques; adult/student/child €8.50/4/free; 10am-12.30pm & 3.30-6.30pm Wed-Mon) Laid out in 1905 for Lord Radcliffe, governor of Malta, the terraces of the Val Rahmeh overflow with exotic fruit-tree collections, including the only European specimen of the Easter Island tree *Sophora toromiro,* now extinct on the island.

Festivals & Events

Fête du Citron STREET CARNIVAL
(Lemon Festival; www.feteducitron.com; Feb) Menton's quirky two-week Fête du Citron sees sculptures and decorative floats made from tonnes of lemons weave processions along the seafront. Afterwards, the monumental lemon creations are dismantled and the fruit sold off at bargain prices in front of Palais de l'Europe. Each year the festival follows a different theme.

Sleeping

Accommodation gets booked up months in advance for the Fête du Citron in February (prices also soar), so plan ahead.

TOP CHOICE **Hôtel Napoléon** BOUTIQUE HOTEL €€
(04 93 35 89 50; www.napoleon-menton.com; 29 porte de France; s/d from €139/149;) Standing tall on the seafront, the Napoléon is Menton's most stylish option. Everything from the pool, the restaurant-bar and the back garden (a heaven of freshness in summer) has been beautifully designed. Rooms come in shades of beige and red; all are equipped with iPod docking stations. Sea-facing rooms also have balconies but are a little noisier because of the traffic.

The two top floor suites (one decorated with Cocteau memorabilia) are sensational, with floor-to-ceiling windows, larger balconies and sea views from the bath!

Ibis Styles Menton DESIGN HOTEL €€
(04 92 10 95 25; www.accorhotels.com; 10 rue Villarey; d/q €110/140;) A great choice in the centre of town, the All Seasons is a minimalist affair, with an all-white decor brightened up by one painted wall in each room (turquoise, red, pink etc, different on each floor). Bathrooms are beautifully designed and the staff are charming. Rates include buffet breakfast.

Rooms from the 2nd floor up have balconies and the family rooms on the top floor have fantastic views.

Hôtel Lemon HOTEL €
(04 93 28 63 63; www.hotel-lemon.com; 10 rue Albert 1er; s/d/tr/q €55/59/75/115;) Housed in a nicely renovated 19th-century villa, Hôtel Lemon has spacious, minimalist rooms in shades of white and funky bright-red or lemon-yellow bathrooms. Wi-fi currently only works on the ground floor.

Eating

La Table d'Oc SOUTHWESTERN FRENCH €€
(04 92 15 14 57; 2 rue du vieux Collège; mains €14-23, menus €18-23;) This modern bistro does a brisk trade in southwestern cuisine, with cassoulet (a bean stew), duck and foie gras gracing the menu, all of which must be accompanied by fine wine (Bordeaux, of course – available by the glass, pitcher or bottle). It is very popular, so book.

A Braïjade Méridiounale TRADITIONAL FRENCH €€
(www.abraijade.fr; 66 rue longue; menu €34, mains €18-25; Thu-Tue) In a beautiful stone-walled dining room framed by heavy wooden beams, A Braïjade is the only restaurant in the old town and has made the best of it. The house speciality is flambé skewers (the kebab is flambéed at your table). The *menu*, which includes an aperitif, glass of local wine and digestive, is good value.

LEMON TREATS

Limoncello, lemon-infused olive oil, lemon preserve, lemon wine and lemon syrup (for squash) are just some of the delicious products you'll be able to sample and buy at the family-run **Au Pays du Citron** (www.aupaysducitron.fr; 24 rue St Michel). Products are also available online.

WORTH A TRIP

ITALY FLITS

Menton literally sits on the border with Italy so getting two countries out of your Côte d'Azur holiday is not only easy but highly recommended.

The perfect excuse is the **all-day Friday market in Ventimiglia** (Vintimille in French), the border town on the Italian side. The market sprawls over 1km along the seafront and is popular with French shoppers for its cheap fruit and veg and lovely deli counters (mozzarella-stuffed peppers, sun-dried tomatoes etc). It is also renowned for bargain leather goods and cheap fashion. There is a lot of counterfeit here, which French customs take very seriously: you risk a fine and confiscation of your goods.

Once you've shopped, head to the fabulous **Pasta & Basta** (☎+39 184 230878; 20/A Via Marconi, Maria San Giuseppe, Ventimiglia; mains €15-20; ⏰lunch & dinner Tue-Sun, lunch Mon; 🖉) for lunch. The modern restaurant, opposite the future port (completion slated for 2013), serves copious portions of utterly delicous homemade pasta. Cross the footbridge from the market and keep going along the seafront until you reach the 'port'.

Ventimiglia is at the end of the French SNCF network; there are half-hourly trains to/from Monaco (€4, 25 minutes), Nice (€7, 45 minutes) and Cannes (€11.60, 1½ hours).

Sucre & Salés CAFE €
(8 promenade Maréchal Leclerc; cakes/sandwiches €3/5; ⏰6.30am-8pm; 📶) Conveniently located opposite the bus station, Sucre & Salés is a contemporary spot to enjoy a coffee, cake or well-stuffed baguette.

Information

Tourist Office (☎04 92 41 76 76; www.tourisme-menton.fr; 8 av Boyer; ⏰9am-7pm)

Getting There & Away

Bus 100 (€1, every 15 minutes) goes to Nice (1½ hours) via Monaco (40 minutes) and the Corniche Inférieure. Bus 110 links Menton with Nice-Côte d'Azur airport (€18, one hour, hourly).

There are regular train services (half-hourly) to Ventimiglia in Italy (€2.30, nine minutes), Monaco (€2, 11 minutes) and Nice (€4.80, 35 minutes).

Ste-Agnès & Gorbio

POP 1223

Ste-Agnès' claim to fame – Europe's highest seaside village – is not for nothing: sitting snug on a rocky outcrop at 780m, the village looks spectacular and commands dramatic views of the area. For the most breathtaking panorama, climb the 200 or so steps to the rubbly 12th-century **château ruins** (admission by donation; ⏰10am-6pm) with their intriguing flower beds, based on allegorical gardens found in medieval French poetry.

The drawbridged entrance to the huge underground **Fort Ste-Agnès** (adult/child €5/3; ⏰10.30am-12.30pm & 3-7pm Tue-Sun Jun-Sep, 2.30-5.30pm Sat & Sun Oct-May) sits at the top of the village. The 2500-sq-metre defence was built between 1932 and 1938 as part of the 240km-long Maginot line, a series of fortifications intended to give France time to mobilise its army if attacked. The fort is in good condition: it was maintained throughout the Cold War as a nuclear fallout shelter and the army only moved out in 1990. Interestingly, it is thanks to this active military history that the village of Ste-Agnès is so picturesque today: all new developments were prohibited in the village during the army's presence, a measure that the village has since maintained.

A well-signposted path leads to the neighbouring village of **Gorbio**, another pretty Provençal village. Just 2km as the crow flies from Ste-Agnès, it is much more convoluted to get there by car, so walking is a good option. Allow one hour on the way down, and 1¼ hours back up, particularly if you've had lunch at the exquisite **Beau Séjour** (☎04 93 41 46 15; place du Village, Gorbio; lunch/dinner menu €27/40, mains €17-25; ⏰lunch & dinner Thu-Tue Apr-Oct). The stuff of Provençal lunch dreams, 'Beautiful Stay' serves up local fare in a buttermilk house overlooking the village square. Inside, the dining room, which looks like it's straight out of a glossy design magazine, proffers panoramic views of the tumbling vale. No credit cards.

Cannes & Around

Includes »

Best Places to Eat

» Sea Sens (p88)
» La Colombe d'Or (p97)
» Mantel (p88)
» L'Affable (p88)
» Bistrot Gourmand Clovis (p101)

Best Places to Stay

» Les Cabanes d'Orion (p96)
» La Maison du Frêne (p98)
» Hôtel Le Canberra (p85)
» La Cascade (p99)
» Le Mas des Cigales (p100)

Why Go?

There are few areas in the world where you can go from opulent luxury to remote rural life within 45 minutes. The area around Cannes is one of them, so you can look forward to walking deserted trails or talking to an olive-oil producer by day and dining in decadent style by night (oh the restaurants of Cannes...). Equally captivating is the region's rich art heritage: every 20th-century great – Matisse, Picasso, Renoir, F Scott Fitzgerald – seems to have stopped here for inspiration, and left a little something behind: a chapel here, a museum there, an art studio. The Massif de l'Estérel, with its rugged beauty and top-rated walks, offers yet another facet of the region, and one that stays relatively low key year-round.

Driving Distances (km)

	Antibes	Biot	Cannes	Grasse	Mougins	St-Raphaël
Biot	7					
Cannes	13	16				
Grasse	28	16	21			
Mougins	14	13	6	11		
St-Raphaël	53	50	37	55	38	
Vence	20	15	31	26	25	68

Getting Around

There are two strategies to visiting this part of the world, and they revolve around where you stay. If you're staying in Cannes or Antibes, you can use the excellent bus network to do day trips around the area and limit car rental for the most rural areas. If, however, you decide to stay in a village or somewhere more isolated, you'll definitely need a car, if only to find somewhere for dinner.

THREE PERFECT DAYS

Day 1: Robinson Crusoe Meets Marilyn Monroe

Pack a picnic and jump on a boat to Île Ste-Marguerite: explore the Fort Royal (p90) and enjoy a long stroll across the island's woodland. Plump yourself on a cove for lunch and enjoy a spot of swimming or sunbathing. Get the boat back to Cannes mid afternoon and walk up to Le Suquet (p84), Cannes' historic quarter. Book for dinner at Mantel (p88) or Sea Sens (p88) and round out the evening with an atmospheric walk along La Croisette (p84).

Day 2: Art Trail

Retrace the steps of famous 20th-century artists. Head to the Fondation Maeght (p96) in St-Paul de Vence and lunch under a Matisse or a Léger at the legendary La Colombe d'Or (p97). Digest among St Paul's exquisite pebbled alleyways and art galleries, and finish the day with a visit to Matisse's masterpiece, the Chapelle du Rosaire (p97) in Vence.

Day 3: Natural Wonder

Spend a day exploring the wonderful Arrière-Pays. Drive to the Domaine des Courmettes (p100) and take one of the scenic walks around the nature reserve; pick from one of the area's gorgeous restaurants and spend the rest of the afternoon motoring around the scenic gorges. Plan a stop at Confiserie Florian (p99) to stock up on traditional sweets and chocolates, and another at Gourdon (p98) for unbeatable views of the valley.

Advance Planning

Many of the most fun activities in the region only take place on certain days of the week or month. Check dates notably for perfume workshops in Grasse and the Palais des Festivals guided tours in Cannes.

Cannes is an important conference centre and when an event swings into town (there are a dozen or so during the year, including the film festival), hotels are generally booked up solid and prices soar, so plan ahead.

DON'T MISS

Picasso spent many years on the Riviera: trail him at the Musée Picasso in Antibes and the Musée Picasso La Guerre et la Paix in Vallauris.

Best Scenic Walks

- » Sentier du Littoral (p106)
- » Chemin du Paradis (p98)
- » Domaine des Courmettes (p100)
- » Cap Roux (p106)
- » Cap d'Antibes (p92)

Best Tours

- » Snorkelling at Corniche de l'Estérel (p106)
- » Perfumery tour (p102)
- » Flower farm visit (p100)
- » Goat's cheese tasting at La Ferme des Courmettes (p100)
- » Wine and olive oil tour at Domaine Saint-Joseph (p100)
- » Catamaran cruise from Cannes (p84)

Resources

- » **Côte d'Azur Tourisme** (www.cotedazur-tourisme.com) Excellent regional guide run by Côte d'Azur tourism professionals
- » **Cannes.travel** (www.cannes.travel) The city's official web portal
- » **Guides RandOxygène** (www.randoxygene.org) Essential for anyone who loves walking.

Cannes & Around Highlights

1 Of all the exceptional 20th-century art to be found in the region, **Fondation Maeght** (p96) in St-Paul de Vence remains the very best

2 A mattress on the beach, fine dining and exclusive partying, enjoy **Cannes'** (p84) hedonistic lifestyle

3 Drive around the stunning **Gorges du Loup** (p98)

4 Delve into **Grasse's** (p101) perfumery industry

5 Admire priceless antiques and modern masterpieces at Mougins' new **Musée d'Art Classique** (p104)

6 Enjoy the blue, green and crimson contrasts of the Corniche de l'Estérel along the **Sentier du Littoral** (p106)

7 Meet local producers (cheese, flower, wine, olive oil) in pretty **Tourrettes-sur-Loup** (p100)

8 Enjoy views of the Alps and ogle millionaires' mansions at **Cap d'Antibes** (p92)

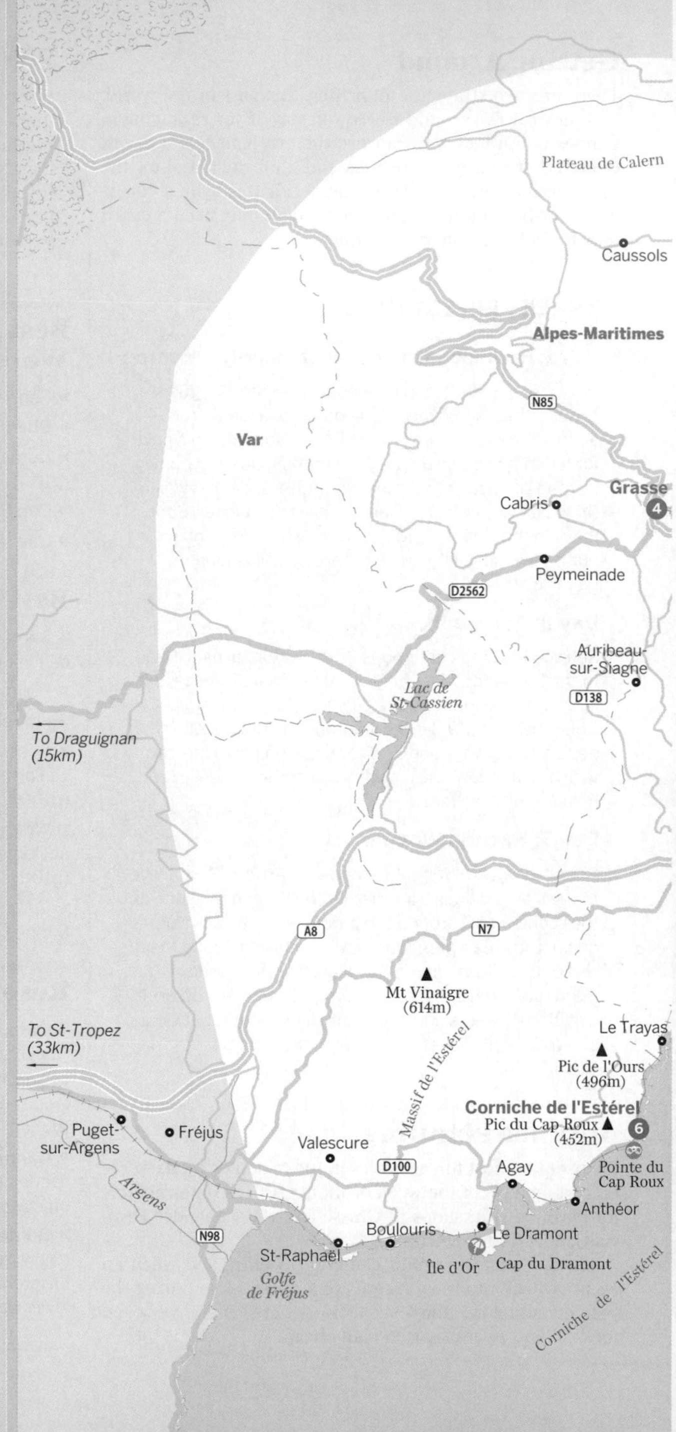

0 10 km
0 5 miles
Gréolières
Coursegoules
Loup
Cipières
D603
D2
Bramafan
Col de Vence (963m)
Baou des Blancs (673m)
N202
Cantaron
Courmes
St-Jeannet
Gorges du Loup
3
Tourrettes-sur-Loup
La Gaude
Courmettes
Gourdon
7
Vence
D2210
Var
Le Bar-sur-Loup
Pont du Loup
D6
St-Paul de Vence
St-Isidore
1
La Colle Loubière (337m)
Nice
La Colle-sur-Loup
N98
St-Laurent-du-Var
Châteauneuf de Grasse
D2085
Roquefort-les-Pins
Opio
Cagnes-sur-Mer
To Corsica
Villeneuve-Loubet
Cros de Cagnes
D3
Valbonne
D9
D4
Villeneuve-Loubet-Plage
N85
Mouans-Sartoux
D103
Sophia Antipolis
Biot
Musée d'Art Classique
A8
Mougins
5
Vallauris
Antibes
N7
Le Cannet
Golfe-Juan
D109
Pointe Bacon
Mandelieu-La Napoule
Cannes
2
Juan-les-Pins
8
Cap d'Antibes
Plage de la Garoupe
Golfe Juan
N98
Golfe de Napoule
Cap d'Antibes
La Napoule
Île Ste-Marguerite
Théoule-sur-Mer
Île St-Honorat
Îles de Lérins
La Galère
Miramar
MEDITERRANEAN SEA

CANNES TO BIOT

Cannes

POP 74,445

Walking among the couture shops and palaces of La Croisette, you'd be forgiven for thinking that the global downturn was all media hype. There is as much wealth and glamour as ever, and admiring Ferraris and Porsches and celebrity spotting on the liner-sized yachts are still favourite Cannes pastimes.

For those who aren't seduced by Cannes' hedonistic air, there's enough natural beauty to make a trip worthwhile: the harbour, the bay, the clutch of islands off the coast and the old quarter, Le Suquet, all spring into life on a sunny day.

As for the world-famous film festival, it is unfortunately not the most visitor-friendly event: think stratospheric prices and insider-only attendance. It is, however, celebrity spotting at its very best!

Sights & Activities

La Croisette ARCHITECTURE

The multi-starred hotels and couture shops that line the famous bd de la Croisette (aka La Croisette) may be the preserve of the rich and famous, but anyone can enjoy the palm-shaded promenade and take in the atmosphere. In fact, it's a favourite amongst Cannois (natives of Cannes), particularly at night when it's lit with bright colours.

There are great views of the bay and nearby Estérel mountains, and stunning art deco architecture among the seafront palaces, such as the **Martinez** or the legendary **Carlton InterContinental** – its twin cupolas were modelled on the breasts of the courtesan La Belle Otéro, infamous for her string of lovers – Tsar Nicholas II and Britain's King Edward VII among them.

Not so elegant but imposing nonetheless is the **Palais des Festivals** (Festival Palace; blvd de la Croisette) at the western end of the prom, host of the world's most glamorous film festival. Climb the red carpet, walk down the auditorium, tread the stage and learn about cinema's most glamorous event and its numerous anecdotes on a Palais des Festivals **guided tour** (adult/child €3/free; 1½hr; guided tours 2.30pm Jun-Apr). The tourist-office-run tours take place several times a month, except in May. Check dates on the office's website (visits in English are sometimes available). Tickets can only be booked in person at the tourist office.

After posing for a photograph on the 22 steps leading up to the cinema entrance, wander along allée des Étoiles du Cinéma, a path of celebrity hand imprints in the pavement.

Le Vieux Port & Le Suquet HISTORIC QUARTER

On the western side of the Palais des Festivals lies the real Cannes. The yachts that frame the **Vieux Port** (Old Port) are the only reminder that this is where celebrities holiday, but they don't seem to impress the pensioners playing pétanque on **square Lord Brougham**. Follow **rue St-Antoine** and snake your way up **Le Suquet**, Cannes's oldest district, for great views of the bay.

For local folklore head to **Marché Forville** (7am-1pm Tue-Sun), a couple of blocks back from the port. It's one of the most important markets in the region and the supplier of choice for restaurants (and for your picnic!).

Trans Côte d'Azur BOAT TOUR

(04 92 98 71 30; www.trans-cote-azur.com; quai Max Laubeuf) From June to September, Trans Côte d'Azur runs day trips to St-Tropez (adult/child €44/32 return) and Monaco (€48.50/32), an ideal way to avoid congested roads to these popular spots and relax among scenic landscapes instead. Panoramic cruises taking in the dramatic contrasts of the Estérel's red cliffs, green forests and intense azure waters are another must (€26.50/16.50).

Beaches BEACHES

Cannes is blessed with sandy beaches, although much of the stretch along bd de la Croisette is taken up by private beaches. This arrangement leaves only a small strip of free sand near the Palais des Festivals for the bathing hoi polloi; the much bigger **Plage du Midi** (blvd Jean Hibert) and **Plage de la Bocca**, west of Vieux Port, are also free.

Rates for private beaches range from €15 to €25 at the relaxed and family-friendly **Plage Vegaluna** (04 93 43 67 05; www.vegaluna.com; La Croisette; 9.30am-7pm;), water sports available, to €34/30/38 for the blue loungers on the front row/other rows/pier of the super-stylish **Z Plage** (9.30am-6pm May-Sep), the beach of Hôtel Martinez. Book ahead.

STARRING AT CANNES

For 12 days in May, all eyes turn to Cannes, centre of the cinematic universe, where more than 33,000 producers, distributors, directors, publicists, stars and hangers-on descend to buy, sell or promote more than 2000 films. As the premier film event of the year, the festival (p85) attracts around 4000 journalists from around the world.

At the centre of the whirlwind is the colossal, 60,000-sq-metre Palais des Festivals, where the official selections are screened. The palace opened in 1982, replacing the original Palais des Festival – since demolished. The inaugural festival was scheduled for 1 September 1939, as a response to Mussolini's Fascist propaganda film festival in Venice, but Hitler's invasion of Poland brought the festival to an abrupt end. It restarted in 1946 – and the rest is history.

Over the years the festival split into 'in competition' and 'out of competition' sections. The goal of 'in competition' films is the prestigious Palme d'Or, awarded by the jury and its president to the film that best 'serves the evolution of cinematic art'. Notable winners include Francis Ford Coppola's *Apocalypse Now* (1979), Quentin Tarantino's cult *Pulp Fiction* (1994) and American activist Michael Moore's anti-Bush-administration polemic *Fahrenheit 9/11* (2004). More recent winners include *La Classe* (2008), a film by Laurent Cantet about teaching in tough Parisian suburbs, and *Amour* (2012), the story of an ailing elderly couple by Michael Haneke.

The vast majority of films are 'out of competition'. Behind the scenes the **Marché du Film** (www.marchedufilm.com) sees nearly $1 billion worth of business negotiated in distribution deals. And it's this hard-core commerce, combined with all the televised Tinseltown glitz, that gives the film festival its special magic.

Tickets to the film festival are off limits to average Joes. What you can get are free tickets to selected individual films, usually after their first screening. Invitations must be picked up on the day at **Espace Cannes Cinéphiles** (La Pantiéro; ⏲9am-5.30pm) and are limited.

Festivals & Events

Cannes lives for music in the summer so come prepared to party hard.

Festival de Cannes FILM FESTIVAL
(www.festival-cannes.com; ⏲May) You won't get in, but it's fun because you see all the celebs walking around. And unlike the Oscars, you can get close to the red carpet without tickets.

FREE **Festival d'Art Pyrotechnique** FIREWORKS
(www.festival-pyrotechnique-cannes.com; ⏲Jul & Aug) Around 200,000 people cram onto the Croisette every summer to admire the outstanding fireworks display over the Bay of Cannes. Magical. Held on six nights from July to August.

Les Plages Électroniques MUSIC FESTIVAL
(www.plages-electroniques.com; €8; ⏲Jul & Aug) DJs spin on the sand at the Plage du Palais des Festivals during this relaxed festival. Held once a week for five or six weeks.

Festival Pantiero MUSIC FESTIVAL
(www.festivalpantiero.com; 4-night pass €55; ⏲early Aug) Electronic-music and indie-rock festival on the terrace of the Palais des Festivals; very cool.

Sleeping

Cannes is an important conference centre and hotels fill up with every event, so try to plan ahead if you want to stay in the city. Search and book accommodation online with **Cannes Hôtel Booking** (www.cannes-hotel-reservation.fr), run by the tourist office; and check out **Riviera Pebbles** (www.rivierapebbles.com) for apartments in Cannes and Antibes.

TOP CHOICE **Hôtel Le Canberra** BOUTIQUE HOTEL €€€
(☎04 97 06 95 00; www.hotel-cannes-canberra.com; 120 rue d'Antibes; d from €255; ❄@📶🏊) This boutique stunner, just a couple of blocks back from La Croisette, is the epitome of Cannes glamour: designer grey rooms with splashes of candy pink, sexy black-marble bathrooms with coloured lighting, heated pool (April to October) in a bamboo-filled garden, intimate atmosphere (there are just 35 rooms) and impeccable service. Rooms overlooking rue d'Antibes are cheaper.

Cannes

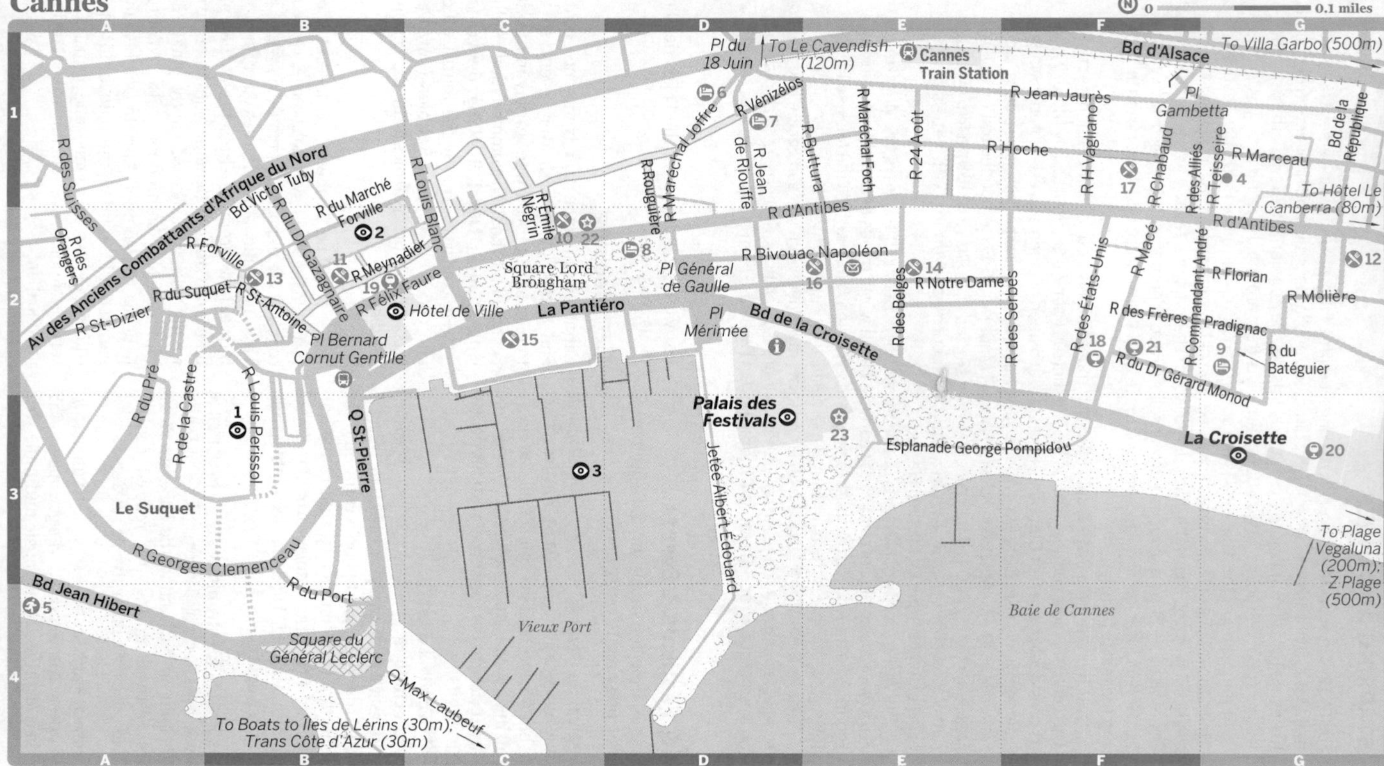
0 200 m
0 0.1 miles
Pl du 18 Juin
To Le Cavendish (120m)
Cannes Train Station
Bd d'Alsace
To Villa Garbo (500m)
R Jean Jaurès
Pl Gambetta
Bd de la République
R des Suisses
R des Orangers
Av des Anciens Combattants d'Afrique du Nord
Bd Victor Tuby
R du Dr Gazagnaire
R du Marché Forville
R Louis Blanc
R Émile Négrin
R Rouguière
R Maréchal Joffre
R Vénizélos
R Jean de Riouffe
R Buttura
R Maréchal Foch
R 24 Août
R Hoche
R H Vagliano
R Chabaud
R des Alliés
R Teisseire
R Marceau
To Hôtel Le Canberra (80m)
R d'Antibes
R Forville
R Meynadier
R du Suquet
R St-Antoine
R Félix Faure
R St-Dizier
Square Lord Brougham
Pl Général de Gaulle
R Bivouac Napoléon
R Notre Dame
R des Belges
R des Serbes
R des États-Unis
R Macé
R Commandant André
R Florian
R Molière
R des Frères Pradignac
R du Batéguier
R du Dr Gérard Monod
Hôtel de Ville
La Pantiéro
Pl Mérimée
Bd de la Croisette
Pl Bernard Cornut Gentille
R du Pré
R de la Castre
R Louis Perissol
Q St-Pierre
Palais des Festivals
Esplanade George Pompidou
La Croisette
Le Suquet
R Georges Clemenceau
R du Port
Jetée Albert Édouard
To Plage Vegaluna (200m); Z Plage (500m)
Bd Jean Hibert
Vieux Port
Baie de Cannes
Square du Général Leclerc
Q Max Laubeuf
To Boats to Îles de Lérins (30m); Trans Côte d'Azur (30m)

Cannes

Top Sights
- La Croisette G3
- Palais des Festivals D3

Sights
1. Le Suquet B3
2. Marché Forville B2
3. Vieux Port C3

Activities, Courses & Tours
4. Les Apprentis Gourmets G1
5. Plage du Midi A4

Sleeping
6. Hôtel 7e Art D1
7. Hôtel Alnéa D1
- Hôtel Le Mistral ..... (see 14)
8. Hôtel Splendid D2
9. Le Romanesque G2

Eating
10. Au Martin Pêcheur C2
11. Aux Bons Enfants B2
12. L'Affable G2
13. Mantel B2
- New York New York ..... (see 8)
14. Petit Paris E2
15. PhilCat C2
16. Sea Sens E2
17. Volupté F1

Drinking
18. Black Pearl F2
19. Byron B2
20. Le Cercle G3
21. Le Sun 7 ..... F2

Entertainment
22. Cinéma Les Arcades C2
23. Le Palais E3

Le Romanesque BOUTIQUE HOTEL €€
(☎04 93 68 04 20; 10 rue du Batéguier; s/d/tr €89/109/149; ❄📶) Every room is individually decorated at this eight-room boutique charmer in the heart of the Carré d'Or nightlife district (book a back room if you're a light sleeper). Favourite rooms include Charlotte, with its sun-drenched bath; and Elizabeth, the former maid's quarters, with low, sloping beamed ceilings. Gay-friendly. Great service.

Hôtel 7e Art BOUTIQUE HOTEL €
(☎04 93 68 66 66; www.7arthotel.com; 23 rue Maréchal Joffre; s €68, d €60-98; ❄📶) Hôtel 7e Art has put boutique style within reach of budgeters. The owners schooled in Switzerland and got the basics right, with great beds, sparkling-clean baths and excellent soundproofing. The snappy design of putty-coloured walls, padded headboards and pop art, and perks like iPod docks in every room, far exceed what you'd expect at this price.

Villa Garbo BOUTIQUE HOTEL €€€
(☎04 93 46 66 00; www.villagarbo-cannes.com; 62 bd d'Alsace; ste from €400; ❄@📶👪) For outstanding style and service, look no further than the Villa Garbo. The spacious studios and suites, all equipped with kitchenettes, are decked out in grey/fuchsia or chocolate/orange and finished to the highest standards (Egyptian cotton sheets, iPod docking stations, king-size beds, open bar every night). The biggest downside of this excellent establishment is its location at a very busy junction.

Hôtel Le Mistral BOUTIQUE HOTEL €€
(☎04 93 39 91 46; www.mistral-hotel.com; 13 rue des Belges; d from €89; ❄📶) This small boutique hotel wins the Palme d'Or for best value in town: rooms are decked out in flattering red and plum tones, bathrooms feature lovely designer fittings, there are sea views from the top floor and the hotel is a mere 50m from La Croisette.

Hôtel Alnéa HOTEL €€
(☎04 93 68 77 77; www.hotel-alnea.com; 20 rue Jean de Riouffe; s/d €70/90; ❄📶) A breath of fresh air in a town of stars, Noémi and Cédric have put their heart and soul into their hotel, with bright, colourful rooms, original paintings and numerous little details such as the afternoon coffee break, the self-service minibar and the bike or boules (to play pétanque) loans. No elevator.

Hôtel Splendid BOUTIQUE HOTEL €€€
(☎04 97 06 22 22; www.splendid-hotel-cannes.com; 4-6 rue Félix Faure; s/d from €160/190; ❄) This elaborate 1871 building has everything it takes to rival the nearby palaces – beautifully decorated rooms, vintage furniture, old-world feel with creature comforts,

fabulous location, stunning views. A handful of rooms equipped with kitchenettes are ideal for longer stays and families.

Hôtel Montaigne BOUTIQUE HOTEL €€
(☎04 97 06 03 40; www.hotel-montaigne.eu; 4 rue Montaigne; d €100-160;) The Montaigne reopened in 2012 after extensive renovations with a fresh, minimalist look and a new spa to boot. Rooms are spacious and bright, and the decor is the same throughout: a palette of beige and burgundy. Families are well catered for with communicating rooms and kitchenettes.

Le Cavendish BOUTIQUE HOTEL €€€
(☎04 97 06 26 00; www.cavendish-cannes.com; 11 bd Carnot; d from €235;) The belle époque facade and period features of Le Cavendish will delight those in search of historic charm. Rooms are definitely modern in comfort but classic in looks, with pastel shades and heavy fabrics. The hotel is located on a busy boulevard – light sleepers, ask for a room at the back.

Eating

Most private beaches have restaurants: they come into their own on sunny days but you'll definitely pay for the privilege of eating *les pieds dans l'eau* (by the sea). Among the better beach restaurants are Le Vegaluna (p84) and **Le Miramar** (www.miramar-plage.fr; Bd de la Croisette;). Expect to pay around €25 to €30 for a main of grilled fish or meat, or a gourmet salad.

TOP CHOICE **Sea Sens** FUSION €€€
(☎04 63 36 05 06; www.five-hotel-cannes.com; Five Hotel & Spa, 1 rue Notre Dame; 2-/3-course lunch menu €29/39, mains €26-55;) Perched on the 5th floor of the Five Hotel, the Sea Sens is Cannes' latest food sensation. Run by the brilliant Pourcel brothers, with pastry-chef wonder Jérôme de Oliveira in charge of desserts, it serves divine food blending French gastronomy and Asian elegance, with panoramic views of Le Suquet and Cannes' rooftops on the side. De Oliveira's signature dessert, 'Onde de Choc', a pear-shaped chocolate tower filled with chocolate and praline, is simply out of this world. Come here for lunch to make the best of the great-value menus.

L'Affable MODERN FRENCH €€€
(☎04 93 68 02 09; www.restaurant-laffable.fr; 5 rue Lafontaine; lunch/dinner menu €26/40, mains €34-38;) Modern French cuisine has never tasted so good. Everything from the ingredients, the cooking and the presentation is done to perfection, whether it be the roasted veal with its vegetable medley, the seared sea bream with white butter and asparagus, or the house speciality, the Grand Marnier soufflé, which arrives practically ballooning at your table. Booking essential.

Mantel MODERN EUROPEAN €€
(☎04 93 39 13 10; www.restaurantmantel.com; 22 rue St-Antoine; menus €25-38; ⊙Fri-Mon, dinner Tue & Thu) Discover why Noël Mantel is the hotshot of the Cannois gastronomic scene at his refined old-town restaurant. Service is stellar and the seasonal cuisine divine: try the wonderfully tender glazed veal shank in balsamic vinegar, or the original poached octopus *bourride*-style. Best of all though, you get not one but two desserts from dessert chef Christian Gonthier, who bakes the bread and prepares the sweets served with coffee.

Aux Bons Enfants TRADITIONAL FRENCH €€
(80 rue Meynadier; menus €23; ⊙Tue-Sat) A people's-choice place since 1935, this informal restaurant cooks up wonderful regional dishes such as aioli *garni* (aioli with vegetables), *daube* (a Provençal beef stew) and *rascasse meunière* (pan-fried rockfish), all in a convivial atmosphere. Make no plans for the afternoon after lunching here. No credit cards and no booking.

PhilCat DELICATESSEN €
(La Pantiéro; sandwiches & salads €4-6.50; ⊙8.30am-5pm) Don't be put off by Phillipe and Catherine's unassuming prefab cabin on the Pantiéro: this is Cannes' best lunch house. Huge salads, made to order, are piled high with delicious fresh ingredients. Or if you're *really* hungry, try one of their phenomenal *pan bagna* (a moist sandwich bursting with Provençal flavours).

Au Martin Pêcheur PROVENÇAL €€
(4 rue Émile Négrin; 2-course lunch menu €14, mains €17-25; ⊙lunch Tue-Sat, dinner Thu-Sat) This unassuming, family-run restaurant is the place to come for great fish. Mother-and-son duo Christel and Maxime prepare traditional and Provençal recipes with whatever the sea has given them that day, from poached sea bass to grilled sea bream. There are always a couple of meat options too.

Petit Paris BRASSERIE €€
(www.le-petitparis.fr; 13 rue des Belges; mains €15-38; ⊙7.30am-1am;) Entirely refurbished

over the 2011–12 winter, the Petit Paris really looks like a Parisian brasserie, albeit a very glamorous one. Like any brasserie worth its French fries, it serves food all day.

New York New York BRASSERIE **€€**
(1 allée Liberté; mains €10-36; ⏲8am-2am; 📶📝📋) The latest venture of the Bâoli nightclub, this new grill house has become a hit with Cannes' young crowd who love the huge burgers, tender steaks, wood-fired pizzas, budget-friendly prices and the industrial chic decor.

Volupté CAFE **€**
(32 rue Hoche; snacks €5, mains €15-18; ⏲9am-7.30pm) Young and beautiful things come here to sip fragrant teas and nibble on *tartines* (a slice of bread with toppings) and salads.

Drinking & Entertainment

Bars around the 'magic square' (the area bordered by rue Commandant André, rue des Frères Pradignac, rue du Batéguier and rue du Dr Gérard Monod) tend to be young, trendy and pretty rowdy. For a more sophisticated atmosphere, try the beach or top hotel bars. Pick up the free monthly *Le Mois à Cannes* for full event listings at the tourist office. It's worth knowing that going out in Cannes is taken very seriously, so dress to impress if you'd like to get in the most-sought-after clubs and events.

Le Sun 7 COCKTAIL BAR
(5 rue du Dr Gérard Monod; ⏲9pm-2.30am; 📶) An unpretentious, happening place, Le Sun 7 attracts a pretty young crowd keen to knock down a few drinks and shake their stuff at the weekend. It's more laid-back on weeknights.

Le Cercle BAR
(Le Grand Hôtel, 45 bd de la Croisette; 📶) The bar of Le Grand Hôtel is a great place for a couple of quiet drinks. The lounge is a cosy space (there's a pianist most nights) but it's the garden that really does it: with its giant fairy lights, views of La Croisette and the sea, it's divine on summer evenings.

Byron PUB
(www.byroncannes.com; 49 rue Félix Faure) There's something of the old traditional pub at the Byron, but the fancy chandeliers, DJ booths and wide screens are definitely more Cannes than the Costwolds. It serves decent food too.

Black Pearl BAR
(www.blackpearlcannes.com; 22 rue Macé) Beautiful, brash and up for it is how you could summarise both the Black Pearl and its clientele. Alas, the music is too loud to talk past 11pm and the space too small to dance.

Le Bâoli NIGHTCLUB
(☎04 93 43 03 43; www.lebaoli.com; Port Pierre Canto, bd de la Croisette; ⏲8pm-6am Thu-Sat) This is Cannes' coolest, trendiest and most selective nightspot. So selective in fact that your entire posse may not get in unless you're dressed to the nines. The Bâoli is part club, part restaurant, so the only way to ensure you'll get in is to book a table and make a night of it.

Le Palais NIGHTCLUB
(www.palais-club.com; Palais des Festivals, bd de la Croisette; cover charge €25-60; ⏲midnight-dawn Jul & Aug) This ephemeral nightclub (it's open only for 50 nights each year) has become the hottest ticket in DJ land, a combination of the most happening names in music and its spectacular setting at the heart of the Palais des Festivals. It's the VIPs' favourite spot so door policy is pretty tight: no guys without girls and only fabulous-looking people.

Cinéma Les Arcades CINEMA
(77 rue Félix Faure) Catch a movie in English.

DON'T MISS

LES APPRENTIS GOURMETS

Part restaurant, part cooking school is probably the best way to describe this boutique kitchen in the heart of Cannes. Cooking classes tend to be short (one to two hours, €32 to €69) and focus on themes or menus (take-away at the end of the class), but **Les Apprentis Gourmets** (☎04 93 38 78 76; www.lesapprentisgourmets.fr; 6 rue Teisseire) flagship product is its express lunch formula: a €15, 30-minute lesson to cook one main, which you then eat with your fellow cooks on the mezzanine above the kitchen (and they throw in the dessert for free). Great fun, cheap and accessible, even if cooking is your domestic nemesis!

Information

There is a free wi-fi hotspot at the **Hôtel de Ville** (town hall).

Tourist Office (☎04 92 99 84 22; www.cannes.travel; Palais des Festivals, bd de la Croisette; ⏲9am-7pm) There's also a tourist office annexe on av Jean Jaurès (open 9am to 1pm and 2pm to 6pm Monday to Saturday).

Getting There & Around

BUS TAM (www.cg06.fr/fr) runs express services to Nice (bus 200, €1, 1½ hours, every 15 minutes), Nice-Côte d'Azur airport (bus 210, €16.50, 50 minutes, half-hourly), Mougins (bus 600, €1, 20 minutes, every 20 minutes) and Grasse (bus 600, €1, 45 minutes). The electric Elo Bus (€1) follows a loop that takes in the **bus station** (Place Cornut-Gentille), the Croisette, rue d'Antibes and the train station. It has no set stops, just flag it down as it passes.

BICYCLE & CAR Mistral Location (☎04 93 39 33 60; www.mistral-location.com; 4 rue Georges Clemenceau) rents out bicycles/scooters/cars for €16/35/52 per day. You'll find the usual car-hire companies at the train station , too.

PARKING Street parking is limited to two hours in the centre. Car parks such as **Parking Palais des Festivals** (Palais des Festivals), **Parking Forville** (Rue Forville) or **Parking Gare SNCF** (Rue Jean Jaurès); train station) have no time restrictions but are expensive (€2.70 per hour).

TRAIN Cannes is well connected to Nice (€6.40, 40 minutes), Antibes (€2.70, 12 minutes), Monaco (€8.70, one hour) and St-Raphaël (€6.70, 30 minutes), with services every 20 minutes or so. There are half-hourly trains to Marseille (€28.40, two hours).

Îles de Lérins

The two islands making up Lérins – Île Ste-Marguerite and Île St-Honorat – lie within a 20-minute boat ride of Cannes. Tiny and traffic-free, they're oases of peace and tranquillity, a world away from the hustle and bustle of the Riviera.

Camping is forbidden, and there are no hotels and only a couple of eating options, so bring a picnic and a good supply of drinking water.

Boats for the islands leave Cannes from quai des Îles, at the end of quai Laubeuf on the western side of the harbour. **Riviera Lines** (www.riviera-lines.com; adult/child €11.50/6 return) run ferries to Île Ste-Marguerite (adult/child €12/7.50 return), while **Compagnie Planaria** (www.cannes-ilesdelerins.com; adult/child €12/6) operates boats to Île St-Honorat (adult/child €13/6 return).

In St-Raphaël, Les Bateaux de St-Raphaël (p107) also runs excursions to Île Ste-Marguerite.

ÎLE STE-MARGUERITE

Covered in sweet-smelling eucalyptus and pine, Ste-Marguerite makes a wonderful day trip from Cannes. Its shores are an endless succession of castaway beaches ideal for picnics, and there are numerous **walking** trails.

The island served as a strategic defence post for centuries. **Fort Royal** (Île Ste-Marguerite; adult/child €6/3; ⏲10.30am-1.15pm & 2.15-5.45pm Tue-Sun), built in the 17th century by Richelieu and later fortified by Vauban, today houses the **Musée de la Mer**, with exhibits on the island's Greco-Roman history, artefacts from the numerous shipwrecks littering the shores and a small aquarium focusing on Mediterranean fauna and flora.

You can also visit the cells of the former **state prison**, where the most famous inmate was the Man in the Iron Mask, and walk around the compound, which boasts grand **views** of the coast.

ÎLE ST-HONORAT

Forested St-Honorat was once the site of a powerful monastery founded in the 5th century. Now it's home to 25 Cistercian monks who own the island but welcome visitors. At 1.5km by 400m, St-Honorat is the smallest (and most southerly) of the two Lérins islands.

The **Monastère Fortifié**, guarding the island's southern shores, is all that remains of the original monastery. Built in 1073 to protect the monks from pirate attacks, the monastery's entrance stood 4m above ground level and was accessible only by ladder (later replaced by the stone staircase evident today). The elegant arches of the vaulted prayer cloister on the 1st floor date from the 15th century, and there's a magnificent panorama of the coast from the donjon terrace.

In front of the donjon is the walled, 19th-century **Abbaye Notre Dame de Lérins**, built around a medieval cloister. In the souvenir shop you can buy the 50%-alcohol **Lérina**, a ruby-red, lemon-yellow or pea-green liqueur concocted from 44 different herbs. The monks also produce wine from their small **vineyard**.

Antibes-Juan-les-Pins

POP 76,580

With its boat-bedecked port, 16th-century ramparts and narrow cobblestone streets festooned with flowers, lovely Antibes is the quintessential Mediterranean town. Picasso, Max Ernst and Nicolas de Staël

Antibes

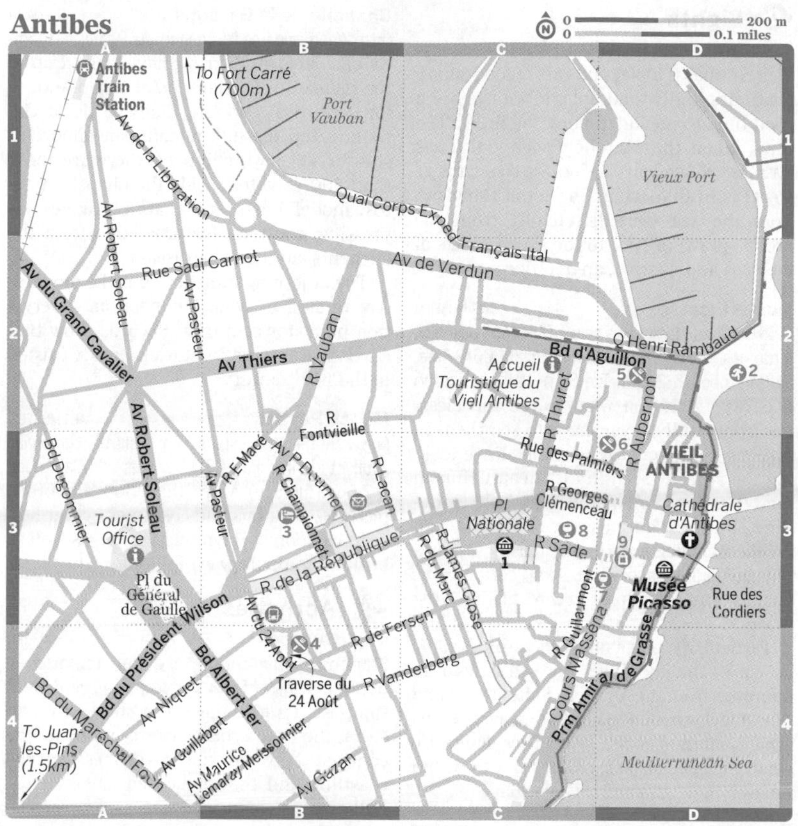

Antibes

Top Sights
Musée Picasso D3

Sights
1 Musée Peynet C3

Activities, Courses & Tours
2 Plage de la Gravette D2

Sleeping
3 Le Relais du Postillon B3

Eating
4 La Badiane B4
5 La Ferme au Foie Gras D2
6 Le Broc en Bouche D3

Drinking
7 Balade en Provence D3
8 Les Sens C3

Shopping
9 Marché Provençal D3

were captivated by Antibes, as was a restless Graham Greene (1904–91), who settled here with his lover, Yvonne Cloetta, from 1966 until the year before his death.

Greater Antibes embraces Cap d'Antibes, an exclusive green cape studded with luxurious mansions, and the modern beach resort of Juan-les-Pins. The latter is known for its 2km-long sandy beach and its nightlife, a legacy of the sizzling 1920s when Americans swung into town with their jazz music and oh-so-brief swimsuits.

Sights

Vieil Antibes HISTORIC QUARTER

Vieil Antibes is a pleasant mix of food shops, boutiques and restaurants. Mornings are a good time to meander along the little alleyways, when the **Marché Provençal** (cours Masséna; ⌚7am-1pm Tue-Sun Sep-Jun, daily Jul & Aug) is in full swing. Check out the views from the sea walls, stretching from the urban sprawl of Nice to the snowy peaks of the Alps and nearby Cap d'Antibes.

Musée Picasso ART MUSEUM

(www.antibes-juanlespins.com; Château Grimaldi, 4 rue des Cordiers; adult/student/child €6/3/free; ⌚10am-noon & 2-6pm Tue-Sun) Pablo Picasso once wrote, 'If you want to see the Picassos from Antibes, you have to see them in Antibes'. Spectacularly positioned overlooking the sea, 14th-century Château Grimaldi served as Picasso's studio from July to December 1946. The museum now houses an excellent collection of the master's paintings, lithographs, drawings and ceramics, as well as a photographic record of the artist at work.

Particularly poignant is Picasso's *La Joie de Vivre* (The Joy of Life), one in a series of 25 paintings from the Antipolis Suite. The young flower girl, surrounded by flute-playing fauns and mountain goats, symbolises Françoise Gilot, Picasso's 23-year-old lover, with whom he lived in neighbouring Golfe-Juan.

Fort Carré HISTORIC SITE

(rte du Bord de Mer; guided tour only adult/student/child €3/1.50/free; ⌚10am-6pm Tue-Sun Jul & Aug, 10am-4.30pm Tue-Sun Sep-Jun) The impregnable 16th-century Fort Carré, enlarged by Vauban in the 17th century, dominates the approach to Antibes from Nice. It served as a border defence post until 1860 when Nice, until then in Italian hands, became French. Regrettably, the tours are rather rushed and the explanations superficial; tours depart half-hourly. Some guides speak English.

BARGAIN BOX

If you intend to visit all of Antibes' museums, buy a combined ticket (€10). It's valid for seven days and can be purchased from the museums or the tourist office.

Chapelle de la Garoupe CHURCH

(http://garoupe.free.fr; chemin du Phare; ⌚10am-noon & 2.30-5pm) Pilgrims have walked up to the plateau of La Garoupe at Cap d'Antibes for centuries, and the Chapelle de la Garoupe, atop the hill, remains an important site for local worshippers: there are more than 300 ex-votos inside the chapel – photos, model boats and marble plaques expressing gratitude for protection from the elements, accidents or diseases.

The adjoining **lighthouse** is the modern-day version of what has been an observation point for centuries. Records show that a wooden observation tower already existed in the 16th century.

Musée Peynet ART MUSEUM

(www.antibes-juanlespins.com; place Nationale; adult/student/child €3/1.50/free; ⌚10am-noon & 2-6pm Tue-Sun) More than 300 humorous pictures, cartoons and costumes by Antibes-born cartoonist Raymond Peynet, as well as brilliant temporary exhibitions.

Activities

Cap d'Antibes WALKING

Starting from the pretty but relentlessly popular **Plage de la Garoupe**, a scenic and signposted **path** skirts the shores to **Cap Gros**, the cape's southeastern-most tip. The contrast between the ruggedness of the coastline and the manicured lawns of the millionaires' mansions are typical of the cape. Signs on chemin des Douaniers and avenue de Beaumont take you back to the beach.

The southwestern tip of the cape is crowned by legendary **Hôtel du Cap Eden Roc**. Dating from 1870, it hit the big time just after WWI when a literary salon held here one summer (previous guests had come for the winter season only) was attended by Hemingway, Picasso et al. The icing on the cake was the immortalisation of the hotel (as the thinly disguised, fictional Hôtel des Étrangers) by F Scott Fitzgerald in his novel *Tender Is the Night* (1934).

Artists & the Mediterranean Sea WALKING TOUR

(www.antibesjuanlespins.com; adult/student/child €7/3.50/free) Antibes has a rich and complex history: not only does it go back a very long way (more than 25 centuries), it has also inspired numerous artists. The **tourist office** (www.antibesjuanlespins.com) runs 1½-

THE MAN IN THE IRON MASK

The Man in the Iron Mask was imprisoned by Louis XIV (r 1661–1715) in the fortress on Île Ste-Marguerite from around 1687 until 1698, when he was transferred to the Bastille in Paris. Only the king knew the identity of the man behind the mask, prompting a rich pageant of myth and legend to be woven around the ill-fated inmate.

More than 60 suggested identities have been showered on the masked prisoner, among them the Duke of Monmouth (actually beheaded under James II), the Comte de Vermandois (son of Louis XIV, said to have died from smallpox in 1683) and the king's brother (a twin or an illegitimate older brother). Some theorists claimed the Man in the Iron Mask was actually a woman.

hour tours: one of the Vieil Antibes and another on artists (Graham Greene, Picasso, Prévert, F Scott Fitzgerald, among others) and the Mediterranean Sea.

Beaches SWIMMING
(sun-lounges per day from €21) Right in the centre of Antibes, you'll find **Plage de la Gravette** (quai Henri Rambaud), a small patch of sand by the *remparts* (ramparts). Twenty minutes out of town is **Plage de la Salis**, with unbeatable views of old Antibes and the Alps. For a more party-like atmosphere, opt for **Juan-les-Pins**.

The stretch of coast between Plage de la Salis and Cap d'Antibes, especially the section around **Pointe Bacon**, is fringed with rocks coves, where snorkellers frolic in clear waters. On the cape itself, **Plage de la Garoupe** was famously first raked clear of seaweed in 1922 by Cole Porter and American artist Gerald Murphy to create a sandy beach. Far from an idyllic paradise today, it is packed with sun lounges.

Festivals & Events

July is *the* party month in Antibes and Juan-les-Pins. The headline event is Juan's jazz festival but a number of fringe music festivals are also picking up.

Jazz à Juan MUSIC FESTIVAL
(www.jazzajuan.fr; Jul) This major festival in mid-July celebrated its 50th edition in 2010. Every jazz great has performed here, and Jazz à Juan continues to attract big music names. The Off fringe festival is the perfect backup option if you haven't managed to get tickets for the main event: amongst the Off highlights include the Jazz à Juan Revelations, where unknown artists get a shot at fame, impromptu concerts and free, scheduled performances from jazz big names.

Sleeping

Hôtel La Jabotte B&B €€
(04 93 61 45 89; www.jabotte.com; 13 av Max Maurey; s/d €124/142;) A hotel with a *chambre d'hôte* (B&B) feel, La Jabotte is Antibes' hidden gem. Just 50m from the sea (and 20 minutes' walk from Vieil Antibes), its 10 Provençal rooms all look out onto an exquisite patio where breakfast is served from spring to autumn. Much of the decor is the work of Yves, who runs La Jabotte with Claude. Rates include breakfast.

Le Relais du Postillon HOTEL €€
(04 93 34 20 77; www.relaisdupostillon.com; 8 rue Championnet; d €73-134;) Housed in a 17th-century coach house, the great value Postillon is in the heart of the old town. The owners did a huge amount of works in 2012: out went the outdated carpet and bathrooms, in came laminate floors and fresh new bathrooms. The decor has thankfully retained its Provençal charm and the welcome is as warm as ever.

Relais International de la Jeunesse HOSTEL €
(04 93 81 27 63; www.clajsud.fr; 272 bd de la Garoupe; dm €20; Apr-Oct;) In the most perfect of Mediterranean locations, with sea views the envy of neighbouring millionaires, this basic but friendly hostel is particularly popular with 'yachties' looking for their next job in Antibes' port. Rates include sheets and breakfast. There is a daily lockout between 11am and 5pm.

Eating

TOP CHOICE **Le Broc en Bouche** MODERN FRENCH €€
(04 93 34 75 60; 8 rue des Palmiers; mains €15-30; lunch Thu-Tue, dinner Thu-Mon) No two chairs, tables or lights are the same at this lovely bistro: instead, every item has been

lovingly sourced from antique shops and car-boot sales, giving the place a sophisticated but cosy vintage feel. The charming Flo and Fred have put the same level of care and imagination into their cuisine, artfully combining Provençal and oriental flavours.

La Ferme au Foie Gras DELICATESSEN €
(www.vente-foie-gras.net; 35 rue Aubernon; sandwiches €3.50-7; ⌚8am-6pm Tue-Sun) Now, this is our idea of what a good sandwich should be like: filled with foie gras or smoked duck breast, onion chutney or fig jam, truffle cheese and fresh salad. And many people seem to think the same: a queue snakes from the tiny counter of La Ferme every lunchtime.

La Badiane FUSION €
(3 Traverse du 24 Août; mains €11-13; ⌚lunch Mon-Fri) Salmon tartare (raw and marinated), fresh pesto lasagne and scrumptious quiches are just some of the treats you can eat at this cute lunch house behind Antibes' bus station. Everything is fresh, dishes are presented with care and you won't find better value for a sit-down lunch.

Drinking & Entertainment

In Antibes, pedestrian bd d'Aguillon heaves with merrily piddled Anglophones falling out of the busy 'English' and 'Irish' pubs.

TOP CHOICE **Balade en Provence** ABSINTHE BAR
(25 cours Masséna; ⌚6pm-2am) Flirt with the green fairy at this dedicated absinthe bar in the vaulted basement of an olive-oil shop. It's the only one of its kind in France, with an original 1860 zinc bar, five round tables and all the accessories (four-tapped water fountain, sugar cubes etc).

Pick from 25 absinthe varieties (€4 per glass) and let the knowledgeable staff debunk some of the myths shrouding this much reviled spirit. And don't worry, if you're really not keen, there are plenty of other beverages on offer.

Les Sens WINE BAR
(☎04 93 74 57 06; 10 rue Sade; ⌚10am-midnight Tue-Sat) Wine shop by day and wine bar by night, Les Sens is a 21st-century cellar: the decor is more designer shop than vaulted basement with its lime-green walls, mezzanine bar and lounge music, but the advice is excellent all the same, with a great selection of local and French wines.

Pearl La Siesta NIGHTCLUB
(rte du Bord de Mer; cover €15-20; ⌚7pm-5am Thu-Sat) This legendary establishment is famous up and down the coast for its beachside nightclub (Le Pearl) and all-night dancing under the stars. Open from early June to mid-September only, you can still party at the indoor bar-lounge (Le Flamingo) during the rest of the year.

Information

Accueil Touristique du Vieil Antibes (☎04 93 34 65 65; 32 bd d'Aguillon; ⌚10am-noon & 1-6pm Mon-Sat)

Tourist Office (☎04 97 23 11 11; www.antibesjuanlespins.com; 55 bd Charles Guillaumont; ⌚9am-noon & 2-6pm Mon-Sat, 10am-12.30pm & 2.30-5pm Sun)

Getting There & Away

BUS The Nice–Cannes service (bus 200, €1) stops by the tourist office. Local bus services (€1) for Opio, Vence and St-Paul de Vence leave from the **bus station** (place Guynemer).

CAR Vieil Antibes is mostly pedestrianised, so park outside the centre and walk in. There are several car parks along the port on av de Verdun. The only free car park is a 20-minute walk from town behind Fort Carré.

TRAIN Antibes' train station is on the main line between Nice (€4.20, 30 minutes, five hourly) and Cannes (€2.70, 10 minutes, five hourly).

Biot

POP 9353

This charming 15th-century hilltop village was once an important pottery-manufacturing centre specialising in large earthenware oil and wine containers. Metal containers brought an end to this, but Biot is still active in handicraft production, especially glassmaking. The dynamic **tourist office** (☎04 93 65 78 00; www.biot.fr; 46 rue St-Sébastien; ⌚9am-noon & 2-6pm Mon-Fri, 2-6pm Sat & Sun) has various itineraries to discover this arts heritage (downloadable as the Visit Biot app).

The village was also the one-time headquarters (1209–1387) of the Knights Templars, then the Knights of Malta: the picturesque **place des Arcades**, dating from the 13th and 14th centuries, is a reminder of this illustrious past.

Biot's main attractions are located outside the historic village, however. The famous **Verrerie de Biot** (☎04 93 65 03 00; www.verreriebiot.com; chemin des Combes; admission

WORTH A TRIP

VALLAURIS

Picasso (1881–1973) discovered ceramics in the small potters' village of Vallauris in 1947. Attracted by its artistic vibe, he settled in Vallauris between 1948 and 1955. During that time, he produced some 4000 ceramics (many on display at the Musée Picasso, p92, in Antibes) as well as his last great political composition, the *Chapelle La Guerre et La Paix* (*War and Peace Chapel*), a collection of dramatic murals painted on plywood panels and tacked to the walls of a disused 12th-century chapel. It is now part of the **Musée Picasso La Guerre et la Paix** (☎04 93 64 71 83; www.musee-picasso-vallauris.fr; Place de la Libération; adult/child €3.25/free; ⌚10am-12pm & 2-5pm Wed-Mon), which also runs various contemporary-art exhibitions.

Picasso left Vallauris another gift: a dour bronze figure clutching a sheep, *L'Homme au Mouton*, now on place Paul Isnard (adjoining place de la Libération). But his biggest legacy was the revival of the ceramics industry in Vallauris, an activity that might have died out had it not been for the 'Picasso effect'.

free, 45-min guided tour €6; ⌚9.30am-6pm Mon-Sat, 10.30am-1.30pm & 2.30-6.30pm Sun) is at the foot of the village and within walking distance. Its bubbled glass is produced by rolling molten glass into baking soda; bubbles from the chemical reaction are then trapped by a second layer of glass. You can watch skilled glass-blowers at work and browse the adjacent art galleries and shop.

About 1.5km in the direction of Antibes sits the **Musée National Fernand Léger** (www.musee-fernandleger.fr; Chemin du Val de Pome; adult/child €5.50/free; ⌚10am-6pm Tue-Sun May-Oct, to 5pm Nov-Apr). It presents a thorough overview of Fernand Léger's work and life: his brush with cubism, his ongoing interest in architecture, society and cinema, and the influence of his stays in America. The free audio guide (which can also be downloaded as an app) is an essential companion to the visit. The museum is signposted (in brown); bus 10 between Antibes and Biot stops nearby (at stop Musée Fernand Léger).

THE ARRIÈRE-PAYS

The 'coast' in Côte d'Azur is what many people come to see, but the *arrière-pays* (hinterland) has a charm of its own. Less crowded and incredibly varied, it has something for everyone, from keen walkers to culture vultures and foodies.

St-Paul de Vence

POP 3540

Once upon a time, St-Paul de Vence was a small medieval village atop a hill looking out to sea. Then came the likes of Chagall and Picasso in post-war years, followed by showbiz stars such as Yves Montand and Roger Moore, and St-Paul shot to fame. The village is now home to dozens of art galleries as well as the exceptional Fondation Maeght.

The village's tiny cobbled lanes get overwhelmingly crowded in high season – come early or late to beat the rush.

Sights

The Village HISTORIC QUARTER

Strolling the narrow streets is how most visitors pass time in St-Paul. The village has been beautifully preserved and the panoramas from the ramparts are stunning. The main artery, rue Grande, is lined with **art galleries**. The highest point in the village is occupied by the **Église Collégiale**; the adjoining **Chapelle des Pénitents Blancs** was redecorated by Belgian artist Folon.

Many more artists lived or passed through St-Paul de Vence, amongst them Soutine, Léger, Cocteau, Matisse and Chagall. The latter is buried with his wife Vava in the **cemetery** at the village's southern end (immediately to the right as you enter). The dynamic **tourist office** (☎04 93 32 86 95; www.saint-pauldevence.com; 2 rue Grande; ⌚10am-7pm) runs a series of informative, themed **guided tours** (1½ hours, adult/child €5/free) that delve into this illustrious past. Book ahead; tours are available in English.

Across from the entrance to the fortified village, the **pétanque pitch**, where many a star has had a spin, is the hub of village life. The tourist office rents out balls (€2) and can organise **pétanque lessons** (€5 per person).

DON'T MISS

MUSÉE RENOIR & MUSÉE ESCOFFIER

Except for their historic centres, the sprawling towns of Villeneuve-Loubet and Cagnes lack charm. Two cultural highlights make them worth the detour, however. Le Domaine des Collettes, today the evocative **Musée Renoir** (☎04 93 20 61 07; Chemin des Colettes, Cagnes-sur-Mer), was home and studio to an arthritis-crippled Pierre-Auguste Renoir (1841–1919), who lived here with his wife and three sons from 1907 until his death.

Works of his on display include *Les Grandes Baigneuses* (The Women Bathers; 1892), a reworking of the 1887 original, and rooms are dotted with photographs and personal possessions. The magnificent olive and citrus groves are as much an attraction as the museum itself. Many visitors set up their own easel to paint. The museum was closed at the time of writing for a major refurbishment and planned to reopen in summer 2013.

Equally wonderful, but in a completely different genre, is the **Musée Escoffier de l'Art Culinaire** (Escoffier Museum of Culinary Arts; www.fondation-escoffier.org; 3 rue Auguste Escoffier; adult/student/child €5/2.50/free; ⌚2-7pm Jul & Aug, to 6pm Sep-Jun), which retraces the history of modern gastronomy. Escoffier (1846–1935), inventor of the pêche Melba and dried potato among other things, was France's first great chef and a celebrity amongst Europe's well heeled.

The museum includes beautiful period furniture and 'appliances', hilarious period cartoons that ridiculed the notion of cooking as an art, and a fascinating wall chronology retracing the history of cooking and chefs from prehistory to nowadays (alas in French only).

Fondation Maeght ART MUSEUM
(www.fondation-maeght.com; 623 chemin des Gardettes; adult/student/child €14/9/free; ⌚10am-6pm) The region's finest art museum, Fondation Maeght was created in 1964 by art collectors Aimé and Marguerite Maeght. Its collection of 20th-century works is one of the largest in Europe. It is exhibited on a rotating basis, which, along with the excellent temporary exhibitions, guarantees you'll rarely see the same thing twice. Find the *fondation* 500m downhill from the village.

The building was designed by Josep Lluís Sert and is a masterpiece in itself, integrating the works of the very best: a Giacometti courtyard, Miró sculptures dotted across the terraced gardens, coloured-glass windows by Braque and mosaics by Chagall and Tal-Coat.

St-Paul's tourist office (p95) runs guided tours (adult/child €5/free); you'll need to book ahead.

Sleeping

Although St-Paul has a good selection of hotels, we have also listed here a couple of options in the pretty village of La Colle-sur-Loup, a mere five minutes' drive from St Paul.

TOP CHOICE **Les Cabanes d'Orion** B&B €€€
(☎06 75 45 18 64; www.orionbb.com; Impasse des Peupliers, 2436 chemin du Malvan, St-Paul de Vence; d €260;) Dragonflies flit above water lilies in the emerald-green swimming pool (filtered naturally), while guests slumber amid a chorus of frogs and cicadas in luxurious cedar-wood treehouses perched in the trees at this enchanting, ecofriendly B&B. Children are well catered for with mini-*cabanes* in two of the treehouses. There is a minimum three-night stay from April to October.

In winter, Orion offers special cocooning packages, with sauna sessions and gourmet baskets complete with organic hot meals and champagne for a cosy night in.

La Forge B&B €€
(☎04 93 89 73 34; www.laforgedhauterives.com; 44 rue Yves Klein, La Colle sur Loup; d €115-170;) It seems hard to believe that this exquisite *maison d'hôte*, with its beautiful stone walls and romantic decor, was once a forge. Anne and Patrick have turned the 18th-century building at the heart of La Colle sur Loup into a delicious Provençal halt: opt for Bois de Charme or Bois d'Amarante for their gorgeous terraces.

Villa St Maxime B&B €€€
(☎04 93 32 76 00; www.villa-st-maxime.com; 390 rte de la Colle, St-Paul de Vence; d €205-265 ; ⌚Mar-Nov;) Run by an American couple, this *maison d'hôte* is vast and full of archi-

tectural flair. Highlights include the show-stopping sliding glass roof, champagne breakfast cooked up by a sabre-wielding John (he'll happily show you how) and the unbeatable views of hilltop St-Paul and the Med. Unusually, rates include evening drinks.

L'Abbaye BOUTIQUE HOTEL **€€€**
(04 93 32 68 34; www.hotelabbaye.com; 541 bd Honoré Teisseire, La Colle sur Loup; s/d €110/190;) A superb boutique hotel inside an 11th-century abbey. Each of the 15 rooms has been decorated with a glamorous palette of black and white and kitted out with designer furniture. The (deconsecrated) chapel, a masterpiece of Roman architecture, has also been daringly converted into a contemporary bar-lounge space.

Les Vergers de Saint-Paul BOUTIQUE HOTEL **€€**
(04 93 32 94 24; www.vergersdesaintpaul.com; 940 rte de la Colle, St-Paul de Vence; d €155-170;) This elegant hotel has something of a belle époque feel about it, with the art deco stripy fabrics, parquet floors, resplendent white facade and wrought-iron balconies. There is a splendid pool too, with assorted loungers. We prefer the rooms in the main building to those in the annexe.

La Colombe d'Or HISTORIC HOTEL **€€€**
(04 93 32 80 02; www.la-colombe-dor.com; place de Gaulle; r from €250-430; closed Nov-Christmas;) This world-famous inn could double as the Fondation Maeght's annexe: La Colombe d'Or (located outside the walls, at the entrance of the village) was the party HQ of many 20th-century artists (Chagall, Braque, Matisse, Picasso etc), who often paid for their meals in kind, resulting in an incredible private art collection. Every room houses unique art and vintage furniture, as do the dining room and garden. Hotel guests get access to the lovely pool, which is heated year-round and crowned by a Calder mobile.

Eating

TOP CHOICE **La Colombe d'Or** TRADITIONAL FRENCH **€€€**
(04 93 32 80 02; www.la-colombe-dor.com; place de Gaulle; mains €30-55; lunch & dinner mid-Dec–Oct;) A Léger mosaic here, a Picasso painting there: these are just some of the original modern artworks at the Golden Dove, the legendary restaurant where impoverished artists paid for meals with their creations. Dining is beneath fig trees in summer or in the art-filled dining room in winter, and the cuisine is surprisingly uncomplicated (terrines, rabbit stew, beef carpaccio). Book well ahead. The restaurant is also a hotel (p97).

Le Tilleul MODERN FRENCH **€€**
(04 93 32 80 36; place du Tilleul; menu €25, mains €18-25; lunch & dinner;) Under the shade of a big lime blossom (linden) tree, Le Tilleul is a gem. Considering its location on the *remparts*, it could have easily plumbed the depths of a typical tourist trap; instead, divine and beautifully presented dishes such as saffron mussel gratin with melting leeks grace your table. A minimum of €30 is required for card payments.

Getting There & Around

St-Paul is served by bus 400 running between Nice (€1, one hour, at least hourly) and Vence (€1, 15 minutes). The town is closed to traffic, but there are several car parks (€2.20 per hour) surrounding the village.

Vence

POP 19,377

Despite its well-preserved medieval centre, visitors often skip Vieux Vence altogether to head straight to Matisse's otherworldly Chapelle du Rosaire. Yet Vence deserves more than a flying visit. It's worth spending a little time here, if only to appreciate its comparatively quiet medieval streets and enjoy some of its gastronomic gems.

The **tourist office** (04 93 58 06 38; www.ville-vence.fr; 8 place du Grand Jardin; 9am-7pm Mon-Sat, 10am-6pm Sun Jul & Aug, 9am-6pm Mon-Sat Sep, Oct & Mar-Jun, 9am-5pm Mon-Sat Nov-Mar) has several good leaflets for self-guided tours in and around Vence. A fruit-and-veg market fills place du Jardin several mornings a week, with antiques on Wednesday.

Sights

TOP CHOICE **Chapelle du Rosaire** ARCHITECTURE
(Rosary Chapel; www.vence.fr/the-rosaire-chapel.html; 466 av Henri Matisse; adult/child €4/2; 2-5.30pm Mon, Wed & Sat, 10-11.30am & 2-5.30pm Tue & Thu) An ailing Henri Matisse moved to Vence in 1943, where he fell under the care of his former nurse and model Monique Bourgeois, who had since become a Dominican nun. She persuaded him to design this extraordinary chapel for her community. 'This work required four years of exclusive and relentless attention, and it is the fruit of my whole working life.

Despite all its imperfections, I consider it my masterpiece,' he said.

From the road, all you can see are the blue-and-white ceramic roof tiles and a wrought-iron cross and bell tower. Inside, light floods through the glorious **stained-glass windows**, painting stark white walls with glowing blues, greens and yellows (symbolising respectively water/the sky, plants/life, the sun/God's presence).

A line image of the **Virgin Mary** and child is painted on white ceramic tiles on the northern interior wall. The western wall is dominated by the bolder **Chemin de Croix** (Stations of the Cross). **St Dominic** overlooks the altar. Matisse also designed the chapel's stone altar, candlesticks, cross and the priests' vestments (displayed in an adjoining hall).

The Vieux Vence HISTORIC QUARTER

Much of the historical centre dates back to the 13th century. The **Romanesque cathedral** on the eastern side of the square was built in the 11th century on the site of an old Roman temple. It contains Chagall's **mosaic** of Moses (1979), appropriately watching over the baptismal font.

The daring **Fondation Émile Hugues** (☎04 93 24 24 23; 2 place du Frêne; adult/child €5/free; ⏲10am-12.30pm & 2-6pm Tue-Sun), with its wonderful 20th-century art exhibitions, inside the imposing Château de Villeneuve, is a nice contrast to Vence's historic quarter.

Sleeping & Eating

TOP CHOICE **La Maison du Frêne** B&B €€€

(☎04 93 24 37 83; www.lamaisondufrene.com; 1 place du Frêne; d €190; ⏲Feb-Dec; ❄📶) This arty guesthouse is quite astonishing. Yes, that Niki de Saint Phalle is an original. And yes, the César too. It's an essential sleepover for true art lovers, if only to enjoy the superb rooms with their classic or contemporary looks and original works. Owners and avid art collectors Thierry and Guy are a mine of information on the local art scene.

TOP CHOICE **Le 2** B&B €€

(☎04 93 24 42 58; www.le2avence.fr; 2 rue des Portiques; d €90-150; ❄📶) This 'bed & bistro', as it's tagged itself, is a welcome addition to staid Vence. Nicolas and his family (who also own La Maison du Frêne) have turned this medieval town house into a hip new establishment offering four very modern rooms, a bistro serving one *plat du jour* (€11) and a pocket-sized cellar featuring local musicians several nights a week. Value and atmosphere guaranteed.

La Litote MODERN FRENCH €€

(☎04 93 24 27 82; www.lalitote.fr; 5 rue de l'Évêché; menus €17.50-28; ⏲lunch Tue-Sun, dinner Tue-Sat) In an area where the bar is set very high, chef Stéphane Furlan still manages to surprise and delight diners with a regularly changing menu that favours quality rather than quantity. Dine al fresco on a little square at the back of the cathedral, or inside the stone-wall dining room with its open fire.

Les Bacchanales GASTRONOMIC €€€

(☎04 93 24 19 19; www.lesbacchanales.com; 247 av de Provence; lunch/dinner menu from €35/55; ⏲lunch & dinner Thu-Mon) Chef Christophe Dufau has found the perfect home in this elegant 1930s town house. It allows him to combine his two passions in life: food (creative, seasonal and divine) and art (the restaurant features daring original works).

Getting There & Around

Bus 400 to and from Nice (€1, 1¼ hours, at least hourly) stops on place du Grand Jardin. Medieval Vence is pedestrian; you can park on place du Grand Jardin or in the streets leading to the historical centre.

Around Vence

The Pays Vençois is an enticing mix of fertile land, rocky heights and quirky attractions. A car is essential to get around.

LES GORGES DU LOUP

A combination of perilously perched villages, sheer cliffs, waterfalls, densely wooded slopes and gushing river, the Gorges du Loup is a scenic and surprisingly unspoiled place. People come here mostly for the spectacular drive and great walking trails. The Guides RandOxygène (p289) have excellent walk suggestions.

The highlight of the western side of the gorges (the D3) is the outstanding village of **Gourdon** (population 445). The panorama from **place Victoria** sweeps 80km of coastline from Nice to Théoule-sur-Mer.

On the eastern side, off the D2210, stands the tiny village of **Courmes** (population 99), reached by a single, winding lane. There isn't much to see here but it is the most atmospheric place to lunch or spend the night. Further south along the gorge is the hamlet of

Pont du Loup. Standing over the Loup River, under what's left of the old **railway bridge** (bombed during WWII), this is where villagers from Gourdon used to come and cultivate flowers and fruit trees. Access to Gourdon was via the **chemin du Paradis**, a track that still exists and is very popular with walkers.

Testimony to this fertile past is sweet factory **Confiserie Florian** (04 93 59 32 91; www.confiserieflorian.com; 9am-noon & 2-6.30pm), where jasmine jam, candied clementines and crystallised flowers such as violets or roses are cooked up in a 19th-century flour mill. Free 10-minute tours show you how and finish in the factory shop where you can sample the goods.

If the unusual flavours of the *confiserie* have piqued your curiosity, try the cooking classes of **Atelier de la Cuisine des Fleurs** (The Flowers' Cooking Workshop; 04 92 11 06 94; www.la-cuisine-des-fleurs.com; 16 Pont du Loup; 1-/3-course-meal lesson €15/80), run by chef Yves Terrillon. The original menus change monthly according to flowers (violet in March, centifolia rose in May, verbena in August etc). Lessons are fun, very hands-on and take place in Yves' airy, 1st-floor kitchen. L'Atelier also runs a great kids' class where little ones (from the age of eight) can learn to bake their own birthday cake or prepare funky sandwiches for picnics.

Further down Le Pont du Loup, on the D2210, hilltop **Le Bar-sur-Loup** (population 2853) pops onto the horizon. Bitter orange trees are cultivated in terraces around the beautifully intact medieval village. There are some great walks from the village and the tourist office (in the town hall) has put together a leaflet with three itineraries in English.

Sleeping & Eating

If you're keen to stay somewhere to get away from it all, you've come to the right place. The only downside is that unless you eat where you stay (often possible, thankfully), you'll have quite a drive to go out. Day trippers will revel in the scenic drives and great lunch options though.

TOP CHOICE La Cascade B&B €

(04 93 09 65 85; www.gitedelacascade.com; 635 chemin de la Cascade, Courmes; d/tr/q €75/80/130;) It really doesn't come much better than La Cascade for rural idyll. This stunning B&B is an old sheepfold sitting snug in 4 hectares of land, complete with forest, ponds, swimming pool, pétanque pitch and the most awesome views of the Gorges du Loup.

In summer, you'll never believe it's high season in these remote mountains, and in winter, cosying up by the fire in such surroundings is a joy. The *table d'hôte* (€22 for a three-course meal, including drinks) is another highlight.

L'Hostellerie du Château HISTORIC HOTEL €€€

(04 93 42 41 10; www.lhostellerieduchateau.com; 6-8 place Francis Paulet, Le Bar-sur-Loup; d from €180; Feb-Oct;) It's hard to imagine that Bar-sur-Loup's majestic 15th-century castle lay in ruins for more than two centuries. Renovated between 2003 and 2005, it now hosts six huge, regal rooms with château-like, rustic furniture. There are great views of the surrounding valleys. Rates include breakfast.

TOP CHOICE Auberge de Courmes MODERN FRENCH €€

(04 93 77 64 70; www.aubergedecourmes.com; 3 rue des Platanes, Courmes; mains €13.50, 3-course menu €23;) Sitting in the middle of the hamlet of Courmes, at the foot of the mountains, the terrace of this charming village inn is an atmospheric place for a long lunch. Run by a young family, it offers a daily choice of two starters, two mains and two desserts. It's very popular with walkers at the weekend, so book.

There are also five small, simple rooms (double with half-board €110); there are no TVs in the rooms but who needs one when the deer roam the village at night and the fireflies put on a show (in June)?

L'École des Filles MODERN FRENCH €€

(04 93 09 40 20; www.restaurantecoledesfilles.fr; 380 av Amiral de Grasse, Le Bar-sur-Loup; mains €25, 2-/3-/4-course menu €35/39/45; lunch Tue-Sun, dinner Tue-Sat) As the name suggests, this is the village's former girls' school and what makes it so special is that it has retained the charm of an old village school: in winter, meals are served in the 'classrooms', with their stone walls and patchwork of colourful cushions and crockery; while in summer, the old playground becomes a lively terrace. The creative menu changes weekly.

Le Bigaradier GASTRONOMIC €€€

(04 93 42 41 10; www.lhostellerieduchateau.com; 6-8 place Francis Paulet, Le Bar-sur-Loup; lunch/dinner menu €29/62; lunch & dinner Wed-Sat, lunch Sun Feb-Nov) Lunch on the village square or dine on the spectacular terrace

DON'T MISS

CREATE YOUR OWN SCENT

It can take months, sometimes years, for a 'nose' (perfumers who, after 10 years' training, can identify up to 3000 smells) to create a perfume. And you'll understand why once you sit down in front of a mind-boggling array of essences: the number of combinations is dizzying. Perfume workshops won't turn you into a perfumer overnight, but the olfactory education they offer is fascinating – and great fun.

Molinard (p103) runs a fantastic 90-minute workshop (€69) in its Grasse factory where you can create your own perfume. Perfumer Céline will quiz you about the scents you like – and dislike – talk you through the structure of the perfume (base, heart and head notes), explain the rules of perfume etiquette (bannish liberal spraying!) and help you through the more subtle blends of your creations. 'Graduates' leave with a stylish (and refillable) 130mL bottle of their perfume.

of Le Bigaradier, L'Hostellerie du Château's superb restaurant. The menu is a great combination of high-brow gastronomy and Provençal flavours. In winter, meals are served in the panoramic dining room, with plunging views of the valley.

TOURRETTES-SUR-LOUP

POP 4207

Dubbed the 'city of violets' after its signature flower, Tourrettes is a postcard-perfect, 15th-century hilltop village. Walking around the medieval village won't take you more than half an hour or so; other attractions are in the surrounding area.

Sights & Activities

There are some great walks to do around Tourrettes, many with panoramic views. *Promenades & Randonnées Balisées* (in French) is a useful leaflet produced by the **tourist office** (04 93 24 18 93; www.tourrettessurloup.com; 2 place de La Libération; 9.30am-12.30pm & 2.30-6.30pm Mon-Sat), with 14 itineraries ranging from easy 1½-hour strolls to heartier walks to local summits or neighbouring villages. Also good is Guides RandOxygène (p289), with a great selection of itineraries in the Pays Vençois section.

La Ferme des Courmettes FARM
(04 93 59 31 93; www.chevredescourmettes.com; rte des Courmettes; 9am-12.30pm & 4-6pm) An organic goat's cheese producer, Les Courmettes welcomes visitors. If you'd like to see the goats being milked, come around 4.30pm between March and October. To organise a tasting and a tour of the farm (one hour, €56 for up to 10 people, available in English), book ahead. The cheeses are absolutely divine and incredibly diverse in taste.

Find the farm 4km up rte des Courmettes, signposted off the D2210, about halfway between Tourrettes and Pont du Loup.

Bastide aux Violettes FLOWER PRODUCER
(Quartier de la Ferrage; 10am-12.30pm & 1.30-5pm Tue-Sat) To find out more about Tourettes' famous violet, head to the Bastide aux Violettes, 10 minutes' walk from the centre of Tourrettes. This modern space takes you through the history of the flower, its uses and cultivation (you can see fields).

Domaine des Courmettes WALKING
(04 92 11 02 32; www.courmettes.com; rte des Courmettes; 9.30am-8pm Apr-Oct, 10am-5pm Fri-Wed Nov-Mar) This nature reserve on the lofty Plateau des Courmettes is home to millennia-old holly oaks and rare birds. There are three lovely trails to explore the reserve; they all start from the visitor centre, which is in a beautiful old farmhouse. There is a small cafe too that sells freshly baked bread at the weekend.

Domaine Saint-Joseph WINERY
(04 93 58 81 31; 160 chemin des Vignes; 9am-noon & 2.30-7pm Mon-Sat) The friendly owners of this small winery and olive-oil producer will happily show you around their estate and answer questions about wine and olive-oil production. You can taste and/or buy their wines (red, white and rosé) and excellent olive oil (part of Nice AOP; Appelation d'Origine Protégée certifies the origin and quality of the oil).

The Domaine is 2km southwest of Tourrettes, signposted off rte de Grasse.

Sleeping & Eating

TOP CHOICE **Le Mas des Cigales** B&B €€
(04 93 59 25 73; www.lemasdescigales.com; 1673 rte des Quenières; d €118;) With its pretty Provençal *mas* (farmhouse), tumbling garden, picture-perfect pool, sweeping

views and amazing breakfast spread, it is likely you'll never want to leave this fabulous *chambre d'hôte* – particularly now that Stefaan and Véronique have taken over and added their warm welcome to this idyllic spot. They've notably started offering *table d'hôte* (evening meals €25-30).

Active types will love the tennis courts, pétanque pitch and bicycles, while those keen for a more relaxing afternoon will prefer the spa and view-commanding loungers.

TOP CHOICE Bistrot Gourmand Clovis MODERN FRENCH €€
(☎04 93 58 87 04; www.clovis-gourmand.fr; 21 grand rue; 2-/3-course menu €28/32; ⏰lunch & dinner Wed-Sun; ✎) Awarded its first Michelin star in 2012, this gourmet bistro in the heart of Tourrettes is immensely popular, both for its great atmosphere and elegant cuisine. Booking essential.

COL DE VENCE

The northbound D2 from Vence leads to photogenic **Coursegoules**, a hilltop village with 11th-century castle ruins and fortifications, via Col de Vence (963m), a mountain pass offering good views of the *baous* (rocky promontories) typical of this region.

The landscape across these lofty plateaux is very arid, a far cry from the orchards and lush valleys around the Loup River. A number of trails criss-cross the area; walkers should use Guides RandOxygène (p289) for itinerary suggestions (paper copies available at tourist offices).

Grasse

POP 53,150

It is the abundance of water in the hills that helped turn Grasse into a perfume centre. Tanners, who needed reliable water supplies to clean their hides, first settled here in the Middle Ages. With the advent of perfumed gloves in the 1500s, the art of perfumery took shape. Glove makers split from the tanners and set up lucrative perfumeries. New irrigation techniques allowed flower growing to boom, sealing Grasse's reputation as the world fragrance capital.

Today, Grasse is still surrounded by jasmine, centifolia roses, mimosa, orange blossom and violet fields, but the industry, which counts some 30 perfumeries, is rather discreet, with only a handful offering tours of their facilities.

Sights & Activities

Attractions in Grasse focus on its celebrated perfume industry, a nice change from traditional sights and activities.

TOP CHOICE Musée International de la Parfumerie PERFUME MUSEUM
(MIP; www.museesdegrasse.com; 2 bd du Jeu de Ballon; adult/child €3/free; ⏰11am-6pm Wed-Mon; 👪) This whizz-bang museum is a work of art. Housed in renovated 18th-century mansion, daringly enlarged with a modern glass structure, it retraces three millennia of perfume history through a brilliant mix of artefacts, bottles, videos, vintage posters,

LOCAL KNOWLEDGE

CORINNE MARIE-TOSELLO, PERFUMER IN GRASSE

Corinne Marie-Tosello has two routes to work: one through olive groves, the other one through fields overlooking the sea. Most people would revel in the view, but Corinne revels in the smells: she runs the 'olfactory training' of perfumery Fragonard's staff (scent identification, production process, types of perfumes etc) and also works as an olfactory consultant (she advises on scents for incense, candles and so on).

Apart from the perfumeries, where else can you learn about Grasse's perfume industry? The flower fields around Grasse, such as the Bastide aux Violettes (p100), the Domaine de Manon (p103) or the Jardins du MIP (p104), are wonderful. You see where the flowers come from and get a chance to meet the people who grow them.

Any fragrant walks in the region? St-Honorat (p90) is an olfactory paradise, with eucalyptus, pine trees, dry wood and vine. I would also recommend the Estérel (p105) in May, when the maquis shrub *cistus* is in bloom.

Where would you recommend for lunch? In Grasse I like the Café des Musées (p103) – the decor is very Fragonard and it has delicious ice creams. In Cannes I like Vegaluna (p84): the chef cooks with fresh, seasonal products, and the atmosphere is very relaxed.

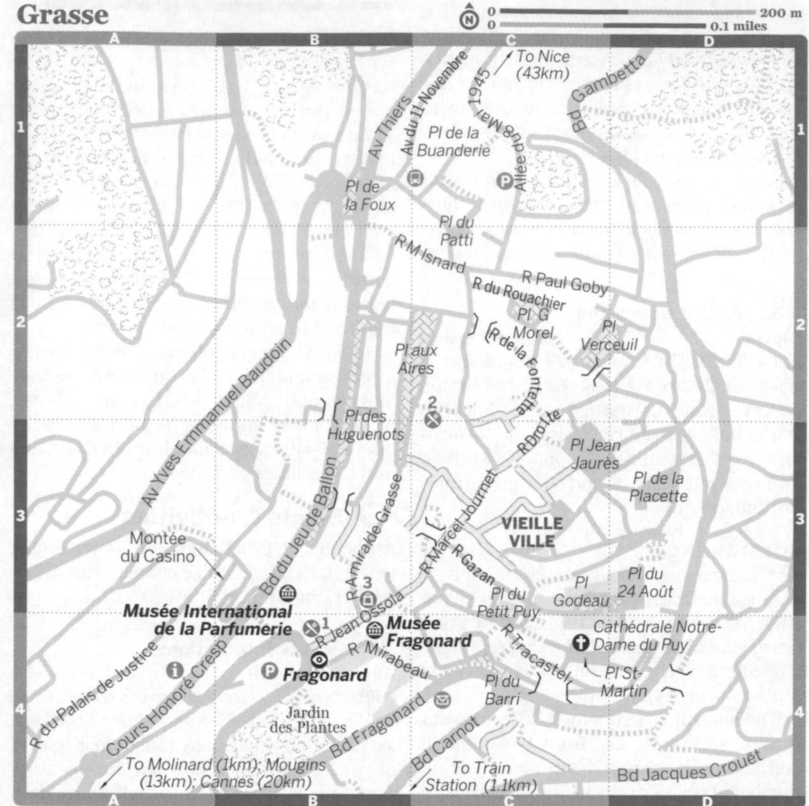

Grasse

Top Sights

- Fragonard B4
- Musée Fragonard B4
- Musée International de la Parfumerie B3

Eating

1 Café des Musées B4
2 Lou Candeloun C2

Shopping

3 Fragonard Maison B3

olfactive stations and explanatory panels (in French and English), all beautifully presented. The museum offers interesting insights into how the industry developed in Grasse.

Kids are well catered for with dedicated multimedia stations throughout, a fragrant garden, a film testing your sense of smell and the reproduction of a 19th-century perfume shop.

Musée Fragonard ART MUSEUM
(www.fragonard.com; 14 rue Ossola; admission free; ⌚10am-6pm) This tiny but fantastic private museum houses France's second-largest collection of works by Grassois painter Jean-Honoré Fragonard (1732–1806). There are 15 major works, beautifully exhibited in a renovated 18th-century town house (admire the splendid ceiling fresco in the entrance hall) and complemented by the paintings of Marguerite Gérard (1761–1837), Fragonard's sister-in-law and protégée, and Jean-Baptiste Mallet (1759–1835), another painter native of Grasse.

Perfumeries PERFUMERIES
Three well-known perfumeries run free guided tours of their facilities: **Fragonard** (www.fragonard.com; 20 blvd Fragonard; ⌚9am-6pm

Feb-Oct, 9am-12.30pm & 2-6pm Nov-Jan), **Molinard** (www.molinard.com; 60 bd Victor Hugo; ⊙9.30am-12.30pm & 2-6pm) and **Galimard** (www.galimard.com; 73 rte de Cannes; ⊙9am-12.30pm & 2-6pm). You're taken through every stage of perfume production, from extraction and distillation to the work of the 'nose'. Tours leave every 15 to 30 minutes and are available in a number of languages.

Visits end in the perfumeries' showrooms where you can buy fragrances (much cheaper than couture perfumes, where 60% of what you pay is packaging).

Domaine de Manon FARM

(☎06 12 18 02 69; www.le-domaine-de-manon.com; 36 chemin du Servan, Plascassier; admission €6) Curious noses can combine a perfumery session with a (literal) field trip to this wonderful flower farm. Centifolia rose and jasmine have been cultivated here for three generations and Carole Biancalana, the current producer, will take you on a tour of her fields and explain how the flowers are grown and processed. The Domaine's production is sold exclusively to haute-couture label Dior.

Tours only take place during flowering and are held on Tuesday at 10am between May and mid-June for rose, and on Tuesday at 9am between August and mid-October for jasmine; ring ahead to double-check since exact times vary from year to year, depending on flowering.

The *domaine* is located 7km southeast of the centre of Grasse, in the small village of Plascassier (officially part of Grasse). Head in the direction of Valbonne along the D4 as you leave Grasse, and then follow signs for 'Vieux Village' when you get to Plascassier. The *domaine* will be on your left, opposite a hair salon.

Sleeping & Eating

There is a dire lack of decent accommodation in Grasse so you'll have to get out of the city for a good night's sleep.

Le Mas du Naoc B&B €€

(☎04 93 60 63 13; www.lemasdunaoc.com; 580 chemin du Migranié, Cabris; d €135-160;) This renovated and vine-covered 18th-century pad in Cabris slumbers in the shade of century-old olive, jasmine, fig and orange trees, and fits the 'quintessentially Provençal' bill perfectly. Soft natural hues dress Sandra and Jérôme Maingret's four lovely rooms, and the coastal panorama from the pool is inspirational. No children under the age of seven. Find the Mas 4km from Grasse, signposted off the D4 to Cabris.

Café des Musées MODERN FRENCH €

(1 rue Jean Ossola; mains €9-13; ⊙8am-6pm) This gorgeous cafe is the perfect place to stop for a spot of lunch (lovely salads, carefully crafted daily specials, soup or pasta of the day) or indulge in a gourmet coffee break (pastry with coffee or tea €7.50) between sights.

Lou Candeloun MODERN FRENCH €€

(www.loucandeloun.eresto.net; 5 rue des Fabreries; lunch menu €19, dinner menu €30-57; ⊙lunch Mon-Sat, dinner Tue-Sat) Tucked down the most unassuming alleyway, this is the gourmet choice in Grasse. Chef Alexis Mayroux changes his menu regularly to match the mood of market stalls. So whatever season you're in town, you'll be in for a treat, and always with a great wine to match.

Shopping

Fragonard Maison HOMEWARES

(www.fragonard.com; 2 rue Amiral de Grasse; ⊙10am-7pm) Perfumery Fragonard now has an extensive range of homewares blending Provençal prints with contemporary designs. You'll find bags, tablecloths, bed linen and beautiful accessories in its boutique, as well as candles and soaps from its main product stream.

Information

Tourist Office (☎04 93 36 66 66; www.grasse.fr; 22 cours Honoré Cresp; ⊙9am-7pm Mon-Sat, 9am-1pm & 2-6pm Sun) Has information on accommodation. There's also an annexe of the tourist office on place de la Foux.

Getting There & Around

BUS Bus 600 goes to Cannes (50 minutes, every 20 minutes) via Mouans-Sartoux (25 minutes) and Mougins (30 minutes). Bus 500 goes to Nice (1½ hours, hourly). All buses leave from the **bus station** (place de la Buanderie); fares are €1.

CAR Grasse's one-way street system is maddening and often congested, so park as soon as you can and walk. If arriving from Nice, park at Parking Notre Dame des Fleurs. If arriving from Cannes, park at Parking Honoré Cresp. Allow €1.70 per hour.

TRAIN The station is out of town but linked to the centre by buses 2, 3, 4 and 5 (€1). There are regular services to Nice (€9.20, 1¼ hours, hourly) via Cannes (€4, 30 minutes).

Mougins & Mouans-Sartoux

Pinprick Vieux Mougins looks almost too perfect to be real. Picasso discovered the medieval village in 1935 with lover Dora Marr and lived here with his final love, Jacqueline Roque, from 1961 until his death. Mougins (population 19,929) has since become something of an elite location with prestigious hotel-restaurants, the country's most-sought-after international school and Sophia Antipolis (France's Silicon Valley) nearby.

Mouans-Sartoux (population 10,490), for its part, is not so picturesque but has a couple of great sights.

Sights

TOP CHOICE Musée d'Art Classique de Mougins ART MUSEUM
(www.mouginsmusee.com; 32 rue Commandeur, Mougins; adult/student/child €15/8/5; ⏲9.30am-8.30pm daily Apr-Oct, to 7pm Tue-Sun Nov-Mar) The brainchild of compulsive art collector and British entrepreneur Christian Levett, this outstanding museum contains 600 works spanning 5000 years of history. The collection aims to show how ancient civilisations inspired neoclassical, modern and contemporary art, so you'll therefore find antiquities juxtaposed with seminal modern works. Not only is it a brilliant idea, it has also been brilliantly executed.

One of the museum's most stunning displays is a window exhibiting an antique Roman Venus in white marble standing next to a resin and plaster-cast *Venus* by Yves Klein in signature blue, with a surreal, giraffe-necked statue by Dalí and the *Birth of Venus* by Andy Warhol in the background. Other highlights include *The Lagre Sphinx*, a drawing by Jean Cocteau, sitting alongside exquisitely decorated sarcophagus and portraits by Picasso that beautifully echo those in the museum's stunning mosaics.

The collection is organised by civilisations – Rome, Greece and Egypt each get a floor – and the top floor is dedicated to armoury. There are fantastic explanatory panels in French and English throughout and excellent interactive displays bringing to life the helmets, spears and shields of the armoury collection.

TOP CHOICE Les Jardins du MIP GARDEN
(www.museesdegrasse.com; 979 chemin des Gourettes, Mouans-Sartoux; adult/child €3/free; ⏲10am-6pm Apr-Oct) Opened in 2012 by the Musée International de la Parfumerie (p101) in Grasse, these gardens beautifully complement the museum's collection by offering an insight into the plants used in perfumery. Visitors are actively encouraged to pick, rub and smell their way around. The gardens are organised by olfactive families (woody, floral, ambered, *fougère* etc); informative leaflets are available and gardeners will happily answer questions.

The leaflets tell you about how each plant is used, the part (root, leaf, flower) that is the most fragrant and famous perfumes it is used in. There are photos to help you identify the plants and explanations are available in English. The gardens are at their best in spring.

The gardens are accessible by public transport (stop Les Jardins du MIP). Take bus 20 or 21, which run between Grasse bus station and Mouans-Sartoux.

Musée de la Photographie André Villers PHOTOGRAPHY MUSEUM
(Porte Sarrazine, Mougins; admission free; ⏲10am-12.30pm & 2-7pm Tue-Fri, 11am-7pm Sat & Sun) The small but perfectly formed Musée de la Photographie has some fascinating black-and-white photos of Picasso, snapped by celebrated photographers such as André Villers and Jacques Henri Lartigue. It also hosts regular exhibitions on anything from fashion to war photography.

Espace de l'Art Concret ART MUSEUM
(www.espacedelartconcret.fr; place Suzanne de Villeneuve, Mouans-Sartoux; adult/child €5/free; ⏲11am-7pm Jul & Aug, noon-6pm Wed-Sun Sep-Jun) Modern-art and architecture lovers shouldn't miss this contemporary-art centre, housed in the 16th-century **Château de Mouans** and the purpose-built **Donation Albers-Honegger** extension, a brilliant and brilliantly controversial lime-

COMBINED TICKET

If you're planning on visiting both the Musée International de la Parfumerie and the Jardins du MIP, you can buy a combined ticket for €5, which includes a bus ticket between Grasse and the gardens (bus 20 or 21).

green concrete block ferociously clashing with its historic surroundings. All the old familiars (Eduardo Chillida, Yves Klein, Andy Warhol, César, Philippe Starck) are here, along with lesser-known practitioners and temporary exhibitions.

Sleeping

Les Rosées B&B €€€

(☎04 92 92 29 64; www.lesrosees.com; 238 chemin de Font Neuve, Mougins; d €220-320;) Chic and authentic is its tagline, and it couldn't be more accurate. This stunning, 400-year-old stone manor house with five romantic suites, pool, spa and century-old olive trees is a gem. The decor is a stunning mix of modern and vintage (so much so that the owners now have their own interior-design venture), and breakfast is a copious organic affair.

The Serguey suite, with its glass fireplace (watch the open fire from your lounge or bathtub), is simply divine for winter breaks, while Isadora, with its stunning terrace, is the pick of the house in summer.

Le Mas de Mougins B&B €€

(☎04 93 75 77 46; www.lemasdemougins.com; 91 av du Général de Gaulle, Mougins; d €145;) Run with flair by the formidable Joël and Sonia, this lovely B&B gets rave reviews from travellers for its five-star hospitality and epic communal breakfasts (juices, homemade pastries, breads, cheese, cold meats, eggs, you name it) served by the pool. The location is great for exploring the area but the traffic noise may be off-putting for those seeking relaxation.

Eating & Drinking

Le Rendez-Vous de Mougins MODERN FRENCH €€

(☎04 93 75 87 47; www.au-rendez-vous-mougins.fr; place du Commandant Lamy, Mougins; lunch/dinner menu €15.80/23.50, mains €16-28; ⏰lunch Mon-Sat, dinner Tue-Sat;) At the heart of Mougins' old village, guarded by a mighty plane tree, Le Rendez-Vous is one of the best-value restaurants you'll find in this neck of the woods. The sun-kissed cuisine is fresh, generous and mostly sourced at the Marché Forville in Cannes: think marinated sardines with sun-dried tomatoes or glacé nougat with lavender honey and citrus coulis. Booking essential.

Le Mas Candille GASTRONOMIC €€€

(☎04 92 28 43 43; bd Clément Rebuffel, Mougins; menu of the day €69, mains €40-60; ⏰lunch & dinner) Le Mas Candille's reputation is starting to travel as far as chef Serge Gouloumès has: originally from Gascony (the foie gras *tatin* with armagnac is his trademark dish), his culinary career has taken him to faraway climes, an experience that has enriched his Mediterranean cuisine with exotic flavours. The setting couldn't be more idyllic either, with spectacular views of Grasse and the Alps.

The Mas Candille also offers cooking courses (four hours, €195), which include a tour of Marché Forville in Cannes and advice from the restaurant's sommelier about matching food and wine.

La Cave de Mougins WINE BAR

(www.lacavedemougins.com; 50 av Charles Mallet, Mougins; ⏰11am-11pm Tue-Sat) The cellar of this fabulous wine bar is worth the detour, and not just for its hundreds of vintages, but also for its stunning vaulted ceiling, events-packed calendar (tastings, meet-the-winemakers evenings, little concerts etc) and atmospheric terrace. During the day, it doubles up as a deli so that you can nibble on pâté and cheese platters with a glass of wine.

Information

Mougins' **tourist office** (☎04 93 75 87 67; www.mougins.fr; 18 bd Courteline; ⏰9.30am-5pm Mon-Sat Oct-Jun, to 6pm daily Jul-Sep), located at the entrance of the old village, can give you a map of the historic centre so that you can wander around. Alternatively, smartphone users can download the excellent Mougins Tourisme app (in French only) complete with audio guide, maps and special offers.

Getting There & Around

Bus 600 (€1, every 20 minutes) between Cannes and Grasse stops in Mougins and Mouans-Sartoux. The old town in Mougins is pedestrian only; there is plenty of free parking on the outskirts.

MASSIF DE L'ESTÉREL

The efficient **Centrale de Réservation Estérel Côte d'Azur** (☎04 94 19 10 60; www.esterel-cotedazur.com; 72 rue Waldeck Rousseau) can help with bookings in this area.

Corniche de l'Estérel

A walk or drive along the winding Corniche de l'Estérel (also called Corniche d'Or, 'Golden Coast'; the N98) is not to be missed and is an attraction in its own right. In fact it was one of the reasons the road was opened by the Touring Club de France in 1903. The views are spectacular and small summer resorts and dreamy inlets (perfect for swimming), all of which are accessible by bus or train, are dotted along its 30km length. The most dramatic stretch is between Anthéor and Théoule-sur-Mer, where the tortuous, narrow N98 skirts through sparsely built areas.

Activities

With its lush green Mediterranean forests, intensely red peaks and sterling sea views, the Estérel is a walker's paradise. Local tourist offices have leaflets detailing the most popular walks, including Pic de l'Ours (496m) and Pic du Cap Roux (452m), but buy IGN's Carte de Randonnée (1:25,000) No 3544ET Fréjus, Saint-Raphaël & Corniche de l'Estérel if you're planning more serious walks.

Those preferring a more informed wander can opt for a three-hour guided walk with a forest ranger from the Office National des Forêts (National Forestry Office, adult/child €10/6, in French only; book with the tourist office) or guided walks with a nature guide from the tourist office (p105) (€10 to €15, English available).

Access to the range is generally prohibited on windy or particularly hot days because of fire risks, so check with the tourist office before setting off.

Diving & Snorkelling DIVING

The Estérel is a leading dive centre: with numerous WWII shipwrecks and pristine waters, it's a prime area for underwater exploration. Much of the coast along the corniche is protected too, so the fauna and flora is some of the best around. Among the most reputable diving clubs are the multilingual **Centre de Plongée Île d'Or** (☎04 94 82 73 67; www.dive.fr; 986 bd 36ème Division du Texas, Agay) and the family-friendly **Euro Plongée** (☎04 94 19 03 26; www.europlongee.fr; Port de Boulouris).

Both clubs offer individual dives as well as courses (Club de Plongée Île d'Or is CMAS and PADI accredited). Euro Plongée also runs great two-hour snorkelling tours (€25). They're fantastic for families, and kids will love spotting starfish, sea anemones, urchins and other colourful Mediterranean residents.

Sentier du Littoral WALKING

Running 11km between Port Santa Lucia (the track starts behind the naval works) and Agay, this coastal path (yellow markers) takes in some of the most scenic spots in the area. It takes roughly 4½ hours to complete, but from May to October you could make a day out of it by stopping at some of the idyllic beaches scattered along the way.

You can choose to walk smaller sections. The most scenic is around **Cap Dramont**, crowned by a semaphore, which you can do as a loop from **Plage du Débarquement**. This long sandy beach is where the 36th US Infantry Division landed on 15 August 1944. The large memorial park has a car park easily accessible from the N98.

Beaches SWIMMING

With its 36km of coastline, the corniche has more than 30 beaches running the gamut of beach possibilities: sandy, pebbly, nudist, covelike, you name it. But wherever you go, the sea remains that crystal-clear turquoise and deep blue, an irresistible invitation to swim.

Best for activities (beach volleyball, kids' clubs, water sports etc) are **Plage d'Agay** and **Plage Beaurivage**. For a scenic swim off a sandy beach, the beaches along the **Rade d'Agay** are perfect, while the section of coast between Anthéor and Le Trayas is famed for its jewel-like *calanques* (tiny coves) and brilliant **snorkelling**. The landscape here is much more rugged, with many coves only accessible by boat.

Sleeping & Eating

Villa Matuzia PROVENÇAL €€

(☎04 94 82 79 95; www.matuzia.com; 15 bd Ste Guitte, Agay; mains €19-26, lunch/dinner menu €20/29; ⊙lunch & dinner Wed-Sun; ❄📶) Hands down the best option to eat in the Estérel is Villa Matuzia, a lovely Provençal house set 200m from the sea in Agay. It serves elaborate Mediterranean cuisine (complete with appetizers and petits fours) and the setting is charming: a cosy dining room in winter and a lush terrace for summer days.

It also has two small bedrooms (double €75, including breakfast), each with its little patio.

ℹ Getting There & Around

BUS Bus 8 runs between St Raphaël and Agay, stopping at Le Dramont on the way; three services a day go all the way to Le Trayas. Tickets cost €1.10.

CAR The corniche gets very busy in summer: if you need to go somewhere, as opposed to enjoy a scenic drive, take the inland N7 or the A8 motorway.

TRAIN Mandelieu-La Napoule, Le Trayas, Agay, Le Dramont and Boulouris all have stations on the St Raphaël–Nice line but only a handful of services each day stop there.

St-Raphaël

POP 34,867

St-Raphaël is a good base to explore the Estérel rather than a destination in itself. The very dynamic **tourist office** (☎04 94 19 52 52; www.saint-raphael.com; 99 Quai Albert 1er; ⏰9am-7pm Jul & Aug, 9am-12.30pm & 2-6.30pm Mon-Sat Sep-Jun) can help you book activities in the region.

A great way to discover the coast is to board **Les Bateaux de St-Raphaël** (www.bateauxsaintraphael.com; Quai Nomy, St-Raphaël; ⏰Apr-Oct) for a scenic cruise along the Corniche de l'Estérel (adult/child €16/10, 1¼ hours). The company also runs boat services to St-Tropez (adult/child €24/14, crossing time one hour) and Ste-Marguerite in the Îles de Lérins (full day adult/child €25/14, half-day €20/12, crossing time 1¼ hours).

The pick of accommodation in town is **L'Hirondelle Blanche** (☎04 94 11 84 03; www.hirondelle-blanche.fr; 533 av des Chèvreteuilles, Santa Lucia; d €99-170), an elegant early 20th-century villa with six rooms near the port of Santa Lucia. Run by avuncular artist George, the house is full of charm, with paintings and books everywhere. The romantic rooms have all been individually decorated and those on the ground and 1st floor have sea views. There is a little traffic noise from the road, but the double-glazing keeps the rooms quiet at night. Unusually for a B&B, breakfast is not included in the price to give guests greater flexibility.

For dinner, head to **Les Charavins** (☎04 94 95 03 76; 36 rue Charabois; mains €18-26; ⏰dinner Thu-Tue, lunch Thu, Fri, Mon & Tue). This jolly wine-bar-cum-restaurant serves traditional French fare such as frogs' legs, onion soup and steak with Béarnaise sauce. The atmosphere is relaxed and, as you'll have guessed from the hundreds of bottles lining the walls, wine gets pride of place on the menu. Interestingly, it's BYO on Tuesday, although with such connoisseurs in the room, you'll have to be confident with your choice!

There are regular trains from St-Raphaël to Nice (€11.20, 1¼ hours, half-hourly), Cannes (€6.70, 30 minutes, half-hourly), Les Arcs Draguignan (€5.40, 15 minutes, hourly) and Marseille (€24, 1½ hours, hourly). Bus 4 goes to Fréjus old town (€1.10) from St Raphaël bus station.

Fréjus

POP 52,953

Settled by Massiliots (Greek colonists from Marseille) and colonised by Julius Caesar around 49 BC as Forum Julii, Fréjus is a quiet place. The appealing old town is a maze of pastel buildings, shady plazas and winding alleys, climaxing with extraordinary medieval paintings in an episcopal complex wedged between a trio of market squares.

Sights

All sights in Fréjus are open 9.30am to 12.30pm and 2pm to 5pm Tuesday to Sunday November to March, and to 6.30pm April to October.

Le Groupe Épiscopal CATHEDRAL

(58 rue de Fleury; adult/child €5/free) Fréjus' star sight is the Groupe Épiscopal, built on the foundations of a Roman temple. At the heart of the complex is an 11th- and 12th-century **cathedral**, one of the first Gothic buildings in the region, and a **cloister** featuring rare 14th- and 15th-century painted wooden ceiling panels depicting angels, devils, hunters, acrobats and monsters in vivid comic-book fashion.

The meaning and origin of these sci-fi like creatures is unknown. Only 500 of the original 1200 frames survive. If you can, bring binoculars for a better view or rent a pair at the ticket desk for €1.

Before you enter the cathedral, make sure you take a peek at the octagonal 5th-century **baptistery** (which incorporates eight Roman columns into its structure) on your left-hand

CENT SAVER

A seven-day **Fréjus Pass** (€4.60) covers admission to the Roman amphitheatre and theatre, archaeological museum and Cocteau's chapel (otherwise, it's €2 per sight). To visit the Groupe Épiscopal as well, buy a seven-day **Fréjus Pass Intégral** (€6.60) instead. Participating sights sell passes, except the Groupe Épiscopal.

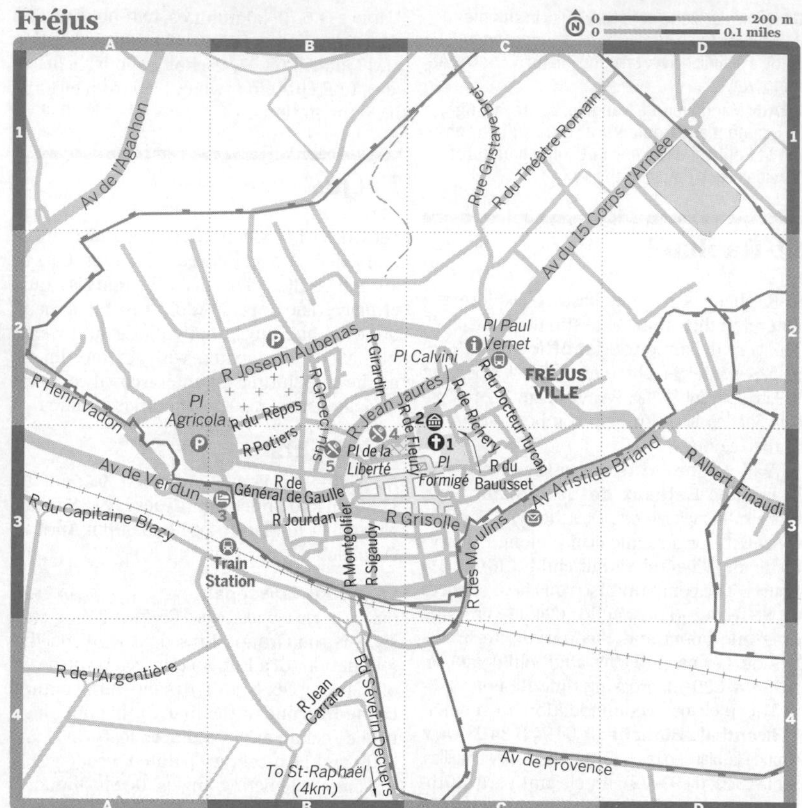

Fréjus

Sights

1 Le Groupe Épiscopal C3
2 Musée Archéologique C2

Sleeping

3 L'Aréna B3

Eating

4 Le Poivrier B3
5 Maison de la Tarte B3

side: it is one of the oldest Christian buildings in France, and is exceptionally well preserved.

Musée Archéologique ARCHAEOLOGY MUSEUM

(place Calvini; adult/child €2/free) The small but fascinating Musée Archéologique features treasures unearthed in and around Fréjus, from everyday objects (including many pottery items – Fréjus was an important production centre in Roman times) to rare finds such as a double-faced marble statue of Hermes, a head of Jupiter and a stunning 3rd-century mosaic depicting a leopard.

Roman Ruins ROMAN SITES

Fréjus' Roman ruins are not as well preserved as those found in Arles or Orange, but their abundance bears witness to the importance of Forum Julii, with its strategic location on Via Aurelia and its port. The best way to appreciate this heritage is to join the **guided tours** (adult/child €6/free) run by the **tourist office** (☎04 94 51 83 83; www.frejus.fr; 249 rue Jean Jaurès; ⏰9.30am-noon & 2-6pm Mon-Sat).

At the southeastern edge of the old city is the 3rd-century Porte d'Orée, the only remaining arcade of monumental Roman thermal baths. North of the old town are the ruins of a Théâtre Romain. Part of the stage and the theatre's outer walls are all that remain. Similarly, crumbling outer walls are all that are left of the 1st-century **arènes** (amphitheatre), which once sat 10,000 and has now been entirely renovated as a modern outdoor venue.

Northeast, towards La Tour de Mare, you'll pass a section of a 40km-long **aqueduct**, which once carried water to Roman Fréjus.

Chapelle Cocteau ART MUSEUM
(Chapelle Notre Dame de Jérusalem; rte de Cannes) This was one of the last pieces of work embarked upon by Jean Cocteau (1889–1963), best known for the fishermen's chapel he decorated in Villefranche-sur-Mer. Cocteau began work on Chapelle Notre Dame in Fréjus in 1961, but it remained incomplete until the artist's legal heir, Édouard Dermit, finished his former companion's work in 1988.

The chapel is about 5km northeast of the old city, in the quarter of La Tour de Mare (served by bus 13), on the N7 towards Cannes.

Sleeping & Eating

L'Aréna HOTEL €€
(☎04 94 17 09 40; www.hotel-frejus-arena.com; 145 rue du Général de Gaulle; d/tr €145/195;) This hotel, with its sienna-coloured walls and lush garden, is a very pleasant option, ideally located to explore Fréjus' Roman ruins. The Provençal decor is starting to age but the rooms remain comfortable. Those in the Jasmine annexe are more spacious but there is no lift in that building. The duplex are ideal for families (with two single beds on a mezzanine).

Auberge de Jeunesse Fréjus St Raphaël HOSTEL €
(☎04 94 53 18 75; www.fuaj.org; chemin du Counillier; dm €19.60; ⊙Mar-Oct;) A rambling, pretty-basic HI-affiliated hostel set in 10 hectares of pine trees, where you can also pitch your tent. Take bus 7 from St-Raphaël or Fréjus train stations to stop Les Chênes, then cross the roundabout and take chemin du Counillier on your left (600m). There is a daily lockout between noon and 5.30pm. Rates include breakfast and sheets.

Le Poivrier FUSION €
(☎04 94 52 28 50; 52 place Paul Albert Février; mains €12-16, 2-course lunch menu €17; ⊙lunch Tue-Sat, dinner Fri & Sat) Tucked away on one of Fréjus' pretty market squares, you'd never guess from the cute al fresco set up that downstairs is a grandiose vaulted dining room with a monumental fireplace. Nowadays, Le Poivrier is a wonderful address serving exquisitely fresh dishes inspired from local traditions and faraway climes.

Maison de la Tarte BOULANGERIE €
(33 rue Jean Jaurès; ⊙7am-7pm Mon-Sat Aug-Jun;) If you're planning a picnic, stop at this mouth-watering bakery. Tarts of every kind (lemon meringue, pear and chocolate, apricot, almond etc), sold by the slice for €2.60, fill the front window and back shelves. Inside, you'll also find the usual breads and pastries as well as sandwiches.

Getting There & Away

BUS Bus 4 links Fréjus' humble **bus station** (Place Vernet) with St-Raphaël bus station (€1.10).

CAR Parking du Clos de la Tour, on the edge of the old town, is free.

TRAIN The main train station in the area is St-Raphaël-Valescure, in St-Raphaël.

St-Tropez to Toulon

Includes »

Best Places to Eat

- » Chez Bruno (p126)
- » Auberge de l'Omède (p122)
- » Le Clos des Vignes (p127)
- » Logis du Guetteur (p125)

Best Places to Stay

- » Hôtel Lou Cagnard (p115)
- » Hôtel de la Tour (p136)
- » Hôtel Bellevue (p130)
- » Hôtel des Deux Rocs (p123)

Why Go?

Sizzling St-Tropez lives up to its reputation as a mythical fishing port with magnificent sex appeal. While away the days strolling the village and people-watching in the Place des Lices, or sipping a cappuccino alongside the yacht-lined quay. Then head out exploring the peninsula's soul-stirring coastal paths, chichi beach clubs, and vine-knitted capes. When you're ready to move out of the limelight, you'll be enveloped by nature in the Massif des Maures, where thick chestnut groves harbour small villages and surprising vistas. The main trio of islands in the Îles d'Hyères offer a splendid, quiet coastal escape. Inland, in the Haut-Var, meander through stone villages each with its own character and history, and meet the laid-back people who maintain an unpretentious but enviable way of life. Oh, and allow plenty of time to dine well.

Driving Distances (km)

	Bandol	Collobrieres	Draguignan	Hyéres	St-Tropez
Collobrieres	72				
Draguignan	103	56			
Hyéres	39	30	82		
St-Tropez	97	30	52	50	
Toulon	20	38	83	18	68

Getting Around

Airport arrivals don't need to navigate big-city Toulon; the airport is east, near Hyères beaches. Driving into St-Tropez at high season can take hours; arrive by boat. Driving and cycling routes are abundant; highlights include the coastal Corniche des Maures, the Route des Crêtes from Bormes-les-Mimosas, and the roads in the Massif des Maures and the Haut-Var. Having your own wheels helps in the interior. Coastal destinations are served by bus and train.

THREE PERFECT DAYS

Day 1: St-Tropez Style

In St-Tropez mooch around place des Lices with its marvellous market, followed by a portside coffee at Sartre's Sénéquier (p119) and a stroll along the coastal path (p115). Devote the afternoon to art and shopping, and come dusk, motor to Plage de Gigaro, where Couleurs Jardin (p122) beckons for a beautiful dinner on the sand.

Day 2: Travel to Eat

Enjoy a morning pottering around the hilltop market of Ramatuelle, then lunch on grilled fish by the sea at Chez Camille (p122) or between vines at Auberge de l'Ournède (p122). Drive inland through the Massif des Maures to taste sweet chestnuts in Collobrières and dine rustic at La Petite Fontaine (p129). If it's winter, delve instead into Aups' truffle market and dine at Chez Bruno (p126).

Day 3: A Wine-Lover's Trail

Head to Maison des Vins Côtes de Provence (p125) in Les Arcs-sur-Argens, for all things wine. Then visit Chapelle de Ste-Roseline (p125) and the neighbouring winery and vineyards to the east, near La Motte. Dine at Domaine de la Maurette (p125) in a humble auberge next to sweeping vines. Alternatively, discover the matchless Appellation d'Origine Protégée (AOP) reds of Bandol, and sup at Domaine de Terrebrune (p137).

Marvelous Markets

» **Monday** Bormes-les-Mimosas, Port Grimaud

» **Tuesday** Bandol, Callas, Cotignac, Fayence, Hyères, Lorgues, St-Tropez

» **Wednesday** Bormes-les-Mimosas, La Garde Freinet, Salernes, Sanary-sur-Mer

» **Thursday** Aups, Bargemon, Callas, Collobrières, Fayence, Grimaud, Hyères, Port Grimaud, Ramatuelle

» **Friday** Entrecasteaux, La Motte, Port Grimaud

» **Saturday** Carcès, Claviers, Cogolin, Draguignan, Fayence, Hyères, St-Tropez

» **Sunday** Ampus, Cavalière (all-day flea market), Collobrières, La Garde Freinet, Port Grimaud, Ramatuelle, Salernes, Vidauban

DON'T MISS

Les Rencontres du Parc are breathtaking, free and twice-monthly nature hikes. Organised from April to October by the Maison du Parc (p133) on Île de Porquerolles: birdwatching, discovering bats, owls and marine life.

Best Escapes

» Domaine du Rayol (p129)

» Île de Porquerolles (p131) & Île de Port-Cros (p133)

» Haut-Var (p123)

Best Tours & Courses

» **Peninsula Nature Walks** Ramatuelle tourist office organises guided coastal and vineyard nature walks.

» **Snorkelling** Domaine du Rayol and Hyères tourist office offer guided snorkelling.

» **Château de Berne** (www.chateauberne.com; chemin de Berne) Presents truffle-hunting, cooking courses, watercolour-painting, perfume-creation and jazz picnics.

Resources

» **Vins de Provence** (www.vinsdeprovence.com) Wine.

» **Visit Var** (www.visitvar.fr) Information on the Var region.

» **Maisons d'Hôtes du Var** (www.mhvprovence.com) Stylish B&Bs.

» **Pays des Maures** (http://en.maures.latitude-gallimard.com) Official site for the Massif des Maures.

St-Tropez to Toulon Highlights

1. Frolic with celebrities in **St-Tropez** (p114) during high season, and soak up the golden light in winter
2. Find your way through the Massif des Maures to serene **Monastère de la Verne** (p129)
3. Roam the tranquil back roads of the **Haut-Var** (p123) and its tiny hilltop villages
4. Take a dramatic cape-to-cape walk around the **St-Tropez peninsula** (p121)
5. Spend the day wandering (or snorkeling) at the lush Mediterranean garden at **Domaine du Rayol** (p129)
6. Enjoy the island paradise of **Île de Porquerolles** (p131)
7. Go nuts on sweet chestnuts in **Collobrières** (p128)
8. Promenade on the quay at **Sanary-sur-Mer** (p136) and taste **Bandol** (p137) wines

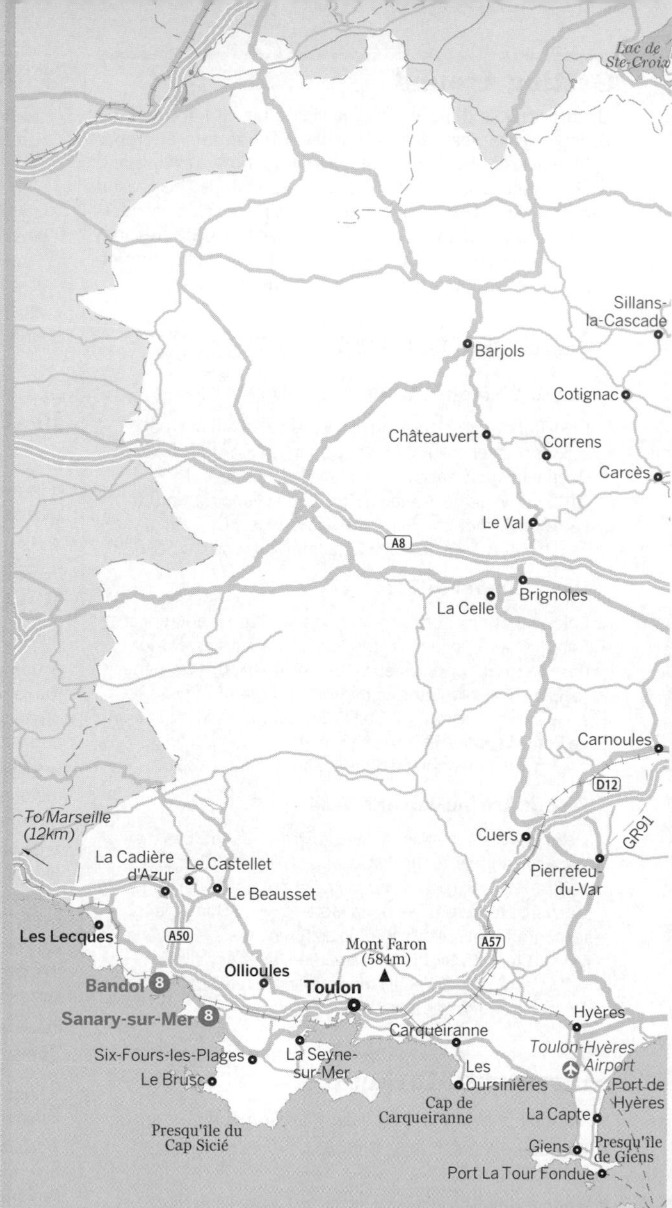

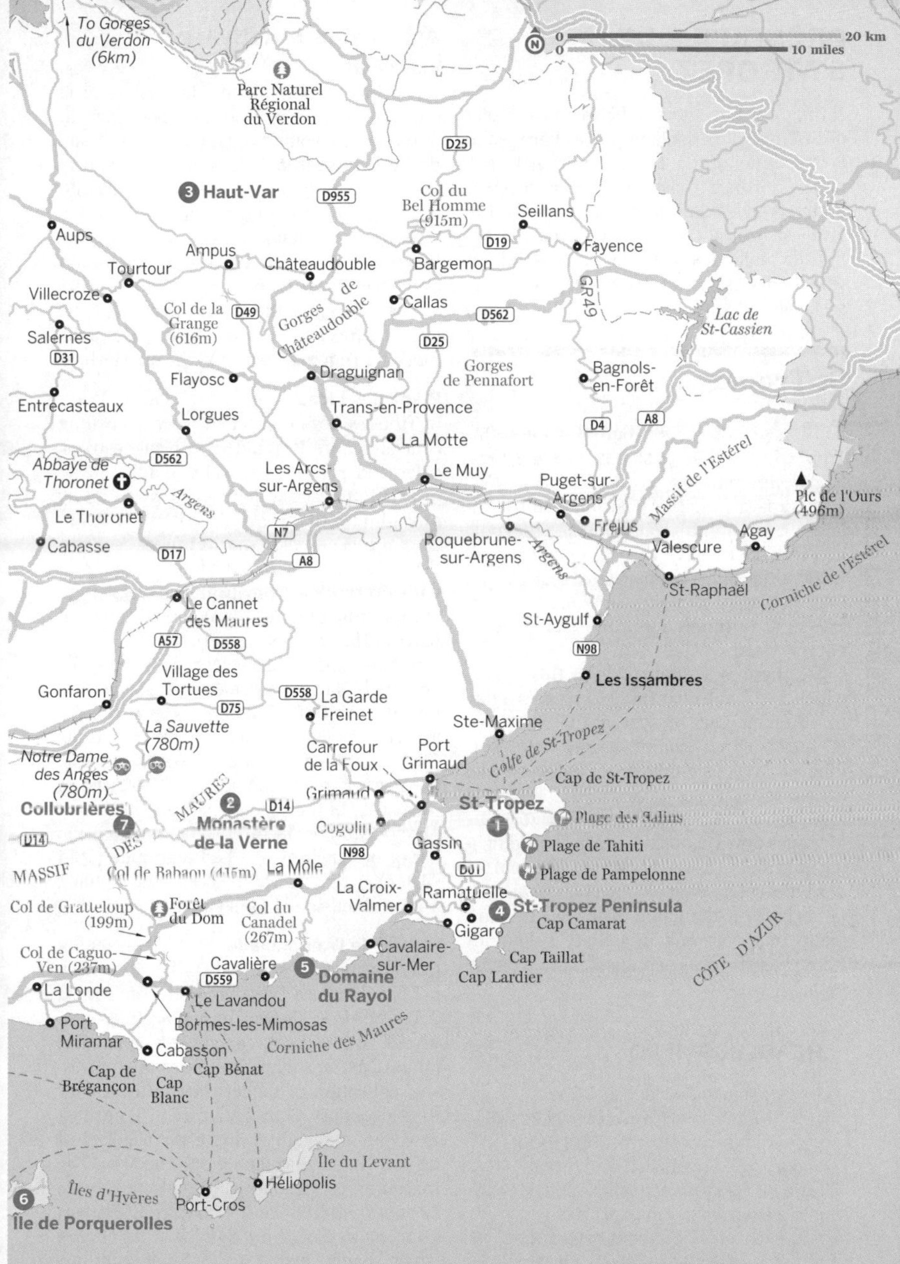

To Gorges du Verdon (6km)
0 20 km
0 10 miles
Parc Naturel Régional du Verdon
D25
3 Haut-Var
D955
Col du Bel Homme (915m)
Seillans
Aups
D19
Fayence
Ampus
Châteaudouble
Bargemon
Tourtour
GR49
Villecroze
Gorges de Châteaudouble
Callas
Col de la Grange (616m)
D49
D562
Lac de St-Cassien
Salernes
D25
D31
Gorges de Pennafort
Draguignan
Bagnols-en-Forêt
Flayosc
Entrecasteaux
Trans-en-Provence
Lorgues
D4
A8
La Motte
Abbaye de Thoronet
D562
Le Muy
Massif de l'Estérel
Les Arcs-sur-Argens
Puget-sur-Argens
Pic de l'Ours (496m)
Argens
Le Thoronet
Fréjus
N7
Roquebrune-sur-Argens
Valescure
Agay
Cabasse
D17
A8
Argens
St-Raphaël
Corniche de l'Estérel
Le Cannet des Maures
St-Aygulf
A57
D558
N98
Village des Tortues
Les Issambres
Gonfaron
D558
La Garde Freinet
D75
La Sauvette (780m)
Ste-Maxime
Notre Dame des Anges (780m)
Carrefour de la Foux
Port Grimaud
Golfe de St-Tropez
Cap de St-Tropez
Grimaud
MAURES
2
D14
St-Tropez
Collobrières
Plage des Salins
7
Monastère de la Verne
Cogolin
1
D14
DES
Gassin
Plage de Tahiti
N98
MASSIF
Col de Babaou (415m)
La Môle
D61
Plage de Pampelonne
La Croix-Valmer
Ramatuelle
Col de Gratteloup (199m)
Forêt du Dom
Col du Canadel (267m)
4 St-Tropez Peninsula
Cap Camarat
Gigaro
Col de Caguo-Ven (237m)
Cavalaire-sur-Mer
Cavalière
5 Domaine du Rayol
Cap Taillat
D559
Cap Lardier
CÔTE D'AZUR
La Londe
Le Lavandou
Port Miramar
Bormes-les-Mimosas
Corniche des Maures
Cabasson
Cap de Brégançon
Cap Bénat
Cap Blanc
Île du Levant
Îles d'Hyères
Héliopolis
6
Port-Cros
Île de Porquerolles
MEDITERRANEAN SEA

PRESQU'ÎLE DE ST-TROPEZ

Jutting out into the sea, between the Golfe de St-Tropez and the Baie de Cavalaire, is the St-Tropez peninsula. From swanky St-Tropez on the northern coast, fine-sand beaches of buttercream yellow and gold – easily the loveliest on the Côte d'Azur – ring the peninsula. Inland, the flower-dressed hilltop villages of Gassin and Ramatuelle charm the socks off millions.

St-Tropez

POP 4986

Pouting sexpot Brigitte Bardot came to St-Tropez in the '50s to star in *Et Dieu Créa la Femme* (*And God Created Woman*; 1956) and transformed the peaceful fishing village overnight into a sizzling jet-set favourite. Tropeziens have thrived on their sexy image ever since: at the Vieux Port, yachts like spaceships jostle for millionaire moorings, and infinitely more tourists jostle to admire them.

Yet there is a serene side to this village which is trampled by 100,000 visitors a day in summer. Out of season the St-Tropez of mesmerising quaint beauty and 'sardine scales glistening like pearls on the cobblestones' that charmed Guy de Maupassant (1850–93) comes to life. Meander down cobbled lanes in the old fishing quarter of La Ponche, sip pastis at a place des Lices cafe, watch old men play *pétanque* (a variant on the game of bowls) beneath plane trees, or walk in solitary splendour from beach to beach along the coastal path.

HEADLESS HERO

A grisly legend provided St-Tropez with its name in AD 68. After beheading a Roman officer named Torpes for becoming a Christian, the emperor Nero packed the decapitated body into a small boat, along with a dog and a rooster who were to devour his remains. Miraculously, the body came ashore in St-Tropez un-nibbled, and the village adopted the headless Torpes as its saint.

Sights & Activities

Vieux Port PORT

Yachts line the harbour and chic visitors stroll the quays at the picturesque old port. In front of the sable-coloured town houses, the **Bailli de Suffren statue**, cast from a 19th-century cannon, peers out to sea. The bailiff (1729–88) was a sailor who fought with a Tropezien crew against Britain and Prussia during the Seven Years War. As much of an institution as the bailiff is portside cafe Sénéquier (p119).

Duck beneath the archway, next to the tourist office, to uncover St-Tropez's daily morning **fish market**, on place aux Herbes.

Place des Lices VILLAGE SQUARE

St-Tropez's legendary and very charming central square is studded with plane trees, cafes and *pétanque* players. Simply sitting on a cafe terrace watching the world go by or jostling with the crowds at its extravaganza of a twice-weekly **market** (place des Lices; 8am-1pm Tue & Sat), which is jam-packed with everything from fruit and veggies to antique mirrors and flip-flops, are integral parts of the St-Tropez experience.

Artists and intellectuals have met for decades in the famous Café des Arts, now simply called **Le Café** (04 94 97 44 69; www.lecafe.fr; place des Lices; lunch/dinner menus €18/30; lunch & dinner daily) – not to be confused with the newer, green-canopied Café des Arts on the corner of the square). Aspiring *pétanque* players can borrow a set of boules from the bar or buy their own at **La Palanquée** (04 94 97 41 41; bd Louis Blanc). Locals tend to hang on the other side of the square.

Musée de l'Annonciade ART MUSEUM

(place Grammont; adult/child €6/4; 10am-noon & 2-6pm Wed-Mon Oct & Dec-May, 10am-noon & 3-7pm Wed-Mon Jun-Sep) In a gracefully converted 16th-century chapel, this small but famous art museum showcases an impressive collection of modern art infused with that legendary Côte d'Azur light. Pointillist Paul Signac bought a house in St-Tropez in 1892 and introduced others to the area. The museum's collection includes his *St-Tropez, Le Quai* (1899) and *Vue de St-Tropez, Coucher de Soleil au Bois de Pins* (1896), which hangs juxtaposed with a window-view of contemporary St-Tropez.

Vuillard, Bonnard and Maurice Denis (the self-named 'Nabis' group) have a room to themselves. Fauvist collections include

Derain and Matisse, who spent the summer of 1904 here. Cubists George Braque and Picasso are also represented.

La Ponche HISTORIC QUARTER

Shrug off the hustle of the port in St-Tropez's ramshackle fishing quarter, La Ponche, northeast of the Vieux Port. From the southern end of quai Frédéric Mistral, place Garrezio sprawls east from 10th-century **Tour Suffren** to place de l'Hôtel de Ville. From here, rue Guichard leads southeast to sweet-chiming **Église de St-Tropez** (place de l'Ormeau), a St-Trop landmark built in 1785 in Italian baroque style. Inside is the bust of St Torpes, honoured during Les Bravades des Espagnols.

Follow rue du Portail Neuf south to **Chapelle de la Miséricorde** (rue de la Miséricorde), built in 1645 with a pretty bell tower and colourful tiled dome.

Citadelle de St-Tropez HISTORIC SITE

(admission €2.50; ⌚10am-6.30pm) Built in 1602 to defend the coast against Spain, the citadel dominates the hillside overlooking St-Tropez to the east. The views (and peacocks!) are fantastic. Its dungeons shelter a **Musée Naval**, dedicated to the town's maritime history and the Allied landings in August 1944.

Beaches BEACH

About 4km southeast of town is the start of **Plage de Tahiti** and its continuation, the famous **Plage de Pampelonne**, studded with St-Tropez's most legendary drinking and dining haunts.

Just east of St-Tropez, **Plage des Salins** (rte des Salins) is a long, wide sandy beach at the southern foot of **Cap des Salins**.

At the northern end of Plage des Salins, on a rock jutting out to sea, is the **tomb** of Émile Olivier (1825–1913), who served as first minister to Napoléon III until his exile in 1870. It looks out towards **La Tête de Chien** (Dog's Head), named after the legendary dog who declined to eat St Torpes' remains.

Further south, **Pointe du Capon** (S of La Tête de Chien) is a beautiful cape criss-crossed with walking trails.

Sentier du Littoral WALKING

A spectacular coastal path wends its way past rocky outcrops and hidden bays 35km south from St-Tropez, around the Presqu'île de St-Tropez to the beach at Cavalaire-sur-Mer and beyond to Le Lavandou (60km). In St-Tropez the yellow-flagged path starts at La Ponche, immediately east of Tour du Portalet, and curves around Port des Pêcheurs, past St-Tropez's citadel. It then leads past the walled **Cimitière Marin** (marine cemetery) to the tiny **Plage des Graniers** and beyond.

The tourist office has maps with distances and walking times (eg to Plage des Salins, 8.5km, 2½ hours).

Tours

Les Bateaux Verts BOAT TOUR

(☎04 94 49 29 39; www.bateauxverts.com; quai Jean Jaurès) Boat trips around **Baie des Cannebiers** (dubbed 'Bay of Stars' after the celebrity villas dotting its coast) are advertised on billboards along quai Suffren at the Vieux Port. From April to September Les Bateaux Verts trips include Baie des Cannebiers (adult/child €9/5); Calanques de l'Estérel (€20/12); Caps Camarat, Taillat and Lardier (€20/12); Cannes (€35/22); Îles de Lérins (€35/22); Port-Cros (€35/22) and Porquerolles (€39/25).

Festivals & Events

Les Bravades RELIGIOUS FESTIVAL

Since 1558 Tropeziens have turned out in traditional costume to watch an ear-splitting army of 140 musket-firing *bravadeurs* parade with a bust of St Torpes. Les Bravades (Provençal for 'bravery') is held 16 to 18 May.

Les Bravades des Espagnols STREET CARNIVAL

Blazing guns and colourful processions on 15 June celebrate victory over the 21 Spanish galleons that attacked in 1637.

Sleeping

St-Tropez is no shoestring destination, but campgrounds sit southeast along Plage de Pampelonne. Most hotels close occasionally in winter; the tourist office lists what's open, and has a list of B&Bs. If you're driving, double-check the parking arrangements.

TOP CHOICE **Hôtel Lou Cagnard** PENSION **€€**

(☎04 94 97 04 24; www.hotel-lou-cagnard.com; 18 av Paul Roussel; d €75-156; ⌚Jan-Oct; ❄📶) Book well ahead for this great-value courtyard charmer shaded by lemon and fig trees and owned by schooled hoteliers. This pretty Provençal house with lavender shutters has its very own jasmine-scented garden, strung with fairy lights at night. Bright, beautifully clean rooms are decorated with painted Provençal furniture. Five have ground-floor

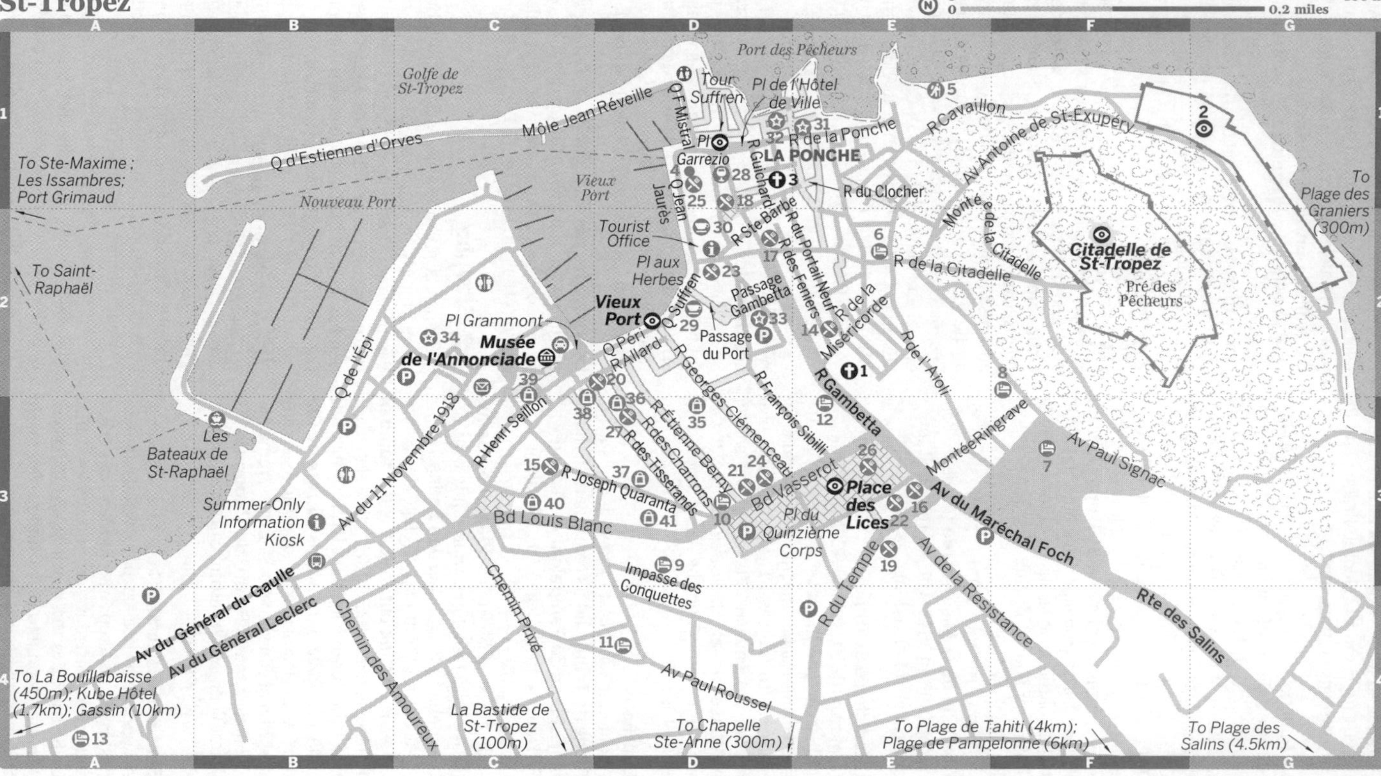
St-Tropez
Golfe de St-Tropez
Port des Pêcheurs
Vieux Port
Nouveau Port
Môle Jean Réveille
Q d'Estienne d'Orves
To Ste-Maxime; Les Issambres; Port Grimaud
To Saint-Raphaël
Les Bateaux de St-Raphaël
Summer-Only Information Kiosk
Tourist Office
Tour Suffren
Pl de l'Hôtel de Ville
Pl Garrezio
LA PONCHE
R de la Ponche
R Guichard
R du Clocher
R Ste Barbe
R du Portail Neuf
R des Feniers
R de la Miséricorde
R de la Citadelle
Monté e de la Citadelle
Citadelle de St-Tropez
Pré des Pêcheurs
R Cavaillon
Av Antoine de St-Exupéry
To Plage des Graniers (300m)
Q F Mistral
Q Jean Jaurès
Pl aux Herbes
Q Suffren
Passage Gambetta
Passage du Port
Vieux Port
Q Péri
R Allard
Pl Grammont
Musée de l'Annonciade
Q de l'Épi
R Georges Clémenceau
R François Sibilli
R Gambetta
R de l' Aïoli
Montée Ringrave
Av Paul Signac
R Henri Seillon
R Étienne Berny
R des Charrons
R des Tisserands
R Joseph Quaranta
Bd Vasserot
Place des Lices
Pl du Quinzième Corps
Av du 11 Novembre 1918
Bd Louis Blanc
Av du Maréchal Foch
Av de la Résistance
R du Temple
Rte des Salins
Impasse des Conquettes
Chemin Privé
Chemin des Amoureux
Av Paul Roussel
Av du Général du Gaulle
Av du Général Leclerc
To La Bouillabaisse (450m); Kube Hôtel (1.7km); Gassin (10km)
La Bastide de St-Tropez (100m)
To Chapelle Ste-Anne (300m)
To Plage de Tahiti (4km); Plage de Pampelonne (6km)
To Plage des Salins (4.5km)
400 m
0.2 miles

St-Tropez

Top Sights

	Citadelle de St-Tropez	F2
	Musée de l'Annonciade	C2
	Place des Lices	E3
	Vieux Port	D2

Sights

1	Chapelle de la Miséricorde	E2
2	Cimitière Marin	G1
3	Église de St-Tropez	D1

Activities, Courses & Tours

4	Les Bateaux Verts	D1
5	Sentier du Littoral	E1

Sleeping

6	B Lodge Hôtel	E2
7	Hôtel Byblos	F3
8	Hôtel Ermitage	F2
9	Hôtel Le Colombier	D3
10	Hôtel Les Palmiers	D3
11	Hôtel Lou Cagnard	D4
12	Pan Deï Palais	E3
13	Pastis	A4

Eating

14	Au Caprice des Deux	E2
15	Auberge des Maures	C3
16	Brasserie des Arts	E3
17	Chez Fuchs	D2
18	Chez les Garçons	D1
19	La Ramade	E3
20	La Table du Marché	D2
21	La Tarte Tropézienne	D3
22	Le Café	E3
23	Le Gorille	D2
24	Le Sporting	D3
25	L'Escale Joseph	D1
26	Market	E3
27	Salama	D3

Drinking

28	Au Petit Bar	D1
	Bar at l'Ermitage	(see 8)
	Bar du Port	(see 23)
29	Café de Paris	D2
30	Sénéquier	D2

Entertainment

31	Le Pigeonnier	E1
	Les Caves du Roy	(see 7)
32	L'Esquinade	D1
33	L'Octave Café	D2
34	VIP Room	C2

Shopping

35	Atelier Rondini	D3
36	Benoît Gourmet & Co	D3
37	De l'Une à l'Autre	D3
38	K Jacques	C3
39	K Jacques	C2
40	La Palanquée	C3
41	Le Dépôt	D3

garden terraces. The cheapest rooms have private washbasin and standup bathtub but share a toilet; 15 of the 19 rooms have air-con.

Pastis HOTEL €€€

(☎04 98 12 56 50; www.pastis-st-tropez.com; 61 av du Général Leclerc; d from €200; ❄≋) This stunning town-house-turned-hotel is the brainchild of an English couple besotted with Provence and passionate about modern art. You'll die for the pop art–inspired interior and long for a swim in the emerald-green pool. Every room is beautiful.

Hôtel Le Colombier HOTEL €€

(☎04 94 97 05 31; http://lecolombierhotel.free.fr; impasse des Conquettes; r €84-158, without bath €76; ❄) The Colombier is in an immaculately clean converted house, five minutes' walk from place des Lices. Its fresh, summery decor is feminine and uncluttered, with pale-pink bedrooms and vintage furniture. Not all rooms have air-con. Rooms without baths share a toilet, but have bidet, sink and shower, open to the bedroom; rooms with baths may only have a partial wall separating them from the bedroom.

Hôtel Ermitage BOUTIQUE HOTEL €€€

(☎04 94 27 52 33; www.ermitagehotel.fr; av Paul Signac; r €180-300; ❄@📶) Kate Moss and Lenny Kravitz favour St-Trop's latest rocker crash pad, which draws inspiration from St-Trop in the '50s through '70s: mid-century modern meets disco. Rooms designed by celebs, including Chloë Sevigny, and the hotel's off-the-beaten-path hillside location, with knockout views over town, increase the exclusivity factor.

B Lodge Hôtel HOTEL €€

(☎04 94 97 58 72; www.hotel-b-lodge.com; 23 rue de l'Aïoli; d from €140; ⊙Dec-Oct; ❄📶) Mod-decor rooms are a bit worn but clean, and

GLITZY SLEEPS

In addition to Pastis, Hôtel Ermitage, and Kube Hôtel, St-Tropez is home to other celebrity-studded hangs, with prices to match. In the city centre, fabled **Byblos** (☎04 94 56 68 00; www.byblos.com; av Paul Signac; r from €762; ⊙Apr-Sep; @☎≋) offers A-list luxe, while elegant **Pan Deï Palais** (☎04 94 17 71 71; www.pandei.com; 52 rue Gambetta; d €620-1215; ⊙Dec-Oct) has an Indian-inspired twist. **La Bastide de Saint-Tropez** (☎04 94 55 82 55; www.bastidesaint-tropez.com; rte des Carles; r/apt from €580/1120; ⊙Feb-Dec; ❄☎≋) lies on the edge of the village and is like living in your own sprawling villa.

some have balconies with citadel views. A two-storey duplex sleeps four (€340). Not all rooms have air-con.

Kube Hôtel DESIGN HOTEL €€€
(☎04 94 97 20 00; www.kubehotel.com; 13 chemin de Rogon de la Valette, rte de St-Tropez; r from €390; ❄@☎≋) Why go to a nightclub when you can sleep at one? Kube houses several bars, including IceKube, and neon-black-lit corridors lead to chichi guestrooms with glitter wallpaper. All you need to bring is an attitude. Along the road into town.

Hôtel Les Palmiers BOUTIQUE HOTEL €€
(☎04 94 97 01 61; www.hotel-les-palmiers.com; 26 blvd Vasserot; d €89-189; ❄) In an old villa opposite place des Lices, Les Palmiers has simple rooms around a courtyard. Choose one in the main building rather than the annexe.

Eating

Prices are high: the glamour-dust sprinkled on fish and chips doesn't come cheap! Many restaurants close in winter. Reservations are essential in high season.

Don't leave town without sampling *tarte Tropézienne,* an orange blossom–flavoured double sponge cake filled with thick cream, created by a Polish baker and christened by Brigitte Bardot in the 1950s.

Quai Jean Jaurès is lined with mediocre restaurants with great portside views.

TOP CHOICE **La Tarte Tropézienne** CAFE, BISTRO €
(☎04 94 97 04 69; www.tarte-tropezienne.com; place des Lices; mains €12-17; ⊙7.30am-6.30pm) This cafe or its associated bakery (36 rue Georges Clémenceau), the original creator of *tarte Tropézienne*, are the best places to buy a slice of the local speciality. Upstairs, in the lively, elegant bistro, pick from delicious daily specials, and downstairs salad/sandwich formulas (€6-7).

Le Sporting BRASSERIE €€
(☎04 94 97 00 65; place des Lices; mains €14-24; ⊙8am-1am) There's a bit of everything on the menu at always-packed Le Sporting, but the speciality is hamburger topped with *foie gras* (fattened goose liver) and morel cream sauce. The Brittany-born owner also serves perfect buckwheat crêpes, honest lunch deals (€13), and a simple salad and *croque monsieur*.

Auberge des Maures PROVENÇAL €€
(☎04 94 97 01 50; 4 rue du Docteur Boutin; mains €31-39; ⊙dinner) The town's oldest restaurant remains the locals' choice for always-good, copious portions of earthy Provençal cooking, like *daube* (braised beef stew) or tapenade-stuffed lamb shoulder. Book a table (essential) on the leafy courtyard.

Chez les Garçons MODERN FRENCH €€
(☎04 94 49 42 67; www.chezlesgarcons.com; 11/13 rue du Cépoun; menus €32; ⊙lunch Tue & Sun, dinner daily mid-Feb–Dec) Super-friendly staff serve delicate specialties like a perfectly poached egg with *foie gras*, all under the watchful eyes of Marilyn, Brigitte and Audrey (art on the wall). Also a lively gay bar next door.

Brasserie des Arts MODERN FRENCH €€
(☎04 94 40 27 37; www.brasseriedesarts.com; 5 place des Lices; mains €20) Wedged in a line-up of eating/drinking terraces jockeying for attention on St-Tropez' people-watching square, BA, as it is known, is where the locals go. Out of season ask for a table at the back to experience the real vibe. The fixed three-course gourmet menu is excellent value.

Au Caprice des Deux TRADITIONAL FRENCH €€€
(☎04 94 97 76 78; www.aucapricedesdeux.com; 40 rue du Portail Neuf; menus €58; ⊙lunch & dinner Thu-Sun) This traditional *maison de village* (old stone terraced house) with coffee-coloured wooden shutters is an old-time favourite with locals. Its intimate interior is as traditional as its French cuisine: think beef filet with truffles or duck.

Chez Fuchs PROVENÇAL €€
(☎04 94 97 10 11; 9 rue de la Citadelle; mains €17-25; ⊙lunch & dinner mid-Feb–Dec) Great wines are paired with firmly Provençal cuisine like

stuffed courgettes or artichokes à *la barigoule* (artichokes braised in a tangy white wine broth), in a lively setting.

La Table du Marché BISTRO €€
(☎04 94 97 02 58; www.christophe-leroy.com; 21bis rue Allard; lunch/dinner menus €19.50/29; ⏲lunch & dinner Apr-Oct; ✎) This simple bistro by St-Tropez' savviest chef, Christophe Leroy, is a success story. The lobster gratin and truffle and celery-stuffed ravioli are unforgettable, and vegetarians are properly catered for.

La Ramade BISTRO €
(☎04 94 81 58 67; 3 rue du Temple; menus €15; ⏲lunch & dinner daily Feb–mid-Nov) Simple, unpretentious and a bargain: a rarity in St-Tropez. Dine heartily by the hearth in winter, on the terrace in summer.

Salama MORROCAN €€
(☎04 94 97 59 62; http://formastec.free.fr/salama/; 1 rue des Tisserands; mains €21-39; ⏲dinner daily high season only) Lounge on cushioned exotic furnishings, wash down heavenly scented couscous and *tajines* with fresh mint tea, and finish with a lime sherbet.

Le Gorille CAFE, BAR €
(☎04 94 97 03 93; www.legorille.com; 1 quai Suffren; sandwiches/mains €7/17; ⏲7am-7pm Thu-Tue) This portside hangout gets it name from its previous owner – the short, muscular and apparently very hairy Henri Guérin! Stop here for breakfast or a post-clubbing *croque monsieur* and fries.

L'Escale Joseph MODERN FRENCH €€€
(☎04 94 97 00 63; 9 quai Jean Jaurès; mains €30-50; ⏲noon-3am Tue-Sun) This celebrity-loved portside restaurant with sand on the floor is a place to see and be seen. The food is so-so.

Drinking & Entertainment

Dress to kill. And bring more money than you think you'll need. Many places close in winter, but in summer it's party central seven days a week.

To tap into the local gay scene, hit Chez les Garçons (p118).

Sénequier CAFE
(☎04 94 97 00 90; www.senequier.com; quai Jean Jaurès) Sartre wrote parts of *Les Chemins de la Liberté* (Roads to Freedom) at this portside cafe, in business since 1887. It's a hot spot with boaties, bikers and tourists. Look for the terrace crammed with bright-red tables and director chairs.

ST-TROPEZ BEACH RESTAURANTS

St-Tropez' seaside scene is defined by its restaurants (which blanket the sand), and they're all wildly different. Mattresses (€15 to €20) and parking (€5) are extra. Most open May to September (call ahead); all are marked on the tourist office map. Book lunch (well ahead) at any of the following.

Club 55 (☎04 94 55 55 55; www.leclub55.fr; 43 blvd Patch, Pampelonne; meals €60; ⏲Apr-Oct) The longest-running club dates to the 1950s, and was originally the crew canteen during the filming of *And God Created Woman*. Now it caters to celebs who do *not* want to be seen. Food's nothing special.

Nikki Beach (www.nikkibeach.com/sttropez; rte de l'Epi, Epi Plage) Favoured by dance-on-the-bar celebs (ie Paris Hilton) who want to be seen. Goes til midnight.

Plage des Jumeaux (☎04 94 58 21 80; www.plagedesjumeaux.com; rte de l'Épi, Pampelonne; mains €22-29; ⏲lunch Thu-Mon year-round, lunch & dinner daily Jul & Aug; 👪) First choice for families, with playground equipment and beach toys; tops for seafood.

Aqua Club (☎04 94 79 84 35; www.aqua-club-plage.fr; rte de l'Epi, Pampelonne; mains €22-29; ⏲Jan-Oct) Friendly mixed gay/straight crowd; the most diverse by far.

Moorea Plage (☎04 94 97 18 17; www.moorea-plage-st-tropez.com; rte des Plages, Tahiti; mains €15-29) Ideal for conversation and backgammon; tops for steak.

Liberty Plage (☎04 94 79 80 62; www.plageleliberty.com; chemin des Tamaris, Pampelonne; mains €17-19; ⏲year-round) Clothing optional – eat naked.

Pearl Beach (☎04 98 12 70 70; www.thepearlbeach.com; quartier de la Bouillabaisse; lunch/dinner menus €30/70; ⏲mid-Feb–Dec) and **La Bouillabaisse** (☎04 94 97 54 00; www.alpazurhotels.com; menus €45; ⏲mid-Feb–Oct), on the way into to town on rte de St-Tropez, are family-friendly.

Bar du Port CAFE, BAR
(www.barduport.com; quai Suffren; ⏲7am-3am year-round) Young, happening bar for beautiful people, with chichi decor in shades of white and silver.

Ice Kube THEME BAR
(☎04 94 97 20 00; Kube Hôtel, 13 chemin de Rogon de la Valette, rte de St-Tropez; admission €30; ⏲6.30pm-1am) Reservations are essential at this bar made of ice. Admission gets you four Grey Goose vodka cocktails, which you must consume within 30 minutes. Then you leave. Best between 11pm and 1am.

Bar at l'Ermitage BAR
(Hôtel Ermitage, av Paul Signac; ⏲5pm-midnight) Escape the crowds at the laid-back Ermitage, kitted out in distressed '50s-modern furniture. Knockout views.

Au Petit Bar BAR
(2 rue Sibille) Year-round, cozy and central.

Café de Paris CAFE, BAR
(www.cafedeparis.fr; 15 quai Suffren; ⏲8am-2am) The terrace is *the* place to sport your new strappy sandals at afternoon aperitifs.

L'Esquinade NIGHTCLUB
(☎04 94 97 87 45; rue du Four; ⏲11pm-5am daily Jun-Sep, Sat & Sun only Oct-May) Where the party winds up when you want to dance till dawn. Open year-round and the top choice of *Tropéziens*.

L'Octave Café NIGHTCLUB
(☎04 94 97 22 56; place de la Garonne; ⏲8pm-5am Apr-Oct) Twirl in a cocktail dress at this intimate club with a live band that plays standards and pop – ideal on date night.

BEST BEACHES

» Plage de Pampelonne (p115) – this divine 9km stretch of golden sand is St-Tropez's most legendary, complete with a clutch of fabulous addresses

» Plage du Layet, Cavalière – nudist beach with legendary shabby-chic beach restaurant, Chez Jo (p130)

» Port-Cros and Porquerolles – two islands with ample unspoilt golden sand to romp on

» Plage d'Hyères – a favourite for its fabulous restaurant, with tables over the water

Les Caves du Roy NIGHTCLUB
(Hôtel Byblos, av Paul Signac; ⏲mid-Apr–Sep) Star-studded bar of the infamous Hôtel Byblos.

Le Pigeonnier NIGHTCLUB
(☎04 94 97 84 26; 13 rue de la Ponche) The least flash, with a *tenue intelligemment négligée* (trendy casual) dress code.

VIP Room NIGHTCLUB
(☎04 94 97 14 70; www.viproom.fr; av du 11 Novembre 1918; ⏲Apr-Aug) New York loft-style club at the Nouveau Port; around for eons and still VIP-hot.

Shopping

St-Tropez is loaded with couture boutiques, gourmet food shops and art galleries. For designer vintage, browse **Le Dépôt** (☎04 94 97 80 10; 6 bd Louis Blanc) and **De l'Une à l'Autre** (☎04 98 12 66 14; 6 rue Joseph Quaranta).

Atelier Rondini SANDALS
(☎04 94 97 19 55; www.rondini.fr; 16 rue Georges Clémenceau) Colette brought a pair of sandals from Greece to Atelier Rondini (open since 1927) to be replicated. They're still making the iconic sandals for about €120.

K Jacques SANDALS
(☎04 94 97 41 50; www.kjacques.com; 25 rue Allard) Hand-crafting sandals (€145–220) since 1933 for clients like Picasso and Brigitte Bardot. There's another branch of **K Jacques** (16 rue Seillon) nearby.

Benoît Gourmet & Co FOOD, WINE
(☎04 94 97 73 78; 6 rue des Charrons) Everything gourmet (caviar, Champagne and *foie gras* included).

Information

The English-language brochure *Out and About* is available in area tourist offices, or check www.bay-of-saint-tropez.com.

Pôle de Santé (☎04 98 12 53 08; www.ch-saint-tropez.fr) Nearest hospital, 11km from St-Tropez on the D559 in Gassin.

Police Station (☎04 94 12 70 00; rue François Sibilli)

Tourist Office (☎04 94 97 45 21; www.ot-saint-tropez.com; quai Jean Jaurès; ⏲9.30am-8pm Jul & Aug, 9.30am-12.30pm & 2-7pm Apr-Jun & Sep–mid-Oct, 9.30am-12.30pm & 2-6pm mid-Oct–Mar) Has a kiosk in July and August in Parking du Port.

GETTING TO ST-TROPEZ

During high season, those in the know avoid horrendous four-hour traffic bottlenecks on the one road into St-Tropez (or €40 parking, which is hard to find) by parking in Port Grimaud or Ste-Maxime and taking a shuttle boat (p115).

Getting There & Around

BOAT Services are reduced or cut in winter.

Les Bateaux Verts (p115) runs many shuttle boats. Shuttles connect St-Tropez with Ste-Maxime (one-way/return €7.10/12.70, 15 minutes, operates year-round), Les Issambres (€8.10/14.20, 25 minutes), Marines de Cogolin (€6.50/11.50, 15 minutes) and Port Grimaud (€6.50/11.50, 20 minutes).

Les Bateaux de St-Raphaël (www.bateauxsaintraphael.com) Connects St-Tropez (Nouveau Port) and St-Raphaël (adult/child €14/9).

Taxi de Mer (06 09 57 31 22, 06 09 53 15 47) Boat taxis can be booked for anywhere around St-Tropez.

BUS VarLib (www.varlib.fr) tickets cost €2 from the **bus station** (04 94 56 25 74; av du Général de Gaulle) for anywhere within the Var département (except Toulon-Hyères airport), including Ramatuelle (35 minutes), St-Raphaël (1¼ hours) via Grimaud and Port Grimaud, and Fréjus (one hour). Buses to Toulon (two hours, seven daily, less in summer) stop at Le Lavandou (one hour) and Hyères (1½ hours).

Four daily buses serve Toulon-Hyères airport (€15, 1½ hours).

TAXI The **taxi** (04 94 97 05 27) rank is at the Vieux Port in front of the Musée de l'Annonciade.

BICYCLE Rolling Bikes (04 94 97 09 39; www.rolling-bikes.com; 14 av du Général Leclerc; bikes/scooters/motorcycles from €15/40/120 per day, plus deposit)

The Peninsula

The golden sands of France's chicest beach, **Plage de Pampelonne**, line the peninsula's eastern side. South of St-Tropez unfurl manicured vineyards and quiet narrow lanes dotted with *châteaux* or solitary stone *bastides* (country houses).

Cap Taillat is guarded by the Conservatoire du Littoral and shelters some of France's rarest plant species as well as a population of Hermann tortoises (p128). Cap Lardier, the peninsula's southernmost cape, is protected by the Parc National de Port-Cros.

The Sentier du Littoral (p115) snakes along the entire coastline.

The yield of area **vineyards** – Côtes de Provence wine – can be tasted at châteaux along the D61 and around the peninsula. Tourist offices have lists.

Sights

Ramatuelle VILLAGE

Ramatuelle, a labyrinthine walled village with a tree-studded central square, got its name from 'Rahmatu'llah', meaning 'Divine Gift' – a legacy of the 10th-century Saracen occupation. Jazz and theatre fill the tourist-packed streets during August's **Festival de Ramatuelle** (www.festivalderamatuelle.com) and **Jazz Fest** (www.jazzfestivalramatuelle.com).

FREE **Sémaphore de Camarat** LIGHTHOUSE

(guided tour only Jun-Sep) Pampelonne stretches for 9km from **Cap du Pinet** to **Cap Camarat**, a rocky cape dominated by France's second-tallest lighthouse (110m), operational since 1861, electrified in 1946 and automated from 1977. Scale it for giddy views of St-Tropez and the peninsula. Book tours at Ramatuelle's tourist office.

Gigaro & Cap Lardier BEACHES, CAPE

Seaside hamlet Gigaro harbours a sandy beach, some lovely eating and sleeping options, and a water-sports school. From the far end of the beach, a board maps the Sentier du Littoral (p115) that works its way around the coast to Cap Lardier (4.7km, 1½ hours) and past **Cap Taillat** to L'Escalet (9km, 2¾ hours). From Gigaro, the narrow but drop-dead gorgeous D93 winds inland over the **Col de Collebasse** (129m) to Ramatuelle – a good ride for mountain bikers. **L'Escalet**, accessible by a 2.5km road signposted off the D93, is a pretty little rocky cove.

Gassin VILLAGE

In medieval Gassin, 11km southwest of St-Tropez atop a rocky promontory, narrow streets wend up to the village church (1558). The village's most wowing feature is its 360-degree panoramic view of the peninsula, St-Tropez bay and the Maures forests.

Sleeping

Château de Valmer LUXURY HOTEL €€€

(04 94 55 15 15; www.chateauvalmer.com; btwn La Croix-Valmer & Gigaro; d from €320, treehouse €660; May-Sep;) This fabulous 19th-century wine-producer's mansion is for nature bods with a penchant for luxury.

Sleep above vines in a *cabane perchée* (tree-house), stroll scented vegetable and herb gardens and play hide-and-seek around century-old palm and olive trees.

Ferme Ladouceur B&B €€
(04 94 79 24 95; www.fermeladouceur.com; D61, quartier Les Roullière, Ramatuelle; d incl breakfast €115-125; Apr-Sep) Have breakfast beneath a fig tree at this lovely *chambre d'hôte* in a 19th-century *bastide*. The rustic restaurant (*menu* including wine €42) is open to anyone who fancies an evening taste of good old-fashioned farm cuisine. Find it north of Ramatuelle, signposted off the D61 to St-Tropez.

Les 3 Îles B&B €€€
(04 94 49 03 73; www.3iles.com; rte du Gigaro, Gigaro; d incl breakfast €190-260; mid-Mar–Oct;) The same seductive view of the sea and those golden Îles d'Hyères glistening on the horizon awaits you in each of the eight carefully thought-out rooms and infinity pool. Tropézienne Catherine and husband Jean-Paul are the creative energy behind this faultless, oh-so-chic *maison d'hôte*.

Hôtel Bellovisto PENSION €
(04 94 56 17 30; www.bellovisto.eu; place des Barrys, Gassin; d/tr from €70/110; Apr-Sep;) A large part of the charm of this hilltop hotel is the cafe-clad square with panoramic view on which it resides. The hotel itself is dead simple: local bar on the ground floor displaying local *pétanque* club trophies, and nine rooms up top.

Le Refuge PENSION €€
(04 94 79 67 38, 06 17 95 65 38; plage de Gigaro, Gigaro; d/studio incl breakfast €95/115, d without bath €65; Apr–mid-Oct;) This rustic seaside house sits back off the sand. Ten humble rooms and five studios with kitchenette provide simple sleeping and open onto private little tabled terraces. Proprietors cook up tasty grills at the restaurant of the same name at the start of the coastal path. Wi-fi downstairs.

Eating & Drinking

As in St-Tropez, reservations are essential.

TOP CHOICE **Auberge de l'Oumède** PROVENÇAL €€€
(04 94 44 11 11; www.aubergedeloumede.com; Chemin de l'Oumède; mains €39-59, d from €225; dinner Tue-Sat May–mid-Sep, dinner daily Jul & Aug;) Epicureans come from far and wide to sample Jean-Pierre Frezia's Provençal cuisine served in a sea of vineyards: red mullet and spinach cannelloni, grilled catch of the day and sensational desserts, all accompanied by some very fine wines. Dining at this isolated *bastide* down a single-lane track is indeed a rare treat. It has seven rooms and a pool – handy should you really not want to leave.

Couleurs Jardin SEAFOOD €€
(04 94 79 59 12; Plage de Gigaro, Gigaro; mains €25-30; lunch & dinner Apr-Sep) Eclectic and hip, this imaginative beachside space is *the* place to dine and/or drink. Loll on cushioned seating beneath the trees or pick a table on the terrace with nothing between you and the deep blue sea. Cuisine is fish- and market-fuelled.

Chez Camille SEAFOOD €€€
(04 98 12 68 98; www.chezcamille.fr; rte de Bonne Terrasse, Ramatuelle; menus €43-78; lunch & dinner Wed-Mon Apr-Sep) Deep terracotta walls hide this blue-and-white-tiled fishing cottage dating from 1913. Now into its fourth generation, the beachside restaurant cooks up just one thing over a wood-fuelled grill: fish. From the D93 follow signs for Bonne Terrasse; it's 4km north of Ramatuelle.

Café de l'Ormeau CAFE
(04 94 79 20 20; place du Village, Ramatuelle; mains €8-13; 7am-9pm) Lovely vine-covered cafe terrace for coffee or meals.

Information

Ramatuelle Tourist Office (04 98 12 64 00; www.ramatuelle-tourisme.com; place de l'Ormeau; 9am-1pm & 3-7.30pm Mon-Fri, 10am-1pm & 3-7pm Sat & Sun Jul & Aug, shorter hrs rest of year)

Golfe de St-Tropez

GRIMAUD

This medieval postcard-perfect hilltop village sits 3km inland. It's crowned with the dramatic shell of **Château du Grimaud**, built in the 11th century, fortified in the 15th century, destroyed during the Wars of Religion (1562-98), rebuilt in the 17th century, and wrecked again during the French Revolution. Magical evening concerts are held on the stage within the ruins during the music festival, **Les Grimaldines**, in July and August.

Grimaud's **tourist office** (04 94 55 43 83; www.grimaud-provence.com; 1 bd des Aliziers; 9am-12.30pm & 2.30-6.15pm Mon-Sat), at the foot of the village on the D558, has information on walks, some with a guide. Le Petit Train de Grimaud (p123) serves Port Grimaud.

South of Grimaud along the St-Tropez-bound D61, visit **Caves des Vignerons de Grimaud** (☎04 94 43 20 14; 36 av des Oliviers, D61, Grimaud), a cooperative where you can stock up on Vin de Pays du Var for little more than €2 a litre.

PORT GRIMAUD

The so-called 'Venice of Provence' stands on what was a mosquito-filled swamp in the 1960s. Inside the high wall that barricades the pleasure port from the busy N98, colourful cottages stand gracefully alongside yacht-laden waterways comprising 12km of quays, 7km of canals and mooring space for 3000 luxury yachts. Thursday and Sunday mornings a **market** fills place du Marché, from where a bridge leads to Port Grimaud's modernist **church**, with stained-glass window designed by Vasarely. Red rooftops fan out from atop its **bell tower** (admission €1).

Port Grimaud is jam-packed with overpriced restaurants. Seafood seekers won't do better than highly regarded **La Table du Mareyeur** (☎04 94 56 06 77; www.mareyeur.com; 10-11 place Artisans; lunch/dinner menu €25/55, mains €26-48; ⏲lunch & dinner Mar-Nov).

March to October, two kiosks across the bridge from the church run 20-minute Port Grimaud **boat tours** (adult/child €5/3) and rent four-person **electric boats** (per 30min €20). Shuttle boats (p115) serve St-Tropez.

Le Petit Train de Grimaud (☎06 62 07 65 09; adult/child return €7/4; ⏲6-8 daily, 50min, Apr-Sep) makes a circuit from the port to the inland village, Grimaud.

Buy conserves of all things Provençal – olives, tomatoes, anchovies etc – at **Au Bec Fin** (☎04 94 55 74 43; www.au-bec-fin.com; 2 ave de Valensole, RD98, Cogolin).

The **tourist office** (☎04 94 56 02 01; quai des Fossés; ⏲9am-12.30pm & 2.30-6.15pm Mon-Sat Jun–mid-Sep) sits just outside the main pedestrian entrance to the village on the N98. Cars are forbidden inside the walls.

Buses link Port Grimaud with Grimaud (€1.60, 10 minutes) and St-Tropez (€3.90, 15 minutes).

HAUT-VAR

The northern half of the Var *département* (north of the A8 autoroute), known as the Northern or Upper Var, is vastly different from its coastal counterpart. Peaceful hilltop villages drowse beneath the midday sun, and are within easy reach of the wild Gorges du Verdon. Skip Draguignan, the hard-nosed main town where the French army maintains its largest military base, and head for the hills: lush vineyards, earthy black truffles and a bounty of gastronomic delights. The best way to get around: your own wheels.

ℹ Information

Each village has its own website and excellent tourist offices. Check www.visitvar.fr for details on the whole region. The Haut-Var is divided into sections served by their own tourist boards and governments. Going from Draguignan counterclockwise:

» **Dracénie** (www.tourisme-dracenie.com), including **bus information** (www.tedbus.com)

» **Haut Var-Verdon** (www.haut-var.com)

» **Provence Verte** (www.provenceverte.fr)

» **Coeur du Var** (www.coeurduvar.com)

For area **wine makers** visit www.vinsdeprovence.com. **Le Var Campsites** booklets are available at tourist offices, while **Gîtes de France** (www.gites-de-france-var.fr) has country rentals.

Le Pass Sites Var is a free pass with discounts on admission to 28 abbeys, chapels, gardens and museums in the Var.

Dracénie

BARGEMON

This medieval village juts out onto a promontory, from which you have excellent views across the valley to Claviers. Market day is Thursday. The **tourist office** (☎04 94 47 81 73; www.ot-bargemon.fr; av Pasteur; ⏲8.30am-12.30pm & 2-5pm Mon-Fri) also rents bikes for those who fancy a day cycling.

SEILLANS

Adjoining the Seillans tourist office is a **gallery** (www.seillans.fr; adult/child €2/free; ⏲10am-12.30pm & 2.30-9pm Mon-Sat) of work by Dorothea Tanning and Max Ernst, who lived here in the 1960s and '70s.

TOP CHOICE **Hôtel des Deux Rocs** (☎04 94 76 87 32; www.hoteldeuxrocs.com; 1 place Font d'Amont; d €78-135, menus €40-67; ⏲lunch Wed-Sun, dinner Tue-Sat Feb-Dec), a boutique hotel with fig-flower Fragonard soap in the bathrooms, a fine collection of B&W family photos and a gourmet restaurant, wins the prize hands-down

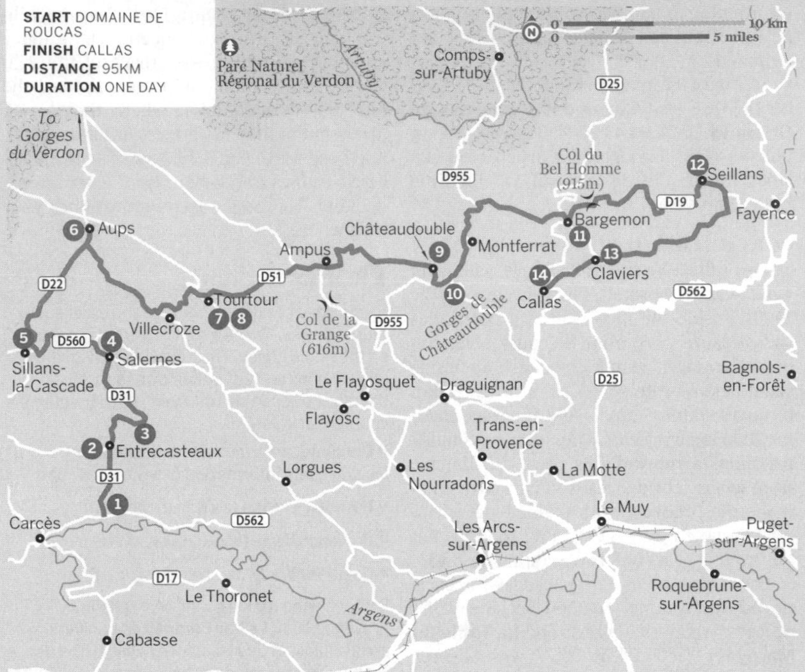

Driving Tour

Haut-Var Hilltop Villages

To find sleepy unspoilt villages teetering on hilltops, from the D562, pick up the northbound D31 towards Entrecasteaux and Salernes. You'll wind past pretty vineyards with dry-stone walls, olive trees and vivid burnt-orange soil. After 1.5km pop into 1 **Domaine de Roucas** for wine tasting. Continuing 4km, hilltop 2 **Entrecasteaux**, with its giant 17th-century château, perches dramatically along the river.

Bear right along the D31 towards Salernes and Aups. Buy honey at *miellerie* 3 **Remy Apiculteur**, 2km north, then drive another wiggly 6km to 4 **Salernes**, where hand-made terracotta tiles called *terres cuites* (literally 'baked earth') have been manufactured since the 18th century. The tourist office has a list of workshops to visit.

In Salernes pick up the westbound D2560 and subsequent D560 to 5 **Sillans-la-Cascade**, on the banks of the River Bresque, a gem of a fortified village with a waterfall. Then it's 9km north along the D22 to 6 **Aups** and another 10km southeast past olive groves and lavender gardens to the typical 'eagle nest' gold-stone village of 7 **Tourtour**. Buy olive oil in the village and, in mid-December, watch olives being pressed in its 17th-century 8 **moulin à huile**; the tourist office runs guided tours of the mill.

Speed 6km further east along the D51 to Ampus and continue east 9km to 9 **Châteaudouble**, an astonishing village clinging to a cliff of the 10 **Gorges de Châteaudouble**.

Just 7km east of here is 11 **Bargemon**, a village with a maze of medieval streets and ramparts to stroll; it hit the headlines when the Beckhams bought a local pad in 2004.

12 **Seillans**, a scenic 12km drive east, is an irresistibly pretty, typical Provençal village with cobbled lanes coiling to its crown, and a village inn, Hôtel des Deux Rocs, that only the stone-hearted will be able to resist.

If you have any gas left in your proverbial tank, you can circle back south (Fayence is best seen from a distance) to 13 **Claviers** and 14 **Callas**, yet more picturesque villages.

for most atmospheric village inn. Scipion, knight of the Flotte d'Agout, lived here in the 17th century. Today, the soulful *bastide* is home to the Malzacs, who run this 13-room hotel with extraordinary panache. Summer dining is alfresco around a fountain.

CALLAS

From the central village square you can get a stunning panorama of the red-rock **Massif de l'Estérel**. The village winds up the hill in a warren of bends. At the southern foot of Callas is **Moulin de Callas** (☎04 94 39 03 20; www.moulindecallas.com; Quartier les Ferrages, Callas; ⏰10am-noon & 2-6pm Mon-Sat), where Nicole and Serge's family have cultivated olives to make oil since 1928. Learn about olive oil (tours are by appointment) and buy in the on-site shop. **Callas Tourist Office** (☎04 94 39 06 77; callastourisme@dracenie.com; place du 18 Juin 1940) has info on the region.

LES ARCS-SUR-ARGENS & LA MOTTE

The extended sprawl around Les Arcs and La Motte is nothing special, but the nearby area (like along the D25) is rich in vineyards and wine tasting opportunities. There are some great restaurants, and the medieval hilltop quarter of Les Arcs is a fun stroll. St Rosaline was born there in 1263 in the 12th century **château** where she later performed the 'miracle of roses', turning bread into roses.

Sights & Activities

TOP CHOICE Chapelle de Ste-Roseline CHURCH
(chemin de Ste-Roseline, Les Arcs-sur-Argens; ⏰2.30-6pm Tue-Sun Feb-Dec) A 1975 mosaic by Marc Chagall illuminates the 13th-century Romanesque Chapelle de Ste-Roseline, 4.5km east of Les Arcs-sur-Argens on the road to La Motte. The church contains the corpse of St Roseline, who was born at the château in Les Arcs in 1263 and became a Carthusian nun and the mother superior here. She experienced numerous visions during her lifetime and was said to be able to curtail demons. She died in 1329. Piano recitals and music concerts are held in the chapel in July and August.

TOP CHOICE Maison des Vins Côtes de Provence WINE TASTING
(☎04 94 99 50 20; www.caveaucp.fr; Les Arcs-sur-Argens; ⏰10am-6pm Mon-Sat, to 5pm Sun) This bacchanalian House of Wines, 2.5km south of Les Arcs-sur-Argens on the westbound N7, is a one-stop shop to taste, learn about and buy (at producers' prices) Côtes de Provence wines. Each week 16 of the 800 different wines from 250 wine estates are selected for tasting. Knowledgeable multilingual staff advise you on the dream dish to eat with each wine.

Château Ste-Roseline WINE TASTING
(☎04 94 99 50 30; www.sainte-roseline.com; Les Arcs-sur-Argens; ⏰9am-12.30pm & 2-6.30pm Mon-Fri, 10am-noon & 2-6pm Sat & Sun) Sample and buy a prestigious *cru classé* (top vintage) wine, produced here since the 14th century. The château adjoins the Chapelle de Ste-Rosaline.

Sleeping & Eating

Le Mas du Péré B&B €€
(☎04 94 84 33 52; www.lemasdupere.com; 280 chemin du Péré, La Motte; d incl breakfast from €89, studio per week from €550; ❄@🏊👪) Signposted from the centre of the village, this is a convenient spot from which to go wine tasting in the region. Perfectly clean, well-appointed rooms in muted tones look out on the pool. Some have dappled terraces, and studios have kitchenettes.

TOP CHOICE Logis du Guetteur TRADITIONAL FRENCH €€
(☎04 94 99 51 10; www.logisduguetteur.com; place du Château, Les Arcs-sur-Argens; 2-/3-course menus from €24/29; ⏰lunch & dinner daily Feb-Dec; ❄📶) This super restaurant perches on the tippety top of Les Arcs in a 12th-century château and watchtower. In winter dine in the renovated *cave* beneath oil paintings of white peacocks and cornucopia, and in summer out on the terrace with views all around. Food is impeccable, service attentive and the ambience one of a kind. Stay over in simple rooms (€130 to €160).

TOP CHOICE Domaine de la Maurette BISTRO, WINE BAR €€
(☎04 94 45 92 82; www.vins-maurette.fr; rte de Callas, La Motte; lunches €13, 3-course menus €24-32; ⏰lunch & dinner) For an authentic Provençal feast, head east out of La Motte, along the D47 to this rustic wine estate on the intersection of the D47 and the D25. Taste and buy wine, and dine on a vine-covered terrace in its roadside inn with attached winery, where the atmosphere of chattering people

dining on wholesome, homemade food is nothing short of electric.

West of Draguignan

LORGUES

Bustling Lorgues is fountain-filled, and the **tourist office** (04 94 73 92 37; www.lorgues-tourisme.fr; 9am-noon & 2-5pm Mon-Sat), near the southern entrance to town, has maps of walks.

The simplest in a trio of great Cistercian abbeys (the other two are Silvacane and Notre-Dame de Sénanque), uninhabited **Abbaye de Thoronet** (04 94 60 43 90; http://thoronet.monuments-nationaux.fr; Le Thoronet; adult/child €7.50/free; 10am-6.30pm Mon-Sat, 10am-noon & 2-6.30pm Sun), 12km southwest of Lorgues, was built between 1160 and 1190. It's remarkable for its ultra-austere architecture: pure proportions, perfectly dressed stone and the subtle fall of light and shadow are where its beauty lies.

France's most famous truffle restaurant, **Chez Bruno** (04 94 85 93 93; www.restaurantbruno.com; rte des Arcs, D10; menus €68-135; lunch & dinner daily Jun–mid-Sep, closed Mon mid-Sep–May), can be found in a country house 2.5km southeast of Lorgues. In his Michelin-starred restaurant, celebrity chef Bruno Clément cooks almost exclusively with those knobbly, pungent delicacies: he goes through an incredible 1000kg of the world's most expensive foodstuff every year. Should you not be able to move after your black-diamond feast, stay in one of Bruno's six lovely **rooms** (rte des Arcs, D10; d from €150).

TOURTOUR

Tourtour is a beautiful amber-stoned village with a churchyard stretching across a promontory offering panoramic views. It makes a handy place to break your journey, stroll the cobbled lanes, or indulge your truffle fancy.

Sleeping & Eating

Maison de la Treille B&B €€
(04 94 70 59 29; www.tourtour.fr; rue Grande 22, Tourtour; d incl breakfast €90; Mar-Nov;) The hefty brass knocker piercing the olive-green front door, the lush bush of lavender outside and the covered breakfast terrace on the top floor immediately catch the eye at this charming *maison d'hôte* in one of the Northern Var's most beautiful hilltop villages.

Les Chênes Verts GASTRONOMIC €€€
(04 94 70 55 06; rte de Villecroze, D51, Tourtour; menus €57; lunch & dinner Thu-Mon Aug-May) It might seem odd that this walled property shuts in June and July. But there is good reason. The Green Oaks is famed for its luxurious truffle cuisine: winter food! The stiff waiters and eclectic decor are hardly wowing, but the cuisine is irreproachable.

L'Alechou BISTRO €
(04 94 70 54 76; 16 rue Grande, Tourtour; mains €9-15; lunch & dinner daily;) On the cuter-than-cute main street, overwhelmingly friendly L'Alechou is a perfect spot for lunch between flowerpots.

Information

Tourtour Tourist Office (04 94 70 59 47; www.tourisme-tourtour.com; montée de St-Dénis)

AUPS

November to late February, those alien-looking nuggets of black fungus can be viewed at the Thursday morning **truffle market** on Aups' central plane-tree-studded square. Truffle hunts and pig-snouting demonstrations lure a crowd on the fourth Sunday in January during Aups' **Journée de la Truffe** (Day of the Truffle).

The **tourist office** (04 94 84 00 69; www.aups-tourisme.com; place Frédéric Mistral; 9am-12.30pm & 3.30-7pm Mon-Sat, 9am-12.30pm Sun), on the central square, has information on other gastronomic festivities and a list of local truffle hunters.

ENTRECASTEAUX

Entrecasteaux, with its giant 17th-century château, old stone houses sun-baked every shade of gold, and fountain-clad square, perches dramatically over a river. Grab a coffee at the green-canopied **Bar Central** (04 94 04 43 53) – you won't get more local than this. The well-lived-in yellow-stone farmhouse at **Domaine de Roucas** (04 94 04 48 14; rte de Carcès; 9am-6pm) welcomes wine tasters. Pick up local honey at **Remy Apiculteur** (04 94 04 45 87; D50, Entrecasteaux), just outside town.

COTIGNAC

POP 2000

Parts of this tiny stone village are built into tuffa cliff faces. The River Cassole carves its heart, and villagers stroll the tree-lined promenade of Cours Gambetta. The Tuesday morning **market** is lively, and the **tourist office** (04 94 04 61 87;

http://ot-cotignac.provenceverte.fr; Pont de la Cassole; ⌚9am-12.30pm & 2-7pm Mon-Sat, 9am-1pm Sun) has maps of walks to chapels and fountains. **Vignobles de Cotignac** (☎04 94 04 60 04; http://vignerons.cotignac-info.com) is the spot to buy the local rosé.

Sleeping & Eating

TOP CHOICE Mas de l'Olivette B&B €€
(☎04 94 80 28 73; www.masdelolivette.com; rte d'Entrecasteaux; d €95, studio per week €800;) The lovely Jean-Claude and Yannick welcome you to their tiny B&B, so much so that it feels like home. The two impeccable, beautifully appointed guest rooms can adjoin for families. The spotless freestanding studio has a kitchen and terrace. Views stretch through the olive groves and bathrooms are kitted out with L'Occitane products.

TOP CHOICE Le Clos des Vignes TRADITIONAL FRENCH €€
(☎04 94 04 72 19; www.restaurant-le-clos-des-vignes.fr; rte Monfort; menus €28-60; ⌚lunch & dinner Tue-Sat) Seek out this farmhouse for the home-cooked cuisine (by husband Jean-Luc) and the warm welcome (by wife Dany). Dining is on the terrace, which is enclosed in winter, and the rhythm is slow and easy. French country life at its finest. Look for the signed dedication by Brad and Angelina, who are patrons and neighbours.

La Table des Coquelicots TRADITIONAL FRENCH €€
(☎04 94 69 46 07; 10 cours Gambetta; lunch/dinner menus €14/27; ⌚lunch & dinner daily) Choose between the elegant, muted-tone dining room or the people-watching terrace under the plane trees. Open year-round, their food is classic...and the profiteroles enormous.

CORRENS

The vineyards surrounding this tiny village 25km west of Le Thoronet on the banks of the River Argens have been organic since 1997. That's when the mayor, himself a wine producer, decided to make Correns' 200 hectares of AOP Côtes de Provence vineyards organic in order to boost the appeal of its vintage.

Correns wine (30% white, 50% rosé and 20% red) has made a name for itself while several other local farmers have turned organic to produce honey, chicken, eggs, olive oil and goats'-milk cheese. Local kids dine on organic meals at the school canteen, and the town hall has in-house expertise in ecofriendly architecture to help villagers 'green' their homes.

Correns **tourist office** (☎04 94 37 21 31; www.correns.fr; 2 rue Cabassonne; ⌚9am-noon & 2-5.30pm Mon-Thu, 2-5.30pm Fri, 9am-noon Sat) has a list of estates where you can taste and buy wine.

The most prestigious of these, **Château de Miraval** (www.miraval.com), was a monastery in the 13th century, then a legendary Miraval recording studio, where Pink Floyd recorded part of *The Wall* in 1979. Unfortunately it shut its doors to passers-by since Brad, Angelina and kids moved into the dreamy gold-stone property on the vast 400-hectare estate in 2008.

Taste and buy Château de Miraval and other big names such as **Domaine de la Grande Pallière** (www.lagrandpalliere.com) at wine cooperative and shop **Vignerons de Correns** (☎04 94 59 59 46; chemin de l'Église; ⌚3.30-7pm Mon-Fri, 10am-12.30 & 3.30-7pm Sat).

At the lovely **Domaine des Aspras** (☎04 94 59 59 70; www.aspras.com; 1.5km southeast of Correns; ⌚11am-12.30pm & 4-7pm Tue-Sat) you can taste in situ and, should you fancy it, rent a six-bedroom *bastide* on the estate.

The wonderfully cool **Vallon Sourn**, where the green waters of the Argens flow peacefully, is perfect for walking and cycling. A scenic drive/ride from the village will get you there: head north on the D45 towards Châteauvert.

Lunch well, and predominantly organicly, at **Auberge du Parc** (☎04 94 59 53 52; www.aubergeduparc.fr; 34 place du Général de Gaulle; menus €35; ⌚lunch & dinner Wed-Mon Mar-Oct), where cuisine is innovative and market-driven, the wine list features the local varieties and mains are as sizeable as the five elegant guest rooms (doubles €130).

LA CELLE

This town is all about the recently restored 12th-century Romanesque **Ancienne Abbaye de la Celle** (☎04 94 72 50 40; La Celle; ⌚tours 2pm Tue & Thu). Forge your way through the urban sprawl to tour the abbey. For a special treat, dine or stay at the fabled **Hostellerie de l'Abbaye de la Celle** (☎04 98 05 14 14; www.abbaye-celle.com; 19 place du Général de Gaulle; lunch menus €46, dinner menus €66-90, d from €340; ⌚lunch & dinner daily, closed Tue & Wed in winter). Top chefs Bruno Clément and Alain Ducasse are the creative energies behind this refined four-star restaurant-hotel. Afterwards try one of the local

DON'T MISS

WONDERFUL ROADWAYS

The D14 runs through Collobrières, the largest town in the massif and chestnut capital of the universe, and is graced with superb panoramas. It's particularly popular with cyclists. Similarly dramatic, the D39 from Collobrières soars north to **Notre Dame des Anges** (780m) before plunging down to Gonfaron. The parallel N98 skims through vineyards and cork oak plantations from St-Tropez to Bormes-les-Mimosas.

From La Môle – where you can find a delicious meal at **Auberge de la Môle** (04 94 49 57 01; place de l'Église; lunch/dinner menus €23/55; lunch & dinner Tue-Sat, lunch Sun) – the breathtakingly narrow **Col du Canadel** (D27) dives dramatically to the coast, dishing up unbeatable views of the Massif des Maures, coastline and offshore islands.

88 vintages at **La Maison des Vins des Coteaux Varois en Provence** (04 94 69 33 18; Abbaye de La Celle, La Celle).

MASSIF DES MAURES

Shrouded by a forest of pine, chestnut and cork oak trees, the Massif des Maures arcs inland between Hyères and Fréjus. Roamed by wild boars, its near-black vegetation gives rise to its name, derived from the Provençal word *mauro* (dark pine wood). Traditional industries (chestnut harvests, cork, pipe-making) are their lifeblood.

La Garde Freinet

Local traditions unfold in the village of La Garde Freinet (topped by 13th-century **ruins of Fort Freinet**) at the environment-driven **Conservatoire du Patrimoine du Freinet** (04 94 43 08 57; www.conservatoiredufreinet.org; Chapelle St-Jean, place de la Mairie, La Garde Freinet; 10am-12.30pm & 2.30-5.30pm Tue-Sat), which hosts exhibitions (flora, fauna, cork harvesting) and organises themed discovery walks (adult/child €9/4.50) and workshops (free to €98; eg art in nature, dry-stone walls, honey-making, forest photography etc). Monthly treks on horseback (adult/child €45/40) and donkey rambles (adult/child €12/10) criss-cross the massif.

Village des Tortues

About 20km north of Collobrières, this **tortoise village** (04 94 78 26 41; www.villagetortues.com; Gonfaron; adult/child €12/8; 9am-7pm Mar-Nov, to 6pm Dec-Feb) protects one of France's most endangered species, the Hermann tortoise (Testudo hermanni). Once common along the Mediterranean coast, it is today found only in the Massif des Maures and Corsica.

The **Station d'Observation et de Protection des Tortues des Maures** (SOPTOM; Maures Tortoise Observation and Protection Station) has a well-documented trail (captions in English) from the tortoise clinic, where wounded tortoises are treated and then released into the Maures, to the egg hatcheries and nurseries, where the young tortoises (a delicacy for preying magpies, rats, foxes and wild boars) spend the first three of their 60 to 100 years.

A great palaeontology trail has vicious-looking models of the tortoise's ancestors lurking among the bushes.

In summer the best time to see the tortoises is in the morning and late afternoon. Watch tortoises hatch from mid-May to the end of June; from November through early March they hibernate.

Collobrières & Around

Hidden in the forest, the leafy village of Collobrières is *the* place to taste chestnuts. Across the 11th-century bridge, the **tourist office** (04 94 48 08 00; www.collobrieres-tourisme.com; bd Charles Caminat; 10am-noon & 2-5pm Tue-Sun, closed Sun & Mon Sep-Jun) can help you join in the October chestnut harvest, celebrated with the **Fête de la Châtaigne**, or join a guided forest walk. They can also give hiking directions to the **Châtaignier de Madame**, the biggest chestnut tree in Provence, with a mighty 10.4m circumference; and the two biggest **menhirs** (each over 3m) in the Var region, now heritage-listed monuments, which were raised between 3000 and 2000 BC. Three shorter walking trails, including a 200m trail to a *châtaigneraie* (chestnut grove), are mapped on the noticeboard outside.

Sights & Activities

TOP CHOICE **Monastère de la Verne** MONASTERY
(☎04 94 43 45 51; http://la.verne.free.fr; near Collobrières; adult/child €6/3; ⊙11am-5pm Wed-Mon Feb-May & Sep-Dec, 11am-6pm Jun-Aug) Majestic, 12th- to 13th-century Monastère de la Verne perches unbelievably on the hip of a mountain deep in the forest, but with a view to the sea. The Carthusian monastery was founded in 1170, possibly on the site of a temple to the goddess Laverna, protector of the bandits who hid in the Maures. The Huguenots destroyed most of the original charterhouse in 1577. Since 1982 the solitary complex has been home to 28 nuns, of the Sisters of Bethlehem.

The monastery's restoration has been a labor of love. A 20-minute video details the work. Highlights include the austere Romanesque church, the prior's cell, complete with a small formal garden and workshop, the bakery and the olive mill. The shop is full of excellent artisanal food, soaps, art and crafts made by the nuns. Walking trails lead from the monastery into its forested surroundings.

From Collobrières, follow rte de Grimaud (D14) east for 6km, then turn right (south) on to the D214 and drive another 6km to the monastery; park at the lot and walk the final section, which is unpaved.

FREE **Musée de la Fabrique** MUSEUM
(⊙9.30am-12.30pm & 2-5pm) This small museum, opposite **Confiserie Azuréenne** (☎04 94 48 07 20; www.confiserieazureenne.com), explains the art of making *marrons glacés* (candied chestnuts), after which you can stock up on chestnut ice cream, *crème de marrons* (chestnut cream), chestnut liqueur, etc in its shop.

Sleeping & Eating

The tourist office lists area *gîtes* (cottages) and B&Bs online.

Hôtel Notre Dame HOTEL €€
(☎04 94 48 07 13; www.hotel-notre-dame.eu; 15 ave de la Libération; d from €98; ❄📶🏊) The town's most high-end option has rooms decorated around rich colour schemes.

Hôtel Les Maures HOTEL €
(☎04 94 48 07 10; www.hoteldesmaures.fr; 19 blvd Lazare Carnot; d €33; ❄📶) This no-frills central hotel is basic but clean.

TOP CHOICE **La Petite Fontaine** REGIONAL CUISINE €€
(☎04 94 48 00 12; place de la République; 3-course/5-course menus €24/31; ⊙lunch & dinner Tue-Sat & lunch Sun Apr-Sep, lunch Tue-Sat & dinner Fri & Sun Oct-Mar) Locals throng here, one of southern France's most charming, relaxed village inns, from miles around to feast on seasonal forest mushrooms and chestnuts at a tree-shaded table. The walls inside are exposed stone, and the fruit tarts for dessert…out of this world. Reservations essential. No credit cards.

Ferme de Peïgros REGIONAL CUISINE €€
(☎04 94 48 03 83; http://fermedepeigros.pagesperso-orange.fr; Col de Babaou; menus €22; ⊙lunch & dinner Jul & Aug) Treat taste buds to wild boar or farm-made chestnut ice cream and grand massif views at this goat farm 1.8km along a gravel track from the top of the Col de Babaou (8km from Collobrières). No credit cards.

CORNICHE DES MAURES

The coastal road, the Corniche des Maures (D559), unwinds beautifully, southwest from La Croix-Valmer to Le Lavandou along a shoreline trimmed with sandy beaches ideal for swimming, sunbathing and windsurfing. Tiny **Plage du Rayol** and **Plage de l'Escale** are particularly enchanting: they're backed by pine trees and have a

DON'T MISS

DOMAINE DU RAYOL

This stunning, lush Mediterranean **garden** (☎04 98 04 44 00; www.domainedurayol.org; av des Belges, Rayol-Canadel-sur-Mer; adult/child €8/6; ⊙9.30am-7.30pm Jul & Aug, to 6.30pm Apr-Jun, Sep & Oct, to 5.30pm Nov-Mar), with plants from all Mediterranean climates the world round, is wonderful for a stroll or a themed nature walk (adult/child €11/6). The dense flora cascade down the hillside from a villa to the sea, and while flowers are at their best in April and May, it's always worth a visit.

In summer, at the estate's gem of a beach, you can snorkle around underwater flora and fauna (adult/child €18/14) with an experienced guide; bookings are essential. Also reserve ahead for open-air musical concerts (€32) or in-depth workshops (€60).

The estate's Café des Jardiniers serves light organic lunches (mains €11) and refreshing hibiscus-peach infusions.

restaurant on the sand. The beautiful beach at **Cavalière** is also home to the hip restaurant **Chez Jo** (04 94 05 85 06; Plage du Layet, Cavalière; lunch May-Sep). Buzzing with barefooted, overly bronzed, sarong-clad beach lovers with a fondness for bathing in the nude and piercings in the most unexpected of places, this sizzling beach restaurant has cuisine straight from the sea.

You'll need a car to travel to Bormes-les-Mimosas and along the Route des Crêtes, but the coastal D559 is on the itinerary of the St-Tropez to Toulon VarLib bus (p121), which stops in most towns, including Le Lavandou (€2).

Bormes-les-Mimosas

POP 6399 / ELEV 180M

This 12th-century village is spectacularly flowered with mimosas in winter, deep-fuchsia bougainvilleas in summer. Its **tourist office** (04 94 01 38 38; www.bormeslesmimosas.com; 1 place Gambetta; 9am-12.30pm & 3-6.30pm daily Apr-Sep, Mon-Sat Oct-Mar) takes bookings for botanical walks (€9) and hikes (€7) with a forest warden in the nearby **Forêt du Dom**.

Old cobbled streets are lined with artists' galleries and boutiques selling traditional Provençal products. At the olive-themed shop **Maison d'Olive** (04 94 46 60 45; www.maison-de-lolive.fr; 5 rue Carnot), buy flavoured olive oils (truffle, lemon, basil), vinegars and aperitifs (pastis and mimosa, fig or melon liqueur) *en VRAC*, meaning take your own bottle to fill or grab one at the shop.

Sleeping & Eating

TOP CHOICE **Hôtel Bellevue** BOUTIQUE HOTEL €€
(04 94 71 15 15; www.bellevuebormes.com; place Gambetta; d €48-74, q €114;) Utterly charming, this sweet hotel has sensational views, spotless, pretty rooms and friendly service. Two rooms are accessible by wheelchair.

Hostellerie du Cigalou HOTEL €€
(04 94 41 51 27; www.hostellerieducigalou.com; place Gambetta; d €140-173;) A plush hotel with fantastic views and dreamy pool.

La Grande Maison des Campaux B&B €€
(04 94 49 55 40; www.lagrandemaisondescampaux.com; 6987 rte du Dom (N98); d incl breakfast €140-160, q €230; Mar-Nov;) This dreamy 17th-century country house languishes in vineyards on the vast 128-hectare Domaine des Campaux. Five rooms evoke a bygone era. Beams are sturdy and age-old, floors are original stone or tile, and linens are crisp white. Find it signposted off the N98 some 6km west of La Môle.

TOP CHOICE **L'Atelier de Cuisine Gourmande** PROVENÇAL €€
(04 94 71 27 80; 4 place Gambetta; menus €28; by reservation) Mireille Gedda offers the most authentic of local cuisine, with flavours from the *terroir*. Her husband serves. Call ahead to see when she's cooking or to take a class (September to June).

Le Lavandou

Once a fishing village, Le Lavandou is a family beach-resort with a small but intact old town and 12km of golden sand. The faux castle on the seafront is the **tourist office** (04 94 00 40 50; www.lelavandou.com; quai Gabriel Péri; 9am-noon & 2.30-6.30pm Mon-Sat). Opposite, boats sail to the Îles des Hyères.

ÎLES D'HYÈRES & ÎLES DU FUN

Legend says gods turned a bunch of swimming princesses into the Îles d'Hyères – and they are magical. Their mica-rich rock, which glitters and gleams in the sunlight, gives them their other name, the Îles d'Or (Islands of Gold).

Porquerolles, at 7km long and 3km wide, is the largest; Île de Port-Cros, in the middle, is a national park; and its eastern sister, Île du Levant, is both an army camp and a nudist colony. Wild camping and cars are forbidden throughout the archipelago.

Dubbed the Îles du Fun, Bendor and Embiez, west of the Îles d'Hyères off Toulon's shores, are more sub-Disney than the stuff of myth.

Islanders refer to the rest of France as the 'continent'.

Getting There & Away

ÎLES DE PORQUEROLLES & DE PORT-CROS Mainland ports are La Tour Fondue, Hyères and Le Lavandou. June to September boats also go to/from Toulon, St-Tropez, Port Miramar, La Croix-Valmer and Cavalaire-sur-Mer.

ÎLE DU LEVANT Ten minutes by boat from Port-Cros. Frequent boats sail year-round from Le Lavandou and Hyères, and in July and

WORTH A TRIP

ROUTES DES CRÊTES

For breathtaking views of the islands, follow Route des Crêtes as it winds its way through maquis-covered hills some 400m above the sea. From Bormes-les-Mimosas, follow the D41 uphill (direction Collobrières) past the Chapelle St-François and, 1.5km north of the village centre, turn immediately right after the sign for Col de Caguo-Ven (237m).

Relais du Vieux Sauvaire (04 94 05 84 22; rte des Crêtes; mains €18-30; lunch & dinner Jun-Sep;) is the hidden gem of these hills. With 180-degree views you could only dream of, this restaurant and pool (most people come here for lunch and then stay all afternoon) is one of a kind. The food is as sunny as the views: pizzas, melon and Parma ham, or whole sea bass in salt crust.

Past the restaurant, Route des Crêtes joins the final leg of the panoramic Col du Canadel road. On the *col* (mountain pass), turn left to plunge into the heart of forested Massif des Maures, or right to the sea and coastal Corniche des Maures (D559).

August from Port Miramar, La Croix-Valmer and Cavalaire-sur-Mer.

ÎLE DE BENDOR Boats sail year-round from Bandol (€8 return); contact 04 94 10 75 93.

ÎLES DES EMBIEZ Boats (www.les-embiez.com; €13.50, 10min) sail year-round from Le Brusc, 5km south of Sanary-sur-Mer. June to September four daily boats (return €10) sail to/from Bandol and Sanary-sur-Mer.

FERRIES Transport Littoral Varois (TLV; 04 94 58 33 76; www.tlv-tvm.com) Year-round boats link **La Tour Fondue** with Île de Porquerolles (return €18, 50 minutes), and **Port d'Hyères** with Île de Port-Cros (return €26, one hour) and Île du Levant (return €26, 90 minutes); going to two islands costs €28. From June to September, weekly boats sail to/from Toulon, St-Tropez, Le Lavandou and Port Miramar near La Londe.

Vedettes Îles d'Or et Le Corsaire (04 94 71 01 02; www.vedettesilesdor.fr; 15 quai Gabriel Péri) From **Le Lavandou**, **Cavalaire-sur-mer** and **La Croix Valmer**, seasonal boats run to/from Île du Levant (return €27, 35 minutes), Île de Port-Cros (€27, 35 minutes) and Île de Porquerolles (€34, 50 minutes). La Croisière Bleue tour (ticket for all three islands €50) and twice-weekly boats to St-Tropez (€50) require reservations.

Île de Porquerolles

POP 250

Despite the huge influx of day trippers (up to 6000 a day in July and August), beautiful Porquerolles is wholly unspoilt: two-thirds of its sandy white beaches, pine woods, maquis and eucalyptus are protected by the Parc National de Port-Cros, and a wide variety of indigenous and tropical flora thrive, including the requien larkspur, which grows nowhere else in the world. April and May are the best months to spot some of the 114 bird species. Pottering along the island's rough unpaved trails on foot or by bicycle, breaking with a picnic lunch on the beach and a dip in crystal-clear turquoise water, is heavenly.

Avoid July and August, when the risk of fire closes the interior of the island and makes some trails inaccessible. In general, smoking is forbidden outside the village.

Sights & Activities

Place d'Armes VILLAGE SQUARE
A tree-shaded *pétanque* pitch dominates central place d'Armes. Music concerts fill **Église Ste-Anne** on its southern side in summer. Day in, day out, this hub of Porquerollais life buzzes with outdoor cafes and ice cream stands and cyclists pedalling to and fro. Once the last of the day-tripper boats has sailed, a Zen lull falls across the square.

Fort Ste-Agathe FORT
(04 94 00 65 41; adult/child €4/2; 10am-noon & 2-6pm May-Sep) This 16th-century fortification contains historical and natural-history exhibits. The tower has lovely island views. Much of the building dates from between 1812 and 1814, when Napoléon had it rebuilt after the British destroyed it in 1793. From place d'Armes, walk uphill along chemin Ste-Agathe (between Villa Ste-Anne and Auberge des Glycines). Admission includes entry to the nearby windmill, **Moulin du Bonheur**.

FREE **Jardin Emanuel Lopez & Conservatoire Botanique National Méditerranéen** GARDEN
(04 94 58 07 24; chemin du Phare; 9.30am-12.30pm & 2-6pm Feb-Oct) This wonderful ornamental garden is planted with magnificent palm varieties, cypress, vanilla and

grenadier trees, cactus and bamboo, sweetly scented jasmine, and every herb known to grow under the Provençal sun. It's also home to the Parc National de Port-Cros Maison du Parc (p133).

Beaches BEACH

Porquerolles' northern coast is laced with beautiful sandy beaches, including **Plage de la Courtade**, a mere 800m walk east from the port (follow the track uphill behind the tourist office). Porquerolles' largest and most beautiful beach, **Plage de Notre Dame**, is 2.5km further east along the same track.

West of the village, **Plage d'Argent**, a good 2km along a potholed track past vineyards, is popular with families because of its summer beachside cafe-restaurant, lifeguards and toilets.

More secluded is **Plage du Langoustier**, a former lobster farm 4.5km from the village on the northern shores of the Presqu'île du Langoustier.

Cliffs line the island's more dangerous southern coast, where swimming and diving is restricted to **Calanque du Brégançonnet** to the east and **Calanque de l'Oustaou de Diou** to the west.

Get maps at the tourist office.

Boats WATERSPORTS

Speedboat-rental outlet Locamarine 75 (p133), at the port, also has kayaks (double kayak half-/full-day rentals €35/45). **Base Nautique** (☎06 60 52 37 06; www.ileo-porquerolles.fr; 1-/3-/6hr kayak rentals €17/35/45) on Plage de la Courtade has kayaks, windsurfers, catamarans and scuba diving.

Cycling CYCLING

The map sold at the tourist office has four cycling itineraries, 6.5km to 13.8km long. More detail is included in the *Guide de Randonnées dans l'Île de Porquerolles* (€6), available at the Maison du Parc (p133).

TRUE LOVE

Three toasters and a towel set just weren't enough. In 1911, newly married Mrs Fournier received the perfect wedding present from hubby François: the island of Porquerolles! Their descendants still own a big piece of the island, including Le Mas du Langoustier.

Vineyards WINE TASTING

Porquerolles' vineyards cover a square kilometre of the western part of the island. The three wine producers offer tastings of their predominantly rosé wines. Framed by a fabulous formation of parasol pines, **Domaine Perzinsky** (☎04 94 58 34 32; ⏲10am-12.30pm & 3.30-7.30pm) is an easy stop en route to Plage d'Argent and requires no reservation. The others are **Domaine de la Courtade** (☎04 94 58 31 44; www.lacourtade.com; ⏲by appt) and **Domaine de l'Île** (☎04 98 04 62 30; www.domainedelile.com; ⏲by appt).

Sleeping & Eating

Accommodation is pricey, limited and gets booked months in advance. The tourist office has details on self-catering apartments/villas and three B&Bs. Prices plummet in the low season. Most hotels also have restaurants.

An admirable picnic of juicy cherries, fresh goat's-milk cheese, etc can be bought from the stands on place d'Armes and the two small grocery stores (they close for two hours just after noon).

TOP CHOICE **L'Oustaou** PENSION €€

(☎04 94 58 30 13; www.oustaou.com; place d'Armes; d from €140, mains €19-23; ⏲Apr-Oct; ❄📶) Superclean rooms with modern decor either face the village square or have marvelous port views. It's lovely for couples, with a hint of romance. Downstairs tuck into modern French standards or burgers.

Auberge des Glycines PENSION €€

(☎04 94 58 30 36; www.auberge-glycines.com; place d'Armes; d per person incl half-board from €139, 3-course menus €29; ❄📶👪) This inn overlooking the village square ranks as highly in the dining stakes as it does in sleeping. Decor is traditional (note the cicada collection hanging on the wall in reception) and dining is *Porquerollaise* – in other words, shoals of fish. Good deals for kids.

Le Mas du Langoustier LUXURY HOTEL €€€

(☎04 94 58 30 09; www.langoustier.com; d per person incl half-board from €215; ⏲May-Oct; ❄📶🏊👪) The 'to die for' choice: guests have been known to drop in by helicopter at this exceptional hotel with a glamorous history (dating to 1931), vineyards, and stunning views from its seaside perch. Everything, from its rooms to two restaurants (one for guests only; four-course menus from €62), is impeccable. Some apartments for families.

ALL AFLOAT

To sleep aboard a sailboat contact **Bateaudhote.fr** (☎06 82 15 93 76; www.bateaudhote.fr; per week €1900) or **Via Skipper** (☎06 03 17 23 67; www.viaskipper.com; per week €1200).

Les Mèdes HOTEL €€
(☎04 94 12 41 24; www.hotel-les-medes.fr; rue de la Douane; d from €94, 4-person apt from €185;) This hotel-residence mixes traditional hotel rooms with self-catering apartments. The icing on the cake: a terraced garden with fountain pool and sun loungers.

Villa Ste-Anne INN €€
(☎04 94 04 63 00; www.sainteanne.com; place d'Armes; d per person incl half-board from €170; Apr-Oct;) The main draw of this typical Porquerollais inn on the square is its terracotta tiled restaurant terrace that overlooks the *pétanque* pitch. Borrow a set of *boules* should you fancy a spin. Indulge in an aperitif and *petit friture* (tiny deep-fried fish dipped in spicy rouille).

Information

Tourist Office (☎04 94 58 33 76; www.porquerolles.com; 9am-6.30pm) Sells maps (€3) marked with cycling and walking paths, as well as plastic guides for snorkellers to identify underwater flora (€20).

Parc National de Port-Cros Maison du Parc (☎04 94 58 07 24; www.portcrosparcnational.fr; Jardin Emanuel Lopez; 9.30am-12.30pm & 2-6pm Feb-Oct) National park office with maps, information and excellent twice-monthly guided walks known as **Les Rencontres du Parc** (free).

Getting Around

BICYCLE Rent at the port or place d'Armes; try **Le Cycle Porquerollais** (☎04 94 58 30 32; www.cycle-porquerollais.com; 1 rue de la Ferme; half-/full day €14/11; year-round).

BOAT TAXI **Locamarine 75** (☎06 09 52 31 19, 04 94 58 35 84; www.locamarine75.com); for **luggage** (☎06 81 67 77 12).

Île de Port-Cros

France's smallest national park, Parc National de Port-Cros, was created in 1963 to protect the 7-sq-km island of Port-Cros and a 13-sq-km zone of water around it.

Until the end of the 19th century, the islanders' vineyards and olive groves ensured their self-sufficiency. Today, high-season tourism is their sustenance. Bring picnic supplies and drinking water; the few port bistros open mid-March to mid-November but there's nothing elsewhere but beauty.

Sights & Activities

Walkers (and birdwatchers) must remain on 30km of marked trails. Fishing, fires, camping, dogs, motorised vehicles and bicycles are not allowed, nor is smoking outside the village.

FREE **Fort de l'Estissac** FORT
(10.30am-12.30pm & 1.30-5.30pm May-Sep) Climb the tower of the imposing 16th-century fort which hosts summer exhibitions.

Walks WALKING
The 15th-century **Fort du Moulin** is the starting point for the **Sentier des Plantes** (Botanical Trail; 4km, 1½ to two hours), a lovely aromatic trail that wends its way past wild lavender and rosemary to **Plage de la Palud** (30 minutes), a beautiful beach on the island's northern shore. A 35-minute **Sentier Sous-Marin** (Underwater Trail; ☎04 94 01 40 70; admission free; mid-Jun–mid-Sep) here allows snorkellers to peer up close at marine life, including 500 algae species and 180 types of fish. Rent equipment from portside diving school **Sun Plongée** (☎04 94 05 90 10; www.sun-plongee.com; mid-Mar–mid-Nov).

From Plage de la Palud, the **Circuit de Port-Man** (four hours) follows the coastline to secluded **Plage de Port-Man** on the island's far northeastern tip before looping back inland.

The demanding **Sentier des Crêtes** (7.5km; three hours) explores the southwest corner of the island and climaxes atop **Mont Vinaigre** (194m).

Sleeping & Eating

Accommodation requires booking months in advance.

Hostellerie Provençale PENSION €€
(☎04 94 05 90 43; www.hostellerie-provencale.com; d per person incl half-board from €145; Apr- Nov;) Run by the island's oldest and largest family since 1921, this bustling portside *hostellerie* (inn) sports five bright rooms facing the water; the best have a balcony. The eye-catching cocktail bar and

restaurant sits on the waterfront with canary-yellow sun umbrellas.

Le Manoir d'Hélène PENSION **€€**
(☎04 94 05 90 52; lemanoir.portcros@wanadoo.fr; d per person incl half-board from €200; ⏲May-Sep; ❄≋) This enchanting 23-room manor with white turreted facade 300m from Port-Cros' port is the exclusive option. Find it nestled in a sweet-smelling eucalyptus grove with outdoor pool, upmarket restaurant and the elegant air of bygone island life.

Information

At the port, the **Maison du Parc** (☎04 94 01 40 70; www.portcrosparcnational.fr) has walking, diving and snorkelling information. It also sells an island map marked with the island's four main trails and guides (in French) to underwater fauna and flora. Its opening hours coincide with boat arrivals.

Île du Levant

Île du Levant, an 8km strip of an island, has a split personality. Ninety percent of it is a closed military camp, and the remaining pocket of **Héliopolis** (on the island's south-western tip) is a nudist colony.

The post office, cafes and hotels are clustered around the central square, place du Village, 1km uphill from the port along rte de l'Ayguade. From place du Village a nature trail leads east into the **Domaine des Arbousiers**, a nature reservation in the eastern part of the colony sheltering rare island plants. The tourist office has information on guided tours.

Baring all is not obligatory except on sandy **Plage Les Grottes**, the main nudist beach east of Port de l'Ayguade. From the port, walk in the direction of **Plage de Sable** Levant along **Sentier Georges Rousseau**, a rocky coastal path. Signs reading 'Nudisme Intégral Obligatoire' mark the moment you have to strip.

Boats dock at **Port de l'Ayguade** near the **tourist information hut** (☎04 94 05 93 52; www.iledulevant.com.fr; ⏲Easter-mid-Sep).

WORTH A TRIP

CAP DE CARQUEIRANNE

Immediately west of Hyères, Cap de Carqueiranne is a partly forested stretch of headland, criss-crossed by tiny lanes. The **coastal path** that edges its way from the town of Carqueiranne is a scenic means of exploring the pretty cape. Reserve ahead at **L'Oursinado** (☎04 94 21 77 06; www.oursinado.com; chemin du Pas des Gardéens; menus €58; ⏲lunch & dinner Thu-Mon, lunch Tue), hidden on a cliff above the tiny port of Les Oursinières. Sit on its tree-framed terrace, gaze down at pounding waves and feast on Toulonnais *bouillabaisse* (order 48 hours in advance), the local version of the legendary Marseille fish stew.

TOULON & AROUND

Relatively unspoilt coastline turns increasingly urban as you head west to Toulon. A final pocket of blue and green surrounds **La Londe** (population 8840), midway between Le Lavandou and Hyères. Explore its olive groves, vineyards and flower gardens on guided walks organised by the **tourist office** (☎04 94 01 53 10; www.ot-lalondelesmaures.fr; ⏲9am-6pm Mon-Sat, 9am-1pm Sun) or hire a bike and wine-taste by pedal power.

Hyères & Presqu'île de Giens

POP 56,020

With its overdose of palm trees, its casino, and medieval Vieille Ville (Old Town) perched on a hillside north of its new town, Hyères retains some of the charm that made it the Côte d'Azur's first resort. The city's real asset, however, is the Presqu'île de Giens (Giens Peninsula).

Sights & Activities

Presqu'île de Giens OUTDOORS
This beach-fringed peninsula briefly became an island in 1811 after huge storms. It is a launch pad for day trips to the Îles d'Hyères and a walker's and spotter's paradise: the protected wetland area harbours amazing birdlife, including pink flamingos, herons, egrets, teals and cormorants. A beautiful **Sentier du Littoral** (Coastal Path) loops the peninsula.

La Capte OUTDOORS
Pink flamingos add a splash of colour to the otherwise barren landscape of La Capte, two narrow sand bars supporting the **Salins des Presquiers** salt pans and a lake 4km south

of Hyères centre. A 1½-hour cycling itinerary (12.5km) loops the salt pans, and the tourist office runs guided bird discovery **nature walks** (adult/child €5/free). Particularly spectacular is the western sand bar road dubbed the **rte du Sel** (Salt Rd), accessible only in summer.

Vieille Ville HISTORIC QUARTER

On the west side of **place Georges Clemenceau**, 13th-century **Porte Massillon** (look for the clock) is the entrance to Hyères' Old Town. West along cobbled rue Massillon is beautiful arcaded **rue des Porches**, with its polished flagstones and collection of boutiques.

The rambling hillside grove of **Parc St-Bernard** abuts **Villa Noailles** (☎04 98 08 01 93; www.villanoailles-hyeres.com; ⊙hrs vary) below, a cubist maze of concrete and glass designed by Robert Mallet-Stevens in 1923 as a winter residence for devoted lover of modern art Vicomte Charles de Noailles.

Back downhill, **Parc Castel Ste-Claire**, a 17th-century convent converted into a private residence, was home to American writer Edith Wharton from 1927. Today it houses the headquarters of the **Parc National de Port-Cros** (☎04 94 12 82 30; www.portcrosparcnational.fr; 50 rue Ste-Claire).

Sleeping

Aged hotels in the Old Town are beaten by great-value ones on Presqu'île de Giens.

Hôtel Bor BOUTIQUE HOTEL €€

(☎04 94 58 02 73; www.hotel-bor.com; 3 allée Émile Gérard, Hyères Beach; d from €130; ⊙Mar-Oct; ❄@📶🏊) This sleek boutique hotel on the sand screams design. Palm trees and potted plants speckle its wood-decking terrace, and sun loungers beg to be used on its pebble beach. Rooms are in muted natural colours.

Hôtel Le Méditerranée HOTEL €

(☎04 94 00 52 70; www.hotel-lemediterranee.com; 8 av de la Méditerranée, Hyères Beach Road; s/d/tr/q from €72/75/90/103; ⊙mid-Jan–mid-Dec; ❄📶👪) This friendly hotel abutting Hyères' horse-racing track is a one-minute walk to the Plage d'Hyères. Bathrooms are modern, rooms are painted in typical Provençal colours and the best has a balcony.

Eating

La Baleine SEAFOOD €€

(☎04 94 57 59 21; 19 quai du Docteur Robin, Port d'Hyères; 3-course menus with wine €26; ⊙lunch & dinner Tue-Sun) The pick of the port-front eateries has a stylish wood terrace and interior tables floating inside a wooden whale-like frame; its menu is fish-driven, modern and creative.

Restaurant Joy FUSION €€

(☎04 94 20 84 98; www.restaurant-joy.com; 24 rue de Limans, Hyères; menus from €35; ⊙lunch & dinner Mon-Sat) This contemporary restaurant is a culinary joy. Fresh, seasonal menu includes ravioli and fantastic cinnamon-spiced *foie gras*.

Information

Hyères Tourist Office (☎04 94 01 84 50; www.hyeres-tourisme.com; 3 av Ambroise Thomas, Hyères; ⊙9am-6pm Mon-Fri, 10am-4pm Sat) Fabulous guided walks.

Getting There & Around

TO/FROM THE AIRPORT Bus 102 (€1.40) links Toulon-Hyères airport (p136), 3km south of Hyères, with the Toulon bus station (40 minutes) via Hyères centre (10 minutes), also served by Bus 63.

BOAT Transport Littoral Varois (☎tel, info 04 94 58 21 81; www.tlv-tvm.com) runs services to Îles d'Hyères.

BUS From the **bus station** (place du Maréchal Joffre), bus 67 (www.reseaumistral.com) goes to the train station (five minutes), Port d'Hyères (€1.40, 15 minutes) and La Tour Fondue (€1.40, 35 minutes).

TAXI Taxis Radio Hyerois (☎04 94 00 60 00; www.taxis-hyeres.com)

TRAIN From the **train station** (place de l'Europe), local trains chug to/from Toulon (€8, 20 minutes). The Marseille–Hyères train (€15, one hour, four daily) stops in Cassis, La Ciotat, Bandol, Ollioules-Sanary and Toulon.

Toulon

POP 167,813

Built around a *rade* (a sheltered bay lined with quays), France's second-largest naval port provokes the reaction a tramp might get in St-Tropez: its seedy rough-cut demeanour just doesn't fit in with the glittering Côte d'Azur. It is not quite as terrible as it once was, though most visitors just pass through, since it is a central transport hub.

Sights

Bateliers de la Côte d'Azur BOAT TRIPS

(☎04 94 05 21 14; www.bateliersdelacotedazur.com; quai Cronstadt) From the port you can take a spin around the *rade*, with a commentary (in French only) on the local events of WWII. In summer, go to the Îles d'Hyères.

Mont Faron MOUNTAIN, ZOO
North of the city, from Mont Faron (584m) you can see Toulon's red-roofed houses and epic port. The tourist office has information on walks. Near the summit, **Mémorial du Débarquement de Provence** (☎04 94 88 08 09; adult/child €4/1; ⏰10am-noon & 2-4.30pm Tue-Sun) commemorates the Allied landings, which took place along the coast here in August 1944. Historical displays and a film form part of this museum.

Téléphérique du Mont Faron (cable car; www.telepherique-faron.com; return adult/child €6.80/4.80; ⏰10am-7pm) ascends the mountain. Kids love **Zoo du Faron** (☎04 94 88 07 89; adult/child €9/5.50; ⏰10am-6.30pm), a wildcat-breeding centre. Combination zoo/cable-car tickets cost €13 for adults, €9 for children.

Musée de la Marine MARITIME MUSEUM
(☎04 94 02 02 01; place Monsenergue; adult/child €5/free; ⏰10am-6pm Wed-Mon) A seafaring museum with models of old sailing ships and paintings illustrating Toulon's history.

Plages du Mourillon BEACH
Good beaches for soaking up some rays are 2km southeast at Mourillon. Take Bus 3 and get off at the Michelet stop.

Sleeping & Eating

Hôtel Little Palace HOTEL €
(☎04 94 92 26 62; www.hotel-littlepalace.com; 6-8 rue Berthelot; s/d €50/62; ❄@📶) The over-the-top Italian-inspired decor lacks authenticity, but Little Palace is well run. No lift.

Le Chantilly BRASSERIE €
(☎04 94 92 24 37; place Puget; mains €10-25; ⏰6.30am-11pm) Going strong since 1907, Le Chantilly will sort you out for food, whatever the time of day.

Information

Tourist Office (www.toulontourisme.com; 12 place Louis Blanc; ⏰9am-6pm Mon-Sat, 9am-1pm Sun)

Getting There & Away

AIR Toulon-Hyères Airport (www.toulon-hyeres.aeroport.fr).

BOAT Ferries to Corsica and Sardinia are run by **Corsica Ferries** (www.corsica-ferries.co.uk; Port de Commerce).

BUS VarLib (www.varlib.fr) buses (€2) operate from the **bus station** (☎04 94 24 60 00; bd de Tessé), next to the train station. Bus 103 to St-Tropez (eight daily) goes via Hyères (35 minutes) and Le Lavandou (one hour).

The tourist office sells a **one-day pass** (www.reseaumistral.com; €6) that includes unlimited travel on local buses (single fare €1.40) and commuter boats, and a return ticket for the Mont Faron Téléphérique.

TRAIN Frequent connections include Marseille (€12, 50 minutes), St-Raphaël (€14, 50 minutes), Cannes (€20, 1¼ hours), Monaco (€26, 2¼ hours) and Nice (€24, 1¾ hours).

TOWARDS MARSEILLE

Sanary-sur-Mer

Pretty-as-a-picture seaside Sanary-sur-Mer is a stroller's dream. Watch the fishers unload their catch on the quay, or admire the traditional fishing boats from one of the seafront cafes. Wednesday's colourful **market** draws crowds from miles around. Shops line interior streets. Novelist Aldous Huxley (1894–1963) called Sanary home in the early 1930s.

Activities

Regard du Vivant DOLPHIN CRUISE
(☎06 10 57 17 11; www.regard-du-vivant.fr; adult/child €75/55) Observe various dolphin species from aboard a boat with naturalist-photographers.

Croix du Sud V BOAT TOUR
(☎06 09 87 47 97; www.croixdusud5.com) Boat tours serve the *calanques* (adult/child from €25/14) and Île de Porquerolles (€36/21).

Sleeping & Eating

TOP CHOICE **Hôtel de la Tour** HOTEL €€
(☎04 94 74 10 10; www.sanary-hoteldelatour.com; Port; d incl breakfast €80-130) Some of the excellent, large rooms in this renovated Victorian-era hotel have awesome portside views. Supermodern bathrooms are spacious, in stone and tile, and the charming decor is clean and inviting. Book ahead.

L'Esplanade SEAFOOD €€
(☎04 94 74 08 56; www.restaurant-esplanade.fr; near Parking de l'Esplanade; 3-course menus from €36; ⏰lunch & dinner Tue-Sat) Dine in portside elegance on the catch of the day.

Le Bard'ô BEACH RESTAURANT €€
(☎04 94 88 42 56; www.le-bardo.com; Plage de Portissol; lunch/dinner menu €18/32; ⊙lunch & dinner daily) Just south of town, on Portissol beach, this seafront club is perfect for everything from leisurely coffees and meals to late-night DJs and live music.

Information

Tourist Office (☎04 94 74 01 04; www.sanarysurmer.com; 1 quai du Levant; ⊙9am-12.30pm & 2-5.30pm Mon-Sat)

Bandol & Around

The built-up town of Bandol, a favourite among French holiday-makers, lends its name to the area's excellent wines. The *appellation* comprises eight neighbouring communities including Le Castellet, Ollioules, Evenos and Sanary-sur-Mer.

Sights & Activities

TOP CHOICE **Maison des Vins** WINE TASTING
(Oenothèque des Vins du Bandol; ☎04 94 29 45 03; www.maisondesvins-bandol.com; place Lucien Artaud, Bandol; ⊙10am-1pm & 3-6.30pm Mon-Sat, 10am-1pm Sun) Bandol's 49 vineyards carefully manage their prized production of red, rosé and white. Pascal Perier, the manager at the Maison des Vins, is a living Bandol encyclopaedia. He provides tastings, keeps a well-supplied shop and can direct you to surrounding vineyards (most require an appointment).

Sentier du Littoral WALKING
This yellow-marked coastal trail runs 12km (allow 3½ to four hours) from Bandol's port to La Madrague in St-Cyr-Les-Lecques, with the beautiful **Calanque de Port d'Alon** roughly halfway.

Sleeping & Eating

TOP CHOICE **Les Quatre Saisons** B&B €€
(☎04 94 25 24 90; www.lesquatresaisons.org; 370 montée des Oliviers, rte du Brûlat (D26), Le Castellet; d €90-130; ❄≋) A few hairpin bends downhill from the medieval hilltop village of Le Castellet, Patrice and Didier have decorated five exquisite rooms in the purest Provençal style. All open on to a central swimming pool. Patrice's *table d'hôte* (€40) is worth every cent.

Golf Hôtel HOTEL €
(☎04 94 29 45 83; www.golfhotel.fr; 10 promenade de la Corniche; d/q from €69/116; ⊙Jan-Nov; ❄) A prime address for beachside sleeping and dining: its restaurant, **La Chipote** (04 94 29 41 62; lunch/dinner menus €19/26; ⊙lunch daily, dinner Mon-Sat) with terrace on the sand, cooks up fresh fish and ace desserts.

Key Largo HOTEL €€
(☎04 94 29 46 93; www.hotel-key-largo.com; 19 corniche Bonaparte; d incl breakfast from €81; ❄) On the point between the port and Renécros beach; some of the basic rooms have sea views.

TOP CHOICE **La Table du Vigneron** RESTAURANT €€
(☎04 94 88 36 19; 724 chemin de la Tourelle, Ollioules; lunch/dinner 3-course menus €25/40; ⊙lunch & dinner Tue-Sat) In Ollioules, at **Domaine de Terrebrune** (☎04 94 74 01 30; www.terrebrune.fr; ⊙9am-12.30pm & 2-6pm Mon-Sat), you can taste their wines and then dine on delicious seasonal country fare at La Table du Vigneron, the estate's traditional *auberge* with alfresco tables overlooking vineyards. Wine by the glass is expensive, but they throw in the champagne with the dessert course. Their new contemporary restaurant in Ollioules village is **L'Atelier du Vigneron** (☎04 94 62 42 34; 348 ave de la Résistance, Ollioules).

L'Assiette des Saveurs FUSION €
(☎04 94 29 80 08; 1 rue Louis Marçon; mains €10) One street back from the busy marina, with its pretty streetside terrace, L'Assiette prepares classic recipes with a cheeky fusion twist.

KV&B MODERN FRENCH €€
(☎04 94 74 25 77; 5 rue de la Paroisse; lunch/dinner 3-course menus €19/29; ⊙lunch & dinner Tue-Sat) The address to enjoy local wine over tapas in a contemporary setting.

Lavender Trail

Pilgrims come from all over to follow the Routes de la Lavande (www.routes-lavande.com), tracking Provence's aromatic purple bloom. In flower from June to August, it usually hits peak splendour in late July. Cruise the fields, visit mountainside distilleries or scoop up all things lavender at abundant local markets.

Abbaye Notre-Dame de Sénanque

1 Follow the winding D177 north of Gordes to this idyllic 12th-century Cistercian abbey (p225), tucked between hills and surrounded by brilliant fields of lavender. Resident monks tend the crops and stock their shop with monk-made goodies.

Château du Bois

2 Provence is dotted with distilleries, but if you make it to tiny Lagarde d'Apt (p229) you're in for a treat: 80 hectares of Lavande des Alpes de Haute Provence, 'true lavender' *(Lavandula angustifolia)*.

Sault

3 The slopes of Mont Ventoux (p209), north of Lagarde d'Apt, make for prime high-altitude lavender. Aim to visit during the Fête de la Lavande (www.saultenprovence.com), usually on 15 August.

Forcalquier

4 Folks come from throughout the region for the booming Monday-morning market in Forcalquier (p241). An embarrassment of riches, the market has vendors selling lavender everything, plus mountain honey, creamy cheeses and handmade sausages.

Plateau de Valensole

5 For sheer heady expansiveness, you can't beat the Plateau de Valensole's carpets of lavender, stretching, dreamlike, as far as the eye can see. Cruise across it on the D6 or D8 east of Manosque, and the A51.

1

DAVID TOMLINSON/GETTY IMAGES ©

2

JEAN-BERNARD CARILLET/GETTY IMAGES ©

Clockwise from top left

Rows of lavender, Sault; Bunches of lavender for sale at a local market; A carpet of purple blooms, Plateau de Valensole

3

BARBARA VAN ZANTEN/GETTY IMAGES ©

Marseille to Aix-en-Provence

Includes »

Best Places to Eat

- » Restaurant Pierre Reboul (p168)
- » La Cantinetta (p157)
- » La Table de Ventabren (p171)
- » Le Café des Épices (p156)
- » Le Petit Verdot (p169)
- » L'Epuisette (p157)

Best Places to Stay

- » Hôtel La Résidence du Vieux Port (p155)
- » L'Épicerie (p167)
- » Le Ryad (p155)
- » Hôtel Vertigo (p155)
- » Casa Honoré (p155)

Why Go?

Radiating out from the Vieux Port, Marseille's irresistible magnetism draws you in to its vibrant, polyglot heart. The city has undergone an extensive facelift for its reign as European Capital of Culture 2013, and now boasts world-class museums, galleries and performing arts. Allow yourself at least 48 hours to take in Marseille's compelling sights, and the dramatic Les Calanques – rocky inlets gashed by the seas of the ice age resulting in the spectacular coastline that snakes southeast to Cassis. Heading north from Marseille, the landscape softens to the green and purple hues of Pays d'Aix (Aix Country) that Cézanne loved so much, with charming, bourgeois Aix-en-Provence at its centre.

Driving Distances (km)

	Aix-en-Provence	Cassis	Marignane (Airport)	Marseille
Cassis	49			
Marignane (Airport)	34	56		
Marseille	34	23	26	
Salon de Provence	34	72	34	30

Getting Around

Unlike most of Provence, which is best seen with your own wheels, you will be grateful in Marseille and Aix-en-Provence *not* to have a car. Driving is difficult, parking expensive. Public transport is super in both cities. To really explore Les Calanques and to drive the jaw-dropping Route des Crêtes near Cassis, though, a car is handy.

THREE PERFECT DAYS

Day 1: Sensory Marseille

Engage in Marseille's frenzy of sights, sounds, smells and flavours: follow the sound of clinking masts to the Vieux Port fish market. Grab a coffee at La Caravelle (p159) and sail to Château d'If (p151). Explore Musée des Civilisations de l'Europe et de la Méditerranée (p145) and get lost in Le Panier (p145). Then take a seaside stroll to Vallon des Auffes for *bouillabaisse* (p157).

Day 2: Gorge on Green

Hike into Les Calanques (p170), booking a table in advance at one of the seaside restaurants. Post-lunch, take a scenic drive around Cassis (p163). Wine taste in the afternoon and sup on sea urchins and crisp white wine at Cassis port.

Day 3: Cézanne Chic

Stroll Aix-en-Provence (p164): from the windy streets of Vieil Aix to its elegant *hôtels particuliers* (private mansions) and the Musée Granet (p165). Follow in the footsteps of Cézanne (p165), then explore Montagne Ste-Victoire (p171). End with a starlit dinner in best-kept secret Ventabren (p171).

Advance Planning

» **Accommodation** The best rooms get snapped up fast – book ahead. Aix-en-Provence fills fast during its fiesta of festivals and at weekends year-round. Its tourist office runs a booking office and, November to March, books hotels offering two nights for the price of one.

» **Sormiou & Morgiou Calanques** To revel in the natural beauty of Marseille's best-known *calanques* at sunset, minus a stiff walk in the searing heat, reserve a table at a Sormiou or Morgiou restaurant, which grants you the right to drive right down to the water's edge.

DON'T MISS

The explosion of galleries (p145) and performing arts events at the Marseille-Provence 2013 European Capital of Culture (www.mp2013.fr) extends from Marseille to Aix-en-Provence and Arles, and promises rich cultural life for years to come.

Best Escapes

» Les Calanques (p161, p164)

» Vauvenargues & Montagne Ste-Victoire (p171)

» Massif de la Ste-Baume (p162)

» Domaine de la Brillane (p171)

Best Tours & Courses

» Aix-en-Provence Walking Tours (p167)

» Calissons du Roy René (p168)

» Sea Kayaking the Calanques (p161)

Resources

» **Marseille City Website** (www.marseille.fr)

» **Marseille Tourisme** (www.marseille-tourisme.com) Tourist office online.

» **Visit Provence** (www.visitprovence.com) Info on Bouches du Rhône département; great itineraries.

» **EuroMéditerranée** (www.euromediterranee.fr) Largest urban renewal project in Europe: Marseille.

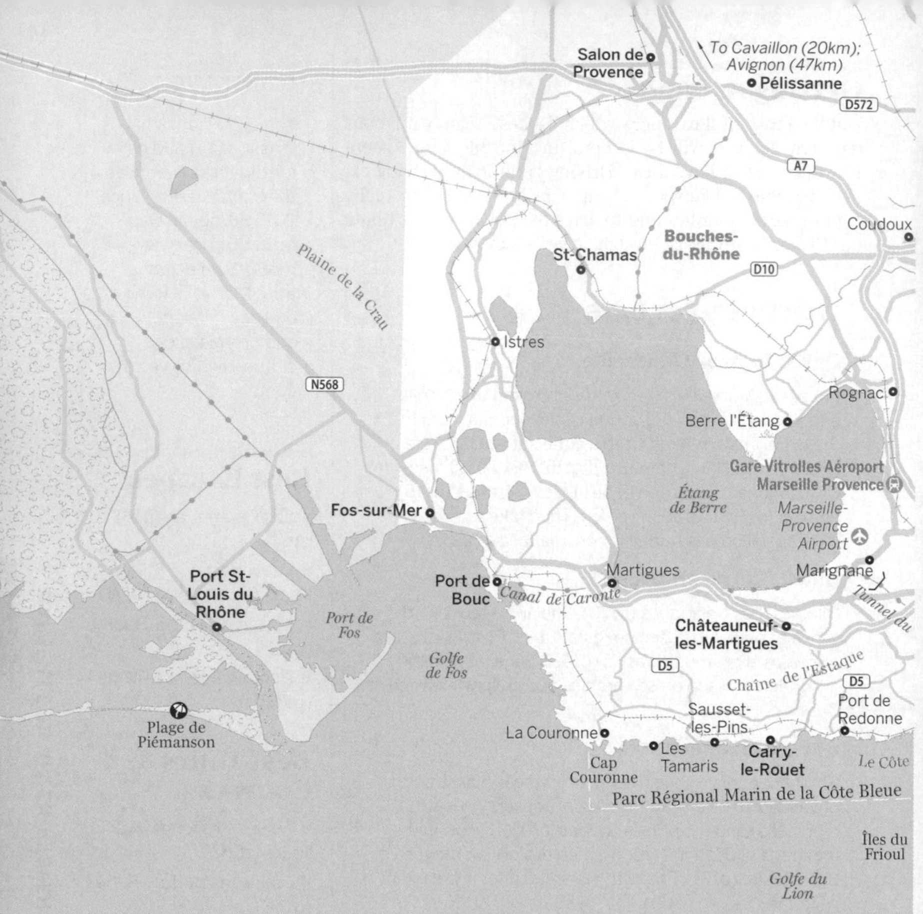

Marseille to Aix-en-Provence Highlights

1. **Restaurant hop** (p156) around Marseille's newest bistros.
2. Peruse the explosion of new **galleries** and **museums** (p145) in Marsellie.
3. Dip into the rocky coves of **Calanque de Sormiou** (p162) and **Calanque de Morgiou** (p162) for gorgeous walks and lunch with sea views.
4. Drive the high-drama **Road of Crests** (p163) before wine tasting at **Cassis** (p163).

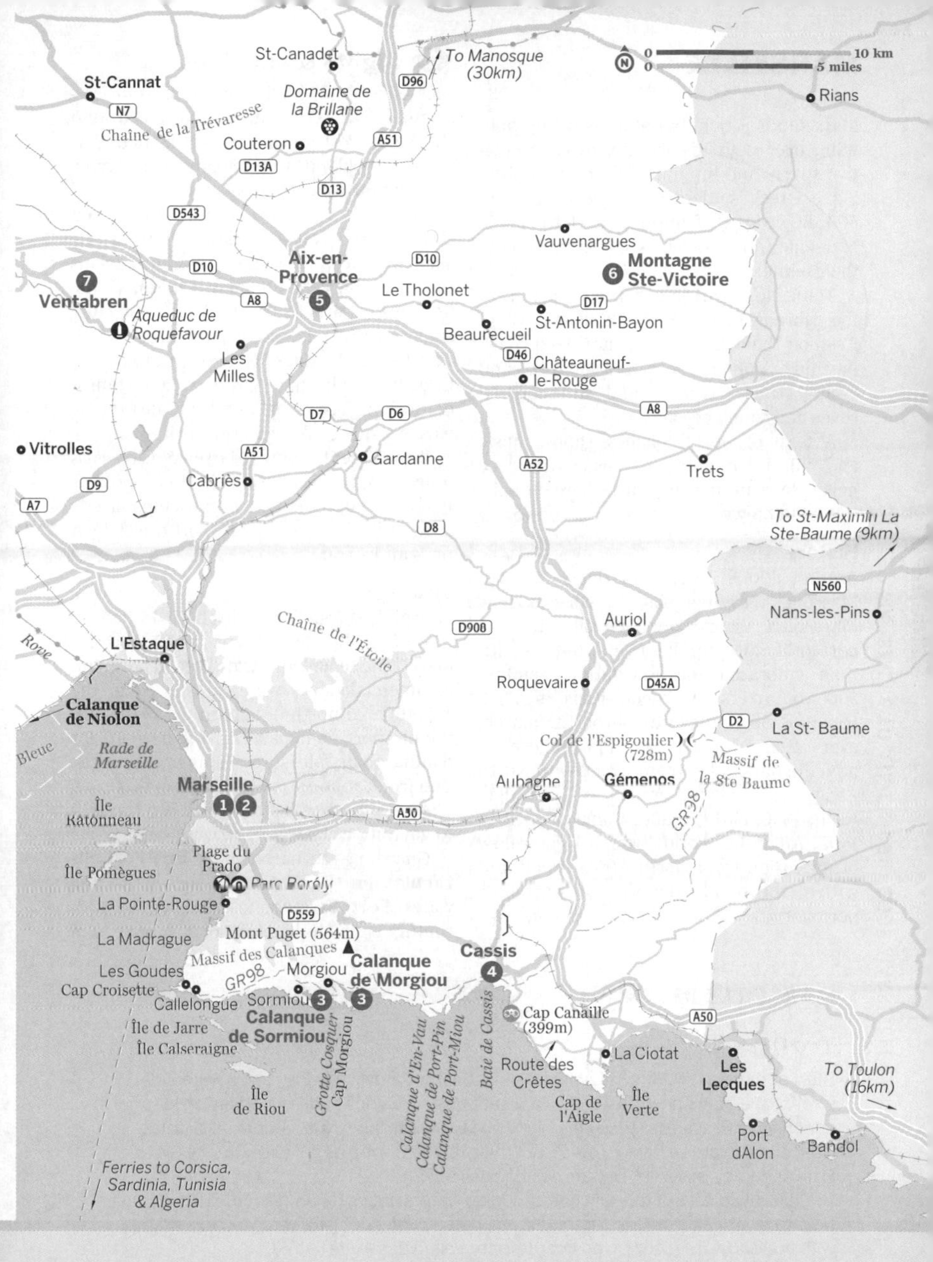

5 Revel in elegant architecture and fine arts in **Aix-en-Provence** (p164).

6 Climb **Montagne Ste-Victoire** (p170), one of Cézanne's inspirations.

7 Feast on a lunch to remember at **La Table de Ventabren** (p171).

MARSEILLE

POP 858,902

Marseille is a rich, pulsating port city bubbling over with history, cutting-edge creative spaces and hip multicultural urbanites. Since Greek settlers came ashore around 600 BC, waves of immigrants have made Marseille (now France's second largest city) their home.

Marseille's maritime heritage thrives at the vibrant Vieux Port (Old Port), where fresh-off-the-boat catches are sold each morning. Along the coast, seaside roads and cycling tracks veer around sun-scorched coves and sandy beaches.

A feast of world cuisines, shops, music and cultural celebrations ensure the pace never slows in this busy city, where the mistral wind blows.

History

Around 600 BC, Greek mariners founded Massilia, a trading post, at what is now Marseille's Vieux Port. Marseille became part of France in the 1480s, but its citizens embraced the Revolution, sending 500 volunteers to defend Paris in 1792. Heading north, they sang a rousing march, ever after dubbed 'La Marseillaise' – now the national anthem. Trade with North Africa escalated after France occupied Algeria in 1830, and the Suez Canal opened in 1869. After the World Wars, a steady flow of migration from North Africa began and with it the rapid expansion of Marseille's periphery.

Sights & Activities

Marseille is divided into 16 *arrondissements* (districts). Sights concentrate around the Vieux Port and Le Panier districts. Dynamic dockland redevelopment is transforming **La Joliette** to the north.

The city's main thoroughfare, **La Canebière** stretches eastwards from the Vieux Port towards the train station. Various morning markets fill **cours Julien** (M Notre Dame du Mont-Cours Julien), an elongated square with a forest of palm trees: fresh flowers on Wednesday and Saturday, antique books alternate Saturdays, and stamps or antique books on Sunday. Cafes on its western side cook up world cuisine.

Buy a cent-saving Marseille City Pass (one-/two-day €22/29) at the tourist office. It covers admission to 15 museums, a city tour, unlimited public-transport travel, boat trips and so on.

Vieux Port HISTORIC QUARTER

(Map p152; M Vieux Port) Ships have docked for more than 26 centuries at the city's birthplace, the colourful Old Port. The main commercial docks were transferred to the Joliette area north of here in the 1840s, but the old port remains a thriving harbour for fishing boats, pleasure yachts and tourists. The free **Cross-Port Ferry** (8am-12.30pm & 1-5pm) in front of the town hall is a fun way to get out on the water, however briefly.

Guarding the harbour are **Bas Fort St-Nicolas** on the south side and, across the water, **Fort St-Jean**, founded in the 13th century by the Knights Hospitaller of St John

MARSEILLE IN...

Two Days

Start at the Vieux Port (p144) with breakfast at La Caravelle (p159) and a waterside stroll to the brand new Musée des Civilisations de l'Europe et de la Méditerranée (p145). Lunch at La Passarelle (p158) then hike up to the Basilique Notre Dame de la Garde (p145) or explore Le Panier (p145), not missing the Centre de la Vieille Charité (p145). Dine at nearby, excellent Le Café des Épices (p156).

On day two, take in magnificent turquoise waters at Les Calanques (p161), or catch a boat to revel in Monte Cristo intrigues at Château d'If (p151). Reward your exploration with *bouillabaisse* (p157) in postcard-pretty Vallon des Auffe (p151).

Four Days

Make art and architecture the centre of the third day, taking in Palais de Longchamp (p150) and other galleries (p145). In the evening, visit Au Petit Nice (p159) in artsy cours Julien for an aperitif, before dinner at La Cantinetta (p157). On the fourth day, take your own picnic and sail to the Îles du Frioul (p151) to lounge in a natural paradise of birdlife and pebble beach and in the evening soak up Marseille's ebullient nightlife (p159).

of Jerusalem, and home of the national **Musée des Civilisations de l'Europe et de la Méditerranée's** (MuCEM; Museum of European & Mediterranean Civilisations; Map p152; ☎04 96 13 80 90; www.mucem.org; ⏱1pm-7pm Wed, Thu & Sat) brand new 40,000-sq-m, state-of-the-art museum.

The port's southern quay is dotted with theatres and bars, and restaurants and cafes buzz until the wee hours a block east on **place Thiars** and **cours Honoré d'Estienne d'Orves**.

Abbaye St-Victor (Map p152; 3 rue de l'Abbaye; ⏱9am-7pm; Ⓜ Vieux Port) is the birthplace of Christianity in Marseille, built on a 3rd-century BC Greek necropolis. Nearby **Musée du Santon** (Map p152; ☎04 91 13 61 36; www.santonsmarcelcarbonel.com; 49 rue Neuve Ste-Catherine; admission free; ⏱10am-12.30pm & 2-6.30pm Tue-Sat) with its boutique and neighbouring **Atelier du Santon** (Map p152; 47 rue Neuve Ste-Catherine) are home to handcrafted tiny kiln-fired figures or santons (from *santoùn* in Provençal, meaning 'little saint'). The custom of creating a nativity scene with figurines dates from the Avignon papacy of John XII (1319–34).

Perched at the peninsula's edge, the **Jardin du Pharo** (Map p148) is a perfect picnic spot and ideal for watching sunsets. See also p146.

TOP CHOICE **Le Panier** HISTORIC QUARTER
(Map p152; Ⓜ Vieux Port) From the Vieux Port, hike north up to this fantastic history-woven quarter, dubbed Marseille's Montmartre as much for its sloping streets as its artsy ambience. In Greek Massilia it was the site of the *agora* (marketplace), hence its name, which means 'the basket'. During WWII the quarter was dynamited and afterwards rebuilt. Today it's a mishmash of lanes hiding artisan shops, *ateliers* (workshops) and terraced houses strung with drying washing.

Its centrepiece is Centre de la Vieille Charité (p145); nearby **Cathédrale de la Major** (Map p152) stands guard between the old and 'new' ports with a 'stripy' facade made of local Cassis stone and green Florentine marble. Creative art exhibitions for kids are held at **Préau des Accoules** (Map p152; ☎04 91 91 52 06; 20 montée des Accoules; admission free; ⏱1.30-5.30pm Wed & Sat) inside an 18th-century Jesuit college.

Centre de la Vieille Charité MUSEUM
(Map p152; 2 rue de la Charité, 2e; both museums adult/student €5/2.50 ; Ⓜ Joliette) In the heart of Le Panier is Centre de la Vieille Charité, built as a charity shelter for the town's poor. Marseille architect and sculptor Pierre Puget (1620–94), born in the house opposite 10 rue du Petit Puits, designed the stunning arched sienna-stone courtyard. The complex now houses rotating exhibitions and the beautiful **Musée d'Archéologie Méditerranéenne** (Museum of Mediterranean Archeology; Map p152; ☎04 91 14 58 59; 2 rue de la Charité, 2e; Ⓜ Joliette) and **Musée d'Arts Africains, Océaniens & Amérindiens** (Museum of African, Oceanic & American Indian Art; Map p152; ☎04 91 14 58 38; 2 rue de la Charité, 2e). It's free to enter the grounds and sunny cafe.

Basilique Notre Dame de la Garde CHURCH
(Montée de la Bonne Mère; Map p148; ⏱7am-7pm, longer hrs summer) Everywhere you go in Marseille, you see the opulent, domed 19th-century Romano-Byzantine basilica occupying Marseille's highest point, La Garde (162m). Built between 1853 and 1864, it is ornamented with coloured marble, murals depicting the safe passage of sailing vessels and superbly restored mosaics. The hilltop gives 360-degree panoramas of the city's sea of terracotta roofs below.

The church's bell tower is crowned by a 9.7m gilded statue of the Virgin Mary on a 12m-high pedestal. Bullet marks and shrapnel scars on the northern facade evidence the fierce fighting of Marseille's Battle of Liberation (15–25 August 1944). It's a 1km walk from the Vieux Port; or take Bus 60 or the tourist-train.

DON'T MISS

ART GALLERIES & MUSEUMS

Marseille's galleries and museums have flourished in recent years. In addition to the many make-overs of local institutions like La Friche La Belle de Mai (p150), Palais de Longchamp (p150) and Musée Cantini (p150), spectacular new facilities have been built for MuCem (p145) and **Fonds Régional d'Art Contemporain** (FRAC; ☎04 91 91 27 55; www.fracpaca.org; 20 bd de Dunkerque; Ⓜ Joliette). The outstanding arts organization **Marseille Expos** (www.marseilleexpos.com) distributes an excellent map of hot galleries plus sponsors the festival **Printemps de l'Art Contemporain** each May. Their website lists what's on.

Vieux Port

AN ITINERARY

Bold and busy and open-armed to the sea, Marseille is France's oldest city. Standing on the quai des Belges it's hard to get a sense of the extent of the old port, a kilometre long on either side, running down to the great bastions of St-Jean and St-Nicolas, which once had their guns trained on the rebellious population rather than out to sea. Immerse yourself in the city's history with this full-day itinerary.

Go early to experience the **fish market** **1**, where you'll swap tall tales with the gregarious vendors. Hungry? Grab a balcony seat at La Caravelle, where views of the Basilique Notre Dame de la Garde accompany your morning coffee. Afterwards, take a **boat trip** **2** to Château d'If, made famous by the Dumas novel *The Count of Monte Cristo*. Alternatively, stay landside and explore the apricot-coloured alleys of **Le Panier** **3**, browsing the exhibits at the **Centre de la Vieille Charité** **4**.

In the afternoon, hop on the free cross-port ferry to the port's south side and wander into the **Abbaye St-Victor** **5** to see the bones of martyrs enshrined in gold. You can then catch the sunset from the stone benches in the **Jardin du Pharo** **6**. As the warm southern evening sets in, join the throngs on cours Honoré d'Estienne d'Orves, where you can drink pastis beneath a giant statue of a lion devouring a man – the **Milo de Croton** **7**.

CAPITAL OF CULTURE 2013

The largest urban renewal project in Europe, the EuroMéditerranée project is rehabilitating the commercial Joliette docks along the same lines as London's Docklands. The city's green-and-white striped Cathédrale de la Major will form its centrepiece. Simultaneously, many of the city's museums and galleries are undergoing ambitious renovations.

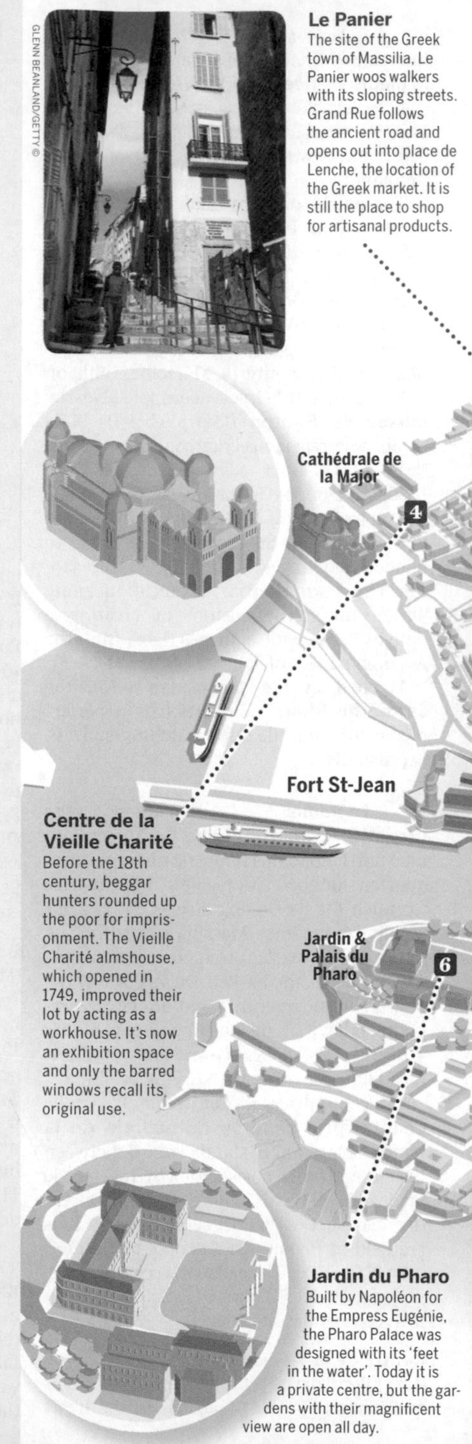

GLENN BEANLAND/GETTY ©

Le Panier
The site of the Greek town of Massilia, Le Panier woos walkers with its sloping streets. Grand Rue follows the ancient road and opens out into place de Lenche, the location of the Greek market. It is still the place to shop for artisanal products.

Centre de la Vieille Charité
Before the 18th century, beggar hunters rounded up the poor for imprisonment. The Vieille Charité almshouse, which opened in 1749, improved their lot by acting as a workhouse. It's now an exhibition space and only the barred windows recall its original use.

Jardin du Pharo
Built by Napoléon for the Empress Eugénie, the Pharo Palace was designed with its 'feet in the water'. Today it is a private centre, but the gardens with their magnificent view are open all day.

TOR EIJSELAND/ALAMY ©

Friouf If Express

Catch the Frioul If Express to Château d'If, France's equivalent to Alcatraz. Prisoners were housed according to class: the poorest at the bottom in windowless dungeons, the wealthiest in paid-for private cells, with windows and a fireplace.

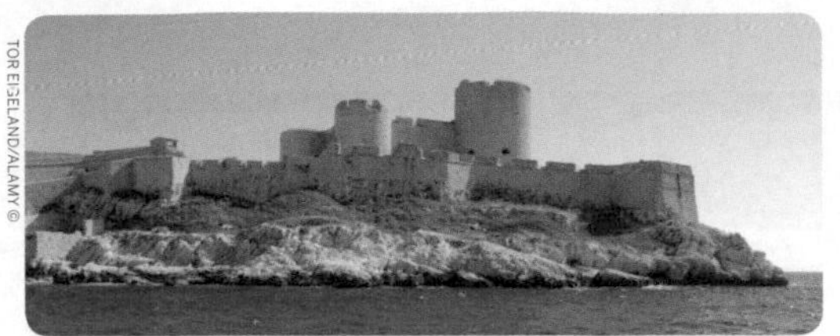

Fish Market

Marseille's small fish market still sets up each morning to hawk the daily catch. Take a lesson in local seafood, spotting sea squirts, scorpion fish, sea urchins and conger eels. Get there before 9am if you're buying.

Milo de Croton

Subversive local artist Pierre Puget carved the savage *Milo de Croton* for Louis XIV. The statue, whose original is in the Louvre, is a meditation on man's pride and shows the Greek Olympian being devoured by a lion, his Olympic cup cast down.

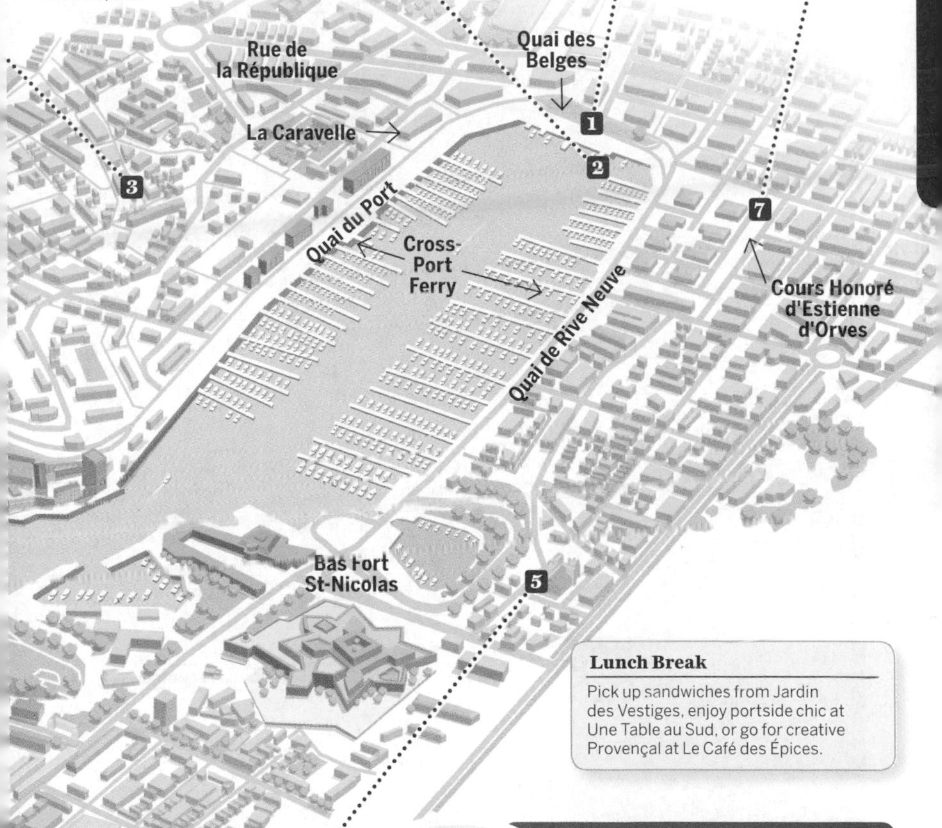

Rue de la République
Quai des Belges
1
La Caravelle
2
3
Quai du Port
Cross-Port Ferry
7
Quai de Rive Neuve
Cours Honoré d'Estienne d'Orves
Bas Fort St-Nicolas
5

Lunch Break

Pick up sandwiches from Jardin des Vestiges, enjoy portside chic at Une Table au Sud, or go for creative Provençal at Le Café des Épices.

Abbaye St-Victor

St-Victor was built (420–30) to house the remains of tortured Christian martyrs. On Candlemas (2 February) the black Madonna is brought up from the crypt and the archbishop blesses the city and the sea.

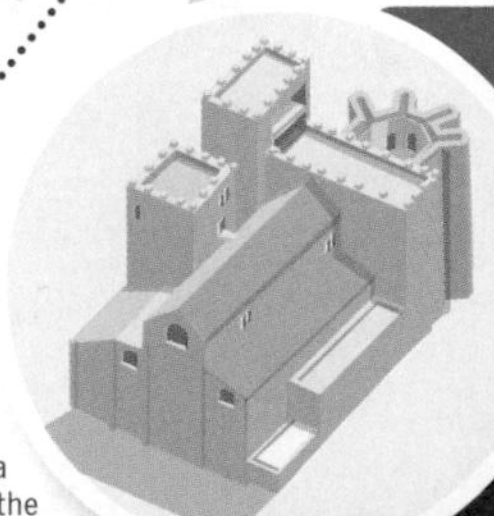

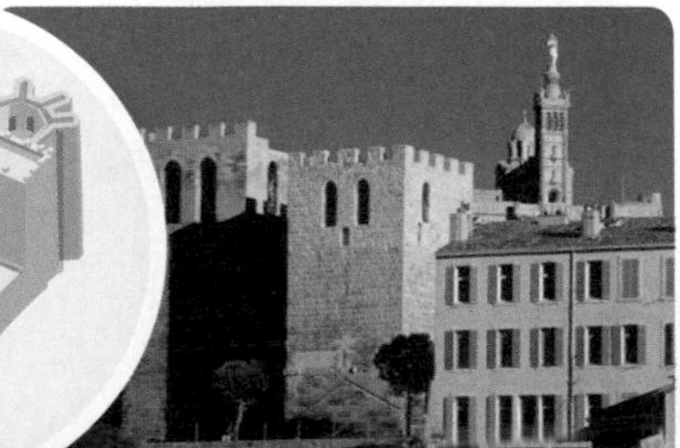

DAN HERRICK/GETTY ©

Marseille

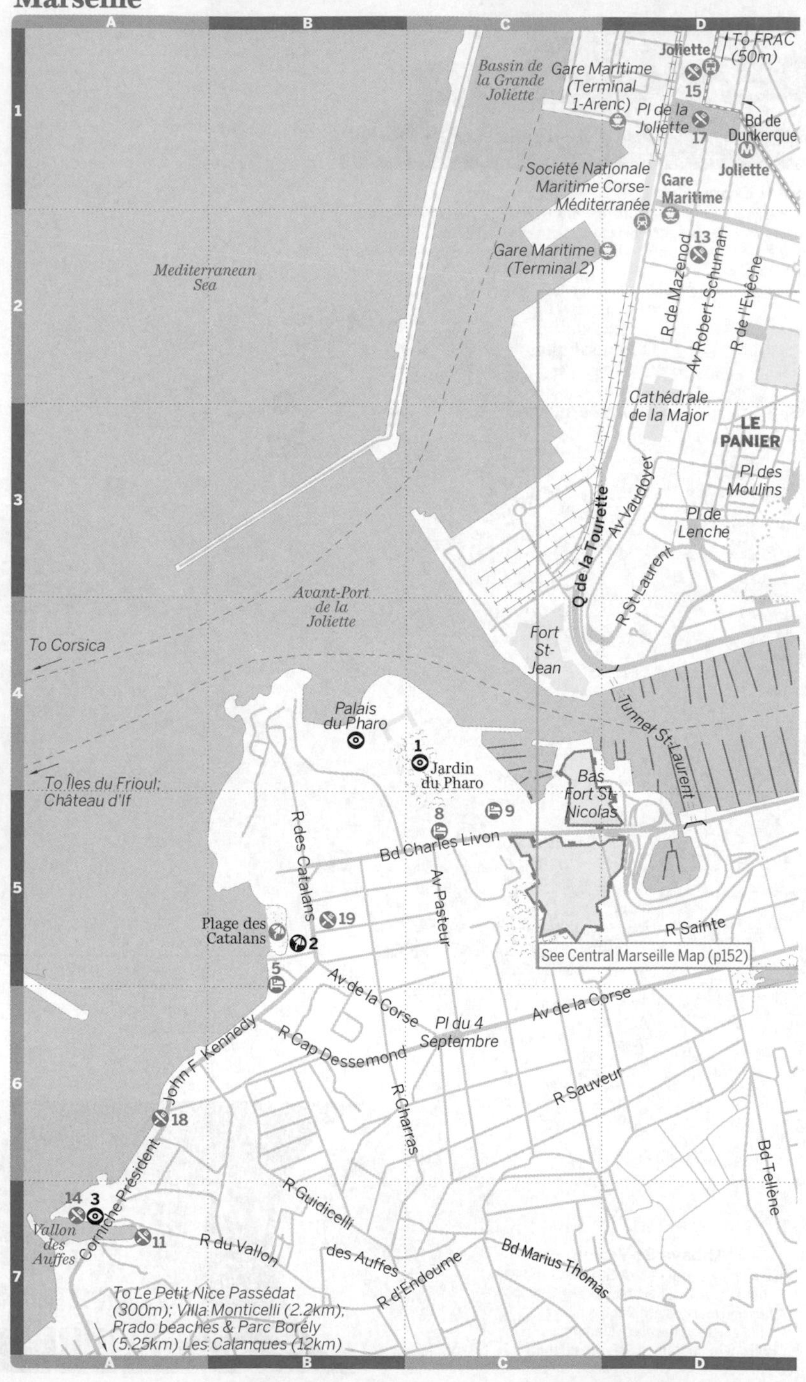
A
B
C
D
1
2
3
4
5
6
7
Bassin de la Grande Joliette
Gare Maritime (Terminal 1-Arenc)
Joliette
To FRAC (50m)
15
Pl de la Joliette
17
Bd de Dunkerque
Joliette
Société Nationale Maritime Corse-Méditerranée
Gare Maritime
13
Gare Maritime (Terminal 2)
Mediterranean Sea
R de Mazenod
Av Robert Schuman
R de l'Evêche
Cathédrale de la Major
LE PANIER
Pl des Moulins
Q de la Tourette
Av Vaudoyer
Pl de Lenche
R St Laurent
Avant-Port de la Joliette
To Corsica
Fort St-Jean
Tunnel St-Laurent
Palais du Pharo
1
Jardin du Pharo
To Îles du Frioul; Château d'If
Bas Fort St-Nicolas
8
9
Bd Charles Livon
R des Catalans
Av Pasteur
19
Plage des Catalans
2
R Sainte
See Central Marseille Map (p152)
5
Av de la Corse
Pl du 4 Septembre
Av de la Corse
R Cap Dessemond
John F Kennedy
R Charras
R Sauveur
18
Corniche Président
Bd Tellène
14
3
Vallon des Auffes
11
R Guidicelli
R du Vallon
des Auffes
R d'Endoume
Bd Marius Thomas
To Le Petit Nice Passédat (300m); Villa Monticelli (2.2km); Prado beaches & Parc Borély (5.25km) Les Calanques (12km)

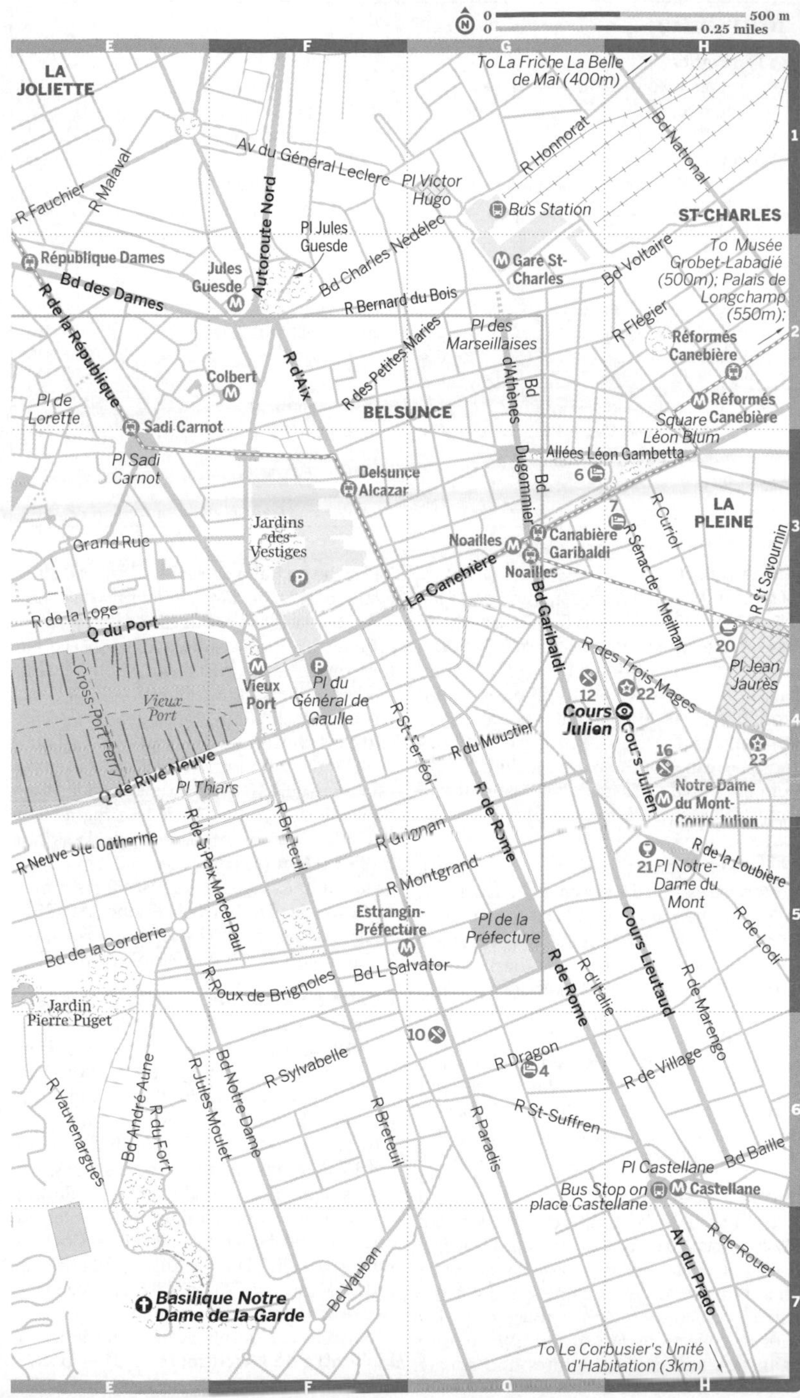

LA JOLIETTE
ST-CHARLES
BELSUNCE
LA PLEINE
To La Friche La Belle de Mai (400m)
To Musée Grobet-Labadié (500m); Palais de Longchamp (550m);
To Le Corbusier's Unité d'Habitation (3km)
Av du Général Leclerc
Pl Victor Hugo
R Honnorat
Bd National
Bus Station
R Fauchier
R Malaval
Autoroute Nord
Pl Jules Guesde
Bd Charles Nédélec
République Dames
Jules Guesde
Gare St-Charles
Bd Voltaire
Bd des Dames
R de la République
R Bernard du Bois
R Flégier
Réformés Canebière
Pl des Marseillaises
R des Petites Maries
R d'Aix
Colbert
Pl de Lorette
Sadi Carnot
Bd d'Athènes
Square Léon Blum
Allées Léon Gambetta
Pl Sadi Carnot
Delsunce Alcazar
Bd Dugommier
R Curiol
Jardins des Vestiges
Grand Rue
Noailles
Canabière Garibaldi
R Sénac de Meilhan
R St Savournin
La Canebière
R de la Loge
Q du Port
Bd Garibaldi
R des Trois Mages
Pl Jean Jaurès
Cross-Port Ferry
Vieux Port
Pl du Général de Gaulle
R St-Ferréol
Cours Julien
R du Moustier
Q de Rive Neuve
Pl Thiars
Notre Dame du Mont-Cours Julien
R Neuve Ste Catherine
R de la Paix Marcel Paul
R Breteuil
R Grignan
R de Rome
R de la Loubière
Pl Notre-Dame du Mont
R Montgrand
Estrangin-Préfecture
Pl de la Préfecture
R de Lodi
Bd de la Corderie
R Roux de Brignoles
Bd L Salvator
R d'Italie
Cours Lieutaud
R de Marengo
Jardin Pierre Puget
R Sylvabelle
R Dragon
R de Village
R Vauvenargues
Bd André Aune
R du Fort
R Jules Moulet
Bd Notre Dame
R Paradis
R St-Suffren
Pl Castellane
Bd Baille
Bus Stop on place Castellane
Castellane
R de Rouet
Av du Prado
Bd Vauban
Basilique Notre Dame de la Garde
1 2 3 4 5 6 7
4 6 7 10 12 16 20 21 22 23
E F G H
0 500 m
0 0.25 miles

Marseille

Musée Cantini ART MUSEUM
(Map p152; ☎04 91 54 77 75; 19 rue Grignan; adult/child €2/1; 10am-5pm Tue-Sun Oct-May, 11am-6pm Tue-Sun Jun-Sep; MEstrangin-Préfecture) Behind grand gates inside a 17th-century *hôtel particulier*, the Musée Cantini has rotating exhibitions. Its permanent collections of 17th- and 18th-century Provençal ceramics and landscapes of the region include André Derain's *Pinède, Cassis* (1907) and Raoul Dufy's *Paysage de l'Estaque* (1908).

FREE **Palais de Longchamp** PALACE, PARK
(Longchamp Palace; bd Philippon; ; Longchamp, MCinq Avenues–Longchamp) The colonnaded Palais de Longchamp and its spectacular fountains were constructed in the 1860s, in part to disguise a water tower at the terminus of an aqueduct from the River Durance. The northern wing houses Marseille's oldest museum, the **Musée des Beaux-Arts**, undergoing renovations at research time and slated to reopen in 2013. The shaded park is one of the centre's few green spaces, popular with local families.

Musée Grobet-Labadié MUSEUM
(☎04 91 62 21 82; 140 bd Longchamp; adult/child €3/2; 11am-6pm Tue-Sun Jun-Sep, 10am-5pm Tue-Sun Oct-May; MCinq Avenues-Longchamp) This intimate museum paints an appealing portrait of elegant 19th-century Marseille with its collections of 13th- to 19th-century paintings, antiques, sculptures and ornate polished wooden floors.

La Friche La Belle de Mai CULTURAL CENTRE
(☎04 95 04 95 04; www.lafriche.org; 41 rue Jobin; 49 stop Jobin) The site of a former sugar-refining plant and subsequent tobacco factory, the theatre, artists' workshops, cinema studios, radio stations, multimedia displays, alfresco installation art, skateboard camps and electro-/world-music parties at La Friche la Belle de Mai are the 'voice' of contemporary Marseille. It underwent an enormous renovation in 2012. Check its program online, view art in the **Galerie de la Friche Belle de Mai** (admission free; 3-7pm Tue-Sat) or lunch in its stylishly industrial restaurant **Les Grandes Tables de la Friche** (☎04 95 04 95 85; www.lesgrandestables.com; 12 rue François Simon; mains €10; 8.30am-8pm Mon-Fri).

L'Unité d'Habitation HISTORIC BUILDING
(La Cité Radieuse; ☎04 91 16 78 00; 280 bd Michelet; 83 or 21 stop Le Corbusier) Visionary International-Style architect Le Corbusier redefined urban living in 1952 with the completion of his vertical 337-apartment 'garden city' also known as La Cité Radieuse (Radiant City). Along its darkened hallways, primary-coloured downlights create a glowing tunnel leading to a mini-supermarket, an architectural bookshop, **Hôtel Le Corbusier** (☎04 91 16 78 00; www.hotellecorbusier.com; 280 bd Michelet; r €70, apt €105-139; 83 or 21 stop Le Corbusier), and a rooftop terrace.

Anyone can stroll around, or lunch at **Le Ventre de l'Architecte** (☎04 91 16 78 23; www.leventredelarchitecte.com; lunch menus €30, dinner menus €60-70; ⌚lunch & dinner Tue-Sat). The aptly named Architect's Tummy takes a contemporary cut on cuisine and proffers distant views of the Med from its balcony. Architecture buffs can book a **guided tour** of a private apartment at the tourist office.

ALONG THE COAST

Mesmerising views of another Marseille unfold along **corniche Président John F Kennedy**, the coastal road that cruises south to small, beach-volleyball-busy **Plage des Catalans** (Map p148; 3 rue des Catalans; ⌚8.30am-6.30pm) and fishing cove **Vallon des Auffes** (Map p148), crammed with boats.

Further south, the vast **Prado beaches**, are marked by Jules Cantini's 1903 marble replica of Michelangelo's *David*. The beaches, all gold sand, were created from backfill from the excavations for Marseille's metro. They have a world-renowned **skate park**. Nearby lies expansive Parc Borély.

Promenade Georges Pompidou continues south to **Cap Croisette**, from where the beautiful *calanques* can be reached on foot. Hipster beach-club addresses are: **La Baie des Singes** (The Bay of Monkeys; ☎04 91 73 68 87; www.la-baie-des-singes.fr; mains €22-26; ⌚lunch & dinner Apr-Oct), with comfy deckchairs overlooking Île Maïre and accessible by boat or on foot along a 500m path between rocks from the Cap Croisette car park; and **La Maronnaise** (☎04 91 73 98 58; rte de la Maronnaise; ⌚Wed-Sat May-early Sep), where 30- and 40-somethings dine, lounge in the sun and dance beneath stars.

To head down the coast, take bus 83 from the Vieux Port. At av du Prado switch to bus 19 to continue further. **La Navette Maritime Vieux Port-Pointe Rouge** (www.rtm.fr; €2.50, good for 1½ hrs on all public transport; ⌚hourly Mar-15 Sep) runs boats between Vieux Port and Pointe Rouge, just to the south of the Prado beaches.

Parc Borély PARK, GALLERY

(av du Parc Borély; 🚌19, 83 stop Parc Borély) Parc Borély encompasses a lake, botanical garden and the just-renovated 18th-century **Château Borély**, hosting art exhibitions.

Musée d'Art Contemporain ART MUSEUM

(Museum of Contemporary Art, MAC; ☎04 91 25 01 07; 69 ave de Haïfa; adult/child €3/2; ⌚11am-6pm Tue-Sun Jun-Sep, 10am-5pm Tue-Sun Oct-May) Creations of Marseille-born sculptor César Baldaccini (1921–98) jostle for white space with Christo, Nice new realists Ben and Klein, and Andy Warhol. From the Prado metro stop take bus 23 or 45 to the Haïfa-Marie-Louise stop.

Château d'If ISLAND, CASTLE

(www.if.monuments-nationaux.fr; adult/child €5/free; ⌚9.30am-6.30pm daily, shorter hours & Tue-Sun winter) Immortalised in Alexandre Dumas' classic 1844 novel *Le Comte de Monte Cristo* (*The Count of Monte Cristo*), 16th-century fortress-turned-prison Château d'If sits on the 30-sq-km island, **Île d'If**, 3.5km west of the Vieux Port. Political prisoners were incarcerated here, along with hundreds of Protestants, the Revolutionary hero Mirabeau, and the Communards of 1871.

Frioul If Express (www.frioul-if-express.com; 1 quai des Belges) boats leave for Château d'If from the Vieux Port. Over 15 daily departures in summer, fewer in winter (€10 return, 20 minutes).

Îles du Frioul ISLANDS

A few hundred metres west of Île d'If are the Îles du Frioul, the barren dyke-linked white-limestone islands of Ratonneau and Pomègues. Sea birds and rare plants thrive on these tiny islands (each about 2.5km long, totalling 200 hectares). Ratonneau has three beaches. Boats to Château d'If also serve the Îles du Frioul (€10 return, 35 minutes).

Tours

Le Grand Tour BUS TOUR

(Map p152; ☎04 91 91 05 82; www.marseillelegrandtour.com; adult/child €18/9; ⌚10am-7pm) Feel the wind in your hair as you travel between key sights and museums aboard a hop-on-hop-off open-topped bus. Tickets sold at the tourist office or on board include a five-language audio guide.

Tourist Train TRAIN TOUR

(Map p152; ☎04 91 25 24 69; www.petit-train-marseille.com; adult/child €7/4; ⌚10am-12.30pm & 2-6pm; Ⓜ Vieux Port) Electric trams with two circular routes: to Notre Dame basilica (year-round) and Le Panier (April to mid-November). Tours last 65 minutes and depart every 30 minutes, less in winter.

Guided Tour WALKING TOUR

(www.resamarseille.com; tours €7; ⌚2pm Sat; Ⓜ Vieux Port) From the tourist office.

FREE **Marseille Provence Greeters** WALKING TOUR

(www.marseilleprovencegreeters.com) There are free walking tours by locals; advance website registration required.

Central Marseille

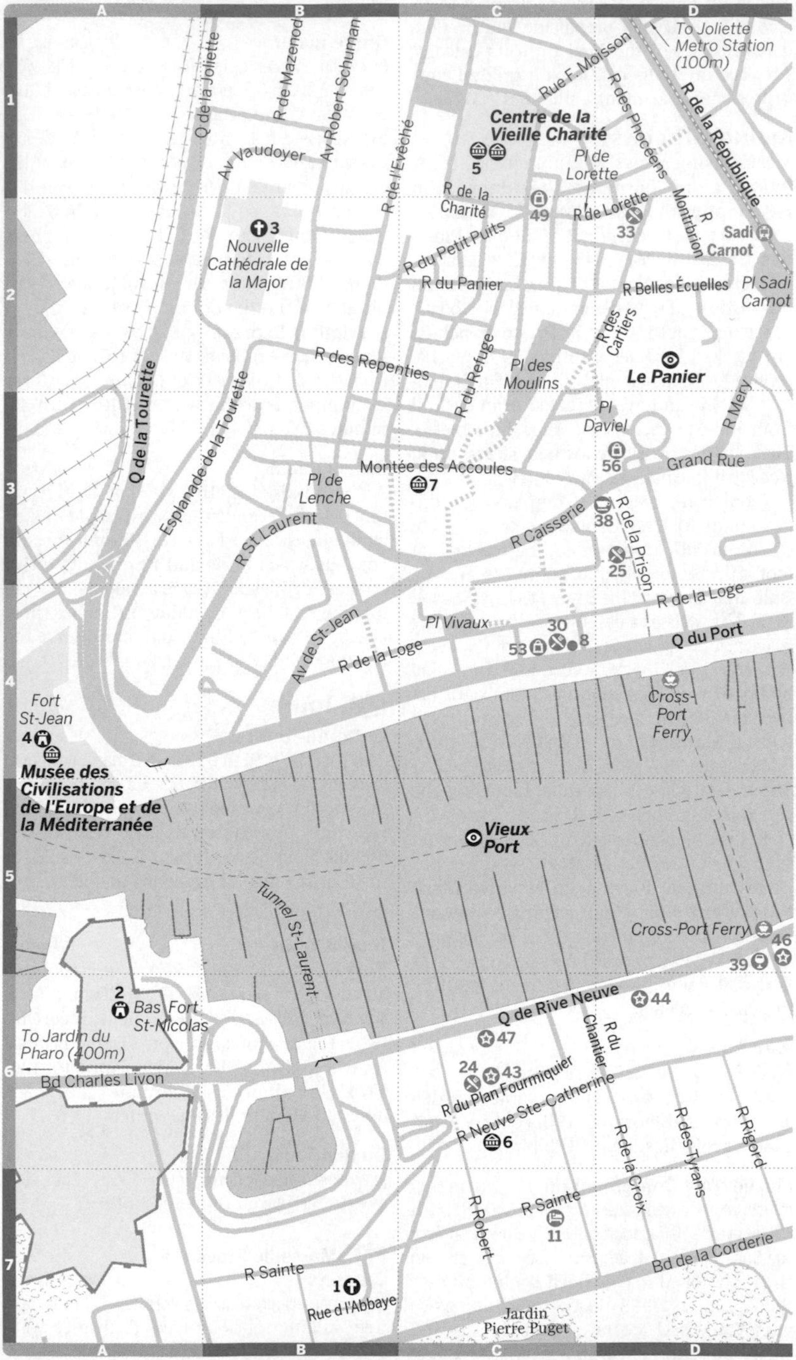

A B C D

1 2 3 4 5 6 7

To Joliette Metro Station (100m)
Rue F Moisson
R des Phocéens
R de la République
Q de la Joliette
R de Mazenod
Av Robert Schuman
Av Vaudoyer
R de l'Evêché
Centre de la Vieille Charité
5
Pl de Lorette
R de la Charité
49
R de Lorette
33
R Montbrion
Sadi Carnot
3
Nouvelle Cathédrale de la Major
R du Petit Puits
R du Panier
R Belles Écuelles
Pl Sadi Carnot
R des Cartiers
R des Repenties
R du Refuge
Pl des Moulins
Le Panier
Q de la Tourette
Esplanade de la Tourette
Pl Daviel
R Mery
Montée des Accoules
7
56
Grand Rue
Pl de Lenche
R St Laurent
R Caisserie
38
R de la Prison
25
R de la Loge
Av de St-Jean
Pl Vivaux
30
53
8
Q du Port
R de la Loge
Cross-Port Ferry
Fort St-Jean
4
Musée des Civilisations de l'Europe et de la Méditerranée
Vieux Port
Tunnel St-Laurent
Cross-Port Ferry
46
39
44
Q de Rive Neuve
R du Chantier
2
Bas Fort St-Nicolas
47
To Jardin du Pharo (400m)
24
43
Bd Charles Livon
R du Plan Fourmiquier
R Neuve Ste-Catherine
6
R de la Croix
R des Tyrans
R Rigord
R Robert
R Sainte
11
Bd de la Corderie
R Sainte
1
Rue d l'Abbaye
Jardin Pierre Puget

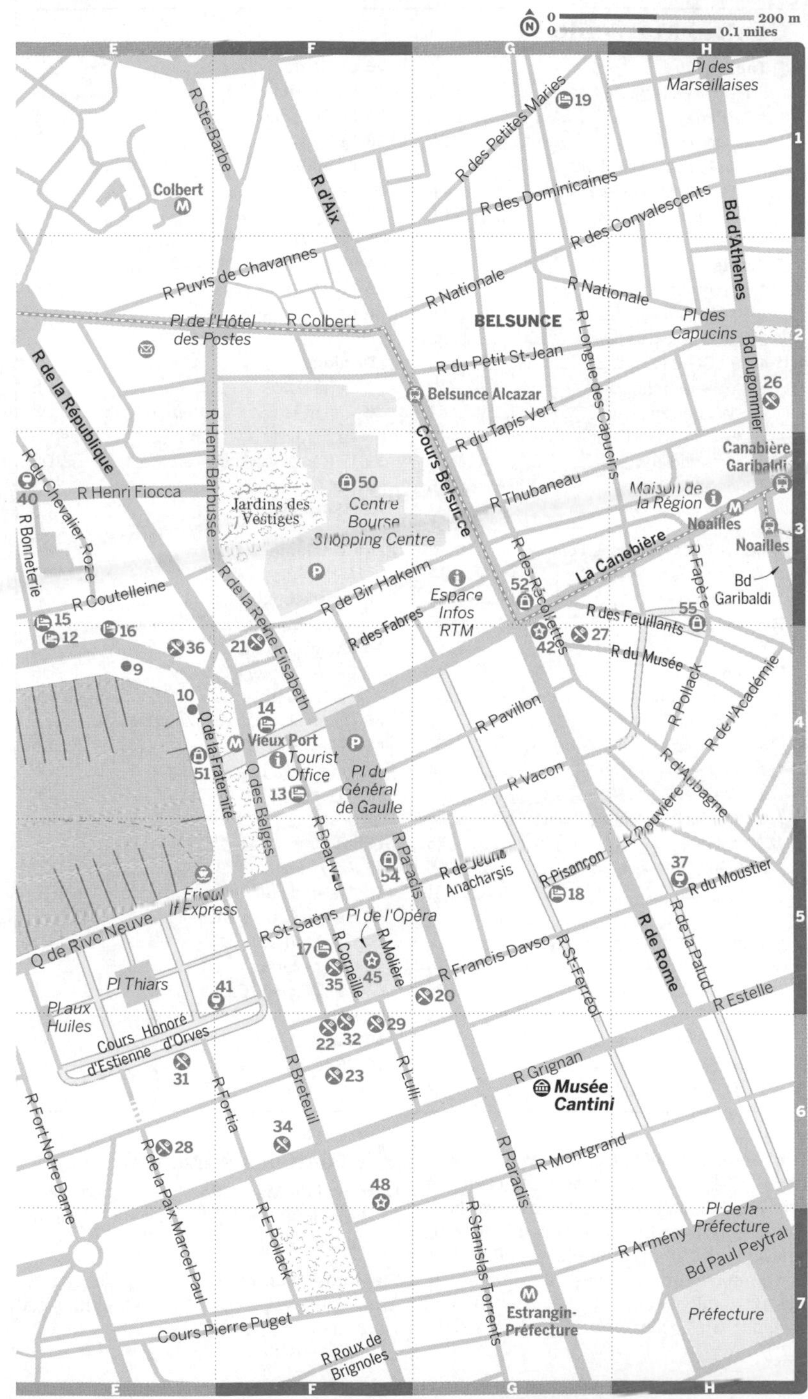
0 200 m
0 0.1 miles
Colbert
R Ste-Barbe
R d'Aix
R des Petites Maries
19
Pl des Marseillaises
R des Dominicaines
R des Convalescents
Bd d'Athènes
R Puvis de Chavannes
R Nationale
BELSUNCE
Pl de l'Hôtel des Postes
R Colbert
Pl des Capucins
R de la République
R du Petit St-Jean
R Longue des Capucins
Bd Dugommier
26
Belsunce Alcazar
R du Tapis Vert
Cours Belsunce
Canabière Garibaldi
R Henri Barbusse
R du Chevalier Roze
40
R Henri Fiocca
50
Jardins des Vestiges
Centre Bourse Shopping Centre
R Thubaneau
Maison de la Région
Noailles
R Bonneterie
R de la Reine Elisabeth
R de Bir Hakeim
La Canebière
R Fapère
Bd Garibaldi
R Coutelleine
Espace Infos RTM
52
R des Récolettes
55
R des Feuillants
15
12
16
36
21
R des Fabres
42
27
R du Musée
9
10
14
R Pavillon
R Pollack
R de l'Académie
Q de la Fraternité
Vieux Port
Tourist Office
Pl du Général de Gaulle
R d'Aubagne
51
Q des Belges
13
R Vacon
R Rouvière
R Beauvau
R Paradis
R de Jeune Anacharsis
R Pisançon
37
R du Moustier
54
Frioul If Express
18
Q de Rive Neuve
R St-Saëns
Pl de l'Opéra
R Corneille
R Molière
R Francis Davso
R St-Ferréol
R de Rome
R de la Palud
17
45
35
Pl Thiars
41
20
R Estelle
Pl aux Huiles
Cours Honoré d'Estienne d'Orves
22
32
29
31
23
R Breteuil
R Lulli
R Grignan
Musée Cantini
R Fort Notre Dame
R Fortia
34
28
R de la Paix Marcel Paul
R Montgrand
48
R E Pollack
R Stanislas Torrents
Pl de la Préfecture
R Armény
Bd Paul Peytral
Estrangin-Préfecture
Préfecture
Cours Pierre Puget
R Roux de Brignoles
E
F
G
H
1
2
3
4
5
6
7

Central Marseille

Top Sights

Centre de la Vieille Charité C1
Le Panier D2
Musée Cantini G6
Musée des Civilisations de l'Europe et de la Méditerranée A4
Vieux Port C5

Sights

1 Abbaye St-Victor B7
2 Bas Fort St-Nicolas A6
3 Cathédrale de la Major B2
4 Fort St-Jean A4
5 Musée d'Archéologie Méditerranéenne C1
Musée d'Arts Africains, Océaniens & Amérindiens ..... (see 5)
6 Musée du Santon C6
7 Préau des Accoules C3

Activities, Courses & Tours

8 Croisières Marseille Calanques C4
9 Le Grand Tour E4
10 Tourist Train E4

Sleeping

11 Casa Honoré C7
12 Hôtel Belle-Vue E4
13 Hôtel Carré du Vieux Port F4
14 Hôtel Escale Oceania F4
15 Hôtel Hermès E3
16 Hôtel La Résidence du Vieux Port E4
17 Hôtel Relax F5
18 Hôtel Saint-Ferréol G5
19 Hôtel Vertigo G1

Eating

20 Boulangerie Aixoise G5
21 Jardin des Vestiges F4
22 La Casertane F6
23 La Part des Anges F6
24 La Passarelle C6
25 Le Café des Épices D3
26 Le Comptoir Dugommier H2
27 Le Femina G4
28 Le Grain de Sel E6
29 Le Mas F6
30 Le Souk C4
31 Les Arcenaulx E6
32 Pain de l'Opéra F6
33 Pizzaria Chez Étienne D2
34 Sylvain Depuichaffray F6
35 Thai Baie F5
36 Une Table au Sud E4

Drinking

37 Caffè Noir H5
38 Cup of Tea D3
La Caravelle ..... (see 12)
39 Le Bar de la Marine D5
40 Les Buvards E3
41 Polikarpov F5

Entertainment

Au Son des Guitars ..... (see 35)
42 Espace Culture G4
Fnac ..... (see 50)
43 La Noche C6
44 Le Trolleybus D6
Ma Demoiselle ..... (see 35)
45 Opéra Municipal de Marseille F5
46 Pelle Mêle D5
47 Théâtre National de Marseille C6
48 XY Le Club F6

Shopping

49 72% Pétanque C2
Atelier du Santon ..... (see 6)
50 Centre Bourse Shopping Centre F3
51 Fish Market E4
52 Garlic Market G3
53 La Maison du Pastis C4
54 Librairie de la Bourse F5
55 Marché des Capucins H3
56 Place aux Huiles D3

Croisières Marseille Calanques BOAT TOUR
(Map p152; www.croisieres-marseille-calanques.com; 74 quai du Port) This outfit runs two-hour return trips from the Vieux Port taking in six *calanques* (family/adult/child €68/22/7); three-hour return trips past 12 *calanques*, to Cassis (family/adult/child €85/28/21); and 1½-hour trips around the Baie de Marseille (€10).

Festivals & Events

Carnaval de Marseille STREET CARNIVAL
(Mar) Mad street carnival with decorated floats; March.

Fiesta des Suds MUSIC FESTIVAL
(www.dock-des-suds.org; Mar) World music at Dock des Suds; March.

Festival de Marseille PERFORMING ARTS
(www.festivaldemarseille.com; ⏲Jul) Three weeks of international dance, theatre, music and art; July.

Five Continents Jazz Festival MUSIC FESTIVAL
(www.festival-jazz-cinq-continents.com; ⏲Jul) Acid jazz, funk and folk music; July.

Foire aux Santonniers CHRISTMAS
(⏲Dec) Since 1803 traditional *santon* makers have flocked to Marseille for this fair; December.

Sleeping

The best rooms in Marseille get snagged fast; reserve ahead. There's also a hotel in Le Corbusier's L'Unité d'Habitation (p150).

TOP CHOICE **Casa Honoré** B&B €€€
(Map p152; ☎04 96 11 01 62; www.casahonore.com; 123 rue Sainte; d incl breakfast €150-200; ❄📶🏊; Ⓜ Vieux Port) Los Angeles meets Marseille at this four-room *maison d'hôte*, built around a central courtyard with lap pool shaded by banana trees. The fashion-forward style reflects the owner's love for contemporary interior design (she has a shop down the block), using disparate elements like black wicker and the occasional cow skull, which come together in one sexy package. One complaint: some bathrooms are partitioned by curtains, not doors.

Le Ryad BOUTIQUE HOTEL €€
(Map p148; ☎04 91 47 74 54; www.leryad.fr; 16 rue Sénac de Meilhan; s €80-105, d €95-125, family €170; 📶👪; 🚊Canebière Garibaldi, ⓂNoailles) With high ceilings, arched alcoves, warm colours and minimalist decor, Le Ryad draws sumptuous influence from Morocco. Beautiful bathrooms, garden-view rooms and great service make up for the sometimes-sketchy neighbourhood. Despite the four-storey walk-up, it's worth booking the top-floor room (Mogador) for its rooftop terrace.

Hôtel Vertigo HOSTEL €
(Map p152; ☎04 91 91 07 11; www.hotelvertigo.fr; 42 rue des Petites Maries; dm/d €25/60; @📶; ⓂGare St-Charles SNCF) This snappy boutique hostel kisses goodbye to dodgy bunks and hospital-like decor. Here it's 'hello' to vintage posters, chrome kitchen, groovy communal spaces and polite multilingual staff. Double rooms are particularly good, some with private terrace. No curfew (or lift). A second, all-dorm facility is closer to the Vieux Port.

Hôtel La Résidence du Vieux Port DESIGN HOTEL €€
(Map p152; ☎04 91 91 91 22; www.hotelmarseille.com; 18 quai du Port; d €125-200, apt €298; ❄@📶; ⓂVieux Port) This top view hotel got a makeover in 2010 in vaguely Jetsons-meets-Mondrian style, with swoop-backed furniture and bold primary colours. Every room looks sharp, and port-side rooms have balconies with views of the old port and Notre Dame.

Mama Shelter DESIGN HOTEL €€
(☎01 43 48 48 48; www.mamashelter.com; 64 rue de la Loubière; d €99-139, q €159, ste €209; ❄📶👪; ⓂNotre Dame du Monte–Cours Julien) The brainchild of Serge Trigano, son of Gilbert (Club Med creator), this affordable-chic new kid on the block opened with a bang in 2012. It sports design by Philippe Starck, nifty extras like Kiehl's bathroom products and free in-room movies. Wheelchair accessible room. Parking €17 per day.

Hôtel Belle-Vue HOTEL €€
(Map p152; ☎04 96 17 05 40; www.hotel-bellevue-marseille.fr; 34 quai du Port; d €84-135; ❄@📶; ⓂVieux Port) Rooms at this old-fashioned hotel are tastefully decorated with mid-budget simplicity, but have million-dollar portside views. Bathrooms have occasional mildew spots, and there's no lift, but La Caravelle, one of Marseille's coolest cafe-bars, is inside.

Sofitel Marseille Vieux Port LUXURY HOTEL €€€
(Map p148; ☎04 91 15 59 55; www.sofitel-marseille vieuxport.com; 36 bd Charles Livon; d from €215; ❄@📶🏊; 🚌83 stop Fort St-Nicolas) Marseille's top full-service hotel commands spectacular views of the sea and the old port. Rooms have all the requisite bells and whistles, from iPod docks to feather beds; some have double-size soaking tubs. Great spa.

Hôtel Escale Oceania HOTEL €€
(Map p152; ☎04 91 90 61 61; www.oceaniahotels.com; 5 La Canebière; d €91-157; ❄📶; ⓂVieux Port) Though rooms run small (you're buying the excellent Vieux Port location) they're fresh and clean. Spotless bathrooms have big walk-in showers. Rooms on the Canebière side sport wrought-iron port-view balconies.

Hôtel Saint-Ferréol HOTEL €€
(Map p152; ☎04 91 33 12 21; www.hotelsaintferreol.com; 19 rue Pisançon; d €99-120; ❄@📶; ⓂVieux Port) On the corner of the city's bustling pedestrianised street, this simple hotel has individually decorated rooms, many inspired

by artists like Van Gogh and Cézanne, with spotless bathrooms and exceptional service.

Villa Monticelli B&B €€
(☎04 91 22 15 20; www.villamonticelli.com; 96 rue du Commandant Rolland; d incl breakfast €105; Rond-Point du Prado, 83 or 19 stop Prado St Giniez) Colette and Jean are passionate about their city and their five exquisite *chambre d'hôte* rooms in their stunning villa are worth the slightly outer-city location. Breakfast of homemade everything is served on the panoramic-view terrace.

Hôtel Le Richelieu HOTEL €
(Map p148; ☎04 91 31 01 92; www.lerichelieu-marseille.com; 52 corniche Président John F Kennedy; d €53-88, tr €91-110; 83) An economical seaside choice with odd-shaped rooms, but the owners keep them looking fresh. The best face the sea, lending a beach-house feel. There's an adjacent beach and shared water-view terrace, but no lift.

Hôtel Edmond Rostand BOUTIQUE HOTEL €€
(Map p148; ☎04 91 37 74 95; www.hoteledmondrostand.com; 31 rue Dragon; s & d €86, tr €127 ; Estrangin-Préfecture) Antique shops surround this good-value hotel in the elegant Quartier des Antiquaires. Though its 16 stylish rooms are a bit worn, some overlook a tiny private garden, others rooftops and Notre Dame de Basilique.

Hôtel Hermès HOTEL €
(Map p152; ☎04 96 11 63 63; www.hotelmarseille.com; 2 rue Bonneterie; s/d from €52/74; Vieux Port) Rooms are small and were under renovation at the time of resarch. A rooftop terrace, for breakfast or drinks, adds value. The nuptial suite (from €104), up a rooftop ladder, has panoramic views.

Hôtel Carré du Vieux Port HOTEL €€
(Map p152; ☎04 91 33 02 33; www.hvpm.fr; 6 rue Beauveau; s/d/tr €95/105/122; Vieux Port) The look is generic modern (think slate walls and low-pile carpeting) but the location is central, rooms fresh and baths spotless. Double-pane windows block noise.

Hôtel Lutétia HOTEL €
(Map p148; ☎04 91 50 81 78; www.hotelmarseille.com; 38 allées Léon Gambetta; s/d/tr €65/72/82; Rèformès-Canabière) Lutétia is a petite house with a thimble-sized lift that whisks guests up to modern, neat-as-a-pin rooms. Bells at the twin-steepled church up the street are a handy wake-up call.

New Hotel of Marseille Pharo LUXURY HOTEL €€€
(Map p148; ☎04 91 31 53 15; www.new-hotel.com; 71 blvd Charles Livon; s/d €225/245; 83, 81) Nestled between the Vieux Port and Plage des Catalans, this striking hotel fuses contemporary design with history. The modern four-storey, 100-room part has a public car park in the basement. Discounts online.

Hôtel Relax HOTEL €
(Map p152; ☎04 91 33 15 87; www.hotelrelax.fr; 4 rue Corneille; s/d/tr €50/65/75; Vieux Port) Overlooking Marseille's Opera House, this simple family-run 20-room hotel lacks good noise insulation and space, but given the location, cleanliness and extras like fridges and hairdryers, it's a bargain. No lift.

Eating

Vieux Port and surrounding pedestrian streets teem with cafe terraces, but choose carefully. For world cuisine, try cours Julien and nearby rue des Trois Mages; **Le Souk** (Map p152; ☎04 91 91 29 29; 100 quai du Port; menu lunch/dinner €13.50/20; lunch & dinner Tue-Sat, lunch Sun; Vieux Port) for Moroccan; and **Le Femina** (Map p152; ☎04 91 54 03 56; 1 rue de Musée; menus €16; lunch & dinner Tue-Sat; Noailles, Canebière Garibaldi) for Algerian. For pizza and couscous under €10, nose around Marché des Capucins (p160).

Le Panier's western fringe flows into the Joliette port area, where inexpensive lunching options like **Le Cafouch aux Saveurs** (Map p148; ☎04 91 31 67 14; www.lecafouch.com; 20 rue Mazenod; quiche menu €10; lunch Mon-Fri; Joliette) fill the surrounding streets and the London-docks-like complex **Les Docks.** (Map p148; 10 place de la Joliette; Joliette)

TOP CHOICE **Le Café des Épices** MODERN FRENCH €€
(Map p152; ☎04 91 91 22 69; www.cafedesepices.com; 4 rue du Lacydon; 3-course lunch/dinner menu €25/40; lunch Tue-Sat, dinner Thu-Fri; Vieux Port) One of Marseille's best young chefs, Arnaud de Grammont, infuses his cooking with a panoply of flavours…think squid ink spaghetti with sesame and perfectly cooked scallops, or tender roasted potatoes with hints of coriander and citrus, topped by the catch of the day. Presentation is impeccable, decor is playful, staff is friendly, and the place fills up reliably. Don't underestimate the desserts either. Saturday lunch is particularly family-friendly on the sunny terrace leading onto an olive-tree lined pedestrianised square. Reservations essential.

La Cantinetta ITALIAN €

(Map p148; ☎04 91 48 10 48; 24 cours Julien; mains €9-19; ⊙Tue-Sat; ⓂNotre Dame du Mont–Cours Julien) The top table at cours Julien serves perfectly al dente housemade pasta, paper-thin prosciutto, marinated vegetables, *bresaola* (air-dried beef) and risotto. Tables in the convivial dining room are cheek by jowl, and everyone seems to know each other. Or escape to the sun-dappled, tiled patio garden. If you're lucky, the gregarious chef-owner, Pierre-Antoine Denis, will regale you with the day's specials. Reservations essential.

Café Populaire NEO-BISTRO €

(Map p148; ☎04 91 02 53 96; 10 rue Paradis; mains €14-16; ⊙lunch & dinner Tue-Sat; ⓂEstrangin-Préfecture) Vintage tables and chairs, old books on the shelf and a fine collection of glass soda bottles all add to the retro air of this 1950s-styled jazz *comptoir* (counter). Plump for a stool at the zinc bar or lounge at a table with a view of the fabulous open kitchen, where simple daily specials like *gambas à la plancha* (fried prawns served on a hot plate) or beetroot and coriander salad are cooked up for a chic crowd.

La Part des Anges BISTRO €

(Map p152; 33 rue Sainte; mains €15; ⊙lunch Mon-Sat, dinner daily) No address buzzes with Marseille's hip, buoyant crowd more than this fabulous all-rounder wine bistro, named after the amount of alcohol that evaporates through a barrel during wine or whisky fermentation: the angels' share *(la part des anges)*. Tables can't be reserved: tell the bartenders you want to eat and take your pick of dozens of wines to try by the glass.

Le Comptoir Dugommier BISTRO €

(Map p152; ☎04 91 62 21 21; www.comptoirdugommier.fr; 14 bd Dugommier; mains €11-12, 3-course menu with drink €20; ⊙7.30am-3.30pm Mon-Wed, 7.30am-1am Thu & Fri; ⓂNoailles, Canebière Garibaldi) Tin molding, wooden floors and vintage signs make a homey escape from the busy street outside. The place gets packed for its downhome French fare, like *andouillette* sausage stewed with artichokes.

Les Pieds dans le Plat MODERN FRENCH €€

(Map p148; ☎04 91 48 74 15; 2 rue Pastoret; lunch/dinner menus €18/35; ⓂNotre Dame du Mont–Cours Julien) Slip into this intimate, cheery restaurant through a small door surrounded by graffiti. The chef incorporates French-Basque and Morrocan influences in his market fresh cuisine. Reservations essential.

Le Grain de Sel MODERN FRENCH €€

(Map p152; ☎04 91 54 47 30; 39 rue de la Paix Marcel Paul; lunch menu €16, mains €17-22; ⊙lunch Tue-Sat, dinner Fri & Sat; ⓂVieux Port) Locals pack this slender bistro for treats like gnocchi with shellfish and fennel or decadent desserts like

BOUILLABAISSE

Originally cooked by fishermen from the scraps of their catch, *bouillabaisse* is Marseille's signature dish. True *bouillabaisse* includes at least four different kinds of fish, and sometimes shellfish, which is why it's served to a minimum of two people. Don't trust tourist-traps that promise cheap *bouillabaisse*; the real McCoy costs about €55 per person and should be reserved 48 hours ahead, enough time to procure the correct ingredients. It's served in two parts: the broth (*soupe de poisson*), rich with tomato, saffron and fennel; and the cooked fish, deboned tableside and presented on a platter. On the side are croutons and *rouille* (a bread-thickened garlic-chilli pepper mayonnaise) and grated cheese, usually gruyère. Spread *rouille* on the crouton, top with cheese, and float it in the soup. Be prepared for a huge meal and tons of garlic.

The most reliable spots for real *bouillabaisse*:

» **L'Epuisette** (Map p148; ☎04 91 52 17 82; www.l-epuisette.com; Vallon des Auffes; €60; ⊙Tue-Sat; 83) The swankest (by far) has a Michelin star and knockout water-level views from an elegantly austere dining room.

» **Le Rhul** (☎04 91 52 01 77; www.lerhul.fr; 269 corniche Président John F Kennedy; €50; 83) This long-standing classic has atmosphere (however kitschy): a 1940s seaside hotel with Mediterranean views.

» **Restaurant Michel** (Chez Michel; Map p148; ☎04 91 52 30 63; http://restaurant-michel-13.fr; 6 rue des Catalans; €60; ⊙dinner nightly) Tops since 1946. Alas, the overly bright dining room lacks romance.

crème brûlée with rum, chestnuts and orange. Reservations essential.

La Casertane ITALIAN, DELICATESSEN €
(Map p152; ☎04 91 54 98 51; 71 rue Francis Davso; pastas €11-12; ⏱lunch Mon-Sat, deli 9am-3pm Mon, 9am-7.30pm Tue-Sat; Ⓜ Vieux Port) Lunch on a mind-boggling array of Italian deli meats and salads, or choose from daily specials, including homemade pastas. Convivial staff and the bustling flow of clientele make for lively meals.

La Passarelle PROVENÇAL €
(Map p152; ☎04 91 33 03 27; www.lapassarelle.com; 52 rue du Plan Fourmiguier; mains €17; ⏱lunch Tue-Sat, dinner Thu-Sat; Ⓜ Vieux Port) Retro tables and chairs sit beneath lime-green parasols on a terrace between veggie and strawberry beds. Everything growing in the walled garden goes into something on Philippe and Patricia's predominantly organic menu, and other products are strictly local.

Pizzaria Chez Étienne MARSEILLAIS €
(Map p152; 43 rue de Lorette; mains €12-15; ⏱Mon-Sat; Ⓜ Colbert) This old Marseillais haunt has the best pizza in town as well as succulent *pavé de boeuf* (beef steak) and scrumptious *supions frits* (pan-fried squid with garlic and parsley). As it's a convivial meeting-point for the neighbourhood, pop in to reserve (there's no phone). No credit cards.

Jardin des Vestiges ARMENIAN, MEDITERRANEAN €
(Map p152; 15 rue Reine Elizabeth; mains €7-13; ⏱9am-6pm Mon-Sat; Ⓜ Vieux Port) This solid budget choice draws on Armenian, Greek and Lebanese in dishes like kebabs, stuffed aubergine, moussaka and tabouleh. Ideal for to-go sandwiches (€4 to €6).

Les Arcenaulx TRADITIONAL FRENCH €€
(Map p152; ☎04 91 54 85 38; www.les-arcenaulx.com; 27 cours Honoré d'Estienne d'Orves; lunch menu €20, mains €17-28; ⏱lunch & dinner Mon-Sat; Ⓜ Vieux Port) Whet appetites with a meander around this cavernous former Louis XIV warehouse with antiquarian/contemporary bookshop and artist studios and galleries. Afterwards dine in grandiose style on sensational dishes evoking old Marseille or visit the neighbouring *salon de thé* (tearoom) for savoury tarts, cakes and ice cream.

Une Table au Sud GASTRONOMIC €€€
(Map p152; ☎04 91 90 63 53; www.unetableausud.com; 2 quai du Port; lunch/dinner menu €36/87; ⏱lunch & dinner Tue-Sat; Ⓜ Vieux Port) It was the *milkshake de bouilleabaisse* that clinched it for us. The inconspicuous entrance brings you to the warmly modern dining room where Chef Lionel Lévy continues to break the modern Mediterranean mould, utilising local ingredients in ever-inventive ways.

Le Mas CLASSIC FRENCH €€
(Map p152; ☎04 91 33 25 90; 4 rue Lulli; mains €22; ⏱11.30am-4pm & 7.30pm-6am Mon-Sat; Ⓜ Estrangin Préfecture) Celebrities' photos line the walls at Marseille's only late-night restaurant, ideal when you've lingered over cocktails. Portions are hearty, flavours rich.

Thai Baie THAI €
(Map p152; ☎04 91 54 15 23; www.thaibaie.com; 6 rue Corneille, Place de l'Opéra; mains €13; ⏱lunch & dinner Mon-Sat; Ⓜ Vieux Port) In the mood for Thai food? Thai Baie is the real deal.

Sylvain Depuichaffray CAFE, BAKERY €
(Map p152; ☎04 91 33 09 75; www.sylvaindepuichaffray.fr; 66 rue Grignan; quiche €3, salads €6; ⏱7am-4pm Mon, 7am-7pm Tue-Sat; Ⓜ Vieux Port) Perfect for a light lunch of quiche or salad followed by a sweet treat.

Pain de l'Opéra BAKERY €
(Map p152; 61 rue Francis Davso; ⏱7am-8pm; Ⓜ Vieux Port) Some of the best pastries near the Vieux Port; also has savoury foods.

Boulangerie Aixoise BAKERY €
(Map p152; ☎04 91 33 93 85; 45 rue Francis Davso; ⏱6.30am-8pm Mon-Sat; Ⓜ Vieux Port) Lines form out the door and onto the red-chaired terrace in front.

ALONG THE COAST

Péron CONTEMPORARY €€€
(Map p148; ☎04 91 52 15 22; www.restaurant-peron.com; 56 corniche Président John F Kennedy; mains €35; ⏱lunch Tue-Sun, dinner Tue-Sat; 🚌83) This designer place set out over the sea is one of the premier addresses in Marseille for a no-holds-barred gastronomic extravaganza. Stunning views unfold over the Med and on your plate, with highlights including lobster risotto and fresh fish.

Chez Aldo SEAFOOD, PIZZA €€
(☎04 91 73 31 55; 27 rue Audemar-Tibido, Port de la Madrague; pizza €10-15, mains €20; ⏱lunch & dinner Tue-Sat, lunch Sun; 🚌19) To blend in with the Marseillais families dining on the coast, share a thin-crust wood-fired pizza to start, followed by fish as a main.

Chez Jeannot MARSEILLAIS €€
(Map p148; ☎04 91 52 11 28; 129 rue du Vallon des Auffes; mains €12-25; ⊙lunch & dinner Tue-Sat, lunch Sun) With a magical setting overlooking the storybook Vallon des Auffes, this affable joint has fresh salads, pasta and shellfish, plus piping-hot pizzas. Fish is so-so.

Au Bord de l'Eau SEAFOOD, PIZZA €€
(☎04 91 72 68 04; www.auborddeleau.eu; 15 rue des Arapèdes, Port de la Madrague; pizza €14, mains €19-25; ⊙lunch Thu-Tue, dinner Thu-Mon, less in low season; ; 19) Chances are, you can thank the fishing boats moored below the sun-drenched terrace for catching the fish on your plate just hours before.

Drinking

La Caravelle BAR
(Map p152; 34 quai du Port; ⊙7am-2am; MVieux Port) Look up or miss this standout, upstairs hideaway, styled with rich wood and leather, zinc bar and yellowing murals. If it's sunny, snag a coveted spot on the portside terrace. Fridays hear live jazz 9pm to midnight. It also does a good breakfast.

Les Buvards WINE BAR
(Map p152; ☎04 91 90 69 98 ; 34 Grand Rue; ⊙10am-1am; MVieux Port, Sadi Carnot) Grand selection of natural wines and munchies.

Longchamp Palace CAFE
(☎04 91 50 76 13; 22 bd Longchamp; ⊙Mon-Sat Sep-Jul; Réformés Canebière) Artsy bustling bistro and lazy coffee shop.

Cup of Tea TEA SALON
(Map p152; ☎04 91 90 84 02; 1 rue Caisserie; ⊙8.30am-7pm Mon-Sat; Sadi-Carnot) Cute cafe with 55 tea varieties and Corsican beer.

Le Bar de la Marine BAR
(Map p152; ☎04 91 54 95 42; 15 quai de Rive Neuve; ⊙7am-1am; MVieux Port) Marcel Pagnol filmed the card-party scenes in *Marius* at this Marseille institution, which draws folks from every walk of life.

Au Petit Nice CAFE, BAR
(Map p148; ☎04 91 48 43 04; 28 place Jean Jaurès; ⊙10am-2am; MNotre Dame du Mont–Cours Julien) Cheap and cheerful: €2 beers in a happening courtyard cafe with a youthful crowd. (This is *not* the hotel of the same name.)

Dame Noir BAR
(Map p148; 30 place Notre-Dame du Mont; ⊙5pm-2am Tue-Sat; MNotre Dame du Mont-Cours Julien) Hip cats spill onto the sidewalk from this bar. DJs spin Thursday to Saturday. No sign; look for the red lights by the door.

GAY & LESBIAN VENUES

The website www.gaymapmarseille.com has coverage of Marseille's and Aix-en-Provence's gay life. Marseille's small scene is a moving target, and only coalesces at weekends. Gay nights happen at various bars, which are generally straight or mixed other nights.

Caffè Noir (Map p152; 3 rue Moustier; MVieux Port) and **Polikarpov** (Map p152; 24 cours Honoré d'Estienne d'Orves; MVieux Port) are reliable addresses for a young, mixed, hard-drinking crowd. Skip Cargo, Caffè Noir's adjoining sauna, for **XY Le Club** (Map p152; www.xy-leclub.com; 66 rue Montgrand; MEstrangin-Préfecture), which only gets busy Sunday afternoons; sometimes it throws mixed parties. Friendly door staff are an excellent resource for what's happening. **Le Trash** (www.trash-bar.com; 28 rue du Berceau; ⊙Fri-Wed; MBaille) is as its name suggests.

Entertainment

Cultural events are covered in *L'Hebdo* (€1.20), available around town, or www.marseillebynight.com and www.journalventilo.fr (all in French). Tickets are sold at *billetteries* (ticket counters) including **Espace Culture** (Map p152; ☎04 96 11 04 60; http://espaceculture.net; 42 La Canebière; MVieux Port), **Fnac** (Map p152; Centre Bourse shopping centre; MVieux Port) and the tourist office (p161). Alternative theatre and stuff for kids are held in a trio of venues on **Passage des Arts**.

Live Music & Nightclubs

Espace Julien LIVE MUSIC
(Map p148; ☎04 91 24 34 10; www.espace-julien.com; 39 cours Julien; MNotre Dame du Mont–Cours Julien) Rock, *opérock,* alternative theatre, reggae, hip-hop, Afro-groove and other cutting-edge entertainment all appear on the bill; the website lists gigs.

Pelle Mêle JAZZ
(Map p152; ☎04 91 54 85 26; 8 place aux Huiles; admission €2; ⊙6pm-1am, closed Sun Oct-Apr; MVieux Port) A thirty-something crowd jives to good jazz at this lively portside bistro.

L'Intermédiaire NIGHTCLUB
(Map p148; 63 place Jean Jaurès; ⏲7pm-2am; Ⓜ Notre Dame du Mont–Cours Julien) Grungy venue with graffitied walls is one of the best for live bands or DJs (usually techno or alternative).

La Noche NIGHTCLUB
(Map p152; www.lanocheclub.com; 40 rue Plan Fourmiguier; ⏲Fri & Sat; Ⓜ Vieux Port) Downstairs, bands play; upstairs, DJs spin everything from electro to salsa.

Le Trolleybus NIGHTCLUB
(Map p152; ☎04 91 54 30 45; 24 quai de Rive Neuve; ⏲Wed-Sat; Ⓜ Vieux Port) Shake it to techno, funk and indie at this tunnel-like club.

Au Son des Guitars NIGHTCLUB
(Map p152; 18 rue Corneille; ⏲Thu-Sun; Ⓜ Vieux Port) Popular with Corsican locals, this club has limited dancing, lots of drinking, and occasionally a Corsican singer. Look sharp.

Ma Demoiselle NIGHTCLUB
(Map p152; 8 rue Corneille; Ⓜ Vieux Port) DJs sometimes play this downstairs girly-girl club.

Theatre

Opéra Municipal de Marseille OPERA
(Map p152; ☎04 91 55 11 10; http://opera.marseille.fr; 2 rue Molière; Ⓜ Vieux Port) Season runs September to June.

AROMATIC MARKETS

» **Fresh Fish Market** (Map p152; quai des Belges; ⏲8am-1pm; Ⓜ Vieux Port) At the old port, circled by hungry seagulls.

» **Marché aux Puces** (av du Cap Pinède; ⏲9am-7pm Sun) Chickens killed to order and African carved animals are among the many colourful sights at this Moroccan-style market. Take bus 35 or 70 from Espace Infos RTM.

» **Marché des Capucins** (Map p152; place des Capucins; ⏲8am-7pm Mon-Sat; Ⓜ Noailles, 🚋Canebière Garibaldi) Fruit, veg, fish and dried goods.

» **Marché de la Joliette** (Map p148; place de la Joliette; ⏲8am-2pm Mon-Fri; Ⓜ Joliette) As above, flowers Monday.

» **Garlic Market** (Map p152; cours Belsunce; ⏲late Jun–late Jul; Ⓜ Vieux Port)

Théâtre National de Marseille THEATRE
(La Criée; Map p152; ☎04 91 54 70 54; www.theatre-lacriee.com; 30 quai de Rive Neuve) Dance and drama, sometimes in English.

Sports

Olympique de Marseille FOOTBALL
Marseille's cherished football team plays at **Stade Vélodrome** (3 bd Michelet; 1hr guided stadium tours in Jul & Aug €5; Ⓜ Rond-Point du Prado). Buy tickets at **OM's Boutique Officielle** (☎04 91 33 20 01; 44 La Canebière; ⏲10am-7pm Mon-Sat; 🚋Canebière Garibaldi, Ⓜ Noailles) for as little as €20.

Shopping

For chic shopping and large chains, stroll west of the Vieux Port to the 6th *arrondissement*, especially pedestrianised rue St-Ferréol. Major chains fill **Centre Bourse** (Map p152) and line rue de la République.

La Maison du Pastis ALCOHOL
(Map p152; 108 quai du Port) Sample over 90 varieties of the region's speciality, pastis (an aniseed-flavoured aperitif), or you could try absinthe.

Place aux Huiles FOOD
(Map p152; www.placeauxhuiles.com; 2 place Daviel; ⏲daily; 🚋Sadi Carnot) Stock up on olive oil, truffles and retro beer La Cagole de Marseille.

72% Pétanque COSMETICS
(Map p152; 10 rue du Petit Puits) Brilliantly coloured scented soaps, such as chocolate.

Librairie de la Bourse BOOKS
(Map p152; ☎04 91 33 63 06; 8 rue Paradis; Ⓜ Vieux Port) Maps and Lonely Planet guides.

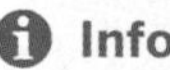

Information

Emergency

Hôpital de la Timone (☎04 91 38 60 00; 264 rue St-Pierre; Ⓜ La Timone) 1km southeast of place Jean Jaurès.

Police (☎04 88 77 58 00; 66-68 La Canebière; ⏲24hr; Ⓜ Estrangin-Préfecture)

Post

Main Post Office (1 place de l'Hôtel des Postes; Ⓜ Colbert) Currency exchange.

Tourist Information

Tourist Office (☎04 91 13 89 00; www.marseille-tourisme.com; 4 La Canebière; ⏲9am-7pm Mon-Sat, 10am-5pm Sun; Ⓜ Vieux Port)

Maison de la Région (61 La Canebière; ⊙11am-6pm Mon-Sat; Ⓜ Vieux Port)

Getting There & Away

Air

Aéroport Marseille-Provence (www.marseille.aeroport.fr) Also called Aéroport Marseille-Marignane; it is located 25km northwest of Marseille in Marignane.

Boat

Passenger-Ferry Terminal (www.marseille-port.fr; Ⓜ Joliette) Located 250m south of place de la Joliette.

Société Nationale Maritime Corse-Méditerranée (SNCM; p295).

Bus

Bus Station (www.lepilote.com; 3 rue Honnorat; Ⓜ Gare St-Charles SNCF) At the back of the train station. Buy tickets here or from the driver. Services to some destinations, including Cassis, use the **stop on place Castellane**, south of the centre.

Eurolines (www.eurolines.com; 3 allées Léon Gambetta) International services.

Car

Avis (☎08 20 61 16 36; www.avis.com)

Europcar (p297)

Train

Gare St-Charles (⊙information 9am-8pm Mon-Sat, tickets 5.15am-10pm daily; Ⓜ Gare St-Charles SNCF) Regular and TGV trains to all over France. In town, buy tickets at the **SNCF Boutique** inside Centre Bourse shopping centre. **Left-luggage office** (from €3.50; ⊙7.30am-10pm) next to platform A.

Getting Around

To/From the Airport

Gare Vitrolles Aéroport Marseille Provence, right by the airport, lies on the Paris, Lyon and Marseille line and has connections throughout the region (Arles, Nîmes, Avignon, Cavaillon). Catch a five-minute shuttle between the airport (platform 2, departs 10 minutes before each train) and the station. Train tickets are sold at the airport.

Shuttle Buses (☎Marseille 04 91 50 59 34, airport 04 42 14 31 27; www.lepilote.com) Link the airport and central train station.

Bicycle

Le Vélo (www.levelo-mpm.fr) Pick up/drop off a bike from 100-plus stations across the city. First 30 minutes are free, €1 for the next 30, and then €1 per hour thereafter. Credit card required to register; instructions in French. Stations dot corniche Président John F Kennedy to Pointe Rouge and the centre.

Boat

Boats run across the Vieux Port (p144), to the offshore islands (p151) and to Pointe Rouge (p151). Tours (p154) go to the *calanques*.

Car

Marseille is a horror for drivers. Central car parks include **Parking Bourse** (rue Reine Elisabeth; Vieux Port) and **Parking de Gaulle** (22 place du Général de Gaulle; Vieux Port) off La Canebière. Expect to pay €2 per hour (€15 per day). Transpass holders can use cheaper **Relais** (www.rtm.fr) parking lots at the city's edge (for less than 24 hour only).

Public Tranport

Marseille has two metro lines (Métro 1 and Métro 2), two tram lines (yellow and green) and an extensive bus network, run by the Régie des Transports Marseillais (RTM). Bus, metro or tram tickets (€1.50) can be used on all public transportation for one hour after they've been time-stamped. A Transpass for one/three/seven days costs €5/10.50/12.

Bus services stop around 9.30pm, when night buses operate until 12.30am. Most start in front of the **Espace Infos RTM** (☎04 91 91 92 10; www.rtm.fr; 6 rue des Fabres; ⊙8.30am-6pm Mon-Fri, 9am-12.30pm & 2-5.30pm Sat; Ⓜ Vieux Port), where you can obtain information, a super transport map and tickets. **Night shuttles** (☎06 27 06 71 23; www.navettelive.blogspot.com; annual membership €15, rides free; ⊙11.45pm-4.30am) operate for people 18 to 30 years old.

The Metro runs from 5am to 10.30pm Monday to Thursday, and until 12.30am Friday to Sunday. Trams run 5am to 1am daily.

Taxi

Taxi Radio Marseille (☎04 91 02 20 20)

Taxis France (☎04 91 49 91 00)

AROUND MARSEILLE

Butting up against Marseille's built-up environs are spectacular stretches of coast hiding crystalline coves, charming towns and celebrated vineyards.

Les Calanques

Marseille abuts the wild and spectacular Calanques, a 20km stretch of high, rocky promontories, rising from brilliant turquoise Mediterranean waters. The sheer cliffs are occasionally interrupted by small idyllic beaches, some impossible to reach without a kayak. The Marseillais cherish the

WORTH A TRIP

MASSIF DE LA STE-BAUME

From Marseille head towards Gémenos, then take eastbound D2 towards 'Vallée St-Pons & La Ste-Baume'. The going gets verdantly dramatic, the road snaking uphill through the scrubby terrain of the Parc Départemental de St-Pons. After 8km, the sea pops on the horizon, then the road climbs to Col de l'Espigoulier (728m), a mountain pass with coastline views. The winding descent is dominated by the Massif de la Ste-Baume.

At the D45a/D2 junction, continue on the D2 to La Ste-Baume (8km), from where a 40-minute forest trail leads to the Grotte de Ste-Madeleine (950m), a mountain cave where Mary Magdalene is said to have spent the last years of her life. Its entrance offers a breathtaking panorama of Montagne Ste-Victoire, Mont Ventoux and the Alps.

Finally, take the D80 northeast via Nans-les-Pins then turn right on the N560 (about 20km all up) to reach the pastel-hued town of St-Maximin La Ste-Baume. Its fabulous Gothic Ste-Madeleine Basilica was built in 1295 as the home of what are claimed to be the relics of Mary Magdalene, discovered in a crypt on the site around 1279. Afterwards lunch in the adjacent convent, now the sumptuous **Hôtel Le Couvent Royal** (☎04 94 86 55 66; www.hotelfp-saintmaximin.com; menu €32).

Calanques, and come to soak up sun or take a long hike. The promontories have been protected since 1975 and shelter an extraordinary wealth of flora and fauna: 900 plant species, Bonelli's eagle, Europe's largest lizard (60cm Eyed Lizard) and longest snake (2m Montpellier snake).

From October to June the best way to see the Calanques (including the 500 sq km of the rugged inland Massif des Calanques) is to hike the many maquis-lined trails. During summer, trails close due to fire danger: take a boat tour (p154), though they don't stop to let you swim; or try negotiating with a fisherman to take you from the Vieux Port (p144). Otherwise, drive or take public transport.

Marseille's tourist office leads guided walks (no kids under eight) and has information about trail closures.

Sea kayaking from Marseille or Cassis is wondrous. **Raskas Kayak** (www.raskas-kayak.com) organises sea-kayaking tours and tourist offices have details of many more guides.

Sights

Calanque de Sormiou INLET

The largest *calanque* hit headlines in 1991 when diver Henri Cosquer from Cassis swam through a 150m-long passage 36m underwater into a cave to find its interior adorned with prehistoric wall-paintings from around 20,000 BC. Now named **Grotte Cosquer**, the cave is a protected historical monument and closed to the public. Many more are believed to exist.

Two seasonal restaurants serve lunch with fabulous views, and require reservations. **Le Château** (☎04 91 25 08 69; mains €18-24; ⊙Apr–mid-Oct) has the best food, **Le Lunch** (☎04 91 25 05 37, 04 91 25 05 39; http://wp.resto.fr/lelunch; mains €16-28; ⊙Apr–mid-Oct) the better view.

By bus take the 23 from Marseilles' Rond-Point du Prado metro stop to La Cayolle stop, from where it is a 3km walk. (Note: Diners with reservations are allowed to drive through; otherwise, the road's open to cars weekdays only, September to June.)

Calanque de Morgiou INLET

The scrubby windswept Cap Morgiou separates Sormiou from Morgiou. Nestled on the eastern side of the cape, this *calanque* has a pretty little port bobbing with fishing boats, and plenty of sheer rock-faces from which climbers dangle. An evening spent at its one restaurant, the delightful **Nautic Bar** (☎04 91 40 06 37; mains €20-25; ⊙lunch & dinner Apr-Oct) is dreamy. No credit cards.

Morgiou beach is a one-hour walk from the car park. The hair-raisingly steep, narrow road (3.5km) is open to motorists Monday to Friday from September to June (daily year-round with a Nautic Bar reservation).

En-Vau, Port-Pin & Port-Miou INLETS

Continuing east along the stone-sculptured coast brings you to **Calanque d'En-Vau**, with emerald waters encased by cliffs and a pebbly beach. Its entrance is guarded by the **Doigt de Dieu** (God's Finger), a giant rock pinnacle. A *steep* three-hour marked trail leads from the car park (closed July to mid-September) on the Col de la Gardiole to En-Vau. The slippery and sheer descents into En-Vau are for the truly hardcore only.

Approaching from the east, it is a solid 1½-hour walk on the GR98 from **Calanque de Port-Miou**, immediately west of Cassis. En route you pass the neighbouring **Calanque de Port-Pin**, a 30-minute walk from Port-Miou. Cassis' tourist office (p164) distributes free maps of the walking trails.

Cassis

POP 7867

Nestled at the foot of a dramatic rocky outcrop crowned by a 14th-century château (now a hotel open only to guests), this little fishing port is all charm, hence the enormous crowds that pile into its **Vieux Port**, play on its shingle beaches, visit its terraced vineyards and sip fabled white Cassis wine.

The town's name comes from the Roman *Carsicis Portus*, meaning 'crowned port', so christened for the rock **Couronne de Charlemagne** (Crown of Charlemagne), which is visible from far out at sea.

Activities

Exploring Les Calanques OUTDOORS

Boats (☎04 42 01 90 83; www.cassis-calanques.com; sq Gilbert Savon) travel to Les Calanques year-round from Quai St-Pierre; buy tickets at the portside kiosk. A 45-minute trip to three *calanques* (Port-Miou, Port-Pin and En-Vau) costs €15/9 per adult/child; a 65-minute trip covering these plus Oule and Devenson is €18/12. No credit cards.

The tourist office (p164) has information on rock climbing, deep-sea diving, sea kayaking and walking (including a one-hour trail to Port-Pin).

Wine Tasting WINERIES

Twelve estates producing the Cassis appellation wines ribbon the hillsides; the tourist office (p164) has a list of suggested itineraries and estates you can visit to taste and buy; most require advance reservation. On the first Sunday in September, the **Ban des Vendanges** celebrates the grape harvest with a Mass, blessing of the vines, traditional dancing, a joyous street procession and tasting alfresco.

Sleeping

Le Clos des Arômes HOTEL €

(☎04 42 01 71 84; www.le-clos-des-aromes.com; 10 rue Abbé Paul Mouton; s/d from €49/69; ❄📶) A short climb uphill from the portside madness, this charming garden hotel is a bit worn, but spotless. Dining at dusk in the courtyard is a peaceful affair. No lift.

Cassis Hostel HOSTEL €

(☎06 85 65 10 92, 09 54 37 99 82; www.cassishostel.com; 4 avenue du Picouveau, Les Heures Claires; dorm/d incl breakfast €29/80; 📶🏊) On the hill above town, this place is simple but has a kitchen, beautiful terrace and pool.

Eating & Drinking

Fleurs de Thym TRADITIONAL FRENCH €€

(☎04 42 01 23 03; www.fleursdethym.com; 5 rue Lamartine; 3-course menu €29; ⊙lunch & dinner Tue-Sat) Provençal specialties with an emphasis on seafood. The tiny, quaint dining room spills onto a flower-filled terrace.

La Poissonnerie SEAFOOD €

(☎04 42 01 71 56; 5 quai JJ Barthélemy; menu du pêcheur €19.90; ⊙lunch Tue-Sun, dinner Tue-Sat Feb-Dec) Run by two brothers (one fishes, one cooks) this locals' favorite offers everything from a humble plate of sardines with a glass of white (€13.90), grilled fish or a *bouillabaisse* (€38.90). No credit cards.

Au Paysan de Cassis MARKET

(☎04 42 01 89 59; 5 rue Séverin) Build a portside picnic at this upmarket greengrocers.

Market MARKET

(place Baragnon; ⊙Wed & Fri) A good option.

Le Chai Cassidain WINE BAR

(☎04 42 01 99 80; 7 rue Séverin Icard; ⊙closed Mon Nov-Mar) Local wines by the glass and often free tastings.

Information

Tourist Office (☎08 92 25 98 92; www.ot-cassis.com; quai des Moulins; ⊙9am-6.30pm

CLIFFHANGERS

Europe's highest maritime cliff, the hollow limestone **Cap Canaille** (399m) towers above the southeastern side of **Baie de Cassis** (Cassis Bay). From the top, captivating views unfold across Cassis and **Mont Puget** (564m), the highest peak in the Massif des Calanques.

Offering equally heart-stopping panoramas, the **Route des Crêtes** (Road of Crests, D141; closed during high winds) wiggles 16km along the clifftops from Cassis to La Ciotat.

AIX-CELLENT

The **Aix City Pass** (€15), valid five days, includes a guided walking tour, admission to the Atelier Paul Cézanne, Jas de Bouffan and Musée Granet and a trip on the mini-tram. The **Cézanne Pass** (€12) covers his three main sights. Buy the passes at the tourist office, or the two Cézanne sights.

Tue-Sat, 9.30-12.30 & 3-6pm Sun, shorter hours low season)

Getting There & Away

Cassis is on the Bandol-Marseille (five daily) and La Ciotat-Aix-en-Provence (three to 12 daily) bus routes; schedules at www.lepilote.com. Buses stop at rond-point du Pressoir, a five-minute walk along av du Professeur René Leriche and rue de l'Arène to the port.

Cassis train station (av de la Gare), 3.5km east of the centre, is on the Marseille-Hyères line. Buses 2, 3 and 4 run to the town centre.

Côte Bleue

The Côte Bleue clambers from Marseille's western edge, past gritty fishing villages, to Cap Couronne. Marine-life-rich waters around the sandy cape are protected by the **Parc Régional Marin de la Côte Bleue**.

The Blue Coast has its own precious trove of **calanques**, which compete with those everyone knows between Marseille and Cassis. At **Calanque de Niolon**, 12km west of L'Estaque, rocky spurs ensnare the perilously perched village of Niolon, which has a handful of cafes and the lovely **Auberge du Mérou** (☎04 91 46 98 69; www.aubergedumerou.fr; 3-course menu €29), with a sea-view terrace.

From the tiny waterside Port du Redonne, a single-track road climbs over to Les Figuières (1km), the Petit Méjean (1.7km) and the Grand Méjean (1.8km). In Grand Méjean you can pick up a stunning 2.1km-long coastal trail to Calanque de l'Érevine.

L'Estaque (www.estaque.com) lured artists from the impressionist, Fauvist and cubist movements. A trail follows in the footsteps of Renoir, Cézanne, Dufy and Braque around the port and shabby old town. On the water's edge buy *chichi frégi* (sugar-coated doughnuts) and *panisses* (chickpea-flour cakes) to munch.

PAYS D'AIX

Picturesque Pays d'Aix (Aix Country), within which oh-so-elegant Aix-en-Provence is ensconced, sits 25km or so north of Marseille.

Aix-en-Provence

POP 141,895

A pocket of left-bank Parisian chic deep in Provence, Aix (pronounced like the letter X) is all class: its leafy boulevards and public squares are lined with 17th- and 18th-century mansions, punctuated by gurgling moss-covered fountains. Haughty stone lions guard its grandest avenue, cafe-laced cours Mirabeau, where fashionable Aixois pose on polished pavement terraces sipping overpriced espresso.

Aix marks the spot where Roman forces enslaved the inhabitants of the Ligurian Celtic stronghold of Entremont, 3km north. In 123 BC the military camp was named Aquae Sextiae (Waters of Sextius) for the thermal springs that still flow today. In the 12th century the counts of Provence proclaimed Aix their capital, which it remained until the Revolution when it was supplanted by Marseille. The city became a centre of culture under arts patron King René (1409–80): painter Paul Cézanne and novelist Émile Zola are its most famous sons.

Aix is a prestigious student hub and is pricier than other Provençal towns.

Sights & Activities

Art, culture and architecture abound in Aix. A stroller's paradise, the highlight is the mostly pedestrian old city, **Vieil Aix**. South of cours Mirabeau, **Quartier Mazarin** was laid out in the 17th century, and is home to some of Aix' finest buildings. **Place des Quatre Dauphins**, with its fish-spouting fountain (1667), is particularly enchanting. Further south still is the peaceful **Parc Jourdan**, home to the town's **Boulodrome Municipal**, where locals gather beneath plane trees to play *pétanque*.

Cours Mirabeau HISTORIC QUARTER

No avenue better epitomises Provence's most graceful city than fountain-studded cours Mirabeau, sprinkled with elegant Renaissance *hôtels particuliers* and crowned with a summertime roof of leafy plane trees. Named after the revolutionary hero Comte de Mirabeau, it was laid out in the 1640s. Cézanne and Zola famously hung out at

Les Deux Garçons (53 cours Mirabeau; 7am-2am), one of a clutch of pavement cafes. It buzzes with people-watchers despite its elevated prices and mediocre food.

Among the most impressive *hôtels particuliers* is **Hôtel d'Espargnet** (1647) at No 38, now home to the university's economics department. Photography and contemporary art gets an airing inside Hôtel de Castillon, now the **Galerie d'Art du Conseil Général des Bouches du Rhône** (04 13 31 50 70; 21bis cours Mirabeau; admission free; 9.30am-1pm & 2-6pm Mon-Sat).

Musée Granet ART MUSEUM
(www.museegranet-aixenprovence.fr; place St-Jean de Malte; adult/child €4/free; 11am-7pm Tue-Sun) Housed in a 17th-century priory of the Knights of Malta, this exceptional museum is named after the Provençal painter François Marius Granet (1775–1849), who donated a large number of works. Its collections include 16th- to 20th-century Italian, Flemish and French works. Modern art reads like a who's-who: Picasso, Léger, Matisse, Monet, Klee, Van Gogh and Giacometti, among others including the museum's pride and joy, nine Cézanne works. Tickets sold to one hour before closing.

Cathédrale St-Sauveur CHURCH
(rue de la Roque; 8am-noon & 2-6pm) Built between 1285 and 1350 in a potpourri of styles, this cathedral includes a Romanesque 12th-century nave in its southern aisle; chapels from the 14th and 15th centuries; and a 5th-century sarcophagus in the apse. More recent additions include the 18th-century gilt Baroque organ. Acoustics make Gregorian chants (4.30pm Sunday) unforgettable. There are cloister tours.

Fondation Victor Vasarely GALLERY
(www.fondationvasarely.fr; 1 av Marcel Pagnol; adult/child €9/4; 10am-1pm & 2-6pm Tue-Sun; 4 or 6 stop Vasarely) This thrilling gallery and national historical monument, 4km west of the city, was designed by Hungarian optical art innovator Victor Vasarely (1906–1907). Though in need of repairs, the building is a masterpiece: 16 interconnecting six-walled galleries, purpose-built to display and reflect the patterning of the artist's 44 acid-trip-ready, floor-to-ceiling geometric artworks.

CÉZANNE SIGHTS

The life of local lad Paul Cézanne (1839–1906) is treasured in Aix. To see where he ate, drank, studied and painted, follow the **Circuit de Cézanne** (Cézanne Trail), marked by footpath-embedded bronze plaques. The informative English-language guide to the plaques, *Cézanne's Footsteps*, is free at the tourist office (p170). A mobile app, City of Cézanne in Aix-en-Provence (€2), is available online.

Cézanne's last studio, **Atelier Paul Cézanne** (www.atelier-cezanne.com; 9 av Paul Cézanne; adult/child €5.50/2; 10am-noon & 2-6pm, closed Sun winter), 1.5km north of the tourist office on a hilltop, was painstakingly preserved (and recreated: not all the tools and still-life models strewn around the single room were his) as it was at the time of his death. Though the studio is inspiring, none of his works hang here. Take bus 1 or 20 to the Atelier Cézanne stop, or walk 1.5km from the centre. A 10-minute walk uphill from the bus stop is the **Terrain des Peintres** (opposite 62 av Paul Cézanne), a terraced garden perfect for a picnic, from where Cézanne, among others, painted the Montagne Ste-Victoire.

Visits to the other two sights must be reserved in advance at the tourist office, which provides transport information. In 1859 Cézanne's father bought **Le Jas de Bouffan** (04 42 16 10 91; adult/child €5.50/2; guided tours 10.30am-5.30pm daily summer, less frequent other times; 6 stop Corsy), a country manor west of Aix centre where Cézanne painted furiously: 36 oils and 17 watercolours in the decades that followed depicting the house, farm and chestnut alley. To get here, take bus 6 from La Rotonde (av Victor Hugo) to the Corsy stop; it's a 20-minute walk from town.

In 1895 Cézanne rented a cabin at **Les Carrières de Bibemus** (Bibémus Quarries; 04 42 16 10 91; adult/child €6.60/3.10; tours 9.45am daily Jun-Sep, 10.30am & 5pm Mon, Wed, Fri & Sun Apr, May & Oct, 3pm Wed & Sat Jan-Mar), on the edge of town, where he painted prolifically and where he did most of his Montagne Ste-Victoire paintings. Atmospheric one-hour tours of the ochre quarry take visitors on foot through the dramatic burnt-orange rocks Cézanne captured so vividly.

Aix-en-Provence

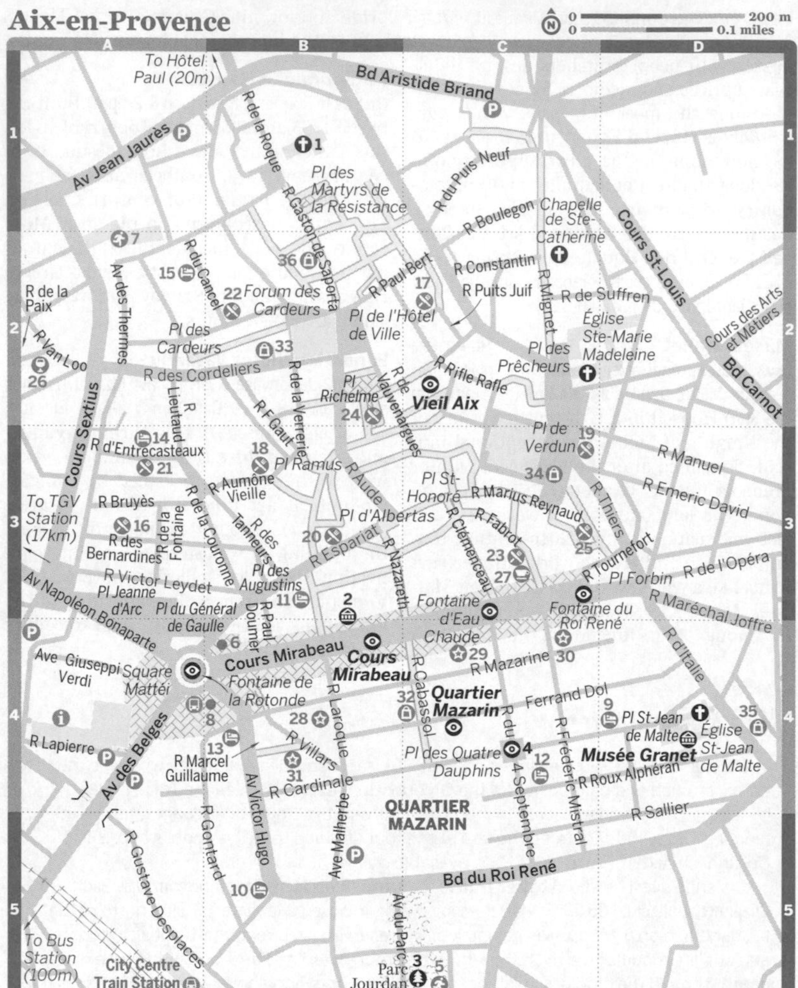

Thermes Sextius SPRINGS

(☎04 42 23 81 82; www.thermes-sextius.com; 55 av des Thermes; day pass €45) These modern thermal spas are on the site of Roman Aquae Sextiae's springs, whose excavated remains are displayed beneath glass in the lobby.

Tours

Tourist Office Tours WALKING TOUR

The tourist office has DIY walking itineraries and runs a packed schedule of guided walking (€8) or bus tours (from €28) in English, such as Retracing Cézanne's Steps. Bus tours include Luberon and Alpilles.

Mini-Tram TRAM TOUR

(☎06 11 54 27 73; www.cpts.fr; €6) Departs place du Général de Gaulle and winds through the Quartier Mazarin, along cours Mirabeau, and around Vieil Aix. Multilingual.

Festivals & Events

Festival d'Aix-en-Provence PERFORMING ARTS

(☎04 34 08 02 17; www.festival-aix.com; ⏲Jul) Month-long festival of classical music, opera, ballet and buskers; July.

Aix-en-Provence

Top Sights

Cours Mirabeau ... B4
Musée Granet ... D4
Quartier Mazarin ... C4
Vieil Aix ... C2

Sights

1 Cathédrale St-Sauveur ... B1
2 Galérie d'Art du Conseil Général des Bouches du Rhône ... B3
3 Parc Jourdan ... C5
4 Place des Quatre Dauphins ... C4

Activities, Courses & Tours

5 Boulodrome Municipal ... C5
6 Mini-Tram ... B4
7 Thermes Sextius ... A2
8 Tourist Office Tours ... B4

Sleeping

9 Hôtel Cardinal ... D4
10 Hôtel Cézanne ... B5
11 Hôtel des Augustins ... B3
12 Hôtel les Quatre Dauphins ... C4
13 Hôtel Saint-Christophe ... B4
14 Le Manoir ... A3
15 L'Épicerie ... A2

Eating

16 Charlotte ... A3
17 Chez Féraud ... C2
18 Jacquou Le Croquant ... B3
19 La Mado ... C3
20 Le Formal ... B3
21 Le Petit Verdot ... A3
22 Le Poivre d'Ane ... B2
23 Pizza Capri ... C3
24 Produce Market ... B2
25 Restaurant Pierre Reboul ... C3

Drinking

26 Le Med Boy ... A2
27 Les Deux Garçons ... C3

Entertainment

28 Ciné Mazarin ... B4
29 Cinéma Renoir ... C4
30 Le Mistral ... C4
31 Le Cézanne ... B4

Shopping

32 Book in Bar ... C4
33 Cave du Félibrige ... B2
34 Flea Market ... C3
35 Place aux Huiles ... D4
36 Roy René ... B2

Sleeping

Hôtel des Augustins HOTEL €€

(04 42 27 28 59; www.hotel-augustins.com; 3 rue de la Masse; r €99-250;) A heartbeat from the hub of Aixois life, this former 15th-century convent with a stained-glass foyer, has volumes of history: for example, Martin Luther stayed here after his excommunication from Rome. Decorated with hand-painted furniture, the largest, most luxurious abodes have Jacuzzis; and two have private terraces beneath the filigreed bell tower.

L'Épicerie B&B €€

(06 08 85 38 68; www.unechambreenville.eu; 12 rue du Cancel; s €80-120, d €100-130;) This intimate B&B is the fabulous creation of born-and-bred Aixois lad, Luc. His breakfast room and *salon de thé* re-creates a 1950s grocery store, and the flowery garden out back is perfect for evening dining (book ahead). Morning meals are veritable feasts. Two rooms accommodate families of four.

Hôtel les Quatre Dauphins BOUTIQUE HOTEL €

(04 42 38 16 39; www.lesquatredauphins.fr; 54 rue Roux Alphéran; s €55-60, d €70-85;) This sweet 13-room hotel, a former private mansion, was redone in 2010 and is fresh and clean, with excellent new bathrooms. The tall terracotta-tiled staircase (no lift) leads to four attic rooms, with sloped beamed ceilings. Wi-fi €5 per 24 hours.

Le Manoir HOTEL €€

(04 42 26 27 20; www.hotelmanoir.com; 8 rue d'Entrecasteux; d €70-92, tr €98-106, q €124; Feb-Dec;) Atmospherically set in a 14th-century cloister, the manor sits in a quiet wedge of the old town. Simple, spotless rooms are spacious. Friendly staff, free parking and breakfasting alfresco in the vaulted cloister round out its offerings.

Hôtel Cézanne BOUTIQUE HOTEL €€€

(04 42 91 11 11; http://cezanne.hotelaix.com; 40 av Victor Hugo; d €179-249;) Aix's hippest hotel is a study in clean lines, with sharp-edged built-in desks and lots of light.

We actually prefer the less expensive 'luxe' rooms, which have the same top-end linens, but more charm. Unfortunately, staff can be surly. Reserve ahead for free parking.

Hôtel Paul HOTEL €
(04 42 23 23 89; hotel.paul@wanadoo.fr; 10 av Pasteur; s/d/tr from €51/52/74;) On the edge of Vieil Aix, this bright, cheery bargain has a sweet garden and a TV lounge. Fans in summer. Wi-fi €1.50 per 30 minutes. Free motorcycle and bike parking. No credit cards.

Hôtel Saint-Christophe HOTEL €€
(04 42 26 01 24; www.hotel-saintchristophe.com; 2 av Victor Hugo; s/d/tr/ste from €84/92/132/174;) The Saint-Christophe is a proper hotel, with a big lobby and helpful staff. Rooms nod to art deco in their styling, and have the standard mid-budget amenities, including good bathrooms; some have terraces, some can sleep four. Parking (€12) by reservation.

Hôtel Cardinal HOTEL €
(04 42 38 32 30; www.hotel-cardinal-aix.com; 24 rue Cardinale; s/d €60/70) Slightly rumpled rooms are quaintly furnished with antiques and tasselled curtains. Six gigantic suites in the annexe up the street, each with a kitchenette and dining room, are ideal for longer stays. Wi-fi €5 per 24 hours.

Auberge de Jeunesse du Jas de Bouffan HOSTEL €
(04 42 20 15 99; www.auberge-jeunesse-aix.fr; 3 av Marcel Pagnol; dm incl breakfast & sheets €19-22; reception 7am-2.30pm & 4.30pm-midnight Feb–mid-Dec) Bare bones dorms are aided by tennis, laundry, bike shed and summer barbecues. Sits 2km west of the centre with the motorway just below.

Camping Arc-en-Ciel CAMPGROUND €
(04 42 26 14 28; www.campingarcenciel.com; rte de Nice; adult/site €6.65/6.20; Apr-Sep; 3 stop Les Trois Sautets) Tranquil wooded hills out back, but a busy motorway in front. It's 2km southeast of town, at Pont des Trois Sautets. No credit cards.

> **SWEET TREAT**
>
> Aix's sweetest treat since King René's wedding banquet in 1473 is the marzipan-like local speciality, *calisson d'Aix*, a small, diamond-shaped, chewy delicacy made on a wafer base with ground almonds and fruit syrup, glazed with icing sugar. Traditional *calissonniers* still make them, including **Roy René** (www.calisson.com; 13 rue Gaston de Saporta) which has a tiny museum. To watch the process first-hand, visit its factory **Calissons du Roy René** (04 42 39 29 90; tours €1; 10am Tue & Thu by appointment), on the city's fringe.

Eating

Aix excels at Provençal cuisine and terraces spill across backstreet squares. Reservations are essential in the restaurants listed below. Eateries on cours Mirabeau are overpriced.

TOP CHOICE **Restaurant Pierre Reboul** GASTRONOMIC €€€
(04 42 20 58 26; www.restaurant-pierre-reboul.com; 11 Petite Rue St-Jean; 3-/7-/12-course menus €42/85/142; lunch Tue-Sat, dinner Wed-Sat, closed late Aug) Aix' newest culinary star invents playful, gorgeous creations...homages to eating. With a minimalist sensibility, in both the relaxed dining room and on the exquisitely-presented plates, Reboul crafts new juxtapositions using fresh, but timeless ingredients.

Think perfectly seared duck with a savoury, unexpectedly Asian-influenced broth, sea foam and tender pasta. The lunch special (€50), includes mineral water, coffee and a glass of perfectly paired wine.

Le Petit Verdot FRENCH €€
(04 42 27 30 12; www.lepetitverdot.fr; 7 rue d'Entrecasteaux; mains €15-25; dinner Mon-Sat, lunch Sat) Delicious menus are designed around what's in season and paired with excellent wines. Meats are often braised all day, vegetables are tender, stewed in delicious broths. Save room for an incandescent dessert. Lively dining occurs around tabletops made of wine crates (expect to talk to your neighbor), and the gregarious owner speaks multiple languages.

Charlotte BISTRO €
(04 42 26 77 56; 32 rue des Bernardines; 2-/3-course menus €15.50/19; lunch & dinner Tue-Sat;) It's all very cosy at Charlotte, where everyone knows everyone. French classics like veal escalope and beef steak fill the handwritten menu, and there are always a couple of imaginative *plats du jour*. In summer everything moves into the garden.

La Mado MODERN FRENCH €€
(Chez Madeleine; ☎04 42 38 28 02; www.lamado-aix.com; 4 place des Prêcheurs; lunch/dinner menus €18/32; ⏰7am-2am daily) This smart daytime cafe and modern restaurant is an unbeatable spot for coffee and fashionable-people watching, or a delicious, relaxed meal. It's been around for years, so the old guard dine while the hipsters shine. The buzzing terrace spills out onto the busy plaza. It also offers oysters and sushi.

Le Formal MODERN FRENCH €€
(☎04 42 27 08 31; www.restaurant-leformal.fr; 32 rue Espariat; lunch menu €21.50, 3-/7-course dinner menus €38/47; ⏰lunch Tue-Fri, dinner Tue-Sat) Chef Jean-Luc Le Formal is making a name for himself in France's foodie circles with his first-class establishment. Impeccably mannered staff serve delicious treats in the vaulted-cellar dining rooms.

Jacquou Le Croquant BISTRO €
(☎04 42 27 37 19; 2 rue de l'Aumône Vielle; 2-course crêpe menu €16, mains from €10; ⏰lunch & dinner daily; 📋) Slide into this tiny, low-key joint for home-cooked, wholesome basics.

Chez Féraud PROVENÇAL €€
(☎04 42 63 07 27; 8 rue Puits Juif; lunch/3-course menus €22/33; ⏰lunch & dinner Tue-Sat Sep-Jul) This elegant, family-run restaurant tucked down a side street is as pretty as a French postcard. The menu features Provençal classics: *soupe au pistou, aubergine en gratin*, red peppers stuffed with *brandade de morue*.

Le Poivre d'Ane CONTEMPORARY €€
(☎04 42 21 32 66; www.restaurantlepoivredane.com; 40 place des Cardeurs; menus €28-45; ⏰dinner Thu-Tue) Locals flock here for affordable, creative, contemporary cuisine in a stylish setting. In summer its tables spill across one of Aix's loveliest pedestrian squares.

Pizza Capri PIZZA €
(☎04 42 38 55 43; 1 rue Fabrot; pizza slice €2.50, pie €8-12.50; ⏰lunch & dinner daily) An Aix institution for piping hot, excellent takeaway pizza. Have them bake yours fresh.

Drinking & Entertainment

The scene is fun, but fickle. *Le Mois à Aix* (free from the tourist office) and listings on www.marseillebynight.com (in French) cover Aix.

For nightlife, hit **rue de la Verrerie** and **place Richelme**. Open-air cafes crowd the city's squares, especially place des Cardeurs, place de Verdun and place de l'Hôtel de Ville.

Aix's student population ensures great cinema (www.lescinemasaixois.com): **Ciné Mazarin** (6 rue Laroque; adult/student €7.50/€6.50), **Cinéma Renoir** (☎08 92 68 72 70; 24 cours Mirabeau; adult/student €7.50/€6.50), and **Le Cézanne** (☎08 92 68 72 70; www.lecezanne.com; 1 rue Marcel Guillaume; adult/student €8.50/€6.70).

Le Med Boy GAY BAR
(www.med-boy.com; 6 rue de la Paix; ⏰9.30pm-2am) Aix's only gay bar packs in stand-and-drink twenty-somethings.

Le Mistral NIGHTCLUB
(3 rue Frédéric Mistral; ⏰midnight-6am Tue-Sat) If anyone's awake past midnight, chances are they'll wind up at this happening basement club, with three bars and a dance floor. DJs spin house, R&B, techno and rap.

Hot Brass LIVE MUSIC
(☎04 42 21 05 57; www.hotbrassaix.com; chemin d'Eguilles) Jazz and other live acts, 6km northwest of town.

Grand Théâtre de Provence PERFORMING ARTS
(☎04 42 91 69 70; www.legrandtheatre.net; 380 av Max Juvénal) State-of-the-art theatre presenting music and opera.

Le Ballet Preljocaj PERFORMING ARTS
(☎04 42 93 48 00; www.preljocaj.org; 530 av Mozart) Performs at the 650-seat Pavillon Noir.

Shopping

Aix's most chic shops cluster along pedestrian rue Marius Reynaud and cours Mirabeau. Allées de Provence has chain stores.

DON'T MISS

MARKETS

» The daily **food market** (place Richelme) has marinated olives, goats' cheese, honey, seafood and other seasonal foods.

» Flower markets fill place des Prêcheurs (Sunday morning) and place de l'Hôtel de Ville (Tuesday, Thursday and Saturday mornings).

» The **flea market** (place de Verdun; ⏰Tue, Thu & Sat mornings) has quirky, vintage items.

Place aux Huiles FOOD, DRINK
(59 rue d'Italie) Provençal goodies like olive oils, chocolates and teas.

Cave du Félibrige FOOD, DRINK
(www.aix-en-provence.com/cave-felibrige; 8 rue des Cordeliers) Splendid array of wines.

Book in Bar BOOKS
(4 rue Cabassol) English bookshop with cafe.

Information

Centre Hospitalier du Pays d'Aix (☎04 42 33 50 00; www.ch-aix.fr; av des Tamaris) Medical services.

Police Station (☎04 42 93 97 00; 10 av de l'Europe)

SOS Médecins (☎04 42 26 24 00) Medical advice.

Tourist Office (☎04 42 16 11 61; www.aixenprovencetourism.com; 37 av Giuseppi Verdi; ⏲8.30am-7pm Mon-Sat, 10am-1pm & 2-6pm Sun, longer in summer) Has tours, sells event tickets.

Getting There & Away

See www.lepilote.com for transport information, and www.info-ler.fr for some regional buses.

AIR Aéroport Marseille-Provence (p161) is 25km southwest and served by regular shuttles.

BUS Aix' **bus station** (☎04 42 91 26 80, 08 91 02 40 25; av de l'Europe) is a 10-minute walk southwest from La Rotonde. Sunday service is limited. Services include Marseille (€5, 35 minutes via autoroute, one hour via D8), Arles (€9.20, 1½ hours), Avignon (€17.40, 1¼ hours) and Toulon (€12, one hour).

TRAIN Tiny **city centre train station**, at the southern end of av Victor Hugo, serves Marseille (€8, 45 minutes).

Aix' **TGV station**, 15km from the centre and accessible by shuttle, serves most of France. To Marseille it's 12 minutes (€8, 20 daily).

Getting Around

Circumnavigating the old town is a nightmare and metered street parking spaces hard to find. Parking lots (about €15 per 24 hours) are plentiful, but if you're staying a few days and want to ditch your car, drop bags at the hotel and park at on the edge of town at **Parc Relais Route des Alpes** (⏲6.30am-9pm Mon-Sat; 🚌1, 23, Mini 3) or **Parc Relais Hauts de Brunet** (24hr €2; 🚌1) and take the free shuttle to the centre.

TO/FROM THE AIRPORT & TGV STATION Half-hourly **shuttles** (☎04 42 93 59 13) link Aix' bus station and the TGV station (€3.70) or the airport (€8) from 4.40am to 10.30pm.

BICYCLE Electric-cycles.fr (☎04 42 39 90 37; www.electric-cycles.fr; 17bis rue Frédéric Mistral; per 1hr/day/week €4/20/90; ⏲closed Mon morning & Sun) rents bikes with electrical motors.

BUS Aix en Bus (☎09 70 80 90 13; www.aixenbus.fr; 27 rue des Cordeliers; 1/10 tickets €1/7, 3-day pass €5; ⏲8.30am-7pm Mon-Sat) runs local buses. Most run until 8pm. La Rotonde is the main hub. The tourist office also has schedules.

» Train station: Minibus 2 serves La Rotonde and cours Mirabeau.

» Vieil Aix Diabline: Electric shuttles circle the old town (€0.50, every 10 minutes Monday to Saturday).

» Night shuttle: Must be 18 to 30 to ride.

TAXI Taxis can be found outside the bus station. Also try **Taxi Mirabeau** (☎04 42 21 61 61) or **Taxi Radio Aixois** (☎04 42 27 71 11).

Around Aix-en-Provence

Mountains immortalised in oil and watercolour by Cézanne, wineries and some fabulous lunches are just a short drive from Aix.

Sights & Activities

TOP CHOICE **Montagne Ste-Victoire** MOUNTAINS
East of Aix towers Cézanne's favourite haunt, the magnificent silvery mountain ridge of Montagne Ste-Victoire, with its dry slopes carpeted in *garrigue* (scented scrub), lower lush pine forests, burnt-orange soil and Coteaux d'Aix-en-Provence vineyards. Many hike the mountain's north side, but the south side, though steeper, is quite beautiful. If you take the D17 along the south side, pick up info on hiking and biking at the **Maison de Ste-Victoire** (☎04 42 66 84 40; www.grandsitesaintevictoire.com; ⏲10am-6pm Mon-Fri, 10.15am-7pm Sat & Sun) in St-Antonin-sur-Bayon. Their restaurant has sandwiches (€3.50). The mountain is closed July and August due to the threat of forest fire (though roads remain open). Driving the loop around Ste-Victoire is gorgeous; or catch bus 110 (www.lepilote.com) from La Rotonde to Payloubier/St-Antonin-sur-Bayon.

TOP CHOICE **Château de Vauvenargues** CASTLE
On the north side of Montagne Ste-Victoire, the D10 passes **Vauvenargues**, home to 14th-century Château de Vauvenargues, where Picasso is buried. The red-brick castle, bought by the artist in 1958 and his home between 1959 and 1961, still belongs to the

WORTH A TRIP

SALON DE PROVENCE

Delve into old town Salon, fortified in the 12th century, from **place Crousillat**, the prettiest square. From 1547 until his death in 1566, the philosopher Nostradamus lived at **Maison de Nostradamus** (☎04 90 56 64 31; 11 rue Nostradamus; adult/child €3.05/2.30; ⏲9am-noon & 2-6pm Mon-Fri, 2-6pm Sat & Sun). His remains lie behind a plaque inside the Gothic 14th-century **Collégiale St-Laurent** (place St-Laurent).

From the turn of the 20th century until the 1950s, soap was a buoyant business thanks to Salon's abundance of olive oil and the palm and copra oils arriving from French colonies. **Savonnerie Marius Fabre** (☎04 90 53 82 75; www.marius-fabre.fr; 148 av Paul Borret; admission with/without tour €3.50/2.50; ⏲8.30am-noon & 2-5.30pm Mon-Thu, to 4pm Fri, guided tours 10.30am Mon & Thu), run by three generations dating from 1900, paints a vivid portrait of the industry with its small museum. **Savonnerie Rampal-Latour** (☎04 90 56 07 28; www.rampal-latour.com; 71 rue Félix Pyat; admission free; ⏲8am-noon & 2-5pm Mon-Fri) offers tours; book at the **tourist office** (☎04 90 56 27 60; www.visitsalondeprovence.com; 56 cours Gimon; ⏲9.30am-6.30pm Mon-Sat, 9.30am-12.30pm Sun Jul & Aug, shorter hrs Sep-Jun). You can buy soap at factory prices in its beautiful 1907 boutique.

The 12th-century **Abbaye de Sainte Croix** (☎04 90 56 24 55; www.relais-chateaux.com/sainte croix; D16, Val de Cuech; d €170-440, menus €52-109; ⏲Apr-Oct; ❄@📶≋), 2km east of Salon, is one of Provence's great historic hotels and a gourmet restaurant.

Picassos. It opened its doors to visitors for a few special months in 2009 to raise money for its restoration, nearing completion at time of research. It is once again closed to the public, but views of it from the sweet village, with Ste-Victoire in the background, are spectacular.

Aqueduc de Roquefavour HISTORIC AQUEDUCT

Take the D64 13km east of Aix, to stroll through the trees beneath Aqueduc de Roquefavour, the world's largest stone aqueduct, built in 1861 to transport water from the River Durance to Marseille. Afterwards lunch at Hôtel-Restaurant Arquier (p171).

Domaine de la Brillane WINERY

(☎06 13 02 67 00, 04 42 54 21 44; www.labrillane.com; 195 rte de Couteron; ⏲9am-1pm Sat & by appointment) Make an appointment at this organic estate to taste esteemed reds and rosés. Find the brilliant ochre-coloured château surrounded by vineyards 7km north of Aix-en-Provence signposted 1km off the northbound D13 from Aix to St-Canadet.

Sleeping & Eating

Hôtel-Restaurant Arquier RESTAURANT €€

(☎04 42 24 20 45; www.arquier-restaurant-hotel.com; 2980 rte du Petit-Moulin; d/q €67/113, lunch buffet €19, menu €29; 📶) This roadside inn gets packed with Aixois enjoying the enormous weekday lunch buffet. Terrace tables proffer a slither view of the Aqueduc de Roquefavour. Stay in simple, comfortable rooms overlooking pleasant greenery.

La Table de Ventabren MODERN FRENCH

(☎04 42 28 79 33; www.latabledeventabren.com; 1 rue Cézanne; menus €41-50; ⏲lunch Wed-Sun, dinner Tue-Sun) Reason itself to visit medeival **Ventabren**, a hilltop village 16km west of Aix-en-Provence, is this one-star Michelin restaurant with a canvas-canopied terrace, magical on starry summer evenings. Inside find exposed stone walls, genial staff and design-led details. Chef Dan Bessoudo creates inventive, wholly modern French dishes and his desserts are out of this world. Afterwards hike uphill to enjoy panoramic views from the ruins of **Château de la Reine Jeanne**.

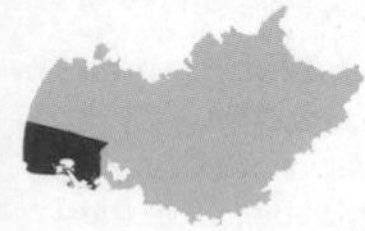

Arles & the Camargue

Includes »

Best Places to Eat

- » L'Atelier (p180)
- » La Chassagnette (p184)
- » L'Autruche (p180)
- » Le Gibolin (p180)
- » Le Mazet du Vaccarès (p184)
- » Restaurant La Telline (p184)
- » Le Cilantro (p180)

Best Places to Stay

- » Hôtel de l'Amphithéâtre (p179)
- » L'Hôtel Particulier (p180)
- » Hôtel de Cacharel (p184)
- » Gîte at Salin de Badon (p182)
- » Le Mas de Peint (p184)

Why Go?

Forget all about time in this hauntingly beautiful part of Provence roamed by black bulls, white horses and pink flamingos. This is slow-go Provence, a timeless wetland chequered with silver salt pans, waterlogged rice paddies and movie-style cowboys. Birds provide the most action on this 780-sq-km delta wedged between the Petit Rhône and Grand Rhône. Grab your binoculars, squat in a shack between bulrushes and know, as another flamingo flits across the setting sun, that these magnificent waters, steeped in legend and lore, have a soul of their own.

The main town of the region, diminutive Arles, is a showstopper. Wander the narrow golden-hued streets that inspired Van Gogh to find the town's lovely restored Roman amphitheatre, top-notch art and history museums, and world-class restaurants. It'll be hard to tear yourself away.

Driving Distances (km)

	Aigues-Mortes	Arles	La Capelière	Le Sambuc	Salin de Giraud
Arles	51				
La Capelière	56	21			
Le Sambuc	62	31	13		
Salin de Giraud	70	38	22	15	
Stes-Maries de la Mer	33	37	41	59	61

Getting Around

Touring the tiny roads criss-crossing this flat, wild region is best done by car or bicycle. The D36 along Étang de Vaccarès' eastern shore and the D85a north of Stes-Maries de la Mer are particularly picturesque. For the Marseille-bound, the Bac de Barcarin provides a car ferry (€5) across the Grand Rhône from Salin de Giraud.

THREE PERFECT DAYS

Day 1: Art & Architecture in Arles

Celts, Greeks and Romans shaped this colourful city, which is chock-a-block with ancient ruins (p176). Spend the day weaving these sites together with the modern legacy of Van Gogh. See what he painted on the banks of the Rhône, on place du Forum (p176) with its yellow cafe, and in the mighty Roman amphitheatre (p176). For modern art, be sure to pop into the magnificent Musée Réattu (p178) and the just-renovated Fondation Vincent van Gogh (p178).

Day 2: Nature Fest

Grab your binoculars and flock with the birds to the southeast corner of this extraordinary wetland. Study its flora at La Capelière (p182) and watch flamingos wade through springtime irises at Salin de Badon. End with a horse trek through purple-flowered sea lavender and brackish lakes at Domaine de la Palissade (p182).

Day 3: A Culinary Tour

Cycle the Digue à la Mer (p182) to Stes-Maries de la Mer for mussels and people-watching at La Cabane aux Coquillages (p186). Or head to Salins de Giraud (p182) for a salt pan tour then lunch at Camarguais inn Estrambord (p184), sheepfold La Chassagnette (p184), or bull farm Le Mas de Peint (p184). Taste wine and rice in the afternoon and dine on local *tellines* (tiny clams) at Restaurant La Telline (p184) or Le Mazet du Vaccarès (p184). Alternatively, return to Arles and choose from its embarrassment of riches.

Advance Planning

» **Mosquitoes** Bring insect repellent. Mosquitoes are savage here.

» **Driving the Camargue** Carry water and binoculars. Get petrol before leaving town.

» **Arles féria (bullfighting festival) tickets** They're snapped up fast.

» **Gîte at Salin de Badon** Bare-bones but nature rich, this prime real estate fills quickly.

» **High-end restaurants** Reserve in advance.

» **Bicycle rental** Companies in Stes-Maries de la Mer deliver bikes to your door for free; book ahead.

DON'T MISS

Plan to be in Arles for the whopping Saturday morning market. Stock up for a picnic, or reserve ahead for a late lunch at one of the outstanding local restaurants.

Best Nature Trails

» Digue à la Mer (p182)

» La Capelière (p182) & Salin de Badon

» Parc Ornithologique du Pont de Gau (p182)

» Musée de la Camargue (p182)

» Domaine de la Palissade (p182)

Best Treks & Safaris

» Camargue Découverte (www.camargue-decouverte.com) Arles-based Jeep-safari company.

» Kayak Vert Camargue (p183)

» La Maison du Guide (www.maisonduguide.camargue.fr)

» Le Mas de Peint (p184)

» Les Cabanes de Cacharel (p183)

Resources

» **Parc Naturel Régional de Camargue** (www.tourisme.ville-arles.fr)

» **Réserve Nationale de Camargue** (www.parc-camargue.fr)

» **Conseil Général des Bouches-du-Rhône** (http://en.tourduvalat.org)

» **Visit Provence** (http://en.tourduvalat.org)

Arles & the Camargue Highlights

1. Discover Roman **Arles** (p176), trail Van Gogh and enjoy some of Provence's finest restaurants
2. Watch rose-pink flamingos at the wondrous bird park, **Le Parc Ornithologique du Pont de Gau** (p182)
3. Spot local flora and fauna from the trails around **La Capelière** (p182) and Salin de Badon
4. Pick a fine restaurant to try in **Le Sambuc** (p184)
5. Gallop like the wind on a horse trek at **Domaine de la Palissade** (p182)
6. Bike along the edge of the world to a 19th-century lighthouse on the **Digue à la Mer** (p182)
7. Birdwatch on the **Étang de Vaccarès** (p182) then dine with lighthouse keepers at legendary **Le Mazet du Vaccarès** (p184)
8. Follow in the footsteps of pilgrims to **Stes-Maries de la Mer** (p184) and its hallowed church

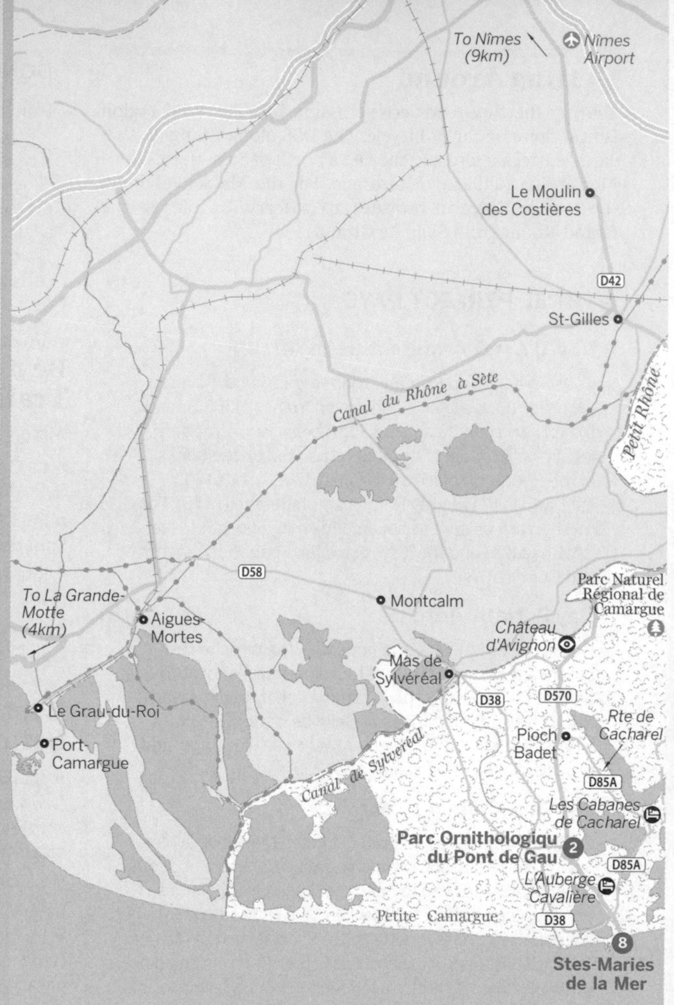

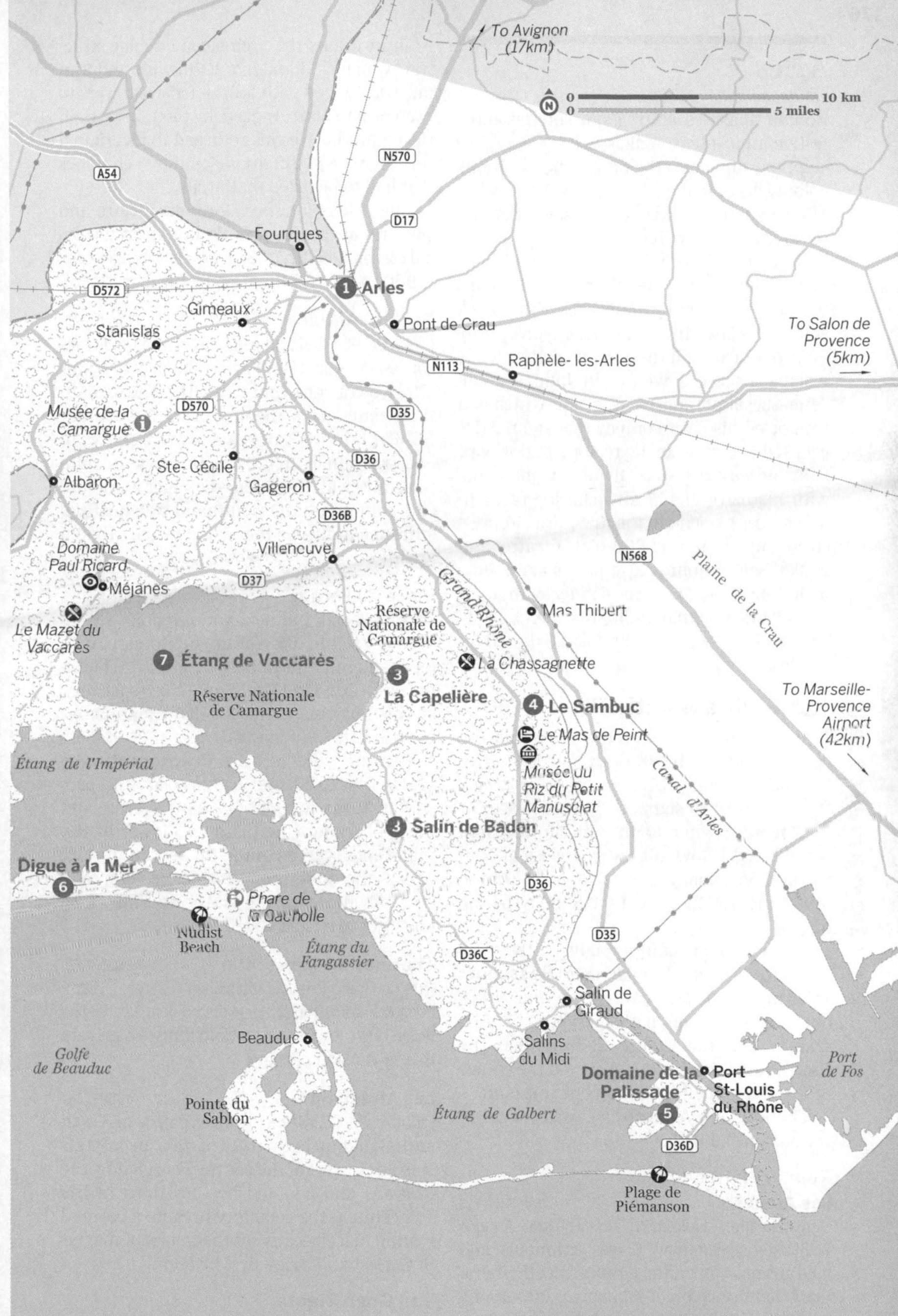
To Avignon (17km)
0 10 km
0 5 miles
N570
A54
D17
Fourques
1 Arles
D572
Gimeaux
Pont de Crau
Stanislas
To Salon de Provence (5km)
N113
Raphèle-les-Arles
Musée de la Camargue
D570
D35
D36
Ste-Cécile
Albaron
Gageron
D36B
Domaine Paul Ricard
Villeneuve
N568
Méjanes
D37
Plaine de la Crau
Grand Rhône
Réserve Nationale de Camargue
Mas Thibert
Le Mazet du Vaccarès
7 Étang de Vaccarès
La Chassagnette
3 La Capelière
Réserve Nationale de Camargue
4 Le Sambuc
To Marseille-Provence Airport (42km)
Le Mas de Peint
Étang de l'Impérial
Musée du Riz du Petit Manusclat
Canal d'Arles
3 Salin de Badon
Digue à la Mer
6
D36
Phare de la Gacholle
Nudist Beach
D35
Étang du Fangassier
D36C
Salin de Giraud
Beauduc
Salins du Midi
Golfe de Beauduc
Domaine de la Palissade
Port St-Louis du Rhône
Port de Fos
Pointe du Sablon
Étang de Galbert
5
D36D
Plage de Piémanson

Arles

POP 54,088

Roman treasures, sultry stone squares and a festive atmosphere makes Arles a seductive stepping stone into the Camargue. And if its colourful sun-baked houses evoke a sense of déjà vu, it's because you've seen them already on a Van Gogh canvas.

Long before the Dutch artist captured starry nights over the Rhône, the Romans had been won over by the charms of the Greek colony Arelate. In 49 BC Arles' prosperity and political standing rose meteorically when it backed a winner in Julius Caesar. After Caesar plundered Marseille, which had supported his rival Pompey the Great, Arles eclipsed Marseille as the region's major port. Soon its citizens were living the high life with gladiator fights and chariot races in magnificent open-air theatres. Still impressively intact, the 12,000-seat theatre and 20,000-seat amphitheatre now stage events including Arles' famous *férias*, with their controversial lethal bullfights, less bloody *courses Camarguaises* and three-day street parties.

Sights & Activities

Arles will soon be graced with a cultural centre designed by world-renowned architect Frank Gehry. Unless otherwise noted, the last entry to sights is 30 minutes prior to closing. Winter hours are shorter than those listed below; places that close at 7pm in summer usually close at 5pm in winter. Museums are free the first Sunday of the month.

Buy a pass for multiple sights at the tourist office or any Roman site: **Passeport Avantage** (€13.50) covers the museums, both theatres, the baths, crypt, Les Alyscamps and the Cloître St-Trophime; the **Passeport Liberté** (€9) gives you the choice of five sights total including one museum.

The **Museon Arlaten** is closed for renovations until 2014.

Roman Sights

Les Arènes ROMAN SITES

(Amphithéâtre; adult/child incl Théâtre Antique €6.50/free; 9am-7pm) Slaves, criminals and wild animals (including giraffes) met their dramatic demise before a jubilant 20,000-strong crowd during Roman gladiatorial displays at Les Arènes, built around the late 1st or early 2nd century AD. During the early medieval Arab invasions the arch-laced circular structure, which is 136m long, 107m wide and 21m tall, was topped with four defensive towers to become a fortress. Indeed, by the 1820s, when the amphitheatre was returned to its original use, there were 212 houses and two churches that had to be razed on the site.

Buy tickets for special events, theatre and concerts at the **Bureau de Location** (Bureau de Location; 08 91 70 03 70; www.arenes-arles.com; 9.30am-noon & 2-6pm Mon-Fri, 10am-1pm Sat).

Théâtre Antique ROMAN SITES

(04 90 96 93 30; bd des Lices; incl in Les Arènes admission; 9am-7pm) Still regularly used for alfresco concerts and plays, the Théâtre Antique dates from the end of the 1st century BC. For hundreds of years it was a source of construction materials, with workers chipping away at the 102m-diameter structure (the column on the right-hand side near the entrance indicates the height of the original arcade).

Place du Forum ROMAN SITES

Just as social, political and religious life revolved around the forum in Roman Arles (spot the remains of a 2nd century AD temple embedded in Hôtel Pinus Nord's facade), so this busy plane-tree-shaded square buzzes with cafe life today.

Beneath your feet are **Cryptoportiques** (adult/child €3.50/free; 9am-noon & 2-7pm), subterranean foundations for the forum and buried arcades (the plaza was lower in Roman times) carved out in the 1st century BC. Access the underground galleries, 89m long and 59m wide, at the **Hôtel de Ville** (Town Hall; place de la République).

Thermes de Constantin ROMAN SITES

(rue du Grand Prieuré; adult/child €3/free; 9am-noon & 2-7pm) Partly preserved Roman baths were built for Emperor Constantine's private use in the 4th century.

Les Alyscamps CEMETERY

(adult/child €3.50/free; 9am-7pm) Van Gogh and Gauguin both painted this necropolis 1km southwest of the centre. Founded by the Romans and adopted by Christians in the 4th century, the cemetery became a coveted resting place because of the tombs of martyr St Genest and Arles' first bishops.

Van Gogh Sights

Though he painted 200-odd canvases in Arles, there are no Van Gogh artworks here today; and Van Gogh's little 'yellow house' on

Arles

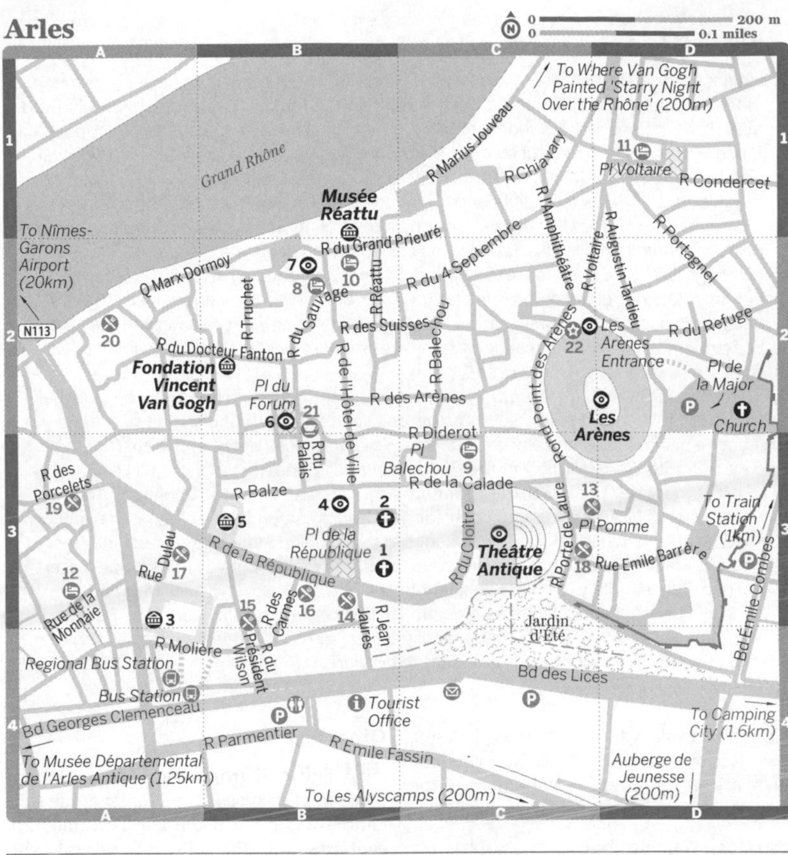

Arles

Top Sights

	Fondation Vincent Van Gogh	B2
	Les Arènes	D2
	Musée Réattu	B1
	Théâtre Antique	C3

Sights

1	Cloître St-Trophime	B3
	Cryptoportiques	(see 6)
2	Église St-Trophime	B3
3	Espace Van Gogh	A3
4	Hôtel de Ville	B3
5	Museon Arlaten	B3
6	Place du Forum	B2
7	Thermes de Constantin	B2

Sleeping

8	Hôtel Arlatan	B2
9	Hôtel de l'Amphithéâtre	C3
10	Hôtel du Musée	B2
11	Le Belvédère Hôtel	D1
12	L'Hôtel Particulier	A3

Eating

13	Au Jardin du Calendal	C3
14	Comptoir du Sud	B3
15	La Mule Blanche	B3
16	L'Atelier	B3
17	L'Autruche	A3
18	Le Cilantro	C3
19	Le Gibolin	A3
20	L'Entrevue	A2

Drinking

21	Café Van Gogh	B2

Entertainment

22	Ticket Office	C2

VINCENT

It's easy to forget that Vincent van Gogh was only 37 when he died, as he appears much older in some of his self-portraits. Born in 1853, the Dutch painter arrived in Arles in 1888 after living in Paris with his younger brother Theo, an art dealer who financially supported Vincent from his own modest income. In Paris he had become acquainted with seminal artists Edgar Degas, Camille Pissarro, Henri de Toulouse-Lautrec and Paul Gauguin.

Revelling in Arles' intense light and bright colours, Van Gogh painted with a burning fervour, unfazed by howling mistrals. During a mistral he would kneel on his canvases and paint horizontally, or lash his easel to iron stakes driven deep into the ground. He sent paintings to Theo for him to try to sell, and dreamed of founding an artists' colony here, but only Gauguin followed up his invitation. Their differing artistic approaches (Gauguin believed in painting from imagination, Van Gogh in painting what he saw) and their artistic temperaments came to a head with the argument in December 1888 that led to Van Gogh lopping off part of his own ear.

In May 1889 Van Gogh voluntarily entered an asylum, Monastère St-Paul de Mausole (p216) in St-Rémy de Provence. During his one year, one week, and one day's confinement he painted 150-odd canvases, including masterpieces like *Starry Night* (not to be confused with *Starry Night over the Rhône*, painted in Arles).

In February 1890 his 1888 Arles-painted work *The Red Vines* was bought by Anne Boch, sister of his friend Eugene Boch, for 400 francs (around €50 today) – the only painting he sold in his lifetime. It now hangs in the Pushkin State Museum of Fine Arts.

On 16 May 1890 Van Gogh moved to Auvers-sur-Oise, just outside Paris, to be closer to Theo. But on 27 July that year he shot himself and died two days later with Theo at his side. Theo subsequently had a breakdown, was committed and died, aged 33, just six months after Vincent. Less than a decade later, Van Gogh's talent started to achieve recognition, with major museums acquiring his work.

place Lamartine, which he painted in 1888, was destroyed during WWII. Nevertheless, there are several ways to pay homage to the master.

Van Gogh Walking Tour WALKING TOUR
Mapped out in a tourist-office brochure (€1 or download it free online), this evocative walking circuit of the city takes in scenes painted by Van Gogh.

Fondation Vincent Van Gogh GALLERY
(☎04 90 49 94 04; www.fondationvangogharles-blog.com; 5 place Honoré Clair; adult/child €6/free; ⏲10am-7pm) This newly renovated gallery houses rotating exhibits and a collection of important modern-day artists, including David Hockney, Francis Bacon and Fernando Botero, paying homage to their distinctive style.

Espace Van Gogh GALLERY
(☎04 90 49 39 39; place Félix Rey) Housed in the former hospital where Van Gogh had his ear stitched and was later locked up (not to be confused with the asylum Monastère St-Paul de Mausole) this gallery houses temporary art exhibitions.

Other Sights

FREE **Église St-Trophime** CHURCH
(place de la République) This Romanesque-style church was built in the late 11th and 12th centuries on the site of several earlier churches. On the western portal the intricately sculpted **tympanum** depicts St Trophime, a late 2nd- or early 3rd-century bishop of Arles, holding a spiral staff. The treasury contains bone fragments of Arles' bishops who were later canonised.

Next door, the evocative 12th- to 14th-century **Cloître St-Trophime** (St-Trophime Cloister; ☎04 90 49 36 36; adult/child €3.50/free; ⏲9am-7pm) hosts excellent exhibitions.

TOP CHOICE **Musée Réattu** ART MUSEUM
(☎04 90 49 37 58; www.museereattu.arles.fr; 10 rue du Grand Prieuré; adult/child €7/free; ⏲10am-12.30pm & 2-6.30pm Tue-Sun) This splendid modern art museum is housed in the exquisitely renovated 15th-century Grand Priory of the Knights of Malta. Among its collections are works by 18th- and 19th-century Provençal artists and two paintings and 57 sketches by Picasso. It hosts wonderfully curated cutting-edge exhibitions.

Musée Départemental Arles Antique ANTIQUITIES MUSEUM
(☎04 13 31 51 03; www.arles-antique.cg13.fr; av de la Première Division Française Libre; adult/child €6/free; ⊙10am-6pm Wed-Mon) This striking, state-of-the-art, cobalt-blue museum perches on the edge of what used to be the Roman chariot racing track (circus), 1.5km southwest of the tourist office. The rich collection of pagan and Christian art includes stunning mosaics. It's also a leading mosaic restoration centre; watch work in progress.

Festivals & Events

Féria d'Arles BULLFIGHTING
(Féria Pascale; www.feriaarles.com; ⊙Easter) Festival held at Easter heralding the start of bullfighting season (bulls in Les Arènes most Sundays in May and June).

Fête des Gardians CULTURAL FESTIVAL
(⊙1 May) Mounted Camargue cowboys parade and hold games; 1 May.

Fêtes d'Arles PERFORMING ARTS
(www.festivarles.com) Dance, theatre, music and poetry for two weeks starting around the end of June.

L'Abrivado des Bernacles BULL PARADE/CONTEST
(www.feriaarles.com) Camargue *gardians* shepherd bulls for 15km from paddock to Les Arènes for the season's most prestigious *course Camarguaise,* the **Cocarde d'Or**. Hundreds of aficionados on bike, scooter, foot and horseback follow the *gardians;* first Monday in July.

Féria du Riz BULLFIGHTING
(www.feriaarles.com; ⊙Sep) Bullfights during week-long festival marking the start of the rice harvest; September.

Sleeping

Arles has reasonably priced, excellent year-round accommodation, which only really fills up during *férias*. Hotels' private parking tends to be pricey.

TOP CHOICE **Hôtel de l'Amphithéâtre** HISTORIC HOTEL €
(☎04 90 96 10 30; www.hotelamphitheatre.fr; 5-7 rue Diderot; s/d/tr/q from €57/67/117/137; ❄@📶) Crimson, chocolate, terracotta and other rich earthy colours dress the exquisite 17th-century stone structure of this stylish hotel, with narrow staircases, roaring fire and alfresco courtyard breakfasts. The romantic suite (€157), with dreamy lilac-walled terrace, overlooks rooftops. Wheelchair access.

Hôtel Arlatan HISTORIC HOTEL €€
(☎04 90 93 56 66; www.hotel-arlatan.fr; 26 rue du Sauvage; d €85-157, apt €177-247; ⊙mid-Mar–mid-Nov; ❄@📶🏊) The heated swimming pool, pretty garden and plush rooms decorated with antique furniture are just some of the things going for this hotel. Add to that a setting steeped in history, with Roman foundations visible through a glass floor in the lobby and 15th-century paintings on one of the lounges' ceilings. Wheelchair access.

A BULLISH AFFAIR

The local Camargue variation of the bull fight, the *course Camarguaise*, sees amateur *razeteurs* (from the word 'shave'), wearing skin-tight white shirts and trousers, get as close as they dare to the *taureau* (bull) to try to snatch rosettes and ribbons tied to the bull's horns, using a *crochet* (a razor-sharp comb) held between their fingers. Their leaps over the arena's barrier as the bull charges make spectators' hearts lurch.

Bulls are bred on a *manade* (bull farm) by *manadiers*, who are helped in their daily chores by *gardians* (Camargue cattle-herding cowboys). These mounted herdsmen parade through Arles during the Fête des Gardians (p179) in May.

Many *manades* also breed the creamy white *cheval de Camargue* (Camargue horse) and some welcome visitors; ask at tourist offices in **Arles** (www.tourisme.ville-arles.fr) and Stes-Maries de la Mer (p186).

A calendar of *courses Camarguaises* is online at the **Fédération Française de la Course Camarguaise** (French Federation of Camargue Bullfights; ☎04 66 26 05 35; www.ffcc.info), with many occurring at the arena in Stes-Maries de la Mer. *Recortadores* (a type of bull-baiting with lots of bull-jumping) also happens during the bullfighting season (Easter to September).

Le Belvédère Hôtel BOUTIQUE HOTEL €
(☎04 90 91 45 94; www.hotellebelvedere-arles.com; 5 place Voltaire; s/d from €65/70; ❄📶) This sleek 17-room hotel is one of the best Arlésian pads. Red-glass chandeliers (and friendly staff) adorn the lobby–breakfast area and the super-clean rooms and bathrooms are fitted out in stylish red, chocolate brown and grey.

Hôtel du Musée BOUTIQUE HOTEL €
(☎04 90 93 88 88; www.hoteldumusee.com; 11 rue du Grand Prieuré; s/d/tr/q from €60/65/90/120; ⊙mid-Mar–Oct; ❄📶) In a fine 17th- to 18th-century building, this impeccable hotel has comfortable rooms, a tiled breakfast room and a sugar-sweet patio garden brimming with pretty blossoms.

L'Hôtel Particulier BOUTIQUE HOTEL €€€
(☎04 90 52 51 40; www.hotel-particulier.com; 4 rue de la Monnaie; d €289-309; ⊙Easter-Oct) This exclusive boutique hotel with restaurant, spa and *hammam* oozes chic charm. From the big black door with heavy knocker to the crisp white linens and minimalist decor, everything about this 18th-century private mansion enchants.

Auberge de Jeunesse HOSTEL €
(☎04 90 96 18 25; www.fuaj.org; 20 av Maréchal Foch; dm incl breakfast & sheets €18.50; ⊙mid-Feb–mid-Dec, reception closed 10am-5pm) This sunlit place, made up of eight-bed dorms, is just 10 minutes' walk from Arles' centre. Its bar closes at 11pm, just like its gates (except during *férias*).

Camping City CAMPGROUND €
(☎04 90 93 08 86; www.camping-city.com; 67 rte de Crau; sites €19; ⊙Apr-Sep) 1.5km southeast on the road to Marseille, Camping City is the closest campground to town. Bike hire and laundry facilities are available and there are supermarkets nearby. To get here, take Bus 2 to the Hermite stop.

Eating

At Arles' enormous Saturday-morning **market** (bd des Lices) Camargue salt, goats' cheese and *saucisson d'Arles* (bull-meat sausage) scent the air. The scene shifts to bd Émile Combes on Wednesday morning. Arles and its environs (p184) are foodie heaven. Reserve ahead; hours are reduced in winter.

TOP CHOICE **L'Atelier** GASTRONOMIC €€€
(☎04 90 91 07 69; www.rabanel.com; 7 rue des Carmes; lunch/dinner menus from €55/95; ⊙lunch & dinner Wed-Sun) Consider this not a meal, but an 'artistic experience'. Every one of the seven or 13 edible works of art is a wondrous composition of flavours, colours and textures, and no two bites are the same. Sit back and revel in Jean-Luc Rabanel's superbly crafted symphony of fresh organic tastes. No wonder this charismatic chef with his own veggie patch has two Michelin stars. Wine pairings are an adventure in themselves.

TOP CHOICE **L'Autruche** MODERN FRENCH €€
(☎04 90 49 73 63; 5 rue Dulau; lunch menus €18, mains €29; ⊙lunch & dinner Tue-Sat) This modern, inviting restaurant run by husband-and-wife team Fabien and Ouria assembles market-fresh dishes to perfection. For example, their Michelin-experienced chef layers thin strips of granny smith apple chutney with a superbly prepared *foie gras*. Extravagant desserts are a treat.

TOP CHOICE **Le Gibolin** BISTRO €€
(☎04 88 65 43 14; 13 rue des Porcelet; menus €25; ⊙lunch & dinner Tue-Sat Sep-Jun) Sup on peerless home-cooking while the friendly patroness bustles between tables, offers ladies fresh roses and her Jack Russell terrier nips at her heels. A wine bar, really, the pairings are *magnifique*. No credit cards.

L'Entrevue MOROCCAN €
(☎04 90 93 37 28; www.lentrevue-restaurant.com; 23 quai Marx Dormoy; mains €14-18; ⊙lunch & dinner daily; 👪) Excellent, heaping bowls of organic *tajines* and couscous are served briskly quay-side.

Le Cilantro PROVENÇAL €€€
(☎04 90 18 25 05; www.restaurantcilantro.com; 31 rue Porte de Laure; mains €41; ⊙lunch Tue-Fri, dinner Tue-Sat; 🍷) Chef Jêrome Laurant, a born-and-bred local lad, runs this hot spot and combines local ingredients with world spices to create accomplished dishes from fresh fish to duck medallions or steak.

Au Jardin du Calendal TRADITIONAL FRENCH €
(☎04 90 96 11 89; 5 rue Porte de Laure; mains €14-18; ⊙noon-7pm Tue-Sun; 📶) The leafy courtyard garden of this hotel (doubles from €120) is perfect for lunching on gourmet salads. Grab breakfast or a snack at its Ōli Pan coffee shop.

La Mule Blanche BISTRO €
(☎04 90 93 98 54; www.restaurant-mule-blanche.com; 8 rue du Président Wilson; mains €13-15;

⏰lunch Tue-Sun, dinner Wed-Sun) Jazz plays inside, but the hottest tables at this soulful bistro are on the pavement terrace.

Comptoir du Sud CAFE €
(☎04 90 96 22 17; 2 rue Jean Jaurès; ⏰10am-5pm Tue-Fri) Gourmet sandwiches (tasty chutneys, succulent meats, *foie gras*) and divine little salads, all at rock-bottom prices, served at a counter.

Drinking & Entertainment

The place du Forum (p176) makes for great cafe sitting. **Café Van Gogh** (11 place du Forum), otherwise called Café de la Nuit, was depicted in Van Gogh's *Café Terrace at Night* (1888). Painted starry-yellow to recreate the painting's feel, it's always packed with tourists.

Roma bands such as Los Reyes and the Gypsy Kings (from Arles no less, discovered while busking in St-Tropez) have performed on the city's streets. Catch Roma bands performing during Stes-Maries de la Mer pilgrimages (p186). Otherwise watch a sangria-fuelled dinner show at **Patio de Camargue** (☎04 90 49 51 76; http://patio.chico.fr; 51bis chemin Barriol; ticket incl dinner €55-70).

The tourist office has lists of what's on.

Information

Both tourist offices organise **walking tours** (with a pass adult/child €6/3, €4.50; ⏰Jul-Sep), like the Van Gogh walking tour (in English, Saturday 11am), and sell maps, cycling itineraries and sightseeing passes (p176).

Tourist Office (main office ☎04 90 18 41 20; esplanade Charles de Gaulle; ⏰9am-6.45pm)

Tourist Office (train station; ☎04 90 43 33 57; ⏰9am-12.30pm & 2.30-5pm Mon-Fri)

Getting There & Around

BUS There are services to Aix-en-Provence (€9, 1½ hours), Stes-Maries de la Mer (€2.50, one hour) and Nîmes (€1.50, one hour) from the **bus station** (☎08 10 00 08 16; www.lepilote.com; 24 bd Georges Clemenceau; ⏰7.30am-4pm Mon-Sat).

Star (☎08 10 00 08 16; ⏰8.30am-noon & 2-5.30pm Mon-Fri) operates local buses from the bus station from 6.30am to 7.30pm Monday to Saturday, and 9.30am to 5.30pm Sunday. Tickets cost €0.80. Free minibuses called Starlets circle the old city every 25 minutes (7.10am to 7.15pm Monday to Saturday).

BICYCLE Europbike (☎06 38 14 49 50; www.europbike-provence.net) Rents bikes and runs tours.

TAXI Call ☎04 90 96 90 03.

TRAIN From the **train station** (av Paulin Talabot) are services to Nîmes (€7.50, 30 minutes), Marseille (€13, 45 minutes) and Avignon (€7, 20 minutes). The closest TGV stations are in Avignon and Nîmes.

Camargue Countryside

Just south of Arles, Provence's rolling landscapes yield to the flat, marshy wilds of the Camargue, famous for teeming birdlife – roughly 500 species. Allow ample time to birdwatch: grey herons, little egrets, shelducks, avocets, oystercatchers and yellow-legged gulls are among the species to spot. King of all is the pink flamingo, which enjoys the expansive wetlands' mild winters.

Equally famous are the Camargue's small white horses; their mellow disposition makes horseback riding the ideal way to explore the region's patchwork of salt pans and rice fields, and meadows dotted with grazing bulls. Bring binoculars and mosquito repellent.

PINK FLAMINGOS

Each year in the Camargue some 10,000 pink or greater flamingo *(Phoenicopterus ruber)* couples nest on the Étang du Fangassier: the 4000-sq-m artificial island, constructed in 1970 as a flamingo-breeding colony, is one of the rare spots in Europe that guarantees the flamingo protection from predators.

This well-dressed bird stands between 1.5m and 2m tall and has an average wing span of 1.9m. When the flamingo feels threatened, its loud hiss is similar to the warning sound made by a goose. Flamingo courtship starts in January, with mating taking place from March to May. Come the end of August or early September, thousands take flight to Spain, Tunisia and Senegal where they winter in warmer climes before returning to the Camargue in February. Some 6000 to 7000 flamingos, however, remain in the Rhône delta year-round.

Enclosed by the Petit Rhône and Grand Rhône rivers, most of the Camargue wetlands fall within the 850-sq-km **Parc Naturel Régional de Camargue** (www.parc-camargue.fr), established in 1970 to preserve the area's fragile ecosystems while sustaining local agriculture. Get information at the Musée de la Camargue (p182).

On the periphery, the 600-sq-km lagoon **Étang de Vaccarès** and nearby peninsulas and islands form the **Réserve Nationale de Camargue** (www.reserve-camargue.org), a nature reserve founded in 1927, with an information centre at La Capelière (p182).

The Camargue's two largest towns are the seaside pilgrim's outpost Stes-Maries de la Mer and, to the northwest, the walled town of Aigues Mortes.

Sights & Activities

Musée de la Camargue MUSEUM
(Musée Camarguais; ☎04 90 97 10 82; www.parc-camargue.fr; Mas du Pont de Rousty; adult/child €4.50/free; ⌚9am-12.30pm & 1-6pm Wed-Mon Feb-Dec) Inside an 1812-built sheep shed, 10km southwest of Arles on the D570, the Camargue Museum paints an exhaustive portrait of traditional life, its exhibitions covering local history, ecosystems, farming techniques, flora and fauna. A 3.5km trail leads to an observation tower with bird's-eye views of the *mas* (farmhouse) and its nature-protected surrounds. The museum is the main information point for the Parc Naturel Régional de Camargue (p182).

Le Parc Ornithologique du Pont de Gau NATURE PARK
(☎04 90 97 82 62; www.parcornithologique.com; Pont du Gau; adult/child €7/4; ⌚9am-sunset) Pink flamingos pirouette overhead and stalk the watery landscape at this bird park, home to every bird species known to set foot in the Camargue. Watch them from 7km of beautiful trails meandering through the site. Find the park on the D570 in Pont du Gau, 4km north of Stes-Maries de la Mer.

FREE **Digue à la Mer** DIKE
The Digue à la Mer is a 2.5m-high dike built in the 19th century to cut the delta off from the sea. A 20km-long walking and cycling track runs along its length, from Stes-Maries de la Mer to the lighthouse at La Gacholle, and footpaths cut down to a couple of lovely sandy beaches. Walking on the fragile sand dunes is forbidden.

The solar-powered **Phare de la Gacholle** (⌚11am-5pm weekends & school holidays), dating to 1882, was automated in the 1960s. Inside the former lighthouse keeper's house, a small exhibition focuses on local birdlife and fishing traditions. The closest you can get by car is two car parks (1km and 5km away) on the eastern side of the Étang de Vaccarès; take the D36B in Le Paradis, 7km west of Salin de Giraud.

TOP CHOICE **La Capelière** NATURE RESERVE
(☎04 90 97 00 97; www.reserve-camargue.org; La Capelière; permits adult/child €3/1.50; ⌚9am-1pm & 2-6pm daily Apr-Sep, 9am-1pm & 2-5pm Wed-Mon Oct-Mar; 🚻) This information centre for the Réserve Nationale de Camargue (p182) sell permits for the observatories and 4.5km of nature trails at wild **Salin de Badon**, former royal salt pans 7km south. True birders must not miss a night in its **gîte** (dorms €12), a cottage with 20 beds over seven rooms, kitchen, toilet and solar electricity. BYO food, drinking water, bedding and mosquito spray. At La Capelière's 1.5km-long **Sentier des Rainettes** (Treefrog Trail) discover flora and fauna native to freshwater marshes.

Domaine de la Palissade NATURE PARK
(☎04 42 86 81 28; www.palissade.fr; rte de la Mer; adult/child €3/free; ⌚9am-5pm or 6pm daily Apr-Oct, 9am-5pm Wed & Sun Nov-Feb) This remote nature centre organises fantastic forays into the marshes on foot and horseback; call ahead to book **horse treks** (1hr adult/child €16/14, 2hr €28/26). It rents binoculars (€2) and has free maps of the estate's three marked walking trails (1km to 8km) through scrubby glasswort, flowering sea lavender (August) and lagoons.

Les Salins de Giraud SALT PANS
(☎04 42 86 70 20; place Péchiney, Salin de Giraud; adult/child/family €8.20/6/24.20; ⌚10am-12.30pm & 2-6pm Apr-Oct) Learn how *sel* (salt) is produced by local *sauniers* (salt farmers) and tour the salt pans on board a **tourist train**.

Château d'Avignon CASTLE
(☎04 90 97 58 60; www.culture-13.fr; rte d'Arles [D570]; adult/child €4/free; ⌚9.45am-5.30pm Wed-Mon Apr-Oct, Fri only Nov-Mar) The park surrounding this 18th-century château is free to wander. The castle itself was owned by Louis Prat-Noilly, a Marseillais merchant, who used it as a hunting lodge.

WORTH A TRIP

AIGUES-MORTES

Actually located over the border from Provence in the Gard *département*, the picturesque town of Aigues-Mortes sits 28km northwest of Stes-Maries de la Mer at the western extremity of the Camargue. Set in flat marshland and encircled by high stone walls, the town was established in the mid-13th century by Louis IX to give the French crown a Mediterranean port under its direct control. Cobbled streets inside the walls are lined with restaurants, cafes and bars, giving it a festive atmosphere and making it a charming spot from which to explore the Camargue.

Scaling the ramparts rewards you with sweeping views. Head to the top of the tower, **Tour de Constance** (adult/child €6.50/free; ⌚10am-7pm May-Aug, 10am-5.30pm Sep-Apr); the 1.6km wall-top walk takes about one hour.

L'Hermitage de St-Antoine (☎06 03 04 34 05; www.hermitagesa.com; 9 bd Intérieur Nord; r incl breakfast €84; ❄) inside the walled town, has three exquisitely appointed rooms, one with a small private terrace. **Hôtel L'Escale** (☎04 66 53 71 14; http://hotel.escale.free.fr; 3 av Tour de Constance; r €40-68, q €75-85; 👪) caters fantastically to budget travellers.

The **tourist office** (☎04 66 53 73 00; www.ot-aiguesmortes.fr; place St-Louis; ⌚9am-noon & 1-6pm) is inside the walled city.

Les Cabanes de Cacharel HORSE RIDING
(☎04 90 97 84 10, 06 11 57 74 75; www.cabanesdecacharel.com; rte de Cacharel; 1/2/3hr horse trek €15/28/40) Farms along route d'Arles (D570) offer *promenades à cheval* (horseback riding) astride white Camargue horses, but a more authentic experience can be had at the less tacky Les Cabanes de Cacharel along the parallel rte de Cacharel (D85A). It also has horse-and-carriage rides (€12/20 per one/two hours).

Domaine Paul Ricard THEME PARK
(☎04 90 97 10 62; www.mejanes.camargue.fr; Méjanes) For kids' pony rides, head to ranch theme-park Domaine Paul Ricard, on the northwestern bank of Étang de Vaccarès, in Méjanes. Drive 14km south along D570 from Arles, turn left along eastbound D37, then right toward Méjanes. It also has bike rental, a restaurant, *courses Camarguaises*, and so on.

Manade Salierène COWBOY COURSE
(☎04 66 86 45 57; www.manadesalierene.com; Mas de Capellane) Get a taste of cowboy life with a one-week *stage de monte gardiane* (Camargue cowboy course). Initiation/perfection courses (€650) include accommodation and meals with the *manadier*'s family.

Boating WATER SPORTS
The marshy Camargue lends itself to exploration by boat. All outfits charge around €10/5 per adult/child for a 1½-hour trip. Find **Camargue Bateau de Promenade** (☎04 90 97 84 72; http://bateau-camargue.com; 5 rue des Launes) and **Quatre Maries** (☎04 90 97 70 10; www.bateaux-4maries.camargue.fr; 36 av Théodore Aubanel) in Stes-Maries de la Mer. **Le Tiki III** (☎04 90 97 81 68; www.tiki3.fr) is a beat-up old paddleboat at the mouth of the Petit Rhône 1.5km west of Stes-Maries.

For canoeing and kayaking on the Petit Rhône, contact **Kayak Vert Camargue** (☎04 66 73 57 17; www.kayakvert-camargue.fr; Mas de Sylvéréal), 14km north of Stes-Maries off the D38.

Cycling BICYCLE TOUR
Bicycles are ideal on the Camargue's flat terrain. East of Stes-Maries de la Mer, seafront paths like Digue à la Mer (p182) are reserved for walkers and cyclists. **Le Vélo Saintois** (☎04 90 97 74 56; www.levelosaintois.camargue.fr; 19 rue de la République, Stes-Maries de la Mer), with an English-language list of cycling routes, rents mountain bikes (per day/three days €15/34). **Le Vélociste** (☎04 90 97 83 26; www.levelociste.fr; place Mireille, Stes-Maries de la Mer) rents and organises cycling-horseback (€36) or cycling-canoeing (€30) packages. Both deliver bikes for free to hotels.

🛏 Sleeping

Ranch-style motel accommodation lines the D570 heading into Stes-Maries de la Mer. The tourist offices list self-catering *cabanes de gardian* (traditional whitewashed cowboy cottages) and farmstays.

TOP CHOICE **Le Mas de Peint** HISTORIC FARMHOUSE €€€
(☎04 90 97 20 62; www.masdepeint.com; Le Sambuc; d/ste from €260/395; ⊙mid-Mar–mid-Nov; ❄📶🏊) Camargue's upmarket *mas* (farmhouse): think chic, gentrified country quarters right out of the pages of design mag *Côte Sud*. The gourmet **restaurant** (3-course dinner menu adult/child €55/29, lunch from €39, canteen mains €17-30; ⊙lunch Sat & Sun, dinner Fri-Wed) with seasonal menus and poolside canteen are open to non-guests. Offerings include horses and bikes to ride, jeep safaris (€60) and Roma music dinners in summer. Reservations essential.

Hôtel de Cacharel FARM PENSION €€
(☎04 90 97 95 44; www.hotel-cacharel.com; rte de Cacharel, D85A; s/d/tr/q from €120/131/142/165; ⊙year-round; @📶🏊) This isolated farmstead balances modern-day comforts with rural authenticity perfectly. Photographic portraits of the bull herder who created the hotel in 1947 give the vintage dining room soul. Priciest rooms look out over the sunrise on the water. The pension's owner is friendly, there are fans for summer and there's wi-fi in reception. It's just north of Stes-Maries de la Mer.

✖ Eating

TOP CHOICE **La Chassagnette** GASTRONOMIC €€€
(☎04 90 97 26 96; www.chassagnette.fr; rte du Sambuc; mains €35; ⊙lunch & dinner Thu-Mon Apr-Jun, Sep & Oct, daily Jul & Aug, Thu-Sun Nov-Mar) Inhaling the scent of sun-ripened tomatoes is one of many pleasures at this 19th-century sheepfold – the ultimate Camargue dine. Alain Ducasse–prodigy Armand Arnal cooks up a constantly changing 100% organic menu, grows much of it himself and woos guests with a mosquito-protected outside terrace. Look for the fork and trowel sign, 12km southeast of Arles on the southbound D36.

TOP CHOICE **Le Mazet du Vaccarès** CAMARGUAIS SEAFOOD €€
(Chez Hélène et Néné; ☎04 90 97 10 79; www.mazetduvaccares.camargue.fr; south of Méjanes; 3-course menu €35; ⊙lunch Fri-Sun, dinner Fri & Sat, closed mid-Aug–mid-Sep & mid-Dec–mid-Jan) Gorging on fish in this legendary lakeside cabin is a feast for the eyes and belly. Memorabilia from Hélène and Néné's days as lighthouse keepers in Beauduc fill the restaurant with soul. The jovial couple cook up one fixed *menu* built from the catch of local fishermen. From Domaine Paul Ricard, it is a signposted 2.5km drive south along pot-holed gravel.

Restaurant La Telline CAMARGUAIS €€
(☎04 90 97 01 75; www.restaurantlatelline.fr; rte de Gageron, Villeneuve; mains €20-25; ⊙lunch & dinner Fri-Mon) Jean-Paul and Florence offer rustic home-cooking in this locals' favourite eatery. No credit cards.

Estrambord CAMARGUAIS €
(☎04 90 97 20 10; www.estrambord.free.fr; Le Sambuc; 3-course menu €13.50-18; ⊙lunch daily) A roadside diner, Camargue-style. Feast on local specialties from seafood to bull.

Stes-Maries de la Mer

POP 2344

This remote seaside outpost has a rough-and-tumble holidaymaker feel, with white-washed buildings crowding dusty streets. During its Roma pilgrimages, street-cooked pans of paella fuel chaotic crowds of carnivalesque guitarists, dancers and mounted cowboys. Stes-Maries de la Mer has a sea-front village **arena** where bullfights and *courses Camarguaises* are held.

◉ Sights & Activities

Stes-Maries de la Mer is fringed by 30km of fine-sand beaches, easily reached by bicycle. Nudist beaches surround the Gacholle lighthouse off the Digue à la Mer (p182).

Église des Stes-Maries CHURCH
(place de l'Église) This 12th- to 15th-century church with its dark, hushed, candle wax-scented atmosphere draws legions of pilgrim Roma to venerate the statue of black Sara, their highly revered patron saint, during the **Pèlerinage des Gitans** (p186). The relics of Sara, along with those of Stes Marie-Salomé and Marie-Jacobé, all found in the crypt by King René in 1448, are enshrined in a painted wooden chest, stashed in the stone wall above the choir. From the church's **rooftop terrace** (€2), a panorama unfolds.

🛏 Sleeping

Most places function April to October.

Hôtel Méditerranée HOTEL €
(☎04 90 97 82 09; www.hotel-mediterranee.camargue.fr; 4 av Frédéric Mistral; d without/with bathroom €42/55, tr/q €75/80; ⊙mid-Mar–Sep; ❄) Handily located in the centre of town is one of the cheapest and most charming accommodations options, festooned with flowerpots. Simple rooms that are seconds from the sea.

START ARLES
FINISH VILLENEUVE
DISTANCE: 85KM
DURATION: ONE DAY

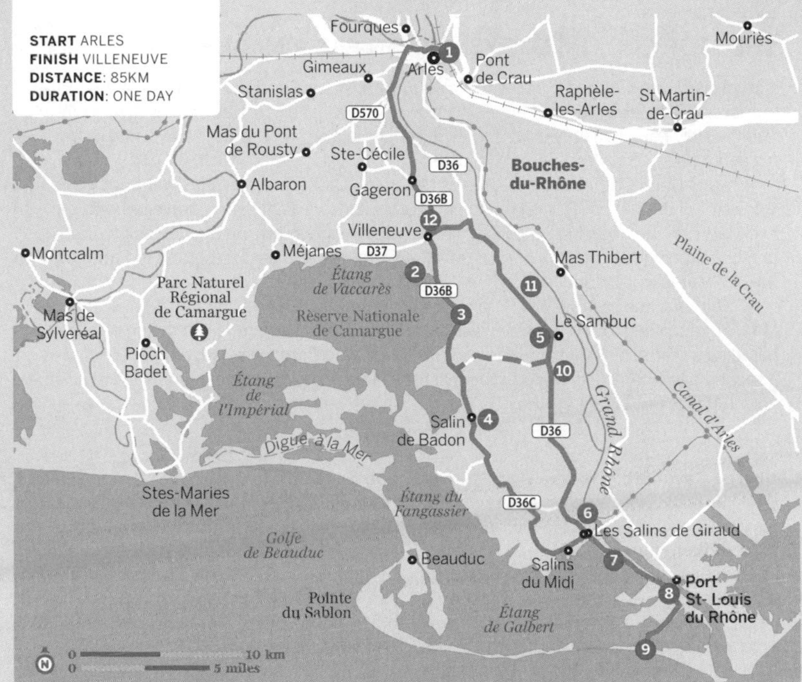

Driving Tour

The Wild Southeast

For a jaunt to the edge of the world, drive south from 1 **Arles** along the D570 (direction Stes-Maries de la Mer). After 2.8km, turn left onto the D36 (direction Le Sambuc and Salin de Giraud) and within seconds you're in the Parc Naturel Régional de Camargue. Four kilometres on, turn right onto the D36B (direction Gageron) and at the crossroads continue straight.

Soon after, the D36B dramatically skims the eastern shores of the 2 **Étang de Vaccarès**. The wetland is at its most savage here and much of the area is off-limits, making the nature trails and wildlife observatories at 3 **La Capelière** particularly precious. Play voyeur as little egrets and grey herons frolic in the marshes and buy a permit for the nature trails at 4 **Salin de Badon** (7km south).

Cut back to 5 **Le Sambuc** for lunch at **La Chassagnette**, **Estrambord** or **Le Mas de Peint**, which also offers horse-riding and jeep tours by appointment.

South along the D36C skip through Salin de Giraud, an unexceptional village that grew up around Europe's largest *salins* (salt pans), producing 800,000 tonnes per year. For the salt mad, visit the 6 **Les Salins de Giraud** museum inside the village saltworks.

More soul-stirring is the windswept panorama of the pans, salt mountains and diggers two kilometres south of the village at the 7 **point de vue** (viewpoint) along the D36D.

The unforgettable final 12km leg of this southbound journey passes pink flamingos wading through water on your way to 8 **Domaine de la Palissade**, a nature centre with walks and horse treks.

The road terminates at 9 **Plage de Piémanson** 3.7km south, where campervans park overnight on the sand.

On the return to Arles along the D36, you can swing into the tiny 10 **Musée du Riz du Petit Manusclat** and 11 **Domaine de Beaujeu**, to learn about and buy local produce. Then dine well at 12 **Restaurant La Telline** in Villeneuve.

THE STORY OF THE MARYS & GITAN PILGRIMAGES

Catholicism first reached European shores in what's now tiny Stes-Maries de la Mer. The stories say that Stes Marie-Salomé and Marie-Jacobé (and some say Mary Magdalene) fled the Holy Land in a little boat and were caught in a storm, drifting at sea until washing ashore here.

Provençal and Catholic lore diverge at this point: Catholicism relates that Sara, patron saint of the *gitans* (Roma Gitano people, also known as gypsies), travelled with the two Marys on the boat. Provençal legend says Sara was already here and was the first person to recognise their holiness. In 1448, skeletal remains said to belong to Sara and the two Marys were found in a crypt in Stes-Maries de la Mer.

Gitans continue to make pilgrimages, **Pèlerinage des Gitans**, here on 24 and 25 May (often staying for up to three weeks), dancing and playing music in the streets, and parading a statue of Sara through town. The Sunday in October closest to the 22nd sees a second pilgrimage dedicated to the two Stes Maries; *courses Camarguaises* are also held at this time.

L'Auberge Cavalière FARM PENSION €€
(☎04 90 97 88 88; www.aubergecavaliere.com; rte d'Arles (D570); d €145-190, tr €145-180; ❄@≋👪) This well-maintained complex of purpose-built thatched-roof cowboy cottages strung along a lake edge woos folks with manicured grounds, pool and a fine **restaurant** (www.aubergecavaliere.com; rte d'Arles [D570]; menus €32-38) with homemade bread, bull steaks and biodynamic produce. Find it set back from the D570 1.5km north of Stes-Maries de la Mer.

Eating

La Cabane aux Coquillages SEAFOOD €
(rue Théodore Aubanel; menus from €18.50; ⏲lunch & dinner daily Mar-Nov) This pocket-sized fish shop has crates of crustaceans piled high inside and a gaggle of sea-blue chairs outside. A glass of dry white and half-a-dozen oysters costs a mere €8.50.

Lou Santen SEAFOOD €
(☎06 30 17 32 49; 21 rue Sadi Carnot; mains €9-15; ⏲May–mid-Sep) Rebuilt each summer for the new season, this beach restaurant is shaded by a typical reed *loupio*. The catch of the day can feel pricey but stick to a finger-licking bowl of *moules frîtes* (mussels and chips) and value is guaranteed.

Information

Tourist Office (☎04 90 97 82 55; www.saintesmaries.com; 5 av Van Gogh; ⏲9am-7pm) Guided walking tours (€7) depart 2pm Tuesday and Friday.

Getting There & Around

Le Vélo Saintois (p183) and Le Vélociste (p183) hire bicycles. Stes-Maries de la Mer has no bus station; buses to/from Arles via Pont du Gau and Mas du Pont de Rousty use the shelter at the northern entrance to town on av d'Arles (the continuation of rte d'Arles and the D570).

Avignon & Around

Includes »

Best Places to Eat

- » L'Oustau de Baumanière (p219)
- » Le Verger des Papes (p201)
- » Moulin à Huile (p206)
- » Le Vivier (p213)
- » Mas de l'Amarine (p217)

Best Places to Stay

- » Hôtel la Mirande (p195)
- » Hôtel Boquier (p195)
- » Hôtel l'Herbier d'Orange (p202)
- » Sous les Figuiers (p217)

Why Go?

Encircled by crenellated ramparts dating back 800 years, Avignon lords above the mighty River Rhône. Its 14th-century hilltop palace – the former seat of popes – defines the skyline and begs exploration, while the narrow streets and leafy squares fanning out beneath it invite wandering.

Rolling countryside, dotted with ancient villages and vineyards that produce some of France's best wines, unfurls outside Avignon. Sample renowned vintages in Châteauneuf-du-Pape, or in the saw-toothed Dentelles de Montmirail. Discover incredibly preserved Roman ruins in Orange, Nîmes and St-Rémy de Provence, and explore medieval streets in Vaison-la-Romaine and Les Baux de Provence.

The glass-green River Sorgue – ready-made for canoeing – connects picturesque towns like L'Isle-sur-la-Sorgue, celebrated for antiques shopping, and Fontaine-de-Vaucluse, the river's mysterious source. Hikers and bikers flock windswept Mont Ventoux, Provence's highest peak, rising from purple lavender fields that perfume the summer breeze.

Driving Distances (km)

	Avignon	Carpentras	Nîmes	Orange	St-Rémy de Provence
Carpentras	25				
Nîmes	42	67			
Orange	27	22	53		
St-Rémy de Provence	20	45	41	48	
Vaison-la-Romaine	46	24	80	28	70

DON'T MISS

Wrapping your head around Avignon means exploring the Palais des Papes (p189). Leave time to wander the adjacent Rocher des Domes Park to take in vistas of the Rhône Valley.

Best Places to Ditch Crowds

» Visite Secrét du Palais des Papes (p189)

» Jardins de l'Abbaye (p199)

» Canoeing the Sorgue (p214)

» Hiking Mont Ventoux (p208)

» Suzette (p206)

Best Tours & Courses

» Avignon Wine Tour (p194)

» La Truffe du Ventoux Truffle Tour (p207)

» Le Marmiton Cooking School (p195)

» Autocars Lieutaud Sightseeing (p194)

Resources

» **Provence Guide** (www.provenceguide.com) Includes lodging specials and itineraries.

» **Avignon Tourism** (www.avignon-tourisme.com) The city's official tourism site.

» **Avignon & Provence** (www.avignon-et-provence.com) Events, dining, lodging.

» **Provence Cycling** (www.provence-cycling.com) Cycling maps and itineraries.

» **Visit Provence** (www.visitprovence.com) Extensive information on the Alpilles.

Getting Around

A car is a nuisance in Avignon – streets are often closed to traffic, and parking garages are expensive – but to see surrounding smaller towns at leisure, you'll need wheels. If you don't want to drive, buses from Avignon serve most villages; trains serve only larger towns and cities, including Orange and L'Isle-sur-la-Sorgue.

THREE PERFECT DAYS

Day 1: Roman Relics

Choose one of three areas to discover incredible Roman ruins. Near chic St-Rémy de Provence, explore Glanum (p216), the remains of a Gallo-Roman town built around a sacred spring. North of Avignon, Orange has the best-preserved Roman theatre in Europe (p202), and is close to France's largest archaeological site, Vaison-la-Romaine (p204). Pont du Gard (p221), the famous three-tiered aqueduct, is half way between Avignon and Nîmes, the latter of which is home to a brilliant Roman amphitheatre, Les Arènes (p219).

Day 2: Cycling and Wine-Tasting the Dentelles de Montmirail

The jagged limestone Dentelles, dotted with sleepy villages and wineries, are ideal for exploring by bicycle. Tourist offices at Vaison-la-Romaine (p206) and Beaumes de Venise (p208) provide detailed back-road route maps tailored to all fitness levels. Worthy destinations include Le Barroux (p207), home to a medieval castle and working monastery; and the little town of Gigondas (p206), where you can sample great reds at cafes and tasting bars lining the sun-dappled village square.

Day 3: The River Sorgue Special

Arrive early to beat the crowds to Fontaine-de-Vaucluse (p214), the River Sorgue's mysterious source. After watching the giant spring bubble up from the earth's depths, float two hours downstream via canoe to L'Isle-sur-la-Sorgue (p212), where you can lunch by the water, then explore antiques shops lining flowery lanes, and admire 18th-century canals and moss-covered waterwheels.

Advance Planning

For the biggest summer festivals, book rooms six months to a year ahead; buy tickets the day they become available.

» Festival d'Avignon

» Les Chorégies d'Orange

» Choralies, Vaison-la-Romaine

» Féria de Pentecôte, Nîmes

AVIGNON

POP 92,454

Ringed by incredibly preserved 800-year-old stone ramparts, graceful Avignon's turn as the seat of papal power bestowed the city with a treasury of magnificent art and architecture, none grander than the massive medieval fortress and papal palace, Palais des Papes. In romantic counterpoint, Pont d'Avignon – of nursery-rhyme fame – spans half the Rhône. Ancient cobbled streets pass inviting boutiques; leafy squares overflow with cafe tables; and in July thousands come for Avignon's renowned performing arts festival.

History

Avignon first gained its ramparts – and reputation for arts and culture – during the 14th century when Pope Clement V fled political turmoil in Rome. From 1309 to 1377, seven French-born popes invested huge sums in the papal palace and offered asylum to Jews and political dissidents. Pope Gregory XI left Avignon in 1376, but his death two years later led to the Great Schism (1378–1417), during which rival popes (up to three at one time) resided at Rome and Avignon, denouncing and excommunicating one another. Even after the matter was settled and an impartial pope, Martin V, established himself in Rome, Avignon remained under papal rule. Avignon and Comtat Venaissin (now the Vaucluse *département*) were ruled by papal legates until 1791.

Sights & Activities

You'll need at least two days in Avignon to visit the major sights: the Palais des Papes, the Pont St-Bénezet and the walled city's lovely cobbled streets. Ticket offices for sights close 30 to 60 minutes before overall closing time.

Palais des Papes PALACE

(Papal Palace; www.palais-des-papes.com; place du Palais; adult/child €6/3; ⏲9am-8pm Jul, 9am-9pm Aug, shorter hours Sep-Jun) The immense Palais des Papes is the world's largest Gothic palace and is a Unesco World Heritage Site. Built when Pope Clement V abandoned Rome in 1309 to settle in Avignon, it was the seat of papal power for 70-odd years. The immense scale, cavernous stone halls and vast courtyards testify to the popes' wealth; the 3m-thick walls, portcullises and watchtowers emphasise their insecurity.

Today, it takes imagination to picture the former luxury of these vast, bare rooms, but PDA-style audio-video guides introduced in 2012 show 2- and 3D imagery of the once sumptuous furnishings. Even without, you can see the splendour in the 14th-century chapel frescoes, painted by Matteo Giovannetti; in the intricate walls of the Pope's bedroom; and in the superb Chambre du Cerf, alive with medieval hunting scenes.

Self-guided tours direct you from lower floors to crenellations; stop for coffee in the sky-high cafe. The guided two-hour **Visite Palais Secret** (Secret Palace Tour) takes you to secret towers, rooftop walkways and hidden chambers; reservations essential. The English-language version (€19.50) runs on Fridays, spring and autumn; the French-language version (€34.50) runs Saturday and Sunday, September to May, and includes brunch.

Check the website for a complete list of opening hours throughout the year.

Place du Palais SQUARE

A golden statue of Virgin Mary (weighing 4.5 tons) stands on the dome of Romanesque **Cathédrale Notre Dame des Doms** (built 1671–72), her outstretched arms protecting the city. Next to the cathedral, hilltop **Rocher des Doms** gardens provide knockout views of the Rhône, Mont Ventoux and Les Alpilles; there's also a **playground**. Opposite the Palais des Papes, the much-photographed building dripping with carvings of fruit and heraldic beasts, is the former 17th-century mint, **Hôtel des Monnaies**.

Pont St-Bénezet BRIDGE

(adult/child €4.50/3.50; ⏲9am-8pm Jul, 9am-9pm Aug, shorter hours Sep-Jun) According to legend, pastor Bénezet had three saintly visions urging him to build a bridge across the Rhône. Completed in 1185, the bridge linked Avignon with Villeneuve-lès-Avignon, controlling trade

AVIGNON PASS

The must-have discount card, *Avignon Passion* provides discounts on museums, tours and monuments in Avignon and Villeneuve-lès-Avignon. The first site you visit costs full price, but each subsequent site will discount admission by 10% to 50%. The pass covers five people and is valid for 15 days. Available from the tourist office and tourist sites.

Avignon & Around Highlights

1. Exploring palaces and ancient streets in **Avignon** (p189)
2. Sampling France's great wines in **Châteauneuf-du-Pape** (p200)
3. Reviving Rome at the **Théâtre Antique** (p202) in Orange
4. Climbing to hilltop medieval **Vaison-la-Romaine** (p204)
5. Paddling beneath famous **Pont du Gard** (p221)
6. Village-hopping the **Dentelles de Montmirail** (p206)
7. Ascending Provence's mightiest peak, **Mont Ventoux** (p208)
8. Antiques-shopping in **L'Isle-sur-la-Sorgue** (p212)
9. Royalty-spotting in **St-Rémy de Provence** (p216)
10. Jousting with ghosts atop **Les Baux de Provence** (p219)

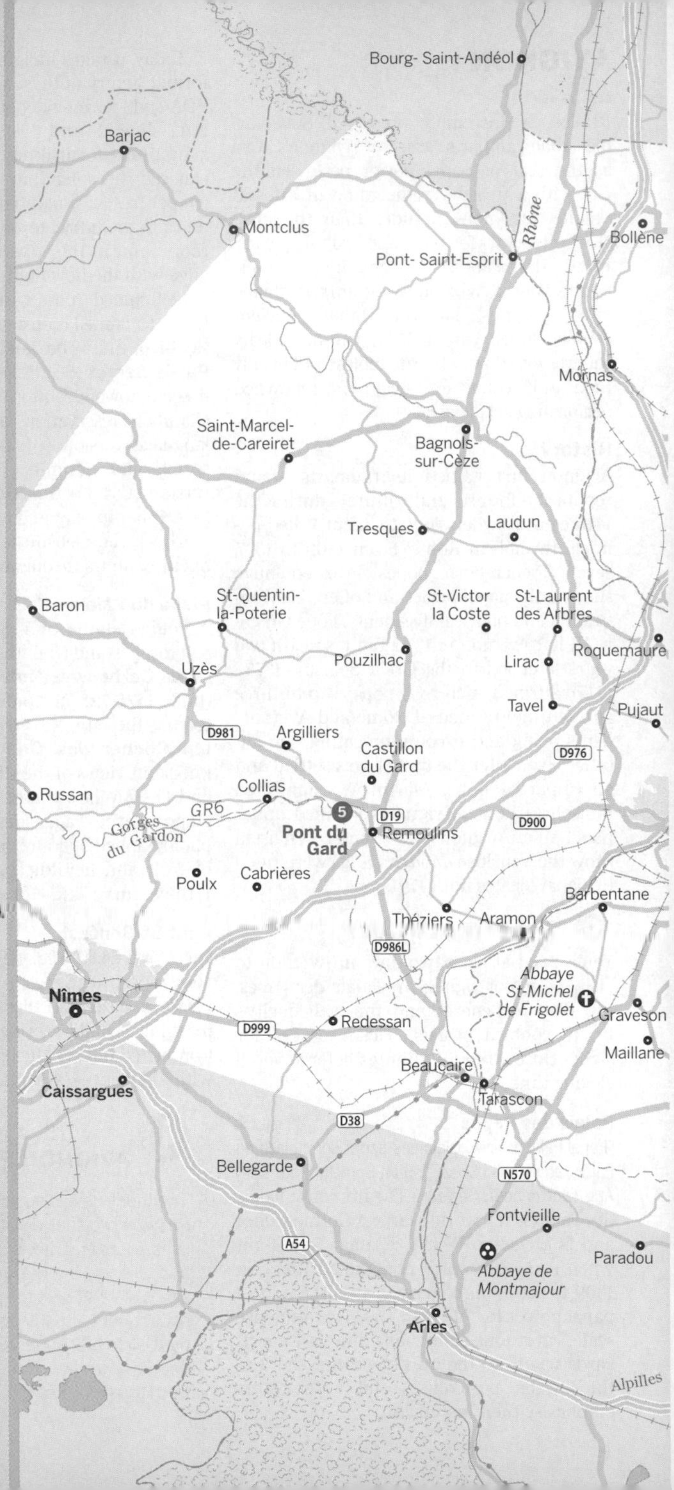

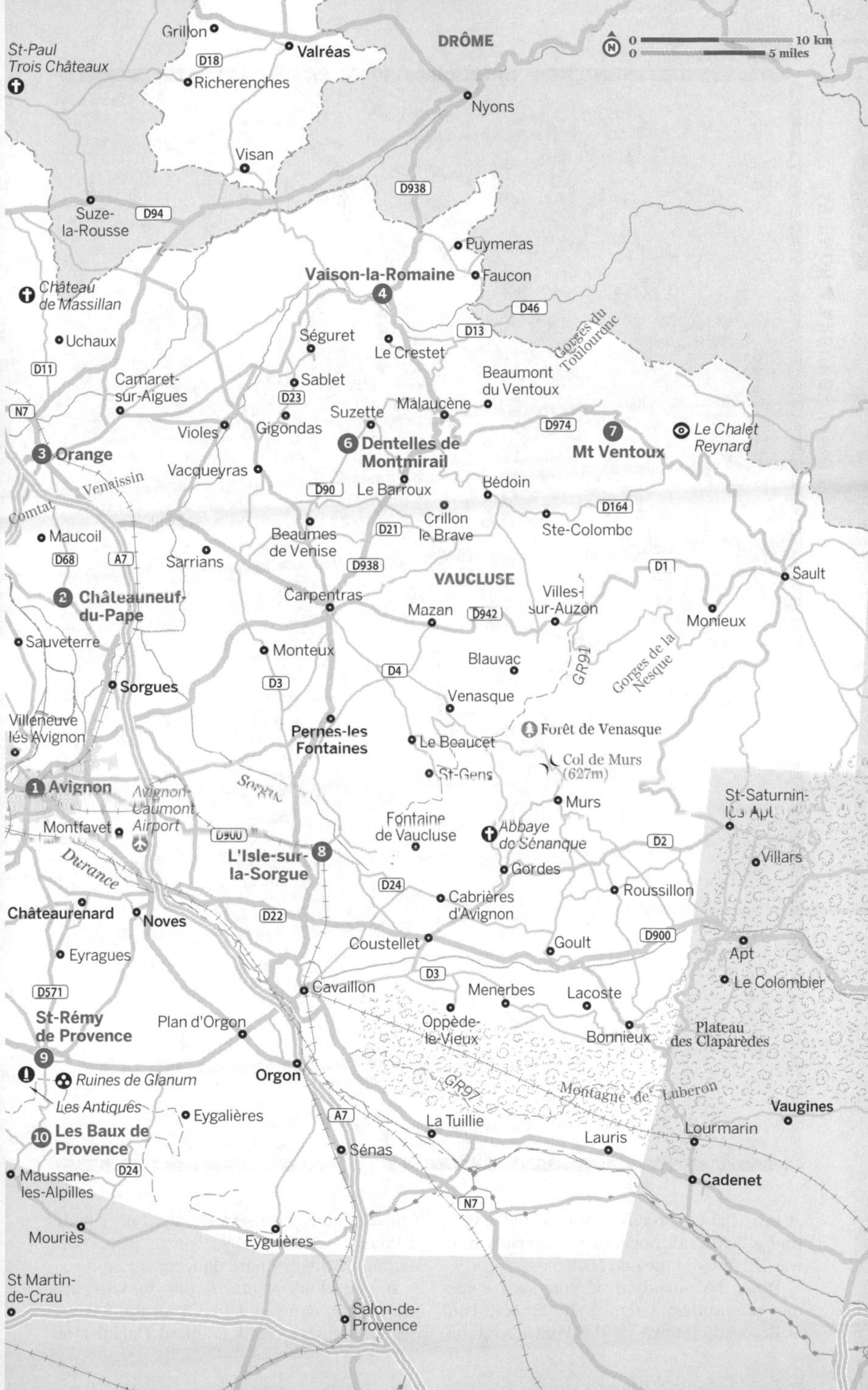

DRÔME
0 10 km
0 5 miles
Grillon
Valréas
St-Paul Trois Châteaux
D18
Richerenches
Nyons
Visan
D938
Suze-la-Rousse
D94
Puymeras
Vaison-la-Romaine
4
Faucon
Château de Massillan
D46
D13
Gorges du Toulourenc
Séguret
Le Crestet
Uchaux
D11
Camaret-sur-Aigues
Sablet
Beaumont du Ventoux
D23
Malaucène
N7
Suzette
Gigondas
D974
Violes
7
Le Chalet Reynard
6 Dentelles de Montmirail
3 Orange
Mt Ventoux
Vacqueyras
Venaissin
Bédoin
D90
Le Barroux
Comtat
D164
Crillon le Brave
Ste-Colombe
Maucoil
D21
Beaumes de Venise
D68
A7
Sarrians
D938
VAUCLUSE
D1
Sault
2 Châteauneuf-du-Pape
Carpentras
Villes-sur-Auzon
Mazan
D942
Monieux
Sauveterre
Monteux
Blauvac
GR91
Gorges de la Nesque
D4
D3
Sorgues
Venasque
Villeneuve lès Avignon
Pernes-les Fontaines
Forêt de Venasque
Le Beaucet
Col de Murs (627m)
St-Gens
1 Avignon
Avignon-Caumont Airport
Sorgue
Murs
St-Saturnin-lès-Apt
Fontaine de Vaucluse
Montfavet
Abbaye de Sénanque
D900
8
L'Isle-sur-la-Sorgue
D2
Villars
Durance
Gordes
D24
Roussillon
Cabrières d'Avignon
Châteaurenard
Noves
D22
Coustellet
Goult
D900
Apt
Eyragues
D3
Le Colombier
Cavaillon
Menerbes
Lacoste
D571
Oppède-le-Vieux
St-Rémy de Provence
Plan d'Orgon
Bonnieux
Plateau des Claparèdes
9
Orgon
Ruines de Glanum
GR97
Montagne de Luberon
Les Antiques
Eygalières
Vaugines
A7
10 Les Baux de Provence
La Tuillie
Lauris
Lourmarin
Sénas
Maussane-les-Alpilles
D24
Cadenet
N7
Mouriès
Eyguières
St Martin-de-Crau
Salon-de-Provence

Avignon

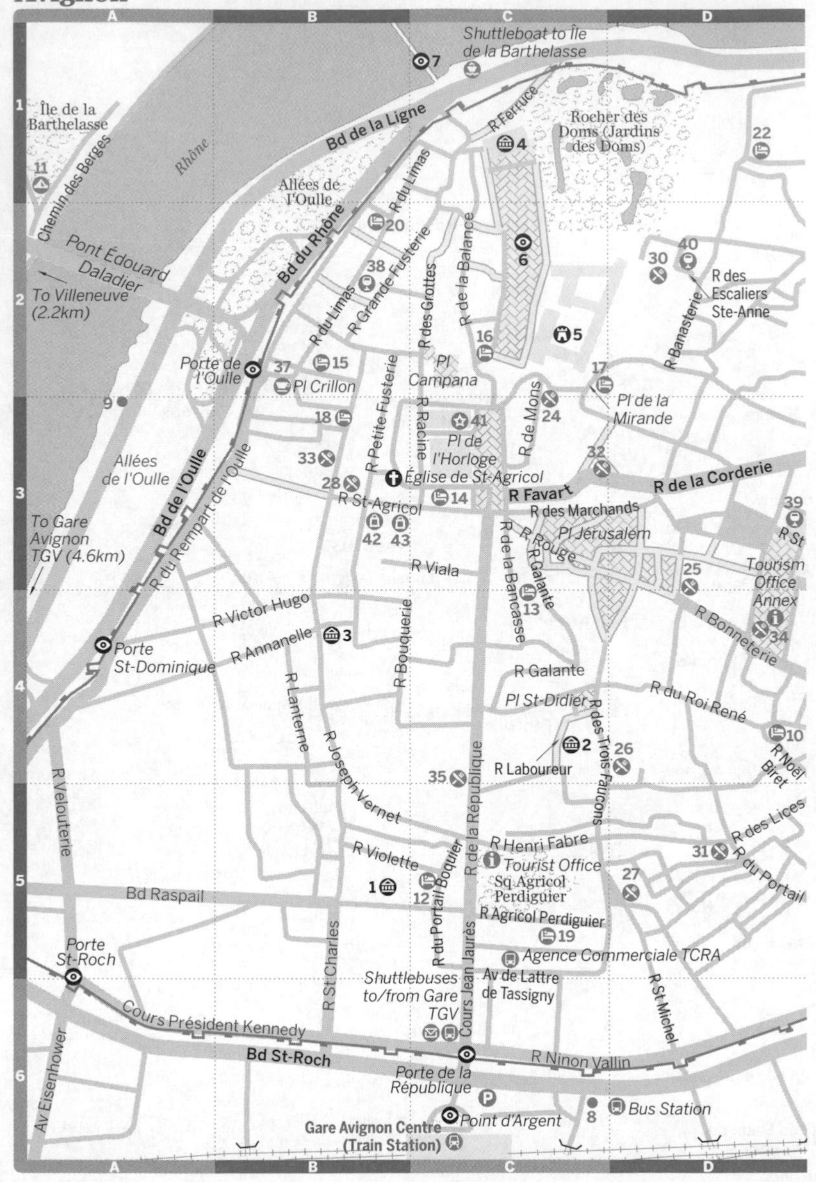

at this vital crossroads. It was rebuilt several times, before all but four of its spans were washed away in the mid-1600s.

Don't be surprised if you spot someone attempting a dance. In France, Pont St-Béezet is known as the Pont d'Avignon, from the chirpy nursery rhyme: 'Sur le pont d'Avignon / L'on y danse, l'on y danse...' (On Avignon Bridge, all are dancing...).

If you don't want to pay to visit the bridge, you can see it free from the Rocher des Doms park, Pont Édouard Daladier or

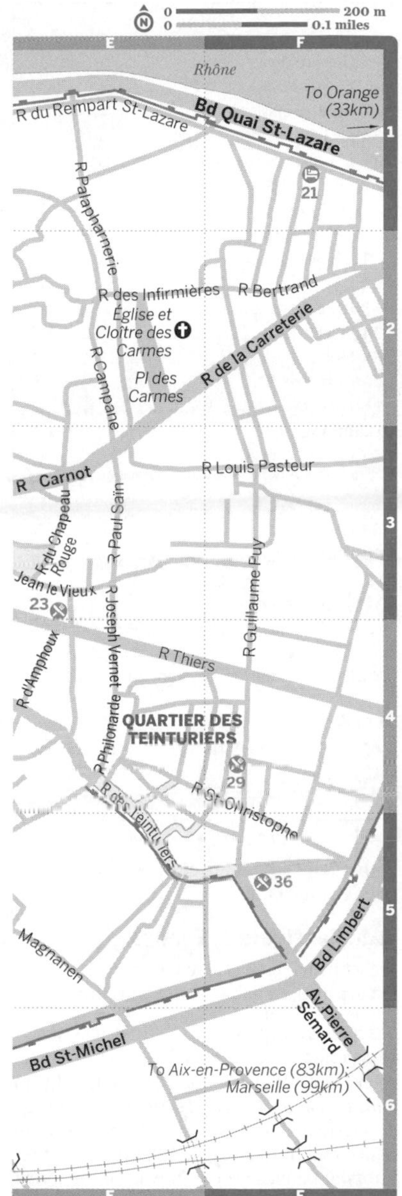

from across the river on the Île de la Barhelasse's chemin des Berges.

City Walks WALK

One of Avignon's chief joys is to wander aimlessly around the photogenic old city. Within its 14th-century **ramparts** lie crooked streets and leafy squares, medieval churches, and handsome houses with ornate doorways. The tourist office has a free map, outlining four different routes, including the **Quartier des Teinturiers**, the former dyers' district, where four waterwheels still turn.

Musée Calvet GALLERY

(☎04 90 86 33 84; 65 rue Joseph Vernet; adult/child €6/3; ⏰10am-1pm & 2-6pm Wed-Mon) The elegant Hôtel de Villeneuve-Martignan (built 1741–54) provides a fitting backdrop for Avignon's fine-arts museum, which has 16th- to 20th-century oil paintings, compelling prehistoric pieces, 15th-century wrought-iron, and the elongated landscapes of Avignonnais artist Joseph Vernet.

Musée du Petit Palais ART MUSEUM

(www.petit-palais.org; place du Palais; adult/child €6/free; ⏰10am-1pm & 2-6pm Wed-Mon) The bishops' palace during the 14th and 15th centuries houses outstanding collections of primitive, pre-Rennaissance, 13th- to 16th-century Italian religious paintings by artists including Botticelli, Carpaccio and Giovanni di Paolo – the most famous is Botticelli's *La Vierge et l'Enfant* (1470).

Musée Angladon GALLERY

(www.angladon.com; 5 rue Laboureur; adult/child €6/4; ⏰1-6pm Tue-Sun Apr-Nov, 1-6pm Wed-Sun Jan-Mar) Tiny Musée Angladon harbours Impressionist treasures including Van Gogh's *Railway Wagons* – look closely and notice that the 'earth' isn't paint but bare canvas. Also displayed are a handful of early Picasso sketches and artworks by Cézanne, Sisley, Manet and Degas; upstairs are antiques and 17th-century paintings.

Collection Lambert GALLERY

(www.collectionlambert.com; 5 rue Violette; adult/student/child €7/5.50/2; ⏰11am-9pm daily Jul & Aug, 11am-6pm Tue-Sun Sep-Jun) Avignon's contemporary-arts museum showcases works from the 1960s to present – from minimalist and conceptual, to video and photography – in stark contrast to the classic 18th-century mansion housing them.

Tours

The tourist office (p198) leads year-round themed guided walks (from €15) in English and French at 10am on varying days from April to October (Saturdays only November to March). It also has good self-guided tour maps.

Avignon

Sights

1 Collection Lambert ... B5
2 Musée Angladon ... C4
3 Musée Calvet ... B4
4 Musée du Petit Palais ... C1
5 Palais des Papes ... C2
6 Place du Palais ... C2
7 Pont St-Bénezet ... C1

Activities, Courses & Tours

8 Autocars Lieutaud ... C6
9 Les Grands Bateaux ... A3

Sleeping

10 Autour du Petit Paradis ... D4
11 Camping & Auberge Bagatelle ... A1
12 Hôtel Boquier ... C5
13 Hôtel de Garlande ... C4
14 Hôtel de l'Horloge ... C3
15 Hôtel d'Europe ... B2
16 Hôtel du Palais des Papes ... C2
17 Hôtel La Mirande ... C2
18 Hôtel Mignon ... B3
19 Hôtel Splendid ... C5
20 Le Limas ... B2
21 Lumani ... F1
22 Villa de Margot ... D1

Eating

23 Au Tout Petit ... E3
24 Christian Etienne ... C3
25 Cuisine du Dimanche ... D3
26 Fou de Fafa ... D4
27 Ginette et Marcel ... D5
28 La Tropézienne ... B3
29 L'Atelier de Damien ... F4
30 Le Grand Café ... D2
Le Lutrin ... (see 16)
Le Marmiton ... (see 17)
31 L'Epice and Love ... D5
32 L'Épicerie ... C3
33 Les 5 Sens ... B3
34 Les Halles ... D4
35 Monoprix ... C4
36 Numéro 75 ... F5

Drinking

37 Cafe la Scène ... B2
Le Cid Café ... (see 14)
38 L'Esclave ... B2
39 Red Sky ... D3
40 Utopia Bar ... D2

Entertainment

AJMI ... (see 30)
Cinéma Utopia ... (see 30)
41 Opéra Théâtre d'Avignon ... C3

Shopping

42 Comtesse du Barry ... B3
43 Oliviers & Co ... B3

Autocars Lieutaud BUS TOUR
(☎04 90 86 36 75; www.cars-lieutaud.fr; 36 bd Saint-Roch; station) Themed half- and full-day tours including wineries, lavender, Roman monuments and Luberon (€45 to €55). For a vintage experience, book the classic convertible Citroën 2CV (from €145).

Les Grands Bateaux BOAT TOUR
(☎04 90 85 62 25; www.mireio.net; allées de l'Oulle; boat tours adult/child €9/5; boat tours 3pm & 4.15pm Apr-Jun & Sep, 2-6pm Jul-Aug) Runs 45-minute boat tours from April to September, looping under the Pont St-Bénezet. For year-round daytime cruises, *Le Mireio* sails to Arles, Châteauneuf-du-Pape and Tarascon. On July and August evenings the company's dinner cruises (8.30pm) draw older crowds with dancing and live entertainment.

Avignon Wine Tour VINEYARD TOUR
(☎06 28 05 33 84; www.avignon-wine-tour.com; per person €80) Visit the region's vinyards with a knowledgable guide, leaving you free to enjoy the wine.

Festivals & Events

Tickets for Festival d'Avignon and Festival Off are also available from FNAC branches.

Festival d'Avignon PERFORMING ARTS
(www.festival-avignon.com; Jul) The three-week Festival d'Avignon, held annually in July, is one of the world's great performing-arts festivals. Over 40 international works of dance and drama play to 100,000-plus spectators at venues around town. Tickets don't go on sale until springtime, but hotels sell out by February.

Festival Off PERFORMING ARTS
(www.avignonleoff.com; Jul) Festival d'Avignon is paralleled by a simultaneous fringe event, Festival Off, with eclectic (and cheaper) experimental programming. La Carte Off (€16) provides 30% discounts.

Sleeping

TOP CHOICE Hôtel La Mirande LUXURY HOTEL €€€

(☎04 90 14 20 20; www.la-mirande.fr; 4 place de la Mirande; d €425-610; ❄@🛜) Avignon's top hotel occupies a converted 16th-century palace with dramatic interiors decked in oriental rugs, gold-threaded tapestries, marble staircases and over-the-top Gallic style. Low-end rooms are small, but still conjure the feeling of staying overnight in someone's private château.

The onsite formal restaurant **Le Marmiton** (4 place de la Mirande; mains from €35, chef's tabe €96) offers cooking classes (from €80) and twice-weekly chef's table (reservations essential); afternoon tea is served (albeit slowly) in the glittering lobby or garden.

TOP CHOICE Le Limas B&B €€

(☎04 90 14 67 19; www.le-limas-avignon.com; 51 rue du Limas; d/tr incl breakfast from €120/200; ❄@) This chic B&B in an 18th-century town house is like something out of *Vogue Living* – everything designers strive for when mixing old and new: state-of-the-art kitchen and minimalist white decor complementing antique fireplaces and 18th-century spiral stairs. Breakfast on the sun-drenched terrace is a treat – as is bubbly owner Marion.

Hôtel d'Europe LUXURY HOTEL €€€

(☎04 90 14 76 76; www.heurope.com; 12 place Crillon; d €190-540; ❄@🛜) For 200 years Hôtel de l'Europe has greeted luminaries from Napoléon to Jacqueline Kennedy Onassis. Service remains excellent, but the glamour has faded – rooms need better lighting and fabrics – but it's a grand address, particularly when you score discounted rates.

Lumani B&B €€

(☎04 90 82 94 11; www.avignon-lumani.com; 37 rue du Rempart St-Lazare; d incl breakfast €100-170; ❄🛜) Art fills this fabulous *maison d'hôte*, a fount of inspiration for painters. Rooms include two suites and there's a fountained garden.

Hôtel Boquier HOTEL €

(☎04 90 82 34 43; www.hotel-boquier.com; 6 rue du Portail Boquier; d €50-70; ❄🛜) The owners' infectious enthusiasm informs this upbeat, colourful, small central hotel; try for themed rooms Morocco or Lavender. Excellent value.

Hôtel de l'Horloge HOTEL €€

(☎04 90 16 42 00; www.hotels-ocre-azur.com; place de l'Horloge; r €95-180; ❄🛜) Most rooms at this super-central, 19th-century stone-walled hotel (with lift) are straightforward (comfortable, all mod cons), but five terrace rooms have the edge with knockout views – room 505 overlooks the Palais des Papes.

Villa de Margot B&B €€

(☎04 90 82 62 34; http://demargot.fr; 24 rue des Trois Colombes; r incl breakfast €110-190; ❄🛜) Charming, quiet old-city address. This 19th-century private home has been converted into an elegant guesthouse with walled garden and rooftop views. Rooms are styled like their names – Oriental, Royal, art deco and Romantic.

Autour du Petit Paradis SELF-CONTAINED €€

(☎04 90 81 00 42; www.autourdupetitparadis.com; 5 rue Noël Antoine Biret; apt nightly €105-180, weekly €650-1050; ❄@🛜) Live like a local in a 17th-century stone house converted into a small apartment-hotel. Scrupulously maintained, each has a kitchenette, ideal for travellers who like style but dislike shelling out for restaurants.

Hôtel de Garlande HISTORIC HOTEL €€

(☎04 90 80 08 85; www.hoteldegarlande.com; 20 rue Galante; d €80-118; ❄🛜) The elegantly decorated rooms in this historic *hôtel particulier* overlook a narrow street, central to everything. Bathrooms sparkle. Note: there's a steep stairway.

Hôtel du Palais des Papes HISTORIC HOTEL €€

(☎04 90 86 04 13; www.hotel-avignon.com; 3 place du Palais; d €88-128; q €138-158; ❄🛜) This traditional small hotel has wrought iron furniture, frescoed ceilings, exposed stone walls, a lift, and (some) views of the Palais des Papes. It has a great on-site Provençal restaurant, **Le Lutrin** (menus €25-38), and some rooms with air-conditioning.

Hôtel Mignon HOTEL €

(☎04 90 82 17 30; www.hotel-mignon.com; 12 rue Joseph Vernet; r incl breakfast €62-84; ❄@🛜) Cute and comfy, with 16 colourful rooms,

SLEEPING: AVIGNON AREA

For stays in July, reserve by January (if not earlier); expect minimum-stay requirements and premium rates. Ask if there's parking – it's usually extra. Most hotels close for several weeks in winter. Orange and Carpentras, both 30 minutes away, are dull by comparison, but make less-expensive bases.

this good-value hotel within the walled city is tops for no-frills budgeteers. Note: it has tiny baths and steep stairs.

Hôtel Splendid HOTEL €
(☎04 90 86 14 46; www.avignon-splendid-hotel.com; 17 rue Agricol Perdiguier; s €48, d €68-78, apt €78-98;) Some rooms at this cyclist-friendly, central small hotel overlook the neighbouring park. The ground-floor flat has a private patio.

La Péniche HOUSEBOAT €
(☎04 90 25 40 61, cell 06 62 37 25 17; www.chambreperiche.fr; chemin île Piot, Île de la Barthelasse; €70-95;) Rock to sleep aboard Avignon's most distinctive *chambre d'hôte*. Moored across the river, a 10-minute walk on Île de la Barthelasse, this four-room barge-houseboat gleams and has a small self-catering kitchen. Extras include a wading pool and free bikes.

Camping & Auberge Bagatelle CAMPGROUND €
(☎04 90 86 30 39; www.campingbagatelle.com; Île de la Barthelasse; tent only per person €6, car per person €13, dm incl breakfast €18; reception 8am-9pm;) Shaded and just 20 minutes' walk from the city centre on an adjacent small island in the Rhône. It has basic two- to eight-bed dorms; sheets cost €2.50 extra.

Eating

Place de l'Horloge is chock-a-block with outdoor brasseries from Easter until mid-November; food is average, but you'll always find a table. Alternatively, Place des Corps Saints is younger, less touristy and a better choice when money's tight.

TOP CHOICE **Cuisine du Dimanche** PROVENÇAL €€
(☎04 90 82 99 10; www.lacuisinedudimanche.com; 31 rue Bonneterie; mains €15-25; daily Jun-Sep, Tue-Sat Oct-May) Spitfire chef Marie shops every morning at Les Halles to find the freshest ingredients for her earthy flavour-packed cooking, and takes no culinary shortcuts. The market-driven menu changes daily, but specialities include scallops and simple roast chicken with pan gravy. The narrow stone-walled dining room is a mishmash of textures - contemporary resin chairs to antique crystal goblets - befitting the chef's eclecticism. Reserve ahead.

L'Atelier de Damien MODERN FRENCH €€
(☎04 90 82 57 35; 54 rue Guillaume Puy; lunch/dinner menus €13.50/26; lunch Mon-Sat, dinner Wed-Sat) Unframed paintings and worn tile floors lend a rough-around-the-edges look to this off-the-tourist-radar restaurant on Avignon's less-glamorous side. Chef Damien Demazure once cooked under Alain Ducasse, and draws inspiration from market-fresh ingredients, combining French with Asian - ginger, lemongrass and coriander are his favorites. Expect excellent fish, foie gras and caramel-candy cake. Reserve.

Fou de Fafa BISTRO €€
(☎04 32 76 35 13; 17 rue des Trois Faucons; menus €22-26; dinner Wed-Sun;) The classic French bistro, Fou de Fafa's strength lies in simplicity - fresh ingredients, bright flavours, and convivial surroundings. Expect a warm welcome (in English!) and fresh spins on classic dishes. Reserve.

L'Epice and Love FRENCH €
(☎04 90 82 45 96; 30 rue des Lices; mains €11-12; dinner Mon-Sat) Tables are cheek by jowl at this tiny bohemian restaurant - our favorite for budget dining - with nothing fancy, just straightforward bistro fare, stews, roasts and other reliably good, home-style French dishes. Cash only.

TOP CHOICE **Christian Etienne** PROVENÇAL €€€
(☎04 90 86 16 50; www.christian-etienne.fr; 10 rue de Mons; lunch menus €31-150, dinner menus €75-150; lunch & dinner Tue-Sat) One of Avignon's top tables, this much-vaunted restaurant occupies a 12th-century palace with a leafy outdoor terrace, adjacent to Palais des Papes. Interiors feel slightly dated, but the refined Provençal cuisine remains exceptional, notably the summertime-only starter-to-dessert tomato menu. Reserve.

Les 5 Sens GASTRONOMIC €€€
(☎04 90 85 26 51; www.restaurantles5sens.com; 18 rue Joseph Vernet; menus lunch €16-21, dinner €39-58; Tue-Sat) Chef Thierry Baucher, one of France's *meilleurs ouvriers* (top chefs), reveals his southwestern origins in specialties like *cassoulet* and foie gras, but skews contemporary Mediterranean in gastronomic dishes such as butternut-squash ravioli with *escargots*. Surroundings are refreshingly unfussy - vaguely French-colonial, with rattan and carved wood - and service is impeccable.

Numéro 75 MODERN FRENCH €€
(☎04 90 27 16 00; www.numero75.fr; 75 rue Guillaume Puy; menus €28.50-34.50, mains €16-25; Mon-Sat) The chic dining room, in the

former mansion of absinthe inventor Jules Pernod, is a fitting backdrop for stylised Mediterranean cooking. Menus change nightly, and include only three mains, but brevity guarantees freshness. On balmy nights, book the courtyard garden.

Le Grand Café MEDITERRANEAN €€
(04 90 86 86 77; www.legrandcafe-restaurant.fr; cour Maria Casarès; lunch/dinner menus €18/28; lunch & dinner Tue-Sat Sep-Apr, Tue-Sun Jun-Aug) Hidden behind the Palais des Papes, this boho-chic bistro-bar with a big terrace adjoins arty Manutention cultural centre. Giant mirrors on rough-hewn walls reflect French actors' portraits and rows of vintage tables. Good-value Provençal menus provide an alternative to more touristy places uphill.

Ginette et Marcel CAFE €
(27 place des Corps Saints; dishes €4-6; 11am-11pm Wed-Mon) *Tartines* (open-faced sandwiches), tarts, salad and soup comprise the menu at this homy cafe with farm tables, vintage floors and big windows overlooking a happening square.

Au Tout Petit MODERN FRENCH €€
(04 90 82 38 86; 4 rue d'Amphoux; menus €11-24; Tue-Sat) The 'Teeny Tiny' packs big flavours into imaginative dishes – tuna Carpaccio with vanilla, apricot *tarte Tatin* with rosemary ice cream – simple cooking that maximises spice. Wine costs just €2.50; lunch is a steal. Reserve.

L'Épicerie BISTRO €€
(04 90 82 74 22; 10 place St-Pierre; lunch/dinner menus from €18/28; daily in summer, Mon-Sat May, Sep & Oct) Tables spill into the cobbled square outside Église St-Pierre – reason enough to linger at this tiny spot, with Mediterranean dishes like lamb *tajine*, spiced beef with vegetable crumble, and *assiette des épicières* (mixed plate). It is closed for winter and the first two weeks of August.

Self-Catering

Les Halles MARKET €
(www.avignon-leshalles.com; place Pie; 7am-1pm Tue-Sun) Over 40 food stalls showcase seasonal Provençal ingredients. There are cooking demonstration on Saturdays at 11am.

La Tropézienne PATISSERIE €
(04 90 86 24 72; 22 rue St-Agricol; 8.30am-7.30pm Mon-Fri, 8.30am-2pm Sat) St-Tropez's famous cream-and-cake *tarte tropézienne,* plus other treats.

Monoprix SUPERMARKET €
(24 rue de la République; 8am-9pm Mon-Sat)

Drinking

Cafes and bars surround place Pie and smaller place des Corps Saint, both great for people-watching.

TOP CHOICE **Utopia Bar** BAR
(4 rue des Escaliers Ste-Anne; noon-midnight) Behind Palais des Papes, adjoining an art-house cinema and jazz-music centre, l'Utopia draws smart crowds to its verandah, lined with red-velvet banquettes, ideal for drinks and light bites pre- or post-theatre.

Cafe la Scène CAFE
(04 90 86 14 70; 19 place Crillon; 9am-1am) On pretty place Crillon, La Scène's outdoor tables are good for drinks and small bites; inside there's a dance floor and cabaret.

Le Cid Café CAFE
(04 90 82 30 38; www.lecidcafe.com; 11 place de l'Horloge; 11am-late) Styled with a nod to the disco era, Le Cid is an upbeat cafe by day, DJ-bar by night.

L'Esclave GAY BAR
(04 90 85 14 91; www.esclavebar.com; 12 rue du Limas; 11pm-dawn Tue-Sun) Avignon's inner-city gay bar gets busy after 11.30pm.

Red Sky PUB
(04 90 85 93 23; rue St-Jean le Vieux; 10am-1am) A bit of London – cherry-red English pub with theme nights and TV sports.

Entertainment

Avignon is the theatre capital of France, with dozens around town. The tourist office has lists.

AJMI LIVE MUSIC
(Association pour le Jazz & la Musique Improvisée; 04 90 86 08 61; www.jazzalajmi.com; 4 rue des Escaliers Ste-Anne; tickets €10-15) Inside La Manutention arts centre, AJMI showcases improvisational jazz at its intimate second-floor (no lift) black-box theatre. There are generally shows on Thursday and Friday evenings and Sunday afternoons.

Opéra Théâtre d'Avignon PERFORMING ARTS
(04 90 82 81 40; www.operatheatredavignon.fr; place de l'Horloge; box office 11am-6pm Tue-Sat) Built in 1847 Avignon's main classical venue presents operas, plays, chamber music and ballet from October to June.

BEST MARKETS

To appreciate Provence's seasonal bounty, visit its markets; most run from 8am to noon. In Nîmes, the covered food market – Les Halles – operates daily; Avignon's operates from Tuesday to Sunday.

» **Monday** Bédoin, Fontvieille

» **Tuesday** Tarascon, Vaison-la-Romaine

» **Wednesday** Malaucène, Sault, St-Rémy de Provence, Valréas

» **Thursday** Beaucaire, L'Isle-sur-la-Sorgue, Maillane, Maussane-les-Alpilles, Orange, Villeneuve-lès-Avignon

» **Friday** Carpentras, Châteauneuf-du-Pape, Fontvieille, Graveson

» **Saturday** Pernes-les-Fontaines, Richerenches, St-Rémy de Provence, Villeneuve-lès-Avignon

» **Sunday** Beaucaire, L'Isle-sur-la-Sorgue

Cinéma Utopia CINEMA
(☎04 90 82 65 36; www.cinemas-utopia.org; 4 rue des Escaliers Ste-Anne) Four-screen art-house cinema showing films in original langauge.

Shopping

Oliviers & Co HOMEWARES
(☎04 90 86 18 41; www.oliviers-co.com; 19 rue St-Agricol; ⏲2-7pm Mon, 10am-7pm Tue-Sat) Fine olive oil and olive oil–based products such as soap, creams and biscuits.

Comtesse du Barry FOOD & WINE
(☎04 90 82 62 92; www.comtessedubarry.com/english/online.asp; 25 rue St-Agricol; ⏲10am-12.30pm & 2.30am-7pm Tue-Sat) Gourmet goodies including fine wine and foie gras.

Information

It's hard to change money at weekends.

Police Station (☎04 32 40 55 55, for emergencies 17; 14 bd St-Roch)

Hôpital Général Henri Duffaut (☎04 32 75 33 33; 305 rue Raoul Follereau) Marked on maps as Hôpital Sud, 2.5km south of the central train station – take bus 3 or 6.

Tourist Office (Main) (41 cours Jean Jaurès; ⏲9am-6pm Mon-Fri, 9am-5pm Sat, 10am-noon Sun Nov-Mar, 9am-6pm Mon-Sat, 10am-5pm Sun Apr-Oct)

Tourist Office Annex (Les Halles; ⏲10am-1pm Fri-Sun)

La Cabine (☎04 90 14 18 20; 15 rue Florence; per 30 min €1; ⏲9am-midnight Mon-Sat) Internet access.

Post Office (☎04 90 27 54 00; cours Président Kennedy; ⏲8am-7pm Mon-Fri, 8am-12pm Sat) Changes currency.

Getting There & Away

Air

Avignon-Caumont Airport (☎04 90 81 51 51; www.avignon.aeroport.fr) 8km southeast of Avignon. Flybe and Cityjet fly direct from UK.

Bus

The underground **bus station** (bd St-Roch; ⏲information window 8am-7pm Mon-Fri, 8am-1pm Sat) is next to the central railway station. Tickets sold on board. For schedules, see www.lepilote.com and www.vaucluse.fr, both with good mobile sites. Long-haul companies **Linebus** (☎04 90 85 30 48; www.linebus.com) and **Eurolines** (☎04 90 85 27 60; www.eurolines.com) have offices at far end of bus platforms.

» Arles €7, 1½ hours

» Carpentras €2, 45 minutes

» Marseille €22, 35 minutes

» Nîmes €1.50, 1¼ hours

» Orange €2, 45 minutes

Car & Motorcycle

Find car-hire agencies at train stations (reserve ahead, especially in July). Narrow, one-way streets and impossible parking make driving within the ramparts difficult: park outside the walls. The city has 900 free spaces at **Parking de L'Ile Piot**, and 1150 at Parking des Italiens, both under surveillance and served by free shuttle bus (hours at TCRA (p199)). On directional signs at intersections, 'P' in yellow means pay lots; 'P' in green, free lots.

Train

Avignon has two train stations. **Gare Avignon TGV**, 4km southwest in Courtine; and **Gare Avignon Centre** (42 bd St-Roch), with multiple daily services to/from: Arles (€6.50, 20 minutes), Orange (€5.50, 22 minutes), Nîmes (€8.50, 30 minutes), Marseille Airport (Vitrolles Station, €16, one to 1½ hours)

Some TGVs to/from Paris (€75, 3½ hours) stop at Gare Avignon Centre, but TGVs to/from Marseille (€29, 35 minutes) and Nice (€52.50, 3¼ hours) only use Gare TGV. From June to September direct **Eurostar** (www.eurostar.com) services operates Saturday to/from London (from €110, six hours).

Luggage storage (*consignes de baggages*; €4.50 per 24 hours) is available only at Gare Avignon Centre.

Getting Around

To/From the Airport

TCRA Bus 21 (€1.50, 20 minutes, Monday to Saturday) runs from the airport to the post office. Taxis cost about €25.

Parking

Parking Gare Centre (04 90 80 74 40; cnr bd St-Roch & bd St-Ruf; 24hr) Massive carpark adjoining central train station.

Local Bus

TCRA (Transports en Commun de la Région d'Avignon; 04 32 74 18 32; www.tcra.fr) Local TCRA bus tickets cost €1.20: buy on board. Buses run from 7am to about 7.40pm (less frequently Sundays, from 8am to 6pm). Main transfer points are Poste (main post office) and place Pie. For Villeneuve-lès-Avignon, take bus 11 (bus 70 on Sundays). For maps and discounted *carnets* of 10 tickets (€9.50), visit TCRA's **Agence Commerciale** (av de Lattre de Tassigny; 8.30am-12.30pm & 1.30-6pm Mon-Fri).

Bicycle & Motorcycle

Vélopop (08 10 45 64 56; www.velopop.fr) This shared-bicycle service has 17 stations around town; pick up a bike at one, return it to another. The first half-hour is free; each additional half-hour is €1. Membership costs €1 per day or €3 per week, plus a refundable deposit of €150, guaranteed to your credit card. Sign up by phone or use credit-card machines at stations.

Provence Bike (04 90 27 92 61; www.provence-bike.com; 7 av St-Ruf; bicycles from per day/week €9/39) Rents city bikes, mountain bikes, scooters and motorcycles.

Taxi

Taxi-Radio Avignon (04 90 82 20 20)

AROUND AVIGNON

Villeneuve-lès-Avignon

POP 12,664

Across the Rhône from Avignon, compact Villeneuve-lès-Avignon has monuments to rival Avignon's with none of the crowds. Meander cloisters of a medieval monastery, take in hilltop views from Fort St-André, and lose yourself in spectacular gardens at Abbaye St-André – reason enough to visit.

Sights

Note that the Avignon Passion discount pass is valid here.

TOP CHOICE Jardins de l'Abbaye GARDEN

(04 90 25 55 95; www.abbaye-saint-andre.com; Fort St-André; adult/child €5/free; 10am-12.30pm & 2-6pm Tue-Sun) Classed as one of France's top 100 gardens, privately owned Jardins de l'Abbaye is built atop the vaults of a 10th-century abbey, within the Fort St-André. Views of Avignon and the Rhône are spectacular. Pathways meander through fragrant roses, iris-studded olive groves, wisteria-covered pergolas, and past the ruins of three ancient churches.

Chartreuse du Val de Bénédiction MONASTERY

(04 90 15 24 24; www.chartreuse.org; 58 rue de la République; adult/child €7.70/free; 9.30am-6.30pm) Shaded from summer's heat, the three cloisters, 24 cells, church, chapels and nook-and-cranny gardens of the Chartreuse du Val de Bénédiction make up France's biggest Carthusian monastery, founded 1352 by Pope Innocent VI, who was buried here 10 years later in an elaborate mausoleum. Today La Chartreuse is a retreat for playwrights on residencies.

Fort St-André FORT

(04 90 25 45 35; adult/child €5.50/free; 10am-12.30pm & 2-6pm) King Philip the Fair (aka Philippe le Bel) wasn't messing around when he built this defensive 14th-century fort on the then-border between France and the Holy Roman Empire: walls are 2m thick! Today you can walk a small section of the ramparts and admire 360-degree views from the Tour des Masques (Wizards' Tower) and Tours Jumelles (Twin Towers).

Tour Philippe-le-Bel LANDMARK

(04 32 70 08 57; adult/child €2.20/free; 10am-12.30pm & 2.30-6.30pm Tue-Sun) King Philip commissioned the Tour Philippe le Bel, 0.5km outside Villeneuve, to control traffic over Pont St-Bénézet to and from Avignon. There are steep steps spiral to the top but climbers are rewarded with stunning river views.

Musée Pierre de Luxembourg MUSEUM

(04 90 27 49 66; 3 rue de la République; adult/child €3.10/free; 10.30am-12.30pm & 2.30-6.30pm Tue-Sun May-Sep, 2-5pm Oct-Dec, Feb & Mar) Inside a 17th-century mansion, this

museum's masterwork is Enguerrand Quarton's *Crowning of the Virgin* (1453), in which angels wrest souls from purgatory. Rounding out the collection are 16th- to 18th-century paintings.

Sleeping & Eating

Find cafes and food shops around place Jean Jaurès, near Musée Pierre de Luxembourg. The tourist office has information on lodging, including several top-end inns.

Écuries des Chartreux SELF-CONTAINED **€**
(☎04 90 25 79 93; www.ecuries-des-chartreux.com; 66 rue de la République; apt d €75-85, q €120; ❄📶) Once part of the neighboring monastery, this historic building has three charming stone-walled good-value studios with kitchenettes. The largest sleeps four. Parking by reservation.

Les Jardins de la Livrée B&B **€€**
(☎04 90 26 05 05; www.la-livree.com; 4bis rue du Camp de Bataille; r €82-120; ❄📶🏊) High-walled gardens and a lovely pool make this town centre, four-room *chambre d'hôte* feel far removed. Free parking.

YMCA-UCJG HOSTEL **€€**
(☎04 90 25 46 20; www.ymca-avignon.com; 7bis chemin de la Justice; dm €36, without bathroom €25; ⏲reception 8.30am-6pm, closed Dec–early Jan; 📶🏊) This spotless hostel is just outside Villeneuve-lès-Avignon, and a 15-minute walk from Avignon. It has some private rooms plus a swimming pool with panoramic views. Sheets are included and there is wheelchair access. Take bus 10 to the Monteau stop.

Information

Tourist Office (☎04 90 25 61 33; www.tourisme-villeneuvelezavignon.fr; 1 place Charles David; ⏲9am-12.30pm & 2-6pm Mon-Fri, to 5pm Sat; also open Sun Jul & Aug) Guided English-language tours in July and August.

Getting There & Away

Bus 11 (70 on Sunday) links Villeneuve-lès-Avignon with Avignon (it's only 2km, but dull walking).

NORTH OF AVIGNON

The vineyards of Châteauneuf-du-Pape are world-renowned and extend north of Avignon to Orange, a small city which is famous for big Roman antiquities. Just east, Vaison-la-Romaine is also rich in ancient treasures, its narrow medieval streets an adventure to explore. Just beyond lie the compact, saw-toothed Dentelles de Montmirail mountains, with small villages known for great wines. Lording over all rises windswept Mont Ventoux, Provence's mighty mountain, a magnet for bicyclists and recognised the world over from the Tour de France.

Châteauneuf-du-Pape

POP 2168

Carpets of vineyards unfurl around tiny, medieval Châteauneuf-du-Pape, epicentre of one of the world's great wine-growing regions. Only a small ruin remains of the château, once the summer residence of Avignon's popes, dismantled for stone after the Revolution, and ultimately bombed by Germans in WWII. Now it belongs to picnickers and day hikers, who ascend the hill for 360-degree panoramas of the Rhône Valley. It's an ideal half-day trip for wine-tasting and lunch before continuing to Orange.

Sights & Activities

The tourist office (p201) has a brochure detailing which wineries allow visits and offer tastings, their fees, and whether they offer English-language tours. Some wineries require appointments: if you're set on some place specific, call ahead.

A car is easiest, but the tourist office also has a brochure detailing a 16km **walking circuit**. Alternatively, hire a bicycle or trot in a **horse-drawn carriage** (☎04 90 70 88 42; la.rebousse@wanadoo.fr; 583 chemin St-Laurent, Courthézon).

Caves du Verger des Papes WINE TASTING
(☎04 90 83 58 08; www.vergerdespapes.com; 4 montée du Château; free tastings; ⏲10am-4pm Tue-Sun Feb–mid-Dec) Beneath the town's namesake château, these small, magnificent wine caves date back 2000 years. The bar carries 80 of the town's 250 labels, with vertical tastings (same vineyard, different years). The prices are excellent with bottles ranging from €19 to €90. English is spoken.

Domaine de la Solitude WINERY
(☎04 90 83 71 45; www.domaine-solitude.com; rte de Bédarides (D192); tastings free, bottles €19-100; ⏲10am-6pm Mon-Fri, Sat & Sun by appointment) Two kilometres east of village, it's worth calling ahead to appreciate Châteauneuf-du-Pape from this family-run estate, cultivated for 600 years by descendants of Pope Urbain

CHÂTEAUNEUF-DU-PAPE WINES: A PRIMER

Thank geology for these luscious wines: when glaciers receded, they left a thick layer of *galets* scattered atop the red-clay soil; these large pebbles trap the Provençal sun, releasing heat after sunset, helping grapes ripen with steady warmth.

The Romans first planted vines here 2000 years ago, but wine-growing took off after Pope John XXII built a castle in 1317, planting vineyards to provide the court with wine. From this papally endorsed beginning, wine production flourished.

Most Châteauneuf-du-Pape is red; only 6% is white (rosé is forbidden). Strict regulations – which formed the basis for the Appellation d'Origine Protégée (AOP) system – govern production. Reds come from 13 grape varieties – grenache is the biggie – and should age five years minimum. The full-bodied whites drink well young (except for all-rousanne varieties) and make an excellent, mineral-y aperitif, hard to find elsewhere (but taste before buying; some may lack acidity).

VIII. You'll receive a warm welcome, in English, as you discover elegant, rounded wines, with supple, never-harsh tannins – the winemaker's signature. Tastings include visits to the barrel cellar.

Château Mont Redon WINERY
(☎04 90 83 72 75; www.chateaumontredon.fr; rte d'Orange (D88); tastings free, bottles €21-31; ⊙9am-7pm) Mont Redon is just 3km from Châteauneuf-du-Pape, and has easy access and gorgeous placement amid sweeping vineyards. Its large size makes it easy for drop-ins, but you may encounter weekend crowds; better to come weekdays, when tastings are served in the stone château. Its respectable wines include an excellent, mineral-y white.

École de Dégustation WINE TASTING
(Tasting School; ☎04 90 83 56 15; www.oenologie-mouriesse.com; 2 rue des Papes; 2hr courses from €40) To appreciate the region's stellar wine, book a two-hour wine-tasting class.

Sleeping & Eating

There's nowhere for a sit-down breakfast, but the village bakery sells croissants.

TOP CHOICE **Le Mas Julien** B&B €€
(☎04 90 34 99 49; www.mas-julien.com; 704 chemin de St Jean, Orange; r incl breakfast €100-115, apt €135; ❄📶≋) A 17th-century stone farmhouse surrounded by vineyards, Le Mas Julien's four rooms blend contemporary and Provençal style, and there's a studio apartment with kitchen that sleeps three. After a day exploring, nothing beats sprawling by the big pool, glass in hand. Between Orange and Châteauneuf-du-Pape, it's ideal base for an extended stay.

Le Verger des Papes RESTAURANT €€
(☎04 90 83 50 40; 4 rue du Château; menus €20-30; ⊙hours vary) Perched beneath the château, above Châteauneuf-du-Pape, Verger des Papes has drop-dead vistas of the Rhône from its stone terrace – ideal for a lingering lunch or romantic dinner (arrive before sunset). Specialties include succulent rack of lamb for two, plus *entrecôte* of beef, served with macaroni-and-cheese spiked with *cèpes*. Park at the château and walk down. Reservations essential.

La Mère Germaine TRADITIONAL FRENCH €€
(☎04 90 22 78 34; www.lameregermaine.fr; place de la Fontaine; menu lunch €18-23, dinner €33-37; ⊙lunch daily, dinner Mon-Sat) Open since 1922, La Mère Germaine is the classic village *auberge*, with fine restaurant and simple **accommodation** (☎04 90 22 78 34; www.lameregermaine.fr; place de la Fontaine; s/d/tr €55/65/90; ❄📶). Good for a date, the dining room has painted-tile floors and vineyard views. Solicitous service includes local wines by the glass, paired well with classic cooking, like foie gras and duck breast. Guestrooms are basic, ideal for budgeteers.

Bernard Castelain CHOCOLATE €
(☎04 90 83 54 71; www.vin-chocolat-castelain.com; rte d'Avignon; ⊙9am-noon & 2-7pm Mon-Sat, daily summer) The specialities at this artisan *chocolatier* include *picholines* (chocolate-covered roasted and cream-and-chocolate-filled *Palets des Papes*.

Information

Tourist Office (☎04 90 83 71 08; www.pays-provence.fr; place du Portail; ⊙9.30am-6pm Mon-Sat, closed lunch & Wed Oct-May)

Getting There & Away

From Avignon (18km, 30 minutes) take D907 north to D17. From Orange (10km, 15 minutes) take D68 south.

Transdev Sud-Est (☎04 32 76 00 40; www.sudest-mobilites.fr) operates limited service to/from Orange (€1.50, 30 minutes, two or three services Monday to Saturday) and Avignon (€2, 60 minutes, one or two services Monday to Saturday), but same-day roundtrips are impossible. Buses stop at intersection of av Louis Pasteur and rue de la Nouvelle Poste.

Orange

POP 30,627

If you see only one Roman site in France, make it Orange. Considering the exceptional beauty of its Roman theatre and monumental archway – both Unesco World Heritage Sites – the ultraconservative town is surprisingly untouristy, and is dead in winter. Accommodation is good value, but it's nearly impossible to find dinner on Sunday or Monday nights.

Sights

TOP CHOICE Théâtre Antique ROMAN SITES

(www.theatre-antique.com; adult/child €8.50/6.50, 2nd child free; ⌚9am-6pm, 9am-4.30pm Nov-Feb) Orange's Roman theatre is France's most impressive Roman site. Its sheer size and age are awe-inspiring: designed for 10,000 spectators, it's believed to have been built during Augustus Caesar's rule (27 BC–AD 14). The 103m-wide, 37m-high stage wall is one of three in the world still standing in entirety (others are in Syria and Turkey) – minus a few mosaics, plus a new roof.

Admission includes a 10-language audioguide and access to **Musée d'Orange** (☎04 90 51 17 60; museum only adult/child €5.50/4.50; ⌚9.15am-7pm summer, shorter hours winter), opposite the theatre, which has unassuming treasures, including portions of the Roman survey registers (precursor to the tax department) and friezes that once formed part of the theatre's scenery.

Come for epic theatrical spectaculars, including the fabulous **Chorégies d'Orange** (www.choregies.asso.fr; tickets €50-240), an international opera festival in July – balmy nights in this millennia-old venue are magical.

Arc de Triomphe ROMAN SITES

(www.theatre-antique.com) Orange's 1st-century AD monumental arch, the Arc de Triomphe, stands on the Via Agrippa, 19m high and wide, and 8m thick. Restored in 2009, its brilliant reliefs commemorate 49BC Roman victories with carvings of chained, naked Gauls.

Colline St-Eutrope GARDEN

For bird's-eye views of the theatre – and phenomenal vistas of Mont Ventoux and the Dentelles – follow montée Philbert de Chalons, or montée Lambert, up Colline St-Eutrope (St Eutrope Hill; elevation 97m), once the Romans' lookout point. En route pass ruins of a 12th-century **château**, once the residence of the princes of Orange.

Sleeping

Hôtel Arène HOTEL €€

(☎04 90 11 40 40; www.hotel-arene.fr; place de Langes; d €88-132; ❄@📶🏊👪) With the best and biggest bathrooms in Orange, the Arène is the closest you'll get to business class. Despite some generic furnishings, the hotel retains individuality, and has an entire floor of hypo-allergenic rooms. Kids love the two heated pools (one indoors, one out); parents appreciate the family-size rooms. Request a remodelled room – but older ones are very comfortable.

Le Glacier HOTEL €€

(☎04 90 34 02 01; www.le-glacier.com; 46 cours Aristide Briand; d €50-110; ❄@📶) All 28 rooms are individually decorated and impeccably maintained by charming owners who pay attention to detail. They also rent bikes (half-/full day €12/16) and have secure, free bike parking.

Hôtel Saint Jean HOTEL €

(☎04 90 51 15 56; www.hotelsaint-jean.com; 1 cours Pourtoules; s €60-70, d €70-85, t €80-100, q €90-120; ❄📶) Simple, spiffy hotel, next to the theatre, with comfortable proportions and colourful Provençal fabrics. Free bike storage, double-pane windows and flat-screen TVs add value.

Hôtel l'Herbier d'Orange HOTEL €

(☎04 90 34 09 23; www.lherbierdorange.com; 8 place aux Herbes; s/d/tr incl breakfast €59/69/79; ❄@📶👪) Friendly enthusiastic owners keep this small, central, basic hotel looking spiffy, with double-pane windows and gleaming bathrooms. Evening aperitif included.

Camping Le Jonquier CAMPGROUND €

(☎04 90 34 49 48; www.campinglejonquier.com; 1321 rue Alexis Carrel; 2 people €20-26; ⌚Easter-Sep; @📶🏊👪) Good for active travellers, this place has a pool, minigolf, tennis, ping pong and a

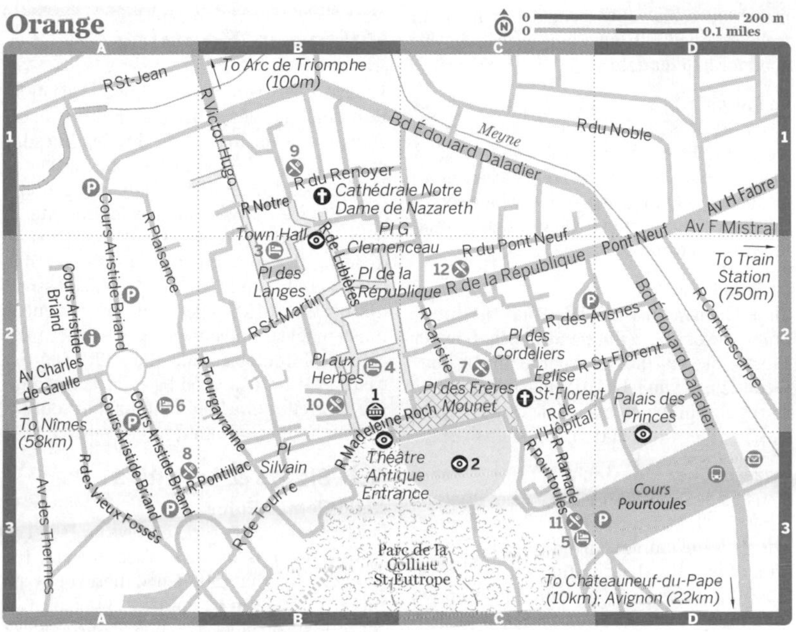

Orange

Sights

1 Musée d'Orange B2
2 Théâtre Antique C3

Sleeping

3 Hôtel Arène B2
4 Hôtel l'Herbier d'Orange B2
5 Hôtel Saint Jean C3
6 Le Glacier A2

Eating

7 À la Maison C2
8 Au Petit Patio A3
9 La Roselière B1
10 Le Forum B2
11 Le Parvis C3
12 Petit Casino C2

hot tub. From Arc de Triomphe, walk 100m north, turn left onto rue du Bourbonnais, then right again at the second roundabout onto rue Alexis Carrel; it's 300m on the left.

Eating

A weekly market fills the town centre on Thursday mornings. Call ahead for all restaurants; for dinner before July performances at Théâtre Antique, book by Easter. For self-catering, there's **Petit Casino** (16 rue de la République).

À la Maison BISTRO €

(☎04 90 60 98 83; 4 place des Cordeliers; lunch menus €12.50-15, dinner menus €25-32, mains €10-16; ⏰Mon-Sat) There's no lovelier spot on a warm night than the leafy fountain courtyard at this simple bistro, which serves consistently good homestyle cooking – but it opens sporadically.

Au Petit Patio TRADITIONAL FRENCH €€

(☎04 90 29 69 27; 58 cours Aristide Briand; lunch menus €18-25, dinner menus €25-35) A good spot for a lingering lunch (menus include wine and coffee) or an indulgent dinner (foie gras is homemade) with excellent service. Au Petit Patio has a charming outdoor terrace, which lacks shade: book inside on hot days.

Le Forum TRADITIONAL FRENCH €€

(☎04 90 34 01 09; 3 rue Mazeau; lunch menus €15-19, dinner menus €29; ⏰lunch Tue-Fri & Sun, dinner Tue-Sun) Classical dishes, like beef fillet with morel sauce, are well executed, but the room feels cramped: sit outside if available. Also good for a quiet date.

Le Parvis GASTRONOMIC €€
(☎04 90 34 82 00; 55 cours Pourtoules; lunch menus €12-19, dinner menus €23-44; ⌚lunch & dinner Tue-Sat, lunch Sun) Nobody speaks above a whisper at Orange's top table, which serves excellent food at good value – never mind the frosty reception.

La Roselière BISTRO €
(3 rue du Renoyer; mains €12-15; ⌚Tue-Sat) Bric-a-brac crowds the ceiling and the chef-owner shouts jokes at diners' expense but by your second glass you'll be laughing along, unless you're shy, in which case don't come. Expect classics like lentils and sausages. Cash only.

Pizzeria Chez Moustache PIZZA €
(☎04 90 34 31 03; Chemin les Peyrières Blanches; pizzas €8-14; ⌚7pm-1am Tue-Sun, lunch Sun; 👪) The only restaurant outside Avignon open after 10pm, this hard-to-find pizzeria has a wood-fired oven, kids' toys and a local crowd that likes to drink. From Orange, go 3km south on rte de Châteauneuf (D68); cross under autoroute, and turn right onto tiny Chemin de la Gironde (look for the sign); keep bearing right.

Information

Tourist Office (☎04 90 34 70 88; www.otorange.fr; 5 cours Aristide Briand; ⌚9am-6.30pm, closed Sun Oct-Mar) Makes hotel bookings.

Post Office (679 bd Édouard Daladier) Changes money.

Getting There & Away

BUS The **bus station** (☎04 90 34 15 59; 201 cours Pourtoules) is at the east end of cours Pourtoules, opposite the post office, on blvd Édouard Daladier. **Trans Vaucluse** (http://vaucluse.fr) buses, operated by **Cars Lieutaud** (www.cars-lieutaud.fr), serve Avignon (€2, 45 minutes) and Vaison-la-Romaine (€2, 45 minutes).

TRAIN Orange's **train station** (www.voyages-sncf.com; av Frédéric Mistral) is 1.5km east of town centre and has services to Avignon (€5.80, 20 minutes), Marseille (€23, 1½ hours), Marseille Airport (Vitrolles station; €20, 1½ hours) and Lyon (€29.30, 2¼ hours).

BICYCLE **Sportaventure** (☎04 90 34 75 08, mobile 06 10 33 56 54; www.velolocation-aventure.com; place de la République; half-day/day/week €12/18/69) Central bike shop; delivers within 20km radius.

Vaison-la-Romaine

POP 6313

Tucked between seven hills, Vaison-la-Romaine has long been a traditional exchange centre: to wit, its thriving Tuesday market. The village's rich Roman legacy is obvious – 20th-century buildings rise alongside France's largest archaeological site. A Roman bridge crosses the River Ouvèze, dividing the contemporary town's pedestrianised centre and the walled, cobbled-street hilltop Cité Médiévale – one of Provence's most magical ancient villages – where the counts of Toulouse built their 12th-century castle. Vaison is a good base for jaunts into the Dentelles or Mont Ventoux, but tourists throng here in summer: reserve ahead.

Sights & Activities

Gallo-Roman Ruins ROMAN SITES
(adult/child €8/3.50; ⌚closed Jan-early Feb) The ruined remains of Vasio Vocontiorum, the Roman city that flourished here between the 6th and 2nd centuries BC, fill two central Vaison sites. Two neighbourhoods of this once-opulent city, Puymin and La Villasse, lie on either side of the tourist office and l'avénue du Général-de-Gaulle. Admission includes a four-language **audioguide** covering the Roman ruins, museum, Cathédrale Notre-Dame and medieval city.

In **Puymin**, see aristocrats' houses, mosaics, the workers' quarter, temple and the still-functioning 6000-seat **Théâtre Antique** (c 20AD). To make sense of the remains (and gather your audioguide), head for the **archaeological museum**, which revives Vaison's Roman past with incredible swag – superb mosaics, carved masks, and statues that include a 3rd-century silver bust and marble renderings of Hadrian and wife Sabina.

The Romans shopped at the colonnaded boutiques and bathed at **La Villasse**, where you'll find **Maison au Dauphin**, which has splendid marble-lined fish ponds.

Admission includes entry to the soothing 12th-century Romanesque cloister at **Cathédrale Notre-Dame de Nazareth** (cloister €1.50; ⌚10am-12.30pm & 2-6pm Mar-Dec), a five-minute walk west of La Villasse and a refuge from summer's heat.

Cité Médiévale HISTORIC QUARTER
Cross the **Pont Romain** (Roman bridge) in the footsteps of frightened medieval peasants, who clambered to the walled city dur-

ing valley conflicts. Steep cobblestone alleyways wend beneath stone ramparts and a 14th-century **belltower**, past romantic fountains and mansions with incredibly carved doorways. Continue uphill to the imposing 12th-century **château** (guided tours in French €2), where your climb is rewarded with eagle-eye vistas.

Cycling Routes BIKING
(www.escapado.fr) Vaison's position is ideal for village-hopping. The tourist office stocks excellent brochures detailing multiple cycling circuits, rated by difficulty, from 26k to 91k.

Festivals & Events

Festival de Vaison-la-Romaine DANCE FESTIVAL
(www.vaison-danses.com) Three-week-long July dance festival held at the Roman Théâtre Antique. Book by April.

Choralies MUSIC FESTIVAL
(www.choralies.fr) Europe's largest choral festival is held in August every three years (2013 and 2016).

Festival des Chœurs Lauréats MUSIC FESTIVAL
(www.festivaldeschoeurslaureats.com; late Jul) The best choirs in Europe; held in late July.

Sleeping

The tourist office has a list of *chambres d'hôte*, self-catering apartments and campgrounds.

Hôtel Le Burrhus DESIGN HOTEL €
(04 90 36 00 11; www.burrhus.com; 1 place de Montfort; d €55-87;) On Vaison's vibrant central square this hotel may look quaint and old, but inside its 38 rooms have ultra-modern decor with designer fittings, original artwork and mosaic bathrooms. No lift. Parking (€7) by reservation.

L'Évêché B&B €€
(04 90 36 13 46; http://eveche.free.fr; rue de l'Évêché; d €92-140) With groaning bookshelves, vaulted ceilings, higgledy-piggledy staircase, intimate salons and exquisite art, this five-room *chambre d'hôte* in the medieval city is fabulously atmospheric. Knowledgeable owners Jean-Loup and Aude also lend bikes.

L'École Buissonière B&B €
(04 90 28 95 19; www.buissonniere-provence.com; D75, Buisson; s €48-52, d €60-70, tr €75-85 q €90-96;) Five minutes north of Vaison in the countryside between Buisson and Villedieu, hosts Monique and John have transformed their stone farmhouse into a tastefully decorated three-bedroom B&B, long on comfort. Breakfast includes homemade jam, and there's an outdoor summer kitchen.

Hostellerie Le Beffroi HISTORIC HOTEL €€
(04 90 36 04 71; www.le-beffroi.com; rue de l'Évêché; d €96-150, tr €180; Apr-Jan;) Within the medieval city's walls, this 1554-built *hostellerie* fills two buildings (the 'newer' one was built in 1690). A fairy-tale hideaway, its rough-hewn stone-and-wood-beamed rooms are small but romantic, and its **restaurant** (www.le-beffroi.com; rue de l'Évêché; menus €28-45; Apr-Jan) opens onto a rose-and-herb garden with kids' swings. Parking €10.

Camping du Théâtre Romain CAMPGROUND €
(04 90 28 78 66; www.camping-theatre.com; chemin de Brusquet; camping per 2 people €21; mid-Mar–mid-Nov;) Opposite the Théâtre Antique. Very sunny, but there's a pool.

Eating

Brasseries on place Montfort vary; restaurants on cours Taulignan are generally better. Dining in Cité Médiévale is limited and pricey.

La Lyriste PROVENÇAL €€
(04 90 36 04 67; 45 cours Taulignan; menus €18-36; Wed-Sun) The contemporary Provençal menu at this charming bistro emphasises seasonal-regional ingredients in dishes ranging from *bourride* (fish stew) to a foie-gras tasting *menu* (€36). In summer book a table on the terrace.

Terrasses de Ninou BISTRO €
(www.lesterrassesdeninou.fr; 3 place Théodore-Aubanel; dishes €7-24; lunch & dinner Apr-Oct, lunch Feb-Apr) The terrace at this simple bistro has stellar views over the river and medieval city. The menu lists simple seasonal dishes; between mealtimes there are crêpes, pizzas and tarts.

Le Bateleur PROVENÇAL €€
(04 90 36 28 04; www.le-bateleur.com; 1 place Théodore Aubanel; menus lunch €17-22, dinner €27-40; lunch Tue-Sun, dinner Tue-Wed & Fri-Sat) The best seats at this simple Provençal dining room overlook the river but you'll need no distractions from the artfully presented quality regional cooking. Lunch includes wine and coffee.

TOP CHOICE **Moulin à Huile** GASTRONOMIC €€€
(☎04 90 36 20 67; www.moulin-huile.com; quai Maréchal Foch; lunch menus €40, dinner menus €60-70; ⊙lunch & dinner Tue-Sat, lunch Sun) Michelin-starred chef Robert Bardot showcases gastronomic prowess in a former olive-oil mill beneath the Cité Médievale. Sample a variety with the €75 tasting menu. In summer dine on the riverside terrace (never mind the plastic chairs). Make a night of it in one of three handsome **guest rooms** (☎04 90 36 20 67; www.moulin-huile.com; quai Maréchal Foch; €130-150).

Information

Tourist Office (☎04 90 36 02 11; www.vaison-ventoux-tourisme.com; place du Chanoine Sautel; ⊙9.30am-noon & 2-5.45pm Mon-Sat year-round, plus 9.30am-noon Sun Apr–mid-Oct) Helps book rooms.

Getting There & Away

BUS Cars Lieutaud (www.cars-lieutaud.fr) buses serve Orange (€2, one hour) and Avignon (€4, via Orange, two hours). **Cars Comtadins** buses serve Carpentras (€2, 45 minutes) and Malaucène (€1, 30 minutes). For schedules see www.vaucluse.fr. The bus stop is on avenue des Choralies, 400m east of the tourist office.

CAR There's parking by the tourist office.

Dentelles de Montmirail

The Dentelle's 8km-long limestone ridge rises abruptly from vineyard-covered plains. Its spires take their name from the *dentelles* (lace) they resemble. Forty kilometres of footpaths wind through the Mediterranean scrub – look for buzzards, eagles and fluorescent-green lizards. Climbers favour the southern face. Around the ridge, find tiny villages famous for wine. The best tourist offices are in Beaumes-de-Venise (p208), Vaison-la-Romaine (p206), and Gigondas (p206).

Getting There & Away

Trans Vaucluse (p204) line 4 connects Orange and Vaison-la-Romaine, via Séguret and Sablet. Line 11 connects Carpentras and Vaison, via Le Barroux.

La COVE (☎08 00 88 15 23; www.transcove.com) buses operate from Monday to Saturday on the Carpentras–Beaumes-de-Venise–Gigondas route, but you must telephone the day before for pick-up.

GIGONDAS

POP 598 / ELEV 282M

Wine cellars and cafes surround the sun-dappled central square of Gigondas, famous for prestigious red wine. The **tourist office** (☎04 90 65 85 46; www.gigondas-dm.fr; rue du Portail; ⊙10am-12.30pm & 2.30-6.30pm Mon-Sat year-round, plus 10am-1pm Sun Jul & Aug) has a list of wineries. In town, **Caveau de Gigondas** (☎04 90 65 82 29; place Gabriel Andéol; ⊙10am-noon & 2-6.30pm) represents 100 small producers and offers free tastings – most bottles cost just €12 to €14. **Wine-tasting** here provides an excellent counterpoint to Châteauneuf-du-Pape: both use the same grapes, but the soil is different.

Above the central square, along the **Cheminement de Sculptures**, enigmatic outdoor sculptures line narrow pathways, leading ever upward to castle ruins, campanile, church and cemetery with stunning vistas.

SÉGURET & AROUND

POP 904, ELEV 250M

Medieval Séguret clings to a hillside above vineyards. Narrow, cobbled streets, lined with flowering vines, wend past a 15th-century fountain, 12th-century church, and uphill to castle ruins (park below the village and walk). Séguret makes a good base for cyclists and hikers, and lovers of quiet countryside.

A wine-producing estate 800m south of Séguret, **Domaine de Cabasse** (☎04 90 46 91 12; www.cabasse.fr; rte de Sablet; d €135; ⊙Apr-Oct; ❄📶🏊) has 12 sunlit rooms, a pretty terrace restaurant, pool, tennis, and wines galore from their barrel-lined cellar. Meals include veggies from the garden: consider half-board.

Good for families, with several quad rooms, cozy 18th-century **La Bastide Bleue** (☎04 90 46 83 43; www.bastidebleue.com; route de Sablet; s/d/tr/q incl breakfast €59/83/116/149; 🏊👪) is simply decorated in classic Provençal style; some rooms have exposed wooden beams. Outside there's a vineyard-view pool. The on-site rustic **restaurant** (☎04 90 46 83 43; www.bastidebleue.com; route de Sablet; menus €22-26; ⊙Thu-Tue Jun-Sept, Thu-Mon Oct-May) serves good regional cooking (reserve).

The weekday classic-French lunch menus at **Les Genêts** (☎04 90 46 84 33; www.restaurant-les-genets.com; D 977, Sablet; menus lunch/dinner €15/28; ⊙lunch & dinner Wed-Sat, lunch Sun & Tue) roadhouse restaurant, 3km south of Séguret, are great value – €14.50 with wine – and everything is fresh. Book a table on the vineyard-view terrace.

SUZETTE

POP 131 / ELEV 425M

Tiny Suzette sits high in the hills between Malaucène and Beaumes-de-Venise, with incredible views that provide perspective on the landscape and make the winding drive worthwhile. Get your bearings at the village-centre *table d'orientation* (orientation plaque).

Ferme le Dégoutaud (04 90 62 99 29; www.degoutaud.fr; route de Malaucène; s €58-62, d €68-72, tr €78-82, q €88-92; weekly cottage rentals from €530;), a 16th-century working farm, has simple, spotless rooms of stone and wood, and self-catering cottages surrounded by spectacular countryside. The farm produces olive oil, honey, jam and organic apricot and cherry juice – sample them at breakfast. Outside there's a summer kitchen and an infinity pool with knockout views. Tops for nature-lovers.

High on a hill, surrounded by vineyards, **Les Coquelicot** (04 90 65 06 94; www.restaurant-les-coquelicots.com; in village centre; mains €14-20; daily Jul-Aug, Thu-Sun Sep-Jun) makes a perfect lunchtime destination when day-tripping the Dentelles, and showcases the flavours of Provence with dishes like lamb with anchovy butter and salt-cod aioli. Book the terrace for incredible views.

LE BARROUX

POP 615 / ELEV 325M

Charming wee Le Barroux clings to a hillside beneath medieval **Château du Barroux** (04 90 62 35 21; www.chateau-du-barroux.com; adult/child €5/free; 10am-7pm Sat & Sun Apr & May, 2.30-7pm Jun, 10am-7pm Jul-Sep, 2-6pm Oct), built in the 12th century to protect the village from Saracen invaders. One of Provence's few castles, its fortunes rose and fell, the last indignity occurring during WWII when retreating Germans set it ablaze – it burned for 10 days. Only ghosts remain in its vast chambers, but it's great fun to explore, especially for kids unaccustomed to such architectural drama.

Two kilometres out of Le Barroux along thread-narrow lanes, hear **Gregorian chants** sung by Benedictine monks at 9.30am daily (10am Sunday and holidays) at **Abbaye Ste-Madeleine** (04 90 62 56 31; www.barroux.org), a Romanesque-style monastery (c 1980s), surrounded by lavender. Its shop carries delicious monk-made almond cake. Hats, miniskirts, bare shoulders and mobile phones forbidden.

For a lazy lunch (and a parking spot), book a terrace table at **Les Géraniums** (04 90 62 41 08; www.hotel-lesgeraniums.com; place de la Croix; menus lunch €18-22, dinner €30-36; Jun-Oct), an old-fashioned country *auberge* with stunning valley views; upstairs are simply furnished, good-value **rooms** (04 90 62 41 08; www.hotel-lesgeraniums.com; place de la Croix; r €65-75; Jun-Oct).

BLACK DIAMONDS

Provence's cloak-and-dagger truffle trade is operated from the back of cars, with payment exclusively in cash. Little known **Richerenches**, a deceptively wealthy village with a medieval Templar fortress, hosts France's largest wholesale truffle market. It's lovely to visit year round, but especially so on Saturday mornings during truffle season (mid-November to mid-March), when the main street fills with furtive *rabassaïres* (truffle hunters), selling to *courtiers* (brokers) representing dealers in Paris, Germany, Italy and beyond.
So covert are the transactions that you are never likely to see a truffle change hands.

Black truffles *(Tuber melanosporum)* cost up to €1000 per kilogram *wholesale*, up to €4000 retail. Although *trufficulteurs* (truffle growers) try tricks like injecting spores into oak roots, humankind has so far been unable to increase crops of this quasi-mystical fungus. Only nature can dictate if it will be a good or bad year – weather is the major determinant of yield.

Richerenches villagers celebrate an annual Truffle Mass in the village church, when parishioners place truffles instead of cash in the collection plate. Then they're auctioned to support the church. The Mass falls on the Sunday nearest 17 January, feast day of Antoine, patron saint of truffle harvesters. (Yes, there's a saint for everything.) Contact Richerenches' **Point Tourisme** (04 90 28 05 34; www.richerenches.fr; rue du Campanile; 2pm-6pm Mon-Sat) for details.

If you want to unearth truffles yourself, **Dominique and Eric Jaumard** (04 90 66 82 21; www.truffes-ventoux.com; La Quinsonne, 634 chemin du Traversier; Oct–mid-Mar) arrange seasonal hunts and year-round walks on their truffle-rich land, 7km southwest of Carpentras, in Monteux. Or you could buy truffles fresh, in season, at weekly regional markets, including Vaison-la-Romaine (Tuesday) and Carpentras (Friday). Store in a sealed jar of rice, which will take on the tubers' heady fragrance.

BEAUMES-DE-VENISE

POP 2185 / ELEV 126M

Snugly sheltered from mistral winds Beaumes-de-Venise is famous for its *or blanc* (white gold) – sweet muscat wines, best drunk young and cold (perfect with Cavaillon melons). Attend tastings at local co-operative **Balma Vénitia** (04 90 12 41 00; www.beaumes-de-venise.com; 228 route de Carpentras; 9am-12.30pm & 2-7pm). The excellent **tourist office** (www.ot-beaumesdevenise.fr; 122 place du Marché; 9am-12pm & 2pm-5pm Mon-Sat) has English-language brochures of wineries.

Taste Beaumes' olive oil at **Moulin à Huile de la Balméenne** (04 90 62 93 77; www.labalmeenne.fr; av Jules Ferry; 9am-noon & 2-7pm daily Apr-Aug, Mon-Sat Sep-Mar), open since 1867. For gifts, consider organic soap from **Savonnerie des Dentelles** (04 90 37 61 80; www.savonnerie-des-dentelles.com; route de Sarrians; Mon-Fri), 1km from Beaumes-de-Venise.

Sprawling 19th-century gardens, vineyards and olive groves surround **Château Juvenal** (04 90 62 31 76; www.chateau-juvenal-provence.com; 120 chemin du Long-Serre, Saint-Hippolyte-le-Graveyron; r €110-170;) manor, with four upmarket rooms, billiards, spa, hot tub and fabulous pool. On Tuesday and Friday evenings there's an excellent *table d'hôte* (€42 with wine; 48-hour advance reservation required). It's 5km west of Beaumes-de-Venise.

Mont Ventoux

The landscape's defining feature, Mont Ventoux (1912m) is nicknamed *le géant de Provence* – Provence's giant. From its peak, clear-day vistas extend to the Alps and Camargue.

Because of the mountain's elevation, every European climate type occurs on its slopes, from Mediterranean on southernmost flanks, to Arctic on exposed its northern ridges. As you ascend the steep gradients – of Tour de France fame – temperatures can plummet 20°C and there's twice the annual precipitation. Relentless mistrals blows 130 days annually, sometimes exceeding 250km/h: bring warm clothes and rain gear year-round.

This unique climatic patchwork supports wildly diverse fauna and flora, protected under Unesco Biosphere Reserve status. Some species live nowhere else, including the snake eagle and several other birds as well as butterflies.

Three principle gateways – Bédoin, Malaucène and Sault – provide services in summer, but they're far apart. You can ascend by road year round, but cannot traverse the summit from 15 November to 15 April.

Sled the south summit at Chalet Reynard, the daytripper's year-round destination for lunch, crêpes and coffee; depart from Bédoin or Sault, not Malaucène. Up the isolated backside, via D974 from Malaucène, the tiny north-facing ski area, Mont Serein, is fun for a few turns, but nothing serious. Snow melts by April – what you see glimmering in summer is limestone.

LAVENDER VS LAVANDIN

When shopping for lavender, understand that the sought-after product is fine lavender (in French, *lavande fine*; in Latin, *Lavandula angustifolia, L. vera, L. officinalis*), not spike lavender (*L. latifolia*) or the hybrid lavandin (*L. hybrida*). The latter are high in camphor, and are used in detergents and paint solvents, not perfume.

Cycling

Tourist offices distribute *Les Itinéraires Ventoux,* a free map detailing eleven itineraries – easy to difficult – highlighting artisanal farms en route. For more cycling trails, see www.lemontventoux.net.

At **Ventoux Bike Park** (www.facebook.com/VentouxBikePark; bike-park access before 2pm €14, after 2pm €10; 9.30am-4.30pm Mar-Nov), near the summit at Chalet Reynard, thrill-seeking bicyclists ascend via rope-tow, then descend ramps and jumps down three trails, beginner to advanced. Bring your own mountain bike; helmet and full-length gloves required. **Bédoin Location** (04 90 65 94 53; www.bedoin-location.fr; place Portail Olivier, Bédoin; Mar-Nov) delivers to the summit, and rents equipment.

Rent bikes from Bédoin Location or **La Route du Ventoux** (04 90 67 07 40; www.larouteduventoux.com; rte du Ventoux, Bédoin; road bikes/mountain bikes/tandems per half-day from €25/15/30; Apr-Nov) in Bédoin, **Ventoux Bikes** (04 90 62 58 19; www.ventoux-bikes.fr; 1 av de Verdun, Malaucène; Apr-Nov) in Malaucène, or **Albion Cycles** (04 90 64 09 32; www.albioncycles.com; rte de St-Trinit, Sault; daily Jul-Aug, Tue-Sun Sep-Jun) in Sault.

Hiking

The GR4 crosses the Dentelles before scaling Mont Ventoux's northern face, where it meets the GR9. Both traverse the ridge. The GR4 branches eastwards to Gorges du Verdon; the GR9 crosses the Vaucluse Mountains to the Luberon. *3140ET Mont Ventoux* map by **IGN** (www.ign.fr) is essential. Bédoin's tourist office (p209) carries a topographic map (€7) detailing 14 walks for all levels; find corresponding trail markers en route.

In July and August tourist offices in Bédoin and Malaucène facilitate night-time up-mountain expeditions to see sunrise (must be over 15 years old).

BÉDOIN

POP 3100 / ELEV 295M

On Mont Ventoux's southwestern flanks, peppy Bédoin is chock-a-block with cafes and shops, and is the most upbeat of the gateways. Its geographic position diminishes the mistral, which contributes to its popularity with cyclists. In July and August the **tourist office** (☎04 90 65 63 95; www.bedoin.org; Espace Marie-Louis Gravier; ⏰9am-12.30pm & 2-6pm Mon-Fri, 9.30am-12.30pm Sat, longer hours in summer), an excellent information source on all regional activities, guides walks into the forest. Market day is Monday.

MALAUCÈNE

POP 2691 / ELEV 377M

Despite deceptively lovely plane-tree-lined streets, Malaucène is dreary, except in summer when hikers and bikers arrive. Its blessing is geographical: on the saddle between Mont Ventoux and the Dentelles, it's well positioned for mountain sorties. Pope Clement V had a second home here in the 14th century: his legacy remains in the Gothic-Romanesque **Église St-Michel & St-Pierre**, constructed in 1309 on the site of an ancient temple. The **tourist office** (☎04 90 65 22 59; http://villagemalaucene.free.fr; place de la Mairie; ⏰9.15am-12.15pm & 2.30-5.30pm Mon-Fri, 9am-noon Sat) stocks information on Mont Ventoux but (surprisingly) not the Dentelles, and keeps erratic hours.

SAULT

POP 1285 / ELEV 800M

At the eastern end of the Mont Ventoux massif, drowsily charming Sault has incredible summertime vistas over lavender fields. Young travellers risk boredom – better to bring grandma. Visit **André Boyer** (☎04 90 64 00 23; place de l'Europe) for honey and almond nougat, family-made since 1887.

WORTH A TRIP

RIVER GORGES DU TOULOURENC

On hot days you can't beat this easy, family-friendly walk beneath Mont Ventoux's wild, northern face. Wear shorts and water shoes, and hike upstream, splashing in calf-deep water, and explore a spectacular, ever-narrowing limestone canyon. By bike, take the tiny road from Malucène to the hamlet of Veaux (roadsigns say 'hameau de Veaux', maps say 'Veaux'); by car, the road via Entrechaux is less winding. Park at the blue bridge over the water. Two hours upstream, there's a Roman bridge – a good turnaround point. Carry food and water.

Sault's **tourist office** (☎04 90 64 01 21; www.saultenprovence.com; av de la Promenade; ⏰9am-noon & 2-5pm Mon Sat), a good resource for Ventoux and Gorges de la Nesque, has lists of artisanal lavender producers such as **GAEC Champelle** (☎04 90 64 01 50; www.gaec-champelle.fr; rte de Ventoux), a roadside farmstand northwest of town whose products include a great gift for cooks: herbes de Provence–infused *fleur de sel* (gourmet salt).

Carpentras & Around

POP 29,709

Carpentras is most inviting on Friday mornings when a massive market fills its streets. Otherwise, it's a slightly down-market agricultural town, with a handful of architectural sites. It makes an inexpensive base. A Greek trading centre and later a Gallo-Roman city, Carpentras became papal territory in 1229, and was shaped by a strong Jewish presence – the 14th-century synagogue is the oldest still operational in France. Its sole Roman remain is a monumental arch.

Sights

Synagogue SYNAGOGUE

(☎04 90 63 39 97; place Juiverie; ⏰10am-noon & 3-5pm Mon-Thu, 10-11.30am & 3-4pm Fri) Carpentras' remarkable synagogue dates to 1367. The wood-panelled prayer hall was rebuilt in 18th-century baroque style; downstairs are ancient bread-baking ovens, used until 1904. Although Jews were initially welcomed into papal territory, by the 17th century they

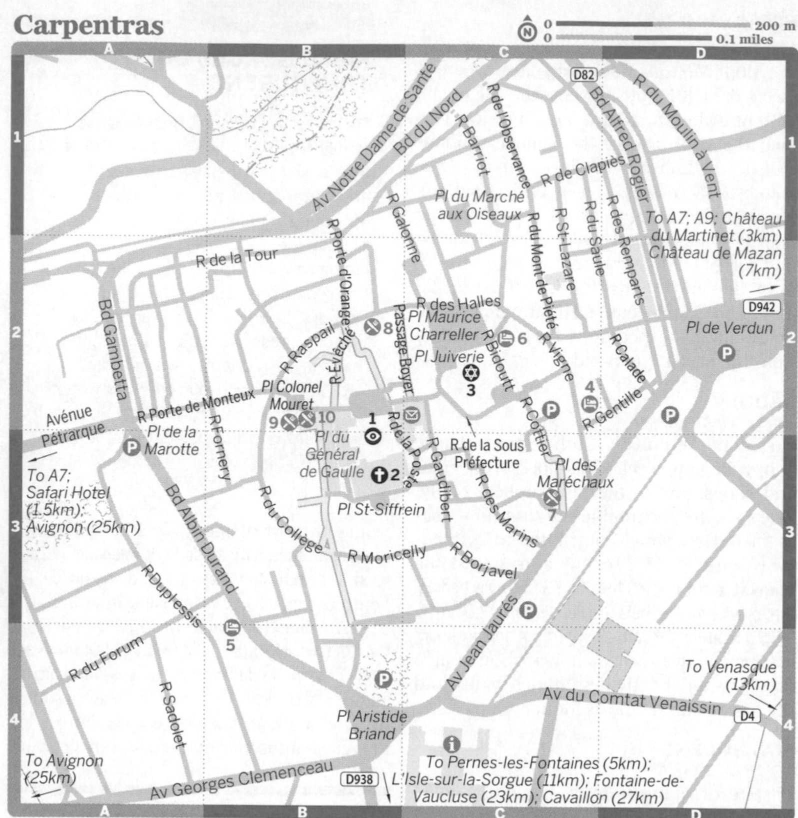

Carpentras

Sights

1	Arc Romain	B3
2	Cathédrale St-Siffrein	B3
3	Synagogue	C2

Sleeping

4	Hôtel du Fiacre	C2
5	Hotel le Comtadin	B4
6	Le Malaga	C2

Eating

7	Chez Serge	C3
8	La Ciboulette	B2
9	La Petite Fontaine	B2
10	Les Palmiers	B2

were forced to live in ghettoes in Avignon, Carpentras, Cavaillon and L'Isle-sur-la-Sorgue. The synagogue is opposite the town hall; its deliberately inconspicuous frontage is marked by a stone plaque inscribed in Hebrew. For access you must ring the doorbell *only* on the half hour, or nobody will answer. Closed on religious holidays.

Cathédrale St-Siffrein CATHEDRAL

(place St-Siffrein; ⌚8am-noon & 2-6pm Mon-Sat, closed during services) Carpentras' cathedral was built between 1405 and 1519 in Méridional (southern French) Gothic style, but it's crowned by a distinctive contemporary bell tower. Its **Trésor d'Art Sacré** (Treasury of Religious Art) holds precious 14th- to 19th-century religious relics that you can see only during the Fête de St-Siffrein (27 November) and on guided walks with the tourist office.

Arc Romain ROMAN SITES

Hidden behind Cathédrale St-Siffrein, the Arc Romain was built under Augustus in the 1st century AD and is decorated with worn carvings of enslaved Gauls.

Sleeping

Hôtel du Fiacre HOTEL €€

(☎04 90 63 03 15; www.hotel-du-fiacre.com; 153 rue Vigne; d €72-110; ⏲reception 8am-9pm; 📶) The faded grandeur of this 18th-century mansion is charming – from marble staircase to canopied beds. Outside there's a lovely sun-dappled courtyard. Good service and value. Parking €7.

Hotel le Comtadin HOTEL €€

(☎04 90 67 75 00; www.le-comtadin.com; 65 bd Albin Durand; s €70-75, d €90-125, t €120-135; ❄📶) Formerly a private mansion, now a fresh-looking midrange small hotel under the Best Western banner, Le Comtadin's best rooms face an interior courtyard; less-expensive rooms face the street, but have double-pane windows. Parking €10.

Château du Martinet LUXURY HOTEL €€€

(☎04 90 63 03 03; www.chateau-du-martinet.fr; 2807 route de Mazan; r incl breakfast €190-295; ⏲Apr-Dec; ❄📶🏊) Live like royalty at this bonafide château, classed a historic monument. Rooms have high ceilings and classical furnishings, downstairs is a spectacular dining room and library, and outside are rambling grounds and pool. Tops for romance.

Château de Mazan HOTEL €€€

(☎04 90 69 62 61; www.chateaudemazan.com; place Napoléon, Mazan; d €140-275, ste €275-400; ⏲Mar-Dec; ❄@🏊) This magnificent 18th-century mansion, 7km east of Carpentras in the village of Mazan, belonged to the Marquis de Sade. Today it houses 30 regal rooms. Its refined haute-cuisine restaurant, **l'Ingénue** (☎04 90 69 62 61; www.chateaudemazan.com; place Napoléon, Mazan; menus lunch/dinner €38/75), merits a special trip.

Safari Hotel HOTEL €€

(☎04 90 63 35 35; www.safarihotel.fr; 1060 av Jean-Henri-Fabre; r €95-120; ❄📶🏊👪) Completely modern, this full-service low-rise tower hotel (with lift) is surprisingly urban with a contemporary, masculine aesthetic, playing to travellers who prefer anonymity. Outside there's a big pool and lawns for kids to play. It's 2km west of town centre.

Le Malaga HOTEL €

(☎04 90 60 57 96, cell 06 16 59 85 59; www.hotel-malaga-carpentras.fr; 37 place Maurice-Charretier; s €35, d €40-45, tr €45-50; 📶) Given the price and city-centre location, the eight no-frill rooms are good value, if a bit threadbare, noisy and lacking in air-con. Downstairs there's a brasserie.

Eating

The Friday market has an incredible 350 stalls. Specialties include *berlingots* (stripy pillow-shaped hard candies) and, in winter, truffles. Restaurant selection is limited.

La Ciboulette PROVENÇAL €€

(☎04 90 60 75 00; 30 place de l'Horloge; lunch/dinner menus from €18/24; ⏲Tue-Sun) Upmarket La Ciboulette has dramatic wood-beamed ceilings and a flowered outdoor patio. The open kitchen uses local ingredients, breathing new life into old classics – save room for lavender *crème brulée*.

Chez Serge PROVENÇAL €€

(☎04 90 63 21 24; www.chez-serge.com; 90 rue Cottier; lunch/dinner menus €17/35; ⏲lunch Sun-Fri, dinner Mon-Sat) This smart little courtyard restaurant plays shabby chic with distressed wood and granite, lending an earthiness that complements the *terroir* cooking: this is the place to sample truffle-based menus.

La Petite Fontaine PROVENÇAL €€

(☎04 90 60 77 83; 17 place du Colonel Mouret; menus lunch/dinner €15/27; ⏲Mon & Tue, Thu-Sat; 📋) On a pedestrianised square with a gurgling fountain this lively bistro doubles as a gourmet deli; expect simple, flavour-rich regional cooking.

Les Palmiers BRASSERIE €

(☎04 90 63 12 31; 77 place du Général de Gaulle; mains from €9; ⏲7am-10pm) This cheap and cheerful brasserie is packed at lunchtime. Tiny tables face a central square, good for people-watching. Expect standards – steak-frites, pasta-pesto, croques monsieurs...

Information

Tourist Office (www.carpentras-ventoux.com; 97 place du 25 Août 1944; tours adult/child €4/2.50; ⏲9.30am-12.30pm & 2-6pm Mon-Sat year-round, plus 9.30am-1pm Sun Jul & Aug) Excellent website; multilingual guided tours from April to September. The free English-language *Discovery Circuit* brochure interprets a *berlingot*-marked walking circuit.

Getting There & Around

BUS The **bus station** (place Terradou) is 150m southwest of the tourist office, which has schedules. Regular services include Avignon (€2, 40 minutes); Orange (€2, 55 minutes); Vaison-la-Romaine (€2, 45 minutes), via Malaucène (€2, 35

WORTH A TRIP

GORGES DE LA NESQUE

Abutting the Forêt de Venasque (and connected via walking-trail GR91), the sheer-walled, 20km-long Gorges de la Nesque is protected as a Unesco Biosphere Reserve. Other than driving or hiking, a novel means of exploring this spectacular limestone canyon (or nearby Mont Ventoux) is alongside a donkey from **Les Ânes des Abeilles** (☎04 90 64 01 52; www.ane-et-rando.com/abeilles/; Col des Abeilles; day/weekend costs from €45/80). Beasts carry up to 40kg (ie, small children or bags).

minutes); Cavailon (€3, 45 minutes); L'Isle-sur-la-Sorgue (€2, 35 minutes); Aix-en-Provence (€11, 1½ hours); Marseille (€15, two hours). Service operated by **Transdev Comtadins** (☎04 90 67 20 25; www.sudest-mobilites.fr) and **Voyages Arnaud** (☎04 90 63 01 82; www.voyages-arnaud-carpentras.com; 8 av Victor-Hugo).

CAR Free parking northeast of tourist office, along av Jean Jaurès.

EAST OF AVIGNON

The small towns between Avignon and the Luberon are defined by water. Pernes-les-Fontaines' aesthetic derives from scores of fountains, some dating to the 15th century; L'Isle-sur-la-Sorgue, famous for antiques trading, is bisected by the glassy River Sorgue; and Fontaine-de-Vaucluse is home to the river's mysterious source.

Pernes-les-Fontaines

POP 10,666

Famous for 40 fountains that splash and gurgle in shady squares and narrow cobbled streets, Pernes-les-Fontaines – once the capital of the Comtat Venaissin – is now a sleepy village of ancient buildings.

Activities

Fountain Walk WALKING TOUR

A free walking-tour map from the **tourist office** (☎04 90 61 31 04; www.tourisme-pernes.fr; place Gabriel Moutte; ⏰9am-1pm & 2-6pm Mon-Sat, 9am-12.30pm Sun Jul & Aug; 9am-1pm & 2-6pm Mon-Fri, 9am-1pm Sat Sept-Jun) details one- and two-hour strolls through quaint streets past historic sights such as **Maison du Costume Comtadin** (☎04 90 61 31 04; rue de la République; free; ⏰hours vary), a 19th-century Provençal costume museum; **Maison Fléchier** (☎04 90 61 31 04; pl Fléchier; free), which displays local crafts; and the gloomy fortified 11th-century **church**. Follow a rough path to the top of the medieval **clock tower** *(tour de l'horloge)* for panoramic views. Among the not-to-miss monumental fountains: grandiose **Fontaine du Cormoran** (pont Notre-Dame, 1761), **Fontaine Reboul** (place Reboul, 15th century) and **Fontaine du Gigot** (rue Victor-Hugo, 1757).

Sleeping & Eating

Mas La Bonoty PROVENÇAL €€

(☎04 90 61 61 09; www.bonoty.com; chemin de la Bonoty; menus lunch €22-48, dinner €32-54; ⏰mid-Dec–mid-Nov;) It's worth getting lost to find this 18th-century farmhouse-hotel, which has earned its reputation as a laudable Provençal restaurant (though owned by an Englishman!). Menus feature hearty fare – thyme-roasted duckling, foie gras and rack of lamb – served on linen in an atmospheric stone-walled dining room. Attractive, simple **rooms** (☎04 90 61 61 09; www.bonoty.com; chemin de la Bonoty; d incl breakfast €75-95;) are available with half-board.

Hôtel Prato-Plage FAMILY HOTEL €

(☎04 90 61 37 75; www.pratoplage.com; rte de Carpentras; d/tr €74/86;) Despite its unpromising location 2km out of town behind an industrial park, this family resort is a wonderful surprise. Seasonal lake and beach (with lifeguard) lend a summer-camp vibe. Spacious rooms are decorated with traditional Provençal furnishings. A good on-site restaurant looks out towards Mont Ventoux. Alas, limited wi-fi.

L'Isle-sur-la-Sorgue

POP 21,000

A moat of flowing river encircles the 'Venice of Provence', with picturesque waterwheels trailing dripping green moss. L'Isle-sur-la-Sorgue's material draw is its upmarket antiques shops (p214), where it is fun to nose around even if you're not buying. L'Isle dates to the 12th century, when fishermen built huts on stilts above what was then a marsh. By the 18th century, canals lined with 70 giant wheels powered silk factories and paper mills.

Sights & Activities

Old Town HISTORIC QUARTER

The tourist office distributes a *Patrimony* brochure revealing the exceptional historical centre. Highlights include the **Collégiale Notre Dame des Anges** (Our Lady of Angels; place de la Liberté; ⏲10am-noon & 3-6pm daily Jul-Sep, Tue-Sat Oct-Jun), whose stately exterior offers no clue of the Baroque theatrics inside – 122 gold angels ushering the Virgin Mary; and a magnificent 1648-built organ, on the left as you face the altar (pipes on the right are mute, purely for visual symmetry).

The former **Jewish quarter** exists in name only – the ghetto's synagogue was destroyed in 1856. The ancient **fishermen's quarter**, a tangle of narrow passageways, dead-ends in L'Isle's eastern corner and retains an apart, town-within-a-town feeling. Dotting the canals are creaking **waterwheels** – the one by the tiny park at ave des Quatre Otages is particularly photogenic.

Museums include quaint **Musée du Jouet & de la Poupée Ancienne** (Ancient Toy & Doll Museum; ☎04 90 20 97 31; 26 rue Carnot; adult/child €3.50/1.50; ⏲11am-6pm Tue-Sun year-round, Sat & Sun Oct-Apr) and **Campredon Centre d'Art** (☎04 90 38 17 41; 20 rue du Docteur Tallet; adult/family/child €6/8/free; ⏲10am-12.30pm & 2-5.30pm Tue-Sat), which mounts temporary exhibitions – mostly contemporary – inside an 18th-century villa.

Partage des Eaux PARK

A country lane runs riverside from old town, 2km east toward serene *partage des eaux* (parting of the waters), where the Sorgue splits into the channels that surround town – ideal for lollygagging on grassy banks, skipping stones, watching birds... Waterside cafes sell ice cream.

Canoë Kayak BOATING

(☎04 90 38 33 22; www.canoe-sur-la-sorgue.com; ave Charles de Gaulle; adult/under 12yr €19/13) Transports you upstream 8km to Fontaine-de-Vaucluse, then you float back downstream in about two hours.

Sleeping

TOP CHOICE **La Prévôté** B&B €€€

(☎04 90 38 57 29; www.la-prevote.fr; 4bis rue Jean-Jacques Rousseau; d incl breakfast €145-210; ⏲closed late Feb–mid-Mar & mid-Nov–early Dec; 📶) Straddling a creek running *through* the house, this former 17th-century convent has been converted into a *très* sexy *chambres d'hôte*, its dreamy rooms decked in luxe style – locally loomed high-thread-count linens, silk draperies and antiques re-upholstered in contemporary fabrics. It also has an excellent gastronomic **restaurant** (☎04 90 38 57 29; www.la-prevote.fr; 4bis rue Jean-Jacques Rousseau; menus lunch €28, dinner €39-58; ⏲Thu-Mon), where Chef Jean-Marie Alloin concocts dishes like foie-gras ravioli, and pear sorbet with thyme-and-rosemary chocolates – *délicieux!*

Hotel Nevons HOTEL €€

(☎04 90 20 72 00; www.hotel-les-nevons.com; 205 chemin des Nevons; d €69-96, tr €115, q €135; ❄@📶≋👪) This modern, generic hotel (with lift) could be anywhere, but its rooms are good value and have gleaming bathrooms renovated in 2011. The rooftop pool has knockout views. A family suite (€145) sleeps five.

Eating

La Villa MODERN FRENCH €€

(☎04 90 38 24 50; www.lavillarestaurant.fr; 682 av Jean Monnet; mains €20-23) Los Angeles meets Provence at hedonistic La Villa where tables line a portico surrounding a swimming pool. Bring a bathing suit and after lunch sunbathe beside sexy Parisians. Come dinnertime everyone dresses sharp, filling the concrete-and-velvet, rustic-chic interior. Up-tempo lounge beats set a lively mood. Midday, expect composed salads, Carpaccios, summer dishes, evenings, tapas and updated classics. Reserve.

Le Vivier GASTRONOMIC €€€

(☎04 90 38 52 80; levivier-restaurant.com; 800 cours Fernande Peyre; menus lunch weekday/weekend €30/45, dinner €45-70; ⏲lunch Tue-Thu & Sun, dinner Tue-Sat mid-Mar–mid-Feb) Outside town swanky Michelin-starred 'Fishpond' is renowned for its imaginative, contemporary cooking. Prime local ingredients appear in dishes like smoked eel with glazed apple, or roasted rabbit with artichoke ravioli, served riverside on the terrace or inside the dining room. Reservations essential.

Le Carré d'Herbes BISTRO €€

(☎04 90 38 23 97; www.lecarredherbes.fr; 13 ave Quatre Otages; menus lunch €17, dinner €24-31; ⏲daily Mar-Sep, Fri-Tue Sep-Mar) An unfussy restaurant among the antiques villages on the main thoroughfare, with lovely patio good for a lingering lunch. Serves market-fresh *menus*. Occasionally hosts live jazz.

Au Chineur BISTRO €€
(☎04 90 38 33 54; 2 esplanade Robert-Vasse; lunch menu €13, dinner mains €14-19; ⏰7am-midnight, Wed-Mon) Antique bric-a-brac hangs from the rafters at this quaiside bistro with excellent people-watching. Expect simple classics and good-value lunches; off-hours find cheese-and-charcuterie plates, tarts and nibbles.

L'Art de Vivre PROVENÇAL €€
(☎04 90 20 18 21; www.lart-devivre.com; 3 rue Molière; menus lunch €13.50-17, dinner €23-27; ⏰lunch Tue-Sun, dinner Tue-Sat; 🅿) Classic Provençal old-town restaurant with ladder-back chairs at wooden tables and ancient wood-beamed ceilings. Serves good-value lunch menus with items like duck confit, roasted veggies with tapenade, and simple grilled steak.

Shopping

Antiques Villages ANTIQUES
(⏰10am-6pm Sat-Mon) If your manor house needs that perfect Louis XV chandelier, look no further. The former mills and factories along L'Isle-sur-la-Sorgue's main road contain seven fascinating-to-explore antiques villages with more than 300 high-end stalls. For bargains, it's better to come in mid-August or at Easter for the **antiques fairs**.

Information

Tourist Office (☎04 90 38 04 78; www.oti-delasorgue.fr; place de la Liberté; ⏰9am-12.30pm & 2.30-6pm Mon-Sat, 9am-12.30pm Sun) Centre of old town.

Getting There & Around

BICYCLE David Bollack (☎06 38 14 49 50; http://veloservices.jimdbo.com; 3 rue du Docteur Dallet; per day from €10) and **Luberon Biking** (☎04 90 90 14 62, cell 06 43 57 58 89; www.luberon-biking.fr; 10 ave de la Gare) rent bicycles (from €18 per day) and deliver to Fontaine-de-Vaucluse; reservations are essential at weekends.

BUS Voyages Raoux buses (www.voyages-raoux.fr) serve Avignon (€2, 40 minutes). Voyages Arnaud buses (p212) serve Carpentras (€2, 30 minutes) and Cavaillon (€3, 30 minutes), via L'Isle-sur-la-Sorgue.

CAR Parking lines the canals; free spaces are rare at weekends.

TRAIN The train station is on ave Julien Guigue. Multiple daily trains serve Marseille (€15, 1½ hours) and Avignon (€5, 30 minutes). Schedules at SNCF (www.voyages-sncf.com).

Fontaine-de-Vaucluse

POP 610

France's most powerful spring surges from beneath the pretty village of Fontaine-de-Vaucluse, at the end of a U-shaped valley beneath limestone cliffs. The miraculous-seeming appearance of this crystal-clear flood draws 1.5 million tourists each year – arrive early, before the deluge; avoid it on Sundays in summer.

Several mini-attractions, from serious to frivolous, cater to the crowds, but the real draw is the springs. Wander beyond the tourist distractions and you quickly sense the peace and beauty that inspired Italian poet Petrarch (1304–74), who wrote his most famous works here – sonnets to his unrequited love, Laura.

Sights & Activities

La Fontaine SPRING
At the foot of craggy cliffs, an easy 1km walk from the village, the River Sorgue surges from the earth's depths. The spring is most dazzling after heavy rain, when water glows azure blue, upwelling at an incredible 90cu metres per second. Jacques Cousteau was among those who attempted to plumb the spring's depths before an unmanned submarine eventually touched base (315m down) in 1985 – but the spring's depths remain largely uncharted.

Canoe to L'Isle-sur-la-Sorgue CANOEING
The glassy Sorgue is a beauty for canoeing on a summer's day. Two companies offer guided or self-guided two-hour trips to L'Isle-sur-la-Sorgue, 8km downstream, from late April to October. Afterwards, you're returned upstream to your car. The trip can also be done in reverse. Contact **Canoë Évasion** (☎04 90 38 26 22; www.canoe-evasion.net; rte de Fontaine de Vaucluse, on the D24 towards Lagnes) or **Kayak Vert** (☎04 90 20 35 44; www.canoe-france.com; Quartier la Baume, 1km out of town on the D25 toward Lagnes).

Musée d'Histoire 1939–1945 WWII MUSEUM
(☎04 90 20 24 00; chemin de la Fontaine; adult/child €3.50/1.50; ⏰10am-6pm Wed-Mon Apr-Oct & Jan-Feb, Sat & Sun Mar, Nov & Dec) Examination of life in occupied France during WWII. Request an English-language brochure.

Sleeping & Eating

Hôtel du Poète HISTORIC HOTEL €€€
(☎04 90 20 34 05; www.hoteldupoete.com; r €95-240; ⏰mid-Feb–Dec; ❄📶🏊) Drift asleep to

THE LEGEND OF ST VÉRAN

Il était une fois – once upon a time – Fontaine-de-Vaucluse was plagued by a vile half-dragon, half-serpent called the Couloubre. Enter St Véran, who slayed the beast and saved the town. A statue outside the village's 11th-century Romanesque church, Église St-Véran, commemorates the slaying. Follow the legend up the cliff to the 13th-century ruins of a castle built to protect the saint's tomb – views are as incredible as the tale.

the sound of rushing water at this elegant small hotel inside a restored mill on the river's banks. By day lollygag poolside in sun-dappled shade on park-like grounds.

Pétrarque et Laure BRASSERIE €€
(☎04 90 20 31 48; place Colonne; lunch/dinner menus from €17/26) Fontaine-de-Vaucluse's restaurants tend towards the *touristiques;* this one is no exception, but manages to serve reasonably priced, good-quality food (try the local trout). The sun-dappled courtyard has mesmerising river views.

Information

Tourist Office (www.oti-delasorgue.fr; Résidence Garcin; ⌚10am-1pm & 2-6pm daily May-Sep, Mon-Sat Oct-Apr) By the bridge, mid-village.

Getting There & Away

BICYCLE The tourist office has an English-language brochure detailing three easy back-roads biking routes. Bike shops in L'Isle-sur-la-Sorgue (p214) (8km west) deliver to Fontaine.

BUS Voyages Raoux (p214) buses serve Avignon (€2, one hour) and L'Isle-sur-la-Sorgue (€1, 20 minutes)

CAR The narrow road to Gordes (14km, 20 minutes) from Fontaine-de-Vaucluse makes a scenic, less-travelled alternative to reach the Luberon. Parking in town costs €3.50.

Pays de Venasque

The seldom-visited, beautiful 'Venasque Country' is perfect for a road trip, a rolling landscape of oak woodlands, dotted with hilltop villages atop rocky promontories, and hundreds of *bories* (domed stone huts from the Bronze Age). The region is famous for its early summer ruby-red cherries.

The **Forêt de Venasque**, criss-crossed by walking trails (including long-distance GR91), lies east of Venasque. Cross the Col de Murs (627m) mountain pass to pretty little **Murs**, and see remains of **Le Mur de la Peste** (Plague Wall), built in 1720 in a vain attempt to stop the plague from entering papal territory. You could also walk into the Luberon from here, calling at Gordes and Abbaye Notre-Dame de Sénanque (p225). The map *Balades en forêts du Ventoux de Venasque et St-Lambert* (€8) outlines several family-friendly walks.

VENASQUE

POP 1001 / ELEV 320M

Tiny Venasque teeters on a rocky spur, its twisting streets and ancient buildings weathered by howling winds. So picturesque are the village and its views that everyone is forever reaching for their cameras. Sights include an ancient **baptistry** (☎04 90 66 62 01; place de l'Église; adult/under 12yr €3/free; ⌚9.15am-noon & 1-6.30am, 9.15am-5pm winter), built in the 6th century on the site of a Roman temple, and a compact **Romanesque church** (Église Notre-Dame; ⌚9.15am-5pm) containing the pride of the village, an unusual late-Gothic Crucifixion painting (1498).

Sleeping & Eating

Les Oliviers B&B €
(☎04 90 66 03 71, cell 06 18 11 32 00; www.lesoliviersvenasque.com; Grand Rue; incl breakfast s €58-68, d €68-78) The three rooms in this pretty stone village house are sunny and fresh, but bathrooms are tiny. Outside there's a brilliant garden with barbecue, fridge and knockout valley views.

Les Remparts PROVENÇAL €€
(☎04 90 66 02 79; www.hotellesremparts.com; rue Haute; menus lunch €16-20, dinner €25-32; ⌚May-mid-Nov; 📶🌶) Built into the city's ramparts, this aptly named restaurant-hotel serves good traditional Provençal cooking, copious lunchtime salads and – *quelle surprise* – a dedicated vegetarian menu. The terrace has stunning valley views: sit outside. There's yummy cherry juice if you're driving. Upstairs are eight spiffy, great-value **rooms** (☎04 90 66 02 79; www.hotellesremparts.com; rue Haute; s/d/tr/q incl breakfast €50/60/78/90).

Information

Venasque Tourist Office (☎04 90 66 11 66; www.tourisme-venasque.com; Grand Rue; ⌚10am-noon & 2-6pm Mon-Sat Apr-Oct) Stocks excellent hiking information.

LES ALPILLES

This silvery chain of low, jagged mountains strung between the rivers Durance and Rhône delineates a *très* chic side of Provence, notably around upmarket St-Rémy de Provence, known for fine restaurants and summertime celebrity-spotting. The entire region is full of gastronomic delights – AOP olive oil, vineyards, Michelin-starred restaurants and truffles. History comes to life at magnificent ruined castles, remnants of medieval feuds, and at one of Provence's best Roman sites, the ancient city of Glanum.

St-Rémy de Provence

POP 10,203

See-and-be-seen St-Rémy has an unfair share of gourmet shops and restaurants – in the spirit of the town's most famous son, prophecy-maker Nostradamus, we predict you'll add a notch to your belt. Come summer, when you may spot Princess Caroline of Monaco at the Wednesday market, the jetset wanders the peripheral boulevard and congregates at place de la République, leaving the quaint historic centre strangely quiet. Many businesses close on Mondays; wintertime is dead.

Sights

Site Archéologique de Glanum ROMAN SITES
(☎04 90 92 23 79; http://glanum.monuments-nationaux.fr; rte des Baux-de-Provence; adult/child €7.50/free, discounted admission with pass €4.50, parking €2.20; ⏰9.30am-6.30pm Apr-Sep, 10am-5pm Oct-Mar, closed Mon Sep-Mar) Spectacular archaeological site Glanum dates to the 3rd century BC. Walking the main street, towards the sacred spring around which Glanum grew, you pass fascinating remains of a once-thriving city, complete with baths, forum, marketplace, temples and houses. Two ancient Roman monuments – a triumphal arch (20AD) and mausoleum (30BC to 20BC) – mark the entrance, 2km south of St-Rémy.

For a panorama over the ruined city, have lunch or drinks at the **Taberna Romana** (☎04 90 92 65 97; www.taberna-romana.com; rte des Baux; menus €16-26; ⏰10am-6.30pm Tue-Sun Apr-Oct), where the cooking revives ancient Roman recipes, including honeyed red wine.

Monastère St-Paul de Mausole HISTORIC SITE
(☎04 90 92 77 00; www.cloitresaintpaul-valetudo.com; entry adult/child €4/3, guided tour €8; ⏰9.30am-7pm Apr-Sep, 10.15am-5pm Oct-Mar, guided tour 10am Tue, Thu, Fri & Sat Easter-Oct) Van Gogh admitted himself to Monastère St-Paul de Mausole in 1889. The asylum's security led to his most productive period – he completed 150-plus drawings and 140 paintings here, including his famous irises. A reconstruction of his room is open to visitors, as are the gardens and Romanesque cloister that feature in several of his works.

For its time, the 19th-century asylum was quite enlightened: Van Gogh was allowed to roam up to a mile away to paint, if accompanied by a staff member. From the monastery entrance a walking trail is marked by colour panels showing where the artist set up his easel. The tourist office runs guided Van Gogh tours in English and French. St-Paul remains a psychiatric institution: an exhibition room sells artwork created by patients.

Musée Estrine
(☎04 90 92 34 72; 8 rue Lucien Estrine; adult/pass €3.20/2.30; ⏰10.30am-12.30pm & 2-6pm Tue-Sun mid-Mar–Nov) Curates changing modern-art exhibitions.

OLIVE OIL MILLS

The Alpilles' southern edge contains some of Provence's best-known *moulins d'huile* (oil mills), where four different types of olives, freshly harvested from November to January, are pummelled and pressed into silken AOP Vallée des Baux-de-Provence oil.

In Maussane-les-Alpilles, the cooperative **Moulin Jean-Marie Cornille** (☎04 90 54 32 37; www.moulin-cornille.com; rue Charloun Rieu; ⏰Mon-Sat) deals directly to the public, though its 200,000L sell out by mid-August. From June to September you can tour the mill at 11am on Tuesdays and Thursdays.

At Mouriès, 6km southeast of Maussane, pop in for tastes of exceptional oils milled at **Moulin Coopératif** (☎04 90 47 53 86; www.moulincoop.com; Quartier Mas Neuf; ⏰closed Sun mornings). The village celebrates a **Fête des Olives Vertes** (Green Olive Festival) in mid-September, and the arrival of the year's new oil with the **Fête des Huiles Nouvelles** in early December.

Musée des Alpilles MUSEUM
(☎04 90 92 68 24; 1 place Favier; adult/child/pass €3/free/2; ⏰10am-6pm Tue-Sun Jun-Sept, 1pm-5.30am Tue-Sat Oct-May) An engaging little museum chronicling the area's rich heritage, with fossils and crafts, bull-fighting exhibits, Augustin Gonfond's painstaking illuminations, and contemporary engravings.

Festivals & Events

Fête de la Transhumance EVENT
On Pentacost Monday thousands of sheep pack the streets before departing to the mountains for winter.

Route des Artistes ART FESTIVAL
(artistes13210.canalblog.com) A hundred professional artists sell works in the streets on one Sunday each month from May to September.

Féria de St-Rémy CULTURAL FESTIVAL
Bull-running, festivities and fireworks; mid-August.

Fête Votive de St-Rémy RELIGIOUS FESTIVAL
A six-day celebration of St-Rémy's patron saint held in late September, with bull fights and parades.

Sleeping

TOP CHOICE **Sous les Figuiers** BOUTIQUE HOTEL €€
(☎04 32 60 15 40; www.hotel-charme-provence.com; 3 av Gabriel Saint-René Taillandier; d €92-154, tr €168; ❄@📶🏊👪) Hidden behind a wall, this single-storey country-chic hotel has 14 art-filled rooms facing a leafy garden – lovely for unwinding after a day's explorations. The owner is a painter (who offers classes by request) and has exquisite taste, marrying design details like velvet and distressed wood, Moroccan textiles and rich colour palates.

Hôtel Canto Cigalo HOTEL €
(☎04 90 92 14 28; www.cantocigalo.com; 8 chemin Canto Cigalo; r €69-89; ❄@📶🏊) This excellent-value, 20-room hotel is a 10-minute stroll from town. Simple and spotlessly clean, its frilly-feminine rooms are decorated in dusty-rose, with wicker and white-wood furniture. Breakfast (€8.50) includes homemade bread and jam. South-facing rooms have air-con.

Fragrance HOTEL €€
(☎04 90 92 35 77; www.fragrance-saintremy.com; 2 rue Emile Daillan; r €90-95; ❄📶🏊) This bright, contemporary two-room *chambre d'hote* brings the outdoors inside with a big wall of glass, opening to a small front yard with a timber-decked lap pool. Thoughtful touches include crisp linens, fresh flowers and homemade breakfast pastries.

ST-RÉMY PASS

This free pass extends discounted admission to Glanum, Monastère St-Paul de Mausole and the town's museums – ask for it at these sites. You will pay full price at the first site, then get discounted admission at the others.

Eating

Les Filles du Pâtissier CAFE €
(☎06 50 61 07 17; 3 place Favier; dishes €8-15; ⏰9am-11pm, variable low-season hours) Tables fill the fountain courtyard outside this upbeat colourful cafe with a daily-changing menu of market-driven salads and tarts. At night it's a wine bar with charcuterie plates and occasional live music.

La Cuisine des Anges BISTRO €€
(☎04 90 92 17 66; www.angesetfees-stremy.com; 4 rue du 8 Mai 1945; lunch/dinner menus €14/27; ⏰lunch Mon-Sat, dinner daily Jun-Aug, lunch & dinner Thu-Sat, dinner Sun Sep-May; ❄📶) Light, simple Provençal dishes derive from organic local ingredients at this cosy village bistro with wood-floored dining room, textured paintings and zinc-topped tables. Upstairs is the cute-as-a-button *chambres d'hôte*, **Le Sommeil des Fées** (☎04 90 92 17 66; www.angesetfees-stremy.com; 4 rue du 8 Mai 1945; r incl breakfast €74-94), with five B&B rooms.

Mas de l'Amarine MODERN FRENCH €€
(☎04 90 94 47 82; www.mas-amarine.com; ancienne voie Aurélia; mains €28-36) Five minutes east of town by car, this fashion-forward *auberge* is filled with contemporary artwork and immaculate details that complement the stylised cooking. Many ingredients come from the magnificent onsite gardens surrounding the former farmhouse. Ideal for a fancy splurge with your sweetheart. Reservations essential. Upstairs are five snappy **rooms** (☎04 90 94 47 82; www.mas-amarine.com; ancienne voie Aurélia; €250-360).

Marc de Passorio GASTRONOMIC €€€
(☎04 90 92 04 40; www.restaurant-marcdepassorio.fr; chemin Canto Cigalo; dining-room menus from €58, bistro €26-32) This refined, Michelin-starred restaurant in mansion-like boutique hotel **Le Vallon de Valruges** (chemin

WORTH A TRIP

TARASCON

The mighty walls of the 15th-century beauty of a castle **Château de Tarascon** (☎04 90 91 01 93; www.tarascon.fr; adult/student/child €7/3/free; ⏲9.30am-5.30pm Oct-May, 9.30am-6.30pm Jun-Sep; last entry 45min before close) rise straight out of the River Rhône. The imposing fortress was built by Louis II to defend Provence's frontier. Today it's a great destination for a half-day trip. Cross the mossy inner courtyard and explore a dainty chapel, ancient pharmacy and carved grotesques, as you make your way up to the crenelated rooftop for stunning river views. The town is refreshingly non-touristy, making it a good-value base for budgeteers. We particularly like **Hôtel de Provence** (☎04 90 91 06 43; www.hotel-provence-tarascon.com; 7 bd Victor Hugo; s €59-65, d €69-85; ❄@📶).

Canto Cigalo; r from €210), combines Provence's best ingredients to create wildly unusual flavours. Even puddings are a wonder – to wit, strawberry sorbet with candied olives. Attached poolside bistro opens for lunch.

Michel Marshall PASTISSERIE **€**
(☎04 90 95 03 54; 2 place Joseph Hilaire) St-Remy's most refined patisserie is an elegant option for afternoon tea.

Shopping

St-Rémy's specialist food shops are usually open until 7pm daily in summer.

Joël Durand CHOCOLATE
(☎04 90 92 38 25; www.chocolat-durand.com; 3 bd Victor Hugo) Among France's top chocolatiers, Provençal herbs and plants – lavender, rosemary, violet and thyme – are used with unexpected flavours, like Earl Grey.

Le Petit Duc FOOD
(☎04 90 92 08 31; www.petit-duc.com; 7 bd Victor Hugo) Biscuits made using ancient Roman, Renaissance, Alpine and Arlésien recipes.

La Cave aux Fromages CHEESE
(☎04 90 92 32 45; 1 place Joseph Hilaire) Thrilling cheese shop with a 12th-century ripening cellar.

Moulin à Huile du Calanquet OLIVE OIL
(☎04 32 60 09 50; www.moulinducalanquet.fr; Vieux Chemin d'Arles) Brother-and-sister-run olive-oil mill located 4.5km southwest of St-Rémy, with tastings and homemade tapenade, fruit juice and jam.

Les Olives: Huiles du Monde/Le Monde de la Truffe OLIVE OIL
(☎04 90 15 02 33; 16 bd Victor Hugo) This place has 30 different oils at its *bar à huiles* (oil bar) and aromatic truffle products.

Information

The websites www.alpilles.com and www.alpilles.fr list information on the region.

Tourist Office (☎04 90 92 05 22; www.saintremy-de-provence.com; place Jean Jaurès; ⏲9am-12.30pm & 2-6.30pm Mon-Sat year-round, plus 10am-12.30pm & 3pm-5pm Sun Jul & Aug) From Easter to October the tourist office runs English-language guided tours (adult/student €8/5), including nature rambles in the Alpilles.

Getting There & Around

BUS Allô Cartreize (☎08 11 88 01 13; www.pilote.com) serves Avignon (€3.10, one hour), Baux de Provence (€2.20, 15 minutes, weekends May to September, daily July and August), Arles (€2.20, 45 minutes, Monday to Saturday) and Cavaillon (€1, 30 minutes).

BICYCLE Rentals and delivery from **Telecycles** (☎04 90 92 83 15; www.telecycles-location.com; 1/3/7 days €19/39/72) and **Vélo-Passion** (☎04 90 92 49 43; www.velopassion.fr).

CAR From Avignon take D571; from Nîmes, the D99. St-Rémy gets packed in summer; there's parking by the tourist office (parking Jean-Jaurès) and north of the periphery (parking Général-de-Gaulle).

Around St-Rémy de Provence

Vineyards and olive groves line valleys below craggy peaks, covered in fragrant Mediterrandean scrub. There are also rugged castles, ancient olive-oil mills, a troglodyte monastery and unusual attractions that dot the countryside.

JARDIN DE L'ALCHIMISTE

East of St-Rémy, in Eygalières, fascinating **Jardin de l'Alchimiste** (Alchemist's Garden; ☎04 90 90 67 67; www.jardin-alchimiste.com;

Mas de la Brune; adult/concession/child €7/5/2; ⏲10am-6pm daily May, 10am-6pm Sat & Sun Jun-Sep) – inspired by the nearby 16th-century house of an alchemist – is planted in arcane medieval patterns, and filled with blossoming trees and herbs reputed to hold mystical properties. It's a magical destination for a Sunday-afternoon drive.

LES BAUX DE PROVENCE

POP 381

Clinging precariously to an ancient limestone *baou* (Provençal for 'rocky spur'), this fortified hilltop village is one of the most visited in France. It's easy to understand why – narrow cobbled streets wend car-free past ancient houses, up to a splendid castle. The **tourist office** (☎04 90 54 34 39; www.lesbauxdeprovence.com; ⏲9.30am-5pm Mon-Fri, 10am-5.30pm Sat & Sun) has information on the few accommodation options.

Sights

Château des Baux CASTLE, RUIN

(www.chateau-baux-provence.com; adult/child €7.60/5.70; ⏲9am-6pm Sep-Jun, 9am-8pm Jul & Aug) The dramatic ruins of Château des Baux crown the village and dominate the landscape. Dating to the 10th century, the castle was largely destroyed in 1633, during the reign of Louis XIII. With maze-like ruins covering 7 hectares, it's a thrilling place to explore – particularly for kids in their toy-soldier phase.

Climb the crumbling towers for incredible views and descend into disused dungeons. Giant medieval weapons dot the site, and pictograms of knights falling from ledges depict cautionary tales about how high you are on the cliffs. The reconstructed trebuchets, ballistas and battering rams are demonstrated several times daily during summer.

Carrières de Lumière LIGHT SHOW

(☎04 90 54 55 56; www.carrieres-lumieres.com; rte de Maillane; adult/student €8/6; ⏲10am-7pm Apr-Sep, 10am-6pm Oct-Dec & Mar) A high-end sound-and-light spectacular, Carrières de Lumière is an odd, strangely thrilling attraction. In the chilly halls of a former limestone quarry, gigantic projections illuminate rough cave walls and floor, accompanied by oration and swelling music in that overly dramatic way the French so love. The show – on Gaugin and Van Gogh, at the time of research – shows famous images in new ways. Dress warmly.

Sleeping & Eating

L'Oustau de Baumanière GASTRONOMIC €€€

(☎04 90 54 33 07; www.oustaudebaumaniere.com; menus €95-150; ✎) A legendary table beneath vaulted stone ceilings, l'Oustau serves rarefied cuisine, including a *très* gourmet vegetarian menu with ingredients from the organic garden outside. Upstairs are luxurious **rooms** (☎04 90 54 33 07; www.oustaudebaumaniere.com; d from €290). Head chef and owner Jean-André Charial's kingdom includes the Michelin-starred restaurant and fancy digs at **La Cabro d'Or** (☎04 90 54 33 21), also in Les Baux. Reservations imperative.

Getting There & Around

CAR Driving is easiest, but parking is hellish. Find metered spaces far down the hill at the village's edge; there's free parking outside Carrières de Lumière (p219). Good luck.

BUS Allô Cartreize (p218) has services to St-Rémy-de-Provence (€2.20, 10 minutes) and Arles (€2.20, 30 minutes) at weekends from May to September and daily in July and August.

Nîmes & Around

NÎMES

POP 144,092

Though not technically Provence, Nîmes' incredible Roman monuments merit a day trip to Languedoc. It's also an important transportation hub for the Camargue. The old town is filled with good shopping, cafes and bars. The Pont du Gard aqueduct, 23km northeast, once supplied the Roman city with water. Now it adorns every postcard rack in the region.

Sights & Activities

Les Arènes ROMAN SITES

(www.arenes-nimes.com; place des Arènes; adult/child €7.90/6; ⏲9am-8pm Jul-Aug, earlier closing at other times) Impressively intact, Nîmes' Roman amphitheatre was once the setting for executions and gladiator fights. Built c AD100 for 24,000 spectators, the interior has four seating tiers and a labyrinth of passages to keep patricians apart from plebs.

COMBO SAVER

Save on Nîmes' three major Roman sites with a **combination ticket** (adult/child €9.90/7.60).

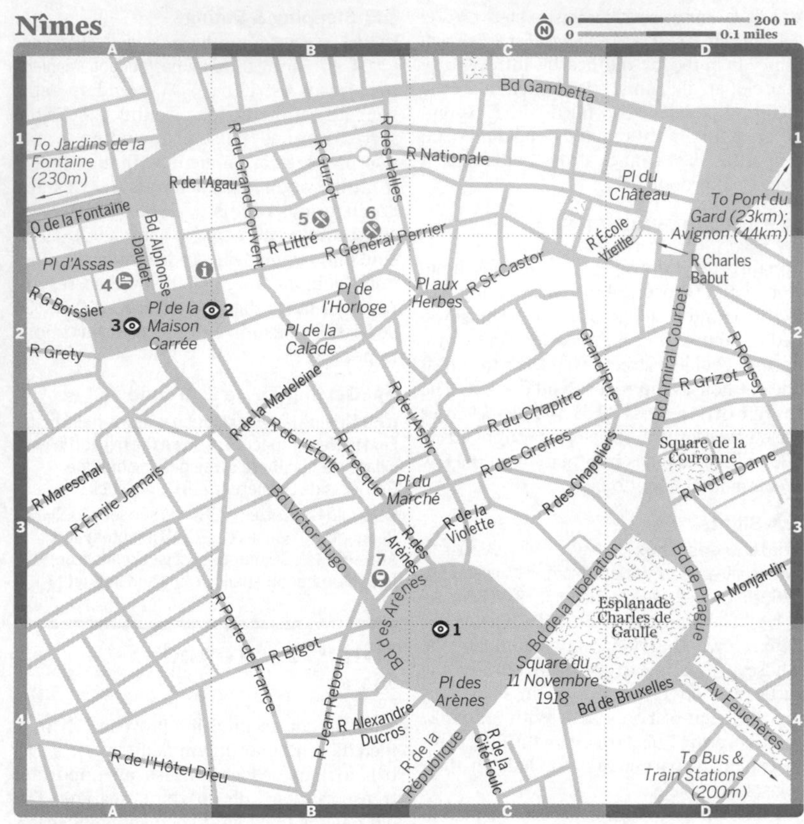

Nîmes

Sights

Carré d'Art ....(see 3)
1 Les Arènes C4
2 Maison Carrée B2
3 Musée d'Art Contemporain A2

Sleeping

4 Royal Hôtel A2

Eating

5 Au Plaisir des Halles B1
Halles Auberge ....(see 6)
6 Les Halles B1

Drinking

7 Grand Café de la Bourse et du Commerce B3

An excellent audioguide brings the dramatic history to life. Year-round, Les Arènes stages plays, concerts and bullfights.

Maison Carrée ROMAN SITES
(place de la Maison Carrée; adult/child €4.60/3.80; ⏲10am-8pm Jul-Aug, earlier closing at other times) This remarkably well-preserved Roman temple was constructed c AD5 to honour Emperor Augustus' two adopted sons. A cheesy 22-minute 3D film, *Héros de Nîmes,* screens every half-hour.

Carré d'Art MUSEUM
(www.carreartmusee.com; place de la Maison Carrée; permanent collection free, exhibitions adult/child €5/3.70; ⏲10am-6pm Tue-Sun) This striking glass-and-steel edifice is home to the **Musée d'Art Contemporain** (place de la Maison Carrée; free; ⏲10am-6pm, closed Monday),

which showcases brilliant works from the 1960s to 1990s.

Jardins de la Fontaine ROMAN SITES
(Tour Magne adult/child €2.80/2.40; Tour Magne 9.30am-6.30pm) One of France's most famous gardens includes the remains of the ancient Roman **Temple de Diane**. A 10-minute uphill walk brings you to Tour Magne, c 15 BC; up its 140 steps, there's a panel interpreting the magnificent panorama.

Festivals & Events

Férias de Nîmes CULTURAL FESTIVAL
Nîmes has two *férias* (bullfighting festivals): five-day *Féria de Pentecôte*, held in June, and three-day harvest-time *Féria des Vendanges*, held in September. Each includes daily *corridas* (bullfights) in which the bull gets killed.

Sleeping & Eating

Place aux Herbes and place du Marché buzz with cafés. **Les Halles** (rue Guizot, rue Général Perrir & rue des Halles; 6.30am-1pm) is Nîmes' vast covered market.

Royal Hôtel HOTEL €
(04 66 58 28 27; www.royalhotel-nimes.com; 3 blvd Alphonse Daudet; r €60-80;) This raffishly bohemian, 21-room hotel is popular with visiting artists. Many rooms overlook dynamic place d'Assas – an exhilarating view, but noisy on summer nights: light-sleepers, book patio rooms.

Grand Café de la Bourse et du Commerce BAR
(bd des Arènes) Opulent 19th-century café, opposite Les Arènes, is great for breakfast, coffee or cocktails.

Halles Auberge TRADITIONAL FRENCH €
(04 66 21 96 70; www.hallesauberge.com; 5 rue des Halles; mains €7-10; Tue-Sun 10.30am-2pm) Inside Les Halles market, this buzzing lunch counter specialises in grilled meats. Great value and a fun alternative to restaurants.

Au Plaisir des Halles TRADITIONAL FRENCH €€
(04 66 36 01 02; 4 rue Littré; mains €24-30; Tue-Sat) Ingredients here are the freshest and lunch three-course *menus* (€20) are excellent value. Consider local-specialty *brandade* (whipped salted codfish). Great list of Languedoc wines.

Information

Tourist Office (04 66 58 38 00; www.ot-nimes.fr; 6 rue Auguste; 8.30am-8pm Mon-Fri, 9am-7pm Sat, 10am-6pm Sun Jul & Aug, shorter hours rest of year) Rents audioguides to central Nîmes (one/two terminals €8/10).

Getting There & Around

A new tram was under construction at the time of research. The Tourist Office has current information.

BUS Bus Station (04 66 38 59 43; rue Ste-Félicité) The bus station adjoins the train station (p221). International operators include **Eurolines** (08 92 89 90 91; www.eurolines.com).

Edgard (www.edgard-transport.fr) Buses anywhere in the Gard *département* cost €1.50, including Villeneuve-lès-Avignon (90 minutes); also serves Avignon (90 minutes).

CAR Nîmes' narrow streets and one-ways render driving confusing. Garages are expensive; watch the clock. Find pay lots by Arènes, Jardins de la Fontaine and Maison Carrée.

TRAIN The **train station** (bd Talabot) is at the southeastern end of av Feuchères. In town, buy tickets at the SNCF Boutique. Services include Avignon (€9, 45 minutes), Arles (€8, 30 minutes) and Aigues-Mortes (€7.60, 45 minutes). TGVs serve Paris (€50 to €100, three hours).

PONT DU GARD

The Romans didn't do anything on a small scale and this awe-inspiring aqueduct is no exception. At 50m, it's the world's highest Roman monument. Walk across for a bird's-eye view over the river.

Sights & Activities

TOP CHOICE **Pont du Gard** ROMAN SITES
(04 66 37 50 99; www.pontdugard.fr; car & up to 5 passengers €18, after 8pm €10, cyclists & walkers free; visitors centre & museum 9am-7pm Jun-Sep, 9am-6pm Mar-May & Sep, 9am-5pm Oct-Feb, parking lots 9am-1am) A Unesco World Heritage Site, this exceptionally well-preserved, three-tiered Roman aqueduct was once part of a 50km-long system of channels, built c 19BC, to move water from nearby Uzès to Nîmes.

DON'T MISS

SUMMER LIGHT

Consider an evening return and see **Pont du Gard** spectacularly illuminated every night in summer, sunset to midnight. The first two weekends in June, a jaw-dropping display of **pyrotechnics and fireworks** showcase the span, starting around 10pm.

The scale is huge: 35 arches comprise its 275m-long upper-tier span, 50m above the River Gard; it once carried 20,000cu metres of water daily.

The visitors centre and main entrance are on the left, northern bank – *rive gauche*; to reach the bridge from parking on either bank requires a 400m walk, with excellent wheelchair access. You can cross the main tier any time, but can tour the upper tier's tunnels only from June to mid-September via **guided tour** (adult/child €10/6; reservations required). The best, least encumbered view is upstream. There's swimming in summer; lifeguards are posted downstream on the *rive droite* (right, southern bank).

Museo de la Romanité ROMAN MUSEUM

(incl in Pont du Gard admission, up to 5 cyclists/walkers €15) The hugely informative high-tech Museum of the Roman World has signage in English. The cinema shows a 15-minute large-screen **film** of the bridge from land and air. Children get their own, dedicated learning area at **Ludo**.

Mémoires de Garrigue WALK

Ditch the crowds along this 1.4km interpretive trail through Mediterranean scrub. Explanatory English-language booklets (€4) interpret the trail.

Canoeing on the River Gard CANOEING

(€20 per person, two hours) For a dramatic arrival, paddle 8km downriver from Collias, 4km west of D981. **Kayak Vert** (☎04 66 22 80 76; www.canoefrance.com/gardon) and **Canoë Le Tourbillon** (☎04 66 22 85 54; www.canoe-le-tourbillon.com), both near the village bridge, rent kayaks and canoes from March/April to October. Allow two hours.

ℹ Getting There & Away

BUS Buses stop on D981, 1km north of the visitors centre. In summer some buses travel to Pont du Gard parking. Edgard (p221) bus B21 operates daily to/from Nîmes; bus A15 from Avignon.

CAR Pont du Gard is 21km northeast of Nîmes and 26km west of Avignon. From autoroute A9, exit 23 at Remoulins, towards Uzès. Park on *rive gauche* for museum and services.

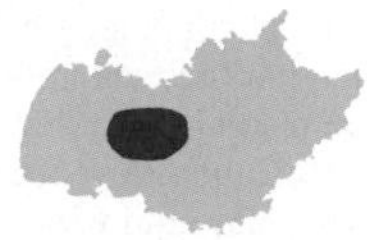

Hill Towns of the Luberon

Includes »

Best Places to Eat

- » Sanglier Paresseux (p233)
- » Véranda (p235)
- » Le Mas Tourteron (p228)
- » Auberge La Fenière (p237)
- » La Table de Pablo (p230)

Best Places to Stay

- » Hôtel La Bastide du Bois Bréant (p235)
- » La Bouquière (p233)
- » Auberge de Presbytère (p232)
- » Hotel Ste-Anne (p231)

Why Go?

Rolling hills dotted with ancient villages define the Luberon Valley. Lush with fruit trees and vineyards, its colours, fragrances and flavours change seasonally. Criss-crossed by country lanes, walking tracks and cycling routes, it is where you come to immerse yourself in nature. And to eat.

The region's capital, Apt, is a central hub, but the Luberon's heart lies in tiny stone villages and the orchard-dotted countryside. Seeing it efficiently requires wheels – motorised or leg-powered.

The valley is delineated by two east–west-trending mountain ranges. On the southern side, the Luberon Mountains are split down the middle by the Combe de Lourmarin gorge, dividing the craggy Petit Luberon in the west from the higher, densely forested Grand Luberon mountains. On the northern side, the Vaucluse Mountains buffer mistral winds, sheltering famous hilltop villages like Gordes and Rousillon, famous for ochre landscapes.

Driving Distances (km)

	Apt	Bonnieux	Cavaillon	Gordes	Lacoste
Bonnieux	10				
Cavaillon	35	25			
Gordes	21	19	17		
Lacoste	15	5	21	23	
Roussillon	13	10	28	9	14

DON'T MISS

To gain perspective on the Luberon's diverse landscapes, explore Rousillon's Sentier des Ocres (p229) and its fiery-orange rock formations. Then contrast it with the lush hilltop woods of the Forêt des Cèdres (p233), high in the hills above Bonnieux, a shady respite on a hot day. For a bird's eye view over the valley, head to Saignon (p232) for mountaintop vistas.

Best Courses

» Reine Sammut (p237) Cooking classes

» Le Mas Perréal (p230) French lessons

» L'Atelier Doré (p236) Painting workshops

Best Lavender Views

» Château du Bois (p229)

» Abbaye Notre-Dame de Sénanque (p225)

» Plateau des Claparèdes (p232)

» Distillerie Les Agnels (p232)

Resources

» **Bienvenue à la Ferme** (www.bienvenue-a-la-ferme.com) Sleep on a farm.

» **Départment de Vaucluse** (www.vaucluse.fr) Bus schedules and fares.

» **Parc Naturel Régional du Luberon** (www.parcduluberon.fr) Information on the natural environment.

» **Vélo Loisir en Luberon** (www.veloloisirluberon.com) Information for cyclists.

Getting Around

The Luberon, an hour from Avignon, is just 60km in length. Car is easiest; bus service limited. Village parking gets difficult in high season. Near-straight D900 bisects the valley, east–west, Cavaillon to Apt, then rises to Haute-Provence and the southern Alps. Secondary roads are slow and winding. Plan to get lost.

THREE PERFECT DAYS

Day 1: Hilltop Villages

Wind your way to Bonnieux (p233) and ascend on foot to its 12th-century church, then learn about bread baking at its museum. Bring a baguette on a two-hour walk in the nearby forest. After picnicking – or lunching in the valley at good-value Café de la Gare (p233) – head to Lacoste (p234) to spot the silhouette of the Marquis de Sade's former château, before ending the afternoon wine tasting in Ménerbes (p234), with big-panorama valley views.

Day 2: Ochre Country Explorer

Begin with a morning drive past lavender fields towards far-flung Rustrel for a walk through candy-coloured rock formations at Colorado Provençal (p228) (avoid wearing white). Shop for olive oil and lunch around St-Saturnin-lès-Apt (p229), then swing west to Gargas (p229) to ooh and ahh at cathedral-like caves at a former ochre quarry (call ahead). End with an amble along the Sentier des Ocres (p229) in rust-coloured Rousillon.
If that's too much driving, head straight to Rousillon (p228), with a late-afternoon drive past Gordes (p225) to see the setting sun turn the grey-white village orange.

Day 3: Mountain Traverse

Get perspective on the mountains by crossing them. Gaze from on high in the tiny village of Saignon (p232), then wind through lavender fields to Buoux, where you can lunch in the garden at Auberge de la Loube (p232) or riverside at Auberge des Seguins (p232). Afterwards, plunge down the Combe de Lourmarin gorge to lively Lourmarin to stroll the château's olive groves and window-shop pretty boutiques. Stay overnight, or cross back over the mountains before sunset.

Getting Away From It All

» **Sunday Brunch in the Mountains** Overlook the Luberon from the terrace of Sanglier Paresseux (p233).

» **Find the Hidden Ice-cream Shop** Ply back roads to find L'Art Glacier (p238), the artisan ice-creamery with hilltop views.

» **Discover Semi-inhabited Ruins** Explore Oppède-le-Vieux (p235), where only a handful of artists live today.

VAUCLUSE MOUNTAINS

Some of Provence's quintessential sights – impossibly pretty villages, beehive-shaped *bories* (primitive dry-limestone dwellings), lavender fields and a stunning Cistercian abbey – lie just a few kilometres apart on the rugged northern side of the Luberon.

Gordes & Around

Like a giant wedding cake rising over the Rivers Sorgue and Calavon, the tiered village of sits spectacularly on the white-rock face of the Vaucluse plateau. Gordes is high on many tourists' must-see lists (notably celebrity Parisians): summer brings a cavalcade of buses, and car parks (€3) are choked. Arrive early or late, or expect to be crammed onto narrow footpaths, dodging tourists and buses. Come sunset, the village glows gold – an eye-popping sight.

Apart from celebrity-spotting, Gordes' star attraction is its 11th-century château, which occasionally hosts exhibitions. Otherwise, there's not much to see. Consider a drive-by: the thrill lies in glimpsing the village from a slight distance.

Sights & Activities

Abbaye Notre-Dame de Sénanque CHURCH
(04 90 72 05 72; www.senanque.fr; guided tour in French adult/student/child/family €7/5/3/20; tours by reservation) Famously framed by lavender in July, the exterior of this isolated Cistercian abbey, 4km northwest of Gordes off the D177, appears on every postcard rack in Provence. The abbey was founded in 1148; it remains inhabited by monks. Reservations essential to visit the austere interior; conservative dress and silence required. It's a 1½-hour walk from Gordes on the GR6 trail, or a slow, winding drive, treacherous in rain.

Village des Bories ARCHITECTURE
(04 90 72 03 48; adult/child €6/4; 9am-sunset) You'll spot beehive-shaped *bories* while buzzing around Provence – 1610 have been counted to date. Explore Village des Bories, 4km southwest of Gordes. Constructed of slivered limestone, *bories* were built during the Bronze Age, inhabited by shepherds until 1839, then abandoned until their restoration in the early 1970s.

Visit early morning or before sunset for an interplay of light and shadow. The lower car park is for buses; go to the hilltop car park, lest you hike uphill in blazing heat.

Moulin des Bouillons RURAL MUSEUM
(04 90 72 22 11; rte de St-Pantaléon; adult/child €5/3.50; 10am-noon & 2-6pm Wed-Mon Apr-Oct) Heading 3.5km south from Gordes along rte de St-Pantaléon (D148), you hit this marvellous rural museum: an olive-oil mill with a 10m-long Gallo-Roman press weighing seven tonnes – reputedly the world's oldest. The adjoining stained-glass museum showcases beautiful translucent mosaics.

Musée de la Lavande LAVENDER MUSEUM
(04 90 76 91 23; www.museedelalavande.com; route D2, Coustellet; adult/child €6/free; 9am-7pm May-Sep, 9am-noon & 2-6pm Oct-Apr) Musée de la Lavande, 7km south of Gordes, in Coustellet, showcases top-end fine lavender. An audio guide and short video (in English) explain the lavender harvest, and giant copper stills reveal extraction methods. The on-site boutique (free admission) is an excellent (if pricey) one-stop shop for quality fine-lavender products, and an easy alternative to driving to distant farms.

Sleeping & Eating

Find cafes and bistros around Gordes' village square. If you're on a budget, carry picnic fixings from Cavaillon

TOP CHOICE **Le Mas de la Béaume** B&B **€€**
(04 90 72 02 96; www.labeaume.com; d €125-100,) In a visually stunning hilltop locale at the village's edge (never mind summertime traffic beyond the garden wall), this impeccable five-room *maison d'hôte* is like a Provençal postcard come to life, with yellow-washed stone-wall rooms decorated with bunches of lavender hanging from wood-beamed ceilings. Beds are dressed in high-thread-count linens, and breakfast is delivered to your room.

> **DINING & ACCOMMODATION**
>
> Make reservations as far ahead as possible for lunch and dinner, lest you go hungry. Every table fills in high season.
>
> Accommodation in the Luberon is limited; much is high end. Save by staying in Cavaillon or Apt. Book well ahead.

Hill Towns of the Luberon Highlights

1 Seeing lavender surrounding **Abbaye Notre-Dame de Sénanque** (p225)

2 Watching white-stone **Gordes** (p225) turn orange at sunset

3 Penetrating ochre landscapes around **Roussillon** (p228)

4 Finding your way to the top of **Bonnieux** (p233)

5 Exploring abandoned **Oppède-le-Vieux** (p235)

6 Getting lost in lavender around **St-Saturnin-lès-Apt** (p229)

7 Strolling fragrant hilltop woods at **Forêt des Cèdres** (p233)

8 Wandering ancient hilltop ruins in **Buoux** (p232)

9 Walking in Peter Mayle's footsteps in **Ménerbes** (p234)

10 Imagining life in the Bronze Age at **Village des Bories** (p225)

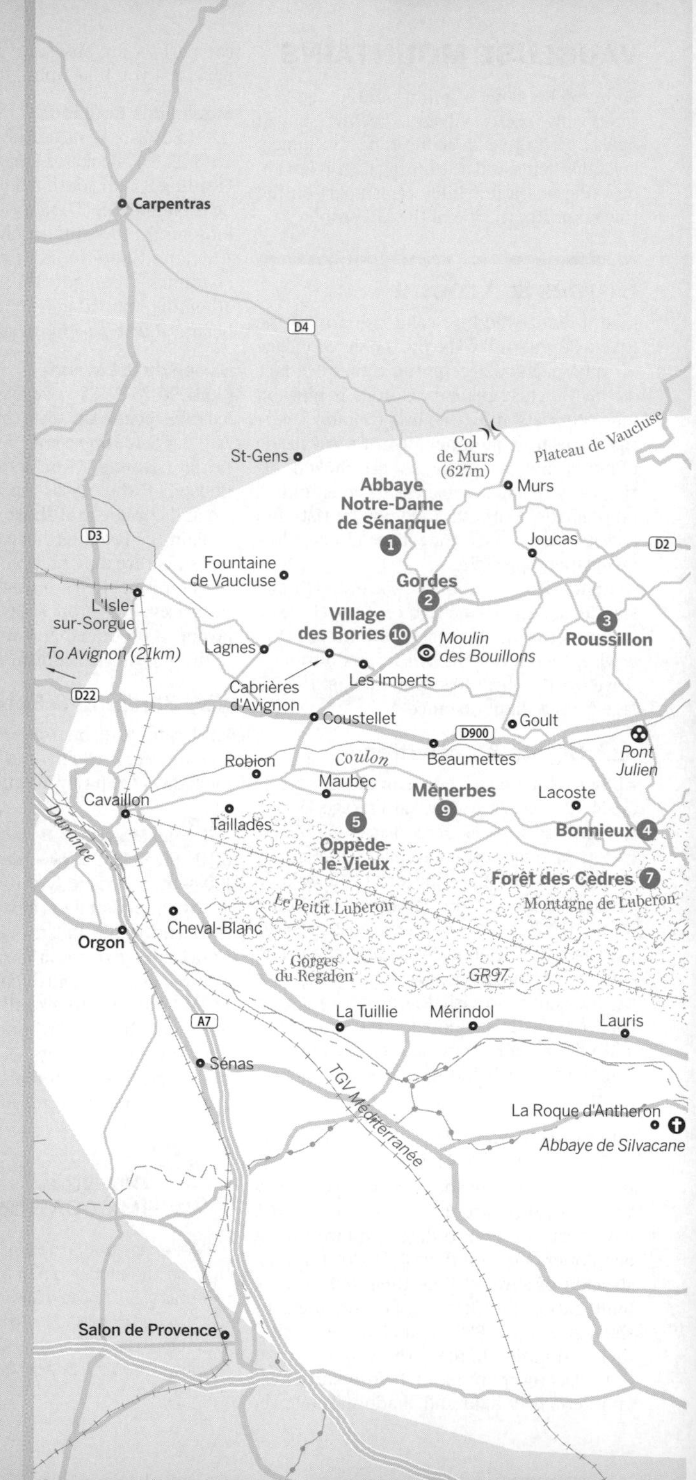

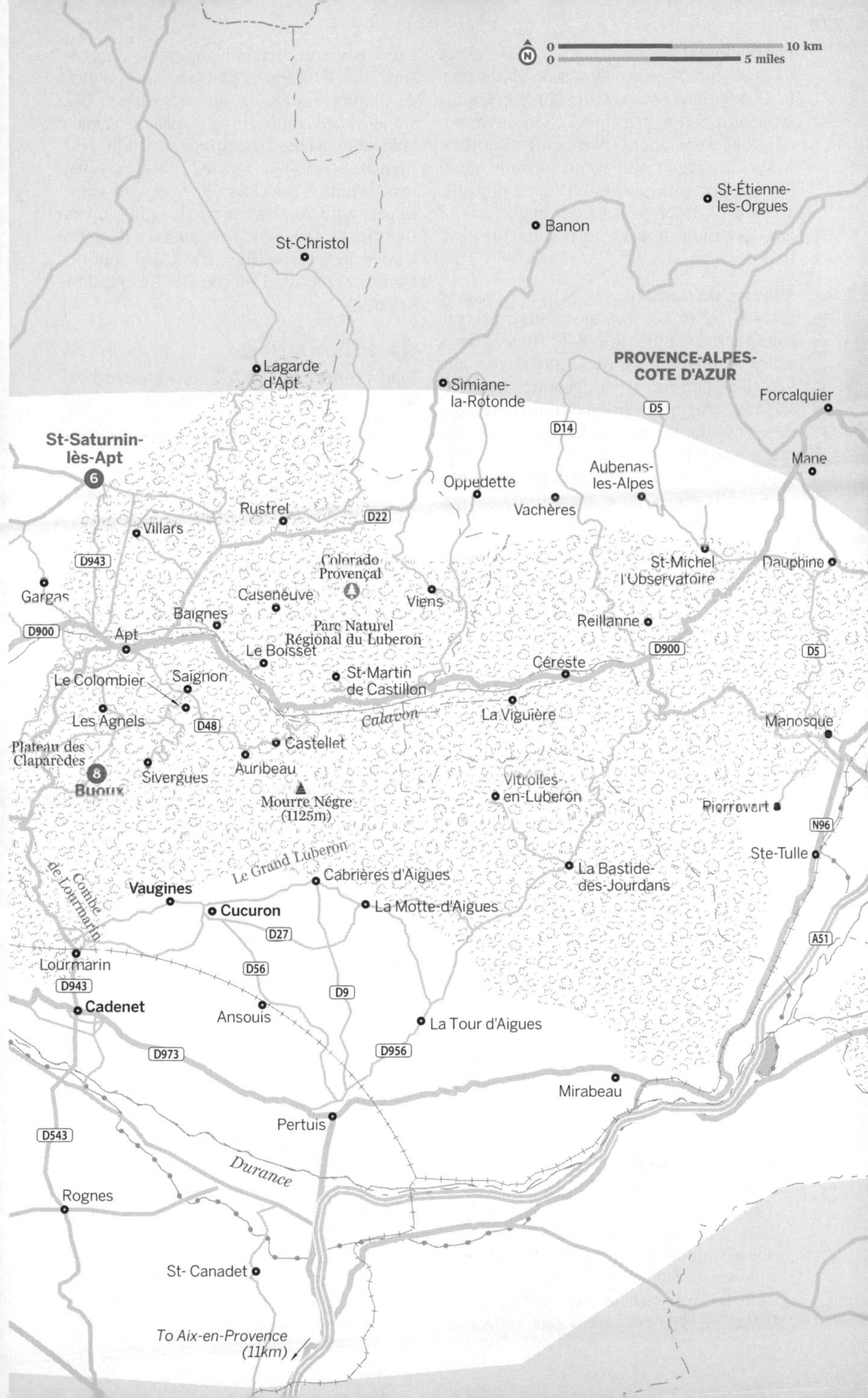

0 10 km
0 5 miles
St-Étienne-les-Orgues
Banon
St-Christol
PROVENCE-ALPES-COTE D'AZUR
Lagarde d'Apt
Simiane-la-Rotonde
Forcalquier
D5
D14
St-Saturnin-lès-Apt
6
Aubenas-les-Alpes
Mane
Oppedette
Vachères
Rustrel
D22
Villars
D943
Colorado Provençal
St-Michel l'Observatoire
Dauphine
Gargas
Caseneuve
Viens
Baignes
Reillanne
D900
Apt
Parc Naturel Régional du Luberon
Le Boisset
D900
D5
Céreste
Le Colombier
Saignon
St-Martin de Castillon
La Viguière
Les Agnels
D48
Calavon
Manosque
Plateau des Claparèdes
Castellet
8
Buoux
Sivergues
Auribeau
Vitrolles-en-Luberon
Mourre Négre (1125m)
N96
Ste-Tulle
Le Grand Luberon
La Bastide-des-Jourdans
Combe de Lourmarin
Cabrières d'Aigues
Vaugines
Cucuron
La Motte-d'Aigues
D27
A51
Lourmarin
D56
D943
D9
Cadenet
Ansouis
La Tour d'Aigues
D973
D956
Mirabeau
Pertuis
D543
Durance
Rognes
St- Canadet
To Aix-en-Provence (11km)

Le Mas Regalade B&B €€
(☎04 90 76 90 79; www.masregalade-luberon.com; D2, Quartier de la Sénancole; d €120-150;) A stone farmhouse on a grassy plain surrounded by oak woodlands, 3.5km south of Gordes, le Mas Regalade's sexy rooms artfully blend the modern with playful antiques. Outside, a vintage Citroën peeks from hedgerows of lavender and rosemary, beyond the big pool. In the country.

Auberge de Carcarille HOTEL €€
(☎04 90 72 02 63; www.auberge-carcarille.com; route d'Apt; d €88-115;) Tucked in a valley 3km east of Gordes, this great-value hotel has spotless rooms, decorated in a conservative mix of traditional and contemporary, with big gardens to roam. The on-site **restaurant** (☎04 90 72 02 63; www.auberge-carcarille.com; route d'Apt; menus lunch €20, dinner €35-50) serves good regional Provençal cooking: consider half-board.

Le Mas Tourteron GASTRONOMIC €€€
(☎04 90 72 00 16; www.mastourteron.com; chemin de St-Blaise; menus from €49; lunch & dinner Wed-Sat, lunch Sun, closed Nov-Mar) The welcome is warm at this countryside auberge, surrounded by flourishing gardens – an ideal destination restaurant for a lazy lunch. The stone-walled dining room has a vaguely boho-chic feeling, befitting chef Elisabeth Bourgeois-Baique's stylised cooking. Husband Phillipe selects from over 200 wines to pair with the seasonally changing, inventive menus. Desserts are legendary. Book the garden in nice weather. It's 3.5km south of Gordes, signposted off the D2. Reservations essential.

Information

Tourist Office (☎04 90 72 02 75; www.gordes-village.com; place du Château; 9am-noon & 2-6pm)

Rousillon

Two millennia ago, the Romans used ochreous earth around Roussillon to make pottery glaze. Today the hilltop village is defined by colour: it's a requirement that villagers tint the façades of their homes with ochre – some 40 different shades, beige to purple. Its visual charms are no secret: arrive early or late.

WORTH A TRIP

THE OCHRE TRAIL: ROUSILLON TO RUSTREL COLORADO PROVENÇAL

Although ochre has been used in the Luberon since Roman times, it wasn't until 1785 that large deposits of the hydrated, oxidised iron-and-clay sands were industrially mined. In 1929, at the peak of the ochre industry, some 40,000 tonnes of ochre was mined around Apt. Traditionally used as a pigment to colour pots and buildings, ochre comes in multiple shades, ranging from pale yellow and vivid orange to fire red and deep purple. Discover these vibrant hues in Roussillon's Sentier des Ocres (p229) or Gargas' ochre quarry (p229).

Further afield, Luberon's biggest ochre site is just outside the tiny village of Rustrel (10km northeast of Apt), gateway to the other-worldly formations of the **Colorado Provençal** (☎04 32 52 09 75; www.colorado-provencal.com; 9am-dusk). Remnant of a quarry, where ochre was mined from the 1880s until 1956, the savage landscape has extraordinary rock formations, notably the fiery upright Cheminée de Fée (Fairy Chimney). It looks like a slice of southwestern USA plunked down in France. Colour-coded trails lead from the car park, signposted south of Rustrel village, off the D22 to Banon. Parking costs €4 (free November to March). A cafe serves lunch in season. The red earth gets blazingly hot in summer: come early, carry water and wear hiking boots and hat.

Consider adding a two-hour visit to **Colorado Aventures** (☎06 78 26 68 91; www.colorado-aventures.com; adult/child €18/14; closed Jan;), a Tarzan-style obstacle course in the red-rock forest, including zip lines rigged through treetops. The site, signposted off the D22, is a rocky 15-minute walk from the car parking; kids must be at least 150cm tall. There's also a good nearby B&B, called **La Forge** (☎04 90 04 92 22; www.laforge.com.fr; Notre-Dame des Anges; d incl breakfast €120; no credit cards), hidden in the forest, inside a dramatic, 1840s vintage iron foundry. In Rustrel, **L'Auberge de Rustréou** (☎04 90 04 90 90; rustreou.hotel@orange.fr; 3 place de la Fête; s/d/tr €48/54-58/63; menus €15-22; Mar-Nov;) has clean, budget rooms and a good Provençal restaurant.

WORTH A TRIP

LAGARDE D'APT

Lagarde d'Apt, 20km northeast of St-Saturnin-lès-Apt, is home to an 800,000-sq-metre lavender farm, **Château du Bois** (☎04 90 76 91 23; www.lechateaudubois.com), where a 2km lavender trail blazes from late June until mid-July when the sweet-smelling flower is harvested. Also in Lagarde d'Apt, beneath some of Europe's darkest night-time skies, the **Observatoire Sirene** (☎04 90 75 04 17; www.obs-sirene.com; day/night/child €10/15-50/free; 👪) reveals astronomical wonders using high-powered telescopes. Reservations essential for star-gazing sessions.

Parking (€3 March to November) is 300m outside the village. Restaurants line main streets; better-value bistros have no view.

Sights & Activities

TOP CHOICE **Sentier des Ocres** WALKING
(Ochre Trail; adult/child €2.50/free; ⏰9am-7.30pm summer, low season closes earlier, closed Jan–mid-Feb) At the edge of the village, groves of chestnut and pine surround sunset-coloured ochre formations, rising on a cliff. A 30-minute to hour-long walk wends through stunning mini-desert landscapes – it's like stepping into a Georgia O'Keeffe painting. Avoid wearing white!

Conservatoire des Ocres et de la Couleur OCHRE MUSEUM
(Ochre & Colour Conservatory; ☎04 90 05 66 69; www.okhra.com; rte d'Apt; guided tours adult/student €6/4.50, combined ticket with Sentier des Ocres €7; ⏰9am-7pm Jul & Aug, 9am-6pm Sep-Jun, closed Mon & Tue Jan & Feb; 👪) This arts centre and historic site examines all things pigment. Occupying a disused ochre factory on the D104 east of Rousillon, it explores the properties of ochre through indoor-outdoor displays and artwork, fun for kids to run around. There's an excellent art and home-decor boutique, carrying extensive shades of powdered pigment. Workshops (some in English) teach colour. Tours run year-round at 2.30pm and 3.30pm; also at 11am and 4.30pm in summer.

Sleeping

Les Passiflores B&B €
(☎04 90 71 43 08; www.passiflores.fr; Les Huguets; d/q incl breakfast €73/120; 📶🏊) Quiet and friendly, this *comme il faut chambre d'hôte* is hidden in the tiny hamlet of Les Huguets, 4km south of Roussillon. Spotless rooms are decorated with pretty flourishes of country-Provençal prints. The four-person suite is excellent value. Outside, the 'pool' is a small filtered pond. *Table d'hôte* (€28) by reservation; includes wine and coffee.

Information

Tourist Office (☎04 90 05 60 25; www.roussillon-provence.com; place de la Poste; ⏰10am-noon & 1.30-5pm Mon-Sat)

St-Saturnin-lès-Apt

POP 2479

About 9km north of Apt, and 10km northeast of Roussillon, St-Saturnin-lès-Apt is refreshingly ungentrified and just beyond the tourist radar. Shops (not boutiques), cafes and bakeries line its cobbled streets. It has marvellous views of the surrounding Vaucluse plateau – climb to the **ruins** atop the village for knockout views. Or find the photogenic **17th-century windmill**, Le Château les Moulins, 1km north, off the D943 toward Sault.

On the edge of the village, see how olives are milled into top-quality olive oil at **Moulin à Huile Jullien** (☎04 90 75 56 24; www.moulin-huile-jullien.com; rte d'Apt, St-Saturnin-lès-Apt; ⏰Mon-Sat, afternoons only Oct-Apr), which also makes excellent honey. Tastings and mill tours are free.

Word of mouth keeps **Le Restaurant L'Estrade** (☎04 90 71 15 75; 6 av Victor Hugo; menus from €15) buzzing. The earthy menu showcases the season's freshest ingredients. Great destination when road-tripping the Luberon. Call ahead.

Around St-Saturnin-lès-Apt

In Gargas, 6km southwest of St-Saturnin-lès-Apt, **Les Mines d'Ocre de Bruoux** (☎04 90 06 22 59; www.minesdebruoux.fr; admission €7.50; ⏰10am-7pm summer, variable rest of year, closed Nov-Mar) is a former ochre mine with

WORTH A TRIP

LUBERON REGIONAL PARK

Egyptian vultures, eagle owls, wild boars, Bonelli's eagles and Etruscan honeysuckle are among the species that call the 1650-sq-km Parc Naturel Régional du Luberon home. Created in 1977 and recognised as a Biosphere Reserve by Unesco in 1997, the park encompasses dense forests, plunging gorges and 67 villages with a combined population of 155,000 people. The GR6, GR9, GR92 and GR97 walking trails cross it, as does a 236km-long **cycling route**.

Information, maps, workshops and guides are available in Apt at the Maison du Parc (p231). Its **Musée de Paléontologie** (Palaeontology Museum; free) provides an historical framework, with prehistoric flora and fauna displays, and a room-size relief of the region showing how the topography fits together.

spectacular spire-filled caves, like a serene mineral church. Visit only on a guided tour; reservations advised.

Surrounded by vineyards, lavender fields and cherry orchards, on a vast 17-acre domain outside St-Saturnin-lès-Apt, **Le Mas Perréal** (☎04 90 75 46 31; www.masperreal.com; Quartier la Fortune; s/d/tr incl breakfast €125/135/175;) is a farmhouse B&B with five charmingly simple rooms, styled with country antiques and Provençal fabrics. Outside there's a heavenly pool and big garden with mountain views. Elisabeth, a long-time French teacher, offers cooking and French lessons (€30 per hour).

Gaining the attention of Michelin, young chef Thomas Gallardo wows diners with inventive gastronomic creations at his tiny, low-key, middle-of-nowhere **La Table de Pablo** (☎04 90 75 45 18; www.latabledepablo.com; Les Petits Cléments, Villars; weekday lunch menus €17-22, dinner & Sun lunch menus €29-55; ⊙lunch Sun-Tue, Thu & Fri, dinner nightly). The clean-lined contemporary-style dining room is comfy enough – it's the food that's exceptional. Also offers cooking courses.

Les Grands Camps (☎04 90 74 67 33; Le Chêne; menus incl wine & coffee €28, children's menus €14; ⊙lunch Sun;) is an unpretentious working farm serving Sunday lunch – four-course feasts of farm-fresh game and charcuterie – near Gargas' ochre quarry. Make reservations. Take the signposted dirt road north from the hamlet Le Chêne.

APT

POP 11,500 / ELEV 250M

The Luberon's principal town, Apt is surrounded on three sides by sharply rising plateaus surrounding a river that runs through town – the gateway to Haute-Provence. Synonymous in France with cherries, and surrounded by orchards, Apt is a natural trading post, and remains a town of services. Its Saturday-morning farmers market is thrilling, but otherwise Apt is where you go to get your car fixed or gather hiking information. A couple of good hotels, restaurants and regional-park dioramas notwithstanding, Apt is dull and decidedly unglam, though not entirely charmless. It makes a good-value base for mid-budget travellers, particularly day hikers and cyclists, who appreciate its location. Up the hill, lavender grows.

Sights

Musée de l'Aventure Industrielle du Pays d'Apt AGRICULTURAL MUSEUM
(Industrial History Museum; ☎04 90 74 95 30; 14 place du Postel; adult/child €4/free; ⊙10am-noon & 3-6.30pm Mon & Wed-Sat year-round, plus 3-7pm Sun Jun-Sep) Gain an appreciation of Apt's artisanal and agricultural roots at this converted candied-fruit factory. The well-curated museum interprets the fruit and candying trade, as well as ochre mining and earthenware production from the 18th century.

Ancienne Cathédrale Ste-Anne CHURCH
(rue Ste-Anne; ⊙9.30am-12.30pm & 2.30-6pm Mon-Fri, 2.30-6pm Sun) The 11th-century Ancienne Cathédrale Ste-Anne houses the relics of St Anne, and 11th- and 12th-century illuminated manuscripts.

FREE **Confiserie Kerry Aptunion** SWEETS FACTORY
(☎04 90 76 31 43; www.lesfleurons-apt.com; D900, Quartier Salignan; ⊙shop 9am-12.30pm & 1.30-6.30pm Mon-Sat Apr-Jun & Sep-Nov, 8.30am-7pm daily Jul, Aug & Dec, closed Jan-Mar) Thirty

tonnes of cherries are candied daily at the world's largest crystallised-fruits factory, 2.5km west of town. Free tastings and tours.

FREE **Fondation Blachère** GALLERY

(☎04 32 52 06 15; www.fondationblachere.org; 384 av des Argiles; free; ⊙2-6.30pm Tue-Sun) A well-curated collection of contemporary African art. Worthwhile 'boutik' with fabrics, jewellery, beads and crafts.

Sleeping

TOP CHOICE **Le Couvent** B&B €€

(☎04 90 04 55 36; www.loucouvent.com; 36 rue Louis Rousset; d €95-130; @☜≋) Behind a garden wall in the cobbled town centre, this enormous five-room *maison d'hôte* occupies a c 17th-century former convent, and offers exceptional value and sense of place; breakfast is served in a vaulted stone dining room. One room has air-con.

TOP CHOICE **Hôtel Sainte-Anne** HOTEL €€

(☎04 90 74 18 04; www.apt-hotel.fr; 62 place Faubourg-du-Ballet; r €79-109; ❄@☜) Lovely seven-room hotel in a 19th-century dwelling, completely redone in 2010. Spotless, crisp-at-the-edges rooms mix modern and traditional furnishings, with exceptional beds and big bathtubs (if small toilets). Little extras include homemade jams and breads, made by the charming proprietor, served at copious breakfasts (€10). Parking €10.

Hôtel le Palais HOTEL €

(☎04 90 04 89 32; www.hotel-le-palais.com; 24bis place Gabriel-Péri; s/d/ste €55/65/95;) Friendly new owners – a young family – are breathing life into this old-fashioned walk-up budget hotel – it's tattered at the edges, but on the upswing and clean. There is wi-fi in the breakfast room.

Eating

Le Fournil du Luberon BOULANGERIE €

(☎04 90 74 20 52; place de la Bouquerie; ⊙7am-7pm Tue-Sat, 7am-1pm Sun) Apt's best bakery makes rustic bread, using local heritage grains, called simply *blé*.

Thym, Te Voilà BISTRO €

(☎04 90 74 28 25; http://thymtevoila.free.fr; 59 rue St-Martin; mains €10-13; ⊙lunch & dinner Tue-Sat;) Earthy, market-driven menus at this colour-splashed bistro, where the Euro-centric cooking reflects the seasons. Tables outside cosy to a pretty, sun-dappled square.

Le Platane MODERN FRENCH €€

(☎04 90 04 74 36; 29 place Jules Ferry; lunch menus €14-16, dinner menus €29;) Everything is made from scratch at this simple, correct restaurant, which uses quality ingredients in its changing French menus. Leafy terrace good on balmy nights.

Information

Maison du Parc (☎04 90 04 42 00; www.parcduluberon.fr; 60 place Jean Jaurès; ⊙8.30am-noon & 1.30-6pm Mon-Fri year-round, plus 9am-noon Sat Apr-Sep) Information and maps for hikes in the surrounding Parc Naturel Régional du Luberon. Outstanding palaeontology exhibits.

Tourist Office (☎04 90 74 03 18; www.luberon-apt.fr; 20 av Philippe de Girard; ⊙9.30am-noon & 2.30-6.30pm Mon-Sat, 9.30am-12.30pm Sun) Excellent source for information about activities, excursions and walks; makes hotel bookings.

Getting There & Around

The **bus station** (250 av de la Libération) is east of the city centre. **Trans Vaucluse** (www.vaucluse.fr) buses go to Aix-en-Provence (€2, two hours), Avignon (€2, 1½ hours) and Cavaillon (€2, 45 minutes).

Rent bikes from **Luberon Cycles** (☎04 86 69 19 00; 86 quai Général Leclerc; bicycle rental half-day/day from €12/16; ⊙9am-noon & 2pm-6pm Mon-Sat).

LE GRAND LUBERON

Marking the great divide between Petit Luberon (to the west) and Grand Luberon (to the east), the deep Combe de Lourmarin cuts a near-perpendicular north–south swathe through the massif, from Bonnieux to Lourmarin – the (winding) back way to Aix-en-Provence. To its east, Le Grand Luberon comprises dramatic gorges, forested peaks and grand fortresses. Come summer, lavender scents the breeze.

HONEY HOUSES

Bees collect nectar from myriad flowers, including *bruyère* (heather), *tilleul* (linden), *châtaignier* (chestnut), *garrigue* (aromatic Mediterranean scrub) and *lavande* (lavender). Tourist offices have lists of mielleries (honey houses), and you'll see signs marked *'miel'*.

Buoux

Dominated by the hilltop ruins of **Fort de Buoux**, the tiny village of Buoux (the 'x' is pronounced softly) sits across the divide from Bonnieux, 8km south of Apt. As a traditional Protestant stronghold, Buoux was destroyed in 1545 and again in 1660. Explore on foot the fort and old village ruins (perilous in places due to loose rocks); painted white arrows mark a return route via a spectacular spiralling staircase cut in the rock.

Local climbing club **Améthyste** (☎04 90 74 05 92; http://amethyste1901.free.fr) organises rock-climbing and walks.

At the base of rocky cliffs in a valley crisscrossed by hiking trails, off-the-beaten-path **Auberge des Seguins** (☎04 90 74 16 37; www.aubergedesseguins.com; dm/d with half-board per person €38/58, lunch/dinner €10/24; ⏲Mar–mid-Nov, lunch & dinner daily May-Sep, no weekday lunch spring & autumn;) feels like summer camp, with two pools (one for kids), fireside game room and convivial dining room. Four stone-walled buildings house simple, great-value rooms (no TVs) and a dorm for budgeteers. The on-site restaurant serves fresh, local produce in its Provençal cooking. It's a winding 2.5km below Buoux.

Auberge de la Loube (☎04 90 74 19 58; lunch/dinner menu from €22/28; ⏲closed Mon, Thu & Jan) is a classic for summertime garden lunches, which start with wicker trays filled with *hors d'oeuvres Provençaux* – tapenade (olive dip), anchoïade (anchovy sauce), quail eggs, sliced melon, fresh figs... Save room for succulent roast lamb, and allow plenty of time to savour the experience, especially at the legendary Sunday-lunch feasts. Cash only (no ATMs in Buoux). Twenty-four-hour advance reservations required. Dapper owner Monsieur Maurice collects 19th-century carriages, drawn by gorgeous horses with impeccably pulled manes – his passion. Look for him rolling around town between mealtimes, and tip your hat his way.

Shaded by tall trees on the banks of Aiguebrun creek, the hideaway country **Auberge de l'Aiguebrun** (☎inn 04 90 04 47 00, restaurant 04 90 71 72 27; www.aubergedelaiguebrun.fr; d €170-290;) serves white-tablecloth meals on its garden terrace to the sound of chirping birds and cascading water – perfect for a lingering lunch or romantic dinner and overnight. Rooms and cottages are pricey, but the sylvan locale is gorgeous. Great pool. It's 6km southeast of Bonnieux, off the D943.

Saignon

POP 1005

Tiny Saignon sits high on rocky flanks, its narrow cobbled streets crowning a hill with incredible vistas of Mont Ventoux and the Luberon. The best reason to come is to stay overnight in a fairytale village hideaway.

Lavender carpets the Plateau des Claparèdes area between Buoux (west), Sivergues (south), Auribeau (east) and Saignon (north). Cycle, walk or drive through the lavender fields and along the northern slopes of Mourre Nègre (1125m), the Luberon's highest point (accessible from Cucuron).

The D113 climbs to idyllic **Distillerie Les Agnels** (☎04 90 74 34 60; www.lesagnels.com; rte de Buoux, btwn Buoux & Apt; free tours mid-Jul–mid-Aug), which distills lavender, cypress and rosemary – stock up on lavender products at the boutique; the small onsite spa has a lavender-scented swimming pool (call ahead).

Dating to the 12th century, **Auberge de Presbytère** (☎09 70 44 64 56; www.auberge-presbytere.com; place de la Fontaine, Saignon; d €65-155; menus €28-38; ⏲restaurant closed Tue;) is a former presbytery that's now a romantic 16-room village inn, with higgledy-

PEDAL POWER

Jaunty blue signs mark the way for the **Autour du Luberon**, a 236km cycling itinerary through the region that leads from one picturesque village to the next. Tourist offices have maps for this, as well as *Les Ocres en Vélo*, another route through ochre country. Decommissioned railway lines near Apt are being redeveloped into cycling paths; to date, 28km exist. Stay tuned. Bicycle club **Vélo Loisir en Luberon** (☎04 92 79 05 82; www.veloloisirluberon.com) has extensive info on everything from where to rent bikes and how to arrange transport of luggage, to the location of toilets en route.

If you can't bear pedalling up all those hills, Sun-E-Bike (p233), in Bonnieux and Gordes, rents electric bicycles; they're not scooters – you have to pedal – but the motor helps significantly with the ascents, putting cycling within reach of non-athletes.

piggledy staircases, low wood-beamed ceilings, and each room (some with air-con) in a different style and shape – book well ahead for the top-floor blue room (€130), with its incredible panoramic terrace. The on-site restaurant, overlooking the moss-covered village fountain, serves classic French fare.

The discreet 16th-century façade at **Chambre de Séjour avec Vue** (☎04 90 04 85 01; www.chambreavecvue.com; rue de la Bourgade; r €80-100; ⏲closed Dec-Feb) belies a fashion-forward interior – this extraordinary guest house–art studio has three guestrooms filled with original contemporary artwork.

High in the hills above Apt, with jaw-dropping vistas, **Sanglier Paresseux** (☎04 90 75 17 70; www.sanglierparesseux.com; Caseneuve; lunch/dinner menus €23/29; ⏲daily Jul & Aug, closed Tue & Sun dinner) tops our list of favourite Luberon restaurants. Its easy style is invitingly casual, and there's no better sunset view than from its west-facing terrace (come for lunch or arrive before dark). The chef's disciplined technique and easy personal charm shine through in refined, unfussy creations, which play off the seasons and showcase regional ingredients. To wit, a winter guinea fowl from up the road, fricasseed with local morels, served bubbling hot in a tiny cocotte, topped with truffles shaved tableside. Impeccable. Our only regret is you can't stay the night. NB: the drive is winding – 10 minutes from Apt, 15 from Saignon.

LE PETIT LUBERON

South of D900, Le Petit Luberon mountains lie west of the Combe de Lourmarin – the north–south divide between Petit and Grand Luberon. Its craggy, silvery-green landscape of scrub is dotted with compact villages overlooking forests, valleys and vineyards.

Bonnieux

Navigating Bonnieux is a little jigsaw puzzle in itself. The tiered village straddles several levels: from place de la Liberté, 86 steps lead to 12th-century **Église Vieille du Haut**. The village has a history of good bread; discover the backstory and symbology at **Musée de la Boulangerie** (☎04 90 75 88 34; 12 rue de la République; adult/student/child €3.50/1.50/free; ⏲10am-12.30pm & 2.30-6pm Wed-Mon Apr-Oct).

Bonnieux extends beyond its hilltop village. Just south (6km via D36, direction Buoux), discover the dense, fragrant **Forêt des Cèdres**, a protected cedar forest with staggering vistas and a lush **botanical trail** (allow two hours), which is shady and cool in summer. North of town (5km on the D36), sample local wines in **Caves de Bonnieux** (☎04 90 75 80 03; www.cave-bonnieux.com; La Gare de Bonnieux; ⏲2.30pm-6pm Mon, 9am-noon & 2.30pm-6pm Tue-Sat).

Sun-e-Bike (☎04 90 74 09 96; www.location-velo-provence.com; 1 av Clovis Hugues, Bonnieux; electric bike per day €35) rents out electric bikes – it also has an office in Gordes.

Sleeping & Eating

TOP CHOICE **La Bouquière** B&B €€
(☎04 90 75 87 17; www.labouquiere.com; chemin des Gardioles; d €90-120) Surrounded by orchards and vineyards, with nary a visible neighbour, this rural hideaway has four country-charming rooms dressed with a mishmash of antiques and Moroccan kilims. All open onto flower-filled gardens and share a kitchen, which you'll be glad for come dark, when it's next to impossible to find the place.

Le Clos du Buis HOTEL, B&B €€
(☎04 90 75 88 48; www.leclosdubuis.fr; rue Victor Hugo, Bonnieux; d €120-138; ⏲closed mid-Feb–mid-Nov; ❄📶🚭) Smack dab in Bonnieux village, this stone townhouse spills onto big terraced gardens, lovely for whiling away the afternoon. The dining room has panoramic views, and there's a self-catering kitchen. One room is wheelchair accessible.

Café de la Gare BRASSERIE €
(☎04 90 75 82 00; La Gare de Bonnieux, 5km northwest of village, off D36; lunch €15-20; ⏲lunch Mon-Sat; 👶) Three-course lunches at this old-fashioned brasserie start with an extensive bar of traditional French salads, followed by the day's main (add €5 for steak, if you dislike the choice), plus wine and dessert. Request the terrace (unless smoke bothers you); kids can play in the grass. Reservations essential. Tricky to find; locate the little road opposite the old train station.

Le Fournil MODERN FRENCH €€
(☎04 90 75 83 62; www.lefournil-bonnieux.com; 5 place Carnot, Bonnieux; lunch menus €23-28, dinner menus €45-49; ⏲closed Mon & Sat lunch & Nov-Mar) On a quiet sun-dappled square, causal-chic Le Fournil's contemporary glass-and-steel interior is carved from rock – a moody backdrop for consistently first-rate, inventive cooking that varies seasonally. It's

pricey, but among Bonnieux's top tables – and you won't soon forget what you ate.

Les Terrasses BRASSERIE €
(☎04 90 75 99 77; cours Elzéar-Pin; mains €7-15; ⏲Thu-Mon, daily in summer) Straddling the roadway, with cliff-side tables overlooking the valley, this brasserie – popular with a younger crowd – serves traditional fare and pizza. Incredible views: sit outside.

Information

Bonnieux Intercommunal Tourist Office (☎04 90 75 91 90; www.tourisme-en-luberon.com; 7 place Carnot, Bonnieux; ⏲9.30am-12.30pm & 2-6.30pm Mon-Fri, 2-6.30pm Sat) Covers the entire Petit Luberon.

Lacoste

POP 436

Its name is unrelated to the brand, but Lacoste, 6.5km west of Bonnieux, does have couturier connections. In 2001 designer Pierre Cardin purchased the 9th-century **Château de Lacoste** (☎06 82 25 36 06; www.demeures-du-luberon.com; adult/student/child €10/7/5; ⏲11am-6pm Jun-Sep) (and much of the village), where the notorious Marquis de Sade (1740–1814) retreated in 1771, when his writings became too scandalous for Paris. The château, where de Sade hosted notorious orgies, was eventually looted by revolutionaries in 1789, and the 45-room palace remained an eerie ruin until Cardin arrived. He created a 1000-seat theatre and opera stage adjacent, open only during July's month-long **Festival de Lacoste** (www.festivaldelacoste.com). In the village, **Espace La Costa** (☎04 90 75 93 12) sells festival tickets (€15 to €150). Starting in 2012, Mr Cardin began allowing visitors inside the château, but only by advance reservation – you can even stay the night. Much of the rest of the village belongs to the US-based Savannah College of Art & Design.

Café de France (☎04 90 75 82 25; chambrescafedefrance@hotmail.fr; village centre, opposite town hall; r without/with bath €38/53; mains €9-14; ⏲Apr-Oct) is a good-value, old-fashioned, nothing-fancy, five-room hotel. Two rooms have fabulous views; four have en-suite bathrooms. Downstairs there's a casual bistro with panoramic vistas. Cash only.

Ménerbes

Scaling steep streets to Ménerbes rewards you with uninterrupted views over Tuscan-like plains. The village's maze of cobbled alleyways lead to a **12th-century church**, and a delicious locale to taste wine.

Ménerbes was made famous by British expat author Peter Mayle, whose books *A Year in Provence* and *Toujours Provence* recount his tales of renovating a farmhouse outside the village in the late 1980s – Monsieur Mayle now lives in Lourmarin.

Sights & Activities

Maison de la Truffe et du Vin WINERY
(House of Truffle & Wine; ☎04 90 72 38 37; www.vin-truffe-luberon.com; place de l'Horloge; ⏲10am-12.30pm & 2.30-6pm daily Apr-Oct, Thu-Sat Nov-Mar) The dramatic Maison de la Truffe et du Vins occupies a 17th-century hospice on the cobbled square. Home to the Brotherhood of Truffles and Wine of the Luberon, it represents 60 domaines, and sells wine at rock-bottom prices. From April to October there's free wine-tasting daily, and a gastronomic restaurant of mixed repute. Winter brings truffle workshops.

Musée du Tire-Bouchon CORKSCREW MUSEUM
(☎04 90 72 41 58; http://domaine-citadelle.com; adult/child €5/free; ⏲9am-noon & 2-7pm Apr-Oct,

MARTYR VILLAGES

The Luberon's pastoral bliss belies a dark history. People of 11 Luberon villages, including Ménerbes, Lacoste and Lourmarin, were brutally massacred on 9 and 10 April 1545, under the terms of the Arrêt de Mérindol, a bill passed by the Aix parliament condemning anyone of Waldensian faith to death. In one village alone (Cabrières d'Avignon), over 700 men were killed, and women were locked in a straw barn and burnt alive.

The Waldenses (Vaudois) were a minority Protestant group who sought refuge in the Luberon hills and other remote parts of France and Italy, following the 1184 excommunication of their leader, Pierre Valdès, from the Catholic Church. What remains of the original castrum in Mérindol guards a memorial to the estimated 3000 murdered and 600 sent to the galleys in the two-day massacre.

10am-noon & 2-5pm Mon-Sat Nov-Mar) A shrine to corkscrews, this quirky museum displays over 1000 of them at Domaine de la Citadelle, a winery on the D3 toward Cavaillon, where you can sample Côtes du Luberon.

Eating

TOP CHOICE **Café Véranda** MODERN FRENCH €€
(04 90 72 33 33; www.cafe-veranda.com; 104 av Marcellin Poncet; lunch mains €10-13, dinner menus €38; lunch Tue-Sun, dinner Tue-Sat) High in the village, Véranda feels effortlessly casual, its candy-striped tablecloths a cheerful complement to the sweeping valley views. The kitchen ekes subtle flavours from seasonal-regional produce – to wit, an elegantly simple truffle omelette. Reservations essential.

Café du Progrès CAFE €
(04 90 72 22 09; place Albert Roure, Ménerbes; menus €13-16; lunch, bar 6am-midnight) Ménerbes' tobacconist-newsagent-bar, Café du Progrès, run by good-humoured Patrick, hasn't changed much since it opened a century ago. Great for a lunchtime *plat du jour*, but arrive early.

Oppède-le-Vieux

Abandoned in 1910, when villagers moved down the hill to the valley to cultivate the plains, this curious little medieval hilltop village (6km southwest of Ménerbes) is today home to a handful of artists (population 20). From the car parks (€3), a wooded path leads to the village's ancient cobbled alleys, up the hillside **ruins**, with formidable valley views – a romantic vantage point on the Luberon's geography (provided it's not hazy). The 16th- to 18th-century church, under constant restoration, hosts concerts during August and celebrates mass in honour of Oppède's patron saint on 10 August. Signs from the car parks also direct you to the **Sentier Vigneron d'Oppède**, a 1½-hour viticulture trail through olive groves, cherry orchards and vineyards; panels explain grape varieties, how to train vines etc.

In the village, get the low-down on local artists at **L'Atelier des Cendres** (04 90 76 75 10; www.denisbouniard.com; 10am-1pm & 3pm-7pm Mon-Sat summer, Mon-Fri winter) gallery, which carries pretty ceramics. **Le Petit Café** (04 90 76 74 01; www.petitcafe.fr; place de la Croix; lunch/dinner menus €18/19-25; closed Tue dinner and Jan-Feb) serves meals and snacks on the old village square.

WINE TASTING

The Luberon is graced with three main wine appellations: the Côtes du Ventoux, the Côtes du Luberon and the Coteaux de Pierrevert. Head to the nearest tourist office and request a map that shows all the local growers, cooperatives and wine cellars. As you traipse through the countryside, you'll always know just where to stop.

Oppède-les-Poulivets (or just Oppède), the new village (population 1250), is 1km north of Oppède-le-Vieux and home to **Les Artisanales en Provence** (09 73 85 63 58, 04 32 52 17 85; http://artisanales-provence.fr/; La Bastide des Minguet, 1367 Route des Petitons; open daily), which sells 40 varieties of farm-made jams and condiments.

Just west of Maubec, on the road to Robion, **Domaine Faverot** (04 90 76 65 16; www.domainefaverot.eu; 771 rte de Robion) is a former silk farm that houses an excellent winery, with good-value prices. If it's quiet, Sally and François eagerly provide behind-the-scenes tours. Four lovely cottages (with swimming pool) overlook the vineyards (doubles per week from €890). Using no chemicals, Domaine Faverot produces only a few thousand cases annually, all of Rhône varietals (syrah, grenache, roussanne) – and at €8 to €13 a bottle, you may want to ship some home!

Shaded by 200-year-old oaks, **Hôtel La Bastide du Bois Bréant** (501 Chemin du Puits de Grandaou, Maubec) is a 2-hectare former truffle plantation sprawled behind an iron gate. The 1825 mansion houses 12 romantic rooms, done in upmarket country-Provençal style. Outside are two cosy *cabanes perchées* – bonafide tree houses (no electricity, but with shower and toilet). The expansive grounds include that rarest of treats in Provence: a heated pool. Table d'hôte costs €28. The valley-floor location is ideal for cycling, and it's halfway between Gordes and Ménerbes – perfectly placed for day trips.

CAVAILLON

POP 24,572

The Luberon's other service town, Cavaillon is synonymous with cantaloupe melons, often simply called 'Cavaillons' in France, regardless of provenance. Melons perfume the early morning Monday market, May to September, and throughout town during July's four-day Fête du Melon. However non-fabulous the town, it's a good-value base for lodging, there's some life after dark, and it's just 25km (30 minutes) from Avignon. On Tuesdays the town shutters.

Sights

Musée Juif Comtadin SYNAGOGUE
(Jewish Museum; ☎04 90 72 26 86; rue Hébraïque; adult/child €3/free; ⊙9.30am-12.30pm & 2-6pm Wed-Mon) Cavaillon's tiny **synagogue** (1772–74) – unusual for its heavily ornamented baroque style – sits above the small Musée Juif Comtadin, which examines the town's Judaic history. No self-guided visits; tours (English and French) every 30 minutes.

Sleeping

TOP CHOICE Le Mas Amandier B&B €
(☎04 90 06 29 60, mobile 06 21 90 80 21; www.mas-des-amandiers.com; 1539 chemin des Puits Neuf; s/d €70-82/77-89;) Surrounded by countryside and centrally located for day trips, this converted 18th-century silk farm has a quiet, easy vibe, which is a reflection on its happy owners – one a famous portrait artist, who painted Pope John Paul II for the Vatican's collection. **Painting courses** (☎04 90 06 29 60; www.lorber.fr; 1539 chemin des Puits Neufs, Cavaillon; 2hr session adult/child €21/17, 20hrs €195/140) are offered in his on-site studio. Big, bright, airy rooms face flower-filled gardens, with a pool and summer kitchen beneath grape arbors.

Hôtel Toppin HOTEL €
(☎04 90 71 30 42; www.hotel-cavaillon.com; 70 cours Léon Gambetta; s/d/tr/q €42-65/55-65/70-90/80-100; @) Lively and colourful, youthful and fun, this small hotel in central Cavaillon is well maintained and has fresh fabrics. Free bike storage (€6 for cars), big buffet breakfast (€9). Choice rooms 108 and 201 have private terraces; there's also a communal sun deck. One room has air-con.

Hôtel du Parc HOTEL €
(☎04 90 71 57 78; www.hotelduparcavaillon.com; 183 place François Tourel; s/d/tr/q €52-59/72-79/82-89/92-99; @) Request a room facing the adjacent public gardens at this kitsch, old-fashioned, family-run hotel. Rooms are overly stencilled and garishly coloured, with circus-peanut-orange bedspreads and electric-blue dressers, but they're clean and good value. Limited wi-fi. Parking €8, breakfast €8.

Eating

Cavaillon is a surprisingly good place to assemble an indulgent picnic basket.

TOP CHOICE Prévôt GASTRONOMIC €€€
(☎04 90 71 32 43; www.restaurant-prevot.com; 353 av de Verdun; lunch menus €25-30, dinner menus €38-85; ⊙Tue-Sat, closed early-late Aug) Cavaillon's top table. Chef Jean-Jacques Prévôt changes his offering seasonally to focus on whatever's in season – in summer, melon-inspired *menus*; in winter, truffles and game meats; asaparagus and artichokes in spring… Also offers classes.

Le Clos Gourmand GROCERY/CAFE €
(☎04 90 78 05 22; 8 place du Clos; ⊙8.15am-12.30pm & 3-7pm Mon-Sat) Gourmet grocery for picnic fixings, with good cheese, charcuterie meats and wine; also serves refreshing Provençal drinks.

Sole e Pan BAKERY/CAFE €
(☎04 90 78 06 54; 61 cours Bournissac; plat du jour €8.50; ⊙7am-7.30pm Wed-Mon) Formerly Chez Auzet, of Peter Mayle fame. Good bakery with multiple varieties of bread, such as walnut-and-Roquefort, olive etc; also good sandwiches and salads served at cafe tables.

BEST MARKETS

The Luberon's markets are particularly thrilling. They generally run 8am to 1pm.

» **Monday** Cadenet, Cavaillon, Lauris

» **Tuesday** Apt (farmers market April to December), Cucuron, Gordes, Lacoste, La Tour d'Aigues, St-Saturnin-lès-Apt

» **Wednesday** Coustellet (from 5.30pm June to August), Gargas, Mérindol, Pertuis

» **Thursday** Allemagne-en-Provence, Allos, Les Salles-sur-Verdon, Montagnac, Roussillon, Sospel

» **Friday** Bonnieux, Lourmarin, Pertuis

» **Saturday** Apt, Cadenet (farmers market May to October), Lauris (2pm to 5pm winter, 5pm to 8pm summer), Manosque, Oppède, Pertuis, Vaugines

» **Sunday** Coustellet (April to December), Vaugines, Villars (June to September)

L'Étoile du Délice CHOCOLATIER €
(☎04 90 78 07 51; www.etoile-delice.fr; 57 place Castil-Blaze; ⊙7am-7.30pm Mon, Tue & Thu-Sat, 7am-1pm Sun) Yannick Jaume – one of France's master *chocolatiers-pâtissiers* – makes sumptuous pastries and chocolates, including a heady melon ganache. Great melon ice cream, too.

Côté Jardin PROVENÇAL €€
(☎04 90 71 33 58; www.cotejardinprovence.com; 49 rue Lamartine; lunch/dinner menus from €13/25; ⊙lunch Mon-Sat, dinner Tue-Sat Apr-Oct, Wed-Sat Nov-Mar) Côté Jardin has beamed ceilings and wicker chairs that set a cosy backdrop for its very fine Provençal cooking. In good weather, book the tiny romantic courtyard.

Information

Cavaillon Tourist Office (☎04 90 71 32 01; www.cavaillon-luberon.com; place François Tourel; ⊙9am-12.30pm & 2-6.30pm Mon-Sat mid-Mar–mid-Oct plus 10am-noon Sun Jul & Aug, 9am-noon & 2-6pm Mon-Fri, 10am-noon Sat mid-Oct–mid-Mar) Information on western Luberon. Arranges tours: melon tasting (adult/child €3/free), hilltop villages (€3) and wine tasting with farmhouse brunch (€40).

Getting There & Around

BUS Bus schedules are posted at the bus station *(gare routière)* on avenue Pierre-Sernard (next to the train station), and at www.lepilote.fr. Voyages Arnaud (p214) serves Carpentras (€2, 40 minutes, daily), via L'Isle-sur-la-Sorgue (€1.50, 20 minutes). Voyages Raoux (p214) serves Avignon (€2, 30 minutes). Allo Cartreize (p218) serves Aix-en-Provence (€4.10, 90 minutes). Transdev Sud-Est (p202) serves Apt (70 minutes), Bonnieux (50 minutes), Ménerbes (30 minutes) and Lacoste (35 minutes), all for €2; NB: the Gordes–Rousillon service is unreliable.

TRAIN The **train station** (www.voyages-sncf.com; place de la Gare) serves Marseille (€14, 90 minutes) and Avignon (€6.60, 30 minutes).

BICYCLE Cyclix Cavaillon (☎04 90 78 07 06; 166 cours Gambetta; day/week from €16/78; ⊙9am-12.15pm & 3-7pm Tue-Sat) Rents bikes and delivers (€0.61 per kilometre return).

SOUTH OF THE LUBERON MOUNTAINS

Lourmarin

At the base of the Combe de Lourmarin and easily accessible, the alluring village of Lourmarin makes for a lovely stroll. Explore the olive groves and herb gardens alongside its Renaissance **Château de Lourmarin** (☎04 90 68 15 23; www.chateau-de-lourmarin.com; adult/child €6/2.50; ⊙10am-6pm Jul & Aug, rest of year generally 10.30am-11.30am & 2.30pm-4.30pm) – the first of its kind built in Provence.

Today home to author Peter Mayle, Lourmarin hosts a lively Friday morning **market**. Unlike many Luberon villages, its pretty streets are flat. Wander past fountains while window-shopping *ateliers* (artisans' workshops) and boutiques lining the main street, rue Henri de Savornin. Lourmarin is the final resting place of Nobel Prize–winning writer Albert Camus (1913–60) and his wife, as well as Henri Bosco (1888–1976), who are all buried in the village cemetery.

Sleeping & Eating

La Cordière B&B €
(☎04 90 68 03 32; www.cordiere.com; rue Albert Camus; r €50-65, studio per week €395-450; 📶) At Lourmarin's centre, this character-rich house, built in 1582, surrounds a tiny flower-filled courtyard, with adjoining summer kitchen for guests. Rooms are filled with atmospheric antiques, and bathrooms are spacious. Also rents three great-value studios, with full kitchen; one has air-con.

Le Mas de Foncaudette B&B €€
(☎04 90 08 42 51; www.foncaudette.com; signposted off the D27 btwn Lourmarin & Puyvert; d/tr/q €95-120/145/160; ⊙Apr-Oct; 📶🏊👪) Friendly Aline welcomes you into her colourful 16th-century farmhouse, surrounding a fig-shaded central courtyard. Some rooms are good for familes. The pool and rambling grounds have glorious valley views.

Café de l'Ormeau CAFE €
(☎04 90 68 02 11; place de l'Ormeau; dishes €4-10; ⊙6.30am-11.30pm) Lourmarin's oldest bar, convivial Café de l'Ormeau has a pavement terrace perfect for sipping *pastis* with locals while watching eye candy stroll by.

TOP CHOICE **Auberge La Fenière** GASTRONOMIC €€€
(☎04 90 68 11 79; www.reinesammut.com; rte de Lourmarin, Cadenet; restaurant lunch/dinner menus from €50/90; 📶🏊) The exquisite domain of Michelin-starred Reine Sammut, who grows a kitchen garden for her outstanding six- and nine-course formal restaurant (lunch/dinner menus from €50/90) and more casual bistro menus (€35). Classes (€75 to €145) demonstrate how to make perfect puff pastry or succulent *andouillette* (pork sausage).

For an indulgent splurge, book dinner and an overnight stay (rooms from €190).

Information

Lourmarin Tourist Office (04 90 68 10 77; www.lourmarin.com; av Philippe de Girard; 10am-12.30pm & 3-6pm Mon-Thu & Sat, 10am-1.30pm & 3-6pm Fri) Leads 10am guided walks (adult/child €4/free) dedicated to Camus (Tuesday), Bosco (Wednesday) and exploring the village (Thursday).

Vaugines & Cucuron

From Lourmarin the D56 shadows the GR97 walking trail 5km east to Vaugines, where Claude Berri's Pagnol films *Manon des Sources* and *Jean de Florette* (1986) were partly shot with the village's horse-chestnut tree as a backdrop.

Cucuron, 2km further east, is the starting point for walks up **Mourre Nègre** (1125m) or an easy one-hour amble through vineyards. Get maps from the tourist office. If you prefer high heels to hiking boots, reserve a table at Michelin-starred **La Petite Maison de Cucuron** (06 68 47 11 02, 04 90 68 21 99; www.lapetitemaisondecucuron.com; place de l'Etang; menus €46-90; Tue-Sun), which also offers cooking classes for €65.

Ansouis

Dubbed one of France's 'most beautiful villages', Ansouis makes a worthy day-trip destination. Visit the **Musée Extraordinaire** (04 90 09 82 64; adult/under 16yr €3.50/1.50; 2-6pm or 7pm;), established by Provençal painter and diver Georges Mazoyer, whose passion for the sea shows in the museum's fossil exhibits and oceanic art. The palatial **Château d'Ansouis** (04 90 09 82 70; adult/6-18yr €6/3; call for hours) can be visited by guided tour; in August it hosts classical-music concerts at its hedged-in courtyard. The table to book in Ansouis: tiny **La Closerie** (04 90 09 90 54; www.lacloserieansouis.com; bd des Platanes; lunch/dinner menus €25/37; lunch Fri-Tue, dinner Fri-Sat & Mon-Tue).

Have an adventure finding **L'Art Glacier** (04 90 77 75 72; Les Hautes Terres hamlet; vary), a worthy drive for ice cream that's art. Michel and Sigrid Perrière hand-craft a heady assortment of flavours, such as lavender or sesame. Find it between Ansouis and La Tour d'Aigues, off the D9, on a hilltop with mountain and valley views (look for signs posted at roundabouts).

Southwest of Lourmarin

Far from madding crowds, spot some 243 species of birds at the **Observatoire Ornithologique**, operated by the Parc Naturel Régional du Luberon, near the Mérindol-Mallemort dam (signposted 1.5km from the roundabout at the entrance to Mérindol on the D973). Watch for herons and great cormorants along the 3km-long bird sanctuary trail (1½ hours), marked with yellow blazes.

Lauris, 10km further east, is a regal hilltop village crowned with an 18th-century **château** surrounded by terraced gardens. Tinctorial plants, many rare, grow in the **Jardin Conservatoire de Plantes Tinctoriales** (04 90 08 40 48; adult/child €7/free; 3pm-7.30pm Tue-Sun Apr-Oct, by appointment Nov-Mar) – workshops explore dyes made from these plants and the little shop carries seeds, pigment and vegetal dyes. Lauris' **tourist office** (04 90 08 39 30; www.laurisenluberon.com; 12 place de l'Église; 9.30am-12.30pm & 2pm-5pm Mon-Fri, plus Sat morning in summer) has details on events at the château.

La Tour d'Aigues is dominated by the 12th- to 15th-century **Château de Tour d'Aigues** (04 90 07 50 33; www.chateau-latourdaigues.com; adult/student/child €5/3/free; 10am-1pm & 3-6pm, closed Sun & Mon mornings). Burned in 1792, it was restored in 1974 and holds outdoor concerts and **Musée des Faïences**, full of 18th-century earthenware.

South of Lauris, 7km southwest of Cadenet, **Abbaye de Silvacane** (04 42 50 41 69; www.abbaye-silvacane.com; adult/child €6.50/4.50; 10am-6pm Jun-Sep, to 1pm & 2-5pm Wed-Mon Oct-May) is one of a trio of medieval Provençal abbeys built by Cistercian monks in austere Romanesque style. Constructed between 1175 and 1230, it hosts **classical concerts** and colonies of bats in its cloister.

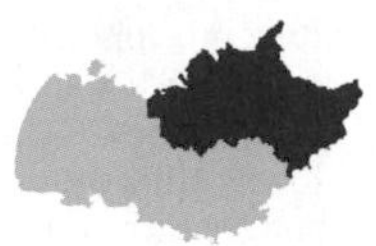

Haute-Provence & the Southern Alps

Includes »

Best Places to Eat

» Auberge-Restaurant le Robur (p256)

» Restaurant Le 9 (p244)

» La Ferme Girerd-Potin (p254)

» La Bastide de Moustiers (p249)

Best Places to Stay

» Moonlight Chalet (p256)

» Les Méans (p253)

» La Bastide de Moustiers (p249)

» Gîte de Chasteuil (p250)

Why Go?

Haute-Provence undulates eastward through lavender fields, from the Luberon toward the Southern Alps – and eventually Italy. North of the Côte d'Azur, the mountains rise in sheer cliffs from the Mediterranean, crowning southeastern France with craggy peaks snow-capped through springtime and creating plunging red-rock river gorges and deep green valleys. You may only have time to carve a small route through this little-visited region of wilderness, but the majestic landscapes are worth the effort: they're an escape from summer's heat, and will change the way you apprehend space.

Haute-Provence's western flanks are marked by several isolated, unspoiled hilltop villages, west of the Vallée de la Durance – the dividing line between foothills and mountains. Magical Moustiers Ste-Marie is the gateway to Europe's largest canyon. In the east, six geographically diverse valleys define Parc National du Mercantour, whose 'Valley of Wonders' wows with 36,000 Bronze Age rock carvings.

Driving Distances (km)

	Barcelonnette	Castellane	Digne-les-Bains	Forcalquier
Castellane	75			
Digne-les-Bains	76	45		
Forcalquier	120	83	48	
Moustiers Ste-Marie	125	35	47	51

DON'T MISS

Dubbed 'Grand Canyon of Europe,' Gorges du Verdon rises toward the Alps, with walls twice as high as the Eiffel Tower. Cycling or driving their precarious rim-side roads provides a dramatic introduction. Pack a picnic.

Best Views

» Roure (p255)
» Vallée de l'Ubaye (p252)
» Belvédère de l'Escalès (p248)
» La Madone d'Utelle (p256)
» Lac d'Allos (p254)

Best Mountain Drives

» Gorges du Verdon (p246)
» Vallée de l'Ubaye (p252)
» Col d'Allos (p253)
» Gorges de Daluis (p254)
» Vallée de la Tinée (p255)

Resources

» **Guides RandOxygène** (www.randoxygene.org) Indispensable outdoor activity guides.

» **La Route Napoléon** (www.route-napoleon.com) Nice to the mountains: Bonaparte's route when he fled Elba – today a brilliant drive.

» **Alpes de Haute-Provence** (www.alpes-haute-provence.com)

Getting Around

Roads are slow and winding, rising and falling precipitously, often without guardrails. Don't pull a Princess Grace. Check weather (*la météo*) before setting out: you'll need snow tyres from October to March, possibly chains. Towns adjacent on maps may be vastly divided in altitude: budget extra time. Many mountain passes (*cols*) close in wintertime, notably around Barcelonnette. Use a good paper map and follow main roads, from autumn to spring. Do *not* trust GPS, which leaves countless motorists stranded on knife-edge routes too narrow to turn around on.

THREE PERFECT DAYS

Day 1: Lavender on the Horizon

Summertime brings to life postcard images of fields of purple lavender, colouring the countryside and perfuming the breeze. Pack a picnic in Forcalquier, then cycle or drive – windows down – to Mane's beautiful 13th-century priory, Prieuré de Salagon (p241). Cross the River Durance toward the little-trafficked D6, along Plateau de Valensole and Provence's greatest concentration of lavender farms. End the day in magical Moustiers Ste-Marie and eat like a king.

Day 2: Grand Canyon Explorer

To beat the crowds, arrive early at the Gorges du Verdon, and set out on a river expedition, day hike or drive above Europe's largest canyon. At day's end, wind up back in Moustiers Ste-Marie to wander its pretty streets and spend another night in comfy digs. Or follow the gorge eastward toward Castellane, where you can overnight in less-glam lodging and better position yourself for tomorrow.

Day 3: High-Mountain Road Trip

Get ready to drive, and head for the dramatic landscapes of Parc National du Mercantour. Make a loop around the red-rock landscapes of Gorges du Cians, then drop down to Nice. If you can add a day, aim instead for dramatic Vallée de l'Ubaye, via Vallée du Haut Verdon (summer only), then loop back to civilisation towards the A51 autoroute (the fast road to Aix, Avignon or Marseille); alternatively from the Ubaye, wind over the mountains from Barcelonnette southeastward, via Vallée de la Tinée, toward Nice.

Advance Planning

» Distances are great, lodgings few. Plan accordingly and make reservations before dark – tourism offices can help if you're stuck.

» Ski towns Pra Loup, Foux d'Allos and Valberg have bargain-priced rooms and apartments in summertime.

PAYS DE FORCALQUIER

Beyond mass tourism's radar, Pays de Forcalquier's expansive landscapes comprise wildflower-tinged countryside and isolated hilltop villages. It's the portal to Haute-Provence from the Luberon, and the fastest way in from Marseille, too. At its heart lies namesake Forcalquier, famous for its market and absinthe. Saffron grows here.

Forcalquier & Around

POP 5000

The area's only town, Forcalquier has an upbeat, slightly bohemian vibe – a hold-over from the 1960s and '70s, when artists and back-to-the-landers arrived and fostered a now-booming organics (*biologiques*) movement. For a taste, time your visit for Monday morning's thrilling **market**, which fills the town's streets. Monday afternoons quieten down; off-season Tuesdays are dead.

Sights & Activities

Old Town HISTORIC QUARTER

Steep steps lead to Forcalquier's gold-topped **citadel** and octagonal chapel, whose **carillon** chimes on Sundays at 11.30am to 12.30pm. As you ascend, peruse **artists' workshops** for pottery and furniture. Pre-Revolution, Forcalquier was the seat of the Comte de Provence and the region's richest town; the legacy remains in ornately carved **wooden doorways** of bourgeois town houses.

Eglise de Châteauneuf CHURCH

For a curative detour, head 800m south of the village of Mane to the Hôtel Mas du Pont Roman, then turn right and either park and walk, or drive 3km, to the Église de Châteauneuf. At the remote, centuries-old hillside church, a church sister, a hermit, concocts natural remedies and makes jam – but she doesn't always reveal herself. If not, consider it an adventure and tick off another church. Bring a picnic.

Ecomusée l'Olivier AGRICULTURE MUSEUM

(☎04 92 72 66 91; www.ecomusee-olivier.com; Ancienne rte de Forcalquier, Volx; adult/child €4/free; ⏲10am-12.30pm & 2-6pm Mon-Fri, 2-6pm Sat, closed Jan;) If all the olive groves around Forcalquier have inspired curiosity, head 15km southeast to Volx to learn about olive oil production and the tree's significance in Mediterranean culture.

TOP CHOICE **Prieuré de Salagon** HISTORIC SITE

(☎04 92 75 70 50; www.musee-de-salagon.com; adult/12-18yr €7/5; ⏲10am-7pm daily Jun-Aug, 10am-6pm Wed-Mon Sep-Apr, closed Jan;) The 13th-century Prieuré de Salagon (4km south of Forcalquier, outside the walled village Mane) is among Provence's most peaceful spots. Wander through medieval herb gardens, fragrant with native lavender, mints and mugworts, and a show garden of world plants. One stone building houses concerts and exhibitions. The inviting bookshop features an extensive children's section.

Couvent des Cordeliers PERFUME MAKING

(☎04 92 72 50 68; www.couventdescordeliers.com) Two-hour workshops (€40 to €50) in perfume-making, wine-tasting, and aromatherapy – some for families – in Forcalquier's 13th-century convent.

Sleeping

TOP CHOICE **Relais d'Elle** B&B €

(☎04 92 75 06 87, cell 06 75 42 33 72; http://relaisdelle.com; rte de la Brillane, Niozelles; s/d/tr/q from €55/62/83/104;) This stately, ivy-covered 1802 stone farmhouse crowns a ridge in big-view countryside about 8km east of Forcalquier. Five rooms and one studio, each with private entrance and some with beamed ceilings, are decorated in smart country-house style. The gracious owners keep horses, which roam below the vast flowered-festooned stone terrace. There's a huge pool and limited wi-fi. Reserve ahead for the *délicieux* all-inclusive *tables d'hôte* (set fixed-price menus; €28).

Bergerie de Beaudine B&B €

(☎04 92 75 01 52; www.gite-labeaudine.com; rte de Limans; s/d/tr €52/62/82;) This genial small B&B is colourfully decorated in simple familial style and has a big yard with pool, outdoor summer kitchen and barbecue. It's 2km from town via the D950 toward Banon. Limited wi-fi. Cash only.

Couvent des Minimes LUXURY HOTEL €€€

(☎04 92 74 77 77; www.couventdesminimes-hotelspa.com; Chemin des Jeux de Maï, Mane; r from €235;) The region's only top-end luxury hotel occupies a converted convent. Entry-level rooms are tiny; book middle category or higher – look online for last-minute half-off sales.

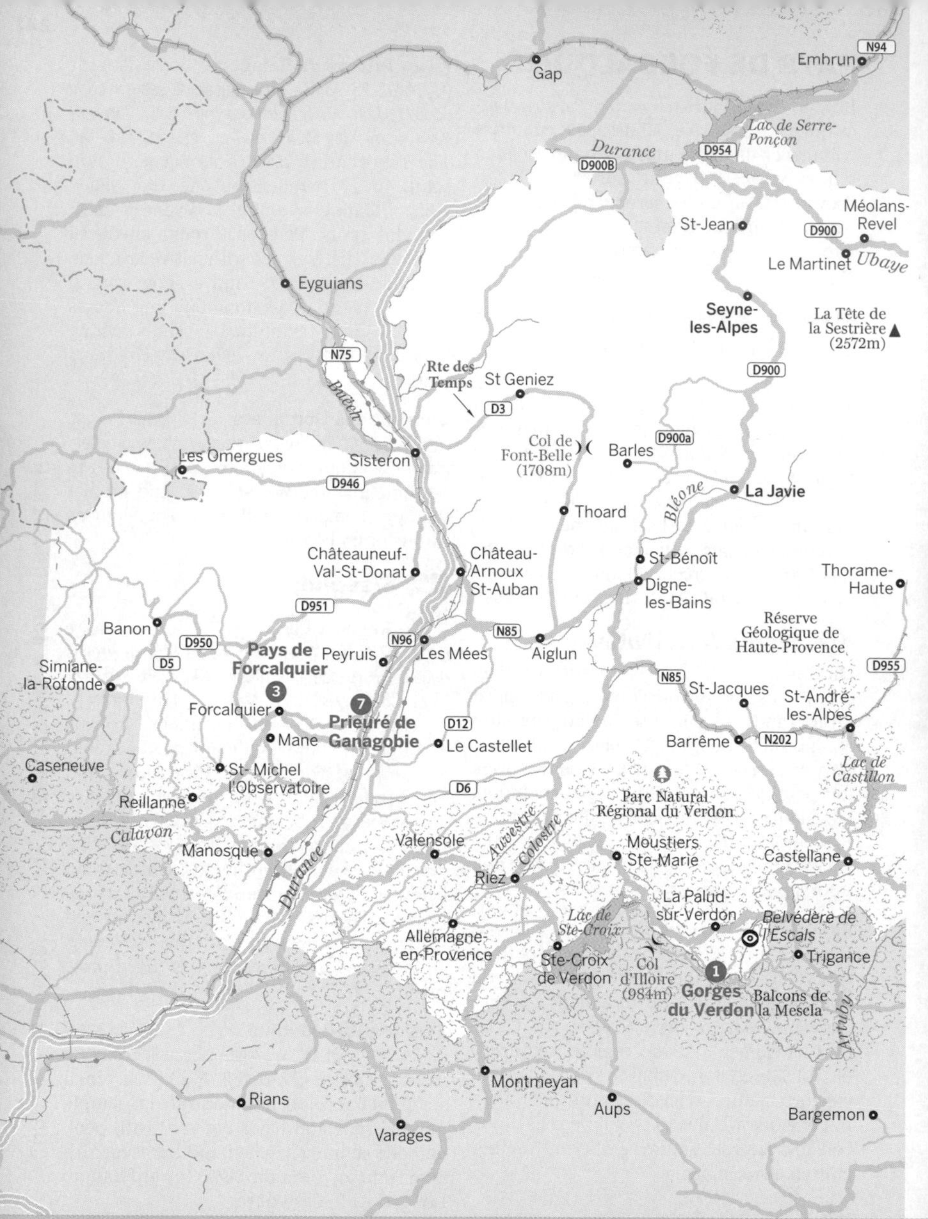

Haute-Provence & the Southern Alps Highlights

1. Plunging through Europe's deepest canyon, **Gorges du Verdon** (p246)
2. Feeling dwarfed by mountain peaks in wild **Vallée de l'Ubaye** (p252)
3. Getting lost on back roads in **Pays de Forcalquier** (p241)
4. Motoring over Europe's highest mountain pass, **Col de Restefond la Bonnette** (p255)
5. Exploring red-rock landscapes in **Gorges de Daluis** (p254)
6. Discovering 3500-year-old rock art in **Vallée des Merveilles** (p257)

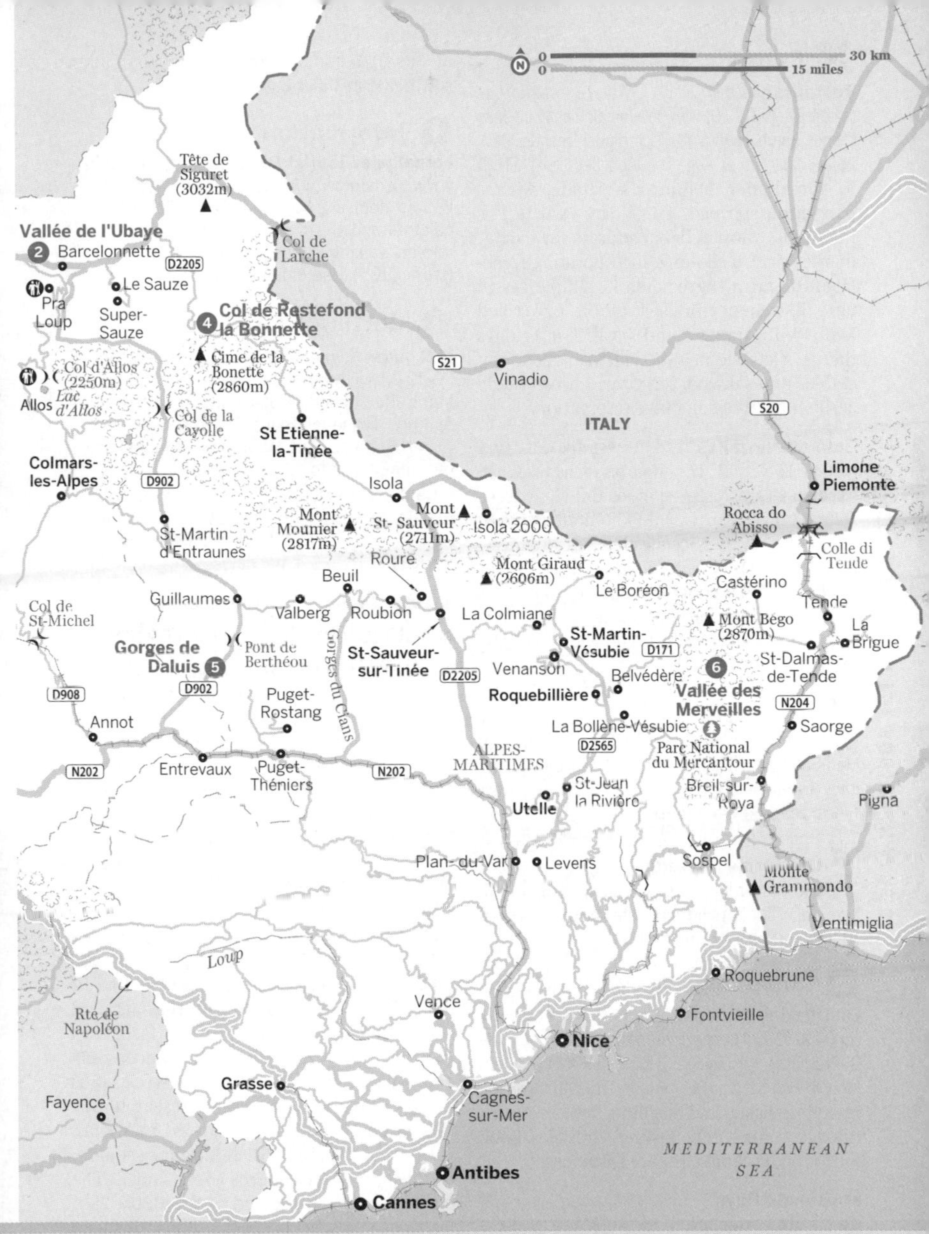

7 Meditating over 12th-century mosaics at **Prieuré de Ganagobie** (p246).

Eating

Restaurant Le 9 PROVENÇAL €€
(☎04 92 75 03 29; www.le9-forcalquier.fr; av Jean Giono; lunch menus €13-18, dinner menus €20-26; ⏲daily Jul & Aug, Thu-Mon Sept-Jun) High in Forcalquier, behind the Citadel with a panoramic terrace, Le 9 (say *luh-nuf*) is the town's most reliable address for earthy, market-driven cooking, incorporating fresh-from-the-farm ingredients in simple bistro fare, like honey-braised rabbit or grilled lamb with tomato and basil. On Fridays there's a classic *grand aïoli* (steamed vegetables and salt cod, served with fresh-made garlic mayonnaise). Make reservations.

Café de Niozelles PROVENÇAL, ITALIAN €
(☎04 92 73 10 17; http://bistrot.niozelles.net; place du Village, Niozelles; mains €12-16; ⏲closed Thu; ❄) Five worthwhile kilometres east of Forcalquier, tiny Niozelles has one business: this convivial *bistrot de pays*, which serves hearty regional cooking – classics like *pieds et paquets* (stuffed sheep's tripe and trotters) and, occasionally, homemade foie gras terrine. Call ahead.

L'Entre d'Eux CAFE €
(23 bd des Martyrs; dishes €5-10; ⏲8.30am-6pm Mon-Sat, to 3pm Wed; ✎) Good for breakfast or easy lunch – salads, cheese plates, etc. Also wine, tea and chocolate.

Unis Verts Paysans MARKET €
(5 place de Verdun; ⏲9am-12.30pm & 3pm-7pm Mon-Sat) Local producers share operation of this excellent organic food shop.

Shopping

Distilleries et Domaines de Provence DRINK
(☎04 92 75 15 41; www.distilleries-provence.com; 9 av St-Promasse, Forcalquier; ⏲10am-12.30pm & 2-6pm Mon & Wed-Sat Apr-Dec) Fiery fragrant spirits, including pastis and absinthe, have been distilled here since 1898. Tastings and sales. Look for the sign marked 'Espace Dégustation'.

Maison du Pays de Haute Provence ARTISANAL PRODUCTS
(☎04 92 75 37 60; rte de Salagon, Mane; ⏲10am-6pm) Small-batch regional products: honey and tapenade, soap and lavender, jewellery and pottery.

Terre d'Oc HOMEWARES
(☎04 92 79 40 20; www.terredoc.com; ⏲9am-7pm Mon-Sat) Handmade candles, essential oils and incense come in pretty wrapped packages at this high-end artisanal factory store, 13km southeast in Villeneuve.

Information

Forcalquier Tourist Office (☎04 92 75 10 02; www.forcalquier.com; 13 place du Bourguet; ⏲9am-noon & 2-6pm Mon-Sat) Office for Forcalquier and all surrounding villages; extensive info on walking, cycling and hot-air ballooning (from €185). Useful iPhone app: 'visit 04'.

Getting There & Around

LER buses (Lignes Express Régionales; ☎08 21 20 22 03; www.info-ler.fr) connect Forcalquier, Mane and St-Michel l'Observatoire, with Apt, Avignon, Digne-les-Bains, Sisteron, Manosque, Aix-en-Provence and Marseille. The tourist office has complete info.

Bachelas Cycles (☎04 92 75 12 47; www.bachelas-cycles.com; 5 blvd de la République) rents mountain, road, tandem and electric bicycles (€18 to €26 per day).

St-Michel l'Observatoire

St-Michel l'Observatoire is famous for starry night skies that are among Europe's darkest. By day it's a cute middle-of-nowhere village. Ascend winding walkways to hilltop overlooks, passing tiny ateliers en route. Uphill from the 12th-century Église Haute, you'll reach a spot with 360-degree panoramas that include the Luberon and the Alps.

Sights & Activities

Observatoire de Haute-Provence OBSERVATORY
(☎04 92 70 64 00; www.obs-hp.fr; adult/child €4.50/2.50; ⏲guided visits 2pm-5pm Tue-Thu Jul & Aug, 2.15pm-4pm Wed Sep-Jun) This national astronomical research centre fascinates with up-close examination of France's only active-use, high-tech 193cm telescope, plus a good film about the centre's research. Buy tickets for the 30-minute guided tour from the ticket office in St-Michel's village square; in July and August, there's a free shuttle. The observatory is at the end of the D305, 2km north of St-Michel l'Observatoire. Call ahead in the low season.

Centre d'Astronomie PLANETARIUM
(☎04 92 76 69 69; www.centre-astro.fr; Plateau du Moulin à Vent; adult/6-16yr €10.50/8.25; ⏲by reservation) From St-Michel l'Observatoire, the eastbound D5 flashes past this astronomy centre, which mounts brilliant planetarium shows and educational workshops.

BISTROTS DE PAYS

A culinary revival is afoot in small towns of Haute-Provence. Ancient tiny villages in the countryside had been dying, following the post-WWII departure of their citizens to seek work in the cities. To rejuvenate these communities, in 1992 the Pays de Forcalquier created a network of country bistros, called **Bistrot de Pays** (www.bistrotdepays.com).

The idea is simple. Member bistros must be in towns with fewer than 2000 inhabitants, with little or no other commerce. They must serve local dishes, made with local products (creating a market for farmers), and remain open morning till night, always offering fresh bread, snacks and morning coffee – making them de facto gathering places. They also provide services nobody else does, specifically tourist information, stamp and newspaper sales. The idea is so successful that the rest of France is adopting it.

There are dozens of such bistros dotting Haute-Provence and the southern Alps, some quite wonderful, such as the Cafe de Niozelles (p244). As you drive around, look for the distinctive colourful Bistrot de Pays logo. If nothing else, stop in for a shot of coffee and hear some village gossip and glimpse the old world coming back to life.

Sleeping & Eating

Hôtel-Restaurant l'Observatoire HOTEL €
(☎04 92 76 63 62; www.hotel-restaurant-lobservatoire.com; place de la Fontaine; s/d/tr/q €52/70/88/109, lunch/dinner menus €18/28; ⌚restaurant closed Sun dinner and Mon; 📶) This reliable restaurant has copious servings of hearty regional cooking; reserve ahead. It's also a well-tended five-room hotel.

La Coupole PROVENÇAL €€
(☎04 92 76 67 01; place Serre; weekday/weekend lunches €13/18, dinner menus €18-25) Well-made provincial French classics – *blanquette de veau* (veal stew), roast venison, house-made rabbit pâté – are served at this small restaurant with a leafy terrace on the town's main square. Reserve ahead.

Banon

POP 940 / ELEV 760M

To sample *fromage* (cheese), follow the D950 25km northwest from Forcalquier to Banon, renowned for *chèvre de Banon* – made from goat's milk and wrapped in a chestnut leaf. En route, you'll pass **Simiane-la-Rotonde**, host village of August's international music festival, *Les Riches Heures Musicales*. In May, Banon celebrates the Fête du Fromage.

The well-known Fromagerie de Banon sells its cheese at Banon's Tuesday-morning market, and at wonderful cheese-and-sausage shop **Chez Melchio** (☎04 92 73 23 05; place de la République; ⌚8am-12.30pm & 2.30-6.30pm Wed-Sun Sep-Jun, 8am-7pm daily Jul-Aug) – unbeatable for picnic supplies. Banon's **tourist office** (☎04 92 72 19 40; www.village-banon.fr; place de la République; ⌚9am-12.30pm & 3-6pm Tue-Sat year-round, plus 10am-noon Sun Jul & Aug) has a list of chèvre farms you can visit. Tuck into cheese-and-charcuterie plates at wine bar and shop **Les Vins au Vert** (☎04 92 75 23 84; www.lesvinsauvert.com; rue Pasteur; mains €12-16; ⌚10am-7pm Wed, 10am-10pm Thu-Sat, 10am-5pm Sun) – make reservations to eat. Bibliophiles: don't miss the village's incredible bookshop, **Le Bleuet** (☎04 92 73 25 85; place St-Just; ⌚9.15am-8pm).

VALLÉE DE LA DURANCE

The River Durance's wide floodplain (affluent of the Rhône) follows portions of Via Domitia – the route from Italy that permitted the Romans to infiltrate all France. Now it's the autoroute's path, fast connector between Alps and coast.

The Durance delimits the Pays de Forcalquier from the southern Alps' western edge. This is a largely rural area of winding back roads and rolling hills. **Manosque** has two lovely fountains and churches, but miles of traffic and suburban nothingness make visiting a nuisance.

Sisteron

Sisteron's stunner is its **citadel** (€6; ⌚9am-7pm Apr-Nov, shorter hours spring & autumn), an imposing 3rd- to 16th-century fortress perched above a transverse valley. The town is a principal travel axis, but it's dead at nighttime. The **tourist office** (☎04 92 61 12 03; www.sisteron.fr; Hôtel de Ville; ⌚9am-7pm Mon-Sat, 10am-5pm Sun Jul-Aug, 9am-noon & 2-6pm Sep-Jun) has details on open-air classical music

MARKET DAYS

Markets generally run 8am to noon.

» **Monday** Forcalquier

» **Tuesday** Breil-sur-Roya, Colmars-les-Alpes

» **Wednesday** Barcelonnette, Castellane, Digne-les-Bains, La Foux d'Allos, La Palud-sur-Verdon, Riez, Sisteron, St-André-les-Alpes, Tende

» **Thursday** Allemagne-en-Provence, Allos, Les Salles-sur-Verdon, Montagnac, Sospel

» **Friday** Colmars-les-Alpes, Entrevaux, Moustiers Ste-Marie, Quinson, Seyne-les-Alpes

» **Saturday** Barcelonnette, Castellane, Digne-les-Bains, Riez, Sisteron, St-André-les-Alpes

» **Sunday** Bauduen (summer), Castellane, La-Palud-sur-Verdon (summer)

» **Daily** St-Martin-Vésubie

concerts of **Festival des Nuits de la Citadelle**, held in mid-July to mid-August.

Musée Terre et Temps (Museum of Earth and Time; ☎04 92 61 61 30; www.resgeol04.org; 6 place Général de Gaulle; ⊙9am-noon & 2-6pm Tue-Sat, closed winter; ♿), occupies a former 17th-century chapel in the town's centre and explores human and geological time. Displays include a Foucault's pendulum, sundials and a water clock. From the museum, drivers can follow the rte du Temps (Time Rd; see also p254).

Roadhouse restaurant-hotel **La Magnanerie** (☎04 92 62 60 11; www.la-magnanerie.net; N85, Aubignosc; lunch menus €19, dinner menus €23-29, r €67-91; ⊙lunch Tue-Sun, dinner Wed-Sat; @📶), 10km south of Sisteron, is good for a white-tablecloth dinner and an overnight on the road between Haute-Provence and points south. Refined cooking; contemporary rooms. Reservations essential.

Les Mées

As you whiz past Les Mées on the autoroute, 22km south of Sisteron, you can't miss the otherworldly Rochers des Mées, rows of 100m-high rocky pinnacles. Legend claims they were once monks, turned to stone for lusting after Saracen women. A walk on the loop trail over them takes 3½ hours.

Ganagobie & Around

Prieuré de Ganagobie (☎04 92 68 00 04; Ganagobie; ⊙3-5pm Tue-Sun), a still-working 10th-century Benedictine monastery 10km south of Les Mées, is isolated, 3km up a winding one-lane road. Stroll among quiet hilltop woods and soak in the ethereal calm surrounding the monastery. The chapel is the only enclosed section open to visitors; its 12th-century floor mosaic (depicting dragons) is the largest of its kind in France. The monk-tended shop stocks soaps, honeys and music made by the monks and houses artefacts found on-site.

Mas Saint-Joseph (☎04 92 62 47 54; www.lemassaintjoseph.com; Châteauneuf-Val-St-Donat; s/d/tr/q €58/64/83/102; ⊙Apr-Oct; 🏊), a converted farmhouse in pastoral country, sits alone atop a wooded hillside (with lots of stairs). Wood beams and stone walls make the whitewashed rooms feel extra special. Hot tub and shared kitchen. The *table d'hôte* (set menu at fixed price; €22) includes wine. It's 10km northwest of Peyruis.

GORGES DU VERDON

Nicknamed the 'Grand Canyon of Europe', the plunging Gorges du Verdon slices a 25km swathe through Haute-Provence's limestone plateau – foothills of the Alps. Under the protection of the Parc Naturel Régional du Verdon since 1997, the gorges create habitat for incredible birds, including the canyon's very own colony of reintroduced griffon vultures.

The spectacular main gorge begins at Rougon, near the confluence of the Verdon and Jabron Rivers; the emerald-green waters wind westward toward Lac de Ste-Croix. The narrow canyon bottom is just 8m to 90m wide. Its walls rise a dizzying 250m to 700m – at their highest, over twice the height of the Eiffel Tower (321m). Overhanging rims widen from 200m to 1500m. See the gorges from above *and* below.

Two jumping-off points are Moustiers Ste-Marie, in the west, and Castellane, in the east. The canyon floors are only accessible by foot or raft. Motorists, equestrians and cyclists can take in staggering panoramas from two vertigo-inducing cliffside roads.

Activities

Cycling & Driving

A complete circuit of the Gorges du Verdon from Moustiers Ste-Marie involves

140km of relentless hairpin turns. Tourist offices provide itineraries. The only village en route is La Palud-sur-Verdon (930m). Expect slow traffic in summer and icy or snowy roads in winter. The rte des Crêtes closes 15 November to 15 March. Watch for falling rocks year-round, and take it easy – opportunities to pass are rare.

Walking & Hiking

Dozens of blazed trails traverse untamed countryside around Castellane and Moustiers. Tourist offices carry the excellent, English-language *Canyon du Verdon* (€4.70), detailing 28 walks, as well as maps of five principal walks (€2.40). You can hike most of the canyon along often-difficult GR4, definitively covered by two IGN maps: No 3442 (Moustiers to Rougon) and No 3542 OT (Rougon to Castellane) – each €10.50. The full route takes two days, but shorter canyon descents are possible.

Bring a torch (flashlight) and drinking water. Camping on gravel beaches is illegal. Don't cross the river, except at bridges, and stay on marked trails, lest you get trapped when the upstream dam opens, which happens twice weekly. Check with tourist offices before embarking.

Outdoor Sports

Castellane is the main water-sports base (April to September, by reservation); its tourist office has detailed lists. At the gorges' eastern end, Lac de Chaudanne has steep-sided banks, but **Lac de Castillon** has gently sloping beaches and waters ideal for swimming and paddle-boating. **St-André-les-Alpes**, on the banks of Lac de Castillon, is France's leading paragliding centre.

Des Guides pour l'Aventure OUTDOOR SPORTS
(06 85 94 46 61; www.guidesaventure.com; Moustiers Ste-Marie; year-round) Expeditions including canyoning (€45/70 per half-/full day), rock-climbing and rafting (€55/75), and 'floating' (€45/90) – river-running with a buoyancy bag strapped to your back.

Aboard Rafting WATER SPORTS
(/fax 04 92 83 76 11; www.rafting-verdon.com) White-water rafting and canyoning trips.

Latitude Challenge BUNGEE JUMPING
(04 91 09 04 10; www.latitude-challenge.fr; jumps €105) Bungee jumps from Europe's highest bungee site, the 182m Pont de l'Artuby (Artuby Bridge). Also skydiving.

COFFEE IN RIEZ

If approaching Gorges du Verdon from the west, you'll pass tiny Riez – a village of red-tile roofs and a good stopover for baguettes and coffee, especially on market days, Wednesday and Saturday.

Aérogliss PARAGLIDING
(04 92 89 11 30; www.aerogliss.com; chemin des Iscles, St-André-les-Alpes; intro flights from €70) Teaches paragliding.

Information

The river rises suddenly when hydroelectric dams upstream are opened, making it impossible to cross. Stay on marked trails! Check water levels and weather before embarking. Roads close due to rock falls and/or snow; watch for falling rocks year-round. Buy petrol whenever you see it.

Castellane Tourist Office (04 92 83 61 14; www.castellane.org; 9am-12.30pm & 2-6.45pm Mon-Sat Mar-Oct, plus 10am-12.30pm Sun Jul & Aug, 9am-noon & 2-5pm Mon-Fri Nov-Feb) Best source for info on river trips and the eastern side of Gorges du Verdon.

Moustiers Ste-Marie Tourist Office (04 92 74 67 84; www.moustiers.fr; daily;) Excellent service, best overall information source and free wi-fi. Hours vary.

Getting Around

Public transport is limited. There's one daily LER bus (p244) between Moustiers, Castellane and Marseille. Daily in July and August, and weekends April to September, Navettes des Gorges **shuttle buses** (€7; www.lapaludsurverdon.com) link Castellane with Point Sublime, La Palud and La Maline (but not Moustiers), returning hikers toward their vehicles. Tourist offices have schedules and detailed information.

Aqua Viva Est (04 92 83 75 74; 12 bd de la République; per half-day €25) Rents bikes in Castellane.

Le Petit Ségriès (04 92 74 68 83; ww.gite-segries.fr; per half-day €13; 9am-7pm) Call ahead for mountain-bike rentals near Moustiers; also guides rides.

Lacs de Ste-Croix & de Quinson

The largest of the lakes in Parc National Régional du Verdon, **Lac de Ste-Croix** (southwest of Moustiers Ste-Marie) is a reservoir, formed 1974, with scads of watercraft –

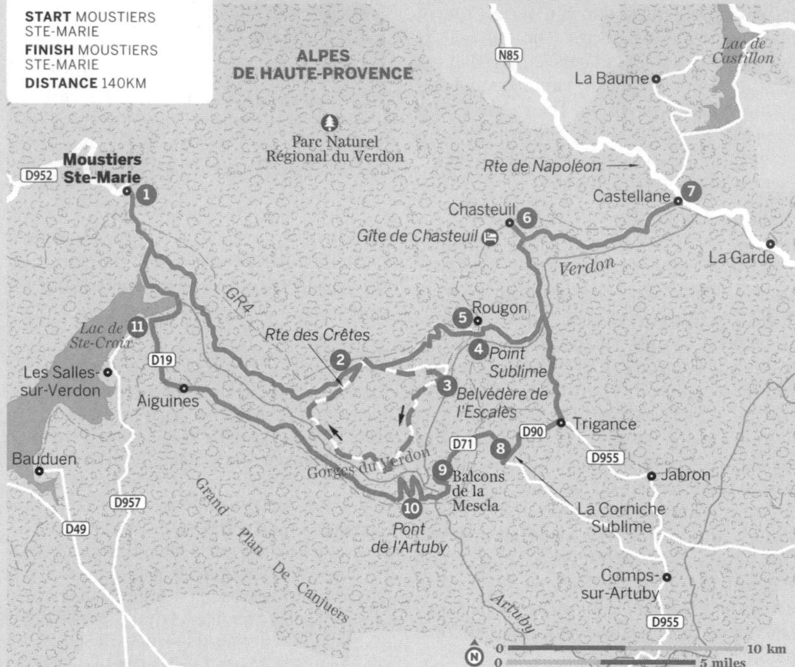

Driving Tour
Gorge Explorer

If you're here in summer, be sure to get an early start. The narrow, winding roads through the gorge slow to a crawl during high-season afternoons, especially on weekends.

Set out from 1 **Moustiers Ste-Marie**, via the Route de Castellane (D52). Aim for the 2 **Route des Crêtes**, a 23km-long loop with 14 lookouts along the northern rim with drop-dead vistas of the plunging river gorge. (Note that there are two turnoffs for the Route des Crêtes. To make the entire loop, take the second turnoff, after the tiny hamlet of La Palud-sur-Verdon. If you're tight on time, or if traffic is terrible, take the first turnoff, see a few overlooks, then turn back towards Moustiers. But pay close attention, as the road soon becomes one-way in the wrong direction.) En route, the most thrilling view is from 3 **Belvédère de l'Escalès** – one of the best places to spot vultures overhead.

After rejoining the D952, the road corkscrews eastward, past 4 **Point Sublime**, which offers a wide view of serrated rock formations falling away to the river. At Point Sublime, from D952, narrow D317 scales 3km northward to the mountain hamlet 5 **Rougon**. Without stops or traffic, that's about two hours' driving. You could rest in Chasteuil, at cosy 6 **Gîte de Chasteuil**, or forge onward. If considering a river expedition – or if you're just passing through, headed to the Côte d'Azur – aim for 7 **Castellane**. Otherwise, return towards Moustiers Ste-Marie (in two hours) along a different, heart-palpitating route, 8 **La Corniche Sublime** (D955 to D90, D71 and D19). It twists along the southern rim, taking in spectacular landmarks including the 9 **Balcons de la Mescla** (Mescla Terraces) and 10 **Pont de l'Artuby** (Artuby Bridge), Europe's highest bridge. On the return to Moustiers Ste-Marie, you'll pass the emerald-green waters of the 11 **Lac de Ste-Croix**.

windsurfers, canoes, kayaks – to rent. Pretty Bauduen sits on its southeastern banks.

Lac de Quinson lies at the southernmost foot of the lower Gorges du Verdon. In Quinson, taxidermy-rich **Musée de la Préhistoire des Gorges du Verdon** (☎04 92 74 09 59; www.museeprehistoire.com; rte de Montmeyan; adult/student/family €7/5/20; ⏱10am-8pm Jul-Aug, 10am-6pm Wed-Mon low season, closed mid-Dec–end Jan; 👪) explores the gorges' natural history and archaeological treasures. From March to October, it organises monthly expeditions to Grotte de la Baume Bonne, a prehistoric cave.

Nearby, **Allemagne-en-Provence** is named for the Roman goddess of fertility Alemona. Her likeness appears on the village's focal point, the turret-topped 12th- to 16th-century **Château d'Allemagne** (☎04 92 77 46 78; www.chateau-allemagne-en-provence.com; guided tours adult/child €7/free; ⏱tours 4pm & 5pm Tue-Sun Jul–mid-Sep, Sat & Sun only Easter-Jun & mid-Sep–Oct) – straight from a fairy tale.

Moustiers Ste-Marie & Around

POP 710 / ELEV 634M

Dubbed 'Étoile de Provence' (Star of Provence), jewel-box Moustiers Ste-Marie crowns towering limestone cliffs, which mark the beginning of the Alps and the end of Haute-Provence's rolling prairies. A 227m-long chain, bearing a shining gold star, is stretched high above the village – a tradition, legend has it, by the Knight of Blacas, who was grateful to have returned safely from the Crusades. Twice a century, the weathered chain snaps, and the star gets replaced, as happened in 1996. In summer, it's clear that Moustiers' charms are no secret.

Sights & Activities

FREE Chapelle Notre Dame de Beauvoir CHURCH

(guided tours adult/child €3/free; ⏱24hr) Lording it over the village, beneath Moustiers' star, this 14th-century church clings to a cliff ledge like an eagle's nest. A steep trail climbs beside a waterfall to the chapel, passing 14 stations of the cross en route. On 8 September, Mass at 5am celebrates the nativity of the Virgin Mary, followed by flutes, drums and breakfast on the square.

Musée de la Faïence POTTERY MUSEUM

(☎04 92 74 61 64; rue Seigneur de la Clue; adult/child €3/free, admission free Tue Jul & Aug; ⏱10am-12.30pm & 2pm-7pm daily Jul & Aug, shorter hr rest of year, closed Jan) When silver was reclaimed by Louis XIV and melted for war, Moustiers' decorative *faïence* (glazed earthenware) graced the dinner tables of Europe's palaces. Today, each Moustiers' 15 ateliers has its own style – from representational to abstract. Antique masterpieces are housed in this little museum, adjacent to the town hall. Village galleries sell new pieces; working ateliers are down the hill – ask the tourist office to direct you to the *meilleurs ouvriers* (French government-listed master craftspeople).

Sleeping & Eating

MOUSTIERS STE-MARIE

La Ferme Rose HOTEL €€

(☎04 92 75 75 75; www.lafermerose.com; chemin de Quinson; d €80-150; ❄📶) An inviting converted farmhouse, now a three-star hotel. Contains quirky collectibles – a Wurlitzer jukebox, display case of coffee grinders – but its dozen room are uncluttered, colourful and airy. Great bathrooms.

Clos des Iris HOTEL €€

(☎04 92 74 63 46; www.closdesiris.fr; chemin de Quinson; r €75-128; ⏱closed Oct-Dec) Good-value nine-room hotel: cosy and sweet, surrounded by quiet gardens.

Clérissy CRÊPERIE €

(☎06 33 34 06 95, 04 92 74 62 67; www.clerissy.fr; place du Chevalier-de-Blacas; dishes €8-12, d/tr incl breakfast €48/58; ⏱daily Jul & Aug, closed Wed low season, closed Nov-Mar) Locals gather on the terrace for pizza, salads, crêpes and pastas. Upstairs are four simple, great-value rooms (reserve ahead). Cash only.

TOP CHOICE La Bastide de Moustiers GASTRONOMIC €€€

(☎04 92 70 47 47; www.bastide-moustiers.com; menus €55-75, d from €240; ❄🏊) This splurge-worthy Provençal nest, domain of legendary chef Alain Ducasse, is famous for fine cuisine – hence the helicopter pad in the garden – and provides a chance to dress for dinner. Rooms are sophisticated and smart, and breakfast is served on a garden-view terrace, in view of scampering baby deer.

TOP CHOICE La Ferme Ste-Cécile GASTRONOMIC €€

(☎04 92 74 64 18; D952; menus €28-38; ⏱lunch Tue-Sat, dinner Tue-Sun, closed Nov–mid-Mar) The delicious culinary surprises, served on the terrace of this authentic *ferme auberge*, may include the thinnest slice of Roquefort and pear warmed in filo pastry, or *foie gras* (fattened goose liver) wrapped in sweet quince. This is a meal for connoisseurs: the fussy chef demands you linger.

La Treille Muscate PROVENÇAL €€
(☎04 92 74 64 31; www.la-treille-muscate.com; place de l'Église; lunch/dinner menus from €20/29; ⊙lunch Fri-Tue, dinner Fri-Wed) This mid-village terrace restaurant has exceptionally good Provençal cooking. Pricy, yes, but wow, the view. Quality assured.

AROUND MOUSTIERS STE-MARIE

TOP CHOICE **Le Petit Ségriès** FARMSTAY €
(☎04 92 74 68 83; www.gite-segries.fr; r incl breakfast €69-79;) Friendly hosts Sylvie and Noël offer five colourful, airy rooms in their rambling farmhouse. Family-style *tables d'hôte* (€21 with wine) – fresh lamb, rabbit, mountain honey – are served at a massive chestnut table. Guided mountain-bike tours (from €65) are also available.

Le Petit Lac CAMPGROUND €
(☎04 92 74 67 11; www.lepetitlac.com; rte du Lac de Ste-Croix; tent per 2 people €15-23, cabins from €47; ⊙camping mid-Jun–Sep, cabins Apr–mid-Oct; @) This activity-oriented lakeside campground also has cute, woodsy eco-cabins (two-night minimum).

Castellane & Around

POP 1539 / ELEV 723M

The cobbled streets of utilitarian **Castellane** are dead off-season but teem in summer, when tourist facilities and water-sports shops reopen. It's along the **Route de Napoléon**, the pre-autoroute highway between Haute-Provence and the Côte d'Azur and a scenic byway between beach and mountains. Castellane's geology is complex and merits investigation if you're the slightest bit geeky.

Chapelle Notre Dame du Roc is perched spectacularly above town on a 184m-high rocky butte, jutting from yawning canyons like a giant tooth. On 15 August (Assumption Day) pilgrims ascend by torchlight for Mass.

Sights

Musée Sirènes et Fossiles PALEONTOLOGY MUSEUM
(☎04 92 83 19 23; www.resgeol04.org; place Marcel Sauvaire; adult/child €4/3; ⊙10am-1pm & 3pm-6.30pm daily Apr, Jul & Aug, Wed, Sat & Sun only May, Jun & Sep, closed Oct-Mar;) Mermaids and fossils feature at this worthwhile paleontology museum; admission includes access to nearby 90-minute, 2km family-friendly walk **Sentier des Siréniens** (Col des Lèques, 6.5km northwest of Castellanne), passing beside 40-million-year-old fossilised rock.

Musée de la Résistance MUSEUM
(☎04 92 83 78 25; rte de Digne; adult/child €4/2; ⊙Apr-Oct by appt) This captivating museum, 1.5km along the road to Digne, is dedicated to heroes of the Resistance. The tourism office will *not* help you find it. Call ahead.

Sleeping & Eating

CASTELLANE

Gîte de Chasteuil B&B €
(☎04 92 83 72 45; www.gitedechasteuil.com; Hameau de Chasteuil; r incl breakfast €58-91; ⊙Mar-Nov) This irresistible *chambre d'hôte* 12km west of Castellane is in a former schoolhouse with gorgeous mountains views – ideal for hikers along GR4, which passes outside. Excellent *table d'hôte* (€20 to €24); reservations are essential.

Nouvel Hôtel Restaurant du Commerce HOTEL €€
(☎04 92 83 61 00; www.hotel-du-commerce-verdon.com; r €75-100; menus €22-28; ⊙Apr-Oct) Castellane's only three-star hotel also has a quality regional Provençal restaurant.

Mas du Verdon B&B €
(☎04 92 83 73 20; www.masduverdon.com; quartier d'Angles; r incl breakfast €55-72; tables d'hôte €22; ⊙Apr-Oct) Hidden 1km south of town on the Verdon's banks, Mas du Verdon is a stone-walled 18th-century farmhouse with five inviting rooms and kindly service. *Tables d'hôte* by reservation May to September.

Auberge du Teillon PROVENÇAL, GASTRONOMIC €€
(☎04 92 83 60 88; www.auberge-teillon.com; D4805, direction Grasse, La Garde; menus €26-38, d €60; ⊙lunch Tue-Sun, dinner Tue-Sat, no lunch Tue Jul & Aug; closed Nov-Mar) Roadside auberge 5km east of Castellane serving the best food this side of Moustiers. Provincial-French classics include housemade pâtés, tender-roasted pigeon and an unusual *tarte tatin au foie gras*. Reservations essential. It also rents simple rooms.

AROUND CASTELLANE

Domaine d'Aiguines TRADITIONAL FRENCH €€
(☎04 92 34 25 72; www.auberge-domaine-aiguines.fr; D119, St-Jacques; menus €22-26;) Peacocks

greet you at this off-the-beaten-path family-operated duck farm and restaurant tucked into a rolling valley. Expect all things *canard*: homemade *foie gras*, confit, sautéed duck breast... Hours vary: call ahead. From Castellane, head 21km north towards Digne; turn right at Barrême, then left onto D119 to St-Jacques. Domaine is also accessible from St-André-les-Alpes: take N202 west 13km, then turn north onto Les Ferrages just before Barrême.

Maison du Saucisson MARKET €
(House of Sausages; ☎04 92 89 03 16; place de Verdun, Saint-André-les-Alpes; ⊙Mon-Sat, plus Sun morning Jul & Aug; Tue-Sat Sep-Jun) Pack a picnic in Saint-André-les-Alpes at Maison du Saucisson, whose 30 varieties of house-made sausage include donkey, ostrich and boar. Also has good pâtés and cheeses.

RÉSERVE GÉOLOGIQUE DE HAUTE-PROVENCE

Footprints of prehistoric birds, outsize ammonites and ram's-horn spiral shells are among the amazing fossils in the 1900-sq-km Réserve Géologique de Haute-Provence. You'll need a detailed regional map (sold at tourist offices) and your own transport to reach the 18 sites, most of which lie around Barles (north) and Barrême (south). An impressive limestone slab with some 500 ammonites sits 3km north of Digne on the road to Barles. The reserve also has museums in Sisteron and Castellane.

Digne-les-Bains

POP 17,680 / ELEV 608M

Despite several worthwhile sights, Digne-les-Bains is dreary – it's where you go to find bureaucrats, hiking information and bus schedules. Its namesake hot springs have become an institutional medical spa.

What's beautiful about Digne lies outside it. This is the foot of the Alps, home to Europe's most diverse population of butterflies, and lavender carpets the mountainsides. **Rando Lavande** (☎04 92 32 27 44; http://randolavande.chez.com; 7 rue de Provence; from €20) organises customised summertime lavender walks and wintertime snowshoeing. The city celebrates August's harvest with the five-day **Corso de la Lavande**.

DON'T MISS

MAISON DE LA GÉOLOGIE

Find time to visit the fascinating Maison de la Géologie in St-Bénoît, 2km north of Digne-les-Bains. Trails lead to **Musée Promenade** (☎04 92 36 70 70; www.resgeol04.org; 10 montée Bernard Dellacasagrande; adult/7-14yr €5/3; ⊙museum 9am-1pm & 2-7pm daily Apr-Oct, closed weekends Nov-Mar, park 24 hr) containing aquariums, insect displays, fossils and plants, placed in evolutionary context, revealing the region's incredible geological significance. Outside, the **Jardin des Papillons** (butterfly garden) attracts more than half of France's butterfly species. The museum is off the road to Barles.

Sights & Activities

FREE **Fondation Alexandra David-Néel** MUSEUM
(☎04 92 31 32 38; www.alexandra-david-neel.org; 27 av Maréchal Juin; ⊙2hr tours 10am, 2pm & 3.30pm) Paris-born writer and philosopher Alexandra David-Néel – among France's great historical figures – was the first woman to enter (in cognito) Tibet's temples. Later she settled in Digne. This museum pays brilliant hommage to both the woman and Tibet. **Journées Tibetaines** (Tibetan Days) happen in August or September.

Musée Gassendi MUSEUM
(☎04 92 31 45 29; www.musee-gassendi.org; place des Récollets; adult/student €4/free; ⊙11am-7pm Apr-Sep, 1.30-5.30pm Oct-Mar, closed Tue) This museum displays compelling contemporary art by Andy Goldsworthy, natural-history exhibits, and works by 16th-century philosopher-scientist Pierre Gassendi.

Via Ferrata du Rocher de Neuf Heures HIKING
(ww.ot-dignelesbains.fr; ⊙6am-8pm high season, 8am-5pm low season) To conquer Digne's *via ferrata* course (p257), gather necessary equipment (€12) from the tourist office (p252), which also has camping info.

Sleeping & Eating

Hôtel Villa Gaïa HISTORIC HOTEL €€
(☎04 92 31 21 60; www.hotelvillagaia.fr; 24 route de Nice; s €55-104, d €72-110; ⊙Apr-Oct) Digne's

HIKING TO SCULPTURES: REFUGE D'ART

In the mountains around Digne, British contemporary artist Andy Goldsworthy has created incredible outdoor sculptures along a 150km hiking circuit through awe-inspiring alpine landscapes. Called the **Refuge d'Art**, the loop passes giant rock hives and cairns that stand like sentinels, and several resurrected ancient stone structures – also artworks – that you can sleep inside (advance arrangements required).

Working with local municipalities and Digne's Musée Gassendi, Goldsworthy plans to keep developing the project as long as he's alive. **Étoile Rando** (www.etoile-rando.com; 6-day hikes €700) guides all-inclusive six-day hikes in English, spending nights in restored ruins and rural *auberges*. Digne's tourist office has information on day hikes to accessible sites, but consider making a longer journey of it.

best place to stay – by far – is an antiques-filled 19th-century villa, 2km west of town. It feels like the private mansion it once was, with Italianate gardens, tennis court, library and grand dining room. *Tables d'hôte* by reservation. Gate shuts at 11pm.

La Chauvinière MEDITERRANEAN €€
(☎04 92 31 40 03; 56 rue de l'Hubac; menus €18-32; ⊙lunch Tue-Sun, dinner Tue-Sat) Reliable old-town restaurant with leafy terrace.

La Taverna ITALIAN, FRENCH €€
(36 bd Gassendi; lunch menus €13-15, dinner menus €17-29) Good for quick lunches – pizzas, pastas, *plats du jour*, copious salads.

ℹ Information

Tourist Office (☎04 92 36 62 62; www.ot-dignelesbains.fr; place du Tampinet; ⊙9am-noon & 2-6pm daily, closed weekends in winter)

Hôpital Digne (☎04 92 30 15 15)

Relais Départemental des Gîtes de France (☎04 92 31 30 40; www.gites-de-france.com; place du Tampinet; ⊙9am-noon & 1-5pm Mon-Fri, 9am-noon Sat) Information on *gîtes* rentals throughout France; adjoins tourist office.

ℹ Getting There & Away

Bus station (☎04 92 31 50 00; place du Tampinet; ⊙9am-12.30pm & 3-6.30pm Mon-Sat) Behind the tourist office, the station is served by LER buses (p244). Helpful routes:

» Marseille (€19, two hours)

» Nice (€19, 2½ hours)

» Castellane (€7, one hour)

» Avignon (€19, 3¼ hours)

» Cavaillon (€16, 2¾ hours)

» Apt (€14, two hours)

» Aix-en-Provence (€15, 2¼)

Touristic Train des Pignes (p61) services Nice.

Vallée de la Blanche

Big Alpine vistas begin at Vallée de la Blanche, 50km north of Digne, straddling above Haute-Provence and Vallée de l'Ubaye. At 1350m, St-Jean-Montclar is famous for bottled spring water (here it flows from the tap) and has a tiny family ski area, but it's better to come in summer and hike. Cute-as-a-button **La Petite Bonnette** (☎06 89 42 36 91, 04 92 31 84 95; www.lapetitebonnette.com; col St-Jean, Montclar; r €60-65) has B&B rooms with knockout views. **Les Alisiers** (☎04 92 35 34 80; www.les-alisiers.fr; St-Jean-Montclar; lunch/dinner menus €15/24; ⊙Thu-Mon) serves alpine comfort food and rents studios.

PARC NATIONAL DU MERCANTOUR

The enormous Mercantour National Park rises north of the Côte d'Azur, east of Haute-Provence, and sprawls nearly 700 sq km (270 sq miles). Its rugged alpine terrain comprises six principal valleys, separated by high peaks.

Vallée de L'Ubaye

The national park's northern edge and least-visited area, spectacular, narrow Ubaye River Valley, runs east–west beneath snow-capped mountains, delimiting the High Alps from Haute-Provence.

The valley's only town, **Barcelonnette** (elevation 1135m), has an unexpected Mexican heritage and exceptional, very un-alpine architecture. From the 18th century until WWII, some 5000 Barcelonnettais emigrated to Mexico to seek their fortunes in silk- and wool-weaving industries; upon their return, they built mansions. One of the most spectacular is **Musée de la Vallée** (☎04 92 81 27 15; 10 av de la Libération; adult/child €3.30/free; ⏰10am-noon & 2.30-7pm daily mid-Jul & Aug, 2.30am-6pm Wed-Sat rest of year, closed mid-Nov–mid-Dec). Cafes surround place Manuel.

Brilliant for outdoor sports, Vallée de l'Ubaye is linked to the outside world via seven mountain passes, destination of hard-core cyclists. In summer, **Le Martinet**, 15km west of Barcelonnette, is a base for mountain-biking and rafting trips; consider outfitter **River** (☎04 92 85 53 99; www.river.fr). Contact the **Bureau des Guides de l'Ubaye** (☎06 86 67 38 73; www.guides-montagne-ubaye.com; rue Manuel, Barcelonnette) to find independent rafting, walking, biking and canyoning guides.

Rising 8.5km southwest of Barcelonnette, ski resort **Pra Loup** (☎04 92 84 10 04; www.praloup.com) has two base areas: **Pra Loup 1500** (sometimes called Les Molanes) and **Pra Loup 1600** (with more infrastructure and nightlife), connected via lifts (when there's snow) with Haut-Verdon ski resort Foux d'Allos. Together they form the Southern Alps' biggest and best snowsports destination. In summer there's brilliant lift-served mountain-biking and hiking.

TOP CHOICE **Les Méans** (☎04 92 81 03 91; www.les-means.com; D900, Méolans-Revel; r/apt incl breakfast from €65/98; 📶), a 15th-century farm, hides a tunnel where knights once escaped into the mountains. Now it's an incredible B&B – heaven for hikers – surrounded by mountains rising 1000m, echoing the cascading river. Outside there's a wood-fired hot tub. Gregarious owners Babette and Frédéric know every hiking and ski trail.

The **Barcelonnette Tourist Office** (☎04 92 81 04 71; www.barcelonnette.net; place Frédéric Mistral; ⏰9am-12.30pm & 1.30am-7.30pm Jul & Aug, 9am-noon & 2-6pm Mon-Sat Sep-Jun) and **Parc National du Mercantour, Barcelonnette Visitors Centre** (☎04 92 81 21 31; www.mercantour.eu; D900; ⏰9am-noon & 2-6pm Jul & Aug only) can help with information.

A car is the easiest way to get around. **Autocars SCAL** (☎04 92 51 06 05; www.scal-amv-voyages.com) operates daily service between Marseille (€25, 4 hours), Digne (€8, 90 minutes), and Barcelonnette. **Autocars Sarlin** (☎04 92 85 50 85; www.autocar-sarlin) buses operate within the valley. Barcelonnette's bus station is at place Aimé Gassier.

Vallée du Haut Verdon

Dizzying Col d'Allos (2250m and snow-blocked in winter) links craggy, narrow Vallée de l'Ubaye with the undulating, wide Haut Verdon, whose south-facing rivercourse glitters beneath Mediterranean sunshine. The River Verdon's source is at La Tête de la Sestrière (2572m).

In wintertime, there's stellar skiing at **Foux d'Allos** (www.valdallos.com); its low-rise base village is cuter than Pra Loup, whose ugly towers lie just beyond the pass. The high-mountain hiking is spectacular. The National Forest Office maintains wilderness cabins, accessible on all inclusive guided hikes with **Retrouvance** (☎05 34 09 82 06; www.retrouvance.onf.fr; 6-day hikes €550) (they even carry your bags). Note: Pra Loup and Foux d'Allos are linked in winter by ski lifts, but the road connecting them is open in summer only.

Nearby tiny **Allos** has a water park (open June to September) with swimming, canoeing and slides. Downstream, the Vauban-fortified village **Colmars-les-Alpes** (elevation 1250m)

ALONG THE MOUNTAIN RAILWAY

Zipping between mountains and sea, the narrow-gauge railway Train des Pignes (p61) is one of Provence's most picturesque trips. Conceived in 1861 and inaugurated in 1911, the line was initially serviced by steam locomotive: the vintage *Train Vapeur* still puffs a few stops around **Puget-Théniers** on Sundays from spring to autumn. Normal-service cars resemble tramway coaches. The alpine views are breathtaking.

Rising to 1000m altitude, the 151km track passes through 50 tunnels, over 16 viaducts and 15 metal bridges along its cliff-hugging journey to Digne-les-Bains, stopping at nearly 50 villages en route. The entire trip from Nice to Digne-les-Bains takes 3¼ hours (€20 one-way). For a taste without overcommitting, consider a trip to **Entrevaux**, 1½ hours from Nice (€10 one way): wander the village, hike or picnic, and return a couple of hours later. Find updated schedules on the website of **Chemins de Fer de Provence** (☎04 97 03 80 80; www.trainprovence.com).

WORTH A TRIP

THOARD

An hour's drive along **la rte du Temps** (Time Rd) transports you through millions of years of geological history. From Sisteron, follow the marked itinerary along D3 to remote St-Geniez, up and over **Col de Font-Belle** (1708m), to the medieval fortified village of Thoard. Roadside interpretive panels explain what you're seeing.

Known regionally for its charcuterie meats, tiny **Thoard** sits atop a rocky promontory, dominated by a 12th-century clocktower. The 2km-long **Balade de Suy** is a signposted walk through village and environs, passing the **Petit Musée des Cuivres** (04 92 31 57 46; www.le-petit-musee-des-cuivres-de-thoard.org; adult/child €3/free; by appointment), a shrine to brass instruments, including a saxophone signed by eponymous Adolphe Sax.The stunningly situated lavender distillery, **Distillerie du Siron** (04 92 34 61 96, 06 25 12 67 17; www.distilleriesiron-lavande.fr; Thoard; admission free; tours by reservation 10am-noon & 2-5pm daily Jul & Aug, by appointment rest of year), up a tiny lane from the village centre, offers free guided summertime tours. Call ahead for lunch or dinner at detour-worthy **Auberge la Bannette** (04 92 34 68 88; www.aubergelabannette.com; Les Prés du Riou, Thoard; menus €22, s/d from €48/53), which serves heaping farm-raised feasts on a vine-shaded mountain-view terrace in summer, or beside a roaring fire winter; it also rents out country-simple, good-value rooms.

was the 14th-century frontier of Savoy; its maze of ancient streets lies beyond never-breached zigzagging ramparts of brilliant geometry. Get a bird's-eye view on the ramparts from the adjacent hilltop fort and little **museum** (place Joseph Girieud; adult/child €3/free; 10am-noon & 3-6.30pm Jul–mid-Sep).

It's worth the trek (and metered traffic) to reach Europe's largest alpine lake, **Lac d'Allos** (2226m; inaccessible from autumn to spring). From Allos, narrow, bumpy D226 climbs 12km to parking; then it's a 40-minute walk. Trail maps are available from the **Parc National du Mercantour hut** (06 32 90 80 24; www.mercantour.eu; Jul & Aug) at the car park. Have lunch (call ahead) or overnight (in dorms) at the rustic **Refuge du Lac d'Allos** (04 92 83 00 24; dm incl breakfast & dinner €40).

Sleeping & Eating

TOP CHOICE **La Ferme Girerd-Potin** TRADITIONAL FRENCH €€
(04 92 83 04 76; www.chambredhotes-valdallos.com; rte de la Foux; menu €29.50; r per person incl breakfast and dinner €42-55; by reservation Oct-Apr, Jul & Aug;) On a working 17th-century farm, high above the Verdon, this cosy *ferme-auberge* grows everything it serves for thrilling rustic-Alpine dinners, served fireside in a candlelit, wood-and-stone dining room. Everything – from vegetables to *foie gras*, bread to cheese – is homemade. Make reservations 24 hours in advance. Upstairs are B&B rooms, some with kitchenette and wood-burning fireplace. The farm is 5km north of Allos.

Attrapeur de Rêve B&B €€
(04 92 83 30 16; www.attrapeurdereves.com; Allos; s/d/q incl breakfast €70/80/100, house per week €450-600;) This romantic mid-village alpine-style B&B has knotty-pine interiors, vaulted ceilings, artworks and Moroccan rugs. It also rents a house.

Les Transhumances B&B, SELF-CONTAINED €
(04 92 83 44 39; www.lestranshumances.fr; Les Espiniers, Colmars-les-Alpes; s/d/tr/q €59/75/90/102, apt €425-600/week;) This quiet 18th-century farm, high above Colmars, has incredible mountain vistas, spotless rooms with wood accents and self-catering apartments. Gentle, kind owners. The guest-only *table d'hôte* (€23) includes wine.

Information

Val d'Allos Tourist Office (04 92 83 02 81; www.valdallos.com; 9am-noon & 2pm-6pm) Covers the entire Haut-Verdon.

Colmars-les-Alpes Tourist Office (04 92 83 41 92; www.colmars-les-alpes.fr; Ancienne Auberge Fleurie; 8am-12.30pm & 2-6.30pm Jul & Aug, 9am-12.15pm & 2-5.45pm Mon-Sat Sep-Jun)

Vallée du Haut-Var

So red is the rock you'd think you were in Arizona. The Gorges de Daluis and Gorges du Cians around Valberg are best explored in a clockwise loop to maximise views. Drive northbound on the D902/D2202, winding at the cliff's edge, dizzyingly high over **Gorges de Daluis**. (The southbound inland lane burrows through 17 viewless tunnels.) Aim for tiny Guillaumes (elevation 800m), a jumping-off point for forays into the red-rock gorges, then Péone, a village beneath rock spires, then Valberg. (Note that Vallée du Haut Var refers to the River Var, not the Var *département*, which lies farther west.)

En route to Guillaumes, vertiginous **Pont de la Mariée**, an 80m-high stone footbridge, crosses the gorge; **Top Jump** (☎04 93 73 50 29; http://topjump.free.fr; jumps €60; ⏲11am-7pm Tue-Sun summer) bungees off. **Pont de Berthéou**, 8km south of Guillaumes on the D2202, is the starting point for **Sentier du Point Sublime** (4km, 1½ hours), an invigorating walk through oak-and-pine forest, past wine-coloured rock formations, to panoramic 'Point Sublime'.

Valberg (elevation 1700m), 13km east of Guillaumes, is a purpose-built, family-oriented ski village lacking charm, but in summer it has good-value apartment rentals, shops, lift-served walking and mountain-biking, and a **luge** (1/3 rides €3.30/8.70). It also has a year-round **national park office**. Kids burn off energy at **Espace Valberg Aventure** (☎04 93 23 24 25; www.valberg.com; admission €10-14; ⏲Jul & Aug; 👪), monkeying around Tarzan-inspired obstacles. Restaurants serve overpriced *raclette* (cheese melted fireside, served over potatoes).

East of Valberg, the spectacular D28 twists eastward along ridge lines to cute **Beuil** (elevation 1450m) – which has several hotels and restaurants, including some that serve good wood-fired pizza. The D28 then cuts south through **Gorges du Cians**, at river level, towards Nice.

The entire 82km loop of both gorges takes 90-plus minutes; from Nice plan four hours round-trip (200km), plus stops. Alternatively, from Beuil continue eastward 24km, via D30, toward tiny **Roubion**, edge of Vallée de la Tinée.

Parc National du Mercantour, Valberg Information Centre (☎04 93 02 58 23; rue Jean Mineur; ⏲9am-noon & 2-6pm Thu-Tue) is Valberg's ranger-staffed year-round information office; there's also the **Valberg Tourist Office** (☎04 93 23 24 25, room reservations 04 93 23 24 32; www.valberg.com; place du Quartier; ⏲9am-noon & 2-6pm).

Vallée de la Tinée

Col de Restefond la Bonette (2802m) – Europe's highest mountain pass – links Vallée de l'Ubaye with plunging Vallée de la Tinée, a steep-sided V-shaped valley lined by towering peaks. In wintertime, when the snowy pass closes, the 149km-long valley can only be accessed via its southern leg from Nice.

At St-Sauveur-sur-Tinée (elevation 490m), the D2205 twists north along the river, near the ski town Isola 2000 – a small resort with ugly architecture, but the region's deepest, driest snow – then to lovely alpine St-Étienne de Tinée (population 1684). If it's crowded, smaller St-Dalmas-le-Selvage is a less-touristed stopover.

Endless hiking trails wind around Cime de la Bonette (2860m). **Ma Vieille École** (☎04 93 03 43 05; www.mavieilleecole.com; D61, Roya; dm €20, half-board per adult/child €39/30; ⏲May-Sep) makes a good rural base with proper table (no credit cards accepted). From D2205, look for the turnoff 5km south of St Etienne-la-Tinée or 9km north of Isola; Roya lies 6km west of D2205.

ROURE

Adjacent on maps to – but 20 hair-rising minutes up switchbacks from – St-Sauveur, tiny Roure (1100m) crowns a pinnacle with vertigo-inducing valley views. From the 1920s

HIGH-MOUNTAIN CYCLING OR DRIVING LOOP

From June to September, connect the following high-mountain passes to make a 150km roller coaster loop that rises and plunges along knife-edged ridge lines and has stupendous Alpine views. Check the weather first, and don't attempt it at night. By car without stopping it takes three hours. A few summertime-only cafes serve lunch, but you should carry water and snacks. Woe betide the carsick. Start in Colmars or Allos:

» D908 north over Col d'Allos (2247m); drop 1000m toward Barcelonnette.

» Ascend D902 south over Col de la Cayolle (2326m); descend D2202 to St Martin d'Entraunes (1009m).

» Ascend Col des Champs (2095m); descend into Colmars (1250m).

THE GREY WOLF

Sustained hunting over 1000 years led to the eventual disappearance of wolves (*Canis lupus*) from France in 1930. Then, in 1992, two 'funny-looking dogs' were spotted near Utelle. Since then, wolves have been making a comeback, loping across the Italian Alps. Unlike the beasts of fairy tales, these wolves are wary – they'll run away if they detect you. However, you're guaranteed a glimpse at the wild animal reserve Wolf Watch at **Alpha** (☎04 93 02 33 69; www.alpha-loup.com; Le Boréon; adult/child €12/10; ⏰10am-6pm; 👪), where you can trek along (easy) trails to spot wolves from viewing huts. In winter, Alpha rents cross-country skis and showshoes for exploring.

until 1961, villagers used a 1850m-long cable to transport items up the mountain; the cable still remains. **Chapelle St-Sebastien** has a sideways-facing clock tower and a sculpture of a figure teetering atop poles over the valley's abyss. Continue uphill to **Arboretum Marcel Kroenlein** (☎09 77 31 68 33; www.arboretum-roure.org; suggested donation adult/child €5/free; ⏰10am-6m; 👪) – pet project of Monaco's Prince Rainier – where 15 steep-sided hectares (1200 to 1500m elev) are planted with mountain flora, adorned with sculptures by Niçois artists.

TOP CHOICE **Auberge-Restaurant le Robur** (www.aubergelerobur.fr; Rour Village) puts gastronomy within reach of mid-budget travelers, and provides mesmerising vistas from its clifftop perch (arrive before sunset). Chef Christophe Billau dazzles with refined, highly stylised cooking, including playful surprises like *foie gras* macaroons. Reservations required. Upstairs are seven spotless rooms with drop-dead views, making this an ideal one-nighter from Nice, 90 minutes away. To arrive on time, budget 30 minutes from St-Sauveur-sur-Tinée.

Visit the **Mercantour National Park Office, St-Étienne-de-Tinée** (☎04 93 02 42 27; quartier de l'Ardon; ⏰Jul & Aug) for info.

Vallée de la Vésubie

The Mercantour's heart, the Vésubie was formerly the private hunting reserve of King Victor Emanuel II of Italy. This kept the land pristine and biologically diverse: the kernel from which the national park grew. Because of Nice's day-trip proximity, this is the park's most-visited sector (depart early). It's also the western gateway to the Merveilles. The following are in south–north order.

The **Gorges de la Vésubie** mark the valley's southern end. For a bird's-eye perspective, head for pilgrimage site **La Madone d'Utelle** (1181m), settled by 9th-century Spanish sailors; it's crowned with a chapel. From mountain village **St-Jean la Rivière** (on the D2565), a stone bridge crosses the River Var, where a steep, winding mountain pass (the D32) leads west to **Utelle** (population 489), 6km northeast of La Madone.

About 18km north of St-Jean, via the D2565, just past the turnoff for La Bollène-Vésubie, you can detour east along the snaking D171 to **Belvédère** (elevation 820m), a hilltop village with a cute dairy museum. In nearby **Roquebillière**, there's a thermal-spring spa for massages and soaks, **Thermes de Berthemont-les-Bains** (☎04 93 03 47 00; www.valvital.eu; from €45; ⏰Apr-Oct).

Principal town and outdoor-activity base **St-Martin-Vésubie** (population 1100, elevation 1000m), an hour from Nice, feels like the Swiss Alps, and there's life after dark. **Escapade Bureau des Guides** (☎04 93 03 31 32; www.guidescapade.com; place du Marché, St-Martin-Vésubie; ⏰Jul & Aug) organises walks, climbs, and canyoning excursions, and guides walks into Vallée des Merveilles (the essential map: IGN No 3741OT). For bird's-eye village views, ascend the D31 to Venanson (elevation 1164m), a rock-perched hamlet above St-Martin.

Gateway to Vallée de la Tinée, the tiny ski station **La Colmiane** rises 1795m, 7km west of St-Martin-Vésubie, with lift-served hiking and mountain biking and (nearby) paragliding; the **tourist office** (☎04 93 23 25 90; www.colmiane.com; ⏰9am-noon & 2pm-6pm) has information. Rent bikes from **Ferrata Sport** (☎04 93 02 80 56) or **Colmiane Sports** (☎04 93 02 87 00; www.colmianesports.com), which also rent equipment for the nearby **via ferrata** course.

Sleeping & Eating

TOP CHOICE **Moonlight Chalet** BOUTIQUE HOTEL €€
(☎06 89 25 36 74; www.moonlightchalet.com; 8 rue Rumplemeyer, Saint-Martin-Vésubie; r incl breakfast €100-130; 👪) Hidden behind the village beside a roaring creek, this splurge-worthy Shangri-la brings the outdoors inside, with

marvellously imaginative, nature-derived details you won't find elsewhere: a round cabin built around a living pine tree, a bathtub of river rocks, sinks carved from tree trunks... Outside there's a spring-fed swimming pond and riverside yoga patch. Three cabins (two with kitchenettes) and two rooms equal quiet. No TVs. Kids welcome.

Le Boréon HOTEL €
(☎04 93 03 20 35; www.hotel-boreon.com; d/tr/q from €68/99/126, half-board per person €64, menus from €23; ⏲closed Nov-Mar; 📶) Magical mountain views unfurl from this secluded Swiss chalet-style hotel 8km north of St-Martin-Vésubie. Ground-floor rooms are cosiest, with pine walls and shared terrace. The restaurant serves alpine specialties.

La Bonne Auberge HOTEL-RESTAURANT €€
(☎04 93 03 20 49; www.labonneauberge06.fr; 98 allée du Verdun; mains €12-19, menus €23-29; s/d/tr/q from €40/55/78/78; ⏲closed mid-Nov–Dec; 📶👪) This small hotel, family run since 1946, has 12 well-kept rooms with pine furnishings. The convivial, atmospheric restaurant serves traditional Provençal classics and live trout. Peek into the bar to see St-Martin's first TV set (circa 1960).

Le Vieux Four PIZZA €
(☎04 93 03 36 06; 3 rue Jacques Barraja; mains €9-14; ⏲hr vary) Wood-fired pizza and *socca* (chickpea crepes). It's tiny: reserve ahead.

Information

Maison du Parc National du Mercantour (Visitor Centre; ☎04 93 03 23 15; rue Serrurier, St-Martin-Vésubie; ⏲9am-noon & 2-6pm mid-June–mid-Sept)

St-Martin-Vésubie Tourist Office (☎04 93 03 21 28; www.saintmartinvesubie.fr; place Félix Faure; ⏲9am-7pm daily Jun-Sep, 9am-noon & 2pm-6pm Mon-Fri Oct-May; 📶)

Getting There & Away

Conseil Général des Alpes-Maritimes (www.cg06.fr) buses (€1) connect Nice with St-Martin-Vésubie (one hour) and La Colmiane (1¼ hours).

Vallée des Merveilles

The 'Valley of Wonders' contains one of the world's most stupendous collections of Bronze Age petroglyphs, dating from between 1800 and 1500 BC, believed to have originated with a Ligurian cult. Effectively an open-air gallery wedged between the Vésubie and Roya Valleys, it comprises over 36,000 prehistoric rock carvings of human figures, bulls and animals, spread 30 sq km around **Mont Bégo** (2870m).

The main access is via the westbound D91 from St-Dalmas-de-Tende, in Vallée de la Roya, to **Castérino**, where there's the summertime-only **national park office** (☎04 93 04 89 79). Alternatively, go via the dead-end D171, which leads north from Roquebillière, in Vallée de la Vésubie.

The engravings are usually snow-covered in winter, rendering snowshoeing useless; the best time is June to October. The entire loop takes two days of strenuous high mountain hiking. Access is mostly restricted so visit with an official guide: inquire at Mercantour National Park visitors centres or Escapade Bureau des Guides (p256).

Vallée de la Roya

Occupied by Italy during WWII, the Roya only became part of France in 1947. **Breil-sur-Roya** is the valley's water-sports base.

VIA FERRATA

During WWI Italian troops moved swiftly through the Dolomites – the natural frontier between Italy and Austria – using iron-rung ladders and steel cables bolted into the mountainside. Today, similar routes known as *via ferrata* (meaning 'iron way' in Italian) allow fit, adventurous tourists, with no specific rock-climbing experience, to scale the rock faces for thrilling Alpine vistas. You need only be in shape and able to walk narrow ledges without getting vertigo.

This region has a clutch of *via ferrata* courses (see www.viaferrata.org and **Les Guides Randoxygène** (http://asp.zone-secure.net/v2/index.jsp?id=105/99/12816) – rigged at dizzying heights – including at Digne-les-Bains, St-Martin-Vésubie and Tende. First-timers can tackle short sections. Equipment hire, guides and tickets are generally handled by local tourist offices.

Roya Évasion (☎04 93 04 91 46; www.royaevasion.com; 1 rue Pasteur) organises kayaking, canyoning and rafting on the River Roya, plus hiking and mountain biking.

The dramatic **Gorges de Saorge**, 9km north of Breil-sur-Roya, lead to fortified **Saorge** (elevation 520m). Perched on sheer cliffs, the village is a maze of tangled streets, with 15th- to 17th-century houses. Franciscan **Monastère de Saorge** (☎04 93 04 55 55; http://saorge.monuments-nationaux.fr/en; ⏲10am-noon & 2-5pm Wed-Mon) has a baroque church with frescoes of St Francis.

Immediately north, the **Gorges de Bergue** lead to **St-Dalmas-de-Tende**, main gateway into Vallée des Merveilles. From St-Dalmas-de-Tende, the D91 winds 10km west to **Lac des Mesches** (1390m), where trails lead into the valley (plan eight hours hiking, round-trip), and 5km further lies **Castérino**, with park information and more northerly trails.

Equally scenic, the eastbound D143 (from St-Dalmas-de-Tende) winds to La Brigue (elevation 770m) then, 4km farther, to **Notre Dame des Fontaines** (admission €2; ⏲10am-12.30pm & 2pm-5.30pm May-Oct) – dubbed Sistine Chapel of the Southern Alps – with brilliantly preserved wall-to-wall 15th-century frescoes, done by Piedmontese painters Jean Canavesio and Jean Baleison.

In **Tende** (population 1890, elevation 830m), which is an easy one-hour train ride from Nice, the free **Musée des Merveilles** (☎04 93 04 32 50; av du 16 Septembre 1947; ⏲10am-6.30pm May–mid-Oct, 10am-5pm mid-Oct–Apr, closed Tue Sep-Jun) explains (in French) the valley's archaeological and historical significance. It also conducts English-language rock-art tours to the Merveilles. Small, sweet **Maison du Miel** (☎04 93 04 76 22; place Lieutenant Kalck; ⏲Jun-Sep) explores regional honey. Find bread and artisanal products along rue de France and av du 16 Septembre 1947; **Fiori delle Alpi** (☎04 93 04 55 05; av du 16 Septembre 1947; ⏲7.30am-8pm) has good sausage and cheese. Tende's tourist office provides details on guided archaeological walks and 4WD trips to **Mont Bégo**, plus outdoor-sports outfitters.

Five kilometres north of Tende, the 1882 **Tunnel de Tende** provides a link to Italy.

Sleeping & Eating

Le Pra Reound B&B €

(☎04 93 04 65 67; chemin St-Jean, La Brigue; s/d €32/40; 📶) Simple, tidy rooms in a valley at La Brigue's eastern edge. Feels like a farm-stay, with orchards and big vistas. Friendly Madame Molinaro makes breakfast (€6), or you can use the self-catering kitchen.

Le Prieuré HOTEL €

(☎04 93 04 75 70; www.leprieure.org; rue Jean Medecin, St-Dalmas-de-Tende; s €56-65, d €64-75, menus €15-22) Rambling 24-room former priory. Request a room overlooking the river and fall asleep to cascading water. The year-round restaurant is among the valley's best.

La Miramonti PIZZERIA €

(☎04 93 04 61 82; www.lemiramonti-restaurant.fr; 5 rue Antoine Vassalo, Tende; menus from €17, d €46; ⏲lunch Tue-Sun, dinner Tue-Sat; 📶📋👪) Wood-fired pizzas and Piedmontese specialities, plus elbow room for kids. Also rents spartan rooms.

Information

Breil-sur-Roya (☎04 93 04 99 76; www.breil-sur-roya.fr; 17 place Biancheri; ⏲hrs vary)

Tende Tourism & Mercantour National Park Office (☎04 93 04 73 71; www.tendemerveilles.com; av du 16 Septembre 1947; ⏲9am-noon & 2-5pm Mon-Sat, 9am-noon Sun)

Getting There & Away

CAR The easiest way from Nice is via autoroute to Ventimiglia, Italy, then north back into France, toward Col de Tende (Italian signs read 'Colle di Tenda'). The tortuous mountain roads around Sospel (especially from the Vésubie) are ideal for motorcyclists but not the faint of heart.

TRAIN Trains (www.voyages-sncf.com) run several times per day along the Nice–Turin line, stopping in Sospel, Breil-sur-Roya, St-Dalmas-de-Tende and Tende.

Understand Provence & the Côte d'Azur

population per sq km

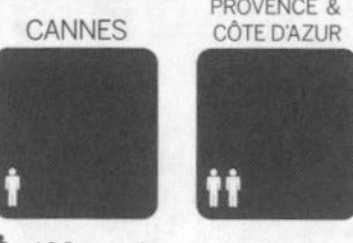

Provence & the Côte d'Azur Today

A Dynamic Region

Provence–Côte d'Azur has always been one of France's economic dynamos. Between 1962 and 1990, it was the country's fastest growing region and its population grew 75%. Although it has lost its leading spot to other regions over the last couple of decades, it still outperforms the national average for economic growth.

Provence–Côte d'Azur is defined in administrative terms as the Provence-Alpes-Côte d'Azur *région*, which is split in six *départements*: Vaucluse (Avignon), Bouches du Rhône (Marseille), Var (St-Tropez), Alpes Maritimes (Nice), Alpes de Haute Provence (Gorges du Verdon) and Hautes Alpes.

The global downturn has taken its toll – unemployment has risen since 2008 – but a number of large-scale projects means the region remains bullish about its prospects: a new highspeed railway line (slated for 2023) is expected to cut transport time between Paris and Nice from five hours and 40 minutes to just four hours; the EuroMéditerranée project in Marseille is breathing new life into the port and dockland area; and Nice has launched a massive regeneration project called Eco-Vallée de la Plaine du Var (west of the city), complete with transport hub, stadium, environmentally friendly housing and a technopole focused on sustainable development. The project, which should be completed by 2018, will generate thousands of jobs and has received state support.

The region also keeps attracting high-profile events: Marseille, Aix and Arles are European Capital of Culture in 2013; Nice will host the Jeux de la Francophonie in September 2013 (the equivalent of the Commonwealth Games) and the Riviera belle may also put another bid to host the 2022 Winter Olympics (it lost to Annecy for the French nomination for the 2018 games, which was eventually won by Pyeongchang in South Korea).

The Price of Fame

All is not rosé wine and never-ending sunshine however. Like most of the developed world, Provence–Côte d'Azur faces the challenge of catering

Top Apps

» **Escapado**, to plan hikes, cycle routes or scenic drives

» **Gallery PACA**, to trail the region's famous painters

» City apps such as **Cannes**, **Biot** and **Mougins**, come complete with walking tours, audio guides and maps

Top Surfs

En Provence (www.enprovence.fr) Inspiration from Provence

La Provence (www.laprovence.com) and **Nice Matin** (www.nicematin.com) Local news

Tourisme PACA (www.tourismepaca.fr) Excellent portal of the regional tourism board

Top Blogs

Best of Nice Blog (www.bestofniceblog.com) Posts on politics, festivals, favourite addresses and more

Provence Post (www.provencepost.com) Reviews and tips by US travel writer Julie Mautner

urban vs rural

(% of population)

if Provence were 100 people

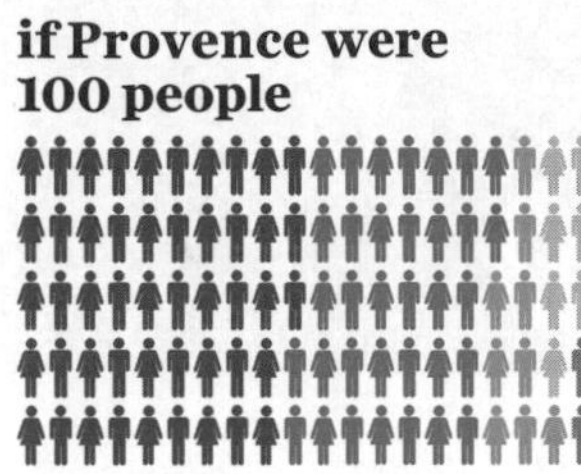

48 would work in Services
34 would work in Public Sector
9 would work in Industry
7 would work in Construction
2 would work in Agriculture

to its ageing population. As well as postwar baby boomers reaching their twilight years, the Riviera has traditionally attracted pensioners in search of a retirement in the sun. The over-60s are already as numerous as the under-19s, and forecasts estimate that their number will grow 57% by 2040, against just 1% for the under-60s. Beyond the issue of pensions, this also means adapting transport, services, housing and health care, all at great public expense.

Which leads to the area's other main challenge: purchasing power. Although Provence and the Côte d'Azur are often portrayed as playgrounds to the wealthy, the reality is rather different. Ordinary Provençaux earn slightly less than the national average, and they have to contend with some of the most expensive real estate in the country, especially in the coastal *départements* (the most populated) where wealthy outsiders (French and foreign alike) love to own holiday homes.

To the Right in Politics

Over the last 30 years or so, Provence and the Côte d'Azur have been a right-wing stronghold. It was here that the extreme-right Front National got its first victories in the 1990s; voters also strongly supported Jean-Marie Le Pen and then his daughter Marine Le Pen in the presidential elections of 2002 and 2012, respectively. In fact, it was in the *département* of Vaucluse that Le Pen got her best results in 2012: 27% of votes.

The political right didn't fare as well as they hoped they would in the June 2012 legislative elections, but two of the three far-right MPs were elected in Provence in Carpentras and Orange.

Restaurant Tips

» Save money by ordering *une carafe d'eau* (a jug of tap water, free).

» *'S'il vous plaît'* – never *garçon* (boy) – is the *only* way to summon a waiter.

» In summer, always book to guarantee a table outside.

Dos & Don'ts

» Take flowers, Champagne or good quality chocolates if invited to someone's house.

» Never discuss money over dinner.

» Don't support Paris-St Germain (PSG), OM's arch enemy.

Tasting Etiquette

» It's OK to spit wine at a tasting: a spittoon or sink is generally available.

» Although tastings are generally free and without obligation, it is polite to buy a bottle if you've tasted a few wines.

History

Prehistoric Man

Provence was inhabited from an exceptionally early age: primitive stone tools more than a million years old were found near Roquebrune-Cap-Martin. Neanderthal hunters occupied the Mediterranean coast from about 90,000 BC to 40,000 BC, living in caves such as Grottes de l'Observatoire in Monaco. Modern humans arrived with creative flair in 30,000 BC. The ornate wall paintings inside the decorated Grotte Cosquer, near Marseille, date from 20,000 BC, while the outstanding collection of 30,000 petroglyphs decorating Mont Bégo in the Vallée des Merveilles date back to 1800–1500 BC.

Archaeologists have found that the people living around Châteauneuf-les-Martigues, northwest of Marseille, about 6000 to 4500 years ago were among the first ever to domesticate wild sheep, allowing them to shift from a nomadic to a settled lifestyle.

Top Prehistoric Sights

» Grottes de l'Observatoire, Monaco

» Vallée des Merveilles

» Musée de la Préhistoire des Gorges du Verdon

» Réserve Géologique de Haute-Provence

Greeks to Romans

Massalia (Marseille) was colonised around 600 BC by Greeks from Phocaea in Asia Minor; from the 4th century BC they established more trading posts along the coast at Antipolis (Antibes), Olbia (Hyères), Athenopolis (St-Tropez), Nikaia (Nice), Monoïkos (Monaco) and Glanum (near St-Rémy-de-Provence). They brought olives and grapevines to the region.

While Hellenic civilisation was developing on the coast, the Celts penetrated northern Provence. They mingled with ancient Ligurians to create a Celto-Ligurian stronghold around Entremont; its influence extended as far south as Draguignan.

In 125 BC the Romans helped the Greeks defend Massalia against invading Celto-Ligurians. Their victory marked the start of the Gallo-Roman era and the creation of Provincia Gallia Transalpina, the first Roman *provincia* (province), from which the name Provence is derived.

TIMELINE

c 90,000 BC

Neanderthal hunters occupy the Mediterranean coast; starting around 30,000 BC Cro-Magnons start decorating their caves.

600 BC

The Greeks colonise Massalia (now Marseille) and establish trading posts along the coast, bringing olive trees and grapevines to the region.

125–126 BC

Romans create Provincia Gallia Transalpina, from which Provence gets its name, and Provence joins the Roman Empire.

The Gallo-Romans

Provincia Gallia Transalpina, later Provincia Narbonensis, embraced all of southern France from the Alps to the Mediterranean and the Pyrenees. In 122 BC the Romans destroyed the Ligurian capital of Entremont and established the Roman stronghold of Aquae Sextiae Salluviorum (Aix-en-Provence) at its foot.

The Roman influence on Provence was tremendous, though it was only after Julius Caesar's conquest of Gaul (58–51 BC) and its consequent integration into the Roman Empire that the region flourished. Massalia, which had retained its independence following the creation of Provincia, was incorporated by Caesar in 49 BC. In 14 BC the still-rebellious Ligurians were defeated by Augustus Caesar, who celebrated by building a monument at La Turbie in 6 BC. Arelate (Arles) became the chosen regional capital.

Under the emperor Augustus, vast amphitheatres were built at Arelate, Nemausus (Nîmes), Forum Julii (Fréjus) and Vasio Vocontiorum (Vaison-la-Romaine). Triumphal arches were raised at Arausio (Orange), Cabelio (Cavaillon), Carpentorate (Carpentras) and Glanum, and a series of aqueducts were constructed. The 275m-long Pont du Gard was part of a 50km-long system of canals built around 19 BC by Agrippa, Augustus' deputy, to bring water from Uzès to Nîmes.

Christianity – brought to the region, according to Provençal legend, by Mary Magdalene, Mary Jacob and Mary Salome, who sailed into Stes-Maries de la Mer in AD 40 – penetrated the region, was adopted by the Romans and continued to spread over the next few hundred years.

CÔTE D'AZUR

The French Riviera: A Cultural History by Julian Hale delves into the modern Côte d'Azur's vibrant past with panache and (Champagne) buckets of anecdotes.

Medieval Provènce

After the collapse of the Roman Empire in AD 476, Provence was invaded by various Germanic tribes. In the early 9th century the Saracens (an umbrella term adopted locally to describe Muslim invaders such as Turks, Moors and Arabs) emerged as a warrior force to be reckoned with. Attacks along the Maures coast, Niçois hinterland and more northern Alps persuaded villagers to take refuge in the hills. Many of Provence's perched, hilltop villages date from this chaotic period. In AD 974 the Saracen fortress at La Garde Freinet was defeated by William the Liberator (Guillaume Le Libérateur), count of Arles, who consequently extended his feudal control over the entire region, marking the return of peace and unity to Provence, which became a marquisate. In 1032 it joined the Holy Roman Empire.

The marquisate of Provence was later split in two: the north fell to the counts of Toulouse from 1125 and the Catalan counts of Barcelona gained control of the southern part (stretching from the Rhône to the River Durance and from the Alps to the sea). This became the county of

400–900

The Roman Empire collapses and Germanic tribes invade Provence; Franks (hence the name 'France') encourage villagers to move uphill to avert Saracen attacks.

974–1032

William the Liberator extends his feudal control over Provence, which becomes a marquisate and joins the Holy Roman Empire.

1309–76

Pope Clément V moves the Holy Seat to Avignon, and nine pontiffs head the Roman Catholic church from there until 1376; 'home' is the Palais des Papes.

1481

King of Naples, Good King René's nephew and successor, Charles III, dies heirless and Provence falls to Louis XI of France.

Provence (Comté de Provence). Raymond Bérenger V (1209–45) was the first Catalan count to reside permanently in Aix (the capital since 1186). In 1229 he conquered Nice and in 1232 he founded Barcelonnette. After Bérenger's death the county passed to the House of Anjou, under which it enjoyed great prosperity.

Ladder of Shadows: Reflecting on Medieval Vestiges in Provence & Languedoc by Gustaf Sobin is a beautiful lyrical narrative on Roman and early Christian relics in southern France.

The Popes

In 1274 Comtat Venaissin (Carpentras and its Vaucluse hinterland) was ceded to Pope Gregory X in Rome. In 1309 French-born Clément V (r 1305–14) moved the papal headquarters from feud-riven Rome to Avignon. A tour of the papal palace illustrates how resplendent a period this was for the city, which hosted nine pontiffs between 1309 and 1376.

The death of Pope Gregory XI led to the Great Schism (1378–1417), during which rival popes resided at Rome and Avignon and spent most of their energies denouncing and excommunicating each other. Even after the schism was settled and a pope established in Rome, Avignon and the Comtat Venaissin remained under papal rule until 1792.

The arts in Provence flourished under the popes. A university was established in Avignon as early as 1303, followed by a university in Aix a century later. In 1327 Italian poet Petrarch (1304–74) encountered his muse, Laura, in Fontaine-de-Vaucluse. During the reign of Good King René, king of Naples (1434–80), French became the courtly language.

French Provence

Top Religious Architecture

- Palais des Papes, Avignon
- Chartreuse du Val de Bénédiction, Villeneuve-lès-Avignon
- Abbaye Notre-Dame de Sénanque, Gordes
- Monastère de la Verne, Collobrières
- Abbaye de Thoronet, Lorgues

In 1481 René's successor, his nephew Charles III, died heirless and Provence was ceded to Louis XI of France. In 1486 the state of Aix ratified Provence's union with France and the centralist policies of the French kings saw the region's autonomy greatly reduced. Aix Parliament, a French administrative body, was created in 1501.

A period of instability ensued, as a visit to the synagogue in Carpentras testifies: Jews living in French Provence fled to ghettos in Carpentras, Pernes-les-Fontaines, L'Isle-sur-la-Sorgue, Cavaillon or Avignon. All were part of the pontifical enclave of Comtat Venaissin, where papal protection remained assured until 1570.

An early victim of the Reformation that swept Europe in the 1530s and the consequent Wars of Religion (1562–98) was the Luberon. In April 1545 the populations of 11 Waldensian (Vaudois) villages in the Luberon were massacred. Numerous clashes followed between the staunchly Catholic Comtat Venaissin and its Huguenot (Protestant) neighbours to the north around Orange.

In 1580 the plague immobilised the region.

The Edict of Nantes in 1598 (which recognised Protestant control of certain areas, including Lourmarin in the Luberon) brought an uneasy

1530s

The Reformation sweeps through France, prompting the core of Catholicism to be questioned.

1539

French (rather than Provençal) is made the official administrative language of Provence.

1545

People of 11 Luberon villages are massacred under the terms of the Arrêt de Mérindol, a bill condemning anyone of Waldensian faith to death.

1560

Nîmes native Jean Nicot (1530–1600) becomes the first to import tobacco into France from Portugal, hence the word 'nicotine'.

peace to the region – until its revocation by Louis XIV in 1685. Full-scale persecution of Protestants ensued.

The close of the century was marked by the French Revolution in 1789: as the National Guard from Marseille marched north to defend the Revolution, a merry tune composed in Strasbourg several months earlier for the war against Prussia – *Chant de Guerre de l'Armée du Rhin* (*War Song of the Rhine Army*) – sprang from their lips. France's stirring national anthem, *La Marseillaise,* was born.

From France to Italy, & Back

Provence was divided into three *départements* (administrative divisions) in 1790: Var, Bouches du Rhône and the Basse-Alpes. Two years later papal Avignon and Comtat Venaissin were annexed by France, making way for the creation of Vaucluse.

In 1793 the Armée du Midi marched into Nice and declared it French territory. France also captured Monaco, until now a recognised independent state ruled by the Grimaldi family. When Toulon was besieged by the English, it was thanks to the efforts of a dashing young Corsican general named Napoléon Bonaparte (Napoléon I) that France recaptured it.

The Reign of Terror that swept through France between September 1793 and July 1794 saw religious freedoms revoked, churches desecrated and cathedrals turned into 'Temples of Reason'. In the secrecy of their homes, people hand-crafted thumbnail-sized biblical figurines, hence the inglorious creation of the *santon* (traditional Provençal figurine).

In 1814 France lost the territories it had seized in 1793. The County of Nice was ceded to Victor Emmanuel I, King of Sardinia. It remained under Sardinian protectorship until 1860, when an agreement between Napoléon III and the House of Savoy helped drive the Austrians from northern Italy, prompting France to repossess Savoy and the area around Nice. In Monaco the Treaty of Paris restored the rights of the Grimaldi royal family; from 1817 until 1860 the principality also fell under the protection of the Sardinian king.

Meanwhile, the Allied restoration of the House of Bourbon to the French throne at the Congress of Vienna (1814–15), following Napoléon I's abdication and exile to Elba, was rudely interrupted by the return of the emperor. Following his escape from Elba in 1815, Napoléon landed at Golfe-Juan on 1 March with a 1200-strong army. He proceeded northwards, passing through Cannes, Grasse, Castellane, Digne-les-Bains and Sisteron en route to his triumphal return to Paris on 20 May. Napoléon's glorious 'Hundred Days' back in power ended with the Battle of Waterloo and his return to exile. He died in 1821.

PLAGUE

In 1720, Marseille was hit by a devastating outbreak of plague. The disease spread from a merchant ship after the city's chief magistrate, owner of the ship's cargo, ignored quarantine measures to ensure his goods made it to the local fair. Half the city's population died.

1562–98

The Wars of Religion see numerous bloody clashes between French Catholics and Protestants (Huguenots).

1598

Bourbon king Henry IV gives French Protestants freedom of conscience with the Edict of Nantes – to the horror of Catholic Paris and Roman Catholicism stronghold Avignon.

» Henry IV - Henry of Bourbon

1720

The Great Plague of Marseille eventually leads to the death of more than half the city's population, and the building of Le Mur de la Peste (Plague Wall).

THE SKY-BLUE COAST

The Côte d'Azur (literally 'Azure Coast') gained its name in 1887 from the first guidebook published on the region. *La Côte d'Azur* was the work of Stéphane Liégeard (1830–1925), a lawyer-cum-aspiring-poet from Burgundy who lived in Cannes. The guide covered the coast from Menton to Hyères and was an instant hit. Its title, a reflection of the coast's clear blue cloudless skies, became the hottest phrase in town and never disappeared. The Côte d'Azur is known as the French Riviera by most Anglophones.

The Belle Époque

The Second Empire (1852–70) brought to the region a revival in all things Provençal, a movement spearheaded by Maillane-born poet Frédéric Mistral. Rapid economic growth was another hallmark: Nice, which had become part of France in 1860, became Europe's fastest-growing city thanks to its booming tourism. The city was particularly popular with the English aristocracy, who followed their queen's example of wintering on the Riviera's shores. European royalty followed soon after. The train line reached Toulon in 1856, followed by Nice in 1864, the same year work started on a coastal road from Nice to Monaco.

In neighbouring Monaco the Grimaldi family gave up its claim over its former territories of Menton and Roquebrune in 1861 in exchange for France's recognition of its status as an independent principality. Four years later Casino de Monte Carlo opened and Monaco leapt from being Europe's poorest state to one of its richest.

The Third Republic ushered in the glittering belle époque, with art nouveau architecture, a whole field of artistic 'isms' including impressionism, and advances in science and engineering. Wealthy French, English, American and Russian tourists and tuberculosis sufferers (for whom the only cure was sunlight and sea air) discovered the coast. The intensity and clarity of the region's colours and light appealed to many painters.

The route that Napoléon followed from Golfe-Juan to Grenoble over the course of his 1815 comeback has become the legendary Route Napoléon. It follows mostly the tortuous and scenic N85 and is especially popular with bikers. For a full itinerary, check www.route-napoleon.com.

WWI & the Roaring Twenties

No blood was spilled on southern French soil during WWI. Soldiers were conscripted from the region however, and the human losses included two out of every 10 Frenchmen between 20 and 45 years of age. With its primarily tourist-based economy, the Côte d'Azur recovered more quickly from the postwar financial crisis than France's more industrial north.

The Côte d'Azur sparkled as an avant-garde centre in the 1920s and 1930s, with artists pushing into the new fields of cubism and surrealism, Le Corbusier rewriting the architectural textbook and foreign writers thronging to the liberal coast.

1789–94

Revolutionaries storm the Bastille, leading to the beheading of Louis XVI and Marie-Antoinette and the Reign of Terror, seeing religious freedoms revoked.

1790–92

Provence is divided into three *départements* (which still exist today); papal Avignon and Comtat Venaissin are annexed by France and Vaucluse is created.

1815

Exiled Napoléon Bonaparte escapes Elba and journeys in secret over the mountains near Digne-les-Bains and Gap to reclaim his title in Paris – it'll only last 100 days.

1848

In 1848 French revolutionaries adopt the red, white and blue tricolour of Martigues near Marseille as their own. France's national flag is born.

The coast's nightlife gained a reputation for being cutting edge, with everything from jazz clubs to striptease. Rail and road access to the south improved: the railway line between Digne-les-Bains and Nice was completed and in 1922, the luxurious *Train Bleu* (Blue Train) made its first run from Calais, via Paris, to the coast. The train only had 1st-class carriages and was quickly dubbed the 'train to paradise'.

The roaring twenties hailed the start of the summer season on the Côte d'Azur. Outdoor swimming pools were built, sandy beaches cleared of seaweed, and sunbathing sprang into fashion after a bronzed Coco Chanel appeared on the coast in 1923, draped over the arm of the Duke of Westminster. France lifted its ban on gambling, prompting the first casino to open on the coast in the Palais de la Méditerranée (today a hotel) on Nice's promenade des Anglais in 1927. With the advent of paid holidays for all French workers in 1936, even more tourists flocked to the region. Second- and 3rd-class seating were added to the *Train Bleu*.

Greatly affected by the plague of phylloxera in the 1880s, vineyards were replanted but struggled: France was overproducing and WWI soldiers preferred red wine to rosé for their rations. With the introduction of AOC labels in the 1930s luck finally turned for Provençal wines.

WWII

With the onset of war, the Côte d'Azur's glory days turned grey. On 3 September 1939 France and Britain declared war on Germany. But following the armistice treaty agreed with Hitler on 22 June 1940, southern France fell into the 'free' Vichy France zone, although Menton and the Vallée de La Roya were occupied by Italians. The Côte d'Azur – particularly Nice – immediately became a safe haven from war-torn occupied France; by 1942 some 43,000 Jews had descended on the coast to seek refuge. Monaco remained neutral for the duration of WWII.

On 11 November 1942 Nazi Germany invaded Vichy France. Provence was at war. At Toulon 73 ships, cruisers, destroyers and submarines – the major part of the French fleet – were scuttled by their crews to prevent the Germans seizing them. Almost immediately, Toulon was overcome by the Germans and Nice was occupied by the Italians. In January 1943 the Marseille quarter of Le Panier was razed, its 40,000 inhabitants be-

ENTER THE BIKINI

Almost called *atome* (French for atom) rather than bikini after its pinprick size, the scanty little two-piece bathing suit was the 1946 creation of Cannes fashion designer Jacques Heim and automotive engineer Louis Réard. Top-and-bottom swimsuits had existed for centuries, but it was the French duo who plumped for the name bikini – after Bikini, an atoll in the Marshall Islands chosen by the USA in 1946 as a testing ground for atomic bombs.

Once wrapped around the curvaceous rear of 1950s sex-bomb Brigitte Bardot on St-Tropez's Plage de Pampelonne, there was no looking back. The bikini was born.

1860

The County of Nice becomes part of French Provence. Meanwhile, European royalty winters in Nice, Europe's fastest-growing city.

1914–18

The human cost of WWI is enormous: of the eight million French men called to arms, 1.3 million are killed and almost one million crippled.

1920s

The Côte d'Azur sparkles as Europe's avant-garde centre and the luxurious *Train Bleu* (Blue Train) makes its first run from Calais to the Mediterranean coast.

1939–45

Nazi Germany occupies France, establishing a puppet state led by ageing WWI hero General Pétain in Vichy; Provence is liberated two months after D-Day.

ing given less than a day's notice to pack up and leave. Those who didn't were sent to Nazi concentration camps. The Resistance movement, particularly strong in Provence, was known in the region as *maquis,* after the Provençal scrub in which people hid.

Two months after D-Day, on 15 August 1944, Allied forces landed on the southern coast at beaches including Le Dramont near St-Raphaël, Cavalaire, Pampelonne and the St-Tropez peninsula. St-Tropez and Provence's hinterland were almost immediately liberated, but it was only after five days of heavy fighting that Allied troops freed Marseille on 28 August (three days after the liberation of Paris). Toulon was liberated on 26 August, a week after French troops first attacked the port.

Italian-occupied areas in the Vallée de La Roya were only returned to France in 1947.

Top WWII Sites

» Plage du Dramont, Corniche de l'Estérel

» Fort Ste-Agnès

» Rade de Toulon

» Mont Faron, Toulon

Les 30 Glorieuses: France's Golden Decades

The 30-odd years following WWII saw unprecedented growth, creativity and optimism in France, and Provence and the Côte d'Azur were no exception. After a false start, Cannes' 1946 international film festival heralded the return to party madness. The 1950s and 1960s saw a succession of society events: the fairy-tale marriage of Monaco's prince to Hollywood film-legend Grace Kelly in 1956; Vadim's filming of *Et Dieu Créa la Femme* (*And God Created Woman*) with a smouldering Brigitte Bardot in St-Tropez the same year; the creation of the bikini; the advent of topless sunbathing (and consequent nipple-covering with bottle tops to prevent arrest for indecent exposure); and Miles Davis, Ella Fitzgerald and Ray Charles appearing at the 1961 Juan-les-Pins jazz festival.

Rapid industrialisation marked the 1960s. A string of five hydroelectric plants was constructed on the banks of the River Durance and in 1964 Électricité de France (EDF), the French electricity company, dug a canal from Manosque to the Étang de Berre. The following year construction work began on a 100-sq-km petrochemical zone and an industrial port at Fos-sur-Mer, southern Europe's most important. The first metro

Villa Air-Bel: WWII, Escape & a House in Marseille by Rosemary Sullivan is a compelling book based on the true story of American heiress Varian Fry, who turned a villa in Marseille into a refuge for Nazi-persecuted artists and intellectuals.

NICE TREATY

No pan-European agreement has been more influential on the future map of Europe than the Treaty of Nice, a landmark treaty thrashed out by the then 15 European Union member states in late December 2000. Enforced from February 2003, the treaty laid the foundations for EU enlargement starting in 2004, determined the institutions necessary for its smooth running and – not without controversy – established a new system of voting in the Council of Ministers for the 25 EU countries from 1 November 2004.

1946

The first international film festival opens at Cannes' old casino, and is a smashing success, helping revive postwar life on the coast.

SERGE DE SAZO/GETTY IMAGES ©

» Festival de Cannes, 1946

1947

Vallée de La Roya, in eastern Provence, which had been occupied by the Italians during WWII, is returned to France.

1956

Rainier Louis Henri Maxence Bertrand Grimaldi, Count of Polignac, aka Prince Rainier III of Monaco, weds his fairy-tale princess, Hollywood film legend Grace Kelly.

line opened in Marseille in 1977 and TGV high-speed trains reached the city in 1981.

From the 1970s mainstream tourism started making inroads into Provence's rural heart. Concrete blocks sprang up along the coast and up on the ski slopes. The small flow of foreigners that had trickled into Provence backwaters to buy crumbling old *mas* (Provençal farmhouses) in the late 1970s had become an uncontrollable torrent by the 1980s. By the turn of the new millennium, the region was welcoming nine million tourists annually.

In 1962 Algeria negotiated its independence from France. Over the next two years, 800,000 *pieds noirs* (literally 'black feet', as Algerian-born French people are known in France) flooded into France, with the majority settling in the south.

Corruption, the Mafia & the Front National

Writer Somerset Maugham had famously described Monaco as 'a sunny place for shady people' but over the course of the 1980s and 1990s, many increasingly felt that this could apply to the region as a whole. Although it was well known that the Italian, Russian and Corsican mafias all operated on the coast, their true extent was revealed after a series of corruption scandals, none more dramatic than the assassination of *député* (member of parliament) Yann Piat in 1994: she was shot in her Hyères constituency following her public denunciation of the Riviera mafia.

The same year, former Nice mayor Jacques Médecin, who had run the city from 1966 to 1990, was found guilty of income-tax evasion and misuse of public funds after being extradited from Uruguay where he'd fled. And in 1995, Bernard Tapie, the flamboyant owner of Olympique de Marseille football club, was found guilty of match fixing and sentenced to two years in jail.

Sophia-Antipolis, the French version of Silicon Valley near Antibes, was created in 1969. It employs more than 30,000 people in four areas: information technologies; earth sciences; health sciences and biotechnology; teaching and research.

Many now think that it was these high-profile corruption cases, combined with economic recession and growing unemployment, that helped fuel the rise of the extreme-right Front National (FN). Led by firebrand Jean-Marie Le Pen, infamous for having described the Holocaust as a 'detail of history', the FN won municipal elections in Toulon, Orange and Marignane in 1995, and Vitrolles in 1997. The party also gained 15.5% of votes in regional elections in 1998 and 14.7% in 2004.

The FN never succeeded in securing the presidency of the Provence-Alpes-Côte d'Azur *région* but Le Pen's success in the first round of presidential elections in 2002 – he landed 16.86% of votes, with its main support base in the south of France – shocked many people. (He eventually lost in the second round, after a massive 80% turnout at the ballot boxes, and 82% of votes in favour of his opponent, Jacques Chirac.)

2000

European leaders meet in Nice to thrash out future EU expansion. Not without controversy, they establish a new system of voting in the Council of Ministers.

2002

The French franc, first minted in 1360, is dumped on the scrap heap of history as the country adopts the euro as its official currency.

2005

After the end of a three-month mourning period for his father, Prince Albert II of Monaco is crowned monarch of the world's second-smallest country.

2008

Marseille and Aix celebrate as they're voted Capital of Culture for 2013, and the cities begin to prepare for hosting the big year of events.

Painters of Provence

Whether it was the search for a refuge, light or more clement weather, it seems that every painter who settled in Provence came here looking for something – and found a lot more than they could have hoped for.

The Impressionists

Van Gogh

Vincent van Gogh (1853–90) arrived in Arles from Paris in 1888; the painter was keen to get away from the excesses of the capital and he settled down quickly. The town, local customs, landscape and unique light all enchanted him and provided much inspiration for his work. By the time he left Arles a year later, he'd done more than 200 oil paintings – including masterpieces such as *Bedroom in Arles* (1888) and *Still Life: Vase with Twelve Sunflowers* (1888) – and over 100 drawings.

The now famous spate with fellow impressionist Paul Gauguin during which Van Gogh cut his own ear off occurred in December 1888. Over the next few months, Van Gogh was in and out of hospital; in May 1889, he decided to voluntarily enter an asylum in St-Rémy de Provence.

His time at the asylum proved to be as productive as his time in Arles. Van Gogh averaged one painting a day during his stay and we owe works such as *Starry Night* (1889) and several haunting self-portraits to this period. Van Gogh left St-Rémy in May 1890 to join his brother Theo in Auvers-sur-Oise; he shot himself two months later.

It is widely acknowledged that Van Gogh's Provençal work represents the height of his art. Unfortunately, Van Gogh's talent was largely unrecognised during his lifetime and few of his paintings remain in the region (Musée Angladon, p193), in Avignon and Musée Granet, p165), in Aix-en-Provence have just a couple of works).

For further biographical information, see p178.

Cézanne Sights

- Atelier Paul Cézanne, Aix-en-Provence
- Le Jas de Bouffan, Aix-en-Provence
- Carrières de Bibemus, Aix-en-Provence
- L'Estaque

Cézanne

Paul Cézanne (1839–1906) is without a doubt the most Provençal of all the impressionists. His work is generally credited with providing a transition from 'traditional' 19th-century art to the radical new art forms of the 20th century, notably cubism.

Cézanne was born in Aix-en-Provence and spent most of his life there, save for a decade in Paris and another ferrying between Provence and the capital. He met writer Émile Zola at school in Aix and the pair remained friends for years – until Zola used Cézanne as the main inspiration for his character Claude Lantet, a failed painter, in his novel *L'Oeuvre* (*The Work*, 1886).

Provence was Cézanne's chief inspiration: the seaside village of L'Estaque, the Bibémus quarries near Aix (said to have inspired his cubist trials by their geometric character) and the family house Jas de Bouffan in Aix appear in dozens of paintings. But it was the Montagne Ste-Victoire that captivated him the most, its radiance, shape and colours depicted in anything from impressionist to cubist styles in no less than 30 oil paintings and 45 water colours.

Sadly, Cézanne's admiration for Provence was not mutual: few of Aix's conservative bourgeoisie appreciated Cézanne's departure from the creed of classical painting and there were even calls for him to leave the city.

In 1902 Cézanne moved into a purpose-built studio, Les Lauves, from where he did much of his painting until his death in 1906. The studio has been left untouched and is one of the most poignant insights into his art.

Renoir

In 1892 impressionist doyen Pierre-Auguste Renoir (1841–1919), started to develop rheumatoid arthritis. The condition gradually worsened and in 1907 doctors ordered Renoir to move to the sunny climes of Cagnes-sur-Mer in a bid to alleviate his pains.

Renoir bought a farm, Les Colettes, where he lived until his death. Far from being a retirement home however, Renoir enjoyed a new lease of life in the south of France and painted vigorously throughout his twilight years. Although he had to adapt his painting technique – he was wheelchair-bound and suffered from ankylosis in his shoulder – many credit his late works with displaying the same joy and radiance that were the hallmark of his earlier (and most famous) works.

Les Colettes is now the Musée Renoir in Cagnes-sur-Mer, where you can see Renoir's studio, a few of his works and the stunning garden; it was undergoing substantial renovations in 2012 and was slated for re-opening in summer 2013.

Matisse Sights

- » Musée Matisse, Nice
- » Chapelle du Rosaire, Vence
- » Cemetery at Monastère de Cimiez, Nice

Matisse

Originally from drab northern France, leading Fauvist exponent Henri Matisse (1869–1954) spent his most creative years lapping up the sunlight and vivacity of the coast in and around Nice.

Matisse travelled to southern France on a number of occasions, including a visit to impressionist Paul Signac in St-Tropez, which inspired *Luxe, Calme et Volupté* (*Luxury, Calm and Tranquility*, 1904). But it was a trip to Nice to cure bronchitis in 1917 that left Matisse smitten – he never really looked back.

Matisse settled in Cimiez, in the hills north of Nice's centre, and it was here that he started experimenting with his *gouaches découpées* (collages

CLASSIC PAINTING

Although Provence and the Côte d'Azur are best known for their relatively modern artistic legacy, the region's reputation as a haven for artists goes back centuries.

In the 14th century Sienese, French and Spanish artists thrived at the papal court in Avignon and created an influential style of mural painting to decorate the palace.

Renaissance painter Louis (Ludovico) Bréa (c1450–1523), often dubbed the 'Fra Angelico Provençal', is best remembered for his signature burgundy colour known as *rouge bréa*.

Two centuries later, it was the rococo influences in his landscapes and the playful and often licentious scenes of his paintings that made Jean-Honoré Fragonard (1732–1806), a native of Grasse, so popular with French aristocrats.

of painted paper cutouts) in the 1940s, after an operation. The famous *Blue Nude* series and *The Snail* epitomise this period.

Matisse's ill health was also a key factor in the creation of his masterpiece, the Chapelle du Rosaire in Vence. The artist had been looked after by a nun during his convalescence and the chapel was his mark of gratitude. Matisse designed everything, from the stained-glass windows to the altar, the structure of the chapel and the robes of the priests. The chapel took four years to complete and was finished in 1951.

Matisse died in Nice in 1954 and is buried in Cimiez's cemetery.

Picasso Sights

» Musée Picasso, Antibes

» Musée Picasso La Guerre et La Paix, Vallauris

» Château de Vauvenargues

» Musée de la Photographie André Villers, Mougins

Picasso

Although Pablo Picasso (1881–1973) moved to the Côte d'Azur rather late in life (the Spanish artist was in his mid-sixties when he moved to Golfe-Juan with his lover Françoise Gilot in 1946), his influence over the region and the region's influence on him were significant.

Antibes & Vallauris

It was following an offer from the curator of Antibes' Château Grimaldi (now the Musée Picasso) that Picasso set up a studio on the third floor of the historic building. Works from this period are characterised by extraordinary postwar *joie de vivre* and Mediterranean mythology.

It was that same year that Picasso visited the nearby potters' village of Vallauris and discovered ceramics. Picasso loved the three-dimensional aspect of the art and experimented endlessly. His method was somewhat unorthodox: he melted clay, used unglazed ceramics and decorated various pieces with relief motifs; he also eschewed traditional floral decorations for a bestiary of his favourite mythological creatures.

Picasso settled in Vallauris in 1948 and although he left in 1955, he carried on working with ceramics until his death. His time in Vallauris wasn't only dedicated to ceramics however; it was here that Picasso got 'his chapel' (arch-rival Matisse had finished his in 1951). It was the chapel of the town's castle, in which he painted *War and Peace* (1952), the last of his monumental creations dedicated to peace, after *Guernica* (1937) and *Massacre in Korea* (1951).

Hungarian-born Victor Vasarely (1908–97), best-known for his bold, colourful geometrical forms and shifting perspectives, had a summer house in Gordes from 1948. He opened a first museum there in 1970 (which closed in 1996) and a second one, Fondation Vasarely, in Aix-en-Provence in 1976, which you can still visit.

Vauvenargues & Mougins

In 1959 Picasso bought the Château de Vauvenargues near Aix-en-Provence. The castle slumbered at the foot of the Montagne Ste-Victoire, depicted so often by Cézanne, whom Picasso greatly admired. It was Cézanne's early studies on cubism that had led Picasso and his peers to launch the cubist movement (which seeks to deconstruct the subject into a system of intersecting planes and present various aspects of it simultaneously); Picasso was also an avid collector of Cézanne's works.

In 1961 Picasso moved to Mougins with his second wife Jacqueline Roque. He had many friends in the area, including photographer André Villers, to whom Picasso gave his first camera and who in turn took numerous portraits of the artist.

Picasso died in Mougins in 1973 and is buried in Château de Vauvenargues, which remains the property of his family.

Modern Art

Chagall

Belorussian painter Marc Chagall (1887–1985) moved to Paris from Russia in 1922. He was well-known for his dazzling palette and the biblical messages in his later works (inspired by his Jewish upbringing in

CONTEMPORARY ART

One look at the portfolio of Documents d'Artistes (www.documentsdartistes.org), an association in Marseille that catalogues and diffuses the work of contemporary regional artists around the world, proves that contemporary art is well and truly alive in Provence: be it tracing a line along the surface of the planet, creating sound installations, or producing inflatable or mechanical art, it is all happening here.

There are many galleries where you can admire contemporary art. In Marseille, make a beeline for exhibition space La Friche La Belle de Mai; in Arles, check the Fondation Vincent van Gogh; or amble the gallery-lined streets of St-Paul de Vence and Mougins.

Russia and trips to Palestine). Chagall managed to escape to the US during WWII and it's upon his return to France in the early 1950s that he settled in St-Paul de Vence on the Côte d'Azur. Both Matisse and Picasso lived in the area at the time and many artists regularly visited; it was this sense of 'artistic colony' that attracted Chagall.

It's acknowledged however, that Provence–Côte d'Azur itself never became inspiration fodder for Chagall. It did offer him a good home, and the incredible Musée National Marc Chagall in Nice attests to the strong bond the artist developed with the region. Chagall is buried in St-Paul de Vence.

New Realism

Provence–Côte d'Azur produced a spate of artists at the forefront of modern art in the middle of the 20th century. Most famous perhaps was Nice-born Yves Klein (1928–62), who stood out for his series of daring monochrome paintings, the distinctive blue he used in many of his works and his experiments in paint application techniques: in his series *Anthropométrie*, paint was 'applied' by women covered from head to toe in paint and writhing naked on the canvas.

Also making a splash in modern-art circles was native Niçois Arman (1928–2005), who became known for his trash-can portraits, made by framing the litter found in the subject's rubbish bin, and Martial Raysse, born in Golfe-Juan in 1936, renowned for pioneering the use of neon in art: his 1964 portrait of *Nissa Bella (Beautiful Nice)* – a flashing blue heart on a human face – is typical.

Yves Klein's famous blue became more than a signature colour: it was actually patented. It is now known in art circles as International Klein Blue (or IKB), a deep, bright hue close to ultramarine.

Klein, Arman and Raysse were amongst the nine people to found New Realism in 1960. The movement was one of several avant-garde trends of the time and was often perceived as the French interpretation of American pop art. In 1961 another prominent Provençal artist, Marseillais César Baldaccini (1921–1998), known for his crushed cars and scrap metal art, joined the New Realists' rank, as did Niki de Saint Phalle (1930–2002), famous for her huge, colourful papier mâché sculptures.

Nice's Musée d'Art Moderne et d'Art Contemporain has one of the best collections of New Realist artists' works; the building itself is a work of art, too.

Cinema & the Arts

The artistic pace in this pocket of southern France has always been fast and furious, fuelled by a constant flux of new arrivals who brought with them new ideas, traditions and precious know-how. Such creative energies have in turn found expression in a variety of mediums and often become international references.

Cinema

Provence and cinema have had a thing going on for more than a century: one of the world's first motion pictures, by the Lumière brothers, premiered in La Ciotat (between Marseille and Toulon) in September 1895. The series of two-minute reels, entitled *L'Arrivée d'un Train en Gare de La Ciotat (The Arrival of a Train at La Ciotat Station)*, made the audience leap out of their seats as the steam train rocketed forward.

Films Starring Provence

» *To Catch a Thief* (1956)

» *Et Dieu Créa la Femme* (1956)

» *Le Gendarme de St-Tropez* (1964)

» *Taxi* (1998)

» *A Good Year* (2006)

Early Days

French film flourished in the 1920s, Nice being catapulted to stardom by Hollywood director Rex Ingram, who bought the city's Victorine film studios in 1925 and transformed them overnight into the hub of European film-making. A big name in the 1930s and '40s was Aubagne-born writer and film-maker Marcel Pagnol, whose career kicked off in 1931 with *Marius*, the first part of his Fanny trilogy, portraying pre-war Marseille. Pagnol's work was famous for his endearing depiction of Provençal people and he remains a local icon.

Cannes & St-Tropez

With the Cannes Film Festival taking off after WWII, French cinema started to diversify. Jean Cocteau (1889–1963) eschewed realism with two masterpieces of cinematic fantasy: *La Belle et la Bête* (*Beauty and the Beast*; 1945) and *Orphée* (*Orpheus*; 1950).

Nouvelle Vague (New Wave) directors made films without big budgets, extravagant sets or big-name stars; many also seemed to have a penchant for the Côte d'Azur. Roger Vadim turned St-Tropez into the hot spot to be with his *Et Dieu Créa la Femme* (*And God Created Woman*; 1956), starring Brigitte Bardot. Jacques Démy's *La Baie des Anges* (*The Bay of Angels*; 1962) is set in Nice, while François Truffaut filmed part of *La Nuit Américaine* (*The American Night*; 1972) in the Victorine studios, the Niçois hinterland and the Vésubie Valley.

Cinema buffs should download the CinePaca app. It lists some 50 films shot on locations across Provence–Côte d'Azur and includes clips of the film in the location and interviews with the actors.

Contemporary Cinema

Provence and the Côte d'Azur continue to inspire and play host to hundreds of films. Action-packed movies such as *The Transporter* (starring Jason

Statham) and the *Taxi* trilogy (by Luc Besson, complete with a home-grown rap soundtrack) take place on the Riviera and Marseille respectively; James Bond drops by Monaco in *GoldenEye*; while cult comedy *Bienvenu Chez les Ch'tis* tells the story of a Provençal public servant being relocated – shock horror – to northern France.

Cannes' eponymous film festival (p85) also guarantees that the limelight of '7th art' keeps shining bright on the region.

Architecture

From old stone villages built on hillocks to cutting-edge glass design: this region covers a fabulous architectural spectrum.

Antiquity

Although there is plenty of evidence suggesting the region was inhabited several thousand years ago, early populations left little in the way of architecture. It was the Massiliots (Greeks) who, from 600 BC, really started building across Provence; the Romans however, took it to a whole new level. Their colossal architectural legacy is a real highlight of travelling to the region, from amphitheatres to aqueducts, arches to temples and baths.

Roman Splendour

» Pont du Gard

» Théâtre Antique, Orange

» Les Arènes, Nîmes

» Trophée des Alpes, La Turbie

» Les Arènes, Arles

Romanesque to Renaissance

A religious revival in the 11th century ushered in Romanesque architecture, so-called because of the Gallo-Roman architectural elements it adopted. Round arches, heavy walls with few windows, and a lack of ornamentation were characteristics of this style, Provence's most famous examples being the 12th-century abbeys in Sénanque and Le Thoronet.

Gothic architecture swapped roundness and simplicity for ribbed vaults, pointed arches, slender verticals, chapels along the nave and chancel, refined decoration and large stained-glass windows. Provence's most important examples of this period are Avignon's Palais des Papes and the Chartreuse du Val de Bénédiction in Villeneuve-lès-Avignon.

The French Renaissance scarcely touched the region – unlike mighty citadel architect Sébastien Le Prestre de Vauban (1633–1707), who notably re-shaped Antibes' star-shaped Fort Carré and Île Ste Marguerite's Fort Royal.

Classical to Modern

Classical architecture fused with painting and sculpture from the end of the 16th to late 18th centuries to create stunning Baroque structures with interiors of great subtlety, refinement and elegance: Chapelle de la Miséricorde in Nice and Marseille's Centre de la Vieille Charité are classics.

Urban 20th-century architecture is the focus of Patrimoine XXe, a label protecting 34 urban landmarks in the Provence-Alpes-Côte d'Azur region. Find the full list of landmarks on www.paca.culture.gouv.fr/dossiers/xxeme/menu.html

Neoclassicism came into its own under Napoléon III, the Palais de Justice and Palais Masséna in Nice demonstrating the renewed interest in classical forms that it exhibited. The true showcase of this era, though, is 1878 Casino de Monte Carlo, designed by French architect Charles Garnier (1825–98). Elegant Aix-en-Provence's fountains and *hôtels particuliers* (private mansions) date from this period, too, as do the intricate wrought-iron campaniles.

The belle époque heralded an eclecticism of decorative stucco friezes, trompe l'œil paintings, glittering wall mosaics, brightly coloured Moorish minarets and Turkish towers.

The three decades following WWII were marked, as in much of Europe, by the rise of modernist architecture – concrete blocks and high-rise towers – partly as a response to pressing housing needs. Marseille's notorious suburbs, Monaco's forest of skyscrapers and the emblematic pyramidal Marina Baie des Anges in Villeneuve-Loubet all date back to this era. Many now bemoan the flurry of constructions that took place in postwar years, and the lack of building regulation (and enforcement) that prevailed at the time.

Top Provençal Reads

- » *The Count of Monte Cristo*, Alexandre Dumas
- » *My Father's Glory*, Marcel Pagnol
- » *A Year in Provence*, Peter Mayle
- » *The Perfume*, Patrick Süskind
- » *Tender is the Night*, F Scott Fitzgerald

Contemporary Architecture

As with every other art form, Provence and the Côte d'Azur have kept innovating in architecture. Mouans-Sartoux's 2004 lime-green Espace de l'Art Concret, designed by Swiss-based architects Annette Gigon and Mike Guyer to complement the village's 16th-century château, has to be the boldest example of late.

Most recent is Rudy Ricciotti's new Musée Jean Cocteau in Menton (he also designed the Pavillon Noir in Aix-en-Provence). The cow-print-like seafront building couldn't contrast more with the old town's Italianate architecture and is an ode to Cocteau's own surrealist style. Another famous contemporary architect to have left his print on Provence-Côte d'Azur is British master Sir Norman Foster, who designed Nîmes' steel-and-glass Carré d'Art, the Musée de la Préhistoire des Gorges du Verdon in Quinson and the new five-storey building for Monaco Yacht Club (scheduled to open in 2013).

Literature

Courtly Love to Prophecies

Lyric poems of courtly love, written by troubadours solely in the Occitan language, dominated medieval Provençal literature.

Provençal life featured in the works of Italian poet Petrarch (1304–74), exiled in 1327 to Avignon, where he met Laura, to whom he dedicated his life's works. Petrarch lived in Fontaine-de-Vaucluse from 1337 to 1353, where he wrote poems and letters about local shepherds, fishermen he met on the banks of the Sorgue, and his pioneering ascent up Mont Ventoux.

In 1555 the philosopher and visionary writer from St-Rémy de Provence, Nostradamus (1503–66), published (in Latin) his prophetic *Centuries* in Salon de Provence, where he lived until his death (from gout, as he had predicted).

LE CORBUSIER

It was rather late in life that Swiss-born Charles-Édouard Jeanneret (1887–1965), alias Le Corbusier, turned to the south of France. He first came to visit his friends Eileen Gray, an Irish designer, and Romanian-born architect Jean Badovici in the 1930s. Gray and Badovici had a very modern seaside villa, E-1027, on Cap-Martin and Le Corbusier was a frequent guest.

Following a spat with Gray in 1938 however, Le Corbusier built his own holiday pad, Le Cabanon. It remained his summer cabin until his death in 1965 (he died of a heart attack whilst swimming).

Le Cabanon is unique because it is a project that Le Corbusier built for himself, but his most revolutionary design is undoubtedly the Marseille concrete apartment block L'Unité d'Habitation. Built between 1947 and 1952 as a low-cost housing project, it comprised 337 apartments arranged inside an elongated block on stilts. The building was considered a coup by architects worldwide (and an aesthetic sacrilege by the Marseillais) and the façade, communal corridors and rooftop terrace of the block have together been protected as an historical monument since 1986.

Le Corbusier is buried with his wife in section J of Roquebrune-Cap-Martin cemetery.

MUSIC

Traditional Provençal music is based on polyphonic chants; as a music form, they have gone out of fashion, although they remain part and parcel of traditional celebrations, notably Christmas and Easter.

Where Provence has really made a contribution to the French contemporary music scene is in rap, jazz and world music, with Marseille's multicultural background proving an inspiration to many artists.

The phenomenal hip-hop lyrics of 1991 smash-hit album, *de la Planète Mars* (*'From Planet Mars'*, Mars being short for Marseille) by rapping legends IAM – France's best-known rap group from Marseille – nudged rap into the mainstream. IAM have since gone on to collaborate with everyone from Beyoncé to film-director Luc Besson. Since that time, the city's music scene has transcended its rap roots.

Cheb Khaled, Cheb Aïssa and Cheb Mami – all from Marseille – have contributed hugely to the development of Algerian raï, encouraging other world-music talents such as Iranian percussionist Bijan Chemiranito, who plays the *zarb* (Persian goblet drum), to thrive.

The Riviera has also fostered a special relationship with jazz music over the years. Nice launched its jazz festival in 1948; Antibes-Juan-les-Pins followed in 1960 after legendary saxophonist Sidney Bechet settled there in the 1950s. Every single jazz great has since played in these festivals (Ella Fitzgerald, Miles Davis, Ray Charles etc) while Marseille has become something of a launching pad for young jazz artists blending traditional rhythms with contemporary influences.

Mistral to Mayle

The 19th century witnessed a revival in Provençal literature, thanks to poet Frédéric Mistral (1830–1914). Mistral set up the literary movement Le Félibrige with six other young Provençal poets in a bid to revive the Provençal dialect and codify its orthography. The result was Provençal dictionary *Lou Trésor dou Félibrige*.

Early-20th-century Provençal literature is dominated by writers depicting their homeland. Jean Giono (1895–1970), from Manosque, blended myth with reality in novels that remain a celebration of the Provençal Alps and their people. Marcel Pagnol wrote about his beloved Marseille and its colourful inhabitants.

Numerous writers passed through or settled in Provence over the course of the 20th century: Colette (1873–1954) lived in St-Tropez from 1927 until 1938; her novel *La Naissance du Jour* (*Break of Day*) evokes an unspoilt St-Tropez. F Scott Fitzgerald enjoyed several stays in the inter-war years; playwright Samuel Beckett sought refuge in Roussillon during WWII; Lawrence Durrell (1912–90) settled in Somières, near Nîmes; and Graham Greene lived in Antibes for many years and even wrote an incendiary pamphlet about political corruption in the 1980s.

Most famous perhaps is Peter Mayle, whose novels about life as an Englishman in Provence have greatly contributed to the popularity of the region among foreign visitors.

Traditional Provençal chants form the root of the powerful percussion-accompanied polyphony by Lo Còr de la Plana (www.myspace.com/locordelaplana), a male choir born in Marseille. Their album, *Tant deman* (2007), is essential listening.

Provence Living

A Question of Identité

In a part of the country where foreigners have always come, gone and invariably stayed, regional identity is not clear cut.

Young, old or salt-and-pepper-haired in between, people do share a staunch loyalty to the hamlet, village, town or city in which they live. People in Marseille have a particularly passionate attachment to their city, a port known for its stereotyped rough-and-tumble inhabitants who are famed among the French for their exaggerations and imaginative fancies, such as the tale about the sardine that blocked Marseille port.

Markedly more Latin in outlook and temperament, Niçois exhibit a common zest for the good life with their Italian neighbours; while law-abiding Monégasques dress up to the nines, don't gossip or break the law. In rural pastures where family trees go back several generations and occupations remain firmly implanted in the soil, identity is deeply rooted in tradition.

Affluent outsiders buying up the region are prompting some traditional village communities to question their own (shifting) identities. With 20% of privately owned homes being *résidences secondaires* (second homes), everyday shops in some villages are struggling to stay open year-round, while property prices in many places have spiralled out of reach of local salaries.

The list of Provence–Côte d'Azur's most famous residents is long and always shifting. Angelina Jolie and Brad Pitt own Château de Miraval in Correns; the Beckhams have a villa in Bargemon; John Malkovich has one in the Luberon; and singer Bono has one in Èze-sur-Mer.

Le Weekend

The working week in Provence is much like any working week in a developed country: plagued with routine, commuting and getting the children to school, albeit with more sunshine than in many places.

The weekend however, is when living in Provence comes into its own. Going to the local *marché* (market) on a weekend morning is a must, not only to pick the finest ingredients for a delicious lunch or dinner, but also to catch up on gossip at the stalls or stop for a coffee at the village cafe.

Sport is another weekend favourite; football, cycling, trekking, sailing, skiing and scuba-diving are all popular in the region. Between April and October many people head to the beach for the afternoon.

Weekends also mean going out, whatever your age: young people pile into the region's bars and nightclubs (the latter don't open until 11pm so partying generally finishes in the wee hours of the morning); older generations dress up to go out for dinner, either at the restaurant or their friends' house, working their way through aperitif, three courses, coffee and *digestif*.

Boules

Pensioners playing boules on a dusty patch of gravel beneath trees seems to be as universal an image of Provençal life as people heading to the market, basket in hand, or sipping a glass of pastis on a cafe terrace.

ENLIGHTENING READS

No titles better provide insight into Provençal living, past and present, than these:

» *Everybody Was So Young* (by Amanda Vaill) Beautiful evocation of an American couple and their glam literary friends in the jazzy 1920s.

» *Côte d'Azur: Inventing the French Riviera* (by Mary Blume) Fabulous portrait of Riviera life: fantasy, escapism, pleasure, fame, eccentricity...

» *Provence A–Z* (by Peter Mayle) The best, the quirkiest, the most curious moments of the 20-odd years this best-selling author has spent in Provence.

» *Provençal Escapes* (by Caroline Clifton-Mogg) Image-driven snoop around beautiful homes in Provence.

» *Words in a French Life: Lessons in Love and Language from the South of France* (by Kristin Espinasse) Daily life in Provence through a series of French words.

Pétanque (Provençal boules) was invented in La Ciotat, near Marseille, in 1910 when arthritis-crippled Jules Le Noir could no longer take the running strides prior to aiming demanded by the *longue boule* game. The local champion thus stood with his feet firmly on the ground – a style that became known as *pieds tanques* (Provençal for 'tied feet', from which '*pétanque*' emerged).

To have a spin yourself (or watch the drama unfold on the village square), here are the rules:

» Two to six people, split into two teams, can play. Each player has three solid metal boules (balls).

» Each team takes it in turn to aim a boule at a tiny wooden ball called a *cochonnet* (jack), the idea being to land the boule as close as possible to it. The team with the closest boule wins the round; points are allocated by totting up how many boules the winner's team has closest to the marker (one point for each boule). The first to notch up 13 wins the match.

» The team throwing the *cochonnet* (initially decided by a coin toss) has to throw it from a small circle scratched in the gravel. It must be hurled 6m to 10m away. Each player aiming a boule must likewise stand in this circle, with both feet planted firmly on the ground.

» Underarm throwing is compulsory. Beyond that, players can roll the boule along the ground (known as *pointer*, literally 'to point') or hurl it high in the air in the hope of it landing smack-bang on top of an opponent's boule, sending it flying out of position. This flamboyant tactic, called *tirer* (literally 'to shoot'), can turn an entire game around in seconds.

L'accent du midi (southern French accent) is one of the most marked regional French accents. Along with its sing-song quality, its most distinctive aspects are the addition of a 'g' sound for words ending in nasal sounds and silent 'e' at the end of words becoming a full on 'euh'.

Football

Long the stronghold, not to mention heart and soul, of French football, Olympique de Marseille (OM; www.om.net) was national champion for four consecutive years between 1989 and 1992, and in 2010; in 1993 it became the first French team to win the European Champions League. It reached the UEFA Cup final in 2004 but hasn't got that far since.

The club has a die-hard fan base and the city has spurned many football greats, chief amongst them Zinedine Zidane, aka Zizou, the midfielder of North African origin who captained France to victory in the 1998 World Cup.

Arsenal manager Arsène Wenger and star striker Thierry Henry both began their careers with the region's other strong club, AS Monaco (ASM).

Provençal Food & Wine

With copious amounts of garlic and olive oil, abundant seafood, fruit and vegetables bursting with flavour and perfectly-chilled rosé, Provençal cuisine is every gourmet's dream. For tips on making the best of it, see p31.

Sunny Gastronomy

Olive Oil

Olive oil is the keystone to Mediterranean cuisine. It moistens every salad, drizzles croutons and cheeses, fries fish and onions, and bakes summer fruit.

There are dozens of varieties, many of which are protected by Appellation d'Origine Protégée (AOP), a label protecting regional know-how and products. There are seven AOPs for olives and olive oil across Provence-Côte d'Azur: Nyons, Baux-de-Provence, Nice, Aix-en-Provence, Nîmes, Haute-Provence and Provence.

Each oil has a distinctive colour, flavour and texture, which can be attributed to the olive variety but also the pressing techniques and maturing processes used.

Olives are picked from November to February. Table olives are harvested first; olives destined to be pressed come last. On average, it takes 5kg of olives to yield 1L of oil.

Tasting Olive Oil

- Domaine Saint-Joseph, Tourrettes-sur-Loup
- Moulin à Huile d'Olive Alziari, Nice
- Moulin de Callas, Callas
- Les Olives: Huiles du Monde/ Le Monde de la Truffe, St-Rémy de Provence

Fruit of the Sea

Provençal cuisine is often described as Mediterranean, and so it's no surprise that a cuisine named after a sea should feature plenty of seafood.

Typical Mediterranean catches include *merlan* (whiting), *St-Pierre* (John Dory), *galinette* (tub gurnard), *daurade* (sea bream) and *rascasse* (scorpion fish). One of the finest however is *loup*, also known as *bar* (sea bass). The local speciality is to cook it *en croûte de sel* (in salt crust – the result is surprisingly unsalty).

BREAD & CHEESE

Just like everywhere else in France, bread and cheese have pride of place in the Mediterranean diet.

Local cheeses are predominantly *chèvre* (goat's cheese), which can be eaten *frais* (fresh, a mild creamy taste) or matured into a tangy, stronger tasting *demi-sec* (semi-dry) or *sec* (dry). Banon cheese, which comes wrapped in chestnut leaves, is well known.

The region's signature bread is picnic favourite *fougasse*, a flat bread stuffed with olives, pancetta or anchovies.

Fish is otherwise served grilled, *à la plancha* (seared), pan-fried with tasty sauces (often butter or cream-based with herbs thrown in) or in stews and soups.

Shellfish is another delight: *crevettes* (prawns) and *gambas* (king prawns) are plentiful, as are oysters, mussels, *oursin* (sea urchin, a delicacy) and *coquilles St-Jacques* (scallops). They're often served in grand-looking *plateaux de fruits de mer* (seafood platters), which make for a truly decadent meal with a bottle of crisp white wine. *Calamar* (calamari) for its part is generally seared or fried.

Best for Seafood

» Le Mazet du Vaccarès, Camargue

» Chez Camille, Ramatuelle

» La Mère Germaine, Villefranche-sur-Mer

» La Cabane aux Coquillages, Stes-Maries de la Mer

» Le Rhul, Marseille

Carnivore's Corner

The meat offering of Provence-Côte d'Azur is as diverse as its seafood: beef, pork and lamb are staples; rabbit is very popular in stews; and game meat is a winter favourite (wild boar and pheasant especially).

Preparation follows the seasons: stews in winter, *grillades* (grilled meat) in summer. Favourites include *sauté de lapin aux olives* (rabbit in a tomato sauce with olives) and *daube* (a beef stew from Nice).

From the Vegetable Patch & the Orchard

Vegetables form the backbone of Provençal cooking. Staples like onions, tomatoes, aubergines (eggplant) and courgettes (squash or zucchini) are stewed alongside green peppers, garlic and various aromatic herbs to produce that perennial Provençal stew favourite, *ratatouille*.

In summer the tomato is king. There are more than 2500 known varieties in the region and they come in all shapes, sizes and colours. They are outstanding in salads (with chunks of goat's cheese, basil leaves and drizzled with olive oil) or *farcies* (stuffed).

Other seasonal wonders include asparagus and artichokes (spring) and courgette flowers (summer). But the culinary highlight of Provence's veggie calendar is the truffle. Dubbed *diamants noirs* (black diamonds) for their value (€500 to €1000 per kilogram), the black truffle (*tuber melanosporum*, a fungi) is found in the Vaucluse and the Var from November to March. Traditionally snouted out by pigs, truffles these days are hunted by dogs. They are trained to sniff out both the black winter truffle and the cheaper, lesser-known white truffle – or summer truffle – between May and August.

Provence also produces marvellous fruit: sun-ripened strawberries, cantaloupe melons, apricots, peaches and nectarines, plums and cherries all grow in abundance and are a riot of flavour (not to mention of colours on the market stands).

Authentic *Herbes de Provence* mixes (they are protected by a label) contain 26% rosemary, 26% savory, 26% oregano, 19% thyme and 3% basil. They tend to be used on grilled meat and fish in Provençal cooking.

Vegetarians & Vegans

In a country where *viande* (meat) once meant 'food' too, it comes as no surprise that vegetarians and vegans are not catered for well. Restaurants that buck the trend are marked with the following icon 🖉.

Otherwise, here are some useful tips to help you make the best of Provençal cuisine:

» Starters are often vegetarian so order two or three starters instead of the usual starter and main.

» Dishes that can easily be customised include pasta, pizza and salads, all very common across Provence–Côte d'Azur.

» Small restaurants serving just a few daily specials will find it harder to accommodate dietary requirements so opt for larger establishments instead.

Strict vegetarians should note that most cheeses in France are made with *lactosérum* (rennet), an enzyme derived from the stomach of a calf or young goat.

Best Food & Wine Pairing

» L'Atelier, Arles

» Le Mas Tourteron, Gordes

» La Cave de l'Origine, Nice

» Le Negresco, Nice

» Le Petit Verdot, Aix-en-Provence

» La Chassagnette, Le Sambuc

Garlicky Goodness

Garlic gives Provençal cuisine its kick, letting rip in a clutch of fantastic sauces, traditionally served to complement *crudités* (raw vegetables), soups and fish dishes.

» *Anchoïade* is a strong anchovy paste laced with garlic and olive oil and delicious served with *bagna cauda* (raw mixed vegetables).

» *Tapenade* is a sharp, black-olive-based dip seasoned with garlic, capers, anchovies and olive oil.

» *Aïoli*, a kind of garlic mayonnaise, is an essential component of *aïoli Provençal complet* – a mountain of vegetables, boiled potatoes, a boiled egg and *coquillages* (small shellfish), all of which are dunked into the pot of *aïoli*.

» Fiery pink *rouille*, a saffron-flavoured *aïoli*, is served with *soupe de poisson* (fish soup), bite-sized toasts – and a garlic clove. Rub the garlic over the toast, spread the *rouille* on top, bite it and breathe fire.

Sweets & Treats

There is plenty to keep sweet-tooths happy. Anise and orange blossoms give *navettes* (canoe-shaped biscuits from Marseille) and *fougassettes* (sweet bread) their distinctive flavours. Almonds are turned into *gâteaux secs aux amandes* (snappy almond biscuits) around Nîmes, and black honey nougat everywhere.

Nice and Apt excel at *fruits confits* (glazed fruits); more decadent is St-Tropez's *tarte Tropézienne*, a cream-filled sandwich cake christened by Brigitte Bardot. A popular dessert in the Vaucluse is cantaloupe melon doused in Muscat de Beaumes de Venise, a local dessert wine.

REGIONAL WINES

APPELLATION	BEST FOR	CHARACTERISTICS
Côtes de Provence	rosé, red	rosé is drunk young; reds can be served young or mature; Correns wines are now a leading organic sub-label
Coteaux d'aix-en-Provence	rosé, red	rosé is dry, Aromatic reds
Coteaux-Varois-En-Provence	red, rosé, white	reds must be drunk mature; rosés and whites are ideal summer meal companions
Côte du Ventoux & Côte du Luberon	red	light and fruity
Gigondas	red	pungent fruit and spice aroma; best drunk mature (seven years or older), hence its relatively high price
Bandol	red, rosé	made with the rare mourvèdre grape; deep-flavoured reds; well-balanced rosés
Cassis	white	crisp; ideal with seafood
Beaumes de Venise	white	a sweet Muscat wine; drunk in aperitif or for dessert
Châteauneuf-du-Pape	red, white	strong (minimum alcohol content 12.5%); full bodied; ages beautifully; mineral flavour; can be drunk both young and aged

Provençal Tipples

Bacchalian Pleasures

Provençal wines are by no means France's most sought-after, but making and tasting them is an art and tradition that bears its own unique and tasty trademark. Most wines carry the name of the château or *domaine* they are produced on.

Before & After Digestion

Aperitifs and *digestifs* (post-dinner drinks) are part and parcel of Provençal dining. The region is home to an array of syrupy, alcoholic beverages; amongst the better known you'll find:

» **Liqueur de Châtaignes** A chestnut liqueur best added to wine for a *kir*.

» **RinQuinQuin** A peach-flavoured aperitif.

» **Vin d'oranges amères** A bitter orange-flavoured aperitif.

» **Vin de noix** Walnut-flavoured aperitif.

» **Farigoule** A thyme-flavoured *digestif*.

» **Verveine** A verbena-flavoured *digestif*.

» **Amandine** An almond *digestif*.

Aperitifs tend to be served on the rocks, whilst *digestifs* are served neat in shot-sized glasses. Many restaurants make their own (as do many entrepreneurial Provençaux!), and it's not unusual for them to offer a glass of complimentary house liqueur at the end of the meal.

Best Wine Shops

» Cave de la Tour, Nice

» La Part des Anges, Marseille

» Cave du Félibrige, Aix-en-Provence

» Les Sens, Antibes

Pastis: the Milk of Provence

When in Provence, do as the Provençaux do: drink pastis. An aniseed-flavoured, 45% alcohol drink, pastis was invented in 1932 in Marseille by industrialist Paul Ricard (1909–97).

WHERE TO TRY/BUY IT	AREA
Maison des Vins Côtes de Provence (p125), Les Arcs-sur-Argens, Vignerons de Correns (p127), Correns, Château Ste-Roseline (p125), Les Arcs-sur-Argens	Haut-Var
Domaine de la Brillane (p171), Aix-en-Provence	Aix-en-Provence
Maison des Vins des Coteaux Varois en Provence (p128), La Celle, Château de Miraval (p127), Correns	Haut-Var
Maison de la Truffe et du Vin (p234), Ménerbes, Caves de Bonnieux (p233), Bonnieux Domaine Faverot (p235), Oppède-le-Vieux	Luberon
Caveau de Gigondas (p206), Gigondas	Dentelles de Montmirail
Maison des Vins (p137), Bandol, Domaine de Terrebrune (p137), Ollioules	Bandol
Le Chai Cassidain (p163), Cassis	Cassis
Balma Venitia (p208), Beaumes-de-Venise	Dentelles de Montmirail
Caves du Verger des Papes (p200), Châteauneuf-du-Pape, Domaine de la Solitude (p200), Châteauneuf-du- Pape	Châteauneuf-du-Pape

CHRISTMAS'S 13 DESSERTS

December in Provence sees families rush home after Mass on Christmas Eve for *Caleno vo Careno*, a traditional feast of 13 desserts – symbolising Jesus and the 12 apostles – at least one bite of each to avoid back luck for the coming year. Among the culinary delights are *pompe à huile* (leavened cake baked in olive oil and flavoured with orange blossom), sweet black and white nougats (made from honey and almonds), dried figs, almonds, walnuts, raisins, pears, apples, oranges or mandarins, dates, quince jam or paste and *calissons d'Aix* (marzipan-like sweets).

Legend has it that the unorthodoxly-named Fast Bastard Gigondas vintage was named after oenologist Thierry Boudinaud allegedly told his English partner Guy Anderson upon tasting the wine: 'Now zat iz what you call eh phet bast-ard'.

Amber-coloured in the bottle, it turns milky white when mixed with water. It is a classic aperitif, but can be drunk any time of day. Bars and cafes serve it straight, allowing you to add the water (five parts water to one part pastis).

A dash of *sirop de menthe* (mint syrup diluted with water) transforms a regular pastis into a *perroquet* (literally 'parrot'). A *tomate* (tomato) is tarted up with one part *grenadine* (pomegranate syrup) and the sweet *Mauresque* is dressed with *orgeat* (a sweet orange and almond syrup).

Leading pastis brands are Pastis 51 and Ricard, both owned by the Ricard empire. Taste them at Marseille's La Maison du Pastis (p160).

Essential pastis etiquette:

» Never order 'a pastis' at the bar – ask for it by brand such as Ricard, Janot or Casanis.

» If you find it too strong, add sugar.

» Bars in Marseille serve pastis in four glass sizes – a *momie* or *mominette* (a dinky shot glass), a *bock* (double-height shot glass), a *tube* (tall thin juice glass) and a *ballon* (like a brandy balloon).

Survival Guide

Directory A–Z

Accommodation

From fairy-tale châteaux to cosy *chambres d'hôte* (B&Bs), Provence's accommodation options tend towards rural and intimate. On the coast, midsize hotels appear, and Monaco is mostly towers. Many lodgings close in winter. All share one detail: tile floors. Pack slippers.

Air-conditioning

Air-conditioning (*la climatisation*, or just *la clime* – pronounced 'cleem') is rare. Don't expect high-power systems, but room air-conditioners of varying force, usually with complicated remote controls – learn their buttons at check-in, not bedtime.

Categories

Hotels in France, by definition, have more than five rooms and are rated by the government with one to five stars, based on amenities. Two stars can be quite comfortable, but usually lack space or extras. Three stars are reliably comfortable, often a town's best lodging. The difference between four and five stars is typically degree of service; top-end hotels are common along the coast, less so in rural Provence. Elevators are rare. So are king-size beds (except at luxury hotels).

Chambres d'hôte (sometimes called *maisons d'hôte*) are, strictly speaking, B&Bs with five or fewer rooms on an individual owner's property. They include breakfast, and vary from bare-bones bedrooms to swanky cottages. All have personality, for better or worse. Some include dinner (*table d'hôtes*) for a fee, a bonus in rural areas with few restaurants; ask when you book. Don't assume B&B necessarily implies old ladies and doilies – they're some of the best accommodation options.

Half-board (aka modified American plan; in French, *demi-pension*) includes breakfast and dinner, and is charged per person, usually at a discount from buying each service separately. *Auberge* means inn. *Gîtes* are weekly house rentals, but *gîtes d'étape* are basic mountain lodges for hikers, often with dorms. *Gîtes de refuge* are mountain huts.

Costs

Rates in this book are for high season. The region gets pricey, particularly along the Côte d'Azur. Some innkeepers drop rates in spring and autumn; many offer discounts (*remises*) for stays beyond two days. Tax costs €0.20 to €1.50 daily. Breakfast is included at *chambres d'hôte*; otherwise, expect to pay €7 to €20. Always ask about parking; it's usually extra. Some inns accept cash only, but the nearest ATM may be far away: plan accordingly. For high-demand destinations such as Avignon, Aix and Monaco, consider staying in less-expensive Orange, Marseille and Nice, then making day trips.

Reservations

Don't just show up in July and August: bookings are essential. Local tourist offices can help, but each is different. Some require bookings be same-day, others require you present in person, others charge a fee. Tourism offices are the best points of contact when you're stuck, but note that officials can't show favouritism to specific businesses: ask pointed questions.

Seasons

Lodging prices vary (hugely) by season.

- » low season: October/November to February/March
- » mid-season: March to May and September/October
- » high season: June to September

Web Resources

- » **Guide de Charme** (www.guidesdecharme.com) Hotels and B&Bs with bags of charm.

> **PRICE RANGES**
>
> The following price ranges in this book apply to a double room with bathroom.
>
> | | |
> |---|---|
> | **€** | under €80 |
> | **€€** | €80-180 |
> | **€€€** | more than €180 |

» **Gîtes de France** (www.gites-de-france-paca.com) For authentic self-catering accommodation.

» **Gîtes Panda** (www.gites-panda.fr) Green arm of Gîtes de France; self-catering and B&Bs near nature reserves.

» **Relais & Château** (www.relaischateaux.com) and **Châteaux & Hôtels Collection** (www.chateauxhotels.com) Two umbrella organisations representing the last cry in luxury.

» **Avignon & Provence** (www.avignon-et-provence.com) Hotels, B&Bs and self-catering options.

» **Fleurs de Soleil** (www.fleursdesoleil.fr) Quality *chambres d'hôte*.

» **Bienvenue à la Ferme** (www.bienvenue-a-la-ferme.com) Farmstays.

Business Hours

We've only listed hours where they differ significantly from the following. We generally list high-season hours. Most businesses close over lunch.

Banks 8/9am-11.30am & 1pm, 1.30/2pm-4.30/5pm Mon-Fri or Tue-Sat

Bars 7pm-1am Mon-Sat

Cafes 7/8am-10/11pm

Nightclubs 10pm-3/4/5am Thu-Sat

Post offices 8.30/9am-5/6pm Mon-Fri, 8am-noon Sat

Restaurants lunch noon-2/3pm, dinner 7/7.30-10/11pm

Shops 9/10am-6.30/7pm Mon/Tue-Sat (sometimes with a break 1-2/2.30pm)

Supermarkets 9am-7/8pm

Other things to be aware of:

» National museums close Tuesday.

» Most businesses close Sunday; exceptions include grocery stores, *boulangeries* (bakeries), florists and businesses for tourists.

» Most businesses close for a month in winter.

» In rural Provence, most businesses open only *Pâques à la Toussaint* (Easter to All Saints' Day, 1 November).

» Restaurants typically close Sunday evening and all day Monday or Tuesday. In rural areas, restaurant service ends early; always call ahead.

Customs

Goods imported and exported within the EU incur no additional taxes, provided duty has already been paid somewhere within the EU and the goods are for personal consumption. Duty-free shopping no longer exists, except upon departure from Europe. For VAT refunds at shops, you'll need your passport number.

Coming from non-EU countries, duty-free adult allowances are 200 cigarettes, 50 cigars, 1L of spirits, 2L of wine, 50mL of perfume, 250mL of eau de toilette and other goods totalling up to €175 (€90 for under 15 years). For details, see www.douane.gouv.fr.

Discount Cards

Many museums and monuments sell *billets jumelés* (combination tickets). Some cities have museum passes. Seniors over 60 or 65 are entitled to discounts on public transport, museums, and cinemas. Train discounts (p299) are available.

French Riviera Pass (www.frenchrivierapass.com) Admission to all of Nice's paying attractions, plus many nearby.

Snowball Pass (www.snowballpass.com) Skiing discounts.

Electricity

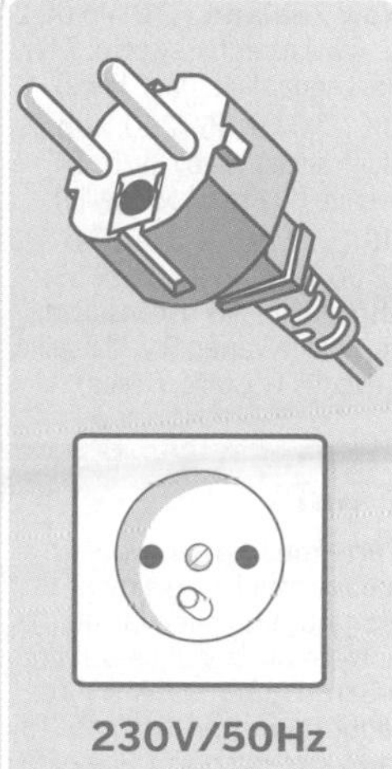

Embassies & Consulates

All foreign embassies are in Paris.

To find consulates or embassies, see www.embassiesabroad.com or look up '*ambassade*' in user-friendly *Pages Jaunes* (Yellow Pages; www.pagesjaunes.fr).

Australia (☎01 40 59 33 00; www.france.embassy.gov.au; 4 rue Jean Rey, Paris)

Germany (☎04 91 16 75 20; www.marseille.diplo.de; 338 avenue du Prado, Marseille)

BOOK YOUR STAY ONLINE

For more accommodation reviews by Lonely Planet authors, check out http://hotels.lonelyplanet.com. You'll find independent reviews, as well as recommendations on the best places to stay. Best of all, you can book online.

Ireland (☎(377) 9315 7045; www.dfa.ie; avenue des Citronniers, Monaco)

Netherlands (☎Marseille 04 91 25 66 64, Nice 04 93 87 52 94; www.amb-pays-bas.fr; 146 rue Paradis, Marseille, 14 rue Rossini, Nice)

New Zealand (☎01 45 00 24 11; www.nzembassy.com; 7 ter, rue Leonard de Vinci, Paris)

UK (☎04 91 15 72 10; http://ukinfrance.fco.gov.uk/fr; 24 avenue du Prado, Marseille)

US (☎Marseille 04 91 54 92 00, Nice 04 93 88 89 55; http://marseille.usconsulate.gov; place Varian Fry, Marseille, 7 avenue Gustave V, Nice)

Food

Carte means menu; *menu* means multicourse meal (sometimes called *formule*). Entrées are appetisers, *plats* are mains. Tap water is free: request *une carafe d'eau* (say, 'ewn kah-*raff* doh'). See p290 for details on tipping. See also Provençal Food & Wine, p280.

Gay & Lesbian Travellers

France is liberal about sexual mores. Provence isn't closeted, but it's conservative. Aix-en-Provence, Nice and Cannes have bars, while Marseille has the biggest gay community and hosts the late-June **Lesbian & Gay Parade** (www.lgpmarseille.fr).

Centre Évolutif Lilith (CEL; ☎06 99 55 06 02; http://celmrs.free.fr; 93 La Canebière) Lesbian socialising, activism.

Gay Map Marseille (www.gaymapmarseille.com) Entertainment, Aix and Marseille

Gay.Provence (☎04 91 84 08 96; www.gay-provence.org) Hotel listings.

FOOD PRICE RANGES

The following prices refer to two-course *menus* – appetiser and main, or main and dessert.

€	under €20
€€	€20 to €40
€€€	more than €40

Health

Before You Go

» Carry medications in original, clearly labelled, containers in carry-on luggage.

» Dental care in France is good; get a pre-departure check-up to minimise risk.

» No vaccinations are required for France, but the World Health Organization recommends travellers be vaccinated against diphtheria, tetanus, measles, mumps, rubella and polio, regardless of destination.

» French tap water is safe to drink, but water from fountains reading '*eau non potable*' is not.

Availability & Cost of Healthcare

» For emergencies, dial ☎15 for ambulance (SAMU) or urgent house call. Or find the nearest *hôpital* or *salles des urgence*. Doctor's offices are *cabinets médicals*.

» For medical referrals and minor illnesses, pharmacists dispense advice and sell medications; look for green neon crosses.

» Doctor visits cost about €25.

» Emergency contraception is available by prescription. Condoms are (*préservatifs*) commonly available.

Insurance

Medical Insurance

EU citizens and those from Switzerland, Iceland, Norway and Liechtenstein are covered for emergencies by the European Health Insurance Card (EHIC), but not for non-emergencies or repatriation. Every family member needs a card. In the UK, applications available from post offices or the Department of Health (www.dh.gov.uk). Seek care from state providers (*conventionnés*); private healthcare is not covered. Pay directly and keep receipts for reimbursement.

Non-Europeans need to determine if your country has reciprocity with France for free medical care. If you need health insurance, strongly consider a policy that covers worst-case scenarios, including emergency medical evacuation. Determine in advance if your insurance pays directly for overseas expenditures, or reimburses you later (it's probably the latter). Keep all documentation.

Travel Insurance

We recommend travel insurance covering theft, loss and medical problems. Some policies exclude dangerous activities, including diving, motorcycling and mountaineering. Read the fine print.

Worldwide travel insurance is available at www.lonelyplanet.com/travel_services. You can buy, extend and claim online, even if you're already on the road.

Purchasing airline tickets with a credit card may provide *limited* travel-accident insurance. Ask your credit-card company.

Internet Access

» Airports have wi-fi, as do hotels, many cafes and some tourist offices.

» In remote valleys of Haute-Provence, it's hard to get online.

» To find wi-fi access, check France-specific www.journaldunet.com/wifi.

» Internet cafes cost €4 to €6 per hour; see On the Road chapters for some locations.

» To access dial-up ISPs via laptop, find telephone plug adaptors at supermarkets.

Language Courses

The government site www.diplomatie.gouv.fr (under 'Francophony') and www.europa-pages.com/france list language schools.

Prices vary greatly. Content can be tailored (for a fee) to your specific needs.

Centre Méditerranéen d'Études Françaises (☎04 93 78 21 59; www.centremed.monte-carlo.mc; chemin des Oliviers, Cap d'Ail) Côte d'Azur language school since 1952.

Legal Matters

» French police have wide powers of search and seizure, and may demand identification at any time, regardless of 'probable cause'.

» Foreigners must be able to prove immigration status (eg passport, visa, residency permit).

» Verbally (or physically) abusing police officers carries hefty fines, even imprisonment.

» You may refuse to sign a police statement, and have the right to request a copy.

» The arrested are innocent until proven guilty, but may be held until trial. The website www.service-public.fr details rights.

» French police are ultrastrict with security. Never leave baggage unattended at airports or stations: suspicious objects may be destroyed.

» French law makes no distinction between 'hard' and 'soft' drugs.

» Penalties for personal use of *stupéfiants* (narcotics; including cannabis) can be a one-year jail sentence and €3750 fine, but may be lessened to a stern talking-to or compulsory rehab.

» Public drunkenness is punishable by a €150 fine. It's illegal to drive with a blood-alcohol concentration (BAC) over 0.05%. Police conduct random breathalyser tests.

» Smoking is illegal in public interiors, including bars and restaurants.

Maps

City Maps

Find maps at *maisons de la presse* (newsagencies), *papeteries* (stationery shops), tourist offices and bookshops. Quality maps cost about €7. The website http://fr.mappy.com has online maps and a journey planner, including tolls and petrol costs.

Free street *plans* (maps) distributed by tourist offices range from superb to useless. Marseille's tourist office has good free city maps, but note the compass rose: north is not at the top of the page.

Blay (www.blayfoldex.com) City-map publishers.

FFRP (www.ffrandonnee.fr) Topographic hiking maps.

Institut Géographique National (IGN; www.ign.fr) Definitive map publishers.

Michelin (sales www.michelin-boutique.com) Brilliant atlases and driving maps.

Driving Maps

Cartographers **Michelin** (http://boutiquecartesetguides.michelin.fr) and **Institut Géographique National** (IGN; www.ign.fr) have online boutiques.

Walking & Cycling Maps

Fédération Française de Randonnée Pédestre (FFRP; French Walking Federation; www.ffrandonnee.fr) publishes detailed French-language topo guides – trail booklets of major routes (eg GRs) with topographic maps.

Several local walking organisations also produce detailed topographic trail guides; ask tourist offices and bookshops.

IGN (IGN; www.ign.fr) publishes brilliant topographical guides and outdoor-sports maps. It also has good mobile apps, though paper is better for serious hiking.

Guides RandOxygène (www.randoxygene.org) is an excellent resource for hiking, mountain-biking, snowshoeing and canyoning, with maps and text; in French.

Money

The euro (€) is the only legal tender in France and Monaco. To track rates and find local exchange bureaux, see http://travelmoney.moneysavingexpert.com.

PRACTICALITIES

» France uses the metric system. To convert kilometres to miles, multiply by 0.6; miles to kilometres, multiply by 1.6.

» Regional news and chat air in English on Monte Carlo–based Riviera Radio (www.rivieraradio.mc).

» French-language regional newspapers are *Nice Matin* (www.nicematin.fr) and *La Provence* (www.laprovence.com).

» English-language regional newspapers are *Riviera Reporter* (www.riviera-reporter.com) and *Riviera Times* (www.rivieratimes.com).

» French TV networks broadcast a second audio program in the program's original language, often English: fiddle with your remote.

ATMs

ATMs (*distributeurs automatiques de billets* or *points d'argent*) are the easiest means of obtaining cash, but banks charge foreign-transaction fees (usually 2% to 3%), plus a per-use ATM charge. Check with your bank. Cirrus and Maestro networks are common.

Credit & Debit Cards

» Notify banks before leaving so they don't freeze your credit cards when foreign charges start posting to your account.

» To avoid fees, investigate prepaid currency cards. Apply before departure, then load with euros. If lost, you pay only €10 and don't lose the funds.

» French credit cards have embedded chips and require a PIN for all transactions.

» North American cards with magnetic stripes don't work on (certain) autoroutes or at unattended 24-hour petrol stations.

» Visa (Carte Bleue – or CB – in France) and MasterCard (Access or Eurocard) are common. American Express less so, but Amex offices provide exchange and travel services.

» Don't assume restaurants take credit cards. Ask first.

Money Changers

» Banks usually charge stiff €3 to €5 fees per foreign-currency transaction – if they change money at all.

» *Bureaux de change* (exchange bureaux) are faster and easier, open longer, and usually have better rates.

» Some post-offices exchange travellers cheques and banknotes, but charge €5 commission for cash; most won't take US$100 bills.

Tipping

By law, restaurants and cafes are *service compris* (15% service included), thus no need to leave a *pourboire* (tip). If you're satisfied with the meal service, it's customary to leave a euro or two on the table.

Bar Round to nearest euro

Hotel housekeepers €1 to €1.50 per day

Porters €1 to €1.50 per bag

Restaurants Generally 2% to 5%; 10% if exceptional

Taxi 10% to 15%

Toilet attendant €0.20 to €0.50

Tour guide €1 to €2 per person

Travellers Cheques

Secure and fee-free, but not widely accepted. Must be converted at exchange bureaux, and rates aren't always favourable.

Public Holidays

French Public Holidays

The following *jours fériés* (public holidays) are observed in France:

New Year's Day (Jour de l'An) 1 January

Easter Sunday & Monday (Pâques & lundi de Pâques) Late March/April

May Day (Fête du Travail) 1 May

Victoire 1945 8 May – celebrates the Allied victory that ended WWII

Ascension Thursday (L'Ascension) May – the 40th day after Easter

Pentecost/Whit Sunday & Whit Monday (Pentecôte & lundi de Pentecôte) Mid-May to mid-June – celebrated seventh Sunday after Easter

Bastille Day/National Day (Fête Nationale) 14 July

Assumption Day (L'Assomption) 15 August

All Saints' Day (La Toussaint) 1 November

Remembrance Day (L'onze Novembre) 11 November – marks WWI armistice

Christmas (Noël) 25 December

Monégasque Public Holidays

Monaco shares the same holidays, except 8 May, 14 July, 11 November. Additionally:

Feast of Ste-Dévote 27 January – Monaco's saint

Corpus Christi June – three weeks after Ascension

National Day (Fête Nationale) 19 November

Immaculate Conception 8 December

Safe Travel

France is a safe destination. Property crimes are a problem, but assault is rare.

France's hunting season runs September to February. Warning signs on trees and fences read '*chasseurs*' or '*chasse gardée*'. Wear bright colours when hiking.

Beaches & Rivers

» Watch for pale-purple jellyfish (stingers) on beaches.

» Major rivers are connected to hydroelectric stations, and flood suddenly when dams open. Ask tourism offices about *l'ouverture des barrages* – commonplace in summer.

» Swimming is prohibited in reservoirs with unstable banks (ie Lac de Ste-Croix, southwest of Gorges du Verdon; Lac de Castillon; and Lac de Chaudanne, northeast of the gorges). Sailing, windsurfing and canoeing are restricted to flagged areas.

Extreme Weather

» Thunderstorms – sometimes violent and dangerous – are commonplace August and September.

» Check weather (*la météo*) before embarking on hikes.

» Carry pocket rain gear and extra layers to prevent hypothermia.

» Year-round, mistral winds can be maddening.

Forest Fires

» For fire emergency, dial 18. Forest fires are common July and August, and spread incredibly fast. July to mid-September, high-risk trails close. Never walk in closed zones. Tourist offices have current information.

» Forests are criss-crossed by fire roads. Signposted DFCI (forest-fire defence team) tracks are closed to motorists, but open to walkers.

» Campfires are forbidden. Barbecues are forbidden in many areas in July and August.

Poisonous Mushrooms

Never eat wild mushrooms until they've been deemed safe by a professional – local pharmacies provide mushroom-identification services.

Theft

» Theft from luggage, pockets, cars, trains and laundrettes is widespread, particularly along the Côte d'Azur. Keep close watch on bags, especially at tourist offices, train and bus stations, outdoor cafes, beaches and overnight train rides (lock your compartment door).

» Leave nothing in parked cars. Carry cash in front pockets or money belt. Beware of pickpockets in crowded tourist areas.

» Common cons: thief finds a gold ring in your path, or lays a newspaper on your restaurant table, or approaches to ask if you speak English. Ignore children with clipboards, especially those playing deaf.

» Don't stare at your smartphone in train stations; conceal it when not using it.

» Lock your passport in the hotel's safe. Carry the passport number (or photocopy) and your driving licence for ID.

» When swimming, take turns sitting with personal effects. On the Prado beaches in Marseille, consider placing valuables in one of the free (staffed) lockers.

» Aggressive theft from cars stopped at red lights is an occasional problem in Marseille, Nice and larger cities; keep doors locked and windows up when idling.

Telephone

Mobile Phones

» French mobile-phone numbers begin with 06 or 07.

» France uses GSM 900/1800, compatible with Europe and Australia, but incompatible with North American GSM 1900 or the Japanese system.

» It's cheaper to buy a French SIM card and prepaid calling plan if you already have a compatible handset, or to buy a temporary phone if you're from North America or Japan, than to use your home plan overseas.

» Unless you have a French bank account for ongoing billing, prepaid calling plans within France are expensive – about €0.50 a call. Texting costs less.

» Buy your phone when you land in Paris, where more salespeople speak English than in Provence.

» SIM cards and phones are available at France's three principal companies: Bouygues (www.bouyguestelecom.fr), Orange (www.orange.fr) and SFR (www.sfr.com).

» Buy recharge cards at newsagents and *tabacs*.

Dialing Codes

» **Calling France (or Monaco) from home** Dial your country's international-access code, then 33 for France (or 377 for Monaco), then the 10-digit number, without the initial zero.

» **Calling abroad from France** Dial 00 for international access, then country code (1 for US, 44 UK, 16 Australia), then area code and local number, minus any initial zeros.

» **Hotel calls** Very expensive and unregulated, usually €0.30 per minute locally.

Phonecards & Payphones

» For instructions on using public phones, push the button engraved with dual flags.

» Public phones accept two kinds of *télécartes* (phonecards) – *cartes à la puce* (magnetic-chip cards), issued by France Télécom for €8 or €15, and *cartes à code* (cards with free access number and prepaid scratch-off code). Find cards at post offices, *tabacs* and newsagents.

» Phonecards with codes have cheaper rates than France Télécom or Country Direct service (which appears on your home bill).

Useful Numbers & Codes

See also p15 for emergency numbers. Free from pay phones.

Directory enquiries 12 or 11 87 12 (€1, plus €0.23 per minute). Not all operators speak English. For help in English with all France Telecom's services, see www.francetelecom.com or call 09 69 36 39 00.

France country code 33

International access code 00

International directory enquiries 118 700

Monaco country code 377

Time

France uses the 24-hour military clock (eg 20.00 is 8pm) and Central European time, one hour ahead of GMT/UTC. During daylight savings (last Sunday in March to last Sunday in

October), France is two hours ahead of GMT/UTC.

Toilets

» Public toilets are signposted *toilettes* or WC. In towns, look for public toilets near the town hall, port, public squares or parking areas.

» Mechanical, coin-operated toilets are free or €0.20. (Never dodge in after the previous user or you'll be doused with disinfectant!) If you exceed 15 minutes, the door automatically opens. Green means *libre* (available); red *occupé* (busy).

» Some older cafes and petrol stations still have hole-in-the-floor Turkish toilets. Provided you hover, they're hygienic, but stand clear when flushing!

» The French are used to unisex facilities.

Tourist Information

Almost every city, town and village has an *office de tourisme* (tourist office run by some unit of local government) or *syndicat d'initiative* (tourist office run by local merchant groups). Both are excellent resources and can provide local maps and accommodation information.

Travellers with Disabilities

France is fast improving its accommodation of the *handicapés* (disabled), but lags behind the standard-setting USA. Footpaths are narrow, streets cobbled, and curb ramps rare. Older public facilities and budget hotels lack lifts. Steep hilltop villages are nightmares for *fauteuil roulant* (wheelchair) navigation.

Ask pointed questions of hoteliers, tourism authorities and restaurateurs. Some two- and many three-star hotels are equipped with lifts, but ensure there are no steps (*aucunes marches*) leading to them. Restaurant bathrooms are often downstairs.

Parking areas have dedicated spots (bring your handicap parking placard). Some beaches are wheelchair-accessible – flagged *handiplages* on city maps – in Cannes, Marseille, Nice, Hyères, Ste-Maxime and Monaco.

Michelin's *Guide Rouge* indicates hotels with lifts and handicap rooms, and **Gîtes de France** (www.gites-de-france-paca.com) provides lists of wheelchair-accessible *gîtes ruraux* and *chambres d'hôte.*

International airports provide wheelchairs by advance arrangement with airlines, but expect to wait (be pushy, if necessary). Trains are wheelchair-accessible; call the **SNCF Accessibilité Service** (☎08 90 64 06 50; www.accessibilite.sncf.com) for information.

Visas

» For up-to-date information on visa requirements see www.diplomatie.gouv.fr.

» EU nationals and citizens of Iceland, Norway and Switzerland need only their passport or national identity card to enter France and work. However, nationals of the 12 countries that joined the EU in 2004 and 2007 are subject to residency and work limitations.

» Citizens of Australia, Canada, Israel, Hong Kong, Japan, Malaysia, New Zealand, Singapore, USA and many Latin American countries need no tourist visa for stays shorter than 90 days.

» Others must apply for a Schengen visa, allowing unlimited travel throughout 26 European countries for a 90-day period. Apply at the consulate of the country that's your first port of entry, or that which will be your principal destination. Among other particulars, you must provide proof of travel and repatriation insurance, and prove you have sufficient money to support yourself.

» Tourist visas *cannot* be extended, except in emergencies (such as medical problems). Leave before your visa expires and reapply from outside France.

Women Travellers

Some French men have given little thought to *harcèlement sexuel* (sexual harassment). Many believe staring at passing ladies is paying a compliment. Suave stares, maybe a whistle, are about as adventurous as most French men get. Women are rarely physically assaulted on streets, or touched in bars.

Rural Provence isn't problematic, but in the dizzying heat of summer, the Côte d'Azur draws people from all over the world, many looking for hook-ups, some totally disrespectful of women. Apply usual common sense when it comes to your safety: remain conscious of your surroundings, avoid entering bars and clubs alone at night, never leave drinks unattended and beware of potentially dangerous surrounds – deserted streets, lonely beaches, dark corners in large stations, night buses in certain districts of Marseille and Nice, and strangers' yachts (seriously).

Topless sunbathing is generally not an issue.

SOS Viol (www.sosviol.com) staffs the national **rape-crisis hotline** (☎08 00 05 95 95) – spearheaded by **SOS Femmes** (www.sosfemmes.com) – and provides online contacts for local services.

Transport

GETTING THERE & AWAY

Since European integration, no checkpoints exist between France and EU countries. The border (*la douane*) now officially roves: you may be asked by border-patrol agents anywhere in France to show papers. Arriving from non-EU countries, you'll need a valid passport (and visa, if applicable) to clear customs. EU citizens need only their identification cards. Flights, cars and tours can be booked online at lonelyplanet.com/bookings.

Air

Tickets are cheapest early spring and late autumn. International departure taxes are included in ticket prices.

Several no-frills airlines (easyJet, Flybe, jet2.com and Ryanair) serve Avignon, Marseille, Nice, Nîmes and Toulon from European destinations.

Airports

Provence has two major airports: Marseille-Provence and Nice Côte d'Azur. Additionally, Avignon-Caumont, Nîmes-Garons and Toulon-Hyères serve limited international destinations.

» **Avignon-Caumont** (☎04 90 81 51 51; www.avignon.aeroport.fr), 8km southeast of Avignon. Flybe and jet2.com seasonally serve UK destinations – Southampton and Exeter, May to September; Birmingham and London City July and August. Check website for other destinations via connection (*vols en correspondance*).

» **Marseille-Provence** (www.marseille.aeroport.fr), 25km northeast of Marseille. Year-round flights between France, Europe, North Africa, Middle East and Canada.

» **Nice-Côte d'Azur** (NCE; ☎08 20 42 33 33; www.nice.aeroport.fr; wifi), 6km west of Nice. Year-round flights to 29 international and 30 French destinations, including many in the UK and Ireland. Daily service to most European cities, plus North Africa, Middle East, New York and Québec.

» **Nîmes-Garons** (☎04 66 70 49 49; www.nimes-aeroport.fr), 15km south of Nîmes, served by Ryanair. London, Liverpool, Brussels and Rome.

» **Toulon-Hyères** (www.toulon-hyeres.aeroport.fr), 25km east of Toulon, serves 10 European cities, some seasonally. Daily flights to Paris (Air France), seasonally to the UK (Ryanair).

Land

Bicycle

European Bike Express (☎(+44) 01430-422 111; www.bike-express.co.uk) transports cyclists and bikes from UK to destinations across France.

Bus

Eurolines (☎08 92 89 90 91; www.eurolines.com) is Europe's largest international bus network, linking Provençal cities such as Nice, Marseille and Avignon, with the rest of Europe. Buses operate

CLIMATE CHANGE & TRAVEL

Every form of transport that relies on carbon-based fuel generates CO_2, the main cause of human-induced climate change. Modern travel is dependent on aeroplanes, which might use less fuel per kilometre per person than most cars but travel much greater distances. The altitude at which aircraft emit gases (including CO_2) and particles also contributes to their climate change impact. Many websites offer 'carbon calculators' that allow people to estimate the carbon emissions generated by their journey and, for those who wish to do so, to offset the impact of the greenhouse gases emitted with contributions to portfolios of climate-friendly initiatives throughout the world. Lonely Planet offsets the carbon footprint of all staff and author travel.

daily in summer, several times a week in winter; advance tickets are required. **Eurolines Pass** (15-/30-day high-season pass €350/460, under 26 €295/380, cheaper mid-Sep-Jun) allows unlimited travel between 51 cities.

Linebùs (☎Avignon 04 90 86 88 67, Barcelona 932 65 07 00, Nîmes 04 66 29 50 62; www.linebus.com) links Avignon (€45, 6½ hours) and Nîmes (€41, 6¼ hours) with Barcelona. Children under 12 discounted 50%.

From within France, it's easiest to reach Provence by train.

Car & Motorcycle

From Paris, consider riding the TGV to Avignon, then picking up a rental car; this shaves four hours off travel time to Provence and spares you urban traffic.

Between the UK and France, high-speed auto-trains by **Eurotunnel** (☎France 08 10 63 03 04, UK 08 443 35 35 35; www.eurotunnel.com) shuttle through the Channel Tunnel between Folkestone and Coquelles (35 minutes, 24 hours, up to four hourly), 5km southwest of Calais. High-season return for car and passengers around £200; for motorcycle and rider, around £80. There are numerous online promotional fares. Advance reservations are required for discounted fares. Note: LPG and CNG tanks are not permitted, and campers and caravans must take ferries.

BRINGING YOUR OWN VEHICLE

To bring your own vehicle, you'll need registration papers, unlimited third-party (liability) insurance and a valid driving licence. In the UK, contact **RAC** (☎08705 722 722; www.rac.co.uk) or **AA** (☎0870 600 0371; www.theaa.com) for advice. In other countries, contact your local automobile association.

Vehicles entering France must display a sticker identifying country of registration. Right-hand-drive vehicles from UK or Ireland must have headlight deflectors to correct the beam's angle, and not blind oncoming traffic. A reflective breakdown triangle and emergency vest must be carried in your car.

DRIVING LICENCE & DOCUMENTATION

All drivers must carry national ID card or passport; valid driving licence (*permis de conduire;* most foreign licences can be used for up to one year); car-ownership papers, called *carte grise* (grey card); and proof of third-party (liability) insurance. If you're stopped by police and lack documents, you risk on-the-spot fines.

Train

Thomas Cook's *European Rail Timetable* (€15), available at Thomas Cook offices and online (www.thomascookpublishing.com), lists train schedules.

The website **The Man in Seat 61** (www.seat61.com) lists timetables and excellent tips.

Rail Europe (☎in Canada 1 800 361 7245, in the UK 0844 848 5848, in the USA 1 800 622 8600; www.raileurope.com) provides good telephone assistance in North America, ideal for first-timers who want help booking.

FROM THE REST OF FRANCE

You can set your watch by France's ultra-efficient trains, operated by state-owned **Société Nationale des Chemins de Fer Français** (SNCF; www.sncf.com) – but its telephone customer service is not effective and it charges you by the minute. Best to book online, or queue patiently at stations or in-town SNCF ticket centres (*boutiques*). SNCF has confusing online sites: the easiest for timetables, fares and reservations is www.voyages-sncf.com.

SNCF's flagship trains are high-speed **Train à Grande Vitesse** (TGV; www.tgv.com). Avignon and Aix-en-Provence have out-of-town TGV stations, distant from city-centre stations served by regional lines.

Sample 1st-/2nd-class single TGV fares between Paris and Provence: Avignon (€145/80, three hours), Marseille (€155/88, 3½ hours), Nice (€180/100, 5½ hours) and Orange (€145/80, 3¼ hours).

SNCF also operates cheaper, slower services. Both *grande ligne* (main line) and **Transport Express Régional** (TER; www.ter-sncf.com) link smaller cities to the TGV network.

Marseille's airport station (Vitrolles) links the airport with regional cities, including Avignon (€16, one hour).

Many towns not on the SNCF network are linked to railheads by buses.

For discounts, see p299.

WITH BICYCLE

Bicycles can be transported as hand luggage when packed into 120cm x 90cm transit bags (available at bike shops). On some main-line trains, flagged with bicycle symbols on timetables, bikes are allowed in luggage vans without being packed down (but not during peak times). On night trains and certain TGVs, bikes can only be transported in a four-bicycle wagon, reserved in advance (€10). See the multilingual SNCF brochure *Guide Train & Vélo* (free), available at stations, or www.velo.sncf.com (in French).

Bagages à domicile (☎3635, then say 'bagages' 41) transports bicycles door-to-door in France, for €80, delivering within 48 hours, excluding Saturday afternoon, Sunday and holidays.

WITH CAR

Motorail AutoTrains carry cars and passengers. Cars are loaded one hour before departure, and unloaded 30 minutes after arrival. Services from Calais to Nice run late May to mid-September, stopping at Avignon and Fréjus (rest of year, cars can be transported via AutoTrain, but you travel separately; see http://autotrain.voyages-sncf.com). Information in the UK available from **Rail Europe** (in Canada 1 800 361 7245, in the UK 0844 848 5848, in the USA 1 800 622 8600; www.raileurope.com). In France, ticketing is handled by SNCF.

FROM ITALY & SPAIN

Nice is the major rail hub, along the busy Barcelona–Rome line.

» Nice–Rome (1st/2nd class around €120/65, plus about €30 for a couchette, nine hours)

» Nice–Barcelona (around €150/110, 10 hours)

Nice–Milan (around €45/30, five hours)

FROM UK

Highly civilised **Eurostar** (in France 08 92 35 35 39, in UK 08432 186 186; www.eurostar.com) whisks between London and Paris in 2¼ hours. Direct seasonal service to Avignon from the UK operates Saturdays, July to early September, from London (six hours) and Ashford (five hours). Otherwise, consider changing trains in Lille, before heading south to Provence, which eliminates the schlep across Paris city centre from Gare du Nord to Gare du Lyon.

Eurostar fares vary hugely. Standard 2nd-class one-way ticket from London to Paris costs £179; from Paris, standard fare to London is €245. But deals cost as little as £79.

Find the best deals by booking non-flexible, return journeys with Saturday-night stayover. Book seven to 14 days ahead – for the best fares, 120 days ahead. Student travel agencies may have youth fares not available from Eurostar.

Discounts are available for Eurail pass holders and people over 60 and under 26 (on day of travel, not booking).

Sea

Giant ferries cross from Nice, Marseille and Toulon to Corsica (France), Sardinia (Italy) and North Africa. Vehicles are allowed; reservations are essential.

From the Rest of France

Ferries from Corsica to Provençal ports are operated by the following companies.

Corsica Ferries (04 95 32 95 95; www.corsicaferries.com) Year-round; Nice and Toulon to Ajaccio, Bastia, Calvi and Île Rousse.

La Méridionale (08 10 20 13 20; www.lameridionale.fr) SNCM subsidiary; year-round between Marseille and Ajaccio, Bastia and Propriano.

SNCM (08 91 70 18 01; www.sncm.fr; 61 bd des Dames; M Joliette) Corsica, Sardinia, Algeria and Tunisia.

From Italy

SNCM runs multiple car ferries weekly, from Marseille to Sardinia (Sardaigne, in French). Sailing time 17 hours. High-season, one-way passage, including tax, costs around €100/120 for armchair/cabin berth. Discounts for passengers under 25 and over 60. Transporting cars costs an extra €110.

Tickets and information available in Provence from SNCM offices. In Sardinia, tickets are sold by SNCM agent **Paglietti Petertours** (079-51 44 77; Corso Vittorio Emanuele 19) in Porto Torres.

From North Africa

Warning: Travel to Algeria is extremely dangerous for foreign tourists. Check your home government's travel advisories.

Algérie Ferries (www.algerieferries.com) and SNCM operate between Marseille and Algiers (from €166, 20 hours).

FERRY SERVICES

COMPANY	ROUTE	WEBSITE
Brittany Ferries	England–Normandy & Brittany, Ireland–Brittany	www.brittany-ferries.co.uk, www.brittanyferries.ie
Celtic Link Ferries	Ireland–Normandy	www.celticlinkferries.com
Condor Ferries	England–Normandy & Brittany, Channel Islands–Brittany	www.condorferries.com
Irish Ferries	Ireland–Normandy & Brittany	www.irishferries.ie, www.shamrock-irlande.com
LD Lines	England–Channel Ports, England–Normandy	www.ldlines.co.uk
Manche Îles Express	Channel Islands–Normandy	www.manches-iles-express.com
Norfolk Line	England–Channel Ports	www.norfolkline.com
P&O Ferries	England–Channel Ports	www.poferries.com

SNCM and Tunisian **CTN** (Compagnie Tunisienne de Navigation; ☎216-135 33 31; www.ctn.com.tn; 122 rue de Yougoslavie, Tunis) operate year-round between Marseille and Tunisia (from €186, 20 to 22 hours).

From UK & Ireland

There are no direct ferries to Provence, but year-round ferries connect the UK and France. Dover to Calais is shortest. Fares fluctuate wildly. Advance purchase is advised.

Foot passengers aren't permitted on Dover–Dunkerque car ferries. On Dover–Calais P&O ferries, foot passengers are permitted only during daytime crossings (and, from Calais to Dover, in the evening); confirm foot-passenger restrictions before purchase. On ferries allowing foot passengers, bicycles are often (but not always) free.

Other ferry routes: Newhaven to Dieppe, Poole to Cherbourg and St-Malo, Portsmouth to Caen/Cherbourg/Le Havre/St-Malo, and Weymouth to St-Malo.

Ferries also connect southern Ireland (Cork and Rosslare) and northern France.

For competitive fares, consider **Ferry Savers** (☎0844-371 8021; www.ferrysavers.co.uk); phone bookings incur fees.

GETTING AROUND

Bicycle

Provence – particularly the Luberon – is eminently cyclable, with back roads lightly travelled. The coast has good cycling paths, but has serious crowds in summer. July and August get blazingly hot. Cycling in national parks is forbidden.

By law, bicycles must have two functioning brakes, bell, red reflector on back, yellow reflectors on pedals. After sunset, and when visibility poor, cyclists must illuminate with a white light in front and red light in rear. Cyclists must ride single file when being overtaken by vehicles or other cyclists.

Most towns have bike-rental outlets; daily cost is around €18.

Useful resource: **Fédération Française de Cyclisme** (☎01 49 35 69 00; www.ffc.fr).

Boat

Canal Boat

Canals connect the Atlantic and Mediterranean and criss-cross France. Canal du Midi – France's most popular, packed in summer – stretches 240km east from Toulouse toward the Camargue and the Canal du Rhône. West of Toulouse, the Canal du Midi connects with the Gardonne River, leading west to the Atlantic Ocean at Bordeaux. It's hard to beat seeing the Rhône or Camargue by boat.

Houseboats and barges accommodate two to 12, and come fully outfitted. Anyone over 18 can pilot, but first-timers must undergo brief training to obtain a temporary pleasure-craft permit (*carte de plaisance*). Speed limit: 6km/h in canals, 10km/h on rivers.

Prices range from €450 to over €3000 weekly. Except for July and August, you can sometimes rent for a weekend, or from Monday to Friday. Advance reservations are essential for holiday periods, long weekends and summertime.

Online rental agencies:

Canal Boat Holidays (www. canalboatholidays.com)

H2olidays (Barging in France; www.barginginfrance.com)

Le Boat (☎in France 04 68 94 42 80, in the UK 0844 463 3594; www.leboat.net) Specifically for Camargue and Rhône.

Rive de France (☎04 67 37 14 60; www.rive-de-france.tm.fr)

Worldwide River Cruise (ww.worldwide-river-cruise.com)

Ferry

Ferries connect coastal communities and offshore islands, notably to/from St-Tropez and St-Raphaël, Port Grimaud and Ste-Maxime in warmer months (generally April to October).

Yacht

One of Europe's largest *ports de plaisance* (pleasure ports) is Port Vauban, Antibes.

Yachts – with or without crew – can be hired at most marinas, including sailing centres at Ste-Maxime and Le Lavandou. For a list of yacht harbours: www.cotedazur-tourisme.com.

For up-to-date marina or harbour-master information, contact **Fédération Française des Ports de Plaisance** (FFPP; ☎01 43 35 26 26; www.ffports-plaisance.com).

Bus

Services and routes are extremely limited in rural areas, where buses primarily transport school children. Bus transport is useful only if you have no car, and the trains don't go where you want, but you may get stuck until the next day. Read schedules carefully. Tourist offices always have schedules.

Autocars (regional buses) are operated by multiple companies, which have offices at *gares routières* (bus stations) in larger towns. One company usually sells tickets for all buses departing from that station.

Car & Motorcycle

Your own vehicle is essential for exploring Provence's smaller towns, many inaccessible by public transport.

Autumn through spring, driving is easy along the Côte d'Azur, but *not* in July and August, when intense traffic chokes all roads and it takes

INTERPRETING SCHEDULES

Transport schedules use abbreviations. The most common:

tlj (tous les jours) daily

sauf except

lun Monday

mar Tuesday

mer Wednesday

jeu Thursday

ven Friday

sam Saturday

dim Sunday

jours fériés holidays

hours to go a few kilometres. For English-language traffic reports, tune to 107.7MHz FM, which updates every 30 minutes in summer.

There are four types of intercity roads, each with alphanumeric designation:

» **Autoroutes** (eg A8) High-speed multi-lane highways with *péages* (tolls)

» **Routes Nationales** (N, RN) National highways

» **Routes Départementales** (D) County roads

» **Routes Communales** (C, V) Tertiary routes

Autoroutes are always fastest (summer traffic notwithstanding), but they're expensive – Marseille to Nice costs €18 in tolls, Paris to Nice €70.

Pay close attention at toll booths: 'CB' (Carte Bleue) indicates credit-card lanes; yellow arrows are exclusively for prepaid drivers; green arrows for cash. If you choose the wrong lane, you'll have to back up – nearly impossible during the summertime.

Traffic information: **Association des Sociétés Françaises d'Autoroutes** (www.autoroutes.fr).

Calculate toll and fuel costs at www.viamichelin.com and www.mappy.fr.

Fuel & Spare Parts

Essence (petrol or gasoline), also called *carburant* (fuel), costs roughly €1.65 a litre, or €1.40 a litre for diesel. *Autoroute* service areas (*aires*) are priciest, but open 24 hours; hypermarkets are cheapest.

Unleaded (*sans plomb*) pump handles are usually green; diesel (*diesel, gazoil* or *gazole*) pumps are yellow.

Many service stations close Saturday afternoon and Sunday, and in small towns during lunch.

Some petrol pumps dispense fuel after-hours, but *only* with chip-and-pin credit cards.

North American credit cards (ie magnetic stripe instead of chip-and-pin) do *not* work at 24-hour pumps. To purchase fuel at night with magnetic-stripe cards, take the *autoroute* or fill up by day.

When travelling mountain regions, keep the tank full.

If your car is *en panne* (broken down), you'll need services for your particular *marque* (make). Peugeot, Renault and Citroën garages are common, but you may have trouble in remote areas finding mechanics to service foreign cars.

Hire

Rentals sell out at peak periods: make advance reservations.

Most companies require drivers be at least 21, have had a driving licence at least one year, and pay with an international credit card (not debit – though debit cards are sometimes allowed if you're willing to pay hefty deposits or purchase zero-deductible insurance). Drivers under 25 usually pay €30 extra daily.

Confirm you understand what's included – insurances, roadside assistance, tax, *kilométrage limité* or *illimité* (limited or unlimited mileage) etc. You may be required to leave a signed, blank credit-card slip as *caution* (deposit). Ensure it's destroyed upon return.

Arranging car hire or fly/drive packages before leaving home means lower-priced options (some only available when purchased overseas), but beware website offers that don't include insurances, lest you double your cost or (worse) be liable for cost of replacing car in the event of an accident.

Automatic transmission rare – reserve well ahead.

All rental cars registered in France have distinctive licence plates, making them instantly identifiable – including to thieves. Never leave anything significant in the car when parked, even in the boot (trunk).

ADA (☎08 25 16 91 69; www.ada.fr)

Auto Europe (☎1 888 223 5555, from France 800 223 55 555; www.autoeurope.com) US-based online hire company

Avis (☎08 20 05 05 05; www.avis.com)

Budget (☎08 25 00 35 64; www.budget.com)

Easycar (☎in France 08 26 10 73 23, in the UK 08710 500 444; www.easycar.com)

Europcar (☎08 25 35 83 58; www.europcar.com)

Hertz (☎08 25 09 13 13; www.hertz.com)

Holiday Autos (☎0871 472 5229; www.holidayautos.co.uk) UK-based online hire company.

National-Citer (☎08 25 16 12 20; www.citer.fr)

Purchase-Repurchase Plans

If you live outside the EU and will be in France (or Europe) from one to six months (up to one year, if studying), by far the cheapest option is to 'purchase' a brand-new car, then 'sell' it back – called *achat-rachat*. You only pay for the time it's in your possession, but the 'temporary transit' (TT) paperwork makes the car legally yours – and it's exempt from huge taxes. Such cars carry red licence plates, instantly identifying drivers as foreigners.

PRIORITÉ À DROITE

Under the *priorité à droite* rule, any car entering an intersection (including a T-junction) from a road on your right has the right of way, unless the intersection is marked '*vous n'avez pas la priorité*' (you do not have right of way), or *cédez le passage* (yield). Drivers may shoot out from intersections directly in front of you: approach with caution! *Priorité à droite* is suspended on priority roads, which are marked by a yellow diamond with white border; it's reinstated when you see a black bar through the yellow diamond.

Eligibility is restricted to non-EU residents (EU citizens are eligible only if they reside outside the EU); minimum age 18 (sometimes 21). You must order at minimum six weeks ahead and prepay your balance before the factory builds your car – and you get to pick the model. Diesel vehicles are more expensive up front, but you pay less for fuel. All plans include unlimited kilometres, 24-hour towing and breakdown service, and comprehensive insurance with zero deductible/excess. Brilliant.

Companies offering *achat-rachat*: **Citroën** (EurocarTT, DriveEurope or EuroPass; www.eurocartt.com), **Peugeot** (Open Europe; www.peugeot-openeurope.com) and **Renault** (Eurodrive; www.renault-eurodrive.com)

Insurance

Car-hire companies provide mandatory third-party (liability) insurance, but other important insurances cost extra, including collision-damage waiver (CDW, *assurance tous risque*), which covers the cost of the vehicle in the event of an accident or theft.

When comparing rates and fine print, find the *franchise* (deductible/excess) cost, which for small cars is around €800 – that's what you pay *in addition to* the cost of the insurance, if the car is damaged or stolen. With many companies, you can reduce the *franchise* by half, perhaps to zero, by paying a supplement of €10 to €16 daily.

Your credit card may cover CDW (only if used at time of rental), but the car-hire company won't know anything about it: verify coverage limitations with your credit-card issuer before leaving home. (Note: In event of incident, you'll have mountains of paperwork to sort with the rental-car company and your credit-card company's guarantor. With CDW, you typically just fill out accident reports, then walk away. Weighthe risks before categorically declining coverage.)

Parking

Provence's ancient villages and cities can be hellish on drivers, with narrow streets, confusing one-way systems and limited parking. Many hotels have no garages: guests drop off bags, then either claim a residents' parking permit from the hotel (if available at all) and find street parking, or hunt down a garage. Ask when reserving.

In city centres, look for 'P' signs to locate parking (often underground); expect to pay about €2.50/20 per hour/day. Alternatively, park outside town centres, then walk.

Road Rules

Enforcement of French traffic laws (see www.securite-routiere.gouv.fr) has been stepped up considerably. Speed cameras are common, as are radar traps, unmarked police vehicles and roadside drug tests. Fines for many infractions are given on the spot; serious violations can lead to confiscation of licence and vehicle. If you have an accident, you will be drug tested.

Speed limits change frequently in the Luberon. If you see a flash, expect a ticket in the mail.

Passenger cars may carry maximum five people. *All* passengers must wear seat belts. Children less than 10kg must travel in backward-facing child seats; children up to 36kg must travel in child seats in the vehicle's rear seat.

Turning right at a red light is illegal.

Only hands-free, speakerphone mobiles are allowed – no handsets, no texting.

British drivers committing offences can receive on-the-spot fines and penalty points to their licences.

Police in Provence rarely speak English – which can be advantageous. Be polite and smile.

Drivers of two-wheeled motorised vehicles (except electric bicycles) must wear helmets. No special licence is required for motorbikes under 50cc.

In forested areas, including Haute-Provence, Massif

SPEED LIMITS

Populated areas 50km/h

Undivided N and D highways 90km/h (80km/h if raining)

Non-autoroute divided highways 110km/h (100km/h if raining)

Autoroutes 130km/h (110km/h if raining, 60km/h if icy)

des Maures and Massif de l'Estérel, unsealed fire roads, signposted DFCI (Défense de la Forêt Contre l'Incendie; forest-fire defence team), are strictly off-limits to private vehicles.

Taxi

Find taxi ranks at train and bus stations, or telephone for radio taxis. Fares are metered, with minimum fare €6; rates are roughly €1.60 per kilometre for one-way journeys.

Train

SNCF's regional network in Provence, served by **TER** (www.ter-sncf.com/paca), comprises two routes: along the coast, with inland track from Cannes to Grasse; and up the interior, Marseille to Aix-en-Provence, Manosque, Sisteron and northward. Narrow-gauge railway **Train des Pignes** (Pine Cone Train; www.trainprovence.com) links Nice with Digne-les-Bains.

TER's website bookings are confusing; use www.voyages-sncf.com to more easily find schedules and fares.

Reservations are not mandatory on most regional trains. In summer, buy tickets in advance to ensure transport.

Two summertime regional passes are available to travellers of all ages, valid July through September. **Carte Bermuda** (€5) is a one-day pass for weekends and holidays, with unlimited 2nd-class travel between Marseille and Miramas. It can't be used on TGVs. **Carte Isabelle** (individual/family of 4 €12/€35) is a one-day pass for unlimited travel along the coast between Fréjus and Ventimiglia, inland between Nice and Tende, and Cannes to Grasse. It can't be used on TGVs, but permits 1st-class travel at no additional cost.

Passes & Costs

Passes are sold at student travel agencies, major train stations within Europe, and at **Rail Europe** (☎in Canada 1 800 361 7245, in the UK 0844 848 5848, in the USA 1 800 622 8600; www.raileurope.com).

For extensive European travel, it may be worth buying a **Eurail** (www.eurail.com) pass, available to non-Europeans; or an **InterRail** (www.interrailnet.com) pass available to Europeans – both valid for unlimited international travel. See **The Man in Seat 61** (www.seat61.com) for pros and cons of rail passes, and whether they make financial sense.

Note: Most passes must be validated at the train station ticket window before your first journey – leave extra time.

> **STAMP IT!**
>
> You must time-stamp your ticket in a *composteur* (free-standing yellow post at the entrance to train platforms) immediately before boarding, or incur hefty fines. Smartphones displaying barcode boarding passes are exempt.

SNCF BOOKINGS, DISCOUNTS & PASSES

» Website www.voyages-sncf.com often has internet-only offers; also an excellent mobile app for booking and electronic ticketing.

» First class costs 20% to 30% more.

» Ticket prices rise with demand: book early.

» Children under four travel free, or €8.50 to anywhere if they need seats. Ages four to 11 travel half-price.

» Travellers aged 12 to 25, and those over 60, receive discounts.

» Choose your seat type when you buy your ticket by clicking '*placement*': '*couloir*' is aisle, '*fenêtre*' window. '*Voitures silences*' are quiet – no mobile phones.

» If plans change, be sure to cancel (*annuler*) your ticket; otherwise you can't collect potential refunds (*remboursements*), assuming your fare type permits refunds.

» *Prem's* are lowest-fare tickets: no changes, no refunds. Limited inventory. Purchase 14 to 90 days ahead. *Bons plans* are last-minute specials; see the '*Dernière Minute*' heading on www.voyages-sncf.com.

» **IDTGV** ('Idée TGV'; www.idtgv.com) offers discounted TGV travel, bookable only online; two carriage types: IDZen and IDZap, the former silent, latter loud. *Loisir Week-end* offers discounts for round-trip travel on weekends, or round trips with a Saturday-night stayover. *Découverte* fares are low-demand 'blue period' trains for people aged 12 to 25, seniors, and adults accompanying children under 12. *Mini-groupe* fares are ideal for three to six travelers on the same booking; requires Saturday night stayover.

Guaranteed discounts of 25% (last-minute booking) to 50% (advance bookings for low-volume 'blue periods') are available with several cards:

Carte 12-25 (www.12-25-sncf.com; €50)

Carte Enfant Plus (www.enfantplus-sncf.com; €71)

Carte Escapades (www.escapades-sncf.com; €76)

Carte Sénior (www.senior-sncf.com; €56)

You must travel significant distance before the following rail passes yield savings:

France Railpass (www.francerailpass.com; 1st/2nd class US$299/242)

Rail One Country Pass (www.interrailnet.com; 5/10/15 days €267/381/422, 12-25yr €175/257/298)

Language

WANT MORE?

For in-depth language information and handy phrases, check out Lonely Planet's *French Phrasebook*. You'll find it at **shop .lonelyplanet.com**, or you can buy Lonely Planet's iPhone phrasebooks at the Apple App Store.

Standard French is taught and spoken throughout France. The heavy southern accent is an important part of regional identity in Provence, but you'll have no trouble being understood anywhere if you stick to standard French, which we've also used in the phrases in this chapter.

The sounds used in spoken French can almost all be found in English. There are a couple of exceptions: nasal vowels (represented in our pronunciation guides by o or u followed by an almost inaudible nasal consonant sound m, n or ng), the 'funny' *u* (ew in our guides) and the deep-in-the-throat *r*. Bearing these few points in mind and reading our pronunciation guides below as if they were English, you'll be understood just fine.

BASICS

French has two words for 'you' – use the polite form *vous* unless you're talking to close friends or children in which case you'd use the informal *tu*. You can also use *tu* when a person invites you to use *tu*.

All nouns in French are either masculine or feminine, and so are the adjectives, articles *le/la* (the) and *un/une* (a), and possessives *mon/ma (my), ton/ta (your)* and *son/sa* (his, her) that go with the nouns. In this chapter we have included masculine and femine forms where necessary, separated by a slash and indicated with 'm/f'.

Hello.	*Bonjour.*	bon·zhoor
Goodbye.	*Au revoir.*	o·rer·vwa
Excuse me.	*Excusez-moi.*	ek·skew·zay·mwa
Sorry.	*Pardon.*	par·don
Yes.	*Oui.*	wee
No.	*Non.*	non
Please.	*S'il vous plaît.*	seel voo play
Thank you.	*Merci.*	mair·see
You're welcome.	*De rien.*	der ree·en

How are you?
Comment allez-vous? ko·mon ta·lay·voo

Fine, and you?
Bien, merci. Et vous? byun mair·see ay voo

You're welcome.
De rien. der ree·en

My name is ...
Je m'appelle ... zher ma·pel ...

What's your name?
Comment vous appelez-vous? ko·mon voo·za·play voo

Do you speak English?
Parlez-vous anglais? par·lay·voo ong·glay

I don't understand.
Je ne comprends pas. zher ner kom·pron pa

ACCOMMODATION

Do you have any rooms available?
Est-ce que vous avez des chambres libres? es·ker voo za·vay day shom·brer lee·brer

How much is it per night/person?
Quel est le prix par nuit/personne? kel ay ler pree par nwee/per·son

Is breakfast included?
Est-ce que le petit déjeuner est inclus? es·ker ler per·tee day·zher·nay ayt en·klew

PROVENÇAL

Despite the bilingual signs that visitors see when they enter most towns and villages, the region's mother tongue – Provençal – is scarcely heard on the street or in the home. Just a handful of older people in rural Provence (Prouvènço) keep alive the rich lyrics and poetic language of their ancestors.

Provençal (*prouvençau* in Provençal) is a dialect of the *langue d'oc* (Occitan), the traditional language of southern France. Its grammar is closer to Catalan (spoken in Spain) than to French. In the grand age of courtly love – the period between the 12th and 14th centuries – Provençal was the literary language of France and northern Spain and was even used as far afield as Italy. Medieval troubadours and poets created melodies and elegant poems, and Provençal blossomed.

The 19th century witnessed a revival of Provençal after its rapid displacement by the *langue d'oïl*, the language of northern France which originated from the vernacular Latin spoken by the Gallo-Romans and gave birth to modern French (*francés* in Provençal). The revival of Provençal was spearheaded by Frédéric Mistral (1830–1914), a poet from Vaucluse, whose works in Provençal won him the 1904 Nobel Prize for Literature.

campsite	*camping*	kom·peeng
dorm	*dortoir*	dor·twar
guest house	*pension*	pon·syon
hotel	*hôtel*	o·tel
youth hostel	*auberge de jeunesse*	o·berzh der zher·nes

a ... room	*une chambre ...*	ewn shom·brer ...
single	*à un lit*	a un lee
double	*avec un grand lit*	a·vek un gron lee
twin	*avec des lits jumeaux*	a·vek day lee zhew·mo

with (a)...	*avec ...*	a·vek ...
air-con	*climatiseur*	klee·ma·tee·zer
bathroom	*une salle de bains*	ewn sal der bun
window	*fenêtre*	fer·nay·trer

DIRECTIONS

Where's ...?
Où est ...? — oo ay ...

What's the address?
Quelle est l'adresse? — kel ay la·dres

Could you write the address, please?
Est-ce que vous pourriez écrire l'adresse, s'il vous plaît? — es·ker voo poo·ryay ay·kreer la·dres seel voo play

Can you show me (on the map)?
Pouvez-vous m'indiquer (sur la carte)? — poo·vay·voo mun·dee·kay (sewr la kart)

at the corner	*au coin*	o kwun
at the traffic lights	*aux feux*	o fer
behind	*derrière*	dair·ryair
in front of	*devant*	der·von
far (from)	*loin (de)*	lwun (der)
left	*gauche*	gosh
near (to)	*près (de)*	pray (der)
next to	*à côté de*	a ko·tay der
opposite	*en face de*	on fas der
right	*droite*	drwat
straight ahead	*tout droit*	too drwa

EATING & DRINKING

What would you recommend?
Qu'est-ce que vous conseillez? — kes·ker voo kon·say·yay

What's in that dish?
Quels sont les ingrédients? — kel son lay zun·gray·dyon

I'm a vegetarian.
Je suis végétarien/végétarienne. — zher swee vay·zhay·ta·ryun/vay·zhay·ta·ryen (m/f)

I don't eat ...
Je ne mange pas ... — zher ner monzh pa ...

Cheers!
Santé! — son·tay

That was delicious.
C'était délicieux! — say·tay day·lee·syer

Please bring the bill.
Apportez-moi l'addition, s'il vous plaît. — a·por·tay·mwa la·dee·syon seel voo play

I'd like to reserve a table for ...	*Je voudrais réserver une table pour ...*	zher voo·dray ray·zair·vay ewn ta·bler poor ...
(eight) o'clock	*(vingt) heures*	(vungt) er
(two) people	*(deux) personnes*	(der) pair·son

Key Words

appetiser	*entrée*	on·tray
bottle	*bouteille*	boo·tay
breakfast	*petit déjeuner*	per·tee day·zher·nay
children's menu	*menu pour enfants*	mer·new poor on·fon
cold	*froid*	frwa
delicatessen	*traiteur*	tray·ter
dinner	*dîner*	dee·nay
dish	*plat*	pla
food	*nourriture*	noo·ree·tewr
fork	*fourchette*	foor·shet
glass	*verre*	vair
grocery store	*épicerie*	ay·pees·ree
highchair	*chaise haute*	shay zot
hot	*chaud*	sho
knife	*couteau*	koo·to
local speciality	*spécialité locale*	spay·sya·lee·tay lo·kal
lunch	*déjeuner*	day·zher·nay
main course	*plat principal*	pla prun·see·pal
market	*marché*	mar·shay
menu (in English)	*carte (en anglais)*	kart (on ong·glay)
plate	*assiette*	a·syet
spoon	*cuillère*	kwee·yair
wine list	*carte des vins*	kart day vun
with/without	*avec/sans*	a·vek/son

Meat & Fish

beef	*bœuf*	berf
chicken	*poulet*	poo·lay
crab	*crabe*	krab
lamb	*agneau*	a·nyo
oyster	*huître*	wee·trer
pork	*porc*	por
snail	*escargot*	es·kar·go
squid	*calmar*	kal·mar
turkey	*dinde*	dund
veal	*veau*	vo

Fruit & Vegetables

apple	*pomme*	pom
apricot	*abricot*	ab·ree·ko
asparagus	*asperge*	a·spairzh
beans	*haricots*	a·ree·ko
beetroot	*betterave*	be·trav
cabbage	*chou*	shoo
cherry	*cerise*	ser·reez
corn	*maïs*	ma·ees
cucumber	*concombre*	kong·kom·brer
grape	*raisin*	ray·zun
lemon	*citron*	see·tron
lettuce	*laitue*	lay·tew
mushroom	*champignon*	shom·pee·nyon
peach	*pêche*	pesh
peas	*petit pois*	per·tee pwa
(red/green) pepper	*poivron (rouge/vert)*	pwa·vron (roozh/vair)
pineapple	*ananas*	a·na·nas
plum	*prune*	prewn
potato	*pomme de terre*	pom der tair
prune	*pruneau*	prew·no
pumpkin	*citrouille*	see·troo·yer
shallot	*échalote*	eh·sha·lot
spinach	*épinards*	eh·pee·nar
strawberry	*fraise*	frez
tomato	*tomate*	to·mat
vegetable	*légume*	lay·gewm

Other

bread	*pain*	pun
butter	*beurre*	ber
cheese	*fromage*	fro·mazh
egg	*œuf*	erf
honey	*miel*	myel
jam	*confiture*	kon·fee·tewr
lentils	*lentilles*	lon·tee·yer
pasta/noodles	*pâtes*	pat
pepper	*poivre*	pwa·vrer
rice	*riz*	ree
salt	*sel*	sel
sugar	*sucre*	sew·krer
vinegar	*vinaigre*	vee·nay·grer

Signs

Entrée	Entrance
Femmes	Women
Fermé	Closed
Hommes	Men
Interdit	Prohibited
Ouvert	Open
Renseignements	Information
Sortie	Exit
Toilettes/WC	Toilets

Drinks

beer	*bière*	bee·yair
coffee	*café*	ka·fay
(orange) juice	*jus (d'orange)*	zhew (do·ronzh)
milk	*lait*	lay
tea	*thé*	tay
(mineral) water	*eau (minérale)*	o (mee·nay·ral)
(red) wine	*vin (rouge)*	vun (roozh)
(white) wine	*vin (blanc)*	vun (blong)

EMERGENCIES

Help!
Au secours! o skoor

I'm lost.
Je suis perdu/perdue. zhe swee·pair·dew (m/f)

Leave me alone!
Fichez-moi la paix! fee·shay·mwa la pay

There's been an accident.
Il y a eu un accident. eel ya ew un ak·see·don

Call a doctor.
Appelez un médecin. a·play un mayd·sun

Call the police.
Appelez la police. a·play la po·lees

I'm ill.
Je suis malade. zher swee ma·lad

It hurts here.
J'ai une douleur ici. zhay ewn doo·ler ee·see

I'm allergic to ...
Je suis allergique ... zher swee za·lair·zheek ...

SHOPPING & SERVICES

I'd like to buy ...
Je voudrais acheter ... zher voo·dray ash·tay ...

May I look at it?
Est-ce que je peux le voir? es·ker zher per ler vwar

I'm just looking.
Je regarde. zher rer·gard

I don't like it.
Cela ne me plaît pas. ser·la ner mer play pa

How much is it?
C'est combien? say kom·byun

It's too expensive.
C'est trop cher. say tro shair

Question Words

How?	*Comment?*	ko·mon
What?	*Quoi?*	kwa
When?	*Quand?*	kon
Where?	*Où?*	oo
Who?	*Qui?*	kee
Why?	*Pourquoi?*	poor·kwa

Can you lower the price?
Vous pouvez baisser le prix? voo poo·vay bay·say ler pree

There's a mistake in the bill.
Il y a une erreur dans la note. eel ya ewn ay·rer don la not

ATM	*guichet automatique de banque*	gee·shay o·to·ma·teek der bonk
credit card	*carte de crédit*	kart der kray·dee
internet cafe	*cybercafé*	see·bair·ka·fay
post office	*bureau de poste*	bew·ro der post
tourist office	*office de tourisme*	o·fees der too·rees·mer

TIME & DATES

What time is it?
Quelle heure est-il? kel er ay til

It's (eight) o'clock.
Il est (huit) heures. il ay (weet) er

It's half past (10).
Il est (dix) heures et demie. il ay (deez) er ay day·mee

morning	*matin*	ma·tun
afternoon	*après-midi*	a·pray·mee·dee
evening	*soir*	swar
yesterday	*hier*	yair
today	*aujourd'hui*	o·zhoor·dwee
tomorrow	*demain*	der·mun

Monday	*lundi*	lun·dee
Tuesday	*mardi*	mar·dee
Wednesday	*mercredi*	mair·krer·dee
Thursday	*jeudi*	zher·dee
Friday	*vendredi*	von·drer·dee
Saturday	*samedi*	sam·dee
Sunday	*dimanche*	dee·monsh

January	*janvier*	zhon·vyay
February	*février*	fayv·ryay
March	*mars*	mars
April	*avril*	a·vreel
May	*mai*	may
June	*juin*	zhwun
July	*juillet*	zhwee·yay
August	*août*	oot
September	*septembre*	sep·tom·brer
October	*octobre*	ok·to·brer
November	*novembre*	no·vom·brer
December	*décembre*	day·som·brer

Numbers

1	*un*	un
2	*deux*	der
3	*trois*	trwa
4	*quatre*	ka·trer
5	*cinq*	sungk
6	*six*	sees
7	*sept*	set
8	*huit*	weet
9	*neuf*	nerf
10	*dix*	dees
20	*vingt*	vung
30	*trente*	tront
40	*quarante*	ka·ront
50	*cinquante*	sung·kont
60	*soixante*	swa·sont
70	*soixante-dix*	swa·son·dees
80	*quatre-vingts*	ka·trer·vung
90	*quatre-vingt-dix*	ka·trer·vung·dees
100	*cent*	son
1000	*mille*	meel

TRANSPORT

Public Transport

boat	*bateau*	ba·to
bus	*bus*	bews
plane	*avion*	a·vyon
train	*train*	trun

I want to go to ...
Je voudrais aller à ... zher voo·dray a·lay a ...

Does it stop at (Amboise)?
Est-ce qu'il s'arrête à (Amboise)? es·kil sa·ret a (om·bwaz)

At what time does it leave/arrive?
À quelle heure est-ce qu'il part/arrive? a kel er es kil par/a·reev

Can you tell me when we get to ...?
Pouvez-vous me dire quand nous arrivons à ...? poo·vay·voo mer deer kon noo za·ree·von a ...

I want to get off here.
Je veux descendre ici. zher ver day·son·drer ee·see

first	*premier*	prer·myay
last	*dernier*	dair·nyay
next	*prochain*	pro·shun

a ... ticket	*un billet ...*	un bee·yay ...
1st-class	*de première classe*	der prem·yair klas
2nd-class	*de deuxième classe*	der der·zyem las
one-way	*simple*	sum·pler
return	*aller et retour*	a·lay ay rer·toor

aisle seat	*côté couloir*	ko·tay kool·war
delayed	*en retard*	on rer·tar
cancelled	*annulé*	a·new·lay
platform	*quai*	kay
ticket office	*guichet*	gee·shay
timetable	*horaire*	o·rair
train station	*gare*	gar
window seat	*côté fenêtre*	ko·tay fe·ne·trer

Driving & Cycling

I'd like to hire a ...	*Je voudrais louer ...*	zher voo·dray loo·way ...
4WD	*un quatre-quatre*	un kat·kat
car	*une voiture*	ewn vwa·tewr
bicycle	*un vélo*	un vay·lo
motorcycle	*une moto*	ewn mo·to

child seat	*siège-enfant*	syezh·on·fon
diesel	*diesel*	dyay·zel
helmet	*casque*	kask
mechanic	*mécanicien*	may·ka·nee·syun
petrol/gas	*essence*	ay·sons
service station	*station-service*	sta·syon·ser·vees

Is this the road to ...?
C'est la route pour ...? say la root poor ...

(How long) Can I park here?
(Combien de temps) Est-ce que je peux stationner ici? (kom·byun der tom) es·ker zher per sta·syo·nay ee·see

The car/motorbike has broken down (at ...).
La voiture/moto est tombée en panne (à ...). la vwa·tewr/mo·to ay tom·bay on pan (a ...)

I have a flat tyre.
Mon pneu est à plat. mom pner ay ta pla

I've run out of petrol.
Je suis en panne d'essence. zher swee zon pan day·sons

I've lost my car keys.
J'ai perdu les clés de ma voiture. zhay per·dew lay klay der ma vwa·tewr

GLOSSARY

Word gender is indicated as (m) masculine or (f) feminine; (pl) indicates plural.

abbaye (f) – abbey

AOP – Appellation d'Origine Protégée (formerly Appellation d'Origine Contrôlée [AOC], still commonly used in France); wines and olive oils that have met stringent government regulations governing where, how and under what conditions the grapes or olives are grown and the wines and olive oils are fermented and bottled

arrondissement (m) – one of several districts into which large cities, such as Marseille, are split

atelier (m) – artisan's workshop

auberge (f) – inn

autoroute (f) – motorway or highway

baie (f) – bay

bastide (f) – country house

billetterie (f) – ticket office or counter

borie (f) – primitive beehive-shaped dwelling, built from dry limestone around 3500 BC

boulangerie (f) – bread shop or bakery

calanque (f) – rocky inlet

carnet (m) – a book of five or 10 bus, tram or metro tickets sold at a reduced rate

cave (f) – wine or cheese cellar

centre (de) hospitalier (m) – hospital

chambre d'hôte (f) – B&B accommodation, usually in a private home

charcuterie (f) – pork butcher's shop and delicatessen; also cold meat

château (m) – castle or stately home

chèvre (m) – goat; also goat's-milk cheese

col (m) – mountain pass

conseil général (m) – general council

corniche (f) – coastal or cliff road

corrida (f) – bullfight

cour (f) – courtyard

course Camarguaise (f) – Camargue-style bullfight

dégustation (f) – the fine art of tasting wine, cheese, olive oil or seafood

département (m) – administrative area (department)

DFCI – Défense de la Forêt Contre l'Incendie; fire road (public access forbidden)

digue (f) – dike

domaine (m) – an estate producing wines

église (f) – church

épicerie (f) – grocery shop

étang (m) – lagoon, pond or lake

faïence (f) – earthenware

féria (f) – bullfighting festival

ferme auberge (f) – family run inn attached to a farm or *château*; farmhouse restaurant

fête (f) – party or festival

formule (f) – fixed main course plus starter or dessert

fromagerie (f) – cheese shop

galets (m) – large smooth stones covering Châteauneuf du Pape vineyards

gardian (m) – Camargue horseman or cattle-herding cowboy

gare (f) – train station

gare maritime (m) – ferry terminal

gare routière (m) – bus station

garrigue (f) – ground cover of aromatic scrub; see also *maquis*

gitan (m) – Roma Gitano person, gypsy

golfe (m) – gulf

grotte (f) – cave

halles (f pl) – covered market; central food market

hôtel de ville (m) – town hall

hôtel particulier (m) – private mansion

jardin (botanique) (m) – (botanic) garden

mairie (f) – town hall

manade (f) – bull farm

maquis (m) – aromatic Provençal scrub; name given to the French Resistance movement; see also *garrigue*

marché (m) – market

mas (m) – Provençal farmhouse

menu (m) – meal at a fixed price with two or more courses

mistral (m) – incessant north wind

monastère (m) – monastery

Monégasque – native of Monaco

moulin à huile (m) – oil mill

musée (m) – museum

navette (f) – shuttle bus, train or boat

Niçois – native of Nice

office du tourisme, office de tourisme (m) – tourist office (run by a unit of local government)

ONF – Office National des Forêts; National Forests Office

parc national (m) – national park

parc naturel régional (m) – regional nature park

pétanque (f) – a Provençal game of boules, similar to lawn bowls

pic (m) – mountain peak
place (f) – square
plage (f) – beach
plan (m) – city map
plat du jour (m) – dish of the day
pont (m) – bridge
porte (f) – gate or door; old-town entrance
préfecture (f) – main town of a *département*
presqu'île (f) – peninsula
prieuré (m) – priory

quai (m) – quay or railway platform
quartier (m) – quarter or district

rade (f) – gulf or harbour
région (m) – administrative region
rond-point (m) – roundabout

salin (m) – salt marsh
santon (m) – traditional Provençal figurine
sentier (m) – trail, footpath
sentier littoral (m) – coastal path
SNCF – Société Nationale des Chemins de Fer Français; state-owned railway company
SNCM – Société Nationale Maritime Corse-Méditerranée; state-owned ferry company linking Corsica and mainland France
stade (m) – stadium

tabac (m) – tobacconist (also sells newspapers, bus tickets etc)
TGV – Train à Grande Vitesse; high-speed train
théâtre antique (m) – Roman theatre

vendange (f) – grape harvest
vieille ville (f) – old town
vieux port (m) – old port
vigneron (m) – winegrower

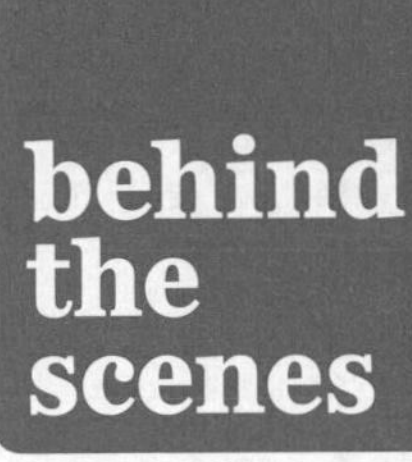

SEND US YOUR FEEDBACK

We love to hear from travellers – your comments keep us on our toes and help make our books better. Our well-travelled team reads every word on what you loved or loathed about this book. Although we cannot reply individually to postal submissions, we always guarantee that your feedback goes straight to the appropriate authors, in time for the next edition. Each person who sends us information is thanked in the next edition – the most useful submissions are rewarded with a selection of digital PDF chapters.

Visit **lonelyplanet.com/contact** to submit your updates and suggestions or to ask for help. Our award-winning website also features inspirational travel stories, news and discussions.

Note: We may edit, reproduce and incorporate your comments in Lonely Planet products such as guidebooks, websites and digital products, so let us know if you don't want your comments reproduced or your name acknowledged. For a copy of our privacy policy visit lonelyplanet.com/privacy.

OUR READERS

Many thanks to the travellers who used the last edition and wrote to us with helpful hints, useful advice and interesting anecdotes: Clare Baynham, Blaž Cugmas, Doug Fleming, Anne Foulsham, Meredith Heyward, Teodor Koranyi

AUTHOR THANKS

Emilie Filou

Big thanks to my parents, who were wonderful travel companions (and sharp critics!); thanks also to Marie-Jo and André Cornet for their hospitality and legendary good humour; Gérard and Florence Rondel for great recommendations in Cannes and elsewhere; Corinne Marie-Tossello for her time and insight; Isabelle Billey-Quéré, Frédérique Tamet and their teams at the tourist office in Nice and Cannes, respectively; my co-authors Alexis and John for elevating Francophilia to new heights; and finally my husband Adolfo, for his unwavering support.

Alexis Averbuck

Boundless thanks to Amy, Rod, Lola and Romy for making Marseille home to me; Cathryn Drake, Céline Emas Jarousseau and Pamela King for sharing the art scene; Tony Popovitch for generously opening Aix-en-Provence to me; Dominique Fouassier for her welcome, and fabulous Var advice; Bettina Hughes for superb gastronomic pointers; Anne-Marie Rohm for St-Tropez insights; Elodie Rothan for super tips; and Samantha Combe for Arles assistance. Special thanks to Jo Cooke for her unflappable editorial guidance and Emilie Filou for leading the author team with wit and *élan*.

John A Vlahides

I owe great thanks to Jo Cooke, Emilie Filou, and Alexis Averbuck, who encouraged me to accept this assignment. I'm so happy they did. In France, I'm grateful for the generosity of spirit of Louis-Paul Astraud, Valère Carlin, Sébastien James, Elodie Rothan, Anne-Marie Rohm, Rabiha Benaissa, Daniela Damiani and Cyril Mazin. Most importantly, I'm grateful to you, dear reader, for riding in my pocket around Provence and the Alps. Thanks for letting me be your guide. Bon voyage!

ACKNOWLEDGMENTS

Climate map data adapted from Peel MC, Finlayson BL & McMahon TA (2007) 'Updated World Map of the Köppen-Geiger Climate Classification', Hydrology and Earth System Sciences, 11, 1633–44.

Illustrations pp68-9, pp146-7 by Javier Zarracina. Cover photograph: Organic lavender rows on the Plateau de Valensole, Douglas Pearson/4Corners.

THIS BOOK

This 7th edition of Lonely Planet's *Provence & the Côte d'Azur* guidebook was researched and written by Emilie Filou, Alexis Averbuck and John A Vlahides. The previous edition was written by Nicola Williams, Alexis Averbuck, Emilie Filou and Fran Parnell. The 5th edition was written by Nicola Williams and Catherine Le Nevez. This guidebook was commissioned in Lonely Planet's London office, and produced by the following:

Commissioning Editor Joanna Cooke
Coordinating Editors Lauren Hunt, Gina Tsarouhas
Coordinating Cartographer Julie Dodkins
Coordinating Layout Designer Katherine Marsh
Managing Editor Annelies Mertens
Senior Editor Andi Jones
Managing Cartographers Shahara Ahmed, Anita Banh, Diana Von Holdt
Managing Layout Designer Jane Hart
Assisting Editors Andrew Bain, Elin Berglund, Cathryn Game, Amy Karafin, Alan Murphy
Assisting Cartographer Chris Tsismetzis
Assisting Layout Designer Yvonne Bischofberger
Cover Research Naomi Parker
Internal Image Research Aude Vauconsant
Illustrator Javier Zarracina
Language Content Branislava Vladisavljevic
Thanks to Dan Austin, Imogen Bannister, Sasha Baskett, Lucy Birchley, David Carroll, Daniel Corbett, Laura Crawford, Ryan Evans, Tobias Gattineau, Chris Girdler, Jennifer Fernández, Larissa Frost, Jouve India, Asha Ioculari, Kate McDonell, Trent Paton, Kirsten Rawlings, Raphael Richards, Averil Robertson, Dianne Schallmeiner, Amanda Sierp, Fiona Siseman, Gerard Walker

index

000 Map pages
000 Photo pages

D

E

F

000 Map pages
000 Photo pages

G

H

I

000 Map pages
000 Photo pages

R

S

T

000 Map pages
000 Photo pages

how to use this book

These symbols will help you find the listings you want:

- Sights
- Beaches
- Activities
- Courses
- Tours
- Festivals & Events
- Sleeping
- Eating
- Drinking
- Entertainment
- Shopping
- Information/Transport

These symbols give you the vital information for each listing:

- Telephone Numbers
- Opening Hours
- Parking
- Nonsmoking
- Air-Conditioning
- Internet Access
- Wi-Fi Access
- Swimming Pool
- Vegetarian Selection
- English Language Menu
- Family Friendly
- Pet-Friendly
- Bus
- Ferry
- Metro
- Subway
- London Tube
- Tram
- Train

Reviews are organised by author preference.

Look out for these icons:

TOP CHOICE Our author's recommendation

FREE No payment required

A green or sustainable option

Our authors have nominated these places as demonstrating a strong commitment to sustainability – for example by supporting local communities and producers, operating in an environmentally friendly way, or supporting conservation projects.

Map Legend

Sights

- Beach
- Buddhist
- Castle
- Christian
- Hindu
- Islamic
- Jewish
- Monument
- Museum/Gallery
- Ruin
- Winery/Vineyard
- Zoo
- Other Sight

Activities, Courses & Tours

- Diving/Snorkelling
- Canoeing/Kayaking
- Skiing
- Surfing
- Swimming/Pool
- Walking
- Windsurfing
- Other Activity/Course/Tour

Sleeping

- Sleeping
- Camping

Eating

- Eating

Drinking

- Drinking
- Cafe

Entertainment

- Entertainment

Shopping

- Shopping

Information

- Post Office
- Tourist Information

Transport

- Airport
- Border Crossing
- Bus
- Cable Car/Funicular
- Cycling
- Ferry
- Monorail
- Parking
- S-Bahn
- Taxi
- Train/Railway
- Tram
- Tube Station
- U-Bahn
- Underground Train Station
- Other Transport

Routes

- Tollway
- Freeway
- Primary
- Secondary
- Tertiary
- Lane
- Unsealed Road
- Plaza/Mall
- Steps
- Tunnel
- Pedestrian Overpass
- Walking Tour
- Walking Tour Detour
- Path

Boundaries

- International
- State/Province
- Disputed
- Regional/Suburb
- Marine Park
- Cliff
- Wall

Population

- Capital (National)
- Capital (State/Province)
- City/Large Town
- Town/Village

Geographic

- Hut/Shelter
- Lighthouse
- Lookout
- Mountain/Volcano
- Oasis
- Park
- Pass
- Picnic Area
- Waterfall

Hydrography

- River/Creek
- Intermittent River
- Swamp/Mangrove
- Reef
- Canal
- Water
- Dry/Salt/Intermittent Lake
- Glacier

Areas

- Beach/Desert
- Cemetery (Christian)
- Cemetery (Other)
- Park/Forest
- Sportsground
- Sight (Building)
- Top Sight (Building)

OUR STORY

A beat-up old car, a few dollars in the pocket and a sense of adventure. In 1972 that's all Tony and Maureen Wheeler needed for the trip of a lifetime – across Europe and Asia overland to Australia. It took several months, and at the end – broke but inspired – they sat at their kitchen table writing and stapling together their first travel guide, *Across Asia on the Cheap*. Within a week they'd sold 1500 copies. Lonely Planet was born.

Today, Lonely Planet has offices in Melbourne, London and Oakland, with more than 600 staff and writers. We share Tony's belief that 'a great guidebook should do three things: inform, educate and amuse'.

OUR WRITERS

Emilie Filou

Coordinating Author; Plan Your Trip; Nice, Monaco & Menton; Cannes & Around; Understand Provence & the Côte d'Azur Emilie was born in Paris but spent most of her childhood holidays roaming the south of France and the Alps. She left France when she was 18 to go travelling and never quite made it back. She studied geography at Oxford and took a grand total of three gap years to see more of Africa, Asia and the Pacific. She has now settled in London, where she works as a freelance journalist specialising in development issues in Africa (she has also contributed to the Lonely Planet guides to Tunisia, West Africa, Africa and Madagascar). She still goes to the Côte d'Azur every summer. You can see more of Emilie's work on www.emiliefilou.com; she tweets at @emiliefilou.

Read more about Emilie at:
lonelyplanet.com/members/emiliefilou

Alexis Averbuck

St-Tropez to Toulon; Marseille to Aix-en-Provence; Arles & the Camargue Alexis Averbuck first came to Provence when she was four and now makes any excuse to visit from her home on Hydra, Greece. Whether careening through hilltop villages in the Haut-Var, sipping wines in Burgundy or château-hopping in the Loire (she has also contributed to Lonely Planet's *France* guide), she immerses herself in all things French. A California native and a travel writer for two decades, Alexis has lived in Antarctica for a year, crossed the Pacific by sailboat and written books on her journeys through Asia and the Americas. Also a painter, she's inspired by each trip to produce new work, both written and visual – see her paintings at www.alexisaverbuck.com.

Read more about Alexis at:
lonelyplanet.com/members/alexisaverbuck

John A Vlahides

Avignon & Around; Hill Towns of the Luberon; Haute-Provence & the Southern Alps; Survival Guide John A Vlahides co-hosts the TV series *Lonely Planet: Roads Less Travelled*, screening on National Geographic Channels International. John worked as a French-English interpreter in Paris, where he studied cooking with the same chefs who trained Julia Child. He's a former luxury-hotel concierge and member of Les Clefs d'Or, the international union of the world's elite concierges. John lives in Northern California, where he sings tenor with the Grammy-winning San Francisco Symphony and spends free time skiing the Sierra Nevada. He looks forward to returning to Provence during tomato season. For more, see johnvlahides.com and twitter.com/JohnVlahides.

Read more about John at:
lonelyplanet.com/members/johnvlahides

Published by Lonely Planet Publications Pty Ltd
ABN 36 005 607 983
7th edition – Jan 2013
ISBN 978 1 74179 915 6

10 9 8 7 6 5 4 3 2 1
Printed in Singapore